Rhodesians Never Die

Peter Godwin is the author of *When a Crocodile Eats the Sun* (2006) and *Mukiwa* (1996). He writes for a number of publications including *The New York Times*, *Time*, *Newsweek* and *National Geographic*. He lives in Manhattan.

Ian Hancock is a Visiting Fellow at the Australian Dictionary of Biography in the Research School of Social Sciences at the Australian National University. He is the author of *White Liberals, Moderates and Radicals in Rhodesia, 1953-1980 (1984)*, *National and Permanent? The Federal Organisation of the Liberal Party of Australia (2000)*, *John Gorton: He Did It His Way (2002)* and *The Liberals: A History of the NSW Division of the Liberal Party (2007)*.

Rhodesians Never Die

THE IMPACT OF WAR AND POLITICAL CHANGE ON WHITE
RHODESIA *c.*1970-1980

PETER GODWIN and IAN HANCOCK

MACMILLAN

First published in 1993 by Oxford University Press

This edition by Pan Macmillan South Africa
Private Bag X19
Northlands
2116
www.panmacmillan.co.za

ISBN-13: 9781770100701

Cover design: Donald Hill of Blue Apple
Printed and bound in South Africa by Pinetown Printers

Rhodesians Never Die

We're all Rhodesians
And we'll fight through thick and thin,
We'll keep our land a free land,
Stop the enemy coming in,
We'll keep them north of the Zambezi
Till that river's running dry,
And this mighty land will prosper
For Rhodesians never die.

Clem Tholet and Andy Dillon

In Memory

Geoffrey Fairbairn
(1924-1980)

and

Jain Godwin
killed in the war,
near Shamva, on 22 April 1978,
aged 27

Foreword

The terrible situation in Zimbabwe conforms in many ways to the very worst of everything white Rhodesians had feared about black 'majority' rule. Today, by almost any index, Zimbabweans – of all races – are far worse off than they were at independence in 1980. Their GDP is lower, their lifespan is now the shortest in the world, health care and schooling have collapsed, and the country is crippled by hyperinflation which is currently ballooning at over 30,000 per cent a month. Robert Mugabe's dictatorial regime – corrupted and corrupting – has debauched Zimbabwe's huge potential, sabotaged the economy, abandoned any pretence of upholding civilised and democratic standards and the rule of law, and effectively declared war on most of its own people.

All of which begs the question: to what extent did white resistance to majority rule contribute to the present disaster?

It is certainly arguable that white Rhodesians must take some of the responsibility for Mugabe and his gang taking power, if not for all that happened thereafter. One assumption in this book is that a transfer of power was both inevitable and imminent. Our argument then, and now, is that UDI in 1965, the declaration of a republic in 1970, the white Rhodesians' own 'war on terror' in the 1970s, their refusal to reach terms with Joshua Nkomo in 1976, and their lukewarm approach to the internal settlement of 1978-9 all worked to prevent a civilised transfer of power and to promote black militancy. White Rhodesia's decision (as immortalised in the song *Rhodesians Never Die*, by Clem Tholet and Andy Dillon) to 'hold on', to 'fight through thick and thin', at once explained and justified the adoption by many blacks of the 'armed struggle', of the 'liberation war'.

ZANU (PF) became the principal party of liberation and Robert Mugabe, elevated by 'the struggle' to the rank of liberation hero, set about cultivating an almost Messianic status. Neither the party nor the man could do wrong. (Even after his North Korean trained 5th Brigade massacred more than 20,000 Matabele civilians in the early 1980s, his reputation emerged almost unscathed, and his people further cowered.) Both benefited from a potent foundation legacy, a form of divine right to rule, and in time, neither the party nor the man could accept it when the electorate grew tired of them.

The continued exploitation of this legacy was blatantly revealed on the brink of the 2002 presidential election. Mugabe then faced his most threatening challenger, Morgan Tsvangirai, the head of the Movement for Democratic Change (MDC). Tsvangirai came up through the trade union movement and, belonging to a younger generation, had not played a direct role in the war for independence. Days before the election, the head of the army, General Vitalis Zvinavashe, went on national TV to warn Zimbabweans that the army would not permit any candidate without direct liberation war credentials to become president of the country. His action amounted to a pre-emptive coup, and showed how far ZANU (PF) would go in manipulating its liberation legacy to remain in office. The 'struggle' also underpins the demonising rhetoric used to identify and brand the 'enemy' – white settler rule and British colonialism – without which the increasingly dictatorial Mugabe would surely have been easier to dislodge, and without which other African governments would have found him easier to criticise.

Given their determined resistance to majority rule – itself understandable in terms of their anxieties and their desire to maintain a privileged existence – the white Rhodesians did contribute to the fulfilment of their own prophecies of doom. Indeed, Ian Smith's government further assisted the execution by bequeathing some useful levers for repressing or stifling dissent, ranging from draconian emergency powers to a strictly controlled media. Even so, it would be drawing too long a bow to hold white Rhodesia responsible for a professed Marxist and 'a man of the people' choosing the path of autocracy, brutality and kleptocracy.

That said, there remains much of abiding interest in the themes pursued in this book: how the Rhodesians fought the guerrilla war and, for a time, held on; how, while constituting just 5 per cent of the population, they managed to dominate the country for 15 years after declaring independence from Britain; and how they did so without destroying it in the process. And there is something all the more poignant about this portrait of a people whose last vestiges have now been so comprehensively swept away – the last largely intact pocket of the white society, the commercial farming communities, were evicted on Mugabe's orders in 2000, accelerating the country's economic collapse. Today, fewer than 30,000 whites remain, down from a high of close to 300,000. And the departing whites are now joined in their Diaspora by many black Zimbabweans fleeing from economic chaos and political repression at home.

Peter Godwin/Ian Hancock November 2007

Preface

This book began its long gestation period in an Oxford pub in the midst of England's winter of early 1979. Two Australian academics decided – just before closing time – that they should write a book about the last years of white Rhodesia. Both had first encountered Rhodesia in the mid-1970s, coming from quite different backgrounds. One was an expert on counter-insurgency who had been in Saigon just before its fall; the other had written about post-independence Uganda. Both disliked racism and minority rule; neither could condemn those whose wrong-headedness had created a terrible little war and yet whose instincts and human qualities were often lovable. The planned study ended abruptly, however, when Geoffrey Fairbairn died in 1980, and Hancock went on to write a very different book about white liberals and moderates in Rhodesia. A chance meeting in 1983 in Harare revived the original idea. Peter Godwin, Rhodesian born and a former, conscripted member of the Security Forces, was himself planning a study of counter-insurgency in Rhodesia in the 1970s. Together, we found that there was remarkable affinity with the assumptions and objectives first expressed in that Oxford pub and, over the next eight years, and in difficult circumstances, we brought our different experiences, materials, and minds to the task of writing this book.

In the process we have collected some enormous debts. Godwin wishes to thank the Beit Trust for a research grant, the Zimbabwe Ministry of Information for access to their archives, and the *Sunday Times* (London) for arranging a sabbatical to allow him to work on the book. Hancock wishes to acknowledge the financial support of the Australian government and of the Australian National University. The staff and the facilities at the National Archives of Zimbabwe, the University Library in Zimbabwe, and the libraries at Rhodes House and Queen Elizabeth House at Oxford provided splendid support. So did all those individuals who gave their time and – in some cases – opened their private papers. No one did more for us than Diana Mitchell. Just one person – a former minister in Ian Smith's government – refused to talk to us. Perhaps we would have preserved our moral absolutes if only more of his kind had been equally offensive. Ian Smith, who does not emerge well in this book, became more likeable as he began to talk more freely and with feeling, even as the authors were concluding that he had failed his own people so badly. Many of his former senior ministers, ordinary supporters of his party, and several who were on and beyond the right-wing fringe were very generous in helping and entertaining two authors who plainly did not share their views.

We are grateful to Clem Tholet for permission to use the words and title of the song he wrote with Andy Dillon.

Susan Allen and Alistair McKenzie provided research assistance; Maree Beer edited the manuscript; Kevin Cowan and Val Lyons prepared the maps; and Nicholas Brown, Bill Craven, George and Helen Godwin, Iain McCalman, Alistair McKenzie, and Phillipa Weeks commented upon, and corrected, the manuscript. We thank them all, while regretting that they cannot be blamed for the faults which follow. We would also like to thank the editorial staff of Oxford University Press for their expert assistance.

We took a long time to produce this book. No doubt a single author would have written it in half the time, and another two authors would have done it differently and better. There are, however, some extenuating circumstances. It is not easy engaging in a joint exercise when the two participants, living and working in different parts of the world, could meet for just eight weeks during the period of serious writing. For what it's worth, they both learnt much in the process. For that, they want to thank each other.

P. G.
I. H.

Contents

List of Maps

List of Tables

List of Abbreviations

ARB	*Africa Research Bulletin*
ACCOR	Associated Chambers of Commerce of Rhodesia
AEU	Amalgamated Engineering Union
ANC	African National Council
ARnI	Association of Rhodesian Industries
BSAP	British South Africa Police
CAT	Civil Action Team
CFU	Commercial Farmers' Union
CID	Criminal Investigation Department
CIO	Central Intelligence Organisation
COMOPS	Combined Operations
CP	Centre Party
CSO	Central Statistical Office
CTs	Communist Terrorists
DAs	District Assistants
DC	District Commissioner
DP	Dominion Party
FRELIMO	Front for the Liberation of Mozambique
FROLIZI	Front for the Liberation of Zimbabwe
ICD	Independence Commemorative Decoration
JOC	Joint Operations Command
K Cars	Kill Cars (helicopter gunships)
MP	Member of Parliament
NATJOC	National Joint Operations Command
NAZ	National Archives of Zimbabwe
NIBMAR	No Independence Before Majority African Rule
NPA	National Pledge Association
NUF	National Unifying Force
OAU	Organisation of African Unity
OC	Officer in Charge
OCC	Operations Co-ordinating Committee
PATU	Police Anti-Terrorist Unit
PF	Patriotic Front
PSYOPS	Psychological Operations
PVs	Protected Villages
RAP	Rhodesian Action Party
RAR	Rhodesian African Rifles

RBC	Rhodesian Broadcasting Corporation
RBC/TV	Rhodesian Broadcasting Corporation/Television
RCA	Rhodesian Constitutional Association
Reps	Salisbury Repertory Players
RF	Rhodesian Front
RLI	Rhodesian Light Infantry
RNFU	Rhodesia National Farmers' Union
RNP	Rhodesia National Party
RP	Rhodesia Party
RRWU	Rhodesia Railway Workers' Union
RTA	Rhodesia Tobacco Association
SAP	South African Police
SAS	Special Air Service
SASCON	Southern Africa Solidarity Conference
sub-JOCs	sub-Joint Operations Commands
TTL	Tribal Trust Land
UANC	United African National Council
UDI	Unilateral Declaration of Independence
UFP	United Federal Party
ZANLA	Zimbabwe African National Liberation Army
ZANU	Zimbabwe African National Union
ZANU(PF)	Zimbabwe African National Union (Patriotic Front)
ZAPU	Zimbabwe African People's Union
ZIPRA	Zimbabwe People's Revolutionary Army
ZUPO	Zimbabwe United People's Organisation

Glossary

RHODESIA: 'Rhodesia' was the 'official' name of the country between 1970 and 1979, and is employed for most of the period covered by this book. Where appropriate, the titles of 'Southern Rhodesia', 'Zimbabwe Rhodesia', and 'Zimbabwe' are also used.

'RHODESIANS' AND 'WHITE RHODESIANS': the term 'Rhodesian(s)' is used here to refer to the whites. Although many Rhodesians resisted the use of 'white' as a prefix, the terms 'Rhodesian(s)', 'white(s)', and 'white Rhodesian(s)' are used interchangeably for stylistic reasons. The terms 'African(s)' or 'black(s)', which are also employed interchangeably, were implicitly excluded from 'Rhodesian(s)' unless they were explicitly included. The terms 'European' (which in the 1969 constitution included members of the Asian and Coloured populations) and 'African' were widely used throughout the 1970s although the Rhodesians began to make more use of 'white' and 'black' as the decade progressed. Ian Smith was certainly one who did so.

'TERRORIST', 'TERRORISTS', 'TERRS': the whites usually referred to the guerrillas (or 'freedom fighters') as 'terrorists' and, where Rhodesian perspectives are relevant, the terms 'terrorist' or 'terrorists' and 'terrs' will be used in this book, and will appear in inverted commas.

Rhodesian and Zimbabwean Place Names

Rhodesia	Zimbabwe
Bindura	Bindura
Bulawayo	Bulawayo
Chipinga	Chipinge
Fort Victoria	Masvingo
Gatooma	Kadoma
Gwelo	Gweru
Hartley	Chegutu
Inyanga	Nyanga
Melsetter	Chimanimani
Marandellas	Marondera
Que Que	Kwekwe
Salisbury	Harare
Shabani	Zvishavane
Sinoia	Chinoyi
Umtali	Mutare
Wankie	Hwange
Zimbabwe Ruins	Great Zimbabwe

Exchange Rates

The Rhodesian currency was decimalised in February 1970.

In February 1970 one Rhodesian dollar was equivalent to £1.00 stg.
In February 1980 one Rhodesian dollar was equivalent to £1.45 stg.

Introduction

I

Most white Rhodesians were bewildered or devastated by the news of Tuesday, 4 March 1980. For weeks they had been expecting to hear that the moderate and pliable Bishop Muzorewa would form the first black government of the new Zimbabwe. A radio announcement, however, confirmed the disturbing rumours of the previous three days: Robert Mugabe, the 'Marxist terrorist',[1] had won an absolute majority in the parliamentary elections.

The Rhodesians[2] had just fought a bitter war against 'terrorism'. Between 1976 and 1979, and much against their inclination, they had (in their view, generously) conceded power to the black majority in the expectation that African rule would be moderate and suitably deferential to white interests. For years Ian Smith, the Rhodesian Prime Minister, had warned his people that they would lose everything if the 'terrorists' came to power. Not surprisingly, many were now convinced that the old Rhodesia would be turned – overnight – into a Marxist state. A few hotheads talked of reprisals, of blowing up the Kariba Dam or sabotaging the coal or gold mines. Others telephoned real-estate agents, took their children out of school, joined the queues for South African visas or for air tickets, or loaded their cars for the drive to the South African border at Beit Bridge. The rest were too stunned to do more than apportion blame. They attributed Mugabe's election victory to intimidation, or to the sinister intervention of the British Foreign Office, or to a conspiracy uniting Western capitalism and Eastern communism. One thing was clear: left to their own devices, those whom Ian Smith once called 'the happiest blacks in the world'[3] would never have voted for such a monstrous evil. So, while Africans danced, jogged, waved branches, and ululated in the streets of Salisbury, and the Security Forces waited impatiently for the order to seize control (an order that never came), white shoppers smiled wanly at the scenes around them, or scuttled by, their faces taut and expressionless.

Yet, by mid-afternoon, the mood was changing. In recent years Salisbury's whites had begun the day depressed about last night's news or worried about the next. But, after several hours of buying or selling, devising new regulations or evading old ones, chasing non-existent spare parts or haggling over petrol coupons, exchanging gossip, going shopping or playing bridge, immediate problems seemed more pressing than longer-term fears. Returning to the suburbs in the evening, and settling down with a drink, perhaps after a swim, a jog, or a set of tennis, white Rhodesians had often decided to 'wait and see'.

On 4 March the shock was too traumatic to be wholly absorbed by the daily round of activity, but the greater calm of the afternoon was strengthened by the evening news. The 'terrorist' leader, introduced on television as 'Comrade Robert Mugabe', promised reconciliation rather than revenge. He would honour the Lancaster House agreement of December 1979, thereby guaranteeing white pension and property rights, and he had invited Lieutenant-General Peter Walls, the Commander of the Security Forces, to head a new integrated army. Within a few minutes the satanic monster of the morning was being

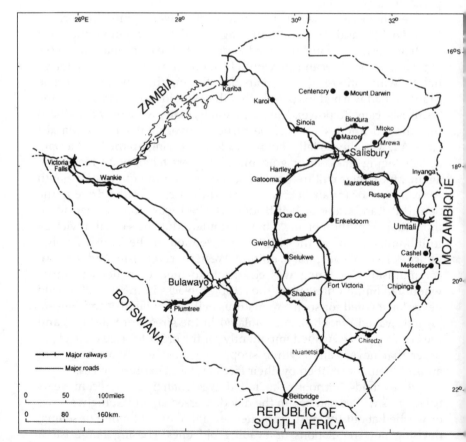

MAP 1.1.   *Rhodesia in 1970*

transformed into a responsible and intelligent Prime Minister-designate. Nonplussed at 10.00 a.m., by the evening the majority of whites wanted to believe that Robert Mugabe, of all people, represented the best hope for restoring peace, stability, and prosperity.

II

There are three immediate points to make about this long day in the history of white Rhodesia. First, wild swings between extreme pessimism and misplaced optimism had not been uncommon during the war in the 1970s. These swings were especially pronounced in Salisbury, a fact which frequently provoked acerbic comment from the rural communities. It seemed that the areas farthest from the fighting were the most vulnerable to rumour and susceptible to uncertainty. The sudden fluctuations in mood reflected both a shallow understanding of changing events in southern Africa and the long-term isolation of Rhodesia from international realities. Most white Rhodesians had become so accustomed to hearing what they wanted to believe, and electing a government that wanted them to believe what it allowed them to hear, that they were often incapable of distinguishing between the ephemeral and the substantial, between fantasy and reality.

Secondly, by 1980, the large majority of white Rhodesians would settle for peace at almost any price. According to the official rhetoric of the 1960s and 1970s, Rhodesia existed in order to defend Western civilisation from the evils of communism and to preserve civilised standards from the anarchy and corruption of black Africa. The election of the Rhodesian Front (RF) government in 1962 and the Unilateral Declaration of Independence (UDI) in 1965 symbolised these objectives. Yet after more than seven years of war and fourteen of sanctions, of intensifying gloom and dashed hopes, the rhetoric had become meaningless to those for whom Rhodesia meant, above all, an agreeable lifestyle. They might detest 'terrorism' and fear communism but, if the election of Robert Mugabe meant the end of the war, and if Mugabe himself was not such a monster after all, then 'things might turn out better than we expected'.

Thirdly, Mugabe's election victory presented the whites with three clear options: they could pack up and leave; they could remain behind, live in the past, and effectively become expatriates in their own country; or they could emigrate with their hearts and minds to the new Zimbabwe. These options were first seriously posed on 24 September 1976 when Ian Smith announced that he had accepted the principle of majority rule. One section of Rhodesian society wanted to continue the war to maintain white power. Other 'good' Rhodesians began to make

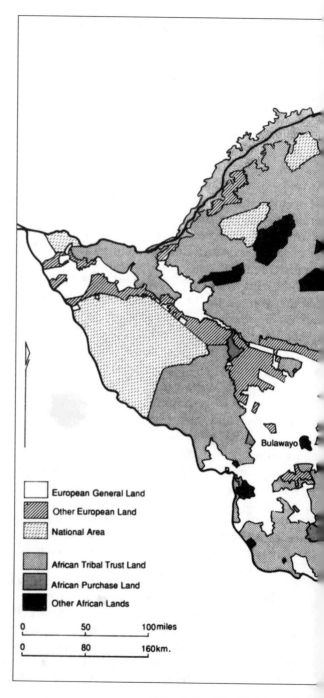

European General Land
Other European Land
National Area

African Tribal Trust Land
African Purchase Land
Other African Lands

Bulawayo

0   50   100 miles
0   80   160 km.

MAP 1.2.   *The Division of Land*

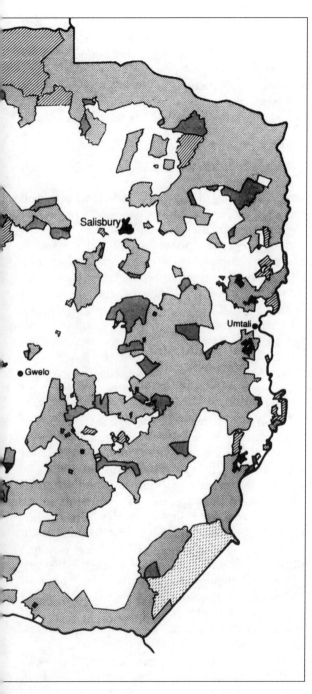

Land Tenure Act, 1 April 1974

the happy discovery that racial separation and white political power were not essential to the maintenance of what they called 'the Rhodesian way of life'. A small minority persisted in believing that political change could mean the introduction of a non-racial democracy. The rest – forming the majority of the whites – alternated between their acceptance of change and their refusal to face its implications. ZANU(PF)'s[4] electoral triumph in 1980 forced that majority to confront a reality it had tried to evade.

Ill

This book endeavours to tell the story of how the Rhodesians, nearly all of them ill-prepared for war and revolutionary change, reacted to the challenge to, and the eventual loss of, their domain. The story begins in 1970 when Rhodesia became a republic, and when the Rhodesians were confident, in control, and even complacent. The new 'world-beater'[5] of a constitution guaranteed their rule for the foreseeable future. The economy was reviving after withstanding the initial shock of the international economic sanctions imposed after UDI. The Security Forces had repelled all the guerrilla attacks emanating from neighbouring Zambia. Petrol rationing had been lifted, a damaging white-led railway strike had been settled, and the Rhodesian cricket team was poised to re-enter the premier grade of the South African Currie Cup competition. Gradually after 1970, and then with gathering pace, Rhodesian authority and confidence crumpled under the strains of war and international pressure. The intensification of the armed struggle after 1972, and its sharp escalation from 1976, eventually divided the entire country into designated operational areas and necessitated the military call-ups which stretched the manpower requirements beyond its white resources. The tightening of economic sanctions from the mid-1970s further hampered Rhodesia's resistance. Following the Portuguese coup of 1974 and the installation of black Marxist governments in Angola and Mozambique, the British, the Americans, and the South Africans insisted upon Rhodesian acceptance and implementation of majority rule. A last-ditch strategem failed when the guerrillas, the African states, and the Western powers all rejected an internal settlement whereby the whites retained considerable formal authority and Bishop Muzorewa led the ill-fated Zimbabwe Rhodesia through the last half of 1979. The story ends on 4 March 1980 when everything seemed lost or, at best, was bound to be very different.

Significantly, on that day, Rhodesians were united only by their sense of shock. The 'national community' was already disintegrating, and from 1980 – deprived of a focus and a purpose – soon fell apart. This process of disintegration had been evident from the mid-1970s. Despite the deliberate cultivation of a patriotic sentiment, the universal rejection of 'terrorism', the determination to prosecute the war, and the formal and informal pressures to conform, the unity of white Rhodesia in the latter part of the 1970s was more apparent than real, and by early 1980 white solidarity was less apparent than confusion and uncertainty. For the war and the political changes of the 1970s had exposed, accentuated, and created sharp divisions within white Rhodesia.

One objective of telling the story is to demonstrate and explain the emergence of these divisions. It will be argued here that Rhodesia did not possess the 'relatively monolithic character'[6] which was the image popularised by its critics and supporters alike. Whether it was regarded as a brave little country[7] or as a nasty racist regime,[8] whether it was supposedly defending Western civilisation or protecting minority privileges, Rhodesia was generally perceived as massed behind Ian Smith and the RF. The 'true' Rhodesians – the descendants of the Pioneers who had founded the country in 1890, the young 'Rhodies' brought up on a history replete with heroes, the ever-faithful worshippers of Ian Smith, and the exiles who now comfort each other at reunions held abroad – all believed that Rhodesians were bound together by a sense of mission and by a shared national identity. The mission might have changed course when Smith began to abandon the RF's founding principles in 1976. But, so the argument went, the Rhodesians had demonstrated their continuing solidarity by giving the RF 85 per cent of the vote in the 1977 elections, by voting overwhelmingly for the majority rule constitution in the referendum of January 1979, and by fighting 'terrorism' all the way until the cease-fire of December 1979. For their part, the critics could interpret the same evidence to argue that, right to the end, the Rhodesians remained solidly behind Smith in trying to maintain their privileged status. Having lost the battle to perpetuate white minority rule, they voted for a new structure that retained their economic control, preserved their jobs, gave them a share of political power, and merely removed the legal barriers to black advancement. Either way, the preferred or assigned image of white Rhodesia presupposed the existence of a 'relatively monolithic' community.

Rhodesian society was probably less differentiated than the white communities of Canada, Australia, New Zealand, and South Africa. Nevertheless, the Rhodesians of the 1970s were not socially or ethnically homogeneous. A few could boast that they belonged to the third generation of Rhodesian-born; the overwhelming majority were either migrants or had been born in the country since the Second World War. A national loyalty had to be invented in the post-UDI years whereas other loyalties – to smaller ethnic, regional, or occupation-based communities – emerged more naturally. The obvious bond was race, and everyday usage testifies to its role in identifying and defining Rhodesian-ness. When most whites referred to 'Rhodesia' they meant 'white Rhodesia', and when they referred to 'Rhodesians' they meant themselves. Blacks were classified either as 'black Rhodesians' – sometimes as 'our black Rhodesians' – or were encompassed by the general phrase 'all Rhodesians'. These racially based attitudes and practice remained at the core of white politics throughout the 1970s. Perhaps for that reason outsiders found it difficult, as well as ideologically unsound, to detect any distinctions within white society over the issue of racial discrimination. On the inside, however, the divisions were real enough. There were the liberals who gallantly defied the white majority in the 1970s and stood up to Ian Smith in the face of derision and ostracism. There were the avowed supremacists and segregationists within the RF who, in the early and mid-1970s, opposed – and even outnumbered – those party members who accepted that Africans would one day govern the country. Thus, while a majority of the electorate revered Ian Smith, a sizeable section of his own party regarded him as a dangerous liberal. In 1977 members of the right wing of the RF broke away to form the Rhodesian Action Party (RAP) and campaigned, unsuccessfully, for racial separation and the retention of white rule. The point is that, although the white electorate rejected the liberal and the segregationist-supremacist models, and although race was a factor in identifying Rhodesian-ness, a common racial identity did not beget uniformity in political behaviour.

One article of faith shared by all Rhodesians in 1970, and one which survived through the 1970s, was a commitment to 'the Rhodesian way of life'. Individuals and families had their own perceptions of what it meant and of what really mattered: perhaps the climate or the education system, the medical services, the cost of living or the sense of self-importance, the pleasant urban amenities or the life of a small farming community. The war and political change in the 1970s forced Rhodesians to decide whether or when the hardships outweighed the benefits. The prospect of black rule, concern about the future of their children, the regular military call-ups, the personal dangers, and the departure of close friends were among the factors which, for thousands, tilted the balance in favour of emigration. And, precisely because the form and depth of commitment to Rhodesia depended so much upon circumstances, and because one of the circumstances was that Rhodesia itself was about to disappear, the national 'community' had become an illusion by March 1980.

Apart from propagating myths about the national 'community', the Rhodesians convinced themselves of many other fallacies or half-truths. They believed, for example, that 'the best counter-insurgency force in the world' was perfectly capable of defeating a contemptible army of 'garden boys'. In 1980 it was customary to argue that Rhodesia never lost the war but was 'defeated' at the conference table by devious British politicians. These claims overlooked the fact that the 'garden boys' were swarming over the entire country by 1979, and ignored the possibility of an eventual military defeat if the war had continued. Another favourite contention was that Rhodesia had 'the best race relations in the world'. Any racial friction, like the war itself, was regarded as the creation of communist-inspired agitators who intimidated the ignorant, non-political black population. Yet, strictly speaking, for most Rhodesians the term 'race relations' was a misnomer; they did not 'relate' to Africans except as masters to servants, and few of them ever understood, or wanted to understand, the motivations, commitment, or the intensity of all those blacks who had actively opposed white rule from the late 1950s.

Further assumptions were that Rhodesians were all rugged individualists, that they were imbued with the adventurous spirit of the Pioneer Column, and that they constituted one of the best-educated societies in the world. The Rhodesians liked to say that they could not, and would not, be pushed around. Yet successive generations had blindly voted for heroes rather than policies and then, lemming like, thousands followed their greatest hero – 'Good Old Smithy' – into the abyss. Fiercely independent, the Rhodesians were easily led, and even more easily deceived. Often quarrelsome, they complained – all the time – but these free spirits acquiesced in the imposition of an intrusive, all-embracing and stifling bureaucracy. Above all, the Rhodesians liked to see themselves as forming one of the last bastions of Western, Christian civilisation. In reality, they practised a Sunday Christianity in 1970; they yielded to moral temptation and, as the war progressed, they broke most of their own codes for civilised behaviour. Instead, therefore, of preserving civilisation, the Rhodesians, isolated as they were, simply took longer to leap from the 1950s to the 1970s.

A second objective, then, in describing white responses to the war and political change is to expose some of the misconceptions held by, and about, the Rhodesians of the 1970s. They were less unified and more self-deluded than is often supposed. Their presumed common characteristics were not necessarily those which determined their actions. Throughout the 1970s the Rhodesians were preoccupied with the largely material needs, activities, and desires of a people living in a semi-detached Western society. They spent more time – before 1977 – living their way of life than they did in defending it, and the lives they lived, and sought to defend, were remarkably ordinary.

The 'big' issues of social discrimination and majority rule rarely intruded into their daily business. Until the mid-1970s most Rhodesians were more interested in the mundane or conventional questions of government intervention in the economy, the degree of bureaucratic control, the level of inflation, the policy of providing cheap food for urban dwellers, the rising cost of farm inputs, the operation of currency regulations, and the standard of education and of the medical services. In 1970 Colin Barlow, an RF back-bencher from Salisbury, indicated what he thought would interest his constituents when he listed the highlights of the 1970 parliamentary year. In order, they were the reduction in direct taxation, the report of the Wild Life Commission, the proposal to include the peri-urban (white) areas in the (white) Salisbury Municipality, the increase of government expenditure on development, the measures taken to assist farmers, the introduction of the Pipeline Bill, the re-zoning of a suburb in the constituency which allowed white girls a choice of two senior schools, and the provision of a greater range of cheaper cars. Barlow reported – briefly – on only two 'big' issues: the need for more white immigrants and the progress being made on the new (white) hospital in Salisbury.[9]

The parish council of All Saints' Anglican Church, Gatooma, held just one 'stormy' political discussion between 1970 and 1980.[10] On 11 June 1970 it supported the Bishop of Mashonaland by nine votes to two in his opposition to the government's apparent determination to separate white priests from their black congregations. The monthly council meetings proceeded for the next ten years to debate matters of much greater importance: the state of the parish finances, the drop in church attendances, the future of the rector's car, and the condition of the church buildings and of the organ. Anglicans everywhere would understand these preoccupations, just as fellow white colonials would appreciate why the Rhodesians were so immersed in planning, achieving, and enjoying material comfort, and in educating their children and confronting everyday issues. A history which is constructed on the principle of listening and observing is bound to discover that the Rhodesians managed to live full lives; that is, when they were not doing the things expected of them like beating their servants or saving Western civilisation.

The undiscovered or ignored dimensions of Rhodesian society constitute an essential part of its recent history. It is not fashionable, however, to explore the territory which lies beyond the main track. What matters at the reunions of 'true' Rhodesians is to remember the hurt of losing a country or to relive past glories. The result is that these Rhodesians perpetuate misconception and fantasy. What matters to the scholarly critics is to condemn the settler state, to bemoan its alleged survival under black rule, and to formulate the theory which correctly locates race and settler capitalism within the framework of class analysis.

This latter approach reduces the white Rhodesians to caricatures and categories, and does so without explaining why they responded in different ways to change in the 1970s, and why many of them – given their assigned roles – behaved so erratically.

There are considerable rewards for paying more attention to what the Rhodesians actually said and did. Their language, rituals, and symbols are fertile sources for their political culture. It has already been suggested that the use of the term 'Rhodesia' had important connotations. Another key word was 'terrorist'. Expanded definitions were not necessary by the mid-1970s unless a white dissident or foreign correspondent had the temerity to refer to 'guerrillas' or, worse still, to 'freedom fighters'. By then, most Rhodesians believed that 'terrorists' were communists, malcontents, and murdering thugs – the Godless embodiment of evil – who made cowardly attacks on defenceless tribesmen and farmers' families, ran away from the Security Forces, and were interested only in personal power or in advancing the cause of Soviet or Chinese communism. The Rhodesians were hardly unique in misunderstanding and misrepresenting their enemies. Nor were they altogether wrong in their assessment of the 'terrorist' methods employed by the guerrillas. Yet historians who do no more than record the persistent usage of the term 'terrorist', or merely shake their heads in dismay or reproach, would overlook a rich mine which lies within their reach. For, by exploring the Rhodesian language, they can draw conclusions about the levels of white ignorance, political sensitivity, and sophistication. They might also locate the deeper recesses where individuals and groups hid their fears and superstitions about the unknown Africa and the allegedly unknowable African mind. And historians will uncover a great truth about white Rhodesia in the 1970s: that opposition to 'terrorism' could unite all except a handful of Rhodesians whereas their racial policies divided them into opposed camps.

Another objective, therefore, is to construct a history which incorporates the diverse dimensions of the Rhodesian experience, which recognises the complexities and contradictions of Rhodesian responses to war and change, and which tries to understand the society from the inside. It is a history which takes seriously what the Rhodesians believed, said, and did, and which recognises that perhaps their worst collective fault was an almost infinite capacity for self-deception.[11]

IV

This history begins with an analysis of what constituted and sustained the Rhodesian way of life in 1970; that is, just before the first major escalation of the war in 1972. It concludes in 1980 with an assessment of how far the war and political change had affected the living standards and outlook of the Rhodesians. The chapters in between are set in chronological sequence, the breaks determined by what, in Rhodesian terms, were considered important landmarks. Some of the principal themes of this story – for instance, the continuing arguments over how best to fight the war and the increasing bureaucratisation of Rhodesian life – are explored through particular subjects such as the protected village system and the administration of the call-up. These subjects are discussed at length in the chapters where they best fit chronologically. Other themes – the growing tensions within white society, the loss of faith and direction, the erosion of life-styles – recur throughout the book.

The approach is unashamedly eclectic and pragmatic. We have borrowed freely from several academic schools and disciplines, eschewed the formal testing of theories, avoided commentaries on the secondary literature, relied upon a narrative structure to establish direction and coherence, and concentrated on the interpretation of primary evidence. Simply, we have tried to write the sort of history which might appeal to a wider audience and with which we feel most comfortable.

There is no suggestion that this approach is inherently superior. The omissions are legion, and nearly all of them are important. We acknowledge the function of literature surveys, the value of locating arguments within their appropriate historiographical context, and the assistance of comparative and theoretical approaches even where an historian might argue that the particular historical circumstances are – when taken together – unique. It is accepted that scholars should now be concentrating on the victors, not least because in 1980, though many 'true' Rhodesians would disagree, ZANU(PF) clearly represented a majority of those who constituted 95 per cent of the population. We feel justified in giving little space to all those settlement talks, the talks about holding talks, and the diplomatic manoeuvres which consumed so much journalistic energy in the 1970s.[12] We acknowledge that others are better able to explain the dynamics of white politics and the class and sectional relationships of white society, or to write the history of the economy and of the impact of economic sanctions, or to provide a detailed account of the military operations and to assess the performance of the Rhodesian Security Forces. We are also conscious that it is impossible to relate everything of significance – even to our own themes – which occurred between 1970 and 1980. It may be thought, for example, that there is a heavy emphasis on Salisbury, where two-fifths of the white population resided, or on the rural communities, which bore the brunt of the war. Equally, it might be noted that the Rhodesian voices which dominate this book are those of the political, economic, and military leaders of the English-speaking white communities. This emphasis reflects our assessment that their views both represented and influenced the values, attitudes, and behaviour of their communities. In any case, the object is not to write a comprehensive history of all the components of white Rhodesia but to discuss the typical views and behaviour of a substantial sample of its English-speaking members.

To many, the significant omission will be that we largely ignore the black majority. The short explanation is that the Rhodesians did much the same. A longer one rests on two assumptions: that the authors are not primarily concerned to investigate either the structure of white society or the dynamics of its internal and external relationships; and that, while the thought and behaviour of an identifiable group (or race or class) may depend in part on external relationships, the group's responses to war and political change can be understood without exploring those relationships. White Rhodesia is examined as a separate entity because, in the minds of nearly all its inhabitants, it existed as one. Perhaps, by decoding the words and actions, it may be possible to uncover the underlying structures of 'Rhodesia' in the 1970s. Our argument is that anyone who chooses to argue such a case should begin by looking at the evidence produced by the Rhodesians themselves. And, given this stress on Rhodesian perspectives, it would not be logical to tell the story of 'the struggle', or to discuss the full social and economic effects of discrimination and exploitation. The corollary is that Rhodesian rather than Zimbabwean nomenclature is more appropriate. The Rhodesians did not defend Mutare or barricade their homesteads around Chipinge or live suburban lives in Gweru, Masvingo, and Harare. They did those things, and more, in Umtali, Chipinga, Gwelo, Fort Victoria, and Salisbury.

Three main types of Rhodesian sources have been used. First, we have relied principally on published material, most of which is readily available in the National Archives of Zimbabwe: the Salisbury, Bulawayo, and regional press, parliamentary debates, the magazines and occasional papers produced by church, employer, trade union, sporting and cultural associations, real estate returns, official propaganda, institutional histories, government and municipal reports and statistics. Extensive use, for instance, is made of parliamentary debates, a source which is normally associated with a narrowly based political history or dismissed as irrelevant in explaining political action. Our view is that speeches in parliament – and especially those of the RF back-bench – encapsulated the language and sentiments of the RF's constituency, while providing an accessible means for others to test our interpretations. Secondly, we used many unpublished papers, including individual holdings of RF documents, secret or confidential Security Force papers which escaped the incinerator in 1979-80, and the manuscript resources of the National Archives. The authors were unable to consult some of the major collections of political and military papers in South Africa which are held in private hands or for which access is restricted.[13] The unpublished sources which were available provided further clues to the values and assumptions of Rhodesians, and did so without substantially modifying the arguments developed from the published material. Finally, the book also draws upon 147 formal interviews, conducted by the authors and by members of the National Archives. Inevitably, the interviews varied considerably in value. Once again, the striking thing was the way in which the oral evidence amplified or echoed themes present in the published sources. One kind of oral evidence, however, stood on its own. All those conversations – direct or overheard – which took place in the bars or at braais,[14] over morning tea or dinner, at rugby and cricket matches, during bouts of rural hospitality, and when discussing the future of a dilapidated vehicle with a succession of car mechanics, were invaluable for introducing us to, or reminding us of, the ways in which the Rhodesians saw themselves, each other, and the world beyond.[15]

V

A basic theme of this book is that the Rhodesians entered the war in a more divided state than many of them appreciated and that, while they appeared to unite in fighting a lost cause and a losing war, the crises of the 1970s revealed, sharpened, and triggered cleavages within white society. The boast that 'Rhodesians Never Die' was as much an act of defiance as an affirmation of reality or a declaration of intentions. More to the point, the assertion of immortality was at once essential to the promotion of a patriotic sentiment, and one of the great delusions. Clem Tholet, Ian Smith's son-in-law, contributed to these words in 1965 when a friend tried to fulfil Rhodesia's need for 'a semi-patriotic song'. The first version did not take off in the year of UDI. In 1973-4, when Tholet thought that the country needed a rallying call, the song was resurrected, the lyrics were rewritten and it became a hit. 'Rhodesians Never Die' then achieved the status of an unofficial national anthem, and was usually sung with more gusto and conviction than the official one which was approved in 1975.[16] It also formed part of that process whereby the Rhodesians invented an identity and a tradition[17] just in time for both to become irrelevant.

1

'We're all Rhodesians'

It has been said of us Rhodesians that we are a nation wandering around the country with short shorts and short stockings . . . playing rugby, tackling hard, drinking hard, swearing hard and enjoying our outdoor life to the full. There is a bit of a ditty which I would like to recall in case hon. members have not heard it. It goes something like this: Rhodesian born, Rhodesian bred; strong in the arm and thick in the head.[1]

Dennis Divaris, the RF Chief Whip and former Mayor of Salisbury, was amused by the image he depicted. He also recognised that it contained an element of truth. Rhodesians did live in an outdoor society; many of them were 'hearties' who enjoyed the physical pleasures of life, who paid little attention to cerebral or spiritual matters, accepted that they inhabited a 'cultural desert',[2] and cheerfully spurned the fashions and sophistication of more ancient worlds. But most Rhodesians in 1970 preferred to see themselves as warm and generous, courageous and fundamentally decent, and as a people who stood up for the basic Western and Christian values which the British had abandoned, the Communists were trying to undermine, and the black Rhodesians were not yet ready to inherit.

The critics looked at Rhodesia and the Rhodesians in a very different light: they saw a society ruled by a privileged caste which exploited the majority black population and presided over an evil racist system, and they saw a people who were arrogant, complacent and oafish, self-deluded, and hypocritical.

Each of these images is incomplete and partly misleading. Divaris, for example, Rhodesian born and bred, and not notably gifted, was speaking in 1973 in favour of a proposal to allocate part of the proceeds of the State Lottery to the National Arts Foundation. Several MPs supported the amendment, and only one opposed giving more money to the 'arty types'. The government, which had set up the state-funded Foundation in 1971 and now wanted to provide funds for sporting bodies, allowed the amendment to pass. Rhodesia was in fact full of the contradictions and paradoxes which mark every society of human beings. The seemingly bovine might also be a tortured spirit, the cultivated might play rugby, the self-effacing may have been a wife-beater. The grubbiest proclaimed that they were embarked upon a civilising mission, and the noblest accepted the system which discriminated on the grounds of race and salved their consciences by practising charity among the discriminated. Some of these inconsistencies were more apparent than real. They reflected variations in temperament rather than conflicting patterns of behaviour across Rhodesian society. More importantly, the large majority of Rhodesians believed that their Rhodesian-ness supplied a common bond which overrode any individual aberrations (and, to make sure that it did, they ostracised and even persecuted dissenting whites).

What, then, constituted Rhodesian-ness in 1970? Was it pervasive, coherent, and enduring? To what extent did reality conform to the preferred self-image? Above all, just who were the Rhodesians?

II

There are two obvious points to make about the Rhodesians in 1970: there were not many of them, and they had not been in the country very long.[3]

According to the official census there were 228,296 Europeans, 15,153 Coloureds, and 8,965 Asians in Rhodesia on 20 March 1969. The separate African census, taken on 29 April, counted 4,846,930 blacks.[4] The Shona constituted about four-fifths of the African population, and the Ndebele and the Kalanga – who resided mainly in the Matabeleland province – made up the rest. Overall, the blacks outnumbered the whites by 21 : 1. Given the higher African birth rate, and the fact that 50 per cent of blacks were under the age of 15, the proportion of whites was bound to decline, and their absolute numbers were much too low to sustain hopes of maintaining a white state.

Three additional sets of figures suggested that any aspirations for a Rhodesian nationhood, or pretence that one already existed, could not be based on the traditional concept of a long and common history.[5] First, only 40.71 per cent (92,934) of the white population in 1969 were Rhodesian born.[6] A total of 21.83 per cent (49,585) were born in South Africa (including South West Africa), 5.50 per cent (12,556) in other African countries (two-thirds of them in Zambia), and 22.98 per cent (52,468) in the United Kingdom. Secondly, over 30 per cent of the white population either held dual citizenship or were formally citizens of another country. More than half the white population could establish a non-Rhodesian citizenship, and a proportion had already done so, giving them an additional or separate loyalty, and a foreign bolt-hole if necessary. Thirdly, nearly one-third of the 130,613 foreign-born white residents in 1969 had arrived in the country since the 1961 Census, and

nearly one-fifth since UDI in 1965. Since almost half the white population (not including children born in Rhodesia) had entered the country
since the Second World War, their Rhodesian roots went no deeper than
twenty-five years. So, although the proportion of Rhodesian-born was
steadily increasing, the statistical evidence raises questions about the
extent and depth of the commitment to Rhodesia. Founded only in 1890,
and in 1970 populated mainly by recent arrivals, white Rhodesia had to
look beyond history to create a sense of Rhodesian patriotism.

The yearly turnover in the white population, proportionately one of
the highest in Western societies,[7] reinforced the need to manufacture a
Rhodesian-ness. From 1961 to 1969 (inclusive) 49,987 white immigrants
entered Rhodesia, and 92,180 departed. This disturbing rate of emigration suggested a vote of no confidence in the country's future as a white-
ruled state. In 1963-4, the collapse of the Central African Federation, the
clouded future of Rhodesia, and a series of disturbances in the African
townships of Bulawayo and Salisbury caused a net loss of nearly 20,000
whites. A further rise in the emigration rate during 1966 was blamed on
the trauma of UDI. On the other hand, the net gain of 13,000 whites in
1967-9 'proved' that the Rhodesian government had successfully
restored political stability and white morale, although the government
could do little to arrest the alarming and increasing disparity in size
between the two main population groups.

Its best hope lay in attracting more white immigrants, and implanting
a sense of loyalty among the newcomers. Both tasks had become easier
by 1970. Apart from tobacco, the economy was steadily improving, there
had been little obvious disruption to the traditional pleasures of living in
Rhodesia, the threat of 'terrorism' had receded, and the government
seemed well in control of the African population.

Three other factors helped to bind arrivals to their new country. First,
the act of emigrating to Rhodesia after 1965 was itself a form of commitment. Legally, Rhodesia was a rebel colony, and the imposition of economic and various political and social sanctions from 1966 had
consigned it to a pariah status. Admittedly, the British and foreign governments maintained offices in Salisbury, loopholes in the sanctions policy were officially approved on humanitarian or educational grounds,
and the lines remained open for outside contact through Portuguese
Mozambique and South Africa. Nevertheless, the decision to migrate to
Rhodesia, even to take up temporary residence, meant accepting a
degree of ostracism, isolation, and political uncertainty and, possibly,
military service in the future.

Secondly, all newcomers experienced an induction into the
prevailing political culture, including those who entered on short-term
contracts and who had no intention of making a longer commitment.

Neighbours welcomed them all with advice about the 'ways' and 'limitations' of the 'munt'[8] or 'Af', extolled the virtues of living in Rhodesia, and reminded them of the miserable world they had left behind.[9] Ben Metcalfe's *A Guide to Farming in Rhodesia* (its cover adorned by a slim, mini-skirted young white woman standing on a lawn next to a healthy, well-endowed bull) assured prospective farmers that the 'good neighbourliness, in the best Christian and pioneer traditions, is the rule throughout Rhodesian farming communities'.[10] A 'good neighbour' in Centenary, for example, would talk tobacco, labour, and politics to the newcomer, and introduce his family to the varied pleasures offered by the country club. Indoctrination was easy to accomplish in the close-knit world of the rural communities, and through the local farmer organisations (though less necessary, because new farmers were a rarity by 1970). There were also innumerable opportunities in the towns to transmit the values of white Rhodesia: in the hotels and clubs, at the braai and the sundowner,[11] the work place or tea on the patio, the sporting days and the recreational evenings. And there was no escaping the message: the government-controlled radio and television constantly reminded Rhodesians of their collective cause.

Thirdly, there was the shared experience which underlay the political culture. Some writers have made much of this point. George Kay, for example, claimed that a common language, environment, and viewpoint (with regard to Africans) 'have given Europeans in Rhodesia a remarkable solidarity which minimises differences of nationality, culture and class. There is, in fact, a Rhodesian nation of Europeans which has an indisputable identity of its own.'[12] Inevitably, and not improperly, arguments of this kind are circular: common interests create a common loyalty which dissolves the differences which are minimal anyway because of the common interests. They also emphasise one facet of white Rhodesia – the apparent, almost uniform, commitment to segregation and white supremacy – at the expense of ethnic, cultural, and class distinctions which, in a different social context, might have been of overriding importance.

A number of commentators have attempted to explain this strong element of consensus by reference to racial solidarity, or to the fusion of class interests within a racial framework, or to the merging or predominance of particular traditions or cultures. The racial unity argument has the advantage of visibility and logic: that is, the whites *appeared* to act in concert as a self-conscious and privileged racial minority and, in view of that minority position, it made sense for them to do so. It can also be argued that a coalition of classes underpinned this racial affinity: that is, the farmers, small local manufacturers, and skilled workers had developed a common interest in exploiting and segregating the African. This coalition certainly formed the support base of the RF in 1962. It came together to fight international capital which was represented by the mining companies, finance houses, and major secondary industries and which opposed rigid segregationist and supremacist policies in favour of the greater incorporation of blacks as wage-earners, consumers, and middle managers.[13] Yet the alliance was always an uneasy one. Conflict within the support base became a factor in the RF's internal quarrels of the 1970s and helps to explain the ultimate failure of a race-based nationalism to preserve the unity of white Rhodesia during the war years. The shared experience of race increasingly had to compete with the specific experience of occupational groupings trying to protect their own interests.

Whatever its basis, most Rhodesians believed in the existence of a Rhodesian identity. George Kay explained its formation in terms of a confluence of the two distinct – southern African and British – traditions. Barry Schutz stressed that the Europeans arriving in Rhodesia before 1921 'carried the attitudes and expectations of British South Africans rather than those of residential British nationals into their new settlement'. Their attitudes congealed into 'a self-centred "Rhodesian-ness"' which appeared to express itself negatively in opposition to Africans, Afrikaners, or non-British Europeans. Applying a variation of the Hartz thesis – that European fragments of the parent society transferred a particular representation of the metropolitan culture – Schutz described Rhodesia as 'a fragment of the fragment': over time, the whites saw themselves as 'British imperials imbued with the sense of the South African frontier; the South African mission; and the South African cultural idea'.[14] Another significant British 'fragment' consisted of former army officers, civil servants, and farmers from the colonial empires of India, East Africa, and Central Africa. Several of the 'refugees' from British India, who arrived in the Eastern Districts from the late 1940s, soon acquired the sobriquet of 'Bengal Chancers', and identified very strongly with the notion of a perpetual white supremacy.

Rhodesia in 1970 was even more of a heterogeneous society than the one McEwan analysed in the early 1960s.[15] Ethnic and religious loyalties were important to a number of white Rhodesians who plainly felt isolated and uncomfortable within the Anglo-Celt hegemony. The Afrikaners, the Jews, and the Greeks were the most prominent of the outsiders. The 1969 Census recorded that there were 18,528 members of the Dutch Reformed Church (representing 8.12 per cent of the white population), 5,194, (2.28 per cent) who professed the Hebrew religion,[16] and 3,784 (1.66 per cent) adherents of the Greek Orthodox Church. Members of these communities frequently disagreed among themselves – a practice traditional and notorious among the Afrikaners,[17] and prompted among the Greeks by differences in origin and by the success of some families in business[18] – but the Jews, Afrikaners, and the Greeks remained collectively conscious of their separation from the mainstream. Hodder-Williams has demonstrated both the importance of the ethnic divide in the Marandellas district (where some 20 per cent of the whites were of Afrikaner stock), and its declining impact in the 1960s when the pressures for white unity overrode some of the discord and separation.[19] The war in the 1970s probably accentuated this process of dissolving English-Afrikaner differences, though many English speakers noted how the Afrikaners were often the first to pull out and migrate south when the war intensified in their area.[20]

The Rhodesians were not, therefore, of common stock, although most were English speaking. They came from different cultural backgrounds, although the colonial, South African, and British inheritance of the English speakers had a longer-term common origin. Their present needs and not their past bound them together in 1970, and committed them to maintain white supremacy and racial separation. Before it can be determined whether or how far this commitment constituted the distinguishing mark of Rhodesian-ness, other factors which affected the Rhodesians' outlook in 1970 warrant examination: namely, where they worked, and where and how they lived.

III

The Rhodesians were not alone among colonials in propagating myths about their pioneering past, or in associating their national identity with conquests over the 'bush' and its inhabitants. Nor did they seem aware of the absurdity of townsmen proclaiming rural values. The fact remained that, like some other colonial societies, Rhodesia soon became highly urbanised. By 1951 two-thirds of all whites lived in eleven towns or cities, and over half of them in either Salisbury or Bulawayo. By 1969 nearly four-fifths of all whites lived in the same eleven towns, almost two-thirds lived in the two major cities, and over two-fifths in Salisbury.[21] In addition, there were thirty-five villages and smaller towns in 1969 – with European populations ranging from 50 to 1,000 – which were mostly mining, administrative, or service centres for the adjoining rural areas.[22]

Each province, district, town, or city seemed to inspire its own sense of identity and loyalty. On suitable occasions Ian Smith liked to call himself a 'white Matabele'. So did Sir Robert Tredgold, a former Chief Justice, whose deepest affections were reserved for Bulawayo and the nearby Matopos Hills, his spiritual refuge from a temporal world he found increasingly distasteful.[23] A proud and envious provincial and

TABLE 1.1. *European Population in the Cities and Towns, 1969*

Town	European population (African population in brackets)	
Bulawayo	49,703	(187,270)
Fort Victoria	2,528	(8,500)
Gatooma	2,319	(22,330)
Gwelo	8,347	(36,840)
Marandellas	2,108	(8,790)
Que Que/Redcliff	4,630	(36,320)
Salisbury	97,764	(280,090)
Shabani	1,553	(14,170)
Sinoia	1,557	(11,560)
Umtali	8,368	(36,300)
Wankie	2,163	(17,980)
TOTAL	181,040	(660,150)

Source: Census of Population, 1969.

rural world looked upon Salisbury as 'Bamba Zonke' (take all), an unhealthy bloodsucker populated by inferior types. Some of Salisbury's own residents – living in the peri-urban areas – angrily endorsed these sentiments in 1970 following the government's decision to absorb the separate Town Management Boards into Greater Salisbury.[24] In 1971, amid some merriment but with underlying determination, and a clear image of their separate character and fealty, the white residents of Gwelo and Umtali celebrated the elevation of their towns into cities.[25]

Rhodesia's rural communities were preoccupied with very practical matters: the prospect of a good rainy season beginning each November, the rising input costs for agriculture, the state of commodity prices, the availability of spares, the now perennial questions of farm viability and crop diversification, the level of taxes and of other government and council charges. There were meetings to attend, of the local Farmers' Association, or of a drama group, or of an RF branch. There were the personal and family matters, the supervision of farm clinics and schools, and the visits to the local country club. They were busy little worlds, even without the intrusion of the 'big' issues of race and politics. They were also the worlds which the rural whites defined as the 'Rhodesia' they sought to defend in the 1970s.

Work provided another focus of identification and division. The 1969 Census classified 102,741 Europeans as 'economically active', of whom one-quarter were employed in the government service, one-third were women, and one-fifth could be described as 'skilled artisans'.[26] A further classification may be seen in Table 1.2. The male artisans formed the largest single occupational group (21,507) and were employed mainly as bricklayers or carpenters (2,546), electrical tradesmen (2,347), machine mechanics (2,127), mechanical fitters (3,466), and transport equipment and plant operators (1,627). A critical section of the machine mechanics group consisted of the motor mechanics (1,783) whose capacity to revive and maintain older vehicles would prove invaluable in sustaining the Rhodesian way of life. Perhaps, however, the most significant development was the growing number of 'production supervisors and general foremen'. This expansion was most obvious in the construction industry where journeymen were assuming supervisory roles over semi-skilled and unskilled black labour, a trend associated with the fragmentation of skilled jobs into parts suitable for cheaper rates.

TABLE 1.2. *European Occupations, 1969*

Occupation	Percentage
Professional and technical	16.9
Administrative and managerial	5.1
Clerical and protective	34.2
Sales workers	10.2
Service workers	3.4
Agricultural, forestry, and related	7.0
Production and related	21.5
Unclassified	1.7
	100.0

Source: Census of Population, 1969.

The female workers were concentrated in the clerical, service, and sales areas and, constituting 62 per cent of the service and 56 per cent of the clerical workers, were employed mainly as teachers, nurses, bookkeepers, telephone operators, secretaries, typists, hairdressers, beauticians, and shop assistants. With the exception of medical practitioners and pharmacists, where women constituted 18 and 31 per cent respectively, the top professions were overwhelmingly male. There were just nine female lawyers, two engineers, and 249 employed in administrative and managerial positions (compared to 321, 1,196, and 4,994 males respectively). The average annual earnings for females were much lower than those for males. In 1969 84 per cent of employed white women, compared with 21 per cent of employed white men, earned less than $2,160 p.a., the highest income grade where females outnumbered males.

The government service was quite open about discriminating on the basis of gender, especially in relation to married women. Single women in established posts were always given preference over married women in promotion and were entitled to better leave, tenure, and holiday benefits. Until 1971, a woman who married while occupying a permanent post in the civil service was required to resign or was discharged. If she wished to stay on, she had to accept a temporary position and the concomitant poorer leave, holiday, and promotion benefits or prospects. An amendment in 1971 allowed a married woman to be placed on the permanent staff – each case would be considered on its merits – but, whereas other officers were required to serve a probationary period of just two years, a married woman who applied for a permanent position was required to serve five years. The Minister for the Public Service explained that a woman had 'to demonstrate over a period of time that she can successfully combine a career and her responsibilities as a housewife'. Her 'prime duty', he said, 'is to her child and to her home'.[27]

The existing histories of white Rhodesia have largely ignored gender discrimination. White women were so much better off than black men that their own inequality seemed inconsequential. More attention has been given to the broader class interests of white labour. Approximately one-quarter of the white work-force qualified as 'recognised employees' under the Industrial Conciliation Act of 1959, and about one-third of eligible workers belonged to a trade union.[28] Formally registered unions were usually organised vertically by industry, and not according to occupation.[29] Each union was required by law to represent only those interests for which it was registered, and the multiracial unions were divided into sections which gave more votes to skilled workers. This 1959 Act was amended in 1971, principally to give the President power to prohibit strikes or lock-outs which were considered to be against the public interest. Although the amended Act appeared to be directed at African trade unions, the white unions regarded provisions of the original bill as tyrannical, and the (white) Trade Union Congress persuaded the Minister of Labour to remove a general prohibition on all strike action.[30] white unionists still felt constrained by informal pressure to avoid strike action during Rhodesia's fight against economic sanctions. Consequently, the white unions were not as militant as their counterparts elsewhere, a fact noted by Howard Bloomfield, a past president of the Trade Union Congress and the President of the Associated Mineworkers, who distinguished Rhodesia's 'responsible' European-led unions from those in Britain with their record for strikes and demarcation disputes.[31]

Even so, there were occasions when the white unions stood up to their private or government employers. When its three-year wage agreement expired in late 1968 the Rhodesia Railway Workers' Union (RRWU), representing some 7,000 members and twenty-eight branches, sought a flat and substantial wage increase.[32] The aim was to offset the cost-of-living increases which were allegedly causing the emergence of a new 'poor white' class in Rhodesia.[33] A similar wage claim was also lodged by the Amalgamated Engineering Union (AEU) on behalf of its 1,500 members. Negotiations between the two unions and the Railways broke down and the matter was referred to the Industrial Tribunal. On 21 October 1969, after months of hearing evidence, including a submission from thirty-four wives of white workers saying they could not afford to feed their families, the Tribunal awarded a backdated increase of 8.5 per cent to all members of both unions. Pat Lennon, the General Secretary of the RRWU, pointed out that a percentage rise was of little benefit to lower-paid workers. The subsequent talks between the RRWU and the Railways collapsed on 3 November and the men began a work-to-rule. The Minister of Transport, Brigadier Andrew Dunlop, introduced Emergency regulations which soon forced a full return to work. Dunlop regarded trade unionism as the antithesis of Westminster democracy, and said later that he refused to allow the nation to be held at 'pistol point' for the benefit of 'a few'.[34] He was supported by his Prime Minister, who warned the unions against intimidating the government, and by the 'patriots' in agriculture, industry, and mining who wanted their goods moved. Confronted by this coalition, the unions accepted an offer which came into operation on 1 January 1970.

The government restored calm by withdrawing the Emergency regulations in February 1970. It also helped that, when the imperious Dunlop retired from politics, he was replaced in the negotiations by the more conciliatory Ian McLean, the Minister of Labour. Resentment within the RRWU was further diverted by an absorbing internal power struggle initiated by the engine drivers who were determined to protect the footplate from the introduction of African firemen paid at cheaper rates. They also wanted to maintain their own pay levels and promotion prospects and to combat the Railways' plan for the single manning of diesels. Convinced that the RRWU was not interested in backing the 'aristocracy' of the industry, the drivers formed their own union in 1971 – the Rhodesian Association of Locomotive Engineers – and engaged in a long battle with the Industrial Registrar and the RRWU to obtain separate recognition under the Industrial Conciliation Act.[35]

Internal union politics were certainly a distraction but some deep-seated fears – which surfaced during the railway dispute – continued to preoccupy and unite many white workers. Some elements in the RRWU and the AEU never lost their conviction that the government had failed to safeguard the position of the European in their industries and, in 1970, they helped to form the right-wing Republican Alliance to oppose the RF.[36] The critical issue was African advancement into unskilled, semi-skilled, and even skilled 'European jobs'. White labour's greatest fear was that employers would continue to 'Africanise' jobs (and, thereby, cheapen them) by fragmenting particular tasks and paying 'African' rates for the unskilled or semi-skilled fragments. Industry leaders replied that the severe shortage in skilled labour could be minimised by further fragmenting of jobs and employing fewer skilled blacks.[37] A conference on manpower in early 1971 nearly broke up after the Associated Chambers of Commerce of Rhodesia (ACCOR) presented a paper claiming that there was a full year's shortfall of manpower to satisfy current demands which could not be met except by further fragmentation.[38] Howard Bloomfield later reminded the government that the white trade unionists had voted the RF into power in 1962 because of its promises to uphold the rate for the job and to oppose fragmentation.[39]

Like most white union leaders, Bloomfield had accepted the notion of African advancement into skilled jobs, provided that those jobs remained intact and that blacks were paid the award rate for journeymen. The lesser-skilled unionists and the RF's right wing wanted to protect all 'European' jobs. John Newington, an ex-RAF Squadron Leader and an MP for a Bulawayo seat since 1962, campaigned relentlessly to preserve the jobs of semi-skilled and unskilled whites – such as wagon examiners, handymen, and storemen – and to ensure that they were paid 'European' wages.[40] Newington attacked the 'pure mercenaries of commerce and industry' and 'protagonists of pure profit' who preferred to employ blacks at cheaper rates. He accused them of forcing what he called the lower-paid '30 per cent' to leave Rhodesia. The aim, he told the RF's annual congress in 1970, was not simply to save a particular job for the skilled artisan but to ensure 'the permanent establishment of the European in Rhodesia'.[41]

The government tried to steer a course between the employers and the unions, and between the employers and its own right wing. Ian McLean, who eventually lined up with the RAP in 1977, was prepared to compromise. The Minister of Labour told the RF congress in 1970 that the inspectors were doing their best to ensure the observance of employment regulations, including the non-employment of under-qualified blacks at cheap rates. The problem was that the government could not afford the army of inspectors needed to ensure 100 per cent compliance. It was obliged to tolerate fragmentation where technological improvement had made it possible, and where industry needed more labour to fulfil its orders. In 1972 McLean claimed that the problem was not one of finding jobs for the unskilled – when there were just 180 whites registered as unemployed each month – but of finding skilled workers to fill the 8-9 per cent vacancy rate.[42]

The owners and managers of capital usually listed this scarcity of skilled labour as one of their main concerns about the post-UDI economy. They also complained to the government about the shortage of foreign exchange, high input costs, and low returns.[43] To an extent, however, their criticisms were offset by the remarkable solidarity of the business, farming, and mining communities in seeking to combat economic sanctions.

Geoff Ellman-Brown explained this commitment in terms of his Rhodesian patriotism. Ellman-Brown was born in Bulawayo in 1910, had attended school at Plumtree, and trained as an accountant. Denying that he was a starry-eyed liberal, he had nonetheless been a minister in the governments of Garfield Todd (1953-8) and Sir Edgar whitehead (1958-62) which had preceded the advent of the RF and which were notably more disposed to African advancement. He refused to join the RF and, unlike many of his friends in the business community, 'never voted for them, never in my life'.[44] By 1970 Ellman-Brown was a company director with interests in sugar, tobacco, banking, insurance, and cement. He was also a principal figure in sanctions-busting operations, and the government rewarded him with the Independence Commemorative Decoration (ICD) for rendering valuable service to Rhodesia. Ellman-Brown insisted that he had acted 'because of the country' and not for the RF, and remarked that 'the main theme of the sanctions period was the amazing unity of people trying to beat sanctions'.[45] His ambivalence was, in fact, typical of many well-placed and more liberal-minded businessmen who propped up the Smith government by successfully breaking the economic blockade. They knew that UDI was a mistake and a disaster, they knew that political change was inevitable and not wholly undesirable, yet they were also patriots who could not accept surrender in the economic war and who were, in the later 1970s, to resent and fear 'Marxist terrorism'.

Although their Rhodesian-ness drew them together in opposition to sanctions, and bound them closer in the later 1970s in seeking a negotiated peace, the owners and managers of capital remained divided over other issues in 1970. The customary distinction drawn between domestic and foreign capital, between the farmers and small manufacturing on the one hand, and mining, finance, and major industrial concerns on the other, was just one and not always the most significant division. Capital was also split over politics. A minority of leading businessmen, including the locally recruited managers of foreign capital, carried their opposition to UDI and their demands for a settlement into opposition politics during the elections of 1970 and 1974. Inevitably, too, there was competition between the various sectors for foreign exchange allocations and import licences. The mining, industrial, and commercial interests looked enviously upon the farmers, and upon the special relationship between the government and the Rhodesia National Farmers' Union (RNFU). That relationship was founded on the close ties between the farmers and the RF, and enhanced by the recognition that the farming communities had borne the brunt of sanctions and that they embodied 'the deepest feelings of nationalism and love of country'.[46] As a result, the farmers obtained financial assistance to cover everything from drought relief to price support.

Competition was also evident within individual sectors. Agriculture was undergoing another crisis in 1970 and there was an 'overall air of despondency'.[47] Less than half the registered white farmers were making a profit, and the resulting tensions were evident at the branch meetings of some eighty Farmers' Associations, and at the annual congresses of the RNFU, the Rhodesia Tobacco Association (RTA), and of the newer commodity associations concerned with cattle, grain, and dairying. The poorer growers criticised the wealthy, commodity representatives attacked each other, the supporters of private enterprise denounced bureaucratic interference and the government's production, pricing, and marketing arrangements, and the farmers grumbled about their own leadership.[48] One internal row became so serious in 1971 that militant ranchers reportedly wanted the Matabeleland branch to secede from the RNFU over the issue of providing cheap stock feed.[49] The tobacco farmers were also sharply divided in 1970-1 over the question of whether to maintain controlled marketing or to restore free auctions.[50] This argument spilt over into a debate about the newly formed Agricultural Development Authority (allegedly 'the Fairy Godmother' of agriculture) which was feared by individuals inside and outside the industry as a socialist measure.

Agriculture politics were both time consuming and divisive in 1970, and individual farmers and their organisations were so absorbed by everyday problems, and by the broader farming issues, that they hardly bothered about the political matters which exercised the minds of outsiders. The same was largely true of the other sectors of the economy. More importantly, perceptions of 'Rhodesia' were being filtered through different experiences. Occupation, locality, and the patriotic war against sanctions were among the factors determining those experiences. At one level, the effect was a heightened sense of Rhodesian-ness. At another, the interpretation and intensity of Rhodesian-ness varied quite markedly.

IV

For all their differences, Rhodesians shared one objective in 1970: to enjoy their way of life. Their understanding of what it entailed, and of how it should be defended, might have diverged. Some felt guilty about its implied racial exclusiveness, or deplored the apparent materialism of its devotees, but there is no evidence of any Europeans emigrating to escape the climate, the servants, the jacarandas, the cheap beef, or the avocados.

Climate was probably the constant factor in all the eulogies about living in Rhodesia: 'Dawn broke on one of those lovely mornings when we pondered on the gift that is bestowed on us in Rhodesia – crisp, bright sunlight, and all around us peace.'[51] Ben Metcalfe pointed out that, despite its location within the tropics, Rhodesia rarely experienced the combination of high temperatures and humidity. The seasons varied from a mild winter of cool nights and sunny days extending from May to August, to the warmer and then hot days of September-October to the (erratic) wet and warm months of November to March, followed by a brief and mild autumn. Metcalfe promised the newcomer that there would be sunshine 'on almost every day of the year'.[52] Although the farmers might have preferred a guarantee of rain during the wet season the immigrant from Britain would probably have forgiven the unreliable rainfall in exchange for the bright days, clean air, and, above all, for the sunshine. It mattered, of course, where people lived. Anyone residing in the lowveld (below 600 metres) in the south-east around Triangle could expect extreme heat in October whereas people could live and work throughout the year in the highveld (above 1,200 metres), on either side of a line stretching north from Bulawayo through Salisbury to Umtali, and have little ground for complaint.[53]

Next to the climate the Rhodesians boasted most about their standard of living, usually overlooking its dependence upon cheap black labour. Potential immigrants were told of the good wages, low prices and taxes, minimal inflation, and good quality housing.[54] While it is difficult to make accurate evaluations of qualities of life, the Rhodesians themselves never doubted that they were better off than the large majority of people who lived in Western societies. Moreover, the superior material circumstances were enhanced by the intangible benefits of removing oneself from 'a troubled world, greatly beset by the vexatious problems of the twentieth century'.[55]

The official propaganda, designed to discourage emigration as much as attract new white immigrants, neglected to mention that access to, and enjoyment of, the material comforts varied considerably according to income, social status, and gender. These variations were highlighted in the 1968 survey conducted by the Central Statistical Office (CSO) which collected 598 budgets from urban white households throughout the country.[56] Each household provided two returns: one covering a daily record of purchases and the other providing general information relating to the family, sources of income, characteristics of the dwelling, regular expenditure, and irregular payments. According to the survey, the average household contained four persons, headed predominantly by artisans or professional people and with a monthly income of $374.61 (the average in Salisbury was $410 and in Bulawayo $354). Some 30 per cent of households received less than $280, and were categorised by the CSO in the lower two of five income groups, both of which spent beyond their earnings in the survey period. Families in these lower categories which, on average, employed 0.9 of a servant, also lived sparingly compared to the 34 per cent of households which earned more than $400 a month and employed 1.5 servants.

The budget surveys, and real-estate statistics,[57] indicate that there were very clear social distinctions in Salisbury. The railway line marked an obvious division. South of the tracks, the white suburbs of Hatfield, Waterfalls, Lochinvar, or Southerton were located near the African townships or Coloured areas. In 1970 the average price for a house in Hatfield, a more desirable location than Waterfalls, was $10,466. Such houses might have attracted first-home buyers, newly married couples, or artisan families who could afford solid three-bedroom bungalows sitting on the acre of land which was the minimum size prescribed by the Salisbury municipality for blocks not connected to mains sewerage.

At the other extreme, across the railway line, the houses in Highlands, Mount Pleasant, and Borrowdale more easily fitted the familiar image of white Rhodesia: large blocks of land, sweeping driveways up the front garden, a pool and perhaps a tennis court, possibly a two-storey home, and certainly more spacious living and sleeping areas. The average sale price in Highlands in 1971 was $18,820. It is a measure of the suburb's social diversity that two of the forty properties sold in 1971 raised over $30,000 each and another three cost less than $9,000. Even this superior white suburb in Salisbury contained housing which was barely adequate for a family of five and which, including some of the mansions in Kew Drive or Orange Grove Drive, were furnished in a style reminiscent of stolid lower middle-class homes of Britain in the inter-war years. Nevertheless, a home in Highlands remained a social aspiration.

More 'typical' were the middling suburbs of the west and the northwest: from the charming Marlborough with its wide and quiet streets and its self-contained centre, to Mabelreign where civil servants, shopkeepers, and artisan families congregated in modern houses on smaller blocks connected to mains sewerage, to the solid and unpretentious homes of Belvedere and Milton Park. Real-estate agents classified Marlborough, where the average price for house sales in 1971 was $13,760, as 'middle of the range' in Salisbury. The most densely populated white suburbs were Avondale or the adjoining Avenues (just north of the city centre) which, though containing some quite substantial mansions, consisted mainly of small bungalows and single- and two-bedroom flats considered ideal for bachelors, widows, and retired folk.

A brief tour of Salisbury's suburbs in 1970, or a perusal of its rental rates or house prices, casts doubt on some of the glib assumptions about lifestyles of urban white Rhodesians. It is true that the average detached house over all the suburbs contained five rooms, and that just 4 per cent contained three rooms or less. Given that 80 per cent of Salisbury's whites went to work in private cars or trucks (three-quarters of them as drivers), it is reasonable to conclude that there was a high level of car ownership.[58] Yet Salisbury's residents did not all live on large blocks. Most who did so lived in suburbs affected by the municipal regulations relating to water-borne sewerage. George Kay noted in a 1974 article that the suburb of Mount Pleasant had 157 detached houses, 85 pools, and no block smaller than one acre. He may not have taken account of the sewerage by-laws or the fact that Mount Pleasant was one of the wealthier suburbs.[59] Even then, just under half of the houses in that suburb did not have pools. In Salisbury as a whole where, in 1969, there were 20,337 detached houses and 6,563 flats occupied by Europeans, one estimate placed the total number of pools at 7,500.[60] Arguably, therefore, life for Salisbury's Rhodesians was certainly comfortable but not uniform,[61] and, for the majority, was not luxurious, except in comparison to life in the African townships.

Social status and access to wealth were, in turn, affected by considerations of gender. Apart from the legal and customary restrictions on employment opportunities and remuneration, white women were also disadvantaged by the divorce laws.[62] The Married Persons' Property Act of 1959 had removed the husband's absolute marital power under the old Roman-Dutch law, and the Act protected a married woman's property from the fraudulent, negligent, or incompetent actions of her husband. Yet, in the absence of a prior agreement establishing a community of property, a woman was not entitled to any assets obtained through her husband's income, had no rights derived from running the marital home, and was forced to bargain with her husband at the time of the divorce. Further, until 1970, a woman not born in Rhodesia, or who was not a Rhodesian citizen, could not obtain a divorce in the Rhodesian courts.

The privileged lifestyle of a white woman was also circumscribed by explicit or subtle reminders that she lived – however willingly – in a male world. She remained dependent upon her husband's monthly earnings and social position, and upon values and perspectives determined by men. A magazine, popular among women in the early 1970s, observed that a wife would be forced to find a job if her husband earned less than $500 a month. Otherwise, she could not afford new dresses, 'hairdos', or visits to the cinema and theatre.[63] No magazine encouraged women who wanted to create an independent career or to assert themselves within the male world. The three women MPs who sat in the parliament between 1922 and 1970, and the many more involved in local government, were duly acknowledged in a book published in 1976 to commemorate the women of Rhodesia.[64] But no mention was made of the more traditional and accepted role of women in white politics: they were expected to answer the telephones, address letters, attend meetings, and sit for hours outside polling stations. The men ran the political parties, determined policy, held the important offices, and selected themselves for parliament.[65] The received wisdom overseas – that the RF cabinet consulted their wives over UDI or constitutional talks, and that Ian Smith was influenced by his more right-wing wife[66] – was probably a fiction. In Rhodesia, as elsewhere, it was expected that men would dominate the public domain.

While exceptional women did exceptional things, most adult white women accepted their roles as wives and mothers. Their principal form of work was house management: that is, white women presided over households where blacks did most of the tedious jobs and often minded their employer's children. Superficially, it seemed a lazy existence: playing cards or tennis, gossiping and drinking tea, shopping, arranging flowers, and organising the servants. The farmers' wives would hardly have recognised themselves in this picture. Nor would the thousands of women in the rural and urban areas who did some of their talking in the Women's Institutes, where they also busied themselves with charitable works. There were over fifty institutes operating throughout the country in 1970, with a nominal (predominantly white) membership exceeding 20,000. During one month branch members sold cakes and needlework, collected toys and clothes for African children, discussed the problems of deserted wives, senior citizens, and the fate of children affected by divorce, attended lectures on skin cancer and African customs, and participated in subcommittees concerned with health, education, social welfare, or international questions.[67] The Institutes never doubted that women had a vital role to play in Rhodesia. Their President told the annual congress on 28 July 1970 that women must use their role as wives and mothers, and as voters, to create a world where tolerance, justice, and humanity prevailed. Women should also have 'the courage' to stand for public office.[68]

A number of Rhodesian women did object to the more blatant presentation of themselves as sex objects. The ladies of Umtali – Presbyterian, Anglican, Catholic, Methodist, Dutch Reformed, and Greek Orthodox – protested in mid-1970 against the 'shameless' writing and photography which depicted a 'false image of womanhood'. They sought 'to add dignity and purity to the attributes of "charm and appeal" as the interpretation of true femininity'.[69] It was an uphill task. The average Rhodesian male was either unconsciously or unashamedly 'sexist'. When discussing the inclusion of certain feminine items on a list of permitted imports, a senior civil servant argued that a man who returned home after working overtime to be greeted by 'a most unattractive-looking old hag of a wife', might ask himself 'What the hell am I doing?' The case was unanswerable: cosmetics, stockings, and foundation garments had to be removed from the list of prohibited imports.[70] Cruder examples may be found in the popular magazines, and especially the union journals, where women were depicted as nagging wives or shapely blondes, as husband-seekers, gold-diggers, or omnipresent mothers-in-law. The jokes belonged to a genre which has amused generations of Western males:

She: Don't you think that blonde looks terrible in that low-cut dress?
He: Not as far as I can see.[71]

The quality of the health service, and a healthy lifestyle, were always placed high among the virtues of the Rhodesian way of life. Again, comparisons are difficult, and contrasts within Rhodesia itself are soon evident. One of the familiar images of white Rhodesians, and one of their own fond illusions, was of a society composed of very fit people. The familiar sights of young men with 'beer guts', of older men straining the seams of safari suits, and of chain-smoking wives with deplorable postures, rarely registered with anyone outside the professional health services. The Secretary of Health was not even sure about the general fitness of the very young. A survey of six Bulawayo schools in 1966 revealed that 60 per cent of boys and 38 per cent of girls had a poor posture, and in 1970 the Secretary urged the introduction of remedial gymnastics. He wrote, 'if present trends in over-nourishment and bad posture continue in the European schoolchild the future Rhodesian will be overweight, flat-footed, knock-kneed and round-shouldered'.[72]

The Secretary was also aware that white society was not much interested in preventative medicine. The dominant concern was to create and maintain curative care in the form of public hospitals, private practice, and flourishing medical aid societies. There was no equivalent of the British National Health Service, a factor which may explain the steady migration of British doctors to the larger urban centres in Rhodesia.

Government subsidies and private insurance funds met over half the cost of European hospital care.[73] whites-only ambulance services, private hospitals, a full range of dental, eye, and ear specialists and of specialist physicians, surgeons, and anaesthetists, and various forms of charitable assistance, completed an enviable medical service for urban Europeans.

Their habits ensured that they would die of causes common to other modern European societies. According to the 1970 *Annual Report* of the Ministry of Health, the two principal killers were cardio- and cerebral vascular disease (accounting for 43 per cent of all registered white deaths) and various forms of cancer (18 per cent). Infant mortality – a high 35 :1,000 in 1950 – had fallen to 19 : 1,000 in 1970 and was continuing to decline. The African rate was much higher (somewhere between 120 and 220 : 1,000) because of the incidence of gastro-enteritis, measles, pneumonia, and nutritional diseases.

The third greatest killer of whites in 1970 was motor vehicle accidents: 120 died on the road in 1970, amounting to 7 per cent of registered white deaths. One newspaper claimed that, on a per-capita basis, there were seven fatal road accidents in Rhodesia for each one in the United States.[74] Apart from Africans walking into (or not properly evading) oncoming traffic in rural areas and on city streets, the main perpetrators and victims of these accidents were the whites. Official reports and the press blamed high speed, intoxication and dangerous driving, a lack of courtesy, and antiquated or inadequately serviced motor vehicles. Newspaper editors, government ministers, the police, and the Automobile Association alternatively pleaded with drivers and condemned them but, until the resumption of petrol rationing in 1974, there was no statistical evidence of saner behaviour.[75]

Nor did the warnings about alcohol consumption appear to make any difference. Twenty-one whites died of cirrhosis of the liver in 1970. A local journalist claimed to have evidence that one in fourteen adult Rhodesians was a confirmed alcoholic needing special medical attention, and quoted an unnamed doctor who said that alcohol was Rhodesia's drug problem.[76] No one was too bothered about cigarettes. The Surgeon-General's report in the United States and all the other published evidence about the effects of smoking might deter individuals, but tobacco remained an important local crop. An editorial in the *Rhodesian Tobacco Journal* for June 1971 suggested that the industry was unmoved by the scientific findings. Referring to 'the so-called evidence of tests on dogs and chimpanzees', the editor insisted that 'no experiments to date had proved a connection between cancer and smoking'. Obviously, in a society where the patriotic tobacco growers had already been battered by sanctions, it would have been treasonable and quite insensitive to have mounted an anti-smoking campaign.

Rhodesians' pride in their health service was matched by their esteem for the education system. They liked visitors to note the corporate spirit of their schools, the cultivation of self-discipline, and the involvement of staff, parents, and pupils in extramural activities.[77] A school magazine editor drew the 'inescapable' conclusion that 'Rhodesian schools – and Chaplin High School in particular – are turning out more pupils each year with a higher academic knowledge than the rest of the world'.[78] Chaplin's most noted 'old boy' – Ian Douglas Smith – would not have disputed this assessment. Convinced that they already constituted an educated elite[79] – largely the result of tight immigration requirements and the rejection of unskilled whites – the Rhodesians looked upon their schools as bastions of traditional values and standards.[80] Not everyone agreed that the desirable standards should be mainly academic. J. A. C. Houlton, the long-serving Secretary of Education, regarded the 'tyranny of formal grammar' and the 'public demand for academic paper qualifications' as barriers to educational enterprise.[81] Houlton argued that it was less important for white apprentices to pass Form II English and Arithmetic than to develop character, good conduct, technical skills, and patience. This view was not shared by Rhodesian employers and parents who wanted the government to maintain the primacy of the 'Three Rs'. High academic standards and moral uprightness would together protect Rhodesia from the marauding liberalism of the 1960s.[82]

Arguments about the desirable emphasis of white education continued into the 1970s, sustained in part by the growing concern that white school-leavers were not interested in becoming artisans.[83] Yet few whites would have disagreed with A. P. Smith, the Minister of Education, when he told the Senate on 5 August 1970 that the 'first priority' was to provide a system of education for Europeans, Asians, and Coloureds 'which is as good as, or better than, can be obtained elsewhere'.[84] In keeping with this approach, recurrent spending on European, Asian, and Coloured education in 1970 amounted to $234-9 per child compared to the $24-48 spent on each African pupil. European children were also generously treated in terms of class sizes. In 1970 there were 248 government and 32 independent primary schools for whites with an average teacher-pupil ratio of 1 : 29 (compared with the average ratio in African primary schools of 1 : 42). These figures compare very favourably with other Western educational systems. So do the examination results: of the 4,248 whites who left school in 1970, 11 per cent had attained two or more A levels.[85]

Compulsory schooling for whites until the age of 15 and the introduction of the O and A level system were factors in raising the general educational standards of white children.[86] Moreover, as there was no real distinction between the values and standards adopted in the state and private schools, there was a common educational experience.[87] Whether Rhodesian children received an education appropriate for living in Africa is another matter. The 1968 *Annual Report* was concerned about the increased enrolment of Portuguese-, Greek-, and Italian-born children and noted only in passing that just 206 children in ten primary schools were learning Shona. In 1970 the Department made some suggestions for studying history at primary level. Standard V pupils were expected to spend half a year on southern Africa – which itself was a considerable advance – but just two of the ten sections of the course were devoted to Africans. The Ndebele featured prominently; the Shona were largely ignored; the personalities for special study were Van Riebeeck, Piet Retief, Livingstone, Rhodes, Jameson, Beit, and Kingsley Fairbridge; and the 'Builders of Rhodesia' were listed as Rhodes, Rudd, Jameson, and Beit.[88] Racial issues were not considered relevant for an inter-house contest on the 'contemporary scene' at Fort Victoria High School in August 1970: instead, the subjects listed were violence, greed, drug-taking, the 'insidious' influence of the mass media, and the 'hoax' of pseudo-intellectualism.[89]

The whites who attended government schools at any time before the late 1970s were, therefore, being educated in partial isolation from their own environment. The society, which was perfectly capable of adopting the new maths and new methods of teaching science at the end of the 1960s, had sent and would continue to send white Rhodesians into the world equipped with abstract ideals of citizenship and a muscular Christianity but without a sensitivity towards, or understanding of, their immediate region.

The University College of Rhodesia, situated in Mount Pleasant, Salisbury, might have rectified some of the deficiencies.[90] For one thing, it was multiracial: in 1970 one-third of its students were black of whom most were enrolled in the humanities and the social sciences. For another, it was able to employ more outsiders and keep in closer touch with the world beyond Rhodesia. But the institution had its own problems after UDI: the RF government ordered deportations of radical staff; RF back-benchers kept attacking 'the little Kremlin on the hill' as a centre of subversion; there were several strikes, dismissals, boycotts, and expulsions; and British critics of UDI campaigned to sever the connections between the University College and the Universities of London and of Birmingham. By 1970 the whites were moving out of the student residences which were becoming black islands in the northern white suburbs. The multiracial dream of the post-war liberals had not survived the tensions of the post-UDI years. More whites wanted to go to South

Africa for higher education, partly because the M-level was sufficient to obtain entry, partly in some cases to escape the supposedly uncongenial atmosphere on the Rhodesian campus, and partly because South African universities could offer a better range of courses and, it was assumed, more acceptable qualifications. At the same time, the University College was finding it harder to attract and hold quality staff – especially in the areas outside the humanities and social sciences – and more of its recruits in the early 1970s were white males who had failed to secure appointments or promotions elsewhere.

V

Defenders of the Rhodesian way of life believed that their lifestyles were at once an advertisement and a fortress for the values which other Western societies had forsaken or neglected. The British exemplified the moral decline of the West: they had abandoned friends who had rallied to the colours in 1914 and 1939; they had lost their faith in democracy and in themselves; and they had given up the fight against communism, atheism, and permissiveness.[91] In contrast, the Rhodesians had preserved the finest of the traditional personal values: restraint, honesty, morality, and a respect for the family. The Rhodesians could have fun without resorting to filth and could enjoy decent culture without taking their clothes off in public. They were proud to be Christian and proud to represent Civilisation in Africa.

They denied, however, that they were dull or provincial. Critics of the arts in Rhodesia, who said they were, usually provoked the response that Rhodesia's cultural achievements were equal to, if not better than, the rest of the world. Locals and visitors were reminded that 'experts' had declared they had not seen better performances in London's West End. In 1970 the Reps company in Salisbury invited Paul Massie from Britain to co-star with a local actor. The historian of Reps remarked that the Salisbury public, 'suffering perhaps from a "laager" mentality brought on by political isolation, seized every chance of proving that the "local boy" could hold his own with the professionals'. The writer, who became a liberal critic of the Smith government, went on to suggest that such 'partisan feelings' probably caused little damage although, in later years, this pleasure of holding one's own in international company was translated into the conviction 'that Rhodesia had nothing to learn from the outside world'.[92]

The Rhodesians worked earnestly in transplanting the traditions of British theatre. In addition to Reps, there were five other dramatic societies in Salisbury, three in Bulawayo and twenty-nine dotted around the country.[93] Although the white Rhodesian was more attracted to 'rib ticklers' and liked 'a good belly laugh', the Reps historian claimed that the public 'would respond to almost any type of play – even Shakespeare – provided it was well done'.[94] Reps was in the best position to oblige. In the early 1970s it could boast a radio announcer who had a gift for comedy, one quality local actor, and a professional producer who could work equally well in tragedy, musical spectaculars, and farce. The other companies were not so privileged and Rhodesia certainly suffered for the lack of a professional theatre and training school. Yet Fort Victoria, in appearance and by tradition a frontier town, raised over $135,000 to build a new theatre and its Drama Circle often won the national contest in the 1970s for the best play of the year. The level of local support was remarkable. Whereas just 5 per cent of Salisbury's white population went to Reps productions, and 10 per cent of the locals attended each production in Umtali, the Drama Circle could attract half of Fort Victoria's white population to each of its plays.[95]

In 1973 the National Arts Foundation commissioned George Maxwell Jackson to report on the general state of the arts in the country.[96] The report looked at ballet, theatre, literature, films, music, art festivals, and eisteddfods. Jackson concluded that there was a widespread lethargy in the arts, attacked the private sector for failing to support the Foundation, and accused the three 'giants' in the field of arts promotion – the university, radio, and television – of being 'either asleep or looking the other way'.[97] Jackson did find much to praise. For him, Rhodesia's showpiece was the gallery in Salisbury (formerly the Rhodesia Gallery and, from 1971, the National Gallery) which had a substantial European collection including works by Van Dyck, Gainsborough, and Reynolds, some sculptures by Rodin, Henry Moore, and Epstein, and graphics by Rembrandt, Goya, and Toulouse-Lautrec. Jackson asserted that 'Rhodesia is famed for its art throughout the world', though he was referring to the Bushman paintings and the Shona sculptures. He wrote warmly of the achievements of the Europeans in ballet after two young dancers, having trained in Rhodesia, joined companies abroad. The report noted that every large centre in the country had a ballet 'school', and that there were fifteen in Salisbury alone. On the other hand, Jackson criticised the country's musical standards, accused the Rhodesian education system of not encouraging the young to play instruments, and claimed that the music schools in Salisbury and Bulawayo lacked sufficient funds.

The survey reveals just how widely the Rhodesians spread their interest in cultural activities. They may have lived in cultural isolation but they were not dying in a cultural desert. In this sense, whether they were the best in the world, or the worst, is immaterial. What matters is

that probably no other transplanted English-speakers had done more –
with similar resources – to reproduce and practise the parent culture.
For all these activities, Rhodesia in 1970 was more obviously an outdoor society. It played – and excelled in – many organised sports: squash,
tennis, swimming, diving, rowing, cricket, athletics, bowls, yachting,
hockey, golf, archery, rugby, and polo. It also fostered a substantial racing
and an associated gambling industry. The government and sporting
bodies publicly emphasised participation rather than performance and
spectating. Games were compulsory in all white schools, and adults in
the cities, towns, and rural areas had several opportunities to play sport.
Still, achievement did matter. Like other colonial societies, which used
sporting achievements to define and enhance national self-esteem, the
Rhodesians deified their heroes and relied upon their national teams to
restore or sustain national morale. Much was expected of the cricketers
and rugby players because, unlike the country's athletes and swimmers
who were already deprived of international competition, their sports
were included in the South African Currie Cup competition. In 1970,
when Craven Week – the prestigious annual rugby competition for
South African schools – was staged in Salisbury, the Cricket Association
successfully lured Mike Proctor to Salisbury to enhance its prospects.
Proctor was a Springbok all-rounder, a fearsome fast bowler and hard-
hitting batsman who had contributed significantly to the recent South
African demolition of the Australians.[98] Two years after his arrival Proctor
declared that Rhodesia was THE place to bring up children', and
defeated Ian Smith in a poll for 'Rhodesian of the Year'. Ultimately,
Proctor failed to deliver a Currie Cup premiership but Rhodesia came
close enough in 1972 to warrant tales of misfortune and accusations of
perfidious South African behaviour.[99]

Another – indoor – form of entertainment would eventually enter the
lives of nearly all Rhodesians. According to the *Annual Report* of the
Rhodesian Broadcasting Corporation for 1971, there were 31,282 sound
and 51,075 combined sound and TV licences in the country. Africans
tended to opt for the cheaper concessionary licences so these figures
suggest that virtually every European household had access to radio. In
Salisbury and Bulawayo – where there were 52,951 European households – some 80 per cent had TV sets, and 79 per cent of all Europeans
in the limited transmission area had access to TV in their homes.[100] They
were the direct beneficiaries of post-UDI international co-operation. The
cabinets were made in Rhodesia and Philips, the London parent company, which had Dutch and South African as well as Rhodesian connections, built the sets at a factory in socialist Yugoslavia.

The viewing choices were limited because the television arm of the
Rhodesian Broadcasting Corporation exercised a monopoly, and because

sanctions and foreign exchange limitations affected its buying capacity. Radio listeners were better served because they could tune in to the BBC, other world services, and to South Africa. The General Service on radio catered for all tastes while concentrating on news, light music, keep-fit programmes, notes for farmers, special sessions for women, and quiz shows. Peak-time viewing on television – between 7.00 p.m. and 9.00 p.m. – was almost completely dominated by old American series. During February-March 1970, the Monday-Wednesday 7.00 p.m.-8.00 p.m. time-slot was occupied, in turn, by the *Red Skelton Show,* the *Danny Kaye Show,* and the *Ed Sullivan Show.* The ratings indicated that some 61 per cent of the potential television audience watched television on weekdays.

And why not? A contributor to *Look and Listen* pointed out that in an ordinary week one could see Dean Martin, Rod Steiger, Gary Cooper, Lucille Ball, Terence Stamp, Peter Finch, Elizabeth Taylor, Sonny and Cher, Ernest Borgnine, Robert Wagner, Frank Sinatra, and Sammy Davis Jnr.[101] Given these opportunities there was no point bemoaning the prohibitive cost of making local programmes or their appalling amateurism, or the inability to buy the more recent products from overseas. TV audiences accepted their diet of trash and recycled favourites, and they were better off than the South Africans who did not yet have television. Besides, the cinemas continued to obtain the latest releases: in February-March 1970 audiences could see *Bonny and Clyde, Bullitt, Rosemary's Baby,* and *Butch Cassidy and the Sundance Kid* (as well as another showing of *Zulu*). Clearly, sanctions had not isolated Rhodesians from the standards of entertainment, and taste expectations, which were common in Britain, the United States, and Australasia.

The Rhodesians were, however, protected from the permissiveness of the 1960s. The State had appointed some formidable guardians to defend the world of *I Love Lucy* from that of *Oh Calcutta.* In 1970 the Chairman of the Censorship Board was John Gaunt. An outspoken and uncouth politician from Northern Rhodesia, Gaunt was elected for the RF in 1962, briefly aspired to succeed Winston Field (Smith's predecessor as RF Prime Minister), and, from 1965, served as the government's representative in South Africa before becoming the country's political watchdog and moral guardian. Gaunt could spot a 'Red' anywhere: in, as well as under, the bed. On the subject of pornography, for example, he detected 'unmistakable signs' of a 'Communist conspiracy', even if he lacked 'concrete proof'.[102] His zeal and powers of detection were infectious. According to a former censor, the Board looked for certain categories: 'promotion of drugs, promotion of perversion, denigration of social and parental authorities, denigration of religion, promotion of atheism'. Not herself a regular church-goer, she regarded the propagation of atheism as 'an integral part of the Communist creed'.[103]

Books and magazines (including manuals and factual material) were usually banned for their sexual or drug connotations.[104] Books banned in 1970 included such titles as *The Upper Pleasure Garden, The Square Root of Sex, Oral Sex Techniques,* and *The Art of Spanking.* The bans extended to Germaine Greer's *The Female Eunuch,* Henry Miller's *The World of Sex,* Montgomery Hyde's *The Other Love,* and Timothy Leary's *Politics of Ecstasy.* The censors were equally harsh on rugby joke books and issues of *Playboy, Penthouse,* and *Cosmopolitan.* Their zeal did not entirely protect the Rhodesians from the *Playboy* cult. On 7 May 1970 the staid *Gwelo Times* displayed four local white 'bunny girls' on its front page. It was an excusable lapse in taste. After all, the ladies were merely trying to raise money for a Christmas Cheer Fund, they were inclined towards solidity, and they were not 'topless'. The anti-communist values of Gwelo's residents remained intact.

Apparently, Marx, Engels, and Lenin were not considered dangerous. Their works were passed while authors such as Ruth First, Shula Marks, Kwame Nkrumah, Nathan Shamuyarira, and Ndabaningi Sithole were all banned by 1970. Perhaps their writings were more likely to appeal to a (gullible) black public. The 1968-9 issue of the more academic *Africa Contemporary Record* was also banned, presumably because it contained material critical of the Rhodesian government. Pornography, however, was perceived as the greater threat and, although the Rhodesians generally acquiesced in the limitations imposed on their freedoms, many were prepared to pay for any titillation which was available. Indeed, the society which, in the early 1970s, officially frowned on sexual display and abnormality, tolerated a 'massage' parlour which operated openly in a Salisbury main street, a lunchtime 'girls-only' male strip show in the Avondale shopping centre, and the overt effeminacy of a popular male media personality. Public morality and private behaviour diverged more sharply and more often than anyone cared to notice or admit.

white girls who 'got into trouble' had always slipped off to Beira or to Europe. By 1970 a psychiatrist in Bulawayo promised assistance by recommending abortions on the basis of broadly defined psychiatric grounds. Between 1962 and 1969 the Bulawayo Central Hospital performed an average of forty-two abortions a year; in 1970 the figure rose to 111 and in 1973 to 156.[105] These 'legal' operations occurred despite the fact that abortion remained a crime under the prevailing Roman-Dutch law. More importantly, the demand existed because the young did not all practise restraint. Homosexuality was also illegal – and, officially, did not occur – but activity inside the closet was not thereby inhibited. Public figures either disguised their inclinations or enjoyed the protection afforded by their status. The stigma remained and homosexuals in Rhodesia relied mostly on their code of silence to avoid persecution.[106] A similar code protected the drug-users. There were just nine registered addicts in Rhodesia in 1970 (their race is unknown) and a mere seventy whites, of whom half were under 21, were arrested in the same year on drug-related offences. The Provincial Welfare Officer for Mashonaland was probably correct in claiming that 'we don't have a drug problem'[107] though the increased use of LSD and 'dagga' (marijuana) after 1970 prompted one RF MP to make unsubstantiated claims of drug abuse and to demand mandatory prison sentences for first-offender drug 'pushers'.[108] Much depended, of course, on how the 'problem' was defined, and on the method of detection. The fact remained that a minority of young Rhodesians did use the less harmful drugs, and many did so in the northern suburbs of Salisbury without attracting the attention of the authorities.

There was one conspicuous and acknowledged divergence between public morality and private behaviour. Having proclaimed the sanctity of marriage, and the centrality of the family, Rhodesians managed to achieve one of the highest divorce rates in the world: by 1970 one in five marriages were dissolved and the rate soon rose above one in four.[109] The law required evidence of fault to sanction divorce, and so the courts repeatedly heard harrowing stories of bereft husbands, beaten wives, drunkenness, infidelity, appalling cruelty, and of bewildered and deprived children. Some patterns suggested that the Rhodesians married in haste and soon repented: a high proportion of divorced females were pregnant before they married, and the highest proportion of separations occurred within five years of marriage. Even so, 40 per cent of divorces took place after at least ten years of marriage.

Apart from breaching the moral code some Rhodesians were also apt to break the law.[110] There were a few convicted molesters and perverts but, like everywhere else, the known statistics probably do not tell the full story. In 1969 a 'well-known' European male, who liked to haunt European female flat-dwellers while covering his face with a white handkerchief, was convicted after his clothing had been identified by a colour photograph taken while he was in the act. In 1970 one European was convicted of raping his 13-month-old daughter and another of the attempted rape of his two young stepdaughters. The more hardened criminal element in Rhodesia was proportionately tiny compared with other societies.[111] The most publicised member of the criminal fraternity was Aiden Diggeden, another 'old boy' of Chaplin High School, and a dedicated thief and audacious escapee. On 6 August 1970 he made yet another – failed – attempt to leave the Salisbury maximum security prison. In the same year Aubrey Fisher was nearing the end of a ten-year spree involving 134 separate acts of fraud which netted over $320,000 to pay his gambling debts. His friends were astounded when the activities of this respectable Bulawayo accountant were revealed in 1972.[112]

Ordinary Rhodesians never thought of themselves as law-breakers. Most of the 36,548 cleared cases of European 'crime' in 1970 consisted of minor traffic offences. Nevertheless, there were 1,086 cases of offences against persons or property, and sixty whites were charged with breaking and entering. There were also 326 reported cases of drunkenness (and another 2,144 involving Africans). Fraud was a continuing problem and even eminent defenders of Western civilisation were tempted into indiscretion. In 1971 T. M. Ellison, ICD, a former Royal Navy officer, a leading pro-republican and RF back-bencher, was forced to resign his seat after his company was found guilty of tampering with sales tax returns.[113] A significant statistic was that in 1969 six persons were charged with serious breaches of Exchange Control regulations. The courts also heard another 145 cases involving transfers of bullion and precious stones. There is further anecdotal evidence of businessmen never being discovered or charged for altering invoices, and of decent and avowedly patriotic men and women engaging in under-the-counter deals to shift funds abroad. A number of Rhodesians, it seems, had little faith in the country's future or little concern for the nation's foreign reserves.

There were unmistakable signs in 1970 that the upright Rhodesians were just like everybody else: they made rules for society which they broke as individuals. It is possible, if unprovable, that the Rhodesians were better than other peoples in observing the codes they professed. But in Rhodesia the conventional rhetoric commanded something more than relative goodness. Self-esteem and self-justification required evidence of *absolute* virtue to contrast Rhodesia with a Western world which had become deeply flawed by permissive morality and left-wing politics. In reality, the achievement fell short of the aspiration.

Officially, Rhodesia remained a Christian country. Ian Smith told Rhodesians in 1965 that UDI had 'struck a blow for the preservation of justice, civilisation and Christianity'.[114] The 1969 constitution began with a dedication: 'The peoples of Rhodesia humbly acclaim the supremacy and omnipotence of Almighty God and acknowledge the ultimate direction by Him of the affairs of men.' Each subsequent session of parliament was opened with prayers and oaths were sworn on the Bible.

Rhodesia's status as a Christian country was confirmed by the white responses to the religious affiliation question asked in the 1969 Census (see Table 1.3). The white Christian affiliation may be further broken down as seen in Table 1.4. Clearly, there was some sort of Protestant

TABLE 1.3. *European Religious Affiliations, 1969*

Category	Number	Percentage
Christian	209,348	91.70
Hebrew	5,194	2.28
Hindu	23	0.01
Muslim	30	0.01
Agnostic or atheist	4,745	2.08
Not stated	8,956	3.92
TOTAL	228,296	100.00

Source: Census of Population, 1969, table 16.

ascendancy whereby the three principal Protestant denominations – the Anglicans, Presbyterians, and (English) Methodists – accounted for more than 60 per cent of Christians and over half the total white population. Although there were few overt signs of sectarianism within white Rhodesia this Protestant emphasis may partly account for Rhodesian

TABLE 1.4. *European Christian Denominations, 1969*

Denomination	Number	Percentage
Anglican	78,573	37.53
Baptist	3,970	1.90
Catholic	[a]33,716	16.10
Dutch Reformed	18,528	8.86
Greek Orthodox	3,784	1.81
Presbyterian	29,478	14.08
Methodist	21,344	10.20
Protestant[b]	3,995	1.90
Other[c]	15,960	7.62
TOTAL	209,348	100.00

Notes
[a] This figure represents two categories: those who described themselves as Roman Catholic (27,246) or as Catholic (6,470).
[b] This category consisted of persons who preferred that title and did not specify a denomination.
[c] This group incuded 1,790 Jehovah's Witnesses and 70 Quakers whose eligible males sought exemption from military service during the 1970s.

Source: Census of Population, 1969, table 16.

hostility to foreign Catholic missionaries, and for the anxiety of lay Catholics to disassociate themselves from the Catholic Commission for Justice and Peace during the war years.

There is no accurate way of measuring the depth of this Christian commitment. One authority claims that the 'devout church-going Christian vote' constituted less than 10 per cent of the electorate, and there is evidence from Anglican sources that Easter and Christmas communicants between 1971 and 1976 accounted for just 10 per cent of the potential communion.[115] Statistics of this kind do not take account of private worship, or evaluate sincerity. Paul Burrough, the Anglican Bishop of Mashonaland between 1968 and 1981, claimed that the white Anglican communion in Rhodesia was more committed than any comparable communion in Britain.[116] Yet the Rhodesians as a whole showed little sign of being profoundly concerned with spiritual matters. The large majority of them called on the clergy to preside over their important rites of passage – baptism, marriage, and burial – and a minority attended the main festivals and observed days of obligation. At critical times a number sought comfort or needed charity. Otherwise, the adherents of the main denominations were fairly relaxed about religious observance.

When Rhodesians used the term 'Christianity' they often did so to delineate or justify a secular world which was anti-communist, democratic, and civilised (that is, white ruled). The official institutions of Christianity – and, notably, the official representatives – were not, in this scheme of things, accorded a special status. A government minister or an RF constituency chairman, the head of a statutory board or a white trade unionist, spoke with equal authority in reminding everyone that Rhodesia was a Christian country which respected traditional moral values. Moreover, the secular authorities could speak without any sense of ambivalence. Whereas the Churches also represented large African congregations, and harboured clergy who openly identified with their African flock, the secular definitions of Christianity could be, and were, unmistakably white Rhodesian.

The Church organisations were either preoccupied with matters which did not relate directly to the 'big' issues of race and politics, or they interpreted those issues in a way which allowed their critics to accuse them of supporting the status quo. The Anglicans, for example, expended much of their energy in 1970 debating the question of whether to permit the remarriage of divorced persons in church.[117] Where the Churches did enter politics they did so with some caution. Most stood up to the government in 1969-70 over the Land Tenure Act. Under the Act which, in replacing the Land Appportionment Act, assigned 45 million acres each to the African and European populations, 'voluntary associations' (including the Churches) could apply to the Minister of Lands for permission to own or lease land. They would have to submit certain details; namely, whether the controlling interest was African or European. Aside from the question of whether the Church should apply to the State for access to land it was already using, the Act raised the possibility of white priests being denied access to their black congregations. Bishop Burrough made the point succinctly: 'By the Land Tenure Act Christ Himself might "own" but not "occupy" His Church, without permission ...'[118] To the Churches, the central objection was State interference in religious affairs; to the government, it was simply a matter of asserting its right to rule over Caesar's world. The Churches were generally less perturbed about institutionalised injustice than about the limitations imposed upon the institutional Church by the State.[119]

The Christian Churches in 1970 were not determining the character and direction of the Christian country. Their ecumenical and firm stand against the 1969 land tenure proposals had disintegrated, and the State was in full control. Deportations had removed some of the troublesome elements, including Guy Clutton-Brock, the Treasurer of the multiracial Cold Comfort Farm Society near Rusape, who insisted that he tried to live by the Gospels which were 'just about the most subversive documents ever written'. Donal Lamont, the turbulent Catholic Bishop of Umtali, refused to be silent and maintained his view that the 'real terrorists' were those who framed the 1969 constitution, though he was disowned by the bulk of the white Catholic laity and by a number of Jesuit priests and Marianhill Fathers.[120] The Anglicans kept complaining about individual injustices without bothering to attack the system. The Dutch Reformed Church had little time for liberalism,[121] and the Presbyterians and Methodists were generally reliable. The State was content because the Churches now professed their political neutrality and said they wanted to concentrate on saving souls and dealing with moral questions.

VI

The Rhodesians shared a pleasant lifestyle which was more varied than is often supposed and less pure than some Rhodesians would have wished. There were pressures to conform but no assurance of uniformity. Yet, to outsiders, the mark of Rhodesian-ness was racial solidarity in defence of privilege and white rule. The question now is whether, superimposed on the distinctions created by ethnicity, birthplace, gender, occupation, class, region, religion, status, and taste, the Rhodesians were drawn together as a race or as a single community by their fear of black majority rule.

According to the local conventional wisdom, about one-third of the Rhodesians believed that the blacks would always be incapable of ruling the country and must, therefore, remain permanently under white rule within a tribal framework. These segregationists and supremacists were the 'racists' of white Rhodesia, although many of them resented the label and were – as individuals – disarmingly benign 'oppressors'. A further quarter of the whites supported African political and economic advancement. At worst, these liberals of white politics – the so-called 'left' – were prone to paternalism and a naive attachment to an impossible non-racial ideal. The remaining whites did not oppose African advancement but hoped to delay its passage into majority rule for as long as possible. The RF, the rallying-point for all those who were not liberals, represented the three-quarters of the white population who were the most afraid or the most intractable. If three-quarters of the population could determine a community position, then clearly the mark of Rhodesian-ness was a combination of fear and prejudice.

The fear is easily explained. The whites lived in the best houses, owned most of the best land, enjoyed a high standard of living, and controlled the executive, the legislature, the judiciary, and the means of coercion. In June 1970 the average annual income for blacks was $312; the figure for whites was $3,104.[122] The Birmingham-born artisan relied upon that disparity to ensure that, while he might not be wealthy, he lived in better circumstances in Rhodesia than his counterparts did back home. So long as his union could protect his job from fragmentation or Africanisation, and so long as the electoral system preserved white rule, then his future was assured. It would be destroyed if the British government imposed a 'settlement' on the Rhodesians, if the black nationalists were allowed to take power, and if a black government 'Africanised' the labour market. The artisan knew what independence had done in black Africa: fear of a similar experience in Rhodesia explained his sense of racial solidarity, and his determination to resist change.

The fear was often expressed through racial jokes which, in turn, were justified by the claim that the story-teller really liked the African, or that the jokes themselves were harmless or misunderstood. When Ian Smith sang the Afrikaans song, 'Bobbejaan, klim die berg' ('Baboon, climb the hill') in front of black university students during an election meeting in 1970, the *African Times* explained that it was just a college rugby song, a folk song, which was not at all political.[123] It was rare for an RF voter to comprehend the hurt caused by racist remarks, just as RF supporters were unable to acknowledge that the government's policies were in any way oppressive or discriminatory. Either they denied the existence of discrimination, or they claimed that the blacks themselves preferred separation. One RF MP explained that Rhodesia's 'harmonious race relations' depended on 'mutual respect', and would be destroyed by an 'orgy of hand-shaking, back-slapping and social integration'.[124] Other RF whites stressed that the black population was way behind in the march of civilisation or observed that blacks in Rhodesia were better off than those who lived north of the Zambezi. Ian Smith's comment to another election meeting in 1970 had become a typical Rhodesian response to criticism: 'Sixty years ago Africans here were uncivilised savages, walking around in skins. They have made tremendous progress but they have an awful long way to go.'[125]

The implication was that, in the meantime, it was both inevitable and acceptable that black earnings and lifestyles would not match those of the whites. Either 'THEY' did not mind, or 'THEY' could not expect any better than to live in workers' compounds, in servants' quarters attached to suburban houses, in townships located near the major white urban centres, or in their Tribal Trust Lands (TTLs). Equally, it was not unreasonable to exclude blacks from white hospitals, schools, bars, swimming pools, cinemas, restaurants, and shops.[126] Custom and the Land Tenure Act were invoked to protect the whites from proximity. Like the South Africans, however, the Rhodesians in 1970 distinguished between local and overseas blacks. The cricket community fell about Gary Sobers when he arrived to take part in a double-wicket competition. The brilliant West Indian all-rounder was photographed laughing with Ian Smith. Although the Rhodesia Herald's editor warned Rhodesians against embarrassing 'Mr Sobers' by making political capital out of the visit, the paper's Sports Editor wrote that Sobers would see how 'colour doesn't matter a damn' and that 'Rhodesians are not bigots with horns growing out of their heads'.[127] It just happened that Ian Smith's government, in part responding to parent demands and perhaps mindful of the dangers of communist subversion,[128] had banned multiracial sporting matches on government school grounds. And the Fort Victoria Town Council would probably have included 'Mr Sobers' in its ban against Africans walking in the local parks where, it was alleged, they were too noisy and engaged in unhealthy practices.[129]

One effect of segregation was to perpetuate the social distance between the races, thereby limiting the opportunities for whites to understand both the ambition for advancement and the fact of it occurring. Social distance, in turn, perpetuated the convenient assumptions that 'the African' was happy to be ruled by his chief or kraal head, that all he wanted was a full belly and a large family, and that he was not interested in what the Rhodesians called 'politics'. The Ministry of Information was not so complacent. Each fortnight in 1970 it distributed 350,000 issues of the African Times with articles printed in English, Shona, or Sindebele denouncing 'terrorism', praising the chiefs, kraal heads, and progressive African farmers, and offering advice for self-improvement. Important whites were forever being photographed in the act of pinning medals on to proud African chests. Whether the *African Times* convinced any blacks to support the government,[130] and whether the Ministry seriously believed that 'our family' of one million black readers spoke affectionately of 'the people's paper',[131] the whites were only too ready to presume that any blacks who opposed the system were malcontents who belonged to a small minority. The Ministry of Internal Affairs encouraged this view in support of its professedly superior understanding of what the African needed. For their part, most Rhodesians were content to allow Internal Affairs – and its trained staff of District Commissioners (DCs), nearly all of them Rhodesian born or locally recruited – to be responsible for controlling the black masses.

At least the DCs could speak an African language and understood something of African customs. Few other whites in 1970 'knew' any blacks except as employees. Fewer still made any serious attempt to understand the Africa which nourished them. Consequently, social distance bred and fed upon dislike and ignorance, and encouraged a polite amusement or bewilderment. The white madams in the suburbs were just sufficiently informed to recount stories of how 'THEY' smelt, were too noisy, demanded hand-outs, breast-fed their children in public, created long queues in the Post Office, never said 'Thank you', or never showed any practical gratitude. A newspaper editor felt obliged to explain to the more sensitive among 'THEM' that, while the European had not invented a suitable word for an adult male worker, the use of the word 'boy' was in no way derogatory or demeaning. Besides, the majority of whites had ceased using words like 'munt' and 'kaffir'.[132] After a senior Internal Affairs official addressed the Sinoia Branch of the Women's Institutes a member wrote:

NOW we know what makes Sixpence 'tick', or at least we thought we did until we got home and found he had watered our seedlings with an old petrol can . .. It was a really enjoyable afternoon with plenty of laughs and we did come away with a better understanding of our Africans.[133]

A few of the white madams even extended their desire for understanding to the suggestion that African languages and customs should be taught as compulsory courses from Standard I, although a further proposal for servants to talk in Shona to the children of the European household was considered impractical.[134]

Occasionally, the fear, dislike, and irritation combined in acts of brutality. Between July and November 1971 four white adult males periodically drove past black pedestrians in Bulawayo and hit them with sticks or threw stones, fracturing several skulls and limbs.[135] Anecdotal evidence suggests that servants and labourers, who were beaten on account of their alleged impudence or incompetence, refused to seek justice in the courts. When the acts of violence did reach the courts the white magistrates were reluctant to let the punishment fit the crime. In 1973 a 20-year-old white received a two-year gaol sentence for raping an African woman. In the same year an African was sentenced to eight strokes with the cane and twelve years in gaol for raping an elderly European woman who had been walking her dogs in Salisbury. 'Racial offences of a sexual nature' evoked strong reactions within the white communities, especially as most of the eighty offences committed in 1970 involved attacks by African males on white women and girls.[136] Not every case was so straightforward. In 1969 an all-white jury freed a white woman who was charged with the murder of her husband's black foreman on their Midlands farm. The jury accepted her plea of self-defence. The intriguing aspect of the case was that the victim was her regular drinking companion on lonely days, and that the two of them – together – had consumed several beers and two bottles of brandy just before she stabbed him to death. In the absence of other, conclusive evidence – save that of an African who had heard the pair arguing – the jury accepted her description of the incident.[137] The fact that it readily did so, and in the process saved the woman (and her husband) from any further embarrassment arising out of her 'scandalous' habits, highlights the inequality before the law in Rhodesia.

For all their sins and for all that the system institutionalised discrimination and exploitation, most white Rhodesians were not racist thugs or heartless beings. A number joined charitable organisations in the spirit of helping those – of all races – less fortunate than themselves.[138] If they were ignorant, afraid, and paternalistic, they were also capable of eschewing reactionary politics. A random survey in Salisbury and Bulawayo, which was conducted by a reputable international firm in 1969, revealed that 61 per cent of whites agreed that Africans should be progressively involved in all aspects of European economic and political life; 57 per cent accepted that discrimination embittered Africans; and 45 per cent thought that majority rule was inevitable.[139] At one level, therefore, ignorance – of their own world and of the world outside, an ignorance born of distance rather than of an innate racism or idiocy – was another mark of Rhodesian-ness. And, as the 1969 sample suggests, this characteristic, like all the others, must be heavily qualified.

VII

This investigation has suggested that Rhodesian society was composed of a number of communities representing different traditions and interests. Despite minority dissent they were fused as a racial group in an outwardly stable society. Diversity was camouflaged by a common commitment to material self-improvement and a pleasant lifestyle. It hardly mattered in 1970 that individuals and families had their own perceptions of what constituted the essence of this Rhodesian way of life. On the other hand, the editor of the *Umtali Post* was worried that Rhodesians lacked a 'concrete national identity'.

What Rhodesia is looking for and desperately needs is national identity. Some Rhodesians are born to it, other people have found it – some prefer not to look.[140]

Presumably the 'true Rhodesians' were those who had acquired this intangible and elusive commodity through birth, or had been inducted into its mysteries by friends or neighbours, or at school or by reading novels,[141] or by listening to 'Good Old Smithy', the RBC, or the songs of Clem Tholet. By the late 1970s, as a result of the war, the 'true Rhodesians' were easier to distinguish, and harder to find. For, by then, those who professed their Rhodesian-ness included many who had discovered that, if its essence had to be defended by personal and material sacrifice, then the Rhodesian way of life had lost its real value.

2

'The even progression of life'

I

Rhodesia became a republic on 2 March 1970, an event which passed almost without notice inside the country. The British Foreign Secretary announced that the assumption of republican status was illegal – just as UDI was unlawful – and warned civil servants that they would be considered to have joined the rebellion if they remained at their desks. There were no mass resignations. The Governor, Sir Humphrey Gibbs, had already left his official residence where he had remained a voluntary prisoner since UDI. Foreign governments closed their consulates, the title 'Royal' was removed from the insignias of the armed services, and the honorary appointments of the Queen and of the Queen Mother were suspended. Ian Smith did mark the occasion by wearing a blue and green striped tie bearing the letters 'COBC' (Commonwealth Old Boys' Club) and the *Rhodesia Herald* dutifully reported the birth of the country's 'first [white] republican' at the Lady Chancellor Maternity Home. But there were no speeches or parades and, though Rhodesia had a new flag, there was no national anthem to arouse patriotic enthusiasm. The government, having failed to provide pomp and circumstance, could hardly blame the local press for showing more interest in the Apollo 13 space mission.[1]

In one sense the low-key reaction was surprising. Eighty-one per cent of the (overwhelmingly white) voters had endorsed the republic at a referendum on 20 June 1969, compared with 72.5 per cent who approved of the new constitution.[2] On the other hand, the government was not anxious to trumpet the cause of separation from the British Crown. Residual loyalties remained strong in Rhodesia, and the Smith cabinet still preferred a constitutional settlement with Britain. Ian Smith had talked with Harold Wilson, the British Prime Minister, in December 1966 on board HMS *Tiger* and in October 1968 on HMS *Fearless*, precisely because he wanted a negotiated and legalised independence.[3] He had distanced himself from the hardline supremacists who argued that a republic was necessary to maintain permanent white rule.

The official restraint was most marked at a ceremony on 16 April held at the former Government House. Clifford Dupont was sworn in as Rhodesia's first President before a small audience of fifty people including Smith, ten of his ministers, the service commanders, three senior civil servants, and three African tribal chiefs. Representatives of the local and foreign press were either barred altogether from the ceremony or were herded into an adjoining room. The government-controlled television service was permitted to record the event but the photographer from the *Rhodesia Herald* was excluded, presumably because he represented the Argus Press which was considered dangerously liberal and even disloyal.[4] Perhaps the government was entitled to be wary of this particular stable. The *Herald* reporter, who was admitted, remarked upon the lack of fanfare, observed that the occasion could hardly be described as 'social' because only one woman (Mrs Dupont) was present, and revealed that the towels in the men's bathroom were still embroidered with crowns.[5]

Dupont, a former London solicitor and a perennial poker player, had been Officer Administering the Government since UDI. In cabinet he had pushed hard for UDI. When on subsequent occasions – on HMS *Tiger* in 1966 and HMS *Fearless* in 1968 – Smith attempted to negotiate a settlement with Harold Wilson, Dupont reputedly campaigned behind the scenes against any agreement which might compromise Rhodesia's independence under white rule.[6] He was not a man to accept a purely titular role, and the swearing-in ceremony gave him the opportunity to lecture on the recent 'decade of turmoil'. Dupont spoke of the violence in the rest of Africa, of the great pressures being placed on the Rhodesian government to accept the unacceptable (black majority rule), and of the attempts by Rhodesians to remain loyal to the monarchy. He insisted that the formal break 'was none of our seeking', and concluded his speech with an observation and a prophecy: 'You have the seeds of greatness in you and I have no doubt that in the years to come these seeds will flourish. I am perfectly confident that with God's help we will overcome any further tests to which we are subjected in the future.'[7]

Dupont spoke the confident language which the RF had been using since its foundation in 1962. The underlying assumption was that a united white community under the RF could survive international pressure and 'terrorist' attack. By 1970 the party had established its ascendancy in white politics and had successfully projected the image at home and abroad of a Rhodesia united under Ian Smith. The RF entered the 1970s, therefore, expecting to nurture 'the seeds of greatness'. Yet it did so divided within itself, uncertain of what policies to follow, almost wilfully ignorant of the damage done by the policies it had adopted, and oblivious of the fact that there was no time to spare. The object of this chapter is to explore these themes through an analysis of the RF and of the political world it had come to dominate.

II

Most Rhodesians in 1970 shared Dupont's confidence. The rebellion of 1965 had survived Harold Wilson's prediction that it would collapse within 'weeks rather than months'.[8] Despite all the difficulties, including the recurring droughts, the economy was apparently entering a minor boom: the shops were reasonably well stocked, more whites were arriving in the country than leaving, and petrol rationing had ended. In addition, a new constitution had been successfully implemented, the government seemed to be well in control of the African population, the black dissidents inside the country were safely incarcerated and the Security Forces had easily repelled all guerrilla incursions. White rule, and the RF, seemed secure, and the editor of the pro-RF *Rhodesian Financial Gazette* prophesied that 'barring violent upheavals instigated from and supported from outside, Mr Smith is here to stay for at least another 10 years'.[9]

Speculation about a settlement, which was renewed after Edward Heath's unexpected victory in the British general election of June 1970, and concern about the immediate future of the agricultural sector and about the long-term effects of sanctions, continued to cause uncertainty in the business community. There was, however, a general optimism about the economy. The politicians were inclined to be extravagant but even the Ministry of Finance was fairly sanguine. Its *Economic Survey* spoke of 'satisfactory progress' in 1970 and, although the rate of real growth had fallen from 9.8 per cent in 1969 to 4.5 per cent (largely because of the drought), the main indicators were encouraging. Apart from agriculture all sectors had recorded improvements in output; manufacturing, construction, and mining were booming; there was a 73 per cent rise in approvals of industrial building plans and a 40 per cent increase for residential plans; and the inflation rate had risen to 3.5 per cent without raising fears about general inflationary pressure.[10] For all its problems, agriculture was making headway with diversification into the production of maize, cotton, wheat, and soya beans. Tobacco, which once contributed 31 per cent of export income, was moving out of the doldrums and selling sufficiently well under the counter for the government to raise the production quotas for the 1971 season. So, while it could be argued that UDI and sanctions had forced the Rhodesians to sell in the cheapest market, and to buy in the dearest, and that sanctions had slowed the rate of growth, the white Rhodesians were convinced that the country had survived the post-UDI crisis and that the economy had benefited from the enforced diversification and import replacement programmes.

The *manner* of Rhodesia's survival mattered as much as the fact. For the Rhodesians liked to depict themselves as participants in an economic war – a life-or-death struggle – from which they had emerged triumphant against overwhelming odds. Victory was sweeter because they had defied Harold Wilson, the United Nations, and the Organisation of African Unity (OAU). The heroes could not be named – to protect the nation's security and 'our friends' overseas – but official decorations and private gossip indicated that leading businessmen and civil servants had done their duty. The 'Scottish Mafia'[11] – David Young of the Treasury and N. H. B. Bruce of the Reserve Bank – were widely praised within government and business circles for their role in maintaining the currency and protecting the nation's reserves. A few, even further removed from the limelight, found satisfaction in posing as James Bond figures. Two prominent Greek businessmen, responsible for shipping minerals, chose the Rhodesian telephone number of 22007. A senior civil servant, later found guilty of corruption, so loved the secretiveness that he was forever arranging meetings under numbered lamp-posts on foreign soil. 'Jack' Malloch, the Second World War veteran, was a more genuine larger-than-life character. His private company flew the 'meat run' around Africa delivering cargoes of Rhodesian beef, and even made night flights into Biafra. To those Rhodesians who knew of Malloch, he embodied the very qualities which they thought were winning the economic war: he was, at once, ingenious, brazen, deft, and inventive.

The reality of sanctions-busting was much less romantic and dangerous. The practitioners were the first to admit that, with the possible exceptions of tobacco and steel, the operation was easy enough to mount.[12] The Portuguese were most co-operative, although their capacity to help was limited because attaching a Mozambique label to Rhodesian chrome would not have fooled anybody. The South Africans were inclined to exact a price but they were also accommodating. Rhodesian minerals could be shipped legitimately by Rhodesian companies legally incorporated in South Africa. It was just a matter of obtaining a certificate from the Johannesburg Chamber of Commerce and appearing before a Commissioner of Oaths with a declaration stating the origin of the goods. The Commissioner could be a South African postmaster, and in the larger post offices there was a special section where an officer simply stamped and signed the form on the information supplied. The top copy was then returned to the Chamber of Commerce and the goods proceeded, bearing a declaration that they had originated in South Africa.

Overseas buyers and sellers were equally co-operative because Rhodesia was a reliable trading partner, and because the favourable terms of trade were a sufficient inducement to disregard UN embargoes and professed government policy. Anti-Rhodesia lobbies regularly exposed some of these sanctions-busting activities, forcing the Rhodesians and their trading partners to open new routes. British MI6 agents sometimes tailed the sanctions-busters across Europe, and various intelligence agents and journalists slipped information out of Rhodesia. Despite this attention, the Rhodesians in 1970 bought, sold, and bartered on both sides of the Atlantic, on both sides of the Iron Curtain, and throughout Africa, the Middle East, and Asia. 'It was all just a matter of business.'[13] The only serious impediment was Rhodesia's capacity to supply or purchase. Sanctions were annoying rather than destructive, and it was tedious rather than exciting trying to break them.

The case for ingenuity can, therefore, be overstated although the confidence in the economy, generated by the success in overcoming sanctions, was a key factor in explaining the general mood of optimism in 1970. Another factor was the belief that Rhodesia's new constitution would protect European rule and provide for long-term stability.

The constitution replaced the previous system of divided rolls,[14] based on franchise qualifications, with two racial rolls: one for Europeans which included Asians and Coloureds, and the other for Africans which demanded lower qualifications. There were to be two chambers: a House of Assembly consisting of fifty members returned on the European roll, eight Africans elected on the African roll (four each from Mashonaland and Matabeleland), and another eight Africans (four each from Mashonaland and Matabeleland) chosen by the chiefs, headmen, and councillors of the TTLs; and a Senate consisting of ten Europeans chosen by the European members of the Assembly, ten Africans chosen by the Council of Chiefs, and three persons of any race selected by the Head of State. Provision was made to increase the African membership of the Assembly to the level of parity by the addition of two members at a time chosen, in turn, by the direct and indirect method, and in proportion to increasing income tax payments made after the African contributions reached 26.5 per cent of the total income assessment of the country. Given that only 986 Africans paid income tax in 1969, and that their contribtutions amounted to 0.5 per cent, the prospect of parity was a distant one.[15] These electoral provisions, including the ceiling of parity, were entrenched in the constitution along with the Land Tenure Act and a clause requiring two-thirds majorities in both houses sitting separately to validate a constitutional amendment.

Liberal whites, black nationalists, and external critics were convinced that the new arrangements and the Land Tenure Act committed

Rhodesia to racial division and confrontation, and to near-permanent white supremacy.[16] Furthermore, between 1965 and 1970, the RF government had carried out the death penalty on convicted 'terrorists', tightened the security legislation by extending the Law and Order (Maintenance) Act,[17] deported dissident whites, and evicted the Tangwena people from their traditional home near Inyanga in accordance with the Land Tenure Act.[18] By contrast, most white Rhodesians considered that any breaches in the rule of law were excusable in the context of the security situation and the economic war, and regarded the RF's legislation and regulations as essential to preserve 'civilised standards'. The government also had to undo the 'damage' caused by the premature liberalism of the former premiers Garfield Todd and Sir Edgar whitehead, to prevent a repetition of the township riots of 1963-4, and to protect the country from its home-grown white liberals, Harold Wilson, the international Left, and the 'terrorists' based in Zambia.

The electorate supported the RF between 1962 and 1970 because it generated confidence in the future of a white Rhodesia, and because the government convinced the electorate that the black population was both content and under control. Internal Affairs assured the whites in 1970 that everything was fine:

Relations between the races in Rhodesia have never been better than they are today ... There has been a steady improvement in race relations since the present [RF] Government was elected. Fear and intimidation have been driven out of the tribal areas, to be replaced by cordiality and co-operation.[19]

For its part, the government was delighted to receive such an unambiguous political endorsement from a crucial department in the 'apolitical' civil service. And it was comforting for everyone to know that the 'ordinary' African was never going to cause any trouble.

III

The electorate entered the 1970s believing that, whatever dangers lay ahead, white Rhodesia was not at serious political or economic risk. The right wing of the RF was not so confident. It was convinced that 'provincialisation' – the RF's policy for separate development within the framework of white supremacy – was essential to secure the future of the whites in Rhodesia. The right's campaign, and Ian Smith's effective resistance, dominated the RF's internal politics between 1968 and 1972. To understand these manoeuvres it is necessary to examine the character and early history of the Rhodesian Front.

The RF was formed in March 1962 to unite several smaller parties or groups on the right of white politics. Three factors prompted this realignment. First, Sir Edgar whitehead's United Federal Party (UFP) government in Southern Rhodesia was planning to repeal the Land Apportionment Act, the precursor of the Land Tenure Act and the cornerstone of white rule. Secondly, the 1961 constitution appeared to pave the way for an African majority within 15-20 years. Thirdly, the Central African Federation, which had been launched in 1953 to link the two Rhodesias and Nyasaland, was on the point of dissolution. The British government was ready to grant full independence to the two northern territories but would probably delay the process in Southern Rhodesia until an African majority assumed power in Salisbury.

The federal and territorial branches of the Dominion Party (DP) were the rock upon which the RF was built. The DP had only just lost the 1958 elections in Southern Rhodesia and, despite a series of splits and personality clashes, and its unattractive racist image, could offer the RF two priceless advantages: a leader and a policy. Winston Field was a gentleman farmer from Marandellas. He may have been imperious and intolerant towards his colleagues but he was the ideal foil against charges that the RF was run by disreputable 'cowboys'. The DP's policy, which underwrote the RF's fifteen founding principles, represented a coherent and emotionally powerful alternative to 'whiteheadism'. Adopting the DP approach, the RF promised to preserve each community's right to maintain its own identity, to preserve proper standards by ensuring that advancement must be on merit, to uphold the principle of the Land Apportionment Act, to oppose compulsory integration, to support the government's right to provide separate amenities for the different races, and to protect skilled workers against cheap labour. Above all, the party promised 'that the Government of Southern Rhodesia will remain in responsible hands', and that it would ensure 'the permanent establishment of the European'.[20]

Much later, RF supporters were to argue about the meaning of the founding principles and whether they constituted Holy Writ. In 1962 the principles merely signalled a rejection of the 'winds of change' sweeping south towards the Zambezi. United in this cause, the party surprised almost everybody (including themselves) by winning 35 of the 50 A-roll constituencies and collecting 56.36 per cent of the vote in the elections of December 1962.[21]

In 1962 the RF won the provincial towns and the mining centres, a majority of the Bulawayo constituencies and all save one of the rural seats. The party then proceeded to win two 'safe' UFP seats in Salisbury in 1964, the 'independence' referendum of November 1964, and, in the general election of May 1965, won all 50 A-roll seats with 77 per cent of the vote. So, by 1965, when the UFP had disintegrated, the RF had clearly established its authority to speak for the white electorate. Having replaced Winston Field with Ian Smith as leader in April 1964, on the ground that Field was not pushing hard enough for UDI, the 'cowboys' were now ready to seize independence. But who were they? The noisy elements created the impression of a party for recent arrivals and the less sophisticated. Barry Schutz noted that several of the party's divisional, constituency, and branch chairmen in Salisbury and Bulawayo were artisans and shopkeepers, and that the activists tended to be South African born or be oriented to South African policies.[22] Yet the government caucus of 1962-5 was not radically different in composition from its UFP predecessor. Whereas some of its most committed supporters were drawn from white labour, only two RF MPs could be described as artisans. Larry Bowman calculated that, in 1965, three-quarters of RF MPs were professional men, farmers, ranchers, managers, or directors. Bowman also noted that the RF drew heavily from among the 'old' Rhodesians: 14 per cent of the RF's 1965 MPs were Rhodesian born compared with an overall total of 5.6 per cent of Rhodesian-born white adults; nearly one-third of the MPs had entered the country before 1942 compared with 18 per cent of the total white population; and, whereas nearly half the white population entered the country between 1952 and 1962, the figure for RF MPs was 28 per cent.[23] Bowman might also have observed that, apart from the greater likelihood of nominating Afrikaner or Greek candidates, the RF followed traditions set by its predecessors in choosing the better-educated, better-known, more respectable candidates to represent the party. The assumption was that Rhodesians would trust a man with a war record or who was a success in his occupation, who was a community leader, and a 'true Rhodesian'. The RF rarely insulted the white electorate by choosing representatives from the lower end of society.

A common view of the party is that it operated 'from the bottom upwards',[24] and that it was united in its opposition to African political advancement and in its support of permanent white rule. Both judgements are misleading. The first is less inaccurate because the RF was certainly democratic in structure and temper. Special provision was made to include extra-parliamentary activists at all levels. In 1965, for example, it was resolved that two of the four vice-presidents, the party chairman, and the deputy chairman should not be MPs. There was considerable traffic between the branches (about 165), and the headquarters in Salisbury. Ordinary branch members (about 15,000 in 1965, and 18,000 in 1968)[25] were encouraged to contact senior party officers and parliamentarians, and could easily do so in a society of small constituencies numbering fewer than 2,000 voters and where MPs and cabinet ministers were readily available. Cementing the democratic structure was the provision that each branch could send at least one delegate to the annual congresses, giving the branches a majority on the body which had the sole authority to amend the party constitution, principles, or policies. Finally, compared to the leisurely practices of other white parties, most RF branches held meetings between elections and could organise a comprehensive and personal canvass of constituencies. The branches which held regular meetings in the rural areas were usually the restive ones, and they often became very critical of government ministers who appeared to ignore them.[26] Seen in this light, the RF was a grass-roots party, a participatory democracy capable of entering all the recesses of the white electorate.

This assessment, however, probably overestimates the level of branch activity between elections.[27] In any case, the RF was governed from the top downwards. The national executive (consisting of the ten officeholders, all the RF MPs and fifty – all non-parliamentary – constituency representatives), the standing committee, and the party officers were in a better position than branch members to influence affairs. Ian Smith's authority over the RF stemmed in part from his day-to-day relations with his well-placed friends on these committees. Moreover, although white Rhodesia was a *de facto* one-party State after 1965, the State and not the party managed the country's affairs. The test was whether the party could implement its policy of provincialisation and, by 1971-2, it was apparent that it could not. Ministers and their civil servants became adept in deflecting demands for tougher segregation laws with arguments about 'legal' and 'technical' complications. When Smith did not want his hardliners to disrupt settlement talks the party took second place to the government. Indeed, if the RF had been ruled from the bottom upwards the history of white Rhodesia in the 1970s might have been very different. The 'small man', who wanted permanent white rule, might have been the foundation of the RF but he never controlled it.

The second judgement – that the RF was monolithic – reflects, in part, more general views about the state of white politics in the post-UDI years. Bowman claimed that, because the regimentation and repression of African life and politics was 'at the very heart of all white politics', there were no meaningful distinctions between or within the white political parties: 'If there is a choice within white politics, it is simply over language (for instance, white rule forever versus white rule for the foreseeable future) or over the best strategy to preserve a commonly accepted goal – the maintenance of the white-dominated political system.'[28] This view is not true of white politics in general and is not even true of the RF. For, within the party, the distinction between 'white rule forever versus white rule for the foreseeable future' became a fundamental one after 1968.

The 'white rule forever' school consisted of those members of the old DP who saw themselves as the heart and soul of the RF. Typical among them was W. J. Cary who assumed a role in the RF as the guardian of the DP's principles. Cary was born into a South African farming family in 1902, was educated in Bloemfontein, and migrated to Southern Rhodesia in 1924 where he took several jobs as an engineer and mine manager before settling upon ranching.[29] He joined the DP, won a Midlands seat in 1958, and committed himself wholeheartedly to the RF's founding principles. He had no time for Winston Field who had dithered over UDI, and not much more for Ian Smith whom he regarded as a 'liberal'. Cary denounced Smith's attempts in 1966 and 1968 to reach a settlement with Harold Wilson, arguing that UDI was not a device to wring more concessions out of the British government. While he denied being a 'racist' – insisting that the African was not innately inferior and disclaiming any intention of keeping him permanently in subjugation – Cary believed that the African was nowhere near ready for political advancement. For him UDI was the guarantee that the present system would remain in force until 'qualified' Rhodesians agreed to change it. In the meantime, the appropriate action was to introduce total political and social segregation along South African lines. Each racial group could then develop at its own pace within the framework of white rule. Under Cary, the 'qualified' Africans would have an interminable time to wait.

Brigadier Andrew Dunlop was another early member of the RF who had DP connections.[30] Born in India in 1907, educated at Wellington and Sandhurst, Dunlop had served in North Africa and Sicily before migrating to Southern Rhodesia after the Second World War and taking up ranching in the Midlands. A military man in appearance, bearing, and thinking, the Brigadier admired patriots and 'fine chaps', had a lot of 'chums' in the British Tory Party, including Julian Amery, Reginald Maudling, and Peter Thorneycroft, and thought of himself as 'conservative though reasonably liberal minded'. On arriving in Southern Rhodesia, Dunlop supported Sir Godfrey Huggins's United Party (the forerunner of the UFP) – 'like everyone else' – but switched to the DP after too many encounters with starry-eyed liberals. In November 1961 'Boss' Lilford sent a circular letter to 250 persons inviting them to form a new political party in opposition to the UFP and the DP.[31] Dunlop responded to the invitation and set up a Que Que branch of the Rhodesia Reform Party whose leader – Ian Smith – was a man he could respect. The new party embodied principles which rejected both the overt racism of the DP and the aggressive multiracialism of the whitehead government. It opposed forced integration and supported political advancement on merit, and it favoured the maintenance of separate facilities for health, education, and residential living, the provision for those who wished to live in a multiracial community, and the amendment rather than the repeal of the Land Apportionment Act. Dunlop was the sort of RF recruit Cary distrusted. Cary had a nose for 'former UFP types', and saw the Rhodesia Reform Party as a modified version of 'whiteheadism' because it accepted the meritocracy principle, failed to support enforced and permanent segregation, and had such a shortened view of 'the foreseeable future'. Even more dangerous were those who had formally represented the UFP or one of its predecessors: men like Desmond Lardner-Burke,[32] a lawyer from Gwelo, or John Wrathall,[33] a Bulawayo accountant, who had once been associated with the very liberal Garfield Todd and who later became leading figures in RF ministries. But Cary's deepest suspicions and loathing were reserved for the man who once abandoned right-wing politics to join the UFP: Ian Douglas Smith.

Smith was born in the mining township of Selukwe in 1919 where his Scottish father worked variously as a butcher, miner, farmer, baker, and garage proprietor. The boy attended the local primary school, was a boarder at Chaplin High School in Gwelo – where he played many sports very well – and began a commerce degree at Rhodes University in South Africa before enlisting in the RAF after the outbreak of war. Assigned to 237 (Rhodesia) Squadron of the RAF, Smith served in North Africa and Italy, crashed one plane on take-off, was shot down in another during an air raid, and served for a period with the Italian partisans. It was not a particularly distinguished career,[34] but the visible war injuries (a face repaired by plastic surgery and left partly expressionless), and his role with the partisans and eventual escape to Britain, were later exaggerated and exploited by the RF to convert him into an heroic figure. Returning to Rhodes, Smith completed his degree, and became an accomplished oarsman and a leader on the campus. Back in Southern Rhodesia he turned to ranching, married a young widow with two small children, and entered parliament in 1948 in opposition to the Huggins policies of gradual integration and government intervention in the economy. Ian Smith was not a spectacular addition to a weak opposition, and he had the good sense to join the newly formed Federal Party to participate in a federation which he distrusted but was prepared to tolerate. He was elected to the first federal parliament, rose to be chief whip of the Federal Party (renamed the UFP), resigned from the party over the 1961 constitution, helped to form the Rhodesia Reform Party, and then joined the coalition which became the RF. After the 1962 elections he became Minister of Finance under Winston Field.

Smith's opponents from the later 1960s liked to remark upon the early signs of relative mediocrity.[35] Friendly commentators emphasised the personal courage and honesty, the considerate and even-tempered nature, and the iron nerve. One biographer drew a distinction between the man and the politician, and detected just one flaw in the former: a tendency to be too loyal.[36] If this characteristic kept the politician aloof from the machinations in April 1964 to replace Winston Field it did not prevent him from steadily removing or downgrading ministers who opposed his policies thereafter. To some critics in the 1960s Smith was narrow-minded and inflexible;[37] and to others he was not the honest man he expected others to be, and was just half the leader his followers wanted. Perhaps his dealings with Harold Wilson and the British civil service had soured the raw colonial and turned him into a devious politician. Perhaps the experience of Winston Field in 1964, and his cabinet's firm rejection of the *Tiger* proposals in 1966, made him so wary that he never led until his followers pointed the way. Whatever the reasons, Ian Smith in 1970 was not a decisive leader of unimpeachable integrity.

He had a curious obsession with honesty. 'Ladies and Gentlemen, let us be honest about this'; this constant refrain from the late 1960s usually signalled a plea to reject a white opposition policy as impractical. It was 'dishonest' to suppose in 1970 that non-racialism or total segregation could work; but it was 'honest' to pretend that white supremacy could survive, unchallenged, in the foreseeable future. It was also 'honest' to contradict oneself – that is, make tactical shifts – provided that the strategy remained constant. So Smith could resign from the UFP over the 1961 constitution and in 1965 seek independence on the basis of that constitution. In November 1966 he could say that Rhodesians prided themselves on having a non-racialist constitution and in May 1968 applaud the future constitution precisely because it would be racialist.[38]

One reason for these apparent somersaults is that Smith was pursuing two objectives in the late 1960s: to secure the 'first prize', a settlement with the British government leading to a legalised independence and the removal of economic sanctions; and to cement white rule in Rhodesia by creating a 'Rhodesia' constitution in line with the RF's 1962 principles.[39] He could not achieve the latter without jeopardising his chances of attaining the former. Yet any settlement with the British government would have to satisfy London's Five Principles – which the majority of RF members opposed – and the prospect of a settlement became all the more unlikely after the inclusion of the Sixth Principle of No Independence Before Majority African Rule (NIBMAR).[40] Despite their bravado about overcoming sanctions, Smith and his ministers knew that Rhodesia's long-term future depended on a return to legality. As a consequence, Smith maintained his contacts with the British government while attempting to restrain his party for the sake of a settlement and, for his party's sake, to produce a constitution capable of preserving white rule in Rhodesia. It was impossible, in these circumstances, to remain consistent and honest.

The important point is that Ian Smith headed a coalition not a monolithic party. It was held together during the late 1960s by its rejection of black rule. According to the *Rhodesian Financial Gazette*, however, there was 'little agreement yet on what future patterns should look like'.[41] One wing of the party elevated the principle of advancement upon merit, had opposed the whitehead government because it was moving too fast, wanted a fair settlement with the British government, and believed that whites should retain control over Rhodesian affairs for a long time to come. Smith, the leader of this faction, was supported by former UFP members of his cabinet, by about half the caucus, and by a majority on the key party committees. The other wing wanted to convert the 'permanent establishment of the European' into permanent white rule, rejected the principle of a non-racial meritocracy, and regarded any settlement talks as mischievous and irrelevant. Cary's views were typical of this faction whose principal supporters were Ralph Nilson, the Party Chairman, Des Frost, his deputy, about one-third of the caucus, and a clear majority among the party activists at the divisional, constituency, and branch level.

IV

The two wings of the RF fought a running battle in 1968-70 over the issues of white supremacy and segregation. The hardline right was defeated because it could not counter Smith's growing authority within the party, and because many on the right were seduced by the prospect of a settlement into abandoning or suspending their deeper convictions.

The first contest was over proposals for a new constitution. A Commission was appointed in March 1967 to devise a constitution 'best suited to the needs of the sovereign independent status of Rhodesia'.[42] Headed by W. R. ('Sam') Whaley,[43] one of Smith's close political *confidants*, the Commission reported in April 1968, rejecting 'both perpetual European domination and ultimate African domination' in favour of the 'ultimate racial parity of political representation'. Weighty arguments and fine details were adduced to support the parity principle and Whaley's attempt to find a separate place for the chiefs and for the Ndebele. The result was a complicated franchise for the lower house which involved the creation of five separate means of election.

Ian Smith, who liked the Whaley proposals,[44] waited for opinions to crystallise. Right-wingers were quick to denounce Whaley by pointing out that the parity principle imposed a limit on white supremacy. Two party committees reached a compromise solution – the Yellow Paper (thus named for the colour of the duplicating paper) which proposed two stages: the first, to last for five years, accepted the parity principle but guaranteed European control; the second replaced parity with three provincial councils (one for whites and two for blacks), and a multiracial national parliament where representation would be determined in proportion to income tax paid. Lord Graham and William Harper, both cabinet ministers and former DP members, rejected the Yellow Paper in favour of racially separate provincial chambers, and a national parliament with a fixed and overwhelming European majority. A debate over the two sets of proposals raged in caucus, the national executive, and in congress between July and September 1968. The Prime Minister threw his full weight behind the Yellow Paper at the September congress which approved this compromise by just eleven votes (217 votes to 206 with 70 abstentions).[45] In the midst of the struggle Smith ejected Harper from the ministry,[46] and Graham resigned from the government after the congress rejected his proposals. Having won a majority and disposed of the 'extremists', Smith joined Harold Wilson on board HMS *Fearless* the following month but refused to make the further concessions necessary to obtain a settlement. The Prime Minister had thwarted his own right wing, without obtaining his first prize.

On 21 November 1968 Ralph Nilson, as Party Chairman, sent one of his regular circular letters to the divisional, constituency, and branch chairmen.[47] He explained that, because the settlement talks had been suspended after *Fearless*, the government was proceeding with its own constitutional proposals. Nilson had supported the Harper-Graham blueprint for the provincialisation of Rhodesian politics and in his circular letter urged the party to choose only those candidates who were committed to implementing separate development. Aware that it might not be possible to entrench separate development in the constitution, he pointed out that apartheid in South Africa had emerged from the 'hearts and brains' of the National Party and not from any constitutional document. Nilson looked to parliament, therefore, to enact what he saw as the RF's central objective of provincialisation. He concluded his letter with a warning: if the parliament failed to implement provincialisation 'I believe that the white man will have no future in Rhodesia'.

The government announced in February 1969 that the Yellow Paper could not be translated into a workable constitution and Smith, with Nilson's support, coaxed the branches into accepting the compromise which became the 1969 constitution.[48] The right, including Nilson, remained dissatisfied. A few had already left the party in 1966-7 over Smith's attempts to negotiate a settlement, and a few more walked out when the RF approved the Yellow Paper. One of the early dissidents was

Wilfred Brooks who edited the monthly journal *Property and Finance*. Brooks had been a fanatical Todd supporter in the later 1950s, experienced an overnight conversion to right-wing politics, and used his paper from the mid-1960s to expose Smith's 'betrayal' of the white man in Rhodesia. Another rebel was Len Idensohn, a municipal employee, who had been the RF's Divisional Chairman of Salisbury East and who was to project himself in the 1970s as the defender of the white race. Inside the RF, the right continued to voice concern about Smith's concessions for the sake of a settlement and regarded the 1969 constitution as a sell-out because it had adopted the hated parity principle. Smith cleverly circumvented them by exploiting the uncertainty about what precisely was being proposed and by assuring the branches that parity was a very distant prospect. Thus thwarted, the right's one remaining avenue of protest was the referendum where many joined the liberals to raise the 'No' vote to 27.52 per cent.[49]

Wilfred Brooks had already worked out that the government had no intention of fully implementing the RF's 1962 principles. He recognised that Smith was either too committed to a settlement or not convinced that extensive segregation and permanent white rule were desirable or possible. Yet the vast majority of RF members in 1969-70 believed that provincialisation – which for them implied separate facilities such as post offices, parks, and hospitals, as well as separate governments and enduring white rule – was the proper and attainable objective. For this reason, congress resolutions supporting provincialisation became the RF's equivalent of a vote for motherhood. At the post-referendum congress in 1969 the pre-eminent Mashonaland Rural Division, backed by the Midlands and Matabeleland Divisions, sponsored a resolution calling on the government to proceed actively with implementation and to report progress to each annual congress.[50] Rowan Cronje, regarded even then as a possible successor to Smith, expressed the general mood of the 1969 congress when he said that provincialisation was 'the crux of the whole future of Rhodesia'. The argument was that, by encouraging Africans to develop a sense of responsibility for their own areas, their political aspirations would be satisfied, the 'African economy' (that is, the TTLs) would be developed, and the separate interests of Europeans and Africans would be safeguarded. Ian Smith made a masterly intervention. He strongly supported the 'stimulating' policy of encouraging -self-government in local affairs and warned that undue-delay might lead – to 'frustration and disenchantment'. He also counselled against haste saying that, while the government was just as enthusiastic as the party, it recognised that the South Africans had taken a long time to set up Bantustans and did not want to hand over responsibilities to people who were not ready for them.

The RF's internal debate continued after the referendum because the party remained formally committed to provincialisation. The right, however, faced three disadvantages. First, the civil service kept supplying the government with evidence that the provincialisation proposals for subdividing the political system on racial grounds were impractical, ill-conceived, costly, and far more complicated than RF congresses envisaged or understood.[51] Secondly, the government had no intention of allowing segregationist policies to prevent a settlement. This attitude sealed the fate of the Property Owners' (Residential Protection) Bill. Originating in 1967 in the desire to exclude Asians and Coloureds (as 'Europeans') from the poorer white ('European') areas of Salisbury and Bulawayo, and strongly promoted by Dennis Divaris on behalf of the Belvedere Residents' Association, the Bill proposed that the President could declare certain areas 'exclusive', thereby denying rights of occupation or ownership to non-white families. Protests from the Asian and Coloured communities and the Churches were matched by strong supporting statements from successive RF congresses. The government, backed by further civil service evidence pointing out the 'technical' difficulties, and realising that no British government could countenance such a racist proposal, dropped the Bill every time the subject became 'inconvenient'. Thirdly, the right was vulnerable to demands that Rhodesia should speak as one voice. The approach of elections in Rhodesia in April 1970 made it necessary to unite the party and the country behind Ian Smith. Ideological purity had to be suspended for the sake of solidarity. And no one felt this more keenly, and with greater regret, than the RF's Party Chairman.

Ralph Nilson, a Mazoe farmer, was a bluff individual who lacked – on his own admission – social finesse and skills in public relations.[52] His brother, Peter, who entered parliament in 1970, travelled with the right wing into the RAP in 1977 and it is highly probable that Ralph, had he lived beyond 1972, would have followed the same course. Alternatively, he might well have led a faction out of the RF much earlier. Yet in 1968-70 the Party Chairman felt bound to reconcile the two pressures exerted upon him. In his circular letter of November 1968 Nilson had warned that the Argus Press was feeding stories to the electorate about the RF being in disarray, and was trying to ridicule the Prime Minister and break the party. Nilson was particularly angry about suggestions that the RF included 'very strong left and right movements' and was dominated by the (notably right-wing) Mashonaland Rural Division.[53] Nor was he pleased about attempts to brand Ian Smith and the South African Prime Minister as 'liberals'. Perhaps, in denying the latter charge, he wanted to deflect right-wing doubts about Smith, or perhaps he just wanted to remind the Prime Minister that 'liberal' was a term of abuse in the RF.

Nilson returned to the criticisms of Smith in his annual report to congress in 1969 when he denied that the Prime Minister and his government 'are selling us down the river'.[54] After all, he said, the country had been pulled back from the brink of disaster in 1962, the government had won overwhelming electoral support and support for the constitution, it had won recognition from the judiciary, 'been an inspiration to many people in the world', 'improved race relations beyond belief, and consolidated Southern Africa 'by repulsing communist infiltration'. Nilson said he was 'no hero worshipper' but he would give credit where it was due.

This man [Smith] has a certain mixture of characteristics of caution, obstinacy, dedication, vision, tenacity and toughness that have evoked rage in some, frustration in others, and admiration and loyalty in most. The plain truth is, I know of no other man who has the physical and mental toughness necessary to have led Rhodesia where it is to-day.

Nilson's warm endorsement of Smith did not inhibit him from attacking the government. His 1969 report pointedly reminded ministers that the RF was put into power by 'the man in the street', the man who first encountered the problems of integration, who could not afford to send his children to South African universities, buy a second car, own his own swimming pool, or pay for residential exclusiveness. Nilson claimed that the UFP had failed precisely because it lost touch with its grass roots, and because it departed from laid down policy and thought it could negotiate with the British government to the advantage of Rhodesia. It was a thinly veiled warning. If the RF could not thrive without Ian Smith, Smith's government would not survive if it abandoned the RF's principles or its natural constituency.

Nilson returned to this theme at the next congress which was held in Salisbury in September 1970.[55] He referred to 'certain signs of restlessness' arising from the feeling that the government had no intention of addressing the problems of 'multiracialism' inherited from its predecessors. Although he spoke again of Smith's 'wise and courageous leadership' he reminded ministers and MPs of their moral and political obligation to implement the party's principles: to do otherwise would 'make a complete nonsense and mockery' of UDI and, after all, 'was UDI not the means of ensuring the future of Rhodesia and has Rhodesia any future without the European?' Nilson's own instincts pointed him clearly towards full separate development, permanent and undiluted white supremacy, and the rejection of any further negotiations with the British. He also had to bow to reality: the electorate probably wanted a settlement, Rhodesia had to remain united, and Smith was the best hope for both. The battler, however, was not going to submit easily. Was it not possible –

he asked Smith – for immediate administrative action to remove 'the small things' which caused humiliation and indignity? The minor aspects of integration attracted considerable attention at the 1969 and 1970 congresses. In 1969 the congress unanimously approved a resolution demanding that the party's ninth principle – opposing compulsory integration and calling for separate facilities – 'be more rigidly enforced'. Some members wanted separate post offices and hospitals, others were worried about evidence of multiracialism on television and of integration in the police and teacher training. A number of divisions submitted resolutions referring to the planned new Salisbury hospital and expressed concern about the provision of facilities for multiracial teaching. Smith assured the delegates that the teaching hospital would provide the best medical service in Rhodesia, save money on overseas training, and avoid the possibility of having to take European patients to an African hospital. He also promised that noisy and unclean Africans visiting the 'selected cases' from the African areas would not inconvenience European patients, and guaranteed that no European patient would be examined by an African medical student. Within a year the Minister of Health was forced to make much the same speech in defending the use of Asian and Coloured sisters in European wards and theatres. He promised that every 'administrative' effort was being made to comply with the RF's ninth principle. The insurmountable problem was the lack of money. Rhodesia, as Nilson himself pointed out in his 1970 report, simply did not have the resources to provide separate facilities in all the 'affected areas'.

One issue which always excited the party faithful and caused ministerial anxiety was black student behaviour at the University College. RF members were quite straightforward about the university's role and status: the government paid most of the bills and, therefore, could and should exert its authority; the university's courses should all be of 'immediate and direct benefit to Rhodesia'; treacherous academics and disobedient (black) students should be dismissed if they questioned European rule and civilisation; the races should have separate residences to protect the hygienic standards of white students. In 1969 the Midlands Division proposed that the government should withhold grants from any student wishing to enrol in Political Science because the humanities and social sciences were responsible for the demonstrations and the general lack of discipline. The Midlands resolution was shelved but in 1970 – in secret session – congress approved a resolution calling for more effective government representation on the University Council and tougher actions against dissident students.[56] John Wrathall, as Minister of Finance, admitted that the government was placed in 'the most difficult position' of being 'a buffer between the public, Congress and the University'. He pleaded for time, knowing that any precipitate action such as imposing government control over the Council 'would not be acceptable to a University worthy of its name'. Ian Smith intervened to protect the university from the barbarians. The graduate of Rhodes University reminded congress of a point missed in the discussion: 'the question of the recognition of the degree from the University'. He did not like the multiracial university: 'we inherited this thing, which was wrong'. Nevertheless, the government had to restore Rhodesians' confidence in their own institution so that parents would not send their children outside the country. By denigrating the university, and by trying to police its activities, the critics were encouraging a brain drain in search of a more respectable institution. They were also undermining one of Rhodesia's claims to be a civilised society.

The RF in 1970 brought together men and women across class, ethnic, and regional lines who had a common interest in supporting UDI, and resisting majority rule and forced integration. RF members also despised or feared the same enemies: African nationalists, 'extreme left' white Rhodesians, foreign missionaries, and devious British politicians. The RF was divided, however, over strategies and tactics, and could easily have splintered at any stage between 1968 and 1970 were it not for the manipulative skills of the party high command and the necessity of presenting a united front to the white electorate and the British government.

V

The party's internal disputes did not affect its capacity to dominate the white electorate. After a sweeping victory in the referendum the RF trounced the newly formed, non-racial Centre Party (CP) in the elections of April 1970. The CP did win 24 per cent of the vote in the sixteen constituencies it contested, and exceeded 30 per cent in five of them. But, with 76 per cent of the popular vote, and all fifty white seats, the RF had a firm grip over white Rhodesia on the eve of the war.

A principal factor in its success was that the party projected itself as the defender of the Rhodesian way of life. The 1970 handbook for candidates and constituency chairmen included a 'suggested draft address' which outlined the RF's case for re-election.[57] It began with the past. Rhodesians were to be reminded of and commended for their 'historic decision' of 1962 'to stand and fight on the Zambezi' by returning a government pledged 'to preserving our European civilisation and to ensuring a permanent home for the white man'. Above all, they were to be reminded of what they had rejected.

We must never forget the plan of our predecessors to hand over to majority rule which, as we all know to-day, would have led Rhodesia back to the days of anarchy and darkness which the pioneers found when they first arrived.

We must never forget the Land Apportionment Act, with its inherent protection for both black and white, was going to be scrapped, destroying the foundation of our security.

We must never forget that the country was in a state of lawlessness with African racialism rampaging and unchecked where it was not always possible for any man of any race to walk in safety.

Remember the petrol bombings, the brutality and intimidation that went with them? [Emphasis in the original]

The RF government had stopped all these 'outrages' and, after dealing patiently with 'an intransigent and deceitful British Government', took the step of UDI in 1965 which, overnight, made Rhodesians 'masters in their own house' and turned the country into a cohesive nation thereby demonstrating a degree of enterprise and ingenuity which 'astounded' the world. The message was that the RF had restored national pride and self-confidence, and should be returned to achieve the remaining 'vital' objectives: 'the total breaking of sanctions; recognition in one form or another; a continual strengthening of our economy, providing not only new opportunity and hope for our own people, but further attractions for still higher immigration, thus securing beyond doubt the western civilisation which we have built.'

The reference to 'our own people' was significant. The RF never disguised the fact that it was a party for white Rhodesia. At the end of the standard speech 'the people of Rhodesia' were to be asked to endorse the RF. Given that, under the 1969 constitution, Africans had no opportunity to vote for or against the RF, the 'people of Rhodesia' were clearly the whites. There was a reference to 'all Rhodesia's people' at the end of a section expressing the RF's 'over-riding' concern for 'racial harmony'. To achieve harmony, the government must take positive action to promote understanding and remove the causes of animosity. No RF speaker in 1970 would be silly enough to suppose that the way to remove antagonism was to end discrimination. Inter-racial strife stemmed from 'the agitation of political opportunists and mischief-makers'. Positive and remedial action depended on the economic development of the TTLs, co-operation with the chiefs 'as the recognised leaders of the vast majority of our African · population', and pursuing the policy of provincialisation whereby responsibility would be delegated (without a lowering of standards) to allow educated Africans to employ their talents to further the interests of their own people.

The *Handbook* also offered some important advice for party canvassers: the 'majority' of male urban voters are small cogs in a large machine; at home they are heads of households and should be respected. Never argue with them, especially in front of the family.

Never launch personal attacks on the opposition and don't be sarcastic or clever or lecture voters at length. Remember that 'the average Rhodesian is inherently courteous' and will respond to courtesy. Never approach him [sic] at meal times or after 9.00 p.m. and note that Rhodesians respond better to 'bread-and-butter' issues than ideology. Candidates were ordered not to depart from party policy, not to be 'extreme' or 'indiscreet', and never to be led too far afield.

The advice reflected a shrewd understanding of the electorate and of its male-dominated households. The party was thorough in its planning, knew how to avoid damage, concentrated on psychological approaches, and cultivated an image of moderation. This latter point was crucial. Whatever outsiders might think, and whatever its own right wing might want, the RF was determined to project itself as the party of common sense which wanted no more than the preservation of decent and civilised society. Professional (by Rhodesian standards) and practical (compared with the CP or the far right), the RF presented itself as the party best equipped to represent Rhodesia.

The *Handbook* did not mention the party's strongest card: Ian Smith. In 1969 the CP commissioned a subsidiary of an international public relations firm to conduct a survey of political attitudes and images.[58] One of its findings was that Smith 'has an exceptionally fine image, the answer in fact to a Public Relations man's prayer'. By contrast Pat Bashford, the Karoi farmer who was president of the CP and a fundamentally decent man, was considered to be 'devious, ineffective, unpopular, unreliable and not very acceptable'. As a result, Bashford was approached just before the 1969 referendum by 'Jock' Anderson, the former Army Commander who had been sacked in 1964 because he could not be trusted to support a rebellion.[59] Anderson wanted Bashford to step down in favour of a man 'of more experience and greater political stature'. There were four possibilities: Geoff Ellman-Brown; Evan Campbell, the Chairman of the Standard Bank and a former High Commissioner to London; Air Vice-Marshal Harold Hawkins, an Australian who was the Rhodesian government representative in South Africa; and John Graylin, a former Federal minister. Modestly, Bashford agreed to stand aside but the four notables remained in the closet arguing that the time was not yet right to make their move. In 1969 they were happy for Pat Bashford to take on someone who seemed unbeatable.

By 1970 Ian Smith was wielding the scalpel and the bludgeon with equal effect. His more illustrious opponents were either scared of him or had already been destroyed. Evan Campbell was one of the victims. Late in 1968, following the collapse of the *Fearless* talks, the captains of commerce, industry, and mining planned that each in turn would come out with a public statement denouncing UDI and calling upon the government to accept the latest British proposals.[60] E. S. Newsom, Chairman of the Rhodesian Iron and Steel Corporation, took the plunge, and Campbell followed. Ellman-Brown was due to speak next when Ian Smith launched a scathing attack on the 'extreme left' and 'the old gang' for wanting to raise the flag of surrender. With one speech he humiliated the leaders of the economy into silence. Smith could be equally brutal with ministerial dissidents. In 1970 he stopped two of them from winning seats in the Senate.[61] A few back-benchers were restive but most of them addressed him deferentially as 'Sir', and referred to him respectfully as 'the old man'. No one, in politics or in business, was anxious to challenge him.

His strength and charisma owed little to oratorical skills. His long-winded speeches and ill-formed sentences were delivered in a dull, flat, nasal monotone. Nor, at first, was Smith much better on television. Harvey Ward, who became Director-General of RBC/TV and was a passionate and unapologetic right-winger, claimed that Smith was 'terrible' on television. Ward took much of the credit for converting an unattractive personality into the 'dour iron man' who took over Rhodesian screens.[62] Des Frost, who left the RF in 1977 and joined the RAP, reproached Ward for doing 'too much of a good job on Ian Smith'.[63] For Ian Smith was successfuly projected on the screen, in RF brochures, and on the platform as the 'true Rhodesian': born and bred in a land he would never leave; committed to Christian values and to the maintenance of civilisation; unyielding in the face of threats and sanctions; shrewd when confronted by British duplicity; always courageous, masculine, and upright. A Smith speech might ramble on incoherently, the wit might be heavy-handed, and the finger jabbing the air might not be timed to match the words. None of this mattered. The image and the message were sufficient, and by 1970 he was invested with an aura which frightened his opponents, induced women of all ages to speak reverently of 'Mr Smith', and mystified those of his critics who thought of him as dishonest and dangerous. Very simply, the true Rhodesian, 'the symbol of the independence struggle',[64] told his audience what it wanted to hear, and they loved him for it.

The depleted and confused state of the liberal opposition also helps to explain the RF's increasing grip on the white electorate. For six years after the RF's first victory in 1962 the 'left' struggled to find a separate and acceptable identity within the framework of white politics.[65] The great defeat had placed it in a dilemma: if the left remained true to its non-racialist principles it would alienate the white electorate without making headway among the African nationalists; if it abandoned non-racialism in order to become a presentable alternative government then it would not differ greatly from the RF. Unable to find an effective role 'the old gang' stumbled along after 1965 in the Rhodesian Constitutional Association (RCA), a non-political association of the effete and the well-spoken. The left's problems were compounded by UDI, and by the RF's ability to equate Rhodesia's survival with its own success. N.A.F. Williams, the chairman of the RCA, highlighted this difficulty in his 1967 annual report: 'if you are anti-Rhodesian Front you are anti-Rhodesia, a confusion which erupts (sic) such words as "traitor"'.[66] There was just one way of retreating with honour: to argue the case for restoring the links with the Crown and for obtaining a legalised independence. The RCA pursued this line after 1965, without making any real impression.

Another organisation pursued similar objectives through high-level contacts with Smith and members of the British government. Forum, which was staffed by the lieutenants of commerce, industry, and mining (and discreetly backed by the captains), tried in 1967-9 to bring the parties to the negotiating table and urged Smith to accept the *Fearless* proposals. Ian Smith repeatedly assured them of his support for their efforts, and of his own attempts to allay RF fears that Forum was an 'extremist' organisation. His attack on Newsom and Campbell, however, and the decision to proceed with the 1969 constitution – coupled with their growing suspicion that the Prime Minister had no intention of dealing with his 'wild boys' – persuaded the business houses that their 'non-party' activities had made no headway.

The Centre Party set out to restore the non-racial ideal in white politics, and fought bravely in the 1969 referendum and the 1970 elections. Formed in 1968 on the initiative of young professional men and women, the party wanted to establish a representative democracy based on a qualified franchise, to remove racial discrimination, install a system of advancement on merit, and to uphold the rule of law. The CP did not support the principle of African majority rule, preferring instead the notion of rule by a non-racial meritocracy. For a brief moment the CP rallied the flagging forces of the left. Unrepentant Tory monarchists and the survivors of whiteheadism joined forces with a new generation of idealists to do battle with the RF. Their alliance did not last long. One section of the new party was more determined to win government, and to negotiate a legalised independence, than to pursue the Rhodes dictum of equal rights for all civilised men. Led initially by Morris Hirsch, the indefatigable little doctor from Que Que and former whitehead *confidant*, the pragmatists argued that the party must accept the reality of white power and try to reform from within. Hirsch walked out of the CP in December 1968 – he left every organisation in a huff when he was outvoted – and Nick McNally, a Salisbury lawyer and good Catholic, assumed the role of advising the left when it was proper to accept the status quo. Accepting reality in 1970 meant working within the framework of parity and the 1969 constitution. This view remained dominant in the party until late in 1971. Not that the CP's opinions counted for much. The referendum and election defeats had reduced the party to a mere talking-shop, incapable of thwarting Ian Smith and the RF.

Periodically, the RF tried to extend its influence by endorsing candidates for municipal elections but even party members preferred to vote for independents. The RF was more successful in cementing its ascendancy by building on extensive personal contacts with key interest groups. Party supporters were prominent in peak associations, and most notably in the RNFU and the RTA whose council members in the late 1960s signalled the extent of their special relationship by joining the RF cabinet in an annual fishing competition.[67] A few farmers, like Pat Bashford, Tim Gibbs, a cattle rancher from Matabeleland and a son of the former Governor, and Roy Asburner, a wealthy tobacco farmer from Raffingora, remained or became active opponents of the RF in 1969-70. Occasionally, the farmer organisations clashed with the government over issues ranging from prices to input costs. But the political and personal loyalties of the majority of farmers – cemented in the Farmers' Associations, the Intensive Conservation Area committees, and the country clubs where known CP figures could feel isolated[68] – assured the RF of a firm if sometimes irritable base in the rural communities. Sustained fights were rare and, in any case, the government usually won because the assertion of state control over the economy after UDI had reduced the power of the RNFU and the RTA to determine an independent course.

The RF was also assured of strong support in the civil service. Rhodesians always argued that one reason for resisting majority rule was that African governments quickly politicised the administration. The neutrality of their own civil service was allegedly protected by the rules prohibiting civil servants from joining political parties and requiring the political parties to address civil servants in separate, closed meetings at election time. Yet absolute neutrality was impossible. Simply by administering the Rhodesian State after 1965 the civil service was participating in the rebellion and helping to keep the RF in power.

A number of senior civil servants went much further. The most notorious among them was Hostes Nicolle, the Secretary for Internal Affairs. Once described as 'virtually another member of the Cabinet',[69] Nicolle sent a memorandum around the Ministry on 5 December 1968 denouncing the 'deadly poison' contained in the British government's *Fearless* proposals.[70] Nicolle wanted to ensure that Provincial and District Commissioners could, in their dealings with both blacks and whites, 'counter some of the wishful thinking and adverse propaganda which appears to be floating around'. The language was highly colourful and hardly judicious, and unusual for men of his status. *Tiger* was a 'hyena' and *Fearless* a 'jackal'; the Privy Council was a 'witchdoctor' and the British were simply untrustworthy and guilty of sharp practice with 'their declared aim of majority rule chaos'. The significant point is that Nicolle's version of the past could have been composed by the Mashonaland Rural Division of the RF: the whites had been leaving Rhodesia before UDI because the country had no clear future except for the black rule which the British were trying to impose; the experience of African rule 'clearly showed' that there would be economic collapse, retrogression, 'the usual civil strife and chaos', and the ejection of whites; those whites who would sell their birthright for a mess of pottage wanted to lift the economy into overdrive while making their fortune and then getting out; those same whites, 'a familiar residue of the past' (presumably 'the old gang'), continued to believe – despite the 'glaring examples' to the contrary – that Africans 'can successfully operate a Government with a sophisticated and enduring civilised economy'.

Hostes Nicolle ran the most important department dealing with the black majority, and did so with assumptions which echoed RF policy documents. His two immediate successors as Secretary were also unashamed RF supporters. On the other hand, it would be a mistake to regard Internal Affairs, or the rest of the civil service, as mere pawns or reproductions of the RF. First, even the supposed hardliners within Internal Affairs had a different conception of 'community development' from the one proposed by the segregationists. Whereas the RF right wing thought in terms of the separate development of distinct racial communities, the visionaries of Internal Affairs hoped to create 'interdependent, self-responsible and self-regulating local governments'.[71] Secondly, even the RF sympathisers – for example, in the Ministry of Local Government – were known to clash with ministers who wanted to implement the latest right-wing policy. The common sense and human decency of civil servants, and non-deliberate bureaucratic delay, saved the country from many lunacies.

Thirdly, although the conspicuous dissidents had resigned or been removed, a few like Ken Flower of the Central Intelligence Organisation (CIO) and Stan O'Donnell, the Secretary for Foreign Affairs, continued to give unwelcome advice. Flower,[72] one of the intriguing characters of this story, had migrated from Britain to Southern Rhodesia in 1937 to become a Mounted Trooper with the British South Africa Police (BSAP). He served in the Horn of Africa during and after the Second World War, returned to the BSAP in 1948 and rose to the rank of Deputy Commissioner with experience in riot control and counter-insurgency.

In 1963 Winston Field, a man he greatly admired but whose RF government he detested, invited him to form CIO. For the next eighteen years
until his retirement in 1981, Flower advised four Prime Ministers – Field,
Smith, Muzorewa, and Mugabe – and, during the 1960s and 1970s,
Organised the infiltration of the guerrilla organisations and maintained
covert external links with Western countries. His attempts in the late
1970s to restrain the warriors and to press for a negotiated settlement
fostered rumours that he was a mole for British intelligence.[73] In 1970 he
lived in the shadows, known to very few Rhodesians. Already, he was
trying to balance an instinctive liberalism with a chess player's view of
war and politics, a policeman's preference for civil action against insurgency, a secret service predilection for intrigue, and a politician's sense
of self-importance. Flower was an intellectual who yearned for more
enlightened company than RF ministers and the higher ranks of the
BSAP and the Army could provide. Convinced he knew how to combat
insurgency, just as he later claimed to know when and how to negotiate
with insurgents, his advice to Ian Smith in 1970 was occasionally circumspect, usually well reasoned, and often irksome.

Overall, the civil service was honest, efficient, and hard-working.
This small society had acquired or produced an elite of considerable
talent. In 1970, of the forty-nine secretaries, deputy-, and under-
secretaries, and members of the Public Services Board, sixteen were
Rhodesian born (most of them attached to Internal Affairs) and another
twelve had been born in South Africa. Seventeen had migrated from
Britain, two from India, and one each from Australia and Northern
Rhodesia. Apart from Internal Affairs, therefore, the upper levels of the
civil service were staffed mainly by post-1945 immigrants from Britain
and South Africa, and by men who had post-secondary education or
been considered sufficiently able and ambitious to be drafted into the
Federal civil service. The cream went into the Treasury where all the
senior staff had overseas qualifications and would have fitted into the
upper levels of any Western administration.[74] Moreover, a handful of the
senior men were to remain in top positions from UDI until Zimbabwe's
independence, a significant factor contributing to the stability and
commitment of Rhodesia's administration, and to Ian Smith's
confidence in his advisers.

The government owed much of its political survival to the loyalty
and efficiency of the civil service. In turn, and despite the battles with
the Public Services Association over pay and conditions,[75] the
government honoured its obligations to the senior appointees by
showering them with decorations and awards.[76] Members of the
statutory boards – dealing with subjects ranging from economic
development to marketing, banking to censorship – did not need any

inducement, although they also received decorations and were paid a few thousand dollars for attendance money. Notions of neutrality hardly applied and, soon after 1962, the RF began stacking the boards with 'reliable' appointments.[77] The party had its own application form which was available to branch members who wanted positions on these boards. Although questions were asked about specific qualifications and experience the form was more concerned with eliciting information about the applicant's party membership and seniority in the party, as well as such personal details as the length of time spent in Rhodesia as a resident and citizen.[78]

It is not known how many appointments were made by this method but notable RF supporters headed or were members of some fifty statutory boards by the mid-1970s,[79] Broadcasting and television proved to be among the most reliable of these quasi-government authorities.[80] The Governors agreed that radio and television had a duty to support the government of the day, that the cornerstone of media policy was 'the preservation of law and order', and that permissiveness and matters of political contention should be avoided. The latter decision was designed to protect the 'credulous and unsophisticated' blacks but did not prevent the Commentary programme in 1970-1 from delivering RF policies to white audiences just after the early evening news. The bias was pronounced and unashamed, with the result that the white radio and television audiences were well informed on two subjects: they knew that the outside world was full of evil, and that Rhodesians were walking along the path of righteousness.

VI

By 1970 the government was firmly in control of black Rhodesia, the RF was firmly in control of white Rhodesia, and the right was determined to take control of the RF. There remained the two unresolved questions of white politics: whether the government would achieve its 'first prize', and whether the segregationists would achieve their South African solution. Both questions were answered definitively, and in the negative, within two years.

The RF caucus shifted further to the right as a result of the 1970 elections. The new parliament contained twenty survivors from 1962, eighteen members elected between 1963 and 1969, and twelve members elected tor the tirst time in 1970, of whom half were to join the RAP in 1977 while another three (all Afrikaners) were certainly on the party's right. One of the new members was Rodney Simmonds who regarded himself as 'typical' of the 1970 intake in wanting to implement the principles of 1962.[81] Simmonds was born in Marandellas in 1925, educated at

Prince Edward School in Salisbury, and served with the Southern Rhodesian Air Force in the Middle East and Europe during the war. After the war he took a degree at Rhodes University before joining the old Native Affairs Department where he rose to the rank of DC. Simmonds spent seventeen years of his service in the Mrewa-Mtoko region where he acquired a reputation for tough action against the nationalists in a notoriously unsettled area. Early in December 1967 he was driving near a store in the Pungwe TTL where he observed an African wearing a straw hat habitually used by restrictees. He arrested the man on suspicion of committing an offence, handcuffed other Africans, beat them about the head with a riding crop, and arrested them for allegedly engaging in illegal political activities and for being insolent towards authority. Charged on five counts of assault and unlawful arrest, Simmonds appeared in court on 20 March 1968 where the magistrate, after praising Simmonds for restoring order in Mrewa, found that he had been 'unnecessarily vicious' and had committed 'a serious abuse of authority'. Simmonds was fined $300, and he resigned from Internal Affairs, convinced that the service had declined once the DCs had lost their magisterial powers.[82]

The reverberations from the Simmonds affair were felt throughout Internal Affairs. His 'union' – the Internal Affairs Association – was astounded that the magistrate had accepted the Africans' version of events, rejected the DC's evidence, and ignored pleas in mitigation supplied by Hostes Nicolle, an RF MP, and by local tribal leaders. Rumours abounded that a 'black book' had been opened listing those members who refused to subscribe to the fund to help Simmonds pay the fine. Meanwhile Simmonds was appointed Administrative Secretary of the RF. In 1970 he won the Mtoko seat with a handsome majority after presenting himself as a man who had demonstrated 'leadership' in the struggle against dissent, who knew how to 'deal' with Africans, and who was wholly committed to racial segregation and permanent white rule.

Simmonds, his fellow back-benchers, and the party headquarters kept prodding the government to introduce provincialisation. They also agitated for additional separate facilities in order to prevent 'racial friction' and the influx of Africans into European residential areas. Caucus members and party officials were particularly critical of ministers and civil servants for their tardiness in promoting white immigration and demanded the payment of higher salaries for Europeans, the removal of Africans from semi-skilled jobs such as driving buses, and the lowering of selection criteria, all to bring more whites into the country and to persuade them to stay.[83] This agitation accelerated after a by-election in August 1971 produced a major swing against the RF. Although the RF retained the Mabelreign seat in Salisbury its majority was reduced to sixty-eight and the party collected just 46 per cent of the votes. Its main opponent was not the Centre Party but the right-wing Candour League whose candidate received 40 per cent of the poll. The by-election was complicated by the Greater Salisbury issue, and the allegedly dictatorial approach of Mark Partridge, the Minister of Local Government and Housing, who had forced the seven Town Management Boards of the peri-urban areas into a more centralised municipality. In addition, there were complaints from tenants and their neighbours about the dilapidated condition of government-owned housing.[84] *Property and Finance* drew its own conclusions from the result: the RF was no longer 'impregnable', and was nearly defeated because it had become 'a centrist party of expedience, similar to the UFP of old'.[85] While the left of white politics continued to argue that the RF was deceiving the electorate by pretending that it *could* achieve permanent European rule,[86] the right attacked the dangerous illusion that the party – under Smith – was even trying to do so.

Des Frost, as the RF's Chairman, shared the right's anxieties. Frost, who had succeeded Nilson, was born in South Africa in 1925. His family was of English and Huguenot extraction, and the young boy spoke Afrikaans at home until he went to high school in Cape Town.[87] After training to be an accountant, Frost served with the South African Army during the Second World War and eventually took up dairying and tobacco farming near Marandellas. He abandoned tobacco in 1964 – he was a conservative in most things, and tobacco was a gamble – and divided his time between farming and RF politics, eventually becoming the chairman of the powerful Mashonaland Rural Division. Unlike so many English-speaking farmers from Marandellas, he communicated easily with the Afrikaners. The press, the white liberals, and the RF faithful regarded him as stern and unbending, as the uncompromising defender of the RF's founding principles. In the event, Frost proved to be gullible and weak, and no match for a tougher, more astute Ian Smith. These flaws were not apparent in 1971. On 7 October he lectured the government during his address to the RF's annual congress. He said that the electorate no longer trusted the government to implement its declared policies, and that the electorate would no longer tolerate multi-racial swimming baths, mixed public facilities, the uncontrolled influx of Africans into urban areas, the population explosion, and the failure to regulate non-white occupancy or ownership in white residential areas.[88]

The government tried to meet these complaints but could not satisfy party demands without damaging the prospects of a rapprochement with Britain. The notable casualty was the Property Owners' (Residential Protection) Bill which went through at least fifteen versions between

1967 and 1973 before lapsing in the face of technical complications and Ian Smith's willingness to sacrifice the Bill for the sake of a settlement. The Bill was eased off the agenda in the latter part of 1971 while Smith pursued his 'secret' talks with Lord Goodman, the chief British negotiator, in his attempt to win the 'first prize'.

These discussions had been proceeding intermittently since November 1970 when Sir Alec Douglas-Home, the Foreign and Commonwealth Secretary, initiated another move to break the impasse. Despite demands at the RF's annual congress in October 1971 for the government to abandon all attempts to reach a settlement with the British, Ian Smith felt sure of his ground in joining Douglas-Home in signing the Anglo-Rhodesian agreement of 24 November 1971. For its part, the British government agreed to recognise an amended version of the 1969 constitution and, in return, the Rhodesians abandoned parity and accepted the principle of ultimate majority rule. The new constitution would include a higher roll for Africans as the mechanism for the eventual introduction of majority rule, reduced qualifications for entering the lower roll, a blocking mechanism to prevent the retrogressive amendment of the entrenched clauses, and a stronger Declaration of Rights. Smith also agreed to appoint a commission to investigate racial discrimination, to review the cases of detainees and restrictees, and to make more unoccupied land available to Africans. The British government promised a matching grant of $100 million over ten years to assist the economic development of the TTLs and African Purchase Areas and to expand African education and housing. Finally, it was agreed that a British-appointed commission would conduct an investigation to determine if the proposals were acceptable to the Rhodesian people as a whole. Normal political activity would be permitted before and during this Test of Acceptability.

The external nationalists and their allies quickly branded the agreement a 'sell-out'.[89] Initial white reactions in Rhodesia were mostly ecstatic.[90] Prices rose on the local share market, the Minister of Foreign Affairs toasted the settlement at the Salisbury Sports Club, Geoff Ellman-Brown said he was 'desperately relieved', a Jewish businessman delivered trays of Rhodesian peaches to Sir Alec's VC-10, and Pat Bashford said it was the best news since VE Day. Sporting administrators were elated at the prospect of re-entering international competition, and the leaders of agriculture, industry, and mining had visions of unlimited expansion following the end of economic sanctions. The *Rhodesia Herald* did warn against excessive rejoicing but, after perusing the document, concluded that the settlement had broadly met the Five Principles in a way 'which need not disrupt the even progression of life here'. The proposals went 'so much down the middle' that the editor predicted that 'a hard core of white Rhodesian reactionaries' and 'a hard core of militant African nationalists' would want to wreck the Test of Acceptability.

Bishop Lamont and Garfield Todd knew that Smith would not will-ingly sign away white control, and were understandably sceptical. Wilfred Brooks, on the right, was outraged by Smith's (albeit, pre-dictable) 'sell-out' of the white man.[91] It is possible that elements in the government were also unhappy about the terms. Ken Flower claimed later that Hostes Nicolle opposed the settlement because he rejected any attempt by political groups to control 'his' Africans.[92] But the most curi-ous aspect about the whole affair was that Smith's white liberal oppo-nents were the strongest Rhodesian advocates of the settlement.

After agonising over its response, the CP eventually decided to cam-paign for a 'Yes' vote during the Test of Acceptability on the grounds that a settlement would bring economic development to the African areas and that it would lead to a direct attack on discrimination. The flaws in the Anglo-Rhodesian agreement were obvious enough. The most critical were that the RF would have the major responsibility for ensuring progress towards majority rule and, in the case of racial discrimination, that the government could not be compelled to implement the recommendations of the investigating commission. Confronted with objections of this kind, the CP argued that the settlement offered a means of avoiding something worse: a bloody war. Its stand soon alien-ated African opinion, though, fortunately for its remaining credibility, few Africans were aware that the CP even tried to persuade the British government to implement the settlement, notwithstanding its rejection by the African majority.[93] It was not a case, however, of the CP revealing its true colours. Party members certainly preferred a gradual approach to change, and they did want to preserve their existing life-styles. But they also had a genuine fear of a violent racial war and regarded the 1971 agreement, however imperfect, as an improvement on the 1969 consti-tution.[94]

The main opposition to the Anglo-Rhodesian agreement was led by the African National Council (ANC). The ANC was launched on 16 December 1971 and united moderate clerics led by Bishop Abel Muzorewa with ZAPU and ZANU elements in a spectacular movement which surprised the government by its momentum.[95] ANC organisers began to follow the Pearce Commission around the country from 11 January 1972 and were immediately successful in rallying crowds of Africans to shout 'No'. On 17 January Smith assured a CP delegation that Lord Pearce would give more weight to opinions expressed in a calm and logical manner than to those presented by 'mass acclamation'.[96] Next day, Garfield Todd and his daughter were detained.[97] The Todds were already marked as pariahs in white Rhodesia for their outspoken opposition to the Anglo-Rhodesian agreement; now they were accused of inciting the rioting and violence which was sweeping through the African townships and the Belingwe TTL.[98]

Des Frost reacted to the demonstrations by telling the Pearce Commission on 4 February that, while the RF had initially accepted the 'package' (with reservations), European opposition had hardened because of African agitation. He bluntly informed the Commission that the sooner it departed 'the sooner we shall be able to return to the peace and tranquillity that Rhodesia has enjoyed for the last decade'.[99] By 10 March, just as the Commission was completing its task, the *Rhodesian Financial Gazette* reported that government and business circles had given up all hope of a 'Yes' vote and were counting on Pearce to decide that intimidation had 'ruled out the possibility of a definitive answer.[100] Instead, on 23 May, the Commission delivered a firm 'No' verdict.

Smith responded to Pearce in a national broadcast delivered on 23 May. Sounding incredulous, aggrieved, and outraged – all at once – he blasted the Commission's 'misinterpretations and misconstructions' and its 'naivety and ineptness'. He accused the Commission of taking the side of 'ex-detainees and unemployed school leavers' and of assuming that 6 per cent of the African population constituted African opinion. He also criticised the British government for insisting on the Test of Acceptability and for ignoring Rhodesian expertise in conducting the exercise. A government statement, issued on the same day, challenged the findings in more detail. Responding to the *Report's* claim that 'the dominant motivation of African rejection' was distrust of the government, the statement argued that the Commission should have discounted the opinions of those who disapproved of the government's policies and distrusted its intentions. After all, the Rhodesians were required to implement the proposals before the settlement could be effected so it was obvious that the Africans who rejected the agreement had not understood its terms.[101] This reply, like much of the statement, was very clever. It also demonstrated just why the Rhodesians were guilty of the only important 'misinterpretations' in 1972. They had elected a government which did not recognise the nature and extent of the African mistrust, or its own responsibility for the failure to achieve a 'Yes' vote, or the need for official action to restore or create the trust necessary to achieve the desired settlement.[102]

A saddened Sir Alex Douglas-Home accepted the Pearce verdict. Begrudgingly, the business community did likewise. The Rhodesian right, on the other hand, was jubilant, even if it meant acknowledging that the African had saved the white man from himself. The bonus was that Smith began to exact his revenge for the Pearce debacle by introducing tighter discriminatory laws. Admittedly, the government rejected the

Property Owners' (Residential Protection) Bill, on the grounds that any such legislation would be too draconian and would mean uprooting Asian and Coloured families. The segregationists had to settle for additions to the General Laws Amendment Act in late 1972 which allowed residents to apply for the registration of restrictive conditions in title deeds. Frustrated over this matter, the right made solid progress in other areas during the latter part of 1972. The Minister of Agriculture assured the RF back-bench on 21 July that qualified Africans would not be appointed to positions of seniority over white officials without his express authority. He made this statement following complaints that a high-ranking white official in Agriculture had advised another European to resign because he was not in sympathy with the department's policy of appointing Africans to senior posts.[103] The Minister of Education told parliament on 22 August that he favoured the segregation of the Halls of Residence at the university.[104] From 29 September the owners of public swimming pools were required to obtain permits for Africans to swim in European areas. From 1 November owners of licensed premises were required to obtain a permit to maintain multi-racial bars and Africans were banned from drinking in European areas after 7.00 p.m. on weekdays, after 1.00 p.m. on Saturdays, and all day on Sunday. At last the RF back-bench could detect signs of progress, reassured by the Minister of Lands and Natural Resources that African families welcomed having 'their fathers at home and not spending their money in hotels'.[105]

It is never easy following the path of purity and righteousness. Ideals can founder when the costs begin to mount. White hoteliers immediately complained about the severe losses incurred through the new drinking laws. One Salisbury hotel allegedly lost one-third of its weekday takings, 80 per cent of its Saturday, and all of its Sunday trade.[106] The hoteliers challenged the regulations and the courts upheld their case, forcing the government to rush amendments through parliament at the end of 1972. Local authorities could not unilaterally change the law. The Fort Victoria Town Council had been forced in 1971-2 to jettison its plans for banning Africans from its parks because of a law which required it to provide alternative facilities for any race denied entry to existing amenities. The Sinoia Town Council was similarly frustrated. On 14 February 1973 it issued a public notice proposing new by-laws requiring the maintenance of separate toilets for whites and the provision of signs clearly indicating which races could use the town's parks, swimming pools, and sports grounds. Within days the council had abandoned the entire enterprise, defeated because the creation of separate and equivalent facilities was too expensive and had raised too many objections.[107]

If the right could take comfort from the government's actions since Pearce – by showing the African just what could be expected for ingratitude and defiance, and by dismantling some of the legacy of multiracialism – the fact remained that Rhodesia could not afford complete segregation. There were some formidable obstacles confronting those who wanted to remove what Ralph Nilson had called 'the small things'.

VII

The Test of Acceptability was an important event in white Rhodesian history. For the African 'No' ended the last major attempt to achieve a settlement when the Rhodesian government was in a strong bargaining position. Not that Ian Smith or the RF seemed aware that anything had changed. A suggestion that Africans would rule the country – sooner or later – was answered with shouts of 'No' at a Farmers' Association meeting in the Eastern Districts in early February 1972.[108] The audience preferred Ian Smith's ingenious idea that the African rejection of the Anglo-Rhodesian agreement amounted to an approval of the 1969 constitution. Meanwhile another, more terrible, disaster had intervened. At 10.30 a.m. on 6 June 1972 three explosions in the No. 2 colliery at the Wankie coalfields ended the lives of 390 Africans and 36 Europeans. Rescuers recovered a few bodies: the remainder were entombed when the colliery was officially closed. Wives and families clung miserably to each other – forgetful, in some cases, of racial background – as a Salvation Army band played 'Abide with Me' at a memorial service. For a brief moment 'all Rhodesians' were united in shock and in grief.

By August, when politics had returned to the front pages, segments of the liberal opposition had formed the Rhodesia Party (RP) to challenge the RF's hold on the white electorate. Recognising the general shift to the right, the RP was primarily interested in obtaining a settlement, calming white fears about political change, and disavowing any association with the non-racialism of the failing Centre Party. The RF backbench was busy setting its own agenda. On 30 October 1972 the Planning and Co-ordinating Committee of the RF caucus reported on 'the problems which face us': namely, how to formulate legislation or take the administrative action necessary for maintaining influx control, preventing Scout or Guide halls from 'falling into African hands', expanding separate facilities for the different races in art galleries and libraries, preventing the promotion of non-Europeans to positions of control over whites, and ensuring that African police and Army accommodation was not sited close to European barracks or white residential areas.[109] Nearly everyone, it seems, was blissfully unaware that the guerrillas had altered their tactics and were now infiltrating the northeast of Rhodesia through Mozambique.

3

'Only a pinprick in our sides'

I

Marc de Borchgrave d'Altena was aged 20 when he arrived in Rhodesia in 1955.[1] The son of a Belgian father and an English mother, De Borchgrave was educated at Marlborough College in England and completed his national service in Malta. After visiting the United States, the young man decided to leave the damp and miserable climate of his native England to become a farm assistant to his brother's godfather near Marandellas. Within three years he had moved to Centenary and, in 1961, leased 1,483 acres of marginal farming land in the hill country on the edge of the Zambezi escarpment. In 1965, the year of UDI, he bought the farm he named Altena and for the next seven years struggled to make a living out of tobacco, maize, and cattle.

By December 1972 De Borchgrave's immediate family consisted of an English-born wife, Margaret, and four young children. Their three-bedroom house, already cramped, was too small when De Borchgrave's mother arrived for a visit, so an itinerant African builder was engaged to add two more rooms. Unknown to the family, the builder was attached to a group of about ten guerrillas who were part of a larger force which had infiltrated the Centenary-Mount Darwin area. Members of Special Branch later claimed that the original orders of each group had pinpointed police posts for attack but, forced to switch tactics by the arrival of an Army convoy, the builder's group decided to hit Altena Farm and then make their escape. This target was probably chosen because the builder could provide detailed plans.[2] His information, however, was deficient in one respect. Marc and Margaret de Borchgrave slept in the tobacco barns, and returned to the house each morning before the builder arrived for work. The two daughters – Ann, aged 8, and Jane who was 9 – occupied the main bedroom. Together with their grandmother, and their two younger brothers, they slept alone in the house, protected by a small hand gun and a recently-mended but flimsy lock on the kitchen door. The dogs were no help, having been banished to the tobacco barn because their barking kept De Borchgrave's mother awake.

At 2.00 a.m. on 21 December 1972 Margaret de Borchgrave woke to a sound which reminded her of a stick being dragged across a corrugated iron roof. Up at the homestead, two AK-47 magazines were being emptied into the centre of the main bedroom. A small grenade also landed on the spot where the De Borchgrave parents normally slept. The two girls, lying in beds on either side of the room, narrowly escaped death or serious injury. Jane received a slight wound in the foot and became the unintended first white casualty of the renewed guerrilla war.

Some thirty seconds of fire announced that ZANU's liberation war had both intensified and changed direction. For six months the guerrillas had been infiltrating the north-east, reaching into the Centenary-Mount Darwin area through the Jesuit-run St Albert's Mission and the TTLs in the Zambezi Valley. Arms were cached, the locals were 'subverted' – with the assistance of spirit mediums – and small bands could now live off and hide among the people.[3] From late December 1972 the guerrillas employed hit-and-run tactics as they attacked white farms, intimidated the black farm labour, mined the dirt roads, and set out to erode the government's authority in the eyes of the tribal African. Although the drought of 1972-3 did not afford the cover of later rainy seasons the guerrillas did enough damage in the north-east between December and the following February to convince the government that it faced something more deadly than originally recognised or admitted. In that period, several farms were attacked and two white occupants died, twenty white and black soldiers were killed or wounded in follow-up operations, and three Lands Inspectors were ambushed in the Mount Darwin area, two of them being murdered and the other taken prisoner.

The Rhodesians soon discovered that the set-piece battles and decisive victories of the 1960s were not to be repeated. Nevertheless, within two years, the Security Forces asserted a kind of mastery over the north-east, or Operation Hurricane as it was designated. They claimed to have killed 524 'terrorists' in action between 1972 and 1974 for the loss of 63 personnel.[4] Some 16 white and 170 black civilians died as a result of the war in that same period. By December 1974, when the South Africans and the Zambians persuaded both sides to implement a cease-fire and to enter negotiations, the Rhodesians believed that less than 100 guerrillas were active in Op Hurricane. The real setbacks had been political and economic. In January 1973 Ian Smith closed the border with Zambia in an attempt to force President Kaunda to remove Rhodesian guerrillas from Zambian territory. The move not only failed, it upset the South Africans and the Portuguese for both political and economic reasons, angered the business community in Salisbury, and hurt the Rhodesian economy.[5] More seriously, the sharp rise in international oil prices from late 1973 sapped vital foreign earnings and forced the

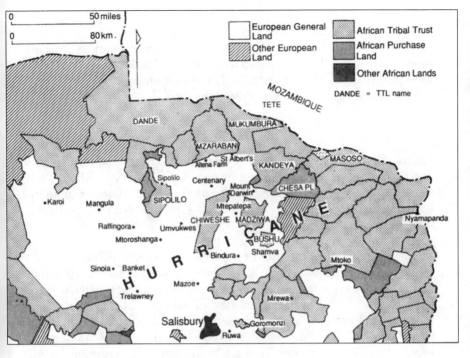

MAP 3.1. *Op Hurricane*

government to reintroduce petrol rationing. Finally, the Lisbon coup of April 1974 effectively removed the weakened Portuguese 'buffer' state of Mozambique, converted it into a Zimbabwe African National Liberation Army (ZANLA)[6] base for operations inside Rhodesia, and convinced Pretoria that Rhodesia had become dispensable within the changed balance of power in southern Africa and an impediment in its quest for better relations with independent black Africa.

Ian Smith was appalled by South Africa's apparent volte-face but he seemed unable or unwilling to read the portents in 1973-4. His own right wing pressed even harder for provincialisation; a few friends urged him to settle with Bishop Muzorewa; the opposition RP called for an all-party conference. Yet, in the two years between Altena and the South African-inspired *'détente'*, which provided him with a last chance to negotiate from a position of strength, Smith merely procrastinated. He accused others of sabotaging the settlement he could not have, while he sabotaged the settlement he did not want. He undermined the Bishop's credibility among younger and more radical Africans, and focused much of his attention on destroying the RP and in uniting the white communities behind his leadership. Throughout this period he indulged in a fantasy which was eagerly shared by a gullible electorate: namely, that a decisive military victory, a revived world economy, and increased dissension among the nationalists would restore Pretoria's sense of common purpose and allow a revitalised white Rhodesia to negotiate with the British for the recognition of the status quo.

II

Reactions to this early phase of the war revealed much about the habits of thought, prejudices, and illusions of white Rhodesians, about their sense of priorities for a civilised society, and about the nature and intensity of community ties. This chapter will explore these themes, beginning with a brief analysis of 'the best counter-insurgency force in the world'.

In December 1972 the Security Forces nominally consisted of 4,700 regular Army and Air Force personnel supported by 10,000 white Territorials,[7] 8,000 members of the BSAP – of whom three-quarters were black – and 35,000 police reservists, of whom three-quarters were white.[8] A system of national service had been in operation since the mid-1950s. In 1972 white males between 18 and 25 years of age were required to undertake 'service training' in either the Army or the Air Force for an initial period of nine months and then could be called up within a period of three years to serve in the Territorials. The government had resisted suggestions to call up 'the good ladies' because a women's military unit would be too expensive.[9] Amendments to the Defence Act in August-September 1972 gave the Minister of Defence authority to extend the initial period to one year and the total liability to six years. The Registrar of Defence Manpower was authorised to draw up a register of all eligible males but although there were severe penalties for non-compliance with the Act, the grounds for exemption were generous – for example, school-leavers could complete university studies before undertaking military service and school teachers, railway workers, and government officials were given a privileged status – and it was possible for fit young men to escape service for minor complaints such as flat feet.

The regular Army had two battalions – the all-white Rhodesian Light Infantry (RLI) – and the white-officered Rhodesian African Rifles (RAR) – and there were two squadrons of the Special Air Service (SAS), one artillery battery, and a squadron of engineers. According to the British *Police Review*, the BSAP had become more of a 'paramilitary' organisation since UDI, as evidenced by the activities of the Police Support Unit (with 240 members in 1972), Special Branch, and Police Anti-Terrorist Unit

(PATU) 'sticks' in counter-insurgency operations.[10] The BSAP was in fact regarded as the principal arm of counter-insurgency operations until after the Altena incident. The Air Force, which played a minor role before 1972, was equipped with 45 combat aircraft comprising 10 Canberra jet bombers, 11 Vampires, 12 Hawker Hunters, and 12 T-52 Provosts. The Air Force also possessed transport and training aircraft and, most importantly for its counter-insurgency operations, 12 Alouette helicopters. Having inherited an Air Force at the break-up of Federation in 1963, and one which was then bigger and more modern than that of the South Africans, the Rhodesians in 1970 had one of the better-equipped air units in Africa.[11] Finally, the Security Forces were supported on the ground by Internal Affairs and by some 3,000 paramilitary South African Police (SAP) who, since 1967, had been operating with the Rhodesians on border patrols.

The government wanted the white electorate to believe that defending the nation was relatively inexpensive. In its *Annual Report* for 1972 the Ministry of Defence boasted that, while defence estimates for 1972-3 had risen by 16 per cent to nearly $24 million, this figure represented just 2.1 per cent of Gross National Product compared with percentages of 2.5 for South Africa, 5.3 for Britain, 7.9 for the United States, and 11.0 for the Soviet Union.[12] The Ministry did not query the value of such unqualified comparisons and completely ignored the security role of the BSAP and Internal Affairs, excluded the Prime Minister's Special Vote which paid for CIO, and took no account of the make-up pay provided for the Territorials. The government wanted to show that a relatively small defence force could defend white Rhodesia while, at the same time, it sought to prepare the electorate for the higher 'premiums' necessary for the 'assured security of this country'. It wanted, in particular, to prepare the public for increased expenditure to overcome the manpower shortages faced by the Army and the police. The European components of both were under-strength because of high wastage and low recruitment rates.[13]

Despite the regular renewal of the State of Emergency, which first came into operation in 1965, white Rhodesians believed that this force was perfectly capable of defeating any conventional invasion or guerrilla infiltration. Their confidence was based upon the failure of 'terrorist' attacks in the late 1960s.[14] After training in Zambia or Tanzania, Ghana, China, or the Soviet Union, the black nationalists had crossed the Zambezi and were soon captured or killed. Seven ZANU insurgents, who had entered Rhodesia to undertake sabotage and attack white farmers and the police, were surrounded near Sinoia on 28 April 1966 and were killed after the Police Commissioner called in four helicopters. The seven are now immortalised as martyrs of the 'Battle of

Chinoyi' and, according to what may be the 'authorised' version of modern Zimbabwean history, their last stand marked the beginning of the 'Second Chimurenga'.[15] It also exemplified the flawed tactics of the early insurgency. ZAPU's efforts were even less threatening. Three times in 1967-8 groups of 80-100 ZAPU guerrillas and members of the South African African National Congress crossed into Rhodesia and were quickly defeated, without seriously challenging white rule.

The Security Forces grew more effective with each counter-insurgency action. Between 1966 and 1968 the Rhodesians lost just 13 men in killing 150 guerrillas and capturing another 292. There were no incidents in 1969, a few minor exchanges at the beginning of 1970, and no contacts during 1971. By then, the Rhodesian authorities were concerned about complacency in a society which regarded the renewal of the State of Emergency and the border patrols of the Zambezi Valley with monumental disinterest. Perhaps Rhodesians would have been more animated if it had become widely known that the RLI was operating inside the Tete Province of Mozambique, and with the full co-operation of the Portuguese authorities.[16] The official explanation for the secrecy was the need to maintain security. Another reason was that the government wanted it both ways: an alert community, prepared to pay for precautionary measures, yet enjoying the 'peace and calm' which characterised 1970-1.[17]

Three other factors underlay the confidence of the early 1970s. First, the divisions between and among the nationalist parties deepened in the late 1960s and were exacerbated with the formation of the Front for the Liberation of Zimbabwe (FROLIZI) on 1 October 1971. The proponents of this 'third force' hoped to unite the factions under a new umbrella. Viewed from Salisbury, the emergence of FROLIZI merely promised the intensification of internecine warfare. This assessment was confirmed when, in July-August 1971, the Zambian government, fed up with the disturbances in the training camps, handed over 129 cadres to the Rhodesian authorities. Secondly, Ken Flower claimed that CIO's penetration of the guerrilla organisations was 'as complete as it could have been. There was virtually nothing we did not know of their inner workings at all levels . . . We knew who had been recruited, where they came from, where they went for training and when they were likely to return.'[18] Black CIO agents posed as recruits, 'turned' guerrillas reported on their comrades, and CIO claimed access to the highest levels of ZANU's hierarchy. Thirdly, the terrain did not hinder counter-insurgency operations. One commentator thought Rhodesia resembled 'a natural fortress': the crocodile-infested Zambezi and Lake Kariba created barriers out of waterways, the Zambezi escarpment was difficult to climb, and there were few natural hide-outs in the open country of the high veld which was mostly visible from the air.[19] These reputed advantages may have been exaggerated. Yet, so long as the guerrillas entered Rhodesia from the Zambian side, their detection would not be too difficult for the border patrols which, in any case, knew where to look. On the other hand, the Rhodesians also faced several disadvantages in the lead-up to Altena. One was the problem encountered by all counter-insurgency forces: in general, the initiative belonged to the insurgents. Extreme right-wing groups in Rhodesia urged the government to balance the odds by attacking the guerrilla base camps in Zambia but, for military as well as political reasons, cross-border raids were considered counter-productive and unnecessary in the early 1970s. Other difficulties included the cost of obtaining spare parts and the inability to buy up-to-date equipment. The more immediate problem was inadequate intelligence. For all Flower's boasting about the penetration of ZANU, CIO was slow in grasping the extent of ZANU's collaboration with the anti-Portuguese FRELIMO (Front for the Liberation of Mozambique) in Tete province. Nor did the Rhodesian authorities as a whole seem to understand the full implications of ZANU's switch in 1969 to a new strategy of avoiding open confrontation in favour of infiltration by small groups to politicise the masses and to store arms and supplies. One inspired plank of this strategy was the use of local spirit mediums to win popular support. Largely unaware of the degree of subversion the Rhodesians were busy attuning themselves for fighting the wrong war. Exercise Countdown, conducted over four days in August, pitted 1,050 regulars and Territorials and 250 vehicles in a conventional battle against an 'enemy' who had 'invaded' the Binga area near Kariba. The Rhodesians 'won' and the Security Force commanders pronounced themselves pleased with an exercise which had highlighted the importance of obtaining better ground cover against 'hostile' Hawker Hunters.[20] It was a lesson which the Rhodesians did not require.

Arguably, their greatest advantage was the limited scope for friction in a society where the military, the bureaucracy, and the politicians came from similar backgrounds.[21] Apart from the soldiers of fortune who, in any case, formed only a tiny minority in 1972 and who attested on the same pay and conditions as everyone else, the white volunteers and conscripts were predominantly either Rhodesian born or long-standing residents.[22] Not surprisingly, the recruits from the schools had already been trained in self-control and had a clear notion of what to defend; and, not surprisingly, the services were pleased because 'morale and discipline have never presented a problem'.[23] The rugby-playing, beer-drinking officer of 1972 was invariably a 'true Rhodesian', and the most senior officers were more likely to support Ian Smith than anyone else. Some resented the obvious implication. The editor of the *Outpost,* who accepted that the police had become more 'paramilitary', denied that they were also 'para-political'. He insisted that the BSAP was there to uphold the law of the land, and that any political opinions were strictly private.[24] No one, it seems, had informed the Police Commissioner of this principle. He wrote in the *Annual Report* for 1972 that the ANC's activities during the Pearce Commission, and the more recent incursions into the north-east, 'serve to underline the fact, amply demontrated in other cities of the world, that densely populated areas are gunpowder kegs which can be exploded by a handful of people using fanatics, malcontents and mobsters to further their political ambitions'.[25]

This statement was typical of an RF response to black political opposition. But the RF's own penetration of the command structure of the Security Forces was a recent development. Ken Flower, General 'Sam' Putterill,[26] and Air Vice-Marshal Hawkins, three of the four members of the Operations Co-ordinating Committee (OCC) from UDI to 1968-9, were opponents of the RF. The compulsory retirement of Putterill and Hawkins, the commitment of successive Police Commissioners to RF policies, and the appointment of 'Archie' Wilson to head the Air Force significantly altered the balance of power. Flower claimed that, from 1969, the OCC 'rarely achieved consensus on any subject which might conflict with government policy'.[27] Flower may have been unhappy about this shift but it mirrored trends elsewhere in white society. The RF had consolidated its hold over the commanding heights of white Rhodesia by 1972, and the Security Forces were not immune because, at all levels, they were made up of those who voted it into government. Within a few years, however, as will be seen in later chapters, the war created its own frictions within the Security Forces which discounted some of the advantages of any political solidarity.

Despite their short histories, the Army and the Air Force already had traditions to reinforce and reflect the courage, independence, and defiance of the 'true Rhodesian'. Every schoolboy (and girl) knew of the exploits of fathers and grandfathers who had rushed to the colours since the 1890s. They had all been taught the story of Allan Wilson's Patrol which, on the banks of the Shangani, had died so bravely in 1893 when outnumbered by Lobengula's 'hordes'. Heroes and heroic moments stalked the Rhodesian past, and the memories weighed heavily upon the present. The airmen, for example, inherited the fine traditions of 237 and 266 (Rhodesia) Squadrons of the RAF, and of 44 (Rhodesia) Squadron of the RAF's Bomber Command.[28] There was the legendary 'Johnnie' Plagis, the son of Greek parents from the Hartley district, whose Spitfire was one of four which launched an attack on 260 enemy aircraft and who managed to survive. Plagis was the most decorated Rhodesian of the Second World War, flying 200 sorties over Malta and Western Europe including D-Day and Arnhem. Hardwicke Holderness was no less brave or foolhardy. A Rhodes Scholar, a handsome and gentle young man, he was awarded a string of decorations before returning to Rhodesia in the hope of making it a harmonious place. 'Archie' Wilson, a former squadron leader in the Second World War and a Bulawayo boy, had a distinguished record with Fighter Command and in the Western Desert. Wilson was replaced in 1973 by the South African-born 'Mick' McLaren, the first Commander who did not serve in the Second World War but who, in the view of professed non-partisans, belonged to the Rhodesian Air Force tradition of 'first-rate-chaps – not like the Army at all'.[29]

The Army commanders in 1972 represented two politico-military traditions: British and Rhodesian. All of them had been trained for 'classical warfare' although some had experience of the counter-insurgency operation in Malaya in the 1950s and of serving in predominantly black units. The Army Commander in 1972 was Lieutenant-General Peter Walls. Rhodesian born, like an increasing number of senior officers, Walls had strong Rhodesian credentials: his mother's parents were Pioneers, and his father had served as Chief of Staff of the Southern Rhodesian Army. Walls had commanded a unit during the Malayan insurgency, attended the British Staff College at Camberley, served in the SAS, commanded the RLI, and had been Chief of Staff since 1968. A stocky man of medium height, Walls was the outdoor and gregarious type who liked to mix with the troops without ever becoming 'just one of the boys'. He was probably the ablest of the senior officers in the 1970s although he never convinced his critics that he deserved to lead more than a battalion or that he was dexterous or tough enough for the politics of high command.

One of Walls's brother officers was Colonel John Hickman, the son of a respected, former Police Commissioner. Hickman won a Military Cross in Malaya, had attended Camberley, commanded the RLI, and was to command Op Hurricane. Short, solid, and a man who lived hard, Hickman possessed greater intellectual gifts than either he or others cared to admit.[30] The received truth in Army circles was that Hickman was envious of Walls and bitterly resented the latter's seniority. The relationship between them did become very strained by the late 1970s but, in 1972, Hickman's immediate career concern was whether he would succeed Walls when the Army Commander retired at the end of his four-year term.

Lieutenant-Colonel 'Derry' MacIntyre was another significant figure in the later 1970s. He always managed to infuse something of the cavalier into the hooligan. MacIntyre commanded the Sipolilo area of

Hurricane where his penchant for chess, derring-do, good malt whisky, and rollicking company secured his standing as a slightly cerebral 'man's man', the sort others would follow. Born in Scotland, MacIntyre conveniently failed a medical course, did his national service, and, after a chance meeting and a drink in a London pub, decided to go soldiering in central Africa instead of farming in Brazil. MacIntyre was 42 at the time of Altena; he had attended Camberley, commanded the RLI, and, like Walls and Hickman, had also commanded black troops. Temperamentally better suited to leading a company into a major skirmish, MacIntyre was a 'stand-up-and-knock-'em-down' warrior who liked to argue that the 'terrs' who avoided contact with his 'troopies' were just 'bloody cowards'. His views, however, expressed the prevailing military and civilian response to the post-Altena war. Even those with experience of Malaya believed that there was a military solution to the insurgency, that the path to victory lay in 'shooting terrs'.[31]

Others were not so sure. Ken Flower insisted later that he had always argued against the official approach.[32] He reproduced notes from 1968-9 which showed how he opposed the RF's policy of separating the races and had warned that, without 'the confidence, trust and mutual support', 'sooner or later the building will collapse'. Flower also recalled how he wanted to fight the post-Altena war by relying mainly upon Internal Affairs, the police, and the pseudo-gangs of the kind used by Ian Henderson in combating Mau Mau in Kenya. It is not clear how hard or how often Flower expressed these views to Ian Smith or the OCC. What is clear is that his emphasis on 'winning the hearts and minds' of the tribespeople, on the use of 'minimum force', and the employment of the civilian rather than the military power, differed sharply from the MacIntyre approach of 'grabbing the balls' and 'letting the hearts and minds follow'. It is also clear that, while paying lip service to the policy of persuasion, the government – having no political solution to offer and having decided that the Army should command counter-insurgency operations – found the MacIntyre approach more congenial. Nevertheless, Flower's approach, supported within Internal Affairs and the police and by many liberals, indicates that the Rhodesians did not enter the war united over strategy or tactics.

These disagreements were largely immaterial in December 1972. On 15 December the editor of the *Rhodesia Herald* congratulated the government on having 'crushed violence and maintained law and order'. On the same day, the Minister of Defence announced plans to extend the initial period of national service from nine to twelve months, and warned Rhodesians that border patrols would have to be increased. The message went unheeded. A few Internal Affairs officials were disturbed by the reluctance of the locals to talk to them. Marc de Borchgrave had noticed a certain restlessness in his compound. On the day before the Altena attack, Archie Dalgleish – whose Whistlefield Farm bordered Altena at one narrow point – reported to the De Borchgraves that he had seen a large Army convoy in the area. But the farmers of the north-east were much more worried about the late rains. Everything else seemed 'normal': Sally Donaldson – the 'Forces' Sweetheart' – had recorded messages to and from 'the boys in the Valley' to be broadcast over Christmas; the Rhodesian cricket team was preparing for its Currie Cup match against South Africa's Eastern Province; the shops in the towns were well stocked and busy. White Rhodesia was looking forward to a relaxed, joyous Christmas.

III

Immediately after the firing ceased at Altena a frightened family assembled inside the house. Marc de Borchgrave went for help and narrowly missed a landmine which had been planted in one of the dirt roads near the farm.[33] The builder reappeared for work on the following day, and offered to repair the damage to the main bedroom. Meanwhile the injured daughter, accompanied by her mother, went to Salisbury for treatment and the rest of the family moved to Dalgleish's two-storey home on Whistlefield Farm. Ann de Borchgrave and her father slept in one of the rooms on the first floor. Early in the morning of 23 December, just after de Borchgrave had turned out the light, a rocket was fired at their window, hit some roof tiling, deflected upwards into the ceiling, and exploded in the room. The girl was severely wounded in the chest and stomach, and was lucky to survive. Her father, who was slightly injured, joined a flushed Dalgleish in firing weapons into the darkness. (At one point they were both fully illuminated by the light which Dalgleish had switched on.)[34] An Army vehicle answered a call for help, set off a landmine, and Corporal Moore later died from the injuries he received. Undeterred by the affair, and claiming to have wounded one in the fight, Dalgleish warned that if 'they' came again he would 'take care of them first and then hand them over to the police'. His one complaint was that Christmas was 'dull' because of the security precautions and, as far as he was concerned, the drought posed the greatest threat to the Centenary farmers.[35] Archie Dalgleish, a proud Scotsman, a former fighter pilot and policeman, had no intention of leaving because a few 'terrorists' had got out of hand.

At first, white Rhodesia was merely outraged. A few 'cowardly terrorists' had assaulted the 'innocent' and the 'defenceless'. There was no immediate awareness of changed circumstances or of a long-term threat.[36] After referring briefly to 'a new problem on a new front', Ian Smith's New Year message for 1973 reassured Rhodesians that the Security Forces had meted out a 'salutary retribution'. The Prime Minister concentrated mainly on what he called Rhodesia's 'Achilles' heel' – the potential for racial discord – and advocated an early settlement as the remedy.[37] For their part, the Centenary farmers were contemptuous as well as indignant. After claiming that 'terrorism' was 'only a pinprick in our sides' Chris Kleynhans, an Afrikaner who farmed near Centenary and was active in the Police Reserve, denounced the 'terrorists' as 'completely useless'. 'All they can do,' he said, 'is come here and shoot at children.'[38] His assessment was premature. On 24 January 1973 his wife died and he was seriously injured in a grenade attack on their farmhouse bedroom. Whether his well-publicised comments had provoked the attack is unknown, although it may be significant that the guerrillas by-passed a conspicuous and exposed social gathering of farmers and Security Force personnel on their way to the Kleynhans farm. Understandably, the Centenary farmers soon ceased to make public remarks about the alleged deficiencies of the 'terrorists'. For all their apparent assurance they were just a little worried that they might be next. Matters had become so serious that the *Sinoia News* abandoned its exclusive concentration on local gossip, tasteless jokes, short stories, and beauty and household hints. From March 1973 it included regular comments from Fred Alexander, a former RF chairman whose parliamentary seat of Sinoia/Umvukwes embraced Centenary, assuring the farmers that the situation was under control.[39]

After recovering from its initial shock the Centenary community turned upon the government for deliberately withholding information about the extent of the 'terrorist' threat. Ian Smith did say on 4 December that, if Rhodesians 'knew the true position', they would not be so complacent about the situation in the north-east.[40] Perhaps if the Prime Minister had shared his secret the farmers might have been better prepared. Marc de Borchgrave made this point very forcibly when Jack Howman, the Minister of Defence, visited him in hospital after the attack on Whistlefield Farm. The criticism resurfaced when, on 30 March 1973, a young Afrikaner farmer was shot dead near Wedza, to the south-east of Salisbury. His father and several other Afrikaner farmers attacked the government for failing to alert the white population to an incursion.[41] Howman's response to De Borchgrave and to the Joubert family was similar: the government did not disclose its information for fear of causing 'alarm and despondency'.[42] The implications of this attitude were twofold. One of them was outlined by Rodney Simmonds in March 1973:

Lack of information is very bad for morale, especially for Rhodesians who ... are notoriously inquisitive. It fosters rumour-mongering which obviously, if let loose amongst fertile minds, can escalate to such an extent as to spread alarm and despondency among normally rational people.[43]

The other implication was that the government did not have faith in the Rhodesian-ness of the Rhodesians. It assumed that if the farmers of Centenary had known of a 'terrorist' presence in late 1972 they might even have run away. The government's next – and inconsistent – line of defence was to admit that it had not known the full extent of infiltration. Warnings could not be given when the information was not available. Fred Alexander adopted this position in claiming that:

on making extensive enquiries ... I have been informed that ground cover exercises were continuous, the Internal Affairs personnel were active ... the police anti-terrorist units sticks ... were very active in that area and yet, in spite of all this, it was a great surprise when the attack came just before Christmas.[44]

The argument was hardly flattering to a government which was supposedly in control. Hilary Squires, another back-bencher and future minister and judge, expressed the mood of the RF caucus when he said that the government was 'caught napping'.[45] A major complaint was that Internal Affairs had failed to monitor or report the extent of subversion in the TTLs of the north-east. John Hickman, who said that the Altena attack was 'a surprise', was particularly scathing about Internal Affairs, citing the case of one DC who was so lazy that a chief from his district in the Zambezi Valley had not seen him for eight years. Hickman described another DC as a 'disaster' who was retained at his post despite having done nothing to earn it.[46] Derry MacIntyre accused Internal Affairs of being lax and ill-informed.[47] Peter Walls, who said that the attack was 'not a surprise', also criticised Internal Affairs and contrasted its performance with that of the Army which, he said, knew what was happening because of its regular patrols in the Valley.[48]

Internal Affairs and the police rejected criticisms of their role. A Provincial Commissioner told a public meeting in December 1975 that Internal Affairs was aware of increased infiltration by August 1972 although he did admit that the seriousness was not apparent until Altena. The problem, as he saw it, was that the government had not given Internal Affairs sufficient resources to provide an adequate cover of the affected areas.[49] Special Branch certainly knew something was wrong. On 4 December 1972 the Branch headquarters in Salisbury issued a memorandum to all its stations recounting examples from the 1960s of 'terrorists' relying upon ancestral spirits and spirit mediums, and cited six instances since March 1972 where mediums had been abducted or recruited. The memorandum also pointed out that the

Dande TTL in the Zambezi Valley had 'special significance for Rhodesian terrorists'. Finally, all stations were urged to give spirit mediums 'maximum possible attention'. Clearly, while Special Branch did not know everything, it knew enough to advise the government that a new kind of problem had arisen in the north-east.[50] One DC, who reportedly told his superiors in mid-1972 that there were signs of unrest and that information was hard to obtain, was advised to remain silent.[51] A former Secretary of Internal Affairs also insisted that the DCs in the north-east were aware of subversive activity in their districts but had to contend with superiors who wanted to hear that their province was peaceful and secure.[52] Evidence from a former head of Special Branch bears out this story. He said that reports of clandestine activity around Bindura were suppressed by the head of Special Branch in the area who did not want to make life more difficult.[53] Significantly, when pressed to explain why the Army's information was not passed on to the government, Walls replied that the cabinet listened only to the advice it wanted to hear.[54]

So the Army blamed Internal Affairs, junior officers blamed their superiors, the farmers blamed Internal Affairs, the police, and St Albert's Mission,[55] and – within the government – everybody blamed CIO. Except for Walls, the accusers stopped short of the real culprits: namely, the politicians who sanctioned the practice of reporting what the authorities wanted to believe. In their defence, the politicians were merely acting on behalf of a society which also wanted to know that everything was under control, and whose assumptions limited its ability to understand what was happening in the north-east. If, indeed, the government was 'caught napping', the underlying explanation is that the cabinet and its senior advisers were Rhodesians. Convinced that nearly all blacks were apolitical and could not be politicised, and contemptuous of their capacity for war or organisation, whites at all levels could not conceive of well-trained guerrillas storing arms and ammunition and merging with the local population to escape detection, or of Africans willingly accepting the promises of 'terrorists' in preference to the civilising presence of white rule. In this sense the particular failures of particular Organisations were less significant than the profound ignorance of all of them. Most whites did not understand that the nationalists were just as resolute as Archie Dalgleish, or that 'the ordinary African' gained much less from Rhodesia than the upstart laird of Whistlefield Farm.

IV

Anger and ignorance, and a concern for self-preservation, underpinned majority Rhodesian attitudes towards the insurgency during 1973. In combination, these reactions also endorsed a particular interpretation of the war, and authorised particular actions for prosecuting it. Not all Rhodesians, however, responded in the same way and, in the months following Altena, differing views began to emerge about the nature and conduct of this new phase.

According to the RF, the war was perpetrated by 'communist-trained and inspired murdering scum', assisted by unemployed youths who were victims of 'total moral weakness', and manipulated by one or more of China, the Soviet Union, the OAU, and the unidentified advocates of one-world government in the United Nations.[56] Interpretations of this kind had two obvious advantages. First, the proponents could dismiss the notion that Rhodesia was fighting a civil war. Even if the 'terrorists' were black Rhodesians they were fighting on behalf of external interests. Secondly, it could be argued that the Rhodesian system was not itself responsible for the war in the north-east. Rhodesia lay midway between the integrationist policies of the Portuguese and South Africa's apartheid and yet the Portuguese were under the most pressure and South Africa the least. As the RF saw it, the specific racial policies were irrelevant because the communists were bent on attacking the most vulnerable targets. This second argument also provided an ingenious defence of the status quo, a clever way of exonerating everything from the 1969 constitution to the pinpricks of racial discrimination. Ian Smith took this position when, on 7 December 1973, he explained why the 'poor tribesman' kept on assisting the 'terrorists'. The tribesman did so, not because there was no common roll or because he could not get a drink at Meikles Hotel in Salisbury after 7.00 p.m., but because the 'terrorist' was holding a gun to his head.[57] Smith had assured a South African journalist in the previous February that 'we have very good relations between black and white in Rhodesia ... amongst the best in the world'.[58] So, the RF would not concede that Rhodesia's racial laws and practice were in any way responsible for the war. When African MPs dared to suggest that racial legislation was responsible, the RF back-bench argued that even to make such a suggestion was proof of communist sympathies. When one RF back-bencher admitted that the European might have 'rubbed them [the Africans] up the wrong way', he countered by insisting that the European 'is a far better co-habiter of this country than the little yellow man to the north'.[59] Anyway, whatever the RF might have done was irrelevant to the origins of communist-inspired war. And wasn't it also true that much more serious disturbances took place in Sir Edgar Whitehead's day?

Allan Savory was one who rejected the RF's interpretation. He had entered parliament in 1968 as a bright young man with a bee in his bonnet about ecology and who, as a Territorial officer, had formed, trained, and commanded the Tracker Combat Unit, read widely on the subject of counter-insurgency, and professed an expertise on guerrilla warfare. Savory left the RF following a dispute with the government over its compulsory acquisition of private holdings at Matetsi in Western Matabeleland.[60] In 1973 he joined the RP as its sole parliamentary representative, and was regarded as an ally by the beleaguered African MPs. Ministers and RF back-benchers found his presence intolerable, and demanded that he recontest his seat in keeping with the promise made by all RF MPs (the so-called 'blood chit') to resign once they left the caucus.

Instead, Savory used parliament in 1973 to challenge the government's interpretation of the war.[61] Although he agreed that the insurgents were 'communist backed' and 'orientated', and that 'the target is the whole of southern Africa', Savory emphasised that the conflict was a 'civil war' being fought between Rhodesians. Much to the annoyance of the RF and the farmers of the north-east, Savory insisted on referring to 'guerrillas' rather than 'terrorists'. He also described ZANU's objectives in 1973 in fairly dispassionate terms: economic disruption, a split between the white allies, hit-and-run assaults on white farms, and rendering the masses at least passive by addressing their real and imagined grievances. Savory urged the government to stress the political rather than the military side of the struggle: to maintain the economy – he opposed the border closure with Zambia – and remove 'petty racialism', avoid a disruptive military saturation of Hurricane and provide collaborators and captured guerrillas with inducements to work for rather than against the Security Forces. For him the issue was simple: 'The side that wins [black support], wins the war.'[62]

This voice of sanity was ignored by a government bent upon a military victory and by a back-bench consumed with anger about the 'evils of terrorism'. There was, in fact, very little sympathy in government or RF circles for 'winning the hearts and minds'. Occasionally a minister would talk of political objectives, of a social and economic policy designed to isolate the civilians from the 'terrorists'. Remarks of this kind were not translated into a coherent or active policy. Nor could they be. For one thing, such a policy implied addressing grievances which did not officially exist. For another, it presupposed spending funds which were unavailable except by shifting resources from white to black Rhodesia, a step which the majority of whites would not have countenanced. According to the government, therefore, and the Security Force commanders, the Centenary farmers and RF spokesmen, the way to eliminate 'terrorism' was to kill 'terrorists', to deny them physical access to the black population, and to punish those Africans who collaborated with the enemy.

This approach meant that the Army began to assume pre-eminence in counter-insurgency operations.[63] A number of sub-Joint Operations

Commands (sub-JOCs) were set up within Op Hurricane where regular meetings involved the senior Army and, perhaps, Air Force officer in the region, and representatives of the uniformed BSAP, Special Branch, and Internal Affairs. The gatherings could become crowded. The roll-call at the weekly meetings of the Mount Darwin sub-JOC, which were held in the DCs office, included the following: 'several' Army officers, three senior uniformed police officers, members of CID and Special Branch, the Flight Commander of the Police Reserve Air Wing, the Area Air Force Commander, and three members of Internal Affairs.[64] Reid Daly called it 'command by committee', but added that if the military man had any 'character' he would take over.[65] By 1974 the senior Army officer present usually had assumed overall authority, a circumstance which caused some anguish in the Centenary and Mount Darwin sub-JOCs. The DCs, in particular, resented this implied and sometimes explicit contempt for their efficiency and status.

The police entered the new phase assuming they were dealing with unconventional crime. Typically, when an elderly British visitor was killed while alone on his son's farm on 4 February 1973, CID opened a murder docket, spent hours drafting a plan of the farm, and, taking advantage of a chance visit by a photographer, set up an elaborate aerial survey.[66] Having been trained to befriend blacks, the police sometimes found it difficult working with Army officers who expected to be cracking heads. Cilliers argues that perhaps the first occasion when the Army did commit itself to civil action – in 1974 it was sent into two TTLs to protect cattle-dipping – the Army saw this operation as an opportunity to kill more 'terrs'.[67] In view of the prevailing assumption of the white electorate in arms – that this war was about killing 'terrorists' – it is hardly surprising that the warriors took control. Nor was it remarkable that men of their background concentrated on 'grabbing the balls'.[68]

A significant manifestation of the hardline policy was the introduction of progressively tougher laws and regulations intended to punish acts of 'terrorism', to deter the recruitment of 'terrorists', and to dissuade Africans in the TTLs from assisting subversive elements. New offences were created, old laws were extended, and penalties were stiffened: in each case the assumption was that 'terrorism' could be contained by intimidation.[69]

On 19 January 1973, one month after Altena, Emergency regulations empowered the government to impose collective punishments on a kraal – including the burning of huts or the confiscation of cattle – where it was suspected that individual members had either directly assisted 'terrorists' or failed to report their presence. Two weeks later the police closed all the beer halls, clinics, schools, butcheries, and stores in Chiweshe as a reprisal for 'terrorist' activity in that TTL. Further regula-

tions promulgated on 15 February raised the maximum penalty from
five to twenty years' imprisonment for individuals caught commiting
these crimes. These regulations were incorporated in amendments to the
Law and Order (Maintenance) Act in the following May while, in
September, the Act was further amended to impose a mandatory sentence of death or life imprisonment for 'terrorist' acts. The September
amendments also imposed a similar penalty for attending training
courses, extended the gaol term for recruiting 'terrorists' to twenty years,
and provided for the forfeiture of property as an additional penalty for
law and order offences. In February 1974 the government gave DCs and
senior police officers power to detain suspects for thirty to sixty days and
to control food supplies and order compulsory labour. All DCs and even
junior Internal Affairs officers were given authority to arrest without
warrant any person suspected of committing an offence under the
Emergency regulations. DCs could also deal summarily with anyone
who, by deed or word of mouth, exposed a DC to 'contempt, ridicule or
disesteem'. Finally, in November 1974, the government introduced a
new offence – of wilfully denying knowledge of 'terrorists' or giving
false information concerning them – while imposing a mandatory death
sentence on any person convicted of recruiting 'terrorists'.

An editorial in the *Rhodesia Herald*, reacting to the regulations of
February 1974, raised two issues.[70] One was posed in the form of a question: 'Why must the Government risk the accusation of fighting terror
with terror? Have all the other means failed?' The editorial argued that
the regulations did 'no good at all to the Government's claim to be fighting for the retention of civilised standards'. In fact the government had
to resist many of its own supporters who regarded 'civilised standards'
as an impediment in the war against 'terrorism'. On 30 March 1973 Ian
Sandeman, a former officer in the Coldstream Guards, suggested that
perhaps 'our methods are a little too civilised and we have too much law
and too little order'. His solution, proposed on the following 26 June,
was trial and punishment by military tribunal and, where the verdict
was guilty, 'the firing squad the next morning'.[71] Delegates to the RF
congress in September 1974 shared Sandeman's view of the courts as too
slow and too lenient. They tried to remove the judicial discretionary
power by imposing a mandatory death sentence on all convicted 'terrorists', while still believing that, so long as the 'terrorists' were convicted
by due legal process, then the rule of law and civilised standards had
been maintained. Desmond Lardner-Burke, as Minister of Justice and
Law and Order, opposed the resolution because of its implied vote of no
confidence in the judiciary. He thought the judges were 'doing an
excellent job'.[72] Evidently he regarded this discretionary power as a
harmless concession to 'civilised standards' because he habitually

increased the severity of penalties, reduced the options available to the courts, rejected pleas for clemency, and ignored charges of brutality levelled against the Security Forces.

The second issue posed by the *Rhodesia Herald* went to the heart of the matter:

The terrorists must be beaten. That is agreed. But the co-operation of the tribesmen is essential if the goal is to be reached. Is the use or threat of these new regulations the only way to get that co-operation?

Most commentators, like the *Herald*, thought that the answer was 'No', and argued that the regulations would probably hinder co-operation. Indeed, by introducing the regulations, the government had effectively given up the struggle to win the allegiance of the African peasantry. Even Mr Justice Hector Macdonald, notorious in nationalist circles as the 'hanging judge', pointed out – when commenting on the amendments of November 1974 – that 'a campaign against terrorists will not be assisted by punishing the innocent victims of terrorism'. Such a law might create the 'dangerous illusion' of defeating 'terrorism' when the effect might be 'to alienate and embitter a substantial section of the community'.[73]

The judge's remarks highlighted the profound differences within the country about the appropriate methods of defeating 'terrorism'. The prevailing view was that a firm hand was more effective than gentle persuasion. Coercion was cheaper, it yielded more immediate results through publicised convictions and executions, and it suited the RF's perception of African societies. When, for example, Allan Savory protested against the collective punishment policy, he was told by an Afrikaner farmer from Karoi – who said he 'knew' the African – that anything less would be 'regarded by the African people very definitely as a weakness'. A townsman from Bulawayo then assured Savory that collective punishment 'was a traditional method understood and practised by the Africans themselves'.[74] Buried in both these replies was the assumption that rural Africans who assisted 'terrorists' were exhibiting moral weakness or plain ingratitude. For these transgressions they must expect, and did expect, retribution. 'Co-operation', therefore, was not essential and, in so far as it mattered, would be extracted rather than induced. Victory for Rhodesia lay in the reassertion of authority over the rural African.

The government's other main attack on 'terrorism' was the creation of Protected Villages (PVs). The foundations were laid when new Emergency powers introduced on 18 May 1973 authorised the movement of African peoples in the north-east into consolidated areas. By late December some 8,000 Africans had been shifted from their homes near the Mozambique border into a holding camp at Gutsa in the Zambezi Valley before being resettled in three sites. The government defended these moves on the ground that the people themselves 'expressed gratitude' for their separation from the 'terrorists' who were intimidating them. On 5 April 1974 it was announced that over 200 tribesmen from the Madziwa TTL south of Mount Darwin had been resettled in an arid area near Beit Bridge – at the other end of the country – as a punishment for assisting 'terrorists'. Then in July 1974 the government lurched into its PV programme. In the coldest month of the year it began moving some 46,960 members of 187 kraals in the Chiweshe TTL into 21 hastily-erected villages within the same area.[75] Speed was the priority because Chiweshe lay between the rich farming areas of Umvukwes, Centenary, Mtepatepa, and Mazoe and stretched to within an hour's drive of Salisbury. Some residents were given a mere two hours' notice and the initial stage of Operation Overload took just three weeks to complete, allowing no time to prepare adequate housing, toilets, electrical power, or running water. Overload II followed soon after, designed to 'rescue' the people of Madziwa TTL from subversive influences and to deprive the 'terrorists' of another sanctuary adjacent to European farms and disturbingly close to urban Rhodesia.[76]

On 17 September 1974 Jack Mussett, then Minister of Internal Affairs, justified the Chiweshe and Madziwa actions as an 'operational imperative' undertaken to separate civilians from the 'terrorists', to stop intimidation, subversion, and co-operation, and to protect black officials and any others who might want to report 'terrorist' movements to the authorities.[77] The PV idea was borrowed from the British in Malaya (where it worked) and from Algeria, Vietnam, and Mozambique (where, generally, it did not). While the Rhodesians insisted that they had learnt from the successes and failures of others, they concentrated almost exclusively on repeating the mistakes. Having physically isolated the civilians, they did not exploit the opportunity of winning their 'hearts and minds'. Perhaps the government had nothing more to promise than night-time protection, piped water, and conveniently-placed schools. Certainly it could not compete with those who promised ultimate access to the white farmlands and black majority rule. And, by taking so long to provide the basic amenities for the people, who were already upset about their separation from crops and grazing lands now sited up to 12 km from their new homes, the government could not even challenge distant dreams with some tangible benefits of living under white rule. The basic problems were that Rhodesia lacked the human and material resources to convert a short-term military exercise into a full economic development programme, and that not enough officials in Internal Affairs, let alone members of the Security Forces or of the RF, believed that political action should accompany the 'operational imperative'. The overriding conviction was that coercion and population control constituted a sufficient as well as a necessary condition for the elimination of 'terrorism'.

Government statements defending the PV programme concentrated on two themes. First, they denied that PVs constituted a form of punishment, although some of the accompanying comments seemed to contradict this proposition. The DC of Chiweshe, for example, issued a pamphlet in Shona and English explaining Operation Overload in terms of the people's failure to report the presence of 'terrorists'. He then asserted that 'the Government has a duty to protect the lives and property of the people and at the moment we are failing to do this. For that reason, and not as a punishment, I require you to move into the protected areas that I am building'.[78] The DC's denial that the PVs were punishment centres was hardly consistent with his initial explanation of their creation. Similarly when, on 17 September 1974, Mussett rejected the claim that PVs were a retribution for assisting 'terrorists', he also said that the people of Chiweshe could have avoided their 'fate' if they 'had given the Government the assistance it was within their power to give'.[79] So, while it was accepted that the 'terrorists' had enforced their will upon 'innocent tribesmen', an entire TTL was made to suffer because a few of the innocents succumbed to the pressure and a few more feared for their safety. Either way, the 'man in the middle'[80] could not win.

Secondly, the government denied that conditions were too harsh or that the people were discontented. L. de Bruijn, the Deputy Secretary of Internal Affairs, claimed that the people in the northern two-thirds of Chiweshe 'moved quite happily' while admitting that the lower third 'were not as happy'.[81] Mussett did concede in his September speech that a move like Chiweshe constituted 'a social upheaval of serious proportions' and that it could be 'a traumatic experience'. This momentary lapse into sensitivity was quickly erased by the next statement: where PVs were necessary for the war effort, 'protected villages we will have, disadvantages and criticisms notwithstanding'. In any case, Mussett believed that the 15 metres square allotted to each family in the PVs were 'for practical purposes ... sufficient'. In the meantime the government was busy installing power and pumped water (two months after Overload began), and it simply lacked the resources to build new houses in the PVs. Nor was the Minister persuaded that the inmates were hostile or upset. Earlier, in answer to a question, he declared that 'the vast majority ... were happy to move and only a few moved with some reluctance'.[82] On 17 September he claimed that people lost heart only when they listened to discontented individuals. In effect he was admitting the existence of discontent but, in a manner characteristic of RF reactions to African protest, blamed a handful of agitators. Nor did it seem important that people were being uplifted from settled homes to live in inadequate shelter. The 'practical purposes' rendered conditions 'sufficient' because the criterion of success was not a better standard of living but the physical isolation of civilian blacks.

All the evidence from non-official sources indicates that the people of Chiweshe and Madziwa disliked their forced removal and detested their new living situation. The African MPs repeated this message, the Catholic bishops led the Churches in condemning the system, and representatives of the Salvation Army's Howard Institute – which was located within Chiweshe and was later closed down by the government – described the conditions in Chiweshe as 'inhumane' and claimed that the 'vast majority' opposed the PV policy.[83] The government invariably ignored comments from these quarters. It should not, however, have dismissed the most savage and authoritative indictment of the early PV system which was written by one of its own officials, J. M. Williamson, the Director of Veterinary Services.[84] Admittedly Williamson was later described by an RP supporter as 'anti-Smith', and he did leak his report to the RP in 1976. Yet, if he was suspect for his liberal tendencies, his most effective criticism of the PV policy was to accuse it of being counter-productive.

In November 1974 Williamson went to three PVs in Chiweshe with two other officials to inspect the livestock facilities. He found that, despite warnings issued in July, the herding arrangements for cattle in the coming rainy season were quite inadequate. He went further and commented on the 'human aspect' of the PVs which he found to be 'an even more serious error of judgement', 'a disgrace to us who purport to value civilised standards'.

Williamson began this section of his report by describing the layout and rules of a 'typical' Chiweshe PV. The village was surrounded by a mesh fence and overhanging barbed wire and had two exit gates each guarded by African District Assistants (DAs) armed with .303 rifles. The perimeter was illuminated all night by powerful electric lights while the 'keep' – an area inside the village which housed the European officer and his African assistants – was separately fenced and protected by earthworks and sandbags. Each family was obliged to erect its own pole-and-dagga thatched huts on its 15 metre square plot as well as a toilet consisting either of a hole in the ground or a 300 mm diameter concrete pipe driven some six feet into the soil. Families were required to remain within the village between 6.00 p.m. and 6.00 a.m. but during the day were permitted to return to their lands some of which were at least five kilometres from the village.

Williamson reported that the PV policy had three objectives or justifications: to provide better educational and medical services, electrical power, and piped water; to create better transport arrangements for crops and more convenient shops; to protect the villagers from infiltration and subversion. Williamson argued that the first objective had already been defeated by the insensitivity and inhumanity of the system, and that the second had become irrelevant because the Africans were losing their crops and livestock and their capacity to buy even the essentials. He highlighted the contrast between life inside and outside the villages, noting that on his way to the PVs he saw 'well constructed brick and iron or brick and thatch groups of huts [which] were the result of years of struggle and effort'. He also saw produce bins, yards, orchards, and kitchens and asked: 'How can these amenities and possessions be accommodated in a stand 15 m x 15 m?' He then asked another question: 'Would any of the European architects of these villages like to live within seven-and-a-half metres of and between two primitive toilets?'

Perhaps sensing that his superiors would not be too sympathetic about the plight of Africans who had collaborated with 'terrorists', or indeed consider that their living conditions constituted any kind of priority, Williamson argued that the policy itself was already self-defeating. He claimed that:

... all the Africans who have been bundled into these camps, see a terrorist victory as their only salvation from their present grim circumstances ... In effect in one fell swoop this policy has most effectively created a pool of resentment which will inevitably cause the whole population to support terrorists at every opportunity.

This 'unrealistic policy' had produced a 'débâcle' which was tying up manpower resources, causing Internal Affairs to bear the odium, and enabling the 'terrorists' to move into other areas because the government had already done their work for them. So, according to Williamson, the third objective had been made redundant.

He was eventually proved right. Opposition to the PVs became so strong and persistent that Bishop Muzorewa's party courted popularity in 1978 by insisting on their abolition. Almost every official analysis of the PVs undertaken after 1974 started with the assumption that the original programme had been hurried, ill-informed, and badly planned.[85]

Nevertheless, from the government's point of view in 1974, the programme was successful once the civilian population had been isolated from the 'terrorists'. Given this criterion, and the tendency to judge everything in terms of 'kills' and 'kill ratios', and of the number of reported incidents and the availability of information, the government happily linked the improved performance of the Security Forces in late

1974 to the introduction of PVs, and – as a consequence – pronounced itself confident of defeating 'terrorism'.

V

The government's prime military objectives in 1973-4 were to reassert physical control and to eliminate 'terrorism'. Its political objective was to obtain a settlement on terms which preserved 'civilised and responsible rule'. Remarkably, neither the renewed war nor the Lisbon coup seemed to change the government's perception of what a settlement might mean, or to inject any note of urgency into its negotiations.

The British government had altered the framework of negotiations to the extent of insisting – after the Pearce disaster – that the races must together agree upon the terms before the British would grant full independence. In other words, Ian Smith had to make a deal with Muzorewa's ANC. Smith repeatedly attacked this stipulation, and treated the Bishop as just another factional leader, less desirable and no more important than the chiefs and the pro-settlement groups with whom he preferred to deal.[86] Nonetheless, the government did talk with the ANC at various stages between September 1972 and mid-1974. These discussions were interspersed with the detention or arrest of 'difficult' ANC personalities, accusations from both sides of delaying tactics and obstinacy, and Smith's clever exploitation of incidents to shift the blame elsewhere or to avoid entering any serious negotiations. Throughout the process, the Rhodesians insisted that the only issue was the implementation of the 1971 terms, and showed no sign in public of accepting that the war, the oil crisis, or the Lisbon coup had affected the situation. Smith's 'final' offer, delivered just six weeks after the change of government in Portugal, was derisory: 6 extra African seats in parliament to give the blacks 22 out of 72. Even this gesture was just an 'advance payment' to be redeemed when the Africans formally qualified under the 1971 agreement for the additional seats. Fortunately for the Bishop, the ANC executive rejected these humiliating terms which he had previously accepted, and Ian Smith retreated, shaking his head, wondering aloud about the sincerity and reliability of the ANC and their London friends.

The initiation and progress of settlement talks were closely related to the exigencies of white politics. On 5 April 1973, for example, Smith intervened in the debate on the security situation to say that 'another opportunity now presents itself to rectify 'the whole tragic and unfortunate mistake' of the Pearce decision.[87] Having again raised hopes of a settlement, and diverted the left and right critics of the government, the Prime Minister then had to explain his failure to achieve one. On 29 June he declared that 'the prospects of a settlement appear to be remote' because the ANC had been encouraged by the British government to spend 'yet another year in cloud-cuckoo land'.[88] The Prime Minister himself had made no offers; he had nothing to give, and nothing could yet be forced out of him.

Instead, he had used the prospect of a settlement to win the Fort Victoria by-election on 18 May against the RP. Smith's contribution to the campaign, acknowledged on all sides to have determined the result, was his call of 'Don't rock the boat'. The virtue of this 'argument' was that it did not require an accompanying policy, merely the affirmation of loyalty to Rhodesia and a willingness to 'leave it to Smithy'. Fort Victoria responded by giving the RF 77 per cent of the vote and shattering the RP's morale.[89] This result, combined with the outrage over the killing of two Canadian girls at Victoria Falls on 16 May by ill-disciplined Zambian soldiers, and by riots in the black townships of Gwelo and Salisbury on 20 May, reinforced Ian Smith's hold over the laager. Riots, murders, and a by-election had become perfect excuses for masterly inactivity.

The RP tried hard to change the direction of Rhodesian politics. Founded by farmers, business, and professional men, by the survivors of 'the old UFP gang' and a new generation of young Rhodesians, the RP claimed that the CP's non-racialism had failed, and that the RF could never achieve a settlement.[90] The new party tried to establish a role in the middle ground. It opposed racial discrimination while acknowledging the right to private association. It called for the restoration of the common roll but insisted on a high qualification franchise. It urged the expansion of African technical education and job opportunities without endangering the position of skilled white workers. The RP represented some familiar liberal values applied to the Rhodesian context: the maintenance of law and order, an independent judiciary, an efficient, non-political civil service, open government, the protection of individual rights, economic development based upon private enterprise. Enlightened capitalism and Westminster democracy (practised by those with the income, education, and property to know how it operated) would together save Rhodesia from the excesses of the RF, the CP, and African nationalism.

The time was certainly opportune. Farmers and businessmen around the country in 1972-3 were calling for the settlement which Ian Smith could not deliver. There was a feeling both on the right and the left of white politics that the RF had 'lost all political direction'.[91] Savory described the RP as a 'young man's party' which offered fresh ideas, new faces, and some hope. The optimism accelerated when the RP reached an agreement with the ANC in July 1973 which affirmed twelve broad if unexceptional objectives. The party then used this agreement during 1974 as evidence of its capacity to secure a settlement. But the RP could not produce anything concrete. The ANC wanted to negotiate with a government, not an opposition, and the white electorate had no intention of creating a government out of an opposition which could not guarantee its future. To succeed, the RP had to convince the white electorate that it would not make the very concessions necessary in order to achieve a settlement. Clearly, Ian Smith did not have a monopoly on dishonesty.

The RP was led by three men – simultaneously – during 1973: Roy Ashburner, a wealthy tobacco farmer from the north east, who had polled well as an independent in the 1970 elections; Morris Hirsch, the medical practitioner from Que Que who had helped to write the 1961 constitution, walked out of the CP in 1969 and now dreamed of the perfect constitutional solution to all of Rhodesia's problems; and Allan Savory whose several shifts in the 1970s kept moving him further to the left of his political friends and, according to his enemies in the RF, took him on to another planet. Savory was the party's 'albatross' and its opportunity. If Ashburner was solid, honourable and uncomprehending, and Hirsch was clever and unpredictable, Savory was the one who attracted attention and support, who argued the unanswerable case in earnest tones, persuaded people to believe in him, and promptly dared them to embrace political oblivion. One of his supporters said of him that 'Savory had the lot: looks, public platform, charisma, the right ideas; he just could not work with others'.[92] Ashburner and Hirsch stormed out of the party in exasperation in October 1973, and from then until May 1974 – when he resigned as leader – the party was constantly covering for Savory's embarrassing tendency to speak his mind.

The classic occasion was a speech he made at Umvukwes on 20 February 1974 at a time when the farmers of the north-east were especially angry about the failure of the Security Forces to defeat 'terrorism'. Fred Alexander had died at the end of 1973, after spending a year trying to calm his constituents, and urging them to support the government's efforts.[93] A by-election for Sinoia/Umvukwes was set for the following 28 February. Four candidates were nominated for the seat: the RF selected Esmond Micklem and the RP chose Strath Brown (both prominent local farmers), Bashford stood for the CP, and Len Idensohn, the RF renegade from the 1960s, was nominated as the candidate promising blood and iron. On 17-18 February three members of the Centenary farming community were killed during ambushes and follow-up operations. Ian Smith and RF ministers were visibly shaken by their subsequent reception at closed and public meetings where a number of farmers rejected the bland assurances and questioned the competence of the Security Forces. Old charges were revived in private conversations: if only, it was said, Colonel Hickman, the Commander of Op Hurricane, had spent as much time chasing 'terrs' as he devoted to the wives and daughters of the region.[94]

When, therefore, Savory spoke at Umvukwes the farming community was angrily questioning the government's capacity to fight 'terrorism'. Instead of simply exploiting the RF's discomfort Savory told his audience that, if the 'guerrillas' laid down their arms, they might be invited to an all-party conference which, alone, could 'save bloodshed and untold suffering'. The *Herald* headline was enough to damn him: 'LET TERRORISTS JOIN TALKS – SAVORY'. The Prime Minister quickly denounced Savory's 'evil and irresponsible suggestion', and the RP's party workers knew immediately that they were losing ground. The RF did not entirely escape the farmers' wrath. Its share of the poll fell by 10 per cent to just 54 per cent; the RP gained 24 per cent and Idensohn won 19 per cent. It was obvious that a collective and determined resistance to 'terrorism' was not sufficient to unite the farming communities at the 'sharp end' in support of common short- and long-term solutions. Yet it was also apparent that a liberal party could not manipulate those divisions by telling some home truths about the future. Savory resigned as party leader soon after the by-election and, by early June, embarrassed his colleagues further when he announced in Hartley that the country faced a choice between a common roll or civil war and that, if he had been born black, he would now be a guerrilla. This latter statement precipitated Savory's departure from the RP.

The emergence of the RP helped Ian Smith to focus on the task he was best able to handle: reasserting the RF's control over the white electorate. He completed this exercise in the general election of July 1974. By then, the CP had been reduced to a small collection of friends and relations (most of them women), and the RP, although receiving more than $50,000 in campaign funds from some major business houses, had lost its impetus and could manage just 22.4 per cent of the vote. For the RF had an unanswerable case, expressed in two slogans: 'No Sell Out' and 'Safeguard Your Future'. There was another factor: Ian Smith. Tim Gibbs, who was chosen to replace Savory, argued that the RF could have nominated 49 tailor's dummies to stand with Smith and still have taken the 50 white seats. He was simply exaggerating a truth accepted on all sides of white politics. Everybody, it seems, agreed that the Prime Minister stood head and shoulders above everyone else.[95]

His one effective opponent was thwarted by an extraordinary decision. Savory stood as an independent for the winnable seat of Highlands North but the RP pursued a personal vendetta against him and nominated its own candidate. The CP's Diana Mitchell was nominated, thereby lining up the liberal candidates against the RF. Savory did well in the circumstances in securing 25 per cent of the votes in a four-way contest.[96] Typically, his defiant riposte to the government was delivered in the RF's own creation. On 5 July he wrote in the *Rhodesian Financial Gazette* that no 'purely European government would win the war', that most Africans supported either ZANU or ZAPU both of which would have to be invited to the conference table, and that the whites should negotiate immediately or they would be left with the 'crumbs' after being forced to join the conference table. The white electorate, which had always preferred Ian Smith's words of comfort and assurance, rejected Savory's unpalatable prophecies.

VI

A cheer squad of Rhodesians, watching in 1973-4 the elaborate game of fortifying prejudice and avoiding reality, tried to inspire the faithful and the faint-hearted with patriotic slogans and assurances. Letter writers, radio and television commentaries, and parliamentary speeches all extolled the brave farmers of the north east – and their wives – and called on all Rhodesians to emulate their fighting spirit.

There was a general acknowledgement of the hardships they faced. One of the problems was financial. The Secretary-Treasurer of the Darwin and Centenary East Mutual Protection Fund Society claimed that the farmers of Centenary East had each spent a minimum of $1,500 on farm security.[97] Two journalists, who travelled in the Centenary-Mount Darwin area in mid-1973, noted the change in lifestyles: families now lived behind electrified security fences, had covered the windows of their houses with steel mesh to stop grenades, and converted their main bedrooms into bomb shelters. Social life was severely limited: evening tennis and squash parties were cancelled, there were no more day return trips to Salisbury, Saturday night parties and amateur dramatics had become distant memories, dinner invitations were extended into overnight stop-overs, and, in Centenary, the village church had been turned into a hospital and the school nursery had closed.[98]

The Centenary community responded to these changes in lifestyle by developing a determination to 'see it through'. There was also a new spirit of fellowship. On 3 April 1973 Delville Vincent was killed on PATU duties. On 22 July some 100 farmers and their families, together with their African labour, turned out for Operation Harvest to help Vincent's family round up the cattle and bring in the maize crop.[99] This sense of fraternity was enhanced after July 1973 by the progressive installation of a radio communication network in the Centenary area.[100] For the Agric-Alert system not only gave farmers and their families a greater sense of security; it also acted as a unifying agent within the separate rural communities. The fully-developed system enabled a farm to raise an alarm on the central station of a particular network and at all other sets on the same network, to call the central station without raising a general alarm, to speak to the central station or to any set on the network, to receive an alarm sent by another set, and to listen to conversations between any two other sets. In turn, the central station could immediately identify which set had raised an alarm, confirm that it had received the signal, raise a general alarm, call all sets simultaneously, and alert available Security Force units. Each network, therefore, became a little Rhodesia, a mutual protection unit where old and new-found friends could be on the line assuring anyone under attack that help was on its way.

A few individuals remained on the outside. Although he played cricket at the Centenary Club, Marc de Borchgrave never quite fitted into the local community. He refused to join the Police Reserve, which was a major bonding factor in the Centenary district, and he had such open and repeated rows with the BSAP that he was almost charged with bringing them into 'disesteem'.[101] His experience, however, was unusual because for most farmers the war, and the local organisations which fought it, or provided comfort to the victims, created friends out of neighbours and communities out of families.

These small farming communities also persevered in trying to maintain an air of normality. It was hard to do so in Centenary but a little easier further south-west in Sinoia where the desire to retain civilised living brought 245 people safely to the Cooksey Memorial Hall on 8 September 1973 to watch a performance of *My Fair Lady*. This 'glittering and enthusiastic audience' cheerfully accepted the absence of appropriate costumes, endured Colonel Pickering's continental accent, and did not mind the substitution of three pianos for an orchestra.[102]

The factors which united the farming communities did not necessarily bind the nation. For the war revealed that not all Rhodesians were patriots, and not all of the patriots were ready for the supreme sacrifice. In March 1973 an RF back-bencher, the right-wing Glaswegian Bill Irvine, claimed that just half of the 3,000 white 'eligibles' for that year were undertaking compulsory national service. Irvine argued that, instead of increasing the period of service to one year – as the government had done just before the attack on Altena Farm – it would be fairer, as well as personally and economically less disruptive, if the initial period remained at nine months and every effort was made to draft the 'eligibles'. He complained that it had been too easy for civil servants, school teachers, and railwaymen to obtain exemptions, and that there was an 'awful lot' of draft dodging. Sympathetic doctors were reportedly providing young men with medical grounds for exemption.

Irvine cited the example of young men crossing the border to South Africa and coming back as 'returning residents'. They knew that Immigration officials were merely required to inform the Registrar of Defence Manpower of 'immigrants' entering the country.[103] The Ministry of Defence rejected the allegation that 'some scores of young men' were shirking their duties.[104] Nevertheless, a substantial minority of eligible white males did legally avoid national service in 1972. Lardner-Burke privately told Allan Savory that he and Jack Howman were 'very concerned' about the reports they were 'constantly receiving' referring to young men who were legally evading their responsibilities.[105] Anecdotal evidence suggests that these young men included sons of outspoken RF supporters. For them, the cause of white Rhodesia mattered less than an uninterrupted, and safe, career path.

The anger about 'draft dodgers' was felt by the conscientious objectors. There was never much sympathy for the 'outsider' and, by 1973, the ritual acknowledgement of a man's principled refusal to kill another counted for very little in the courts or in the society at large. Not one of the thirty-four applicants successfully argued his case for an exemption in 1972.[106] By 1973 the penalties for attempted non-compliance had stiffened. In 1970 an Umtali magistrate fined a Jehovah's Witness $310 (or 130 days' imprisonment) for refusing to do national service.[107] In 1973 another Umtali magistrate called for tougher penalties in the light of the 'new situation'. On 26 June 1973 he gaoled two Jehovah's Witnesses for six months each and, in October, after gaoling two more, ordered a six-month suspended sentence for a juvenile who was to receive ten cuts with a light cane. The magistrate also called on parliament to allow the military to arrest objectors who, he said, should not be allowed to take employment. The judiciary tried to keep matters under control. Speaking on behalf of four other judges, Mr Justice Beck in the High Court condemned the magistrate's caning order as 'objectionable and shocking', criticised the magistrate for speaking of 'the legitimacy of retribution', and pointed out that the order exceeded eight cuts, the limit beyond which whipping amounts to 'the beating of inanimate flesh'. Mr Justice Beck rescinded the order but the caning had already been administered.[108]

Conscientious objection and 'draft dodging' were considered 'un-Rhodesian', and un-Rhodesian attitudes and behaviour could not be tolerated. It was also un-Rhodesian to accuse the Security Forces of brutality,[109] to oppose the arrest of Africans without a warrant, and to pronounce an intention to emigrate. Letter writers abused the local renegades and whingers even more vehemently than they derided those 'ignorant' outsiders who dared to criticise. The Catholic Church, and its priests and nuns from Europe, became a favourite target in 1973-4, largely because of its attacks on the behaviour of the Security Forces. Peter Niesewand, a South African-born Rhodesian citizen and journalist, was another victim, this time of the government's obsession with secrecy and its determination to control the press. He was also disliked by Ian Smith and senior officials in the Information Ministry. Niesewand was detained on 19 February 1973 and subsequently found guilty of breaches of the Official Secrets Act for publicising the poorly-kept secret that the Rhodesian Security Forces had been operating with the Portuguese inside Mozambique since early 1972. Although he was acquitted of every charge on appeal – in a decision which reflects well on the integrity of the Rhodesian judicial system – nothing could save him from the vicious rumours that he was a communist agent and that he knew which Centenary farmers were to be killed by the 'terrorists'.[110] Some of the defenders of Western civilisation painted the word 'TRAITOR' on the road outside his house. Their action typified a growing resentment against real or presumed white dissent and suggested that, like the election of the RF in 1962 and UDI in 1965, the war had sharpened tempers inside white Rhodesia.

VII

The war did not, however, disrupt the pace of life throughout Rhodesia in 1973-4, Incidents which occurred within an hour's drive of Salisbury might have been happening a thousand miles away for all that they affected city dwellers. Gwelo's white residents were even more insulated. The war intruded – briefly – in May 1973 when the *Gwelo Times* reported the death of a retired employee from the Midlands area who was shot near Mount Darwin. There was a bigger story in May of the following year when two airmen were buried in Gwelo after being killed in the north-east. A reporter from the Midlands, after visiting the Centenary area in early 1974, claimed that 'most [Rhodesians] are unaware of the seriousness of the position'. He protested when a television commentary declared that 'terrorism' was being contained. He knew of thirty-nine incidents which occurred near Centenary just before Christmas 1973, and noted that the carol service had to be held in a tobacco grading shed which was ringed by patrols: 'a little different from the same service held that day in Gwelo'.[111]

Rhodesians who had no contact with the north-east could ignore the 'sharp end' because a tight censorship kept them ignorant. At the same time, cabinet ministers, the military chiefs, the Argus Press, and the government-owned radio and television services kept assuring them that they were secure, that the economy was still prospering, that control had been restored in the TTLs, and that the 'terrorist' menace had dissipated.[112] And, given the high 'kill rate' of 1974 there was no good reason for doubting the capacity of the Security Forces to remain 'on top of the situation'. Typically, the methods of success were not advertised. It was not widely known before 1980, for example, that in 1974 CIO had created the notorious Mozambique Resistance Movement in order to exploit anti-FRELIMO dissent in Rhodesia's neighbouring territory.[113] On the other hand, the formation and activities of the Selous Scouts became an open secret. It was decided in late 1973 to build upon the skills of the Army's Tracker Combat Unit by establishing a new unit to operate as 'pseudo gangs'. Commanded by Ron Reid Daly, who had served under Walls in Malaya as a non-commissioned officer, the Scouts, predominantly black in a membership which included several 'turned terrs', quickly established a reputation in 1974 for collecting valuable intelligence about guerrilla movements and for causing confusion among villagers and the genuine ZANLA gangs. The Scouts also located and set up guerrillas for annihilation.[114] Another innovation in 1974 was the grouping of armed helicopters and RLI troops in what became known as 'Fire Force' which was called into action from observation posts on the ground to surround and eradicate ZANLA gangs.[115] These new counter-insurgency tactics not only improved the efficiency in hunting and killing 'terrs': they reinforced the Rhodesian self-image of showing ingenuity and resourcefulness in meeting adversity while giving the Security Forces the confidence that they could eliminate the menace of 'terrorism'.

The propaganda, which stressed the certainty of 'victory', was powerful, and so was the will to believe it. Individuals and the opposition parties simply could not implant a sense of urgency when the Rhodesians were so obviously 'winning the war'. Their solutions were unacceptable, so their analysis was summarily dismissed. Admittedly, the farmers at the 'sharp end', surrounded by their security fences, knew all about the contrary indications: most importantly, that 'the best coimter-insurgency force in the world' had taken far too long to contain a small 'terrorist rabble'. Yet, within a year of Altena, Des Frost had spoken defiantly at the RF's annual congress in 1973:

A settlement of our problems may be necessary for the greater advancement of Rhodesia but certainly is not imperative for our survival ... The Rhodesian Front was formed in 1962 to stop the attempted handover of the country and this remains the basic principle of the RF today.[116]

In December 1974, two years after Altena, most Rhodesians still retained their illusions.

4

'This void in our national life'

The ringmasters of *détente* – Mr Vorster and President Kaunda – soon despaired of the players. The South Africans had persuaded Smith to accept a ceasefire in December 1974 and to release the jailed or detained black nationalists. The Zambians had pushed the nationalists – ZANU, ZAPU, and FROLIZI – into a united front under the banner of Muzorewa's ANC. It was hoped that the subsequent negotiations would produce an acceptable settlement. Instead, the nationalists insisted on immediate black rule, the Rhodesians refused to abandon white supremacy, and neither side had any intention of compromising during 1975. Until one side could be forced to submit, or both forced to trade, the ringmasters had no alternative but to watch the players battle among themselves and with each other to improve their bargaining positions. So, while the Rhodesians and the nationalists accused each other of breaking the truce which neither of them wanted, and blamed each other for delaying the negotiations which everyone considered to be irrelevant, the twelve months following *détente* were spent regrouping the forces in preparation for the next round.

Most white Rhodesians ignored or did not notice much of what happened during 1975. ZANU's National Chairman, Herbert Chitepo, was assassinated in Lusaka on 18 March but CIO's complicity in his murder remained a secret and the Rhodesians dismissed the episode as typical of nationalist in-fighting.[1] Edson Sithole, a clever young lawyer associated with Muzorewa's ANC, mysteriously disappeared in mid-October after being bundled into a car in a Salisbury main street. Public interest in his whereabouts soon waned.[2] Meanwhile, British officials came and went, without attracting much attention. Mozambique's independence on 25 June provoked some comment, although the slight unease within government circles was nothing compared to the disappointment of those who made regular excursions to Beira for the beaches, the wine, and the prawns. Virtually no one in white Rhodesia had any expectations of a settlement when the ringmasters assembled the players on

25 August in a railway carriage perched on the bridge over the Zambezi at Victoria Falls.[3] The talks collapsed on the first day because Smith refused to grant an immunity allowing all the nationalists to attend negotiations inside Rhodesia. The fears of his right wing proved groundless. There were no serious negotiations, and no possibility of concessions. In any event, Smith wanted a postponement while the Security Forces strengthened his hand for any future meetings. The 'Big Push', which was launched in August 1975, and was preceded by a campaign to alert the whites against loose talk, was designed to remove all 'terrorists' from Rhodesian soil.[4] In October 1975 the Security Forces told the press that there were only about thirty left operating in the country.[5]

Two events, however, did startle white Rhodesia. One was the departure of the SAP in August 1975. Relations between the Rhodesian and South African governments had deteriorated sharply at a meeting in Cape Town in the previous February after Mr Vorster discovered that Ian Smith had reneged on an understanding which had underwritten *détente:* namely, that the Rhodesians would accept a common roll based on a qualified franchise and the notion of power-sharing.[6] The special relationship nosedived when the Rhodesians arrested ZANU's Ndabaningi Sithole on 4 March 1975 on the charge of plotting the assassination of his nationalist colleagues. The move appeared calculated to destroy the *détente* negotiations.[7] Having already withdrawn the SAP from forward positions as part of the *détente* exercise, the South Africans resisted all Rhodesian pleas and removed them altogether. It was widely accepted within the Security Forces that the SAP contributed little to border defence, although their presence did relieve pressure on Rhodesian manpower and they did bequeath valuable equipment to the Rhodesians.[8] The primary significance of their removal was the effect on white morale. Sensing the psychological blow of being left alone, P. K. van der Byl, then Minister of Foreign Affairs and Defence, and the local press alternately pleaded for a change of mind and reacted bitterly to the departure.[9]

The other disturbing event was the arrival of the Soviets and Cubans in southern Africa to defend Angola from the South African invasion of November 1975. If most Rhodesians had not realised (and were not told) that thousands of young blacks had crossed into Mozambique during 1975 to join the training camps, they did at least grasp the significance of Eastern bloc involvement in the affairs of southern African. Their world had become so dangerous that, except for the right, they supported Smith's half-hearted attempt to negotiate a separate settlement with Joshua Nkomo's ANC at the end of 1975.[10] Admittedly, Nkomo was a 'terrorist' leader but 'Mr Smith' knew what he was doing (even if it was the opposite of what he had long promised), and it was best, therefore, to allow him to decide.

Two themes stand out in the domestic history of white Rhodesia between 1973 and 1975. First, the war and events in southern Africa were already changing the political agenda and the Rhodesian way of life. Secondly, most Rhodesians reacted to the new circumstances by affirming the dominant values of the past. Neither the world outside nor the threats from the inside figured prominently in the day-to-day outlook of communities whose version of reality had prepared them to enjoy the good and to absorb or deflect the unpleasant. The right and the left tried to inject their own jarring notes of urgency – the one demanding full segregation, the other calling repeatedly for a settlement – but ten years of poor leadership and isolation, self-centredness and provincialism, had imposed a mental inertia.

II

An indication of the pervading sense of unreality in white Rhodesia in 1973-5 may be found in the debates over the settlement issue and racial discrimination.

The right wing of the RF wanted Smith to abandon the quest for a settlement and to implement provincialisation within the framework of UDI or, failing that, to insist that a return to legality presupposed an independence constitution based upon provincialisation. Ted Sutton-Pryce, a former British Army officer and a highly articulate right-winger on the back-bench, echoed Des Frost's 1973 claim that a settlement was not imperative for Rhodesia's survival. Speaking on the eve of the 1974 election, Sutton-Pryce urged the government to concentrate on introducing provincialisation.[11] Frost told the 1974 congress, held just after the elections, that he was 'heartily sick' of hearing about an internal settlement which amounted to handing over to a few 'power-hungry nationalists'.[12] The Party Chairman was aware that Smith did not have any policy at all, and believed that the Prime Minister could not be trusted to stand firm in defence of undiluted white supremacy. Moreover, he was convinced that Smith remained a closet liberal, committed to advancement on merit and to the principle of eventual majority rule.

A number of Frost's political friends had already left the RF because they considered that any settlement was bound to jeopardise the objectives of segregation and permanent white rule. Some joined the fringe right-wing parties which died or fractured within months of successful public launches, victims in part of personality clashes and their attraction for political and social misfits. The best-known after *détente* was the Southern Africa Solidarity Conference (SASCON) which flourished during 1975 and was strongly supported by the early renegades from the RF.[13]

The amiable Lord Graham was a member and so was Wilfred Brooks, singing his own hymn of racial hate. Their common enemies, according to SASCON's Matabeleland chairman, included the Jews, the communists, the Carnegie and Rockefeller Foundations, the World Council of Churches, and the UN.[14] Their friend should have been South Africa but Pretoria had behaved incomprehensibly in supporting *détente*. More disturbingly, white Rhodesia also rejected them. The well-attended rallies of May, August, and December 1975, and the big meetings held in the regional centres during the Smith-Nkomo talks, were not translated into votes. Vitriol and scare tactics simply did not work. Len Idensohn might label Kaunda 'a little monkey', argue that a bomb dropped on the bridge at Victoria Falls would solve all the country's problems (by removing Smith as well as the nationalists), and warn male Rhodesians that the 'terrorists' intended to rape their mothers, daughters, and sisters (but not, apparently, their wives).[15] Most white Rhodesians remained unmoved. They were not 'extremists' and, even where they sympathised with the far right, they were not disposed to follow nonentities. Idensohn and Brooks concluded that the electorate was just apathetic, or had been duped by Smith and brainwashed by the RBC.[16]

Des Frost, and his political friends who remained in the RF, regarded Smith's acceptance of *détente* as the final proof that he had abandoned the faith. The one hope was to force him to implement the policy of provincialisation, and a caucus subcommittee was appointed to devise some new proposals.[17] Its three members belonged to the party's right: Wickus de Kock, the Minister of Information; Ted Sutton-Pryce, a Deputy Minister after the 1974 elections; and Dr Colin Barlow, a dentist and an able young back-bencher. The Prime Minister appeared to give them his blessing, and the three set out to canvass caucus opinion.

On 19 August 1975 51 members gave anonymous answers to ten questions put by the committee.[18] The results indicate both the strength of the right in caucus and the extent of its myopia about current political trends. Forty-six respondents thought that majority rule was not inevitable, two were uncommitted, and just three thought that it would eventuate. Forty-one thought that it was dishonest to continue under the 1969 constitution which allowed for majority rule. While 45 agreed that Africans would not be satisfied with less than majority rule, 29 thought that it would be possible to maintain white control in a central parliament whereas 15 did not and 7 were uncommitted. The 'No' vote on the latter issue might have included both the far right like Rodney Simmonds who believed that having any blacks in the central parliament was the thin edge of the wedge, and more moderate MPs such as Chris Andersen,[19] who saw no future for a permanent white majority. In a firm endorsement of the RF policy towards the chiefs, 43 respondents believed that the best chance of an internal settlement lay through negotiations with the tribal leaders. On the other hand, the far right position (in favour of full partition and confederation) which had been rejected in 1968 received just 13 votes out of the 51.

Heartened by these replies, if not by the vote on confederation, the subcommittee prepared its case for provincialisation, worried only that Ian Smith now seemed bent on sabotaging their efforts. The test was the RF's annual congress in Umtali in September held just after the fiasco at Victoria Falls.[20] It was agreed that Sutton-Pryce should introduce the resolutions proposed by the Salisbury West Division calling for an investigation into setting up a 'Confederation of Rhodesian States' which should become 'the basis of constitutional settlement discussions'. There was another supporting resolution from Mashonaland Rural which attacked *détente* as a 'sad and unprofitable path' and urged the government to stand up to the nationalists and concede nothing. Knowing that Sutton-Pryce was a good performer on the platform, Smith tried to prevent him from speaking, and relented only after two of his loyal senior ministers prevailed upon the Prime Minister to drop the objection. Sutton-Pryce proceeded to sway the delegates with precise argument and passion, and received a standing ovation. Barlow followed him, and left the platform confident of a strong majority. He was followed by a succession of party notables who supported the motion. The exception was Rodney Simmonds who took the impeccably right-wing position of opposing any extension of African political rights.

Just before dinner Ian Smith asked to speak. He began by reminding everyone of what a great country Rhodesia was, and of how important it was to stick together. Then for about forty minutes he rambled and cajoled, poked his finger in the air, lowered his voice to draw the audience towards him, narrowed his eyes, tugged his cuffs, flicked a dry tongue across his lips. He accused his opponents of trying to stab him in the back and told his audience how he would never let them down, how they mustn't stop him from doing his best for Rhodesia, and how, if the motion to provincialise was passed, it would be a vote of no confidence in him and would prevent him from obtaining an honourable settlement. A spellbound congress swayed back behind its leader and gave him a standing ovation. Sutton-Pryce and Barlow were treated as pariahs when they entered the dining-room after the speeches.

The RF's right may have lost the main battle at the 1975 congress but it did make a mark. Des Frost sounded his usual note of warning about ignoring party policy, and demanded that the government make greater efforts to protect European jobs, to spread the call-up net even wider, and to end the 'foreign controlled press monopoly'. He also wanted the government to forget about talking to the ANC ('this rabble who are masters of the art of leading from the rear') and to cease 'losing our country by default' by supporting *détente*. The Party Chairman did not disagree with 'hearts and minds concepts', but argued that they should not be introduced into an area until 'terrorism' had been eliminated and the Security Forces had restored 'full and complete control'.

Frost's blunt and uncompromising sentiments were echoed in several of the resolutions proposed by the party's branches and divisions. Ministerial intervention did deflect some of the anger. As a result, for example, of Lardner-Burke's continued opposition to mandatory death sentences, which was based on judicial advice, the proposal from the Mashonaland Rural and Salisbury West Divisions to impose such sentences was left to lie on the table.[21] The other law and order motions were carried, including one deploring the increasing practice of manning stations with African police, 'particularly during the hours of darkness'. Another resolution, carried unanimously, called on the government to exercise greater supervision over staff in the schools and at the university. Many teachers, according to one speaker, had 'anti-Christian, ultra-liberal and immoral opinions'. Other successful resolutions supported the ban on multi-racial sport in government schools, rejected 'any suggestion of a common roll', and proposed a joint caucus and party committee to examine ways of breaking the Argus Press monopoly. Clearly, the delegates at Umtali in September 1975 had no inkling that within a few months these resolutions would be redundant.

Smith himself did little to enlighten them. His Presidential Address at Umtali confirmed all their prejudices. Everyone else, he said, including (regrettably and inexplicably) the South Africans, practised 'double talk' and employed 'double standards'. He had accepted the *détente* exercise on the basis of three undertakings: that all acts of 'terrorism' would cease; that the South Africans would not withdraw the SAP until 'terrorism' had ceased; and that the released detainees would adopt a low profile in order to help any conference to a successful conclusion. All these undertakings, according to Smith, had been broken; Rhodesia was now in 'a worse situation' because it had lost its position of strength. The 'average tribesman' believed that the government gave in to extremists and that it would be unwise to side with the Security Forces. White morale had been affected leading to 'an unfortunate and unhealthy immigration [*sic*] from Rhodesia'.

Smith was careful not to disclose 'our negotiating stance' and insisted that, for security reasons, he could not reveal 'other details' of the *détente* exercise. He portrayed himself as the reasonable man surrounded by the weak and the perfidious. He fed the RF's thirst for moral superiority by reciting a catalogue of duplicity, murder, and mayhem which 'proved that the rest of the world was uncivilised or untrustworthy. And he concluded by appealing for patience and unity in the 'long haul' ahead. As always, Smith spoke seriously – and at length – without actually saying anything at all.

The right wing of the RF did at least offer an alternative strategy and – theoretically – a secure defence against black rule. Nevertheless, provincialisation had died at Umtali, and Wilfred Brooks was merciless. 'Once again', he wrote, the RF delegates had gone to an annual congress as 'roaring lions' and left as 'neutered lambs'.[22] Others, on the right, thought that Wickus de Kock might stand up to Smith. An Afrikaner farmer from Rusape with good connections in South Africa, De Kock had already been anointed by the Rhodesian press as the heir apparent. High-ranking members of the South African government saw him in a different light, and warned CIO that De Kock would run at the first whiff of grapeshot.[23] Some Afrikaners, they said, would never stand up for Rhodesia. Correct or not, this advice was overshadowed in September-October 1975 by De Kock's own allegations of untrustworthiness. Smith had told the Umtali congress that Mr Vorster was opposed to provincialisation (which De Kock said was untrue), and had criticised the South African government over *détente* (which De Kock thought was unfair). On 16 October De Kock informed caucus and cabinet that he was out of step with the government over its attacks on South Africa and over its misrepresentation of Vorster's position. He also opposed Smith's acceptance of eventual majority rule. Accusing the Prime Minister of being 'a liar and a man without integrity', he tried to resign, was dissuaded from doing so, and then, on 30 October, could take no more and left the government.[24]

Ian Smith took all these criticisms in his stride. He said later that he had never trusted De Kock who, in any case, had wept as he departed, a sure sign that he still admired his leader.[25] Besides, if 'Rusape' meant 'the one who does not give', here was one Afrikaner who ran before the fight. Finally, the Prime Minister retained the unstinting, and unthinking, loyalty of 'the masses'. The wife of a tobacco farmer reportedly said: 'We have heard Mr de Kock's explanation of his decision to resign. My family support Mr Smith and we are 100 per cent behind him. We have not yet heard his side of the story.'[26] She felt that there was no need to complicate matters with a reasoned rebuttal of the De Kock allegations. Mr Smith would know what was best for the laager.

All he lacked was a policy, though the caucus subcommittee was still trying to supply one. The Umtali congress had at least approved further investigations and, in February 1976, the subcommittee delivered its findings. The stated objective was 'to ensure that the Government of Rhodesia remains permanently in responsible hands'. To avoid any misunderstanding, the authors added in brackets: 'which means white hands'. In their view, the trouble with the present situation was that widespread political uncertainty was lowering white confidence and causing people to emigrate. The solution lay in the reassertion of permanent white rule and the removal of a dishonest constitution which allowed for the emergence of majority rule. The subcommittee thus proposed a new structure consisting of three provincial assemblies (European, Shona, and Ndebele) to preside over local authorities, and which themselves would be supervised by a central government where African representation should be fixed to 25 per cent. Outsiders – the subcommittee claimed – might look at the 1969 constitution and think that Africans would eventually rule the country; no one, looking at the proposed constitution, could see any objective other than permanent white control.

The subcommittee had displayed a refreshing candour, and a total misunderstanding of what was possible in early 1976. The left had been more realistic about what was possible in 1975 without being any more successful in pressing its case. The RP sought vainly to interest Smith in 'The Plan', a document published in June 1975 to solve an impasse which the majority of Rhodesians had not quite noticed.[27] 'The Plan' was based on four premises: outside intervention was necessary to bring the parties together; the Rhodesians had to accept the inevitability of majority rule and the black nationalists must abandon demands for an immediate transfer of power; there should be a transitional period of five years; and there must be constitutional safeguards against extremism and 'mob rule'. These proposals, which anticipated some of the principles and details of the eventual transfer of power in 1979-80, indicated that moderate opinion in white Rhodesia, represented by the RP, had accepted that a transfer of power was both inevitable and imminent.

Barriers still remained. Since its inception the RP had been an all-white party seeking to attract white votes. It could not afford to be too honest. In addition, while the mind knew what would happen, the heart was not prepared to say that it should. After all, the RP's members wanted to preserve their pleasant lifestyle, and were sufficiently 'Rhodesian' to be troubled about 'rocking the boat'. There was also a residual naivety. Four RP delegations saw Smith between December 1974 and April 1975 and assumed that the nation's leader – needing, in their words, 'the backing of every moderate Rhodesian' – was genuinely interested in pursuing a preconceived policy for a settlement. The RP failed to grasp the simple fact that Ian Smith did not have a policy at all, beyond the hope of implementing a modified version of the 1971 Agreement. At least, however, the RP had understood what was happening in southern Africa and had correctly predicted the outcome. Nor were its activities restricted to polite gestures within white politics. On the eve of the Victoria Falls conference, the party published advertisements confronting whites with the stark alternatives of a settlement or fighting a prolonged war. The RP's leaders also made several forays beyond Rhodesia in 1974-5 for talks with the so-called Front Line States and the externally-based nationalists.[28]

Like-minded individuals made similar trips. Two prominent farmers from the Umvukwes area – John Strong and Sandy Firks – visited Zambia in early April 1975 where they had a euphoric luncheon with President Kaunda.[29] Firks told their host that every 'intelligent man' acknowledged the inevitability of majority rule, adding that the principle of majority rule should be accepted immediately. According to Firks, 70 per cent of the farming leadership shared this view and, while all the white farmers were capitalists and many were conservative, 'the bulk of the obdurate, reactionary thinking' would be found among the artisans. Firks and Strong told Kaurida what the business community had been saying for a decade: the wealthier and more progressive sections of white Rhodesia could handle political reform. They added, however, that the farmers would fight for their land and, in the absence of a reasonable response from the nationalists, the whole white community would resist. Finally, they reminded Kaunda that Rhodesia possessed one of the most efficient counter-insurgency forces in the world.

The report of this meeting is revealing. At one level, two intelligent RP-minded farmers understood the import of the last few years and were worried about the lack of progress towards a settlement. At another level, they were Rhodesians, determined to defend their country and their own stake within it. Before leaving home, they had contacted the Secretary for Foreign Affairs. He advised them to 'project an image of reasonableness and a sincere wish to achieve a Settlement'. Firks, who believed that Ian Smith was 'a moderate man', the best candidate for implementing a compromise solution, did not require any prompting. He just could not contemplate acting against his own government's wishes.

III

The 'moderate man' had just one morsel to offer. On 8 July 1975 the government finally decided to implement one of the provisions of the 1971 Agreement by appointing the Quenet Commission to inquire into racial discrimination.[30] Opposition political groups reacted predictably. The ANC said it was interested only in talking about a transfer of power, many CP members decided that the exercise was no longer relevant, the RP was delighted, and Len Idensohn, who thought that the whites were the real victims of discrimination, said that he 'could vomit'.[31] It is not

quite clear why the government decided to act. The terms of reference –
'to study and report on ways of removing unnecessary or undesirable
discrimination' – hardly suggested a conversion to radical change. In
any case, the government still believed that some form of discrimination
was either desirable or necessary. Perhaps there was some advantage in
demonstrating flexibility to overseas friends while silencing the liberal
critics at home. Whatever the intention, nothing dangerous was about to
happen; a belated recognition of the causes of dissent in the 1960s, and
the appointment of 'safe' whites and 'sound' Africans to investigate the
matter, would upset the far right without troubling the rest of white
society.

The Commission collected most of its evidence towards the end of
1975 and that material, together with the report which was handed
down in April 1976, provides a useful insight into the discriminatory
basis and attitudes of white Rhodesia.[32]

Frost put the RF position: social mixing led to tension; 'a measure of
separation leads to peaceful co-existence'; racial harmony was 'vital' but
the RF opposed forced integration; 'left-wing elements' were doing a
'disservice' to all communities because integration would lower standards, push the European out of Rhodesia, and end the protection of
unsophisticated Africans in the TTLs.[33] The RF did not argue that the
whites were innately superior. Even SASCON did not make that claim,
preferring to tell the Commission of the 'cultural' origins of Rhodesia's
discriminatory practices and of the inequality of the races evidenced by
the failure of blacks in Africa to generate wealth of their own. At least the
RF delegation and SASCON were being partially candid. They did not
go to the Commission to apologise for, or to deny, a discrimination they
supported.

Some of the other witnesses were more evasive. The Ministry of
Internal Affairs asked to talk to the Commission in private because, like
so many official bodies, it wanted to avoid justifying discrimination in
terms which sounded so 'racist'. Forced to explain the lack of black
appointments, or promotions to senior positions, other officials resorted
to generalised statements about the possibility of 'unpleasantness' arising out of greater social contact. They said that Europeans would not
accept Africans as equals, that blacks were easily intimidated by their
own people, and were not always honest or reliable.[34] On occasions, the
white officials came perilously close to claiming that Africans were inferior, or confessing that cultural differences amounted to racial distinctions. More frequently, they opposed 'forced integration' on the ground
that 'the white community' would not tolerate it.

The evidence of discrimination in the public service was overwhelming. Figures from the Public Services Board showed that Africans mainly

occupied the unskilled and semi-skilled positions where incomes ranged from nearly $67 to $162 a month. Skilled artisans and stenographers received almost $484 a month, and only 19 per cent of them were non-Europeans. Just 12 per cent of established officer posts were held by Africans. Private enterprise was no better although more blacks were now entering lower management positions – in personnel – in the major corporations. A few more blacks had become shop assistants and semi-skilled tradesmen because there were not enough white housewives or artisans to serve in the expanding retail outlets or in the manufacturing industry. The business houses continued to advocate their traditional position. Rio Tinto clashed with the white-led TUC over 'the rate for the job' arguing that the principle was holding down African earnings, wasting manpower, and denying opportunities. No one broached the question of whether the companies might have made a unilateral attack on the question of wages. Certainly something would have to be done. A university study in 1975 had shown that about 80 per cent of black urban workers received incomes which placed them below the poverty line, and that about 85 per cent of blacks employed in agriculture did not earn half the amount necessary to reach it.[35]

The Quertet Commission examined many of the economic disabilities encountered by Africans in Rhodesia in 1975. It was not, however, especially interested in structural factors except, perhaps, for the Land Tenure Act. Much of the time was spent on the 'pinpricks' and on the issues of education and multiracial sport. The latter remained a burning question in 1975. An RF branch sent two delegates from a mining constituency to explain to the Commission that forced integration in school sport would cause strife among lower-income Europeans who were not able to buy segregation. While the Ministry of Education denied that it had directed schools since 1967 to desist from multiracial sport, it agreed that the 'Government's framework' had allowed European pupils to enter Asian or Coloured schools but not vice versa. The Secretary for Education informed the Commission that he had two full cartons of letters condemning multiracial sport. Swimming, in particular, created 'sensitive social problems', not present in other school sports. The Rhodesia Swimming Association was also upset. Banned since 1973 from participation in international swimming because of racial discrimination, the Association wanted to rejoin the world body. It was not helpful in 1975 to have the Minister of Local Government banning non-whites from competing in a gala in Salisbury.

Sport and sporting clubs were at the forefront of racial 'incidents' during 1975. John Newington, the RF back-bencher and Deputy Speaker, resigned from the Bulawayo Municipal Sports Club when it permitted multiracial tennis on its courts.[36] The prospect of Asians just playing tennis on white courts was sufficient; the fact that they would not be admitted as club members or as guests in the club house did not appease him. In Salisbury, an all-white club, which won the country's premier soccer trophy in 1975, continued to ban non-whites from its rooms, including the black president of the Rhodesian Football Association and the Coloured wife of its own goalkeeper. The one concession was a decision to send beer to the changing rooms of visiting multiracial and non-white teams. The goalkeeper decided to leave the country.[37] He would certainly have had the sympathy of the *Rhodesia Herald,* and of all those professional and voluntary associations which told the Quenet Commission that blacks, above all, resented social exclusion. The *Herald* believed that the 'deepest wish' of Africans was 'to be greeted and accepted by white people'. Underlying this claim was a widespread belief among Rhodesians that the war was being fought so that blacks might enter whites-only social clubs. Aware that such demands would upset many of its readers, the *Herald* assured whites that being polite, giving way occasionally, and respecting the existence and rights of other communities did not mean forced integration and would not lead to the 'mongrelisation' feared by the far right.[38] Several unions were still determined to exclude blacks. When Rhodesia Railways set out in 1974-6 to integrate grades and salary scales – for the sake of 'industry rationalisation' – the relevant unions postponed their demarcation disputes and internecine warfare to oppose what they saw as 'job fragmentation' and an attack on 'the rate for the job'. The old fears returned: young whites without a trade or five O levels might as well emigrate; Africans would be employed as Learner Diesel Drivers or Junior Enginemen at wages appropriate to the African economy; a 'Cheap Labour' policy would undermine the standard of living of lower-skilled whites. Management claimed that the unions wanted to control decision-making as well as protect the past. On 19 November 1975, R. A. Blackwell, the Personnel Manager of Rhodesia Railways, told a seminar on industrial relations that the unions were using the 'backdoor approach' to override management attempts to run the railways on sound business lines. Unionists were lobbying MPs, RF officials, and ministries, and he could quote 'dozens of examples' where 'pure obstruction or obstinacy allied to political influences have obstructed the smooth management of the Rhodesia Railways'. Blackwell blamed the older, 'vociferous elements' for the current militancy. These same elements had always opposed the promotion of black skills. They had no intention in 1975 of modifying their stand even though labour scarcity rather than a cheap labour policy was prompting management to introduce more blacks into the lower end of the skilled trades. A new situation might call for a new approach but the white unions, and their

RF connections, remained locked into the old conflicts about cheap labour.[39]

The Churches thought about moral leadership, and pleaded for better understanding and improved race relations. They approched the government to complain about the alleged brutality of the Security Forces, and criticised the Indemnity and Compensation Act of 1975 which protected members of the Security Forces from civil or criminal proceedings for actions done in 'good faith' while suppressing 'terrorism'.[40] The Catholic bishops and the Justice and Peace Commission,[41] following the path of Bishop Lamont, were the most outspoken in denouncing racial discrimination. The Anglicans were more circumspect. Bishop Burrough walked 470 miles through his diocese of Mashonaland during Lent in 1975 to show how his Church listened to and loved its black people.[42] The Bishop of Matabeleland told his synod that the government should promote Africans within the public service and suggested that race relations would improve if only the races would listen to each other. The Anglicans contributed to greater equality by awarding a 45 per cent pay rise to their African clergy in 1975. Father Lewis, 'the high priest of the RF', who had long despaired of the apathy and timidity of his brethren, knew that the white Anglican Communion had rejected his 'extreme' views. The Anglican Church remained, nonetheless, on the side of the status quo. It existed to bear witness to eternal salvation, to the centrality of the Cross and the sacraments, to Man's sin and God's power to redeem. People should change, society should change, but the State must restrain those who identified their 'desires' with justice and right.[43] The State, which had every intention of enforcing restraint, was even less concerned about dismantling the past. A government, which could announce the appointment of the Quenet Commission in a speech condemning 'terrorism' and the ANC, which offered no encouragement in its terms of reference for a frontal assault upon discriminatory attitudes and practices, and whose own delegates to the Commission represented its right wing, had not accepted that the new circumstances of southern Africa called for a radical approach.

IV

While a growing minority of whites might have demanded more urgent action – either to go backwards or forwards – most accepted the Prime Minister's leisurely pace towards nowhere. They did so because of their assumption in 1973-5 that the war was being won, and that any 'difficulties' would soon be overcome. Any disturbing evidence was either hidden away in official documents or was ignored by an unreceptive audience. The annual police reports, for example, recorded a rising incidence of violent crime and an increase in the number of uncleared cases.[44] If the Police Commissioner could attribute these developments to general world trends in crime then most Rhodesians were bound to ignore the pressure being placed on police manpower by the growing black threats to law and order. Underlying the optimism and the complacency was the conviction that, although the government had been forced in 1974 to impose a 10 per cent surcharge on personal and company taxes, the military struggle would not prevent Rhodesia from winning the economic war. There were some worrying moments when undercover transactions were exposed in the press. The most significant led in 1974 to the gaoling of James McIntosh, a British merchant banker, who received fourteen years on a number of charges relating to the passing of secret documents exposing sanctions-busting activities. No one could measure the damage he caused.[45] Despite this reverse, and despite sanctions, the border closure, the rise in oil prices, the advancing world recession, and domestic political uncertainty, the Rhodesian economy performed quite well in 1973-4. A good rainy season, strong prices for minerals and foodstuffs, and the steady growth of manufacturing combined to record a real growth rate of 10 per cent during 1974. Perhaps the signals in 1975 were less auspicious but who could doubt that such a tenacious people would overcome these 'cyclical' problems?

All the forecasts in early 1975 had warned against optimism. Shortages of foreign exchange, enforced cuts in import quotas of more than 50 per cent, uncertainty about Mozambique, port and rail congestion in South Africa, all were factors spreading gloom in informed circles. On 28 April Ian Smith admitted that there would be 'a diminution in economic activity and a slower growth'. He called 1975 'a year of challenge' while insisting that only 'an extreme pessimist' would deny that Rhodesia had 'a very bright future'.[46] The President of ACCOR was more direct when, a few days later, he said that Rhodesia faced 'a very thin year' and that the economy would not regain impetus until there was a settlement.[47] No one, however, wanted to blame the war. After reviewing developments in his area, the President of Umtali's Chamber of Commerce told his annual general meeting on 27 June 1975 that the economic crisis was caused by a world-wide inflation and depression.[48] Nine months later, the official *Economic Survey* for 1975 acknowledged several setbacks: a net decline in Gross Domestic Product for the first time since UDI, a record deficit in the balance of payments, an adverse movement in the terms of trade, and reduced growth rates in agriculture, manufacturing, and mining. In 1982 a former Secretary of the Treasury argued that the second half of 1975 marked a turning-point in the fortunes of the economy because of the sharp fall in foreign exchange earnings. The war did not cause this downturn but its escalation after 1975 prevented any recovery.[49]

General discussions about the economy ignored the war almost entirely. The critics blamed political uncertainty for the worsening situation in 1975, and the government emphasised external factors such as depressed commodity prices, transport difficulties, and world inflation. There was no conspiracy to hide the impact of the guerrilla incursions because there was no obvious connection between them and the worsening economic performance. Yet defence costs were certainly rising. Estimates for all defence items in 1972-3 amounted to $52.3 million and constituted 14.3 per cent of total budget outlays; the estimates for 1975-6 were $120.8 million and accounted for 20.3 per cent of the budget. Another little noticed cost was that an increasing proportion of a rising transport budget was devoted to new roads, bridges, and airfields in or near the 'sharp end'. In 1975 the Secretary of Roads and Road Traffic reported that the Department was building some 500 kilometres of new security roads each year and had been forced to postpone much-needed repairs and new construction elsewhere. The Treasury had to make a special supplement for resurfacing roads in the north-east with bitumen and the Department was losing men and vehicles in landmine incidents.[50] It suited the government to play down these expenses and to treat the war as a minor item in calculating the economic balance sheet. The July budget speech, for example, made only passing references to Hurricane in explaining rising defence costs and the increased expenditure on the TTLs. The objective was a 'normal' budget, notable for its strict housekeeping, small projected deficit ($25 million), and altered personal tax structure. It assumed that, although the 'economic war' would continue, the armed struggle would not. Unknowingly, the Minister of Finance had brought down the last 'non-war' budget in white Rhodesia.[51]

To some extent, estimates of the impact of the war depended on where people lived and what they did. In Umtali shopkeepers lost 'several thousand dollars a month' because of a slow-down in both directions of tourist traffic across the Mozambique border. On the other hand, empty flats and houses were filling up with Portuguese refugees.[52] The tourist industry in general also reported contrasting experiences. In the year before Altena some 352,000 tourists arrived in Rhodesia, 71 per cent of them by car and mostly through Beit Bridge. The Tourist Board disclosed that there was a 25 per cent decline in visitors to Rhodesia in 1973 and began advertising to win back the South African motorist who – it was assumed – was discouraged by 'terrorist' incidents and the high cost of the Rhodesian dollar.[53] The campaign did not save a Juliasdale hotel (situated near Inyanga) which closed in April 1974. The proprietor explained that South Africans were unable to distinguish between the Eastern Highlands and the north-east, and that he had been felled by the 'final blow' of petrol rationing.[54] Yet in 1975 the other hotels of the Eastern Highlands were recording shortages of accommodation in trying to cope with the Rhodesians who were obliged to take their holidays inside the country.[55] By then, the tourist industry was more worried about the increasing level of government interference in its operations which was occurring irrespective of the war. Under the new Tourist Development Act, which was designed to promote the 'orderly development' of the industry, registered hotels were to be strictly supervised, their restaurants were to be separately licensed, and they could be inspected annually by each of four different authorities. Hoteliers who wished to alter their premises would have to meet the separate and potentially conflicting standards set by the Licensing Board and the Tourist Board.[56] Understandably, there were members of the tourist industry in 1975 who believed that bureaucracy rather than 'terrorism' constituted the greater menace.

The farmers, who were the most affected by the worsening economic situation in 1975, did not highlight the war in explaining their difficulties. The hardest hit were the tobacco growers who blamed several factors for the 'crisis of confidence' in their industry: the low yields from the poor 1974-5 season; unfavourable exchange rates forcing up the international price of Rhodesian tobacco; competition from other types of tobacco better suited to changing overseas tastes; the lengthening of the tobacco pipeline in the struggle against sanctions; the higher input costs and falling prices. The 'crisis' was real enough. One-third of tobacco growers recorded a loss at the end of the 1974-5 season. A further third only just covered the costs of production, returned less than their family living requirements, and could not plant another crop without significant financial assistance.[57] Indebtedness was also rising. Tobacco growers owed $79 million in short-term credits in December 1973; by December 1974 the figure had risen to $98 million, and, in March 1975, reached $120 million. The war simply added to these problems. Given that some 50 per cent of tobacco growers farmed in or near the sensitive areas, it was tempting to attach the major blame to 'terrorist' incursions for the exodus of a third of the farmers from the Mtoko district by July 1975.[58] Yet there were few 'desertions' from the richer tobacco farms in equally dangerous areas, suggesting perhaps that profitability and the size of the investment were sufficient antidotes to concerns for personal safety. The editor of their Association's journal had a different explanation for the farmers' steadfastness:

But the great thing about Rhodesians, as the politicians never tire of reminding us, is that we actually thrive on adversity and uncertainty. It brings out the best in us and prevents [*sic*] us from the softness that makes others easy prey to permissiveness.[59]

The other sectors of agriculture were also worried in 1975. Paddy Millar, an RF stalwart and President of the RNFU, reminded the annual congress in July that, while yields and producer prices had fallen across the board, input costs had risen by 43 per cent in the previous eighteen months.[60] Fuels and fertilisers were becoming more expensive just as pressures on foreign reserves were rendering their supply more uncertain. One solution, strongly advocated by the same farmers who attacked inflationary wage and price increases in the non-agricultural sector, was a call for the 'socialistic' policy of helping the 'small farmer' to remain above the 'breadline'. Specifically, the farmers wanted a fixed pre-planting price for their crops which would guarantee a minimum return without restraining their access to higher profits in a buoyant market. Traditionally, the RF tried to balance the competing interests of its rural and urban supporters. Under pressure from the RNFU the government finally relented in 1975 and agreed to a pre-planting price for maize, cotton, wheat, sorghum, groundnuts, and soya beans. The Minister of Agriculture told parliament on 25 July that this was 'one of the most important announcement [*sic*] that had been made in Rhodesia in recent years'.[61] An RF back-bencher, representing the lower-middle-income suburb of Mabelreign in Salisbury, surprised and pleased his rural colleagues by supporting better cash returns for farmers and accepting that urban consumers would have to pay more for food.[62] He was acclaimed for his patriotism and his courage when he was merely acknowledging the reality of the RNFU's lobbying power, the impact of worsening economic conditions upon the farming community, and the conventional wisdom that white Rhodesia needed 'to keep the farmers on the land'.

There were two components of this conventional wisdom: the incontestable assumption that absentee farmers and deserted farms constituted a security risk, and the proposition – uncontested within the farming community – that profitable white farming was indispensable to the economy as a whole. Both themes were evident in discussions at the RNFU annual congress in 1975, the first occasion for a full-scale debate among farmers on the impact of the war. The farmers of Matabeleland were the most anxious. One was worried because thirteen ranching operations owned 34 per cent of the land in the province and one-third of all Matabeleland farmers in 1971 were non-resident. Ranching operations were considered vulnerable to terrorist infiltration because many were owned by overseas companies which installed white managers who, in turn, employed Africans to run the business. Vacant land, non-resident farmers, temporary managers, and African-run operations were all highly undesirable. One answer, expressed by R. K. Harvey from Umvuma, was to adopt 'a communistic attitude' to the 'archaic estates'; that is, to break them up and replace the foreign owners and managers with young farmers or ex-service types. The 'moral fibre of our country' was 'entirely dependent on the fibre of its rural population'; it was essential, therefore, to redress the imbalances in the rural community by a state-supported land settlement scheme.

Fiercely independent, rugged individualists to a man (and woman), the farmers in 1975 turned to the government to finance uneconomic land sub-divisions, to 'Rhodesianise' their community, and to fill the empty white spaces. Ian Smith was there to reassure them, just in case anyone might query their consistency. He told the congress how he admired the individualism and independence of the farmers: they 'have always been the front line of defence against totalitarian doctrines such as Communism, and the even more dangerous encroachment of insidious socialism'. Smith's reasoning was that farmers the world over seemed 'better able to retain a sense of the eternal values'. No one at the congress wanted to dispute his assessment, just as no one – anywhere – could conceivably label as 'socialistic' any policy which merely tried to 'Rhodesianise' farming or to help small, uneconomic white farmers to remain on the land.

If the farmers were worried about the multiplier effects of the world recession, urban Rhodesians were still enjoying a rising standard of living. A household budget survey showed that the average income of European urban households had risen by 88 per cent between 1968 and 1975-6, that average net savings after tax had risen from $72 to $806 a year in the same period, and that just 4 per cent of households (all in the lowest income bracket) spent more than they received.[63] The average European income for Salisbury and Bulawayo was now $8,028; 29 per cent of incomes were over $11,000; about 10 per cent exceeded $17,000 and were subject to the top marginal tax rate of 60 cents in the dollar. It is true that consumer prices were beginning to move sharply. There was an overall rise in the European index from 115.6 in 1970 to 149.2 in 1975 (the African index rose from 112.4 to 144.0), with a sudden jump of 20.4 points in 1974 – 5.[64] The principal increases occurred in foodstuffs, transport, clothing, footwear, and servants' wages. Housing prices also rose significantly in the middle and upper brackets. Whereas houses in the lower-income white suburbs in Salisbury cost an average 14 per cent more in 1975 than 1970, prices increased by 35 per cent in Mabelreign and by 28 per cent in Highlands over the same period.[65] Sales at all levels, however, fell during 1974-5. The confidence of the consumer, and of the investor, had gone down after the continued failure to achieve a settlement and because of the growing political uncertainty throughout southern Africa. But, aside from individual failures and the poorer pensioners, white Rhodesians were much better off in 1975 than they had been in 1970.[66]

And they were not prepared to restrain further claims for greater prosperity. Blatant inequities – within white Rhodesia – could not be tolerated. The public service unions mounted a steady campaign during 1974-5 to eliminate (white) staff shortages and redress the 'imbalance' in salary scales between government and the private sector.[67] Their success, in straitened times, was remarkable: a 17.5 per cent pay rise over 1975-6, an extension of a generous home loan scheme, increases in pension and travelling allowances, higher government contributions to the Dental Aid Scheme, and improved leave conditions for established posts.[68] The unions did not have to press too hard for these gains. The RF's support base included the public service, and the government knew how much its reputation and survival depended upon the maintenance of what it considered to be a skilled, incorruptible administration. It capitulated quickly to the demands of an influential minority which wanted to enhance its privileges at the expense of other whites.

Meanwhile, the problems of private enterprise were exacerbated by the call-ups which were becoming more than a nuisance. The regulations had been tightened during 1973 to catch the school-leavers. Exemptions became harder to obtain and university students were required to seek annual deferments. Industry and commerce began to complain when men over 25 were being called up and were required to serve more frequently. Although the government talked of phasing out call-ups (a favourite theme of RF candidates in the 1974 elections), and of relying upon the regular forces, the Army's image as a 'last resort' career, special circumstances such as the 'Big Push' of August 1975, and the RF's reluctance to raise a large black army meant that the authorities had to increase their demands on young and middle-aged whites. Despite the arrival in the mid-1970s of veterans from Northern Ireland and Vietnam, and rumours about scores of mercenaries joining the RLI, there was no future in relying upon overseas recruitment because the Security Forces insisted that all recruits should be attested on exactly the same terms. Adventurers might get the opportunity to kill but there was little prospect of becoming rich in the process. So the government had to rely upon the local white population. In June 1975 it advertised for women to undertake duties at Army and Air Force bases and received over 1,200 applicants within a few days.[70] On 11 September 1975 it announced that all white males between 25 and 30, without current commitments in the Security Forces, would be called up for 56 days followed, later, by another 28. Whites in the 30-8 age bracket were to be called up for a shorter initial period, and a longer subsequent one, for service in Internal Affairs, the BSAP, or the Police Reserve. White Rhodesia grumbled, and the business houses openly protested.

Reports continued to circulate of some men doing more than their share, and of others escaping altogether, in spite of attempts by the Security Forces from early 1974 'to make the mesh finer still'.[71] During 1975 the Matabeleland Chambers of Commerce and Industries repeatedly objected that men from their province were being called up more often than those from other regions. The oil companies were critical because 62 per cent of their employees were liable for call-up. In November 1975 the banks found that 266 out of their combined white staff of 614 were subject to service. It was a disturbing situation because highly-priced executives were being taken from productive jobs and, as a consequence, firms claimed they were losing business. The farmers were also affected. Many had already objected because they had to leave their own homesteads unprotected while they did call-up duties with the Police Reserve in other areas. Others, apparently unaware of the spirit of solidarity, criticised the diversion of funds and manpower to assist rival tobacco farmers in Centenary. The Makoni Farmers' Association drew attention to the greater financial hardships experienced by their members who were being called away for long periods twice a year to defend the farmers of Centenary who spent just two days a week in the Police Reserve.[72]

These objections to inefficient and inequitable manpower arrangements soon became commonplace. Their appearance before 1976 demonstrated how the war was more disruptive and divisive in the earlier period than many were prepared to admit. If the major factors affecting the economy originated externally, the war was already intruding into the economic and social life of white Rhodesia.

V

There were two developments in 1973-5 which all white Rhodesians were bound to notice: the reintroduction of petrol rationing and the increasing level of emigration.

Following the sharp rise in international oil prices after October 1973, the Rhodesian government launched a media campaign under the slogan of 'Don't Drive Rhodesia Dry'. The objective was a voluntary reduction in private petrol consumption in order to save foreign reserves. The campaign was successful – there was a 30 per cent fall in consumption by the end of December – but the government was obliged to reintroduce rationing to counter 'the spiralling costs of crude oil'.[73]

Rationing was imposed from 1 February 1974. Though the initial scheme was not harsh it quickly tested the patience of those unaccustomed to Rhodesian bureaucracy. Seven classes of vehicle were introduced and motorists and motor cyclists were awarded units (each to the value of 5 litres) according to the weight of the vehicle measured against the distance between home and work. If, for example, a private car weighed 700 kg and the motorist lived 10 km from his office, he was entitled to 55 litres of petrol a month. In addition, the same motorist could claim an annual holiday allowance equivalent to 1,000 km which was considered sufficient for travel within Rhodesia's borders. Special allowances were available for foreign tourists driving foreign-registered vehicles, and for local motorists having 'special compassionate grounds'. Finally, the speed limit and the prescribed hours when petrol could be sold – reduced during the media campaign – were restored to their previous levels.

A *Herald* editorial argued that, while there would be restricted motoring, 'with luck it won't be too bad'.[74] Within three years the initial scheme looked very generous. Abuse and indignation often worked in the early days in persuading harassed, temporary rationing officers that the existing allowance was unjust or inappropriate. The flint-faced pensioners and middle-aged housewives, who occupied the rationing offices in later years, had not yet been summoned to defend the nation's bowsers. Nevertheless, it was frustrating trying to overcome bureaucratic absurdities and delays. An editorial in the *Lomagundi News* pointed out that, because the fuel officer in Sinoia did not have the power to vary allocations, and because variations could not be made without an interview, Sinoia residents had to drive to Salisbury to complain about their allowance.[75] Most of these anomalies were soon ironed out, and it was not necessary to drive Rhodesia dry in order to acquire the right to drive anywhere. And, if the spirit of conserving fuel for Rhodesia had 'long ... vanished' by mid-1975,[76] the restrictions did contribute to the 23 per cent reduction of the white road toll.[77] Moreover, the system established a logic of its own which the habitual docility of the white electorate helped to sustain. Another freedom had been curtailed – in this case, to hop into a car at will and visit friends or a favourite place for a braai – and another, regular encounter with bureaucracy had been institutionalised. By the end of 1975 Rhodesians had become so accustomed to rationing and to haggling for coupons that they simply incorporated the restrictions and the perennial battles into their way of life.

The impact of the war was immediately apparent in the migration statistics. During 1972 Rhodesia had a net gain in European, Asian, and Coloured migration of 8,825; in 1973 the comparable figure was 1,680, and in 1974 it was 599. There was a net loss of 118 in September 1973, the first such loss since 1966. Net losses were also recorded in December

1973, in four months of 1974, and in three months of 1975.[78] An influx of Portuguese settlers from Mozambique helped to retrieve the situation for 1975 – when there was a net gain of 1,930 – but the high departure rates of white Rhodesians continued to alarm the authorities. Emigration rose by 50.5 per cent in the year after Altena, and by over 16 per cent in each of 1974 and 1975. A breakdown of these statistics proved even more disturbing. In terms of age, the major departing categories were the very young, the elderly, and those between 15 and 24. There was a very real fear that, while many of the latter would return upon completing their education, too many would apply their superior qualifications elsewhere. Despite the net gain of males in 1974 in the 25-39 category, and the arrival of discontented, job-seeking skilled tradesmen from Britain and Europe, there was also an overall loss of professional and technical workers. The disturbing fact was that Rhodesia in 1972-5 was losing too many of the right sort, and not gaining enough of those it most needed.

The government was acutely aware of the political and psychological significance of the migration figures. On 1 January 1974 Ian Smith launched 'Settlers '74', a campaign which urged Rhodesians and their friends to submit the names of one million potential immigrants who, in turn, would receive an official brochure outlining the advantages of living in Rhodesia. Smith himself set the tone by contrasting 'warm and inviting' Rhodesia with a Britain of 'widespread unemployment, spiralling inflation, strikes and a cold, wet winter'.[79] African leaders and the Churches protested that this appeal for mass white immigration was insensitive, racist, and unnecessary.[80] The money would be better spent on reducing black unemployment and creating a more skilled black workforce. The worst fears of the protesters proved groundless. Early expectations of acquiring one immigrant for every ten names submitted (that is, an influx of 100,000 new white settlers) were quickly revised downwards to 10,000. By May the government had a list of just 4,200 names. 'Settlers '74' was already a total flop and the government quietly discarded the idea.

The back-bench was not discouraged. Rodney Simmonds wanted to provide assisted holidays to seduce middle-aged adults in the skilled trades and professions to migrate.[81] Archie Wilson, the former Commander of the Air Force, recalled Lord Baden-Powell's dream of a 'spiritual home' for the Boy Scout movement, and urged the creation of a 'Mecca in the Matopos' to which – ultimately – thousands of young settlers might be drawn.[82] Simmonds and Wilson did at least address the question of diminishing migration returns. The government was afraid to do so, partly because 'Settlers '74' was still a fresh, embarrassing memory, and partly because the RF preferred to avoid unpleasant realities. Characteristically, the government was trying to solve a problem whose existence could not be acknowledged outside of confidential meetings. Having assumed that white morale would not survive a bout of honesty, the appropriate response was to pretend that nothing was wrong and that other things were right. This approach was evident in a *Fact Paper* distributed overseas by the Information Section of Foreign Affairs in April 1975.[83] The paper argued that there had always been a high turnover in the white population, that the 'normal pattern' of strong net gains was always restored after periods of political uncertainty, and that the concentration on migration statistics was diverting attention from the natural increase of the white population and the increasing proportion of whites born in southern Africa (from 62 per cent in 1969 to 70 per cent in 1975) who could not accurately be classified as 'settlers'. The argument, relying heavily on evasion and *non sequiturs*, also assumed that 'normality' could be restored under white rule.

Petrol rationing certainly affected lifestyles, and the migration statistics probably influenced morale. Yet any changes in lifestyle or weakening of morale did not noticeably affect the Rhodesians' mental outlook during 1975. The majority never doubted their cause and remained convinced that they would win through. Their stand was reinforced by encouraging words from sympathetic visitors who, themselves, were often located on the fringes of right-wing politics.[84] Rhodesia's broadcasting services contributed to the general myopia by persistently representing the outside world as crippled by depravity, corruption, instability, and cowardice. It was hard to obtain contrary views. The Exchange Control Act and restricted holiday allowances reduced the mental horizons of most Rhodesians to southern Africa. Few of those who did venture out of Africa allowed new experiences to challenge existing prejudices and values. And those who stayed home had neither the means nor the inclination to establish contact with black aspirations. The overall result was that most Rhodesians failed to understand the extent of their isolation and to recognise the dangers confronting them.

Nor was their mental isolation restricted to politics. Defending, as they saw it, the traditional values (which even more of them were abusing in practice by 1975), Rhodesians continued to associate social and cultural change in the West with the growth of permissiveness and with anti-Christian behaviour. Their enforced separation from Western society was, in this sense, lauded rather than deplored. It hardly mattered that the Rhodesians were accused of living in a time warp when they saw themselves protecting a society from destructive change.

In one instance the Rhodesians resisted change because they were freedom-loving patriots. In mid-1975 the Bulawayo City Council attempted to ban smoking in the city's cinemas. Ten thousand signatures from all races were collected in opposition to the move. On 30 July Hilary Squires proposed in parliament that, where the local authorities refused to act, the government should legislate to prohibit smoking in cinemas to protect the rights and the health of the non-smokers.[85] He cited all the health arguments against smoking, and especially against smoking in confined places, and demonstrated how other Western countries had banned the practice in cinemas. Several of his fellow backbenchers argued that the cinemas would lose money. Peter Nilson declared that his wife was a very heavy smoker, and that he liked to take her to the cinema. Ian Sandeman, who represented a tobacco-growing area and who regarded the World Health Organisation as politically suspect, claimed that its evidence was based on foreign tobacco and not the local product which was 'entirely safe for people to smoke'. Dennis Divaris wanted to know why cinemas were being singled out for attention, criticised the government for 'tragic' inaction including the failure to introduce health warnings on cigarette packets, and then voted against the motion. The Minister of Health, Rowan Cronje, intervened only to deliver a five-word infantile interjection ('Ask the Minister of Health'). The whole subject was treated with great hilarity and, although the motion was eventually passed by 29 votes to 15, the ministers abstained and cabinet ignored the outcome.

A prominent liberal had already given the formal justification for doing nothing when he wrote to the press warning that a government-imposed ban would lead to the establishment of 'a fully collectivised socialist state'.[86] Rhodesians – it seems – already had too much experience of regulation, or they wanted to preserve the autonomy of local authorities, or else they so believed in the rights of individuals that self-destruction and the infringement of the rights of others were considered secondary. The argument against centralised state control – however hypocritical in relation to themselves, let alone in relation to the black population – was also a useful cover for those Rhodesians who simply wanted to defend the tobacco industry. Significantly, Squires began his speech by assuring the growers that he wished them to be prosperous. Clearly, therefore, the Rhodesians were not altogether isolated from world trends: they had inherited the inconsistency and hypocrisy which marked the anti-tobacco debates elsewhere. Their special circumstances, however, as heavy smokers in a society where tobacco was cheap and the growers carried political weight, meant that in 1975 those debates were only just beginning.

Another example of resistance, and a further indication of remoteness, was the reaction to the issue of women's liberation. The National Federation of Business and Professional Women published *Profiles of Rhodesian Women* to coincide with the International Women's

Year of 1975. Having adopted the theme – 'Looking towards the 21st century: the full recognition of women as people' – the Federation wanted to feature the development of Rhodesia. There were brief portraits of individuals, including some twenty-five blacks, Coloureds, and Asians. One chapter examined eleven women who worked in business and the professions under the heading 'In a Man's World'. The title reflected Rhodesian assumptions about the division between the public (male) and private (female) domains, while the claim that these eleven women saw their careers as additional 'to their traditional roles of mothers and homemakers' accurately described both their own outlook and the expectations held of them. This outlook was confirmed in 1975 in a poem written by Senator Olive Robertson to mark the Jubilee Year of the Women's Institutes in Rhodesia. The Senator assured women that their overriding devotion to the family and the home was both laudable and self-fulfilling:

> Here is the base and not the boundary
> Of interests and affections,
> These are not prison walls from which she needs
> Escape and liberation,
> This the foundation on which she, herself,
> Can build the living structure of her life
> To its completion.[87]

The Senator was not totally isolated: she knew the arguments and vocabulary of the international sisterhood. She also knew that the 'Man's World', invaded by only a few more women and still endorsed by millions of others, remained secure in the West. She, and Rhodesia, were 'behind' only in the sense of there being an almost total absence of interest in 'women's issues' in 1975. It was fashionable to trivialise or reject the symbols which mattered greatly to liberationists elsewhere. The *Chronicle*, for example, reported that some Bulawayo women liked to be addressed as 'Ms' though largely to avoid the stigma of the unmarried state. The overwhelming majority preferred 'Miss' or 'Mrs' because those titles were more 'feminine'. One informant, who explained this reaction in terms of Rhodesian women being 'too conservative and too isolated', and of not coming into contact 'with modern trends', identified herself as 'Mrs' Jill Hancock.[88] Few Rhodesian women publicly doubted their own importance in the scheme of things. Beyond the family and the home there were the Women's Institutes, the Forces Canteens, and the Border Patrol Welfare Fund, and beyond such good works there was the contribution to the 'Man's World'. When Mrs Daniels addressed a seminar for secretaries and receptionists in Gwelo which had been organised by the Rhodesian Institute of Management, she assured them that women were essential to a well-organised business. They are wanted, she said, because they are methodical and practical, and because 'part and parcel of their make-up' was that they 'worked better for someone other than themselves'.[89]

Young girls were being reminded of their traditional status. A booklet, published just after the conclusion of International Women's Year, examined the range of careers open to young Rhodesians.[90] It pointed out to male school-leavers that they would want to earn enough to support a wife and family, and that they should be sufficiently qualified so that the wife would not need to go out and work. Girls were told that, although a 'career' of being a wife and mother was of 'the greatest importance', it was desirable for a mother of grown-up children, a divorcee, or the wife of a disabled husband to be well qualified so that she could re-enter the workforce. Besides, in 'today's world', women 'are beginning to take their place beside the men'. Almost, but not quite: on 1 August 1975 thirty-five women joined the newly-created Rhodesian Women's Service to operate computers, teleprinters, and radios, or to drive cars, perform clerical duties, or cook. The war had, to a minor extent, opened up one end of a male profession. There was little movement elsewhere. Most jobs listed in the careers booklet – from accountancy to real estate to dental surgery – assumed that the applicants would be male while the 'female' jobs were the familiar ones of nursing, teaching, beauty therapy, bookkeeping, office reception, and secretarial work. Fashion modelling was another possibility: a good figure was 'essential' but good looks 'may not be quite as important' and, in any case, 'wonders can be done with the right make-up and hair style'.

Obviously, the Rhodesian male had nothing to fear. The more worrying outcome of the 'Swinging Sixties' was the increasing volume and variety of challenges to traditional moral values. Fortunately, the official censors were alert to the dangers, and continued to protect innocent adult Rhodesians from literary or pictorial encounters with 'abnormal sex', 'sex for swingers', sex instruction manuals, violence, and drug-taking. By 1975 the Board of Censors had grown tired of outlawing individual issues and decided on a blanket ban of *Penthouse*, *Playboy*, and *Screw*. They were also paying more attention to the 'insidious' influence of record covers, posters, and calendars and of those highbrow 'pornographers' like Gore Vidal, Philip Roth, and James Baldwin.[91] Sometimes they had to make fine distinctions. A Rhodesian of any age could buy a hardback copy of *The Taking of Pelham 123*, the story of the hijacking of a New York underground train. The film was a box office success in Salisbury. Yet the censors banned the paperback edition, on the ground that teenagers were more likely to see it. So while possession was not illegal, it was against the law to buy, borrow, or display the cheaper copy.

Allan Wright, a former magistrate and DC who became Chief Censor in 1973, denied that the Board was a harsh moral guardian. After all, it allowed 70 per cent of films through uncensored and it did not bar 'tasteful nudity'.[92] In 1975 Wright claimed that 75 per cent of the letters sent to the Board complained that it was too lax, and that he had been described as 'a prurient old goat' for passing the Glenda Jackson-George Segal film *A Touch of Class*.[93] An earlier decision to pass *Jesus Christ Superstar* went to the Appeals Board which, with Des Frost's wife as one of its members, upheld the original decision, perhaps providing further evidence that even the most upright could not be relied upon.[94] Evidently the RBC also distrusted the Censorship Board. There were over 200 records passed by the Board which the Corporation either banned altogether or restricted to certain times. The Beatles' song 'Lucy in the Sky with Diamonds' was affected, presumably because of its drug connotations. The banning of Olivia Newton-John and Gene Pitney is harder to explain.

It was time-consuming and unrewarding work saving adults from ever-increasing moral dangers. Allan Wright thought that the censors should be replaced every five years to avoid excessive exposure to 'blue sex' and violence. One crusader who enjoyed the sacred duty was Gene Sulter, a confirmed bachelor and local councillor from Gwelo. He conducted his own campaign in the Midlands against the 'plethora of violence, vice and venereal disease'.[95] His great hate was *Lunicorn*, the Rag magazine produced by Rhodesian university students as part of their annual fund-raising exercise for charity. The humour was, at worst, puerile, but Councillor Sulter managed to have the 1973 issue banned by the Council from sale in Gwelo streets, thereby boosting its receipts by 300 per cent. On 1 June 1974 the councillor took his views to the highest level. He spoke at the opening of a new theatre in Gwelo before a black tie audience which included the Prime Minister and his mother, as well as several cabinet ministers and other dignitaries. Suiter praised the Board of Censors for helping to stem the 'sick, sordid and sexual slush which threatens to overwhelm and undermine western civilisation'.[96] His remarks were followed by a performance of *The Sound of Music*. Two months later Sulter topped the poll in the local elections"

White Rhodesia preferred wholesome, conventional sport and culture, and continued to believe that it was blessed with the highest standards, even if it could not always demonstrate them. On 22 May 1975 Rhodesia was ousted from the Olympic movement. Individuals and teams in other sports were already affected by Rhodesia's exclusion from international competition. At this time, the country boasted a full back in rugby second only to the legendary J. P. R. Williams of Wales, a world-class hockey striker, a champion golfer, a fine women's squash player, and a men's doubles finalist at Wimbledon.[97] It was no consolation to learn that Rhodesians remained in touch with the declining standards of sporting behaviour. In 1975 the umpires complained of cricketers verbally abusing opponents in a manner reminiscent of Ian Chappell's 'ugly Australians'.[98]

Off the field, Reps was flourishing. Its annual ticket sales in 1975 amounted to $120,000 and the annual bar turnover had reached $60,000.[99] An ambitious Arts complex was opened in Avondale and even though the part-time director of the National Gallery, a prominent South African, had attacked the 'fairies' of the art and theatre world and P. K. van der Byl had been scathing about young men prancing upon the stage, the editor of the *Umtali Post* assured Rhodesians that a male who preferred ballet was no less of a man for doing so.[100] Fortunately, watching television was one form of entertainment which did not require proof of manhood or sophisticated taste. Some 83 per cent of European homes within the small transmission area had a television set by 1975; the figures for Salisbury and Bulawayo were 86 and 87 per cent respectively. Inferior sets continued to produce inferior pictures in black and white, and Rhodesia television continued to buy old movies and American serials. In April-May 1975 the favourites were *Bonanza, The Mary Tyler Moore Show,* and *Marcus Welby* MD.[101] Isolation, the RBC/TV Governors, and the Director-General had combined to ensure that Rhodesians were spared anything challenging, dangerous, or subversive.

VI

There were two contradictory tendencies evident in Rhodesian society during 1973-5. First, there were the changes which were introduced or reinforced by the war, by other events in southern Africa, and by the increasing impact of sanctions and movements in the world economy. Secondly, there was the resolute affirmation of the status quo, the determination to preserve 'normality', to resist any kind of reform, to stand firm against the madness of the modern world. Both tendencies were manifest in most aspects of the Rhodesian way of life. Defiance, fostered by isolation, was generally triumphant, although 1975 proved to be the last year when Rhodesians could so confidently resist reality.

It was also the last year when they resisted it together. Despite appearances, the society became more disunited as the war escalated. The strains were already evident in 1975. The *Fact Paper* on migration had provided one explanation by drawing attention to the shifting base of the white population. It was difficult enough to create an elevated community spirit upon the foundations of shared privilege and a common racial identity. It was harder still to establish any sense of community in a society whose past comprised just three generations and whose current membership experienced such a high turnover. War might help to forge new nations but a search-and-destroy mission against 'terrorists', and the largely-secret and mundane battle against sanctions, did not have the heroic or romantic overtones of the Anzac Legend which had promoted a sense of national unity among Australians after 1915.

How, then, could Rhodesians be persuaded to think and act as one people? A republic, a flag, and the story of Allan Wilson's patrol were not enough: the new nation needed an anthem, 'to fill a void in our national life'.[102] On 26 August 1974, after a six-year search and examining hundreds of suggestions, the government chose Beethoven's 'Ode to Joy'. The Minister of Education explained that an anthem must be 'serious but not heavy, dignified but not pretentious [and] most important of all it had to inspire and contain the seeds of national pride'. It was generally agreed that a Rhodesian theme might have been better but the government could wait no longer: it was, in 1974, 'more than ever necessary to reflect the unity of the country and to inspire our fighting men'. The *Herald's* music critic, who pronounced himself 'dumbfounded' by the choice, remarked that 'it is probably the only instance in the world where a melody that has supra-national associations has been plagiarised for nationalistic ends'. The editor of the *Umtali Post*, who noted that the official version of 'Ode to Joy' had been recorded by the South African Broadcasting Corporation, merely hoped that the Rhodesians might contribute something towards their own national anthem.[103]

The government certainly wanted them to do so, and a competition was launched to find some suitable words. On 24 September 1975, exactly one year before Ian Smith announced the nation's surrender, the government published the judges' findings. Mrs Mary Bloom, a South African-born resident of Gwelo, who had previously won an award for naming a cocktail bar in her home town, won the first prize of $500 for her entry.

> Rise, O voices of Rhodesia. God
>   may we Thy bounty share.
> Give us strength to face all
>   danger and, where challenge
>   is, to dare.
> Guide us, Lord, to wise
>   decision, ever of Thy Grace
>   aware.

> Oh, let our hearts beat bravely
>   always, for this our land within
>   Thy care.
> Rise O voices of Rhodesia,
>   bringing her your proud
>   acclaim,
> Grandly echoing through the
>   mountains, rolling over
>   far-flung plain.
> Roaring in the mighty rivers,
>   joining in one grand refrain,
> Ascending to the sunlit
>   heavens, telling of her
>   honoured name.

It hardly mattered that Mrs Bloom's banalities had debased one of Beethoven's greatest triumphs. She had, after all, managed to capture part of the Rhodesian self-image: the notion of the Christian country, the majesty of the land, the need to stand firm. Nor was it her fault that adult whites had barely enough time to learn the lyrics, that an anthem which was meant to express and inspire a sense of national identity was produced just before the nation itself was about to disappear. Filling the 'void in our national life' were the constant appeals to Rhodesian patriotism, the incessant propaganda on radio and television, and the government's repeated assurances; but nothing could save Rhodesia or preserve an absolute solidarity in the face of the new challenges which began in early 1976.

VII

Even so, much of the confidence and the complacency, so marked in 1970, had survived into 1975. The *African Times* was informing its black readership – now claimed to number over two million – that the residents of the protected villages were generally happy. Editorials and news stories in the paper attacked all the nationalist factions, senior chiefs told their people to support the government, and white officials were still being depicted pinning on medals or shaking hands with honoured blacks. African survivors of 'terrorist' mutilations recalled their ordeals at the hands of 'brutal, spiteful men'. One told of how his upper lip had been severed by the 'terrorists' *after* he had co-operated with them. In short, the *African Times* continued to portray a black world in the image preferred by white Rhodesia: it was happy, loyal, and acquiescent, needing only to be reminded of its good fortunes in being governed by civilised men.[104]

Given the widespread (and false) assumption that killing 'terrs', or removing them from Rhodesian soil, constituted a substantial victory, then the guarded optimism of 1975 was not misplaced. The official Rhodesian statistics showed that some 600 'terrorists' had been killed between December 1972 and December 1975, that the 'Big Push' had cleared the country of all but a handful, and that just 106 members of the Security Forces and 17 white civilians had died as a result of the war.[105] Lieutenant-General Walls said that the Security Forces had achieved 'a resounding victory' and would also win the next round 'hands down'.[106] The *Rhodesia Herald* decided, however, to relegate Walls's Christmas message to page 5, thereby hiding his warning of a new 'terrorist' offensive. There was already enough gloomy news to report. Senior pilots were leaving Air Rhodesia because they wanted to fly modern aircraft and more challenging routes, the Christmas buying spree was hampered by the lack of imported goods, the business houses were talking themselves into a depression, four Army officers – including Major-General John Shaw, the Army's Chief of Staff and Walls's probable successor – were killed in a helicopter crash on 23 December.[107] The good news was that the Christmas 1974 road toll of twenty-nine (including all races) was halved in the same period of 1975. It was also worth reporting that, three years after the attack on Altena, Marc and Margaret de Borchgrave had remained on their farm. Outsiders were not to know that the war, among other factors, was placing an intolerable strain upon their marriage.

5

'It is perhaps, the end of the beginning'

I

The white residents of Salisbury debated a very serious matter in early 1976. Should their garbage be collected from inside or outside their gates? A majority on the Municipal Council argued that kerbside collection was both more economical and less unsanitary. In response, several people protested about the inconvenience and the eyesore of stacking kitchen waste on the street. Salisbury's residents were also engrossed in an issue of national importance. On 5 January 1976, eight new cigarette brands, sold in unlined cardboard packets, replaced the existing forty. The government's objective was to save $1 million in foreign currency.[1] A Gatooma resident wrote that the new variety reminded him of wartime 'Gyppo' cigarettes and their 'fine blend of camel dung and khaki weed'. Under pressure, the government agreed in late February to forgo $390,000 by increasing the filter length and allowing foil packaging. It was a stunning victory over the national bureaucracy, and an important reaffirmation of the Rhodesian way of life. Salisbury's residents were less successful. In the same month the Municipality resolved to continue collecting the garbage from outside the gates.[2]

Other issues soon began to assume precedence. On 6 February Ian Smith announced in an evening broadcast that, following 'the most serious incursion that we have yet experienced', the 'eastern front' had been opened.[3] Rumours were already circulating in Salisbury about Cubans and Russians arriving at Beira, and about Soviet tanks and SAM-7 missiles poised for war against Rhodesia. The South Africans made it plain that they could not be relied upon to bail out the Rhodesians in the event of an all-out 'terrorist' war. Then on 3 March Samora Machel closed the Mozambique border, placed his country on a war footing, and seized Rhodesian assets including a quantity of rolling stock. Meanwhile the Smith-Nkomo talks, which had commenced in the previous December, dragged on until 19 March when, after three months or thirteen sessions for a total of twenty-three hours, the parties reached an impasse on what Joshua Nkomo called 'the single and fundamental issue of majority rule now'.[4] A peaceful settlement seemed more remote than ever.

So there was not much for Rhodesians to cheer about in early 1976. The cost of living had risen by 2 per cent in January, the private petrol allocation was cut by 20 per cent following the Mozambique border closure, and the Rhodesian cricket team – despite a fighting two-wicket victory over last year's premiers – could manage only third place on the Currie Cup table. A British journalist was convinced that morale had plummeted, a victim of the South African stance of non-intervention, the cigarette issue, and the shortage of local brandy.[5] Although there were wild swings in morale over the following months the whites tried hard to preserve an air of normality, even as they grumbled about any trivial or substantial interference with the Rhodesian way of life. In June the hotels, restaurants, national parks, and resorts around the country were insisting that it was 'business as usual'. An entertainment guide claimed that it was possible to 'hit town every night of the month in Salisbury and still not get round all the cinemas, theatres, clubs, hotels and restaurants': 'even the most avid hedonist would not go short.[6] More importantly, the number of hedonists was already multiplying: young and middle-aged men were beginning to crowd into the bars and clubs seeking release or trying to forget. And by 24 September, when the South Africans and the Americans had forced Ian Smith into a public surrender to the principle of black majority rule, the morale index was heading rapidly and permanently downwards.

The war invaded every aspect of Rhodesian life during 1976. While the farming communities of the new operational areas – Thrasher in the Eastern Districts, Repulse in the south-east, Tangent in the south-west –constituted the front line, everyone was affected in some way by the escalation of the war between January and September: by the continuous call-up of Territorials from 1 May and the doubling of white Security Force and civilian deaths in a few months; by the introduction of convoys and restricted travel in the operational areas, the blow-out of the defence budget, and the cutting of emigration and holiday allowances; and by the falling morale and depleted manpower resources which accompanied the rise in the net average emigration rate to nearly 800 a month. Although the escalation affected individuals, families, and communities in different ways they all experienced a sense of uncertainty, manifest in the way people lashed out at each other, reacted intemperately to reverses, hunted for scapegoats, and became loudly patriotic. More importantly, the escalation of the war generated and intensified divisions which the illusion of greater solidarity could not conceal.

The government and the Security Forces handled adversity by compounding old mistakes and making new ones, all the time misleading an electorate which begged to hear what it wanted to believe, and preferred not to believe what it could observe. One effect of this mutual deception

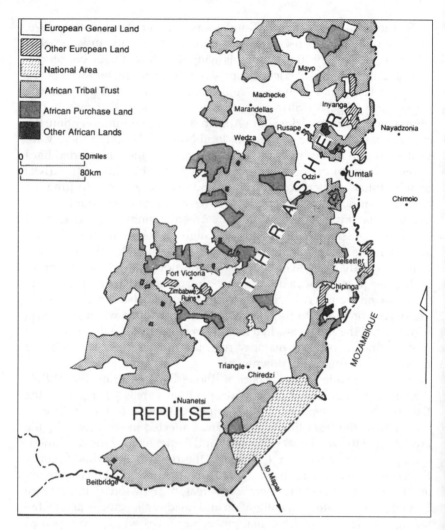

MAP 5.1. *Op Thrasher and Op Repulse*

was that Rhodesians were shocked by Smith's announcement of 24 September. Another was that most drifted or catapulted between reality and fantasy; on the one hand, they accepted that the old Rhodesia was falling apart and could not be sustained; on the other, they were determined to resist change or not to notice it. This ambivalence, the duplicity, the divided loyalties, and the internal conflicts form the main themes of this chapter.

II

The Prime Minister made several statements in February-March 1976 which reflected his dual role as the maker and the spokesman of Rhodesian opinion. His remarks and actions, supported by his ministers and the Security Force commanders, were critical in deceiving a credulous electorate about the dangers ahead.

His broadcast on 6 February, for example, did not reveal the *extent* of the incursion. On 21 January some eighty ZANLA guerrillas were intercepted south of Nyamapanda. Intelligence information suggested that another 800 were poised to enter the country along an arc stretching from Hurricane to Chipinga.[7] Evidently, Smith felt he must prepare his people for bad news without discouraging them by revealing the worst. Above all, he had to remind the whites of their 'national spirit' of resistance.

He began his broadcast, therefore, with the prediction that there would be hit-and-run assaults on white farms, indiscriminate mine-laying, and brutal attacks on innocent tribesmen.[8] He also alerted Rhodesians to the prospect of 'psychological warfare' aimed at persuading them to follow the course of Angola and Mozambique by surrendering 'the reins of Government'. Talking with 'terrorists' would achieve nothing: ZANU was not interested in negotiations and would settle for nothing less than the violent overthrow of the civilised order and its own total domination of the country. Surrender was unthinkable: the 'terrorists' were merely the 'latest spearhead' of 'the steadily advancing communist menace' whose aim was to create a 'saddle' across Africa from Angola to Mozambique, and to use Rhodesia and South West Africa as the 'springboard' for the total domination of southern Africa. Confronted with this prospect Smith despaired of any help from the West:

Regrettably ... we can anticipate that the Western powers, blind to the consequences of their actions, will not only acquiesce, but will join in the chorus orchestrated by the Russian baton. Unfortunately there is no Churchill alive today to bring home to them the folly of such appeasement.

Smith argued that appeasement would have appalling consequences. If, for example, the whites were forced to let go of government, 'nothing would be more certain than the inevitability of civil war between blacks in Rhodesia'. Rhodesians, however, would not capitulate 'to the forces of evil'.

Smith's next set of important statements followed the collapse of his talks with Nkomo. The formal denouement of the negotiations was predictable because Nkomo could not accept less than immediate majority rule and Smith could not yet admit its possibility. Nevertheless, in private, both sides made some important concessions. Nkomo's ANC compromised by not insisting on the prior introduction of a common roll based on a universal franchise; and the government agreed that one-third of the lower house should be black and that a further third should be elected on a common roll high-qualification franchise. Although the Prime Minister did not commit himself to the principle of majority rule, or to a timetable, the ANC left the talks believing that the government had accepted the introduction of majority rule within ten to fifteen years. What Smith did concede was that UDI was negotiable, that power-sharing with blacks was now an option.[9]

Smith's message to his constituency was equivocal. When the talks collapsed, he stunned many commentators by saying that the British government 'should no longer avoid the responsibility which it claims and should now actively assist in resolving the constitutional issue in Rhodesia'. Having accused the British of scuttling earlier talks by their back-door interference, the Prime Minister told a televised press conference on 20 March that he now wanted London to 'come in through the front door'. Smith then addressed two audiences. He told the British, the nationalists, and the moderates in the Rhodesian business and professional community that he would *consider* abandoning UDI, without necessarily agreeing to do so.

If I am satisfied, and it can be shown to me that this or any other decision is necessary in the interests of Rhodesia, I will lend my support to carrying out that decision.

The language was tortuous though the meaning was clear: UDI was not non-negotiable. Smith also spoke to his own people:

I have said before, and I repeat, we are prepared to bring black people into our Government to work with us. I think we have got to accept that in the future Rhodesia is a country for black and white, not white as opposed to black and vice versa. I believe this is wrong thinking for Rhodesia. We have got to try to get people to change their line of thinking if they are still thinking like that. This is outdated in Rhodesia today, (raising his voice) I don't *believe* in majority rule ever in Rhodesia ... not in 1,000 years. I repeat that I believe in black and whites working together. If one day it is white and the next day black I believe we have failed and it will be a disaster for Rhodesia. [emphasis added]

The words may not have been chosen carefully, but there is no excuse for mistaking the message. Ian Smith had advocated, not predicted, the long-term survival of white supremacy and the postponement of black rule. He told his people that, while not wavering in his principled opposition to majority rule, he had not ruled out the possibility of power-sharing in the immediate future.[10] Far from being retrogressive, his statement signalled what, for the RF, was a major concession: the co-option of blacks into the government.

On 22 March Mr Callaghan, the British Foreign Secretary, responded to Smith's invitation in a speech to the House of Commons where he outlined four pre-conditions for Britain's re-entry into negotiations: acceptance of the principle of majority rule; acceptance of a time limit of eighteen months to two years for elections leading to majority rule; acceptance of the NIBMAR principle; agreement that negotiations should not be drawn out. Even Smith's presumed and professed opponents on the left attacked Callaghan for going too far.[11] The *Rhodesia Herald* said that the price was too high, and that Smith had no option except to reject this 'ill-considered assessment'. Tim Gibbs for the RP predicted that 'chaos' would follow the hand-over to majority rule within two years. Des Frost's fears went beyond the matter of timetables. The RF Chairman warned of 'bloody uproar' if the government agreed to any of Callaghan's terms. A government hint, reported in the *Rhodesia Herald* on 23 March, that Frost was 'reflecting his own views', was partly borne out when Smith replied to the Callaghan speech. Despite his denunciation of the proposals as 'hopeless', and his assurance of continued Rhodesian opposition both to NIBMAR and to a 'premature handover to black rule', the Prime Minister emphasised his own commitment to evolutionary change.[12] Smith was engaging in his habitual practice of prevarication and mystification. Yet he was not solely to blame for the failure of his own people to understand that they no longer controlled the pace and direction of change. If, by March 1976, Des Frost could still think that majority rule was avoidable, and if Tim Gibbs could still assume that there was time to apply tests of suitability for the vote, then many Rhodesians were clearly out of touch with the real world.

Their illusions were sustained by a succession of public statements and private briefings in March and April assuring them that the Security Forces were on top of the situation, that the opposition was an unrepresentative rabble, and that normality would soon be restored. P. K. van der Byl, the Minister of Foreign Affairs and Defence, welcomed the international press on 5 March in a tone of mock regret. The journalists, he said, had come to Rhodesia expecting 'if not chaos, certainly wild excitement and confusion'. They were now at a loose end because everything is 'completely normal and calm'. The government had, therefore, 'arranged a number of things to give you something to do'.[13] It was a typical 'PK' performance. Born in Cape Town in 1923, the son of a prominent South African politician in Smuts's party, Van der Byl had passed through Cambridge, Harvard, the Queen's Hussars, and the tobacco industry on the way to becoming a senior Smith minister. Tall, dark, and handsome, his affectations, foppishness, and superior manner infuriated opponents, just as his frankness and wit delighted friends. Probably his major contribution as Minister of Defence was to design his own ceremonial uniform,[14] though he reputedly inspired warmth in the ordinary troopie. Detested by the National Party hierarchy in South Africa – Smith had to leave him at home when making important visits to Pretoria[15] – Van der Byl's major contribution as Minister of Foreign Affairs was to win the hearts and minds of the decadent and powerless European nobility. On this occasion, speaking to the press in March 1976, he was thoroughly enjoying himself.

Major Brian Barrett-Hamilton, the second in command of the RLI, advised a passing-out parade that there were 'not enough ["terrorists"] to go around ... so please get yours early'.[16] Ted Sutton-Pryce, speaking as the Deputy Minister in the Prime Minister's Department, informed a press conference on 26 March that, while 1976 would be one of the 'roughest, toughest years in our history', he faced it with a 'real, calculated sense of optimism'. He minimised the threat by disputing the claims of Western diplomats that 15,000 guerrillas were in training camps in Tanzania and Mozambique: there were 1,500 fully-trained and 6,000 half-trained men outside the country and just 700 inside Rhodesia and, putting, the number in perspective, there were now just 150 more 'terrorists' on Rhodesian soil than ever before. While he admitted that the recent infiltrators may be 'a little better than the tail-end charlies we met last year', he felt certain that Rhodesia could withstand any challenge, including the possibility of Soviet tanks entering the fray: the morale of the nation was high and 'nowhere is it in better shape than in the operational areas'.[17] Sutton-Pryce then told a televised press conference on 10 April that the 'terrorists' and their supporters 'are backing a losing and sterile cause'. Ian Smith said in a radio interview on 15 April that the Security Forces 'are very definitely on top' and, on 27 April, in his first address to the nation since 6 February, the Prime Minister reassured his audience: 'operations against the terrorists are being conducted with the utmost vigour and I have every confidence in the ability of our security forces to meet this threat and to defeat it'.[18]

Smith had three main objectives in his April broadcast. First, he wanted to reply to a statement by Dr Henry Kissinger made in Lusaka on that same day. The American Secretary of State had announced ten proposals for a 'rapid, just and African solution' of the Rhodesian problem. According to Smith, Kissinger had decided to join the campaign 'to exert psychological pressure on Rhodesia'. The Soviet Union had stolen a march on the British and the Americans by its intervention in Angola and now, in order to prevent further Soviet aggression in southern Africa, the West was prepared to back the 'terrorists' and sacrifice

Rhodesia. This analysis served a number of purposes: Smith could recall his forecast on 6 February that the West would be unreliable; he could attack the Western powers for moral weakness and poor political judgement while assuring them of Rhodesia's determination to defend Western civilisation; and he could remind the white electorate of its commitment never to surrender the country to appease the communists and let it become a 'shambles' like Angola and Mozambique.

Secondly, the Prime Minister used the broadcast to change the terms of the public debate about majority rule. Having sounded the note of defiance in response to Kissinger, he said:

Provided we are able to preserve our policy of the maintenance of standards (i.e. Government by the best people, irrespective of colour), I believe the vast majority of thinking Rhodesians will support this philosophy of responsible majority rule.

'Thinking Rhodesians' were those who agreed with Smith (and, in this context, included both blacks and whites). 'Responsible majority rule' represented an advance upon the majority rule he opposed in late March although Smith himself would argue – and his right-wing opponents could only agree – that he had always supported the notion of a meritocracy. The key point is that Smith was trying to divert attention from an argument about the desirability or inevitability of majority rule and to focus on the issue of maintaining standards. In this way he could refute any local accusations of inconsistency, present himself to the West as a reasonable man, and rally the troops in the fight against extreme demands for a sudden transfer of power. In this mood he was bound to lapse into honesty. Towards the end of the speech Smith made an admission which few Rhodesians seemed to notice. After declaring that it was not enough to contain 'terrorism' – it must be 'eradicated' – he said the next year would call for a supreme effort to ensure, in part, 'that we operate from a position of strength'. Smith was not talking about victory, or about maintaining UDI. He was saying that Rhodesia's chances of securing 'responsible majority rule' depended upon its bargaining position which, in turn, depended upon the capacity of the Security Forces to hold the line against 'terrorism'.

The third objective was to spell out his plans for evolutionary change. Smith promised to give the Quenet Report 'immediate and serious consideration', and to appoint four Chiefs to the cabinet and three black MPs as Deputy Ministers. Predictably, but for different reasons, white liberals and right-wingers regarded their appointment on 28 April as futile window-dressing. Whether Smith really believed that this gesture would create a united nation, or persuade 'the potential African leadership ... to nail their colours to the mast', he could have been under no illusion about the response in black Africa or the West. None the less, Smith convinced most of his own constituency that he – and they – had acted with generosity and foresight. Moreover, he had encouraged the belief that there was now time to sit back and see how the experiment worked.

III

Smith's April broadcast warned of a 'big initiative' in the following month. On 1 May Security Force headquarters announced its continuous call-up 'to deal effectively with the recent upsurge in terrorist incursions and to ensure that these would not only be contained but decisively defeated'.[19] From this point, Rhodesians became acutely aware of the intensification and expansion of the war.

One inescapable sign of the escalation was the sharp rise in the casualty figures. When Sutton-Pryce addressed the press conference on 26 March he reported that 114 'terrorists' had been killed since the beginning of the year and that the Security Forces had lost 14 dead. By early June the figures had risen to 253 and 38 respectively. In May, the bloodiest month of the war to that stage, 18 Security Force members were killed and the death ratio with the guerrillas – usually better than 10 : 1 – had fallen to 6 : 1. Overall, 85 Security Force personnel (the majority of them white) died as a result of armed clashes between March and September compared to 89 deaths between December 1972 and February 1976.

Despite the rising casualty figures Derry MacIntyre, the commanding officer of Operation Thrasher, contemptuously dismissed ZANLA as a fighting force of mere 'garden boys' who were perpetrators of a 'bloody shambles'.[20] But how could such a rabble defy the world's best counter-insurgency force, kill so many of its men, and cause such a disruption to lifestyles? Good patriots generally preferred to discuss this question with consenting adults in private.[21] It was bad for morale to admit in public that ZANLA's attacks were becoming bolder and more frequent and that the Security Forces had trouble finding and stopping the 'terrorists'. It was also plainly inadequate to attribute all 'terrorist' successes to FRELIMO participation, and to sneer at the cowardly 'terrs' for refusing to stand and fight (and to forget that they were not required to do so). Try as he might, MacIntyre could not dismiss the rising death and injury toll.[22] Nor could he ignore the conversion of the Eastern Districts into a war zone.

In 1976 the Honde Valley, Chipinga, and the Lowveld became the new and bitterly-contested 'sharp end' of the war. Seven farmers were killed in Thrasher between April and August, farms were 'revved', farm stores robbed, and cars ambushed; and police stations, Army camps, rail lines, and agricultural installations were bombarded with mortars and rockets. Convoys, attended by armed vehicles, were soon operating along many roads in the Eastern Districts, and on the main link from Fort Victoria to the South African border, while dusk-to-dawn curfews were imposed in the area and it became unsafe to travel between the late afternoon and early morning.

Even Umtali was not immune. On Sunday, 8 August, five Umtali men died during a mortar attack on an Army base camp and follow-up operations in the Burma Valley 20 km south of the city. All five were Territorials: one had just married, two were middle-aged, three had played rugby, four were local tradesmen. Men and women wept openly at Sunday church services, and demanded retribution. Within hours Smith approved a long-planned raid on a 'terrorist' base inside Mozambique, and the Selous Scouts achieved their most spectacular assault of the entire war when they invaded Nyadzonia camp later on the same Sunday and killed some 500 ZANLA and FRELIMO personnel and an unknown number of civilians.[23] The action was condemned by Western governments and the South Africans felt obliged to withdraw some fifty of its pilots and an undisclosed number of technicians who were attached to the Rhodesian Air Force. The Rhodesians were unabashed, and defended the raid as the 'hot pursuit' of unprovoked aggression.[24] Pat Bashford of the Centre Party said he could not understand why the government had taken so long to act. Umtali heard the news on 10 August and jubilant whites accosted each other in the street. An editorial in the *Gwelo Times* said it all: '... we can be pushed so far, but not all the way.' Five deaths had been avenged by the slaughter of hundreds.

FRELIMO quickly retaliated. A rocket and mortar attack was launched on Umtali just after 4.30 a.m. on Wednesday, 11 August, and, accompanied by small arms fire, lasted for half an hour. Slight damage was inflicted on government buildings, private houses, and cars without causing serious casualties. About 100 men, women, and children were evacuated to the Thrasher headquarters at the colonial-style Cecil Hotel whose top floors were cleared in case of bombardment. Meanwhile the city's most distinctive landmark – the Cross Kopje, a memorial to the black troops who died in the Second World War – remained a brilliantly-lit range finder. Bishop Lamont, awoken by the noise, said a small prayer, and kept his head down and the lights off. At dawn white schoolboys scavenged for pieces of shrapnel to take home as Chinese souvenirs.

It was all a bit of a lark, though some demonstration of defiance was deemed necessary. Next day, the 66th Umtali Show started on time. The pupils of Umtali Girls' High School, led by their principal sitting in an armed vehicle, and joined by a smaller contingent from the Boys' High School, marched down Main Street singing 'Rhodesians Never Die' and carrying placards bearing messages such as 'Thumbs up for Umtali', 'Rhodesia is Super', and 'We have faith in our soldiers'. Motorists hooted their horns and bystanders clapped as the parade passed into Market Square where the assembly sang 'Mountains All Around Us' and the boys completed the ceremony with their school war cry of 'Shumba'.[25]

Although Umtali was occasionally 'revved' later in the war, it was never subjected to sustained urban guerrilla warfare.[26] Nor was Salisbury. Two grenades exploded in the capital on 20 July without creating panic or dramatically altering lifestyles. Both incidents occurred at about 8.30 p.m. Some sixty people were eating or serving when a grenade hit the Pink Panther restaurant in Manica Road. One man was badly injured, a woman was hit on the leg, and a meat refrigerator, which took the full brunt of the blast, suffered damage to the value of $500. The second grenade was thrown outside La Boheme, a night club which advertised itself as 'the city's strip centre' where bunny girls served drinks to off-duty troopies.[27] The principal casualty of this second attack was the holed petrol tank and shattered windscreen of a car belonging to 'Zillah', the club's resident stripper.[28]

The rising casualty figures, the opening of new operational areas, the expansion of Security Force activities, and the changing lifestyles within the operational areas were all evidence of an escalating war during 1976. It was the extended and intensified call-up, however, which brought the message home to almost every white family.

The call-up system had already been modified in September 1975. Following the mass mobilisation of eligible males on 1 May 1976, the government announced further changes: Territorials, who had not completed three years after their initial training, were required to undertake 'continuous call-up'; males in the 25-38 category were called up for temporary service; and the national service period was extended from twelve to eighteen months. This latter decision obliged the intake, which was due for release on 11 May, to serve an additional six months. Job plans had to be abandoned, or postponed until after November, although the government did promise the next intake that individuals would be released if they could demonstrate a 'proved commitment' to enter a course of higher education in 1977.[29] Then, on 14 May, the government cancelled all exemptions issued before 1 May, and imposed tougher criteria for reassessments and all new cases. In addition, the Military Police and other authorities were empowered to stop males in public places and require them to produce evidence of completing their obligations under the National Service Act. Clearly, the country was now on a more advanced war footing than it had been during the 'Big Push'. And General Walls was relatively frank: the situation 'will get worse before it gets better'.[30]

Amendments to the National Service Act were rushed through parliament in late July to early August to ratify regulations issued under ministerial order and to introduce further conditions: the age of registration was lowered to 16 (the age of entry into service remained at 18); the call-up was formalised into three phases extending from age 18 to 50; the Minister might now 'designate' more units as suitable for meeting the national service obligation; and there were stricter rules requiring employers to submit regular returns so that the authorities could check on the service obligations of employees. Finally, the Act authorised the government to call up Africans who were university students or apprentices. This clause was included to appease the vociferous sections of the white electorate which insisted on the principle that blacks should defend 'their' country. In practice the clause was unnecessary because there were enough black volunteers to justify several more RAR battalions.

Alongside these wider and tougher call-up demands generated by the expanding nature of the war, the government was obliged to take a closer look at the call-up system. There were increased grumbles in early 1976 within the white communities about draft dodging and the inequitable periods of service. By September, the tribulations of the call-up had snowballed into a major issue within white politics.

On 21 April the government appointed a subcommittee to recommend ways and means of improving the system.[31] Reginald Cowper, the Minister of Co-ordination, took the chair. Born in India in 1931, a graduate of the University of Cape Town and a former school principal in Bulawayo, 'Fats' Cowper had entered parliament in 1970. His fastidious manners, 'English' accent, arrogance, and vanity did not inspire much affection within the RF. His above-average intelligence, and not his popularity, had levered him into a talent-starved ministry. Cowper had one overriding conviction: namely, that the way to fight the 'terrorist' war was to mobilise the white population. In the meantime, he was obliged to deal with the questions of equity and efficiency. After examining civilian manpower ussage between 1 January and 31 March 1976, Cowper's supcommittee recommended the formation of an independent body to control call-ups and, having conducted its own survey with manual records, the subcommittee proposed the introduction of computers. The Security Council of cabinet agreed. On 17 May the government established the Directorate of Manpower and accepted the offer of technical assistance from a computer firm to develop a data base. Some 200 people were then employed – as voluntary labour – to obtain statistics, and the Army set up its own Data Processing Unit. The Minister told parliament on 21 July that the Directorate itself had five objectives: to maintain records, direct initial and emergency call-ups, recommend the redistribution and retraining of civilian manpower within the Security Forces, liaise with the private sector to minimise disruption to the economy, and to police exemptions, Cowper also announced that all sets of records were to merge by 16 August, and that two ancillary systems would help employers and immigation officials to check on males liable for registration or service.

Complaints continued to mount.[32] Early rumours that good sportsmen, nervous types, and homosexuals were getting exemptions were swiftly quashed.[33] Yet there was evidence of young men taking elaborate steps to evade the call-up, and there were persistent rumours of the sons of 'good Rhodesians' eagerly pursuing jobs or education abroad. It is impossible to determine whether a decision to leave signified an unwillingness to fight for Rhodesia, or a desire not to interrupt a career. Wing Commander Simmonds, an RAF veteran and RF back-bencher, claimed he had evidence of parents sending their sons abroad for secondary schooling and of whole families migrating just to prevent one son being called up.[34] The headmasters of Plumtree and Falcon, two of the elite schools, identified the desire for a continuous education as the key factor. They predicted that there would be a 40 per cent drop in the number of students taking their A levels in Rhodesia. Many would sit M levels in South Africa and enter South African universities, thereby avoiding a three-year delay in undertaking tertiary training.[35]

Other back-benchers attacked the 'debacle', the 'appalling muddle', and the 'maladministration' of the call-up.[36] They criticised the misuse of skills, the indeterminate periods of call-up, and the lack of adequate make-up pay. They claimed that while the burden 'falls harder and harder on the few', 'many escape this net'. MPs could cite many examples of inefficiency. There was the instance of the Chipinga farmer being called up to serve in Centenary while, at the same time, a Centenary farmer was called up to serve in Chipinga.[37] In another case, a man was called up in Salisbury, travelled to Bulawayo to attend camp, and was promptly ordered back to Salisbury to serve in the Hurricane area. The business community was especially angry. Firms with staff on continuous call-up doubted their capacity to extend 'make-up' pay for the full period of duty. ACCOR and ARnI repeatedly sought meetings with the government to obtain clear guidelines on the obligation to meet the difference between Territorial pay and civilian wages. The personnel manager of African Explosives expressed a greater worry. He described the call-up procedures – whereby key employees were being drafted indefinitely, or where they might return for brief periods and be called up again without notice – as 'a bloody shambles'. There was, he said, no pattern or order, and it had become 'impossible to plan'. Even the professions were affected: some teachers were exempted from service during term, others never saw the inside of a class-room all year.[38]

Apprentices and their families felt particularly aggrieved, and had some outspoken allies on the right of the RF. John Newington recounted the case of one apprentice who was removed from a lecture hall at the Technical College in Bulawayo a few days before he was to sit an examination he could not take for another two years. Newington claimed that, even when such young men eventually qualified as journeymen after a disjointed training, all the good jobs had been taken by Africans.[39] One case attracted considerable publicity. In 1976 Michael Carr was a 23-year-old apprentice electrician. He had completed his national service and was undertaking an advanced course at the Salisbury Polytechnic. Carr had missed an examination because of the continuous call-up, and the Army refused an exemption in exchange for his offer to serve for a longer period. His one hope of recovering lost time lay in sitting the examination as an external student at his own expense and at an indeterminate date. His mother – a Rhodesian-born widow – spoke of her struggle to put her fourth and youngest child through his apprenticeship and argued that, compared to African apprentices and university students, the white apprentices 'seem to be penalised and treated as second-class citizens'. In reply, the Apprenticeship Authority said that Carr and others were not especially disadvantaged, although it admitted that, with 3,000 apprentices out of 3,800 affected by the continuous call-up, the Authority was 'hard-hit' by a problem which 'affects apprentices badly'.[40]

By mid-1976, after months of complaint and unfulfilled promises from government – to say nothing of continuous service and long breaks from farming or small business operations – the white communities of Rhodesia had reached what the RF back-benchers called 'boiling point'.[41] Cowper's Directorate had not solved the problem. The system could not secure equity because it could not secure accurate information. Peter Nilson, a political if not a personal friend of Cowper's, pointed out that his own file was some eight years out of date.[42] Cowper replied that only by assembling wrong information would the authorities be able to get it right. Further problems resulted from a decision to maintain divided responsibility for the call-ups: the Minister, on the advice of the Security Forces, determined how many men were needed and the Directorate decided who could be called up. If, on the surface, the division made sense, the system was fundamentally flawed because the Security Forces and the

Directorate had different objectives: the former needed the best men to fight an escalating war irrespective of their role in the society and their previous periods of service, and the latter had to reconcile military and economic necessities while trying to ensure that all did their fair share. Very simply, a small society, which was afraid to arm blacks in vast numbers, which was unwilling to forsake the Rhodesian way of life for total war, and was unable to service both an economy and a counter-insurgency campaign, could not hope to achieve equity, victory, and economic growth at the same time. What it did achieve was prolonged acrimony and a pronounced increase in bureaucratic endeavour.

IV

The escalation of the war during 1976 had an immediate impact on four sensitive issues in white politics: tourism, emigration, taxes, and travel allowances.

The tourist industry was an early casualty, and Easter 1976 marked the turning-point in its fortunes. Record or near-full bookings were recorded for Easter in Kariba, the Fort Victoria region, and the Eastern Districts. Hoteliers all remarked on the big influx from South Africa.[43] At dusk on Easter Sunday, 18 April, four South Africans on motor cycles were fired upon by a group of about eighteen guerrillas who were holding up three motor cars on the Beit Bridge to Fort Victoria road, 100 km north of the South African border. Three of the motor cyclists were killed. The fourth – a young woman pillion passenger – was injured. Simultaneous attacks on a ranch at Nuanetsi, and the detonation of part of the railway line near Rutenga, forced the government to order the temporary closure of the Beit Bridge road. Within a week the government also introduced the convoy system between Umtali and Hot Springs and from Cashel and Melsetter to the main Umtali road.

P. K. van der Byl dismissed the Easter attacks as 'hardly the most gallant battle since Borodino',[44] and, despite the rumours of a South African exodus and fears of mass cancellations, the tourist industry continued to report a brisk business in the unaffected areas. Yet, within two weeks, the hoteliers of the Eastern Districts, south of Umtali and in the Vumba, were becoming worried. At first, they were reluctant to pinpoint 'terrorism' as the cause of the post-Easter slump.[45] The managing director of Leopard Rock Hotel in the Vumba, with Mozambique clearly visible from its upper windows, blamed the general recession, rising prices, and lack of petrol for the fall in occupation rates at his hotel to about 35 per cent. Others were less reticent. The hotel proprietors noticed that Rhodesians as well as South Africans were avoiding the area 'like the plague'. The Chimanimani Hotel at Melsetter had thirty-six rooms; just two were occupied on Saturday, 1 May. Although the hotel was three-quarters full over Easter, the average occupation rate had fallen to 40 per cent because travel in the area was restricted to convoy traffic. In another case, there were fifteen cancellations because of a 'vicious rumour' that one hotel's camping site had been attacked.

The tourist industry had entered another slump. Any immediate recovery appeared to depend on its ability to attract Rhodesians to the Eastern Highlands. Cheap package tours presented one option. From early August, and for a mere $4, a Salisbury resident could buy a return bus ticket to the Eastern Highlands to stay in a designated hotel. Another scheme involved a special petrol concession to cover the period from 29 July to 30 November. Motorists were permitted extra petrol rations to visit the region stretching from Inyanga to Fort Victoria. Inevitably, there was a bureaucracy to negotiate. White Rhodesians and foreign visitors could not be trusted; they might fill the tank for other purposes. So motorists were required to stay a minimum of three nights at one or more of the designated hotels, fill in a form – called an FR7 – and present a written, confirmed booking to a Rationing Office. An official would then measure the exact number of kilometres on the shortest route between the motorist's home base and the designated hotels, and calculate how much petrol would be needed for the return journey. Any unused petrol coupons had to be returned, and hotels were obliged to report unused bookings. For anyone who did not find the Eastern Highlands particularly appealing the paperwork alone probably acted as a deterrent.

The war in 1976 contributed substantially to a sharp rise in the rate of emigration, thereby generating strains in domestic politics. After a series of monthly losses of around forty, the net departure figure suddenly jumped to 817 in April, the worst result for a single month since 1964.[46] No doubt the April statistics included emigrants who had decided to leave before the escalation. But the net average monthly loss of 771 between May and September pinpointed the worsening security situation as the primary cause of the increase. Understandably, the government tried to play down the effects of the war. The Minister of Immigration told parliament on 5 August that emigrants gave 101 reasons for leaving: better job opportunities, getting married, wanting to retire by the sea.[47] Only 'a very small minority' said they left because of the call-ups. Friends, neighbours, and letters-to-the-editor were less generous or, in their way, more honest. Emigrants who announced their intentions were often accused of being 'faint hearted', of trying to evade call-ups, or lacking the courage to stand and fight.[48] Others just preferred to slip away, pretending to go on holiday and making arrangements from abroad about their property and personal effects. Either way, their departure deprived Rhodesia of young families, skills, and security manpower. Half of those who quit Rhodesia in mid-1976 were in their twenties or thirties and were predominantly drawn from the professions and specialised trades. Worse still, they had publicly delivered a vote of no confidence in Rhodesia's right and capacity to survive. Abused for taking the 'chicken run' or the 'yellow route' (Allan Savory called it 'the wise old owl run'), the emigrants left behind an embattled government scrambling for explanations.

The rising financial costs of the war really began to hurt white Rhodesia from April 1976. Budget calculations had already been upset by the continuing world recession, high oil prices, and lower receipts from company and personal taxation. The surging defence bill forced the Finance Minister in April to double sales tax to 10 per cent and to impose higher duties on alcohol and tobacco. David Smith, the Minister, was promoted from Agriculture in December 1975 after John Wrathall was appointed President to replace the ailing Clifford Dupont. A Scottish-born, self-made farmer and company director, David Smith belonged to what he called 'the practical side' of the RF.[49] His April mini-budget also suggested a certain astuteness: indirect taxes softened the blow for white Rhodesians by deflecting part of it to the African consumer. Nevertheless, cheap food, tobacco, and alcohol were regarded as 'traditional' components of the Rhodesian standard of living. Higher charges were not merely unwelcome; they removed something of the essence.[50]

David Smith's next step was the 1976-7 budget. Handed down on 15 July, it was the clearest, official admission of the impact of the war. Although he was optimistic – the world recession was weakening and the closure of the Mozambique border had not been catastrophic – the Minister admitted that the 'terrorist' war was affecting 'almost every sphere of economic activity' through the extension of military duty. The government needed to increase its total outlays by 22 per cent to $702.8 million in order to offset inflation and to pay the rising defence bill. The Ministry of Defence required an extra 40 per cent ($84.4 million), the police another 23 per cent ($44 million), and the government wanted to create an emergency reserve of $15 million and provide additional funds for Roads, Internal Affairs, and to those who qualified for benefits under the Victims of Terrorism (Compensation) Act. The Minister decided to meet these increased outlays by government borrowings but, in the short term, felt he must deal directly with the mounting costs of invisible items. Unable to reduce the import allocations to commerce and indus-try, having no power to alter externally-imposed transport and freight charges, and refusing to 'shatter irreparably Rhodesia's creditworthi-ness' by restricting the investment income of emigrants or other non-residents, the Minister turned to emigration and foreign travel allowances.

With immediate effect, the government reduced the allowance to each emigrating family from $5,000 to $1,000, and for overseas travel from $400 to $250 a year.[51] More generous terms were available in the fine print – including the provision that the travel allowance could be accumulated over two years – but the blunt message set off a howl of protest. Dennis Divaris, who claimed to know 'the mood of the Rhodesian just as well as anybody else', said that there was 'a lot of concern'.[52] He took five calls on budget night before taking his telephone off the hook. Other RF back-benchers met a similar response, and questioned the necessity or equity of allowing emigrants and overseas investors to receive their full dividends from the country. Letter writers complained to the press that they had become 'detainees'. One spoke of being placed behind the 'Berlin Wall', another described himself as an 'economic prisoner'.[53] Hard luck stories abounded. One young woman said that she would have just $50 to spend on her Switzerland wedding and honeymoon. An old man commented that he faced a lonely retirement because he could not afford to join his son's family abroad. Others complained of having to abandon travel plans and of losing their deposits in the process. A petition called on the government to restore the $400 or allow a two-year accumulation for travel in South Africa: Rhodesians 'need to escape from the tensions of their present situation' and foreign holidays were essential for 'morale' in fighting 'the military and economic war'. Almost immediately, two housewives collected 2,000 signatures and, by the end of the month, the total reached 6,000. Travel agents joined the critics. The Chairman of the Association of Rhodesian Travel Agents reports that his members were the butt of abuse and hostility, and predicted that many agents would go bankrupt. He asked two questions which echoed the sentiments of the protesters: how could anyone enjoy a ten-day holiday in Durban with just $150 (after paying for bed and breakfast), and who would want to spend two weeks in Victoria Falls?[54]

Calmer voices and different interest groups raised other issues. The local hoteliers were certainly not unhappy about the prospect of more Rhodesians spending their holidays within the country. The South Africans were worried – Rhodesians accounted for 25 per cent of their visitors in 1975 and spent R75 million[55] – but the South African Tourist Corporation disputed Rhodesian estimates of holiday costs by claiming that a family of four would do well on $70 a day in Cape Town after their package tour accounted for fares and accommodation in a three-star hotel. A few letter writers considered that the complainants were being unpatriotic. Mrs Sally Bown of Chisipite advised 'the majority of those skedaddling off with their possessions' that they had come to the 'wrong place' in trying to extract what they could. They should, instead, go to black Africa. Others, concerned to defend the reduced holiday allowance, said that only the well off could afford to go anyway. Mrs Beatrice Fairfax-Francklin of Queensdale evoked a more noble spirit. In recalling her days of deprivation in Britain during the war, she said that morale was not affected then, and would not be affected now. Patriotism in fact worked both ways. A good Rhodesian could spend holidays inside the country and sustain the local industry, save valuable dollars in foreign reserves, and so help to buy better weapons for 'our boys'. An equally good Rhodesian – having put up with 'endless restrictions; shortages, spiralling prices; no new cars for years at a time; a call-up reaching deeper and deeper into families, shops, offices, businesses; continuing 10 per cent on income tax etc.' – might also argue that 'the last straw' is the one 'that comes from your own side'.[56]

V

The bitterness and discord engendered by the call-up and the reduced travel allowances were to some extent offset by the unifying effect of the ever-expanding hate list. By mid-1976 the list included the 'terrorists' and 'terrorist collaborators',[57] the Eastern bloc, the OAU, the neighbouring black states, the World Council of Churches, foreign missionaries, the Catholic Commission for Justice and Peace, the liberal opposition parties, the British government, 'the left' (however composed and wherever located), emigrants, conscientious objectors, city dwellers who had an 'eight to four attitude',[58] and Bishop Lamont.

It was bad enough that the 'treacherous and unpatriotic'[59] Catholic Bishop of Umtali consistently blamed the whites for the outbreak and escalation of violence. His 'disloyalty', shared by others on the Rhodesian left, was compounded by a refusal to condemn 'terrorist' atrocities and a readiness to censure every swift response by the Security Forces as 'brutality'. In mid-1976 Lamont queried the frequent and cryptic official references to curfew-breakers being killed in the operational areas and asked if 'trigger happy' soldiers had been killing innocent people.[60] The government denied Lamont's charge, claiming that every effort was made to warn the local population of the curfew and of the consequences of breaking it. Plainly irritated, it accused the Bishop of persistently denigrating soldiers who were 'carrying out their normal duties' of protecting life and property. Irritation exploded into anger when, on 11 August (the day Umtali was mortared), Lamont published an *Open Letter* to the Rhodesian government charging that the government's policies had 'provoked the present disorder', mocked 'the law of Christ', and invalidated any claim to rule except with the consent of 'a small and selfish electorate'. Mark Partridge, the leading Catholic in the government, denounced this 'unbalanced, prejudiced and misleading diatribe'. Clearly, he said, 'the reverend gentleman is either suffering from a mental disorder or is a communist'.[61]

In calmer days Lamont was simply a nuisance. By 1976 his accusations, and his denial of Rhodesia's right to exist, had become deeply offensive to RF-minded Rhodesians. The *Open Letter* was the final, provocative act. On 27 August the Bishop was charged on two counts of failing to report the presence of 'terrorists' and a further two of inciting others to do likewise. The charges related to incidents at Avila Mission near Inyanga between April and June 1976 following Lament's decision to relieve the missionaries of any responsibility for reporting the presence of 'terrorists'. Pleading guilty, Lamont made a marathon speech from the dock. He indicted the State as the cause of the present troubles, and highlighted the dilemma facing the rural missions, caught as they were between the demands of the Security Forces and of the guerrillas. The trial in Umtali, which concluded just before Ian Smith announced the surrender on 24 September, attracted crowds of black and white sympathisers. Evidently, the magistrate saw himself as the standard-bearer for those affronted by the attitudes and actions of foreign missionaries and who wanted vengeance against anyone who could be blamed for the present predicament. He sentenced Lamont to ten years with hard labour, thus making him pay for everything which had gone wrong, and for daring to suggest that the cause itself was both injust and the source of its own destruction.[62]

whites who 'betrayed' Rhodesia were ostracised or silenced. Inevitably, the civilised society demanded even greater retribution for black 'treachery'. Early in 1976 the Security Forces, farmers, RF MPs, and officials urged the government to impose firmer and swifter methods of justice on the 'terrorists' and their 'collaborators'. As a result, special mobile courts were gazetted on 30 April. The Prime Minister defended the procedure on the grounds that orthodox methods were too slow and could not be applied in the area where the offences had been committed. He assured everyone that civilised standards would be maintained. The courts first sat in Umtali in late May and, by 30 July, had imposed thirteen death sentences and a number of long gaol terms.[63] The farmers, however remained dissatisfied because the courts – were occasionally lenient. On 14 June Frank Pitcher was murdered on his property at Mtepatepa (located between Bindura and Mount Darwin). It transpired that 'terrorists' had been living on the farm for two days prior to the killing and that their presence had not been reported by the labour force. Two employees were charged before a special court at Bindura on 8 July, Goldberg Makamba, the farm manager, was sentenced to twenty years' imprisonment and a woman, Fungisayi Gamahoko, received four years of which two and a half were suspended. The RF back-bench, led by Es Micklem, who was Pitcher's MP, criticised the 'slowness' in hearing the case and attacked the sentences for being too light and for discriminating in favour of the woman. Micklem expressed a view then common within the farming community: he might not want the judges to emulate the 'barbaric' practices of black Africa but he did want the mandatory death penalty for those convicted of failing to report the presence of 'terrorists'. Hilary Squires, the Minister of Justice, reminded an unsympathetic back-bench of the remark by a South African judge that 'naturally righteous anger should not preclude judgement'. The majority of MPs ignored Squires, and argued that tougher laws, roughly administered, offered the best answer to the dangers faced by farmers every day.[64] Their demands were partly met on 8 September when new laws authorised mandatory death sentences for the recruitment of 'terrorists', the failure of Africans in authority to report the presence of 'terrorists', and the possession of arms of war.

The intensification of the war had all but eliminated a token commitment to 'winning the hearts and minds'. Geoffrey Fairbairn, a visiting Australian authority on counter-insurgency, attended an Army briefing in Umtali and noted afterwards that the Rhodesians 'have an extermination approach'.[65] John Hickman, now a Major-General, continued to mouth the official orthodoxy. He told the Rhodesian Legion on 8 May that killing or capturing 'terrs' was a misleading way of judging military success. It was a 'battle' for the hearts and minds because, for the 'terrorists' to win, they must gain the support of a substantial section of the population.[66] Ken Flower doubted whether Hickman was really committed to a course of gentle persuasion.[67] Either way, it hardly mattered. Hickman would have had few allies. Lieutenant-Colonel Peter Rich, then Officer Commanding the RLI, said in mid-May that the battalion had a new catch-phrase: 'they just want to go out and slay houts.'[68] The RLI was certainly not the place to look for a tender conscience or a political solution, and its 'search-and-destroy' mentality spread throughout the Security Forces during 1976. A Territorial officer told a British journalist at the end of May that one could forget about the hearts and minds: 'the gloves are off and it is going to be rough on everybody.'[69] And, on 29 July, the Secretary of Law and Order told the graduates at a police passing-out parade that they 'should not be too squeamish in departing from the niceties of established procedures which are appropriate for more normal times'.[70]

Not everybody thought of winning the war by killing 'terrs'. Centre Party whites knew that the war could never be 'won', and that negotiations for immediate and substantial political reforms constituted the only road to peace. They were, however, hesitant about stating this truth, and reluctant to abandon their lingering faith in non-racialism. On 7 May the CP executive resolved that, in future, party members might like to refer to a state of 'non-racial rule in which ultimately Africans will be in the majority'.

The RP was even less robust. Several of its members flirted with another of those implausible creations which, to blacks, seemed designed to circumvent majority rule. The National Pledge Association (NPA) was formed in May 1976 as a 'non-party, non-political' organisation committed to the proposition that Rhodesia would be a happy country if only people would be *nice* to each other. Individuals could signify their desire to be courteous and friendly by signing a pledge to support the removal of discriminatory laws and practice. When RF members complained of a phrase in the original pledge, which called upon the government to enact the Quenet recommendations 'as a matter of the highest priority', the NPA offered an alternative version for those who were worried about telling the government what to do or about making an implicit criticism of past inaction. Some 11,000 signatures were collected – it is not known which pledge was the preferred version or how many blacks signed up – and the NPA achieved its objective of spreading the word about harmony. Perhaps the NPA was just an attempt to focus on the 'pinpricks' of racial discrimination and to divert attention from the question of majority rule. More probably, given the manifest sincerity of its leadership, the NPA was supported by whites who simply had not grasped the political implications of what was then the bloodiest phase of the war, nor possessed the wisdom to recognise the growing irrelevance of their brand of politics.[71]

John Wrathall, the President, had his own solution. He asked that 19 May 1976 be observed as a Day of Prayer. The Protestant churches all over Rhodesia were crowded with peace-lovers between noon and 1.00 p.m. Ian and David Smith went to their Presbyterian church in Salisbury, Wrathall and his wife heard Dean da Costa tell an overflowing congregation at the Anglican cathedral that their prayers were 'for the right ordering of all things for the good of all men in their land', and an African congregation in Waterfalls prayed for 'all who are fighting' after the Revd Bosworth of the African Evangelical Church indicated that it was immaterial 'whether they are security forces or terrorists'.[72] The objective of the Day of Prayer was to ask God to stop the flow of blood, rather than to embroil Him – or His flock – in making political judgements.

No one on 19 May referred publicly to the welling hatred inside white Rhodesia. Instead, it had become fashionable to be committed to racial harmony, though not to integration. Des Frost might continue to denounce forced racial mixing. Coloureds who lived south of the railway line in Salisbury might still be excluded from membership of the Hatfield and Southern Suburbs Ratepayers' Association.[73] But the publication of the Quenet Report on 14 June encouraged middle-of-the-road Rhodesians to believe they had a blueprint for survival. Quenet recommended a return to the common roll, the opening up of white commercial, industrial, and farming land for African purchase, and the abolition of discrimination in hotels, cinemas, restaurants, and cafes. On the other hand, the Commission wanted to retain segregation in swimming pools, urban residential land, and education. Ian Smith said that the government accepted most of the recommendations and Des Frost replied that many of them ran counter to RF principles. Pat Bashford for the CP said that, with the exception of the common roll, all the recommendations failed to touch 'the heart of the problem'. Bashford argued that the removal of racial discrimination offered only a 'temporary palliative'; the cure was to take steps to introduce 'representative government'.[74] Most Rhodesians in mid-1976 had an altogether different view. Either they wanted to win the war first, or they regarded Quenet as a generous offer which they – and the government – were in no hurry to implement. It was often difficult trying to practise good will. The 'Af' was often ungrateful, even obtuse. Mrs A. Williams of Salisbury pointed out to an African letter writer, who had complained about the use of the term 'boy' to describe a male African adult, that 'boy' really meant 'male' and did not imply 'juvenile male'. Sensitive to their feelings, 'very large numbers of Europeans go to a lot of trouble to avoid using the term in front of Africans'. Regrettably, the Africans had not produced 'any practical and acceptable alternative': the term 'garden man' was no substitute until it was clear that a 'garden boy' had come of age, and whites could not be expected to ascertain age in the course of a brief encounter.[75]

VI

Rhodesian reactions to the events of March-September 1976 veered sharply between extreme pessimism and wild optimism. The politicians, the military, and the media tried to bolster confidence with accounts of successes and constant references to the 'best counter-insurgency force in the world'. Almost every day from 4 May, when Peter Walls said that the continuous call-up made him confident of 'fairly quick success',[76] someone of prominence would assure Rhodesians that the Security Forces were 'getting on top of the terrorist menace'.[77] The RBC-RTV and the press were very much involved in this propaganda exercise. Despite its reservations about the government's capacity to achieve a settlement, the much-maligned Argus group joined its RF critics in praising the Security Forces in their battle against 'terrorism'. Stories of courage and commitment from the rural areas, supported by articles about the Security Forces, fostered an image of quiet efficiency and dedication and, above all, of a winning team. Rhodesians were constantly reminded that 'the Rhodesian Army has more experience of terrorist warfare than any other in existence. Its aggressive expertise is without parallel.'[78] Most members of the Security Forces believed in and promoted this image of invincibility. When Geoffrey Fairbairn visited the Thrasher headquarters in Umtali in July he found 'a somewhat astonishing optimism', the by-product of an absolute contempt for the 'terrorist' who was described to him as 'a pretty complete nong in the field of conflict'.[79]

Yet it was hard keeping the truth from the farmers or the Territorials. No one would say so in public – except for the very public act of emigrating – but in private many were prepared to admit that, even if defeat was unlikely, victory was impossible. Fairbairn recorded in his diary that he met a major in PSYOPS (Psychological Operations) and a former British gunnery officer both of whom acknowledged that 'the game was up'. Fairbairn also reported a briefing at Bindura where a Chief Superintendent of the Special Branch said that the situation had become 'very serious' because of widespread subversion, abductions, and all manner of intimidation against Africans identified with the government.[80] Although the international press habitually overplayed stories in 1976 of whites preparing to leave, or behaving as doomed pleasure-seekers,[81] there is ample evidence that, by mid-year, many Rhodesians knew very well that the situation was deteriorating.

If the government could not hide the truth about the war, it quite successfully concealed the extent of the external pressure to settle. The decline in Rhodesian-South African political relations during 1975 continued into 1976 when the South Africans increased their 'arm-twisting' following discussions between Vorster and Dr Kissinger in West Germany on 18-20 June 1976. The Rhodesians were warned that South Africa itself was under such pressure from the United States that Pretoria would support a transfer of power to the black majority. Smith later acknowledged that South Africa's stand was crucial in forcing his acceptance of the Kissinger terms.[82] Yet at no stage did he warn the white electorate about South Africa's attitude. In late June he assured his people that South Africa would resist American pressure because of an 'understanding' between Rhodesia and South Africa to defend Western civilisation in the region.[83] In late July he told Rhodesians that they had faced a more testing time after the break-up of the Federation and just before UDI, and interpreted the West German meeting to mean that the Americans had at last realised the importance of South Africa to the

West.[84] He was certainly worried about the directions of American policy but was adamant that the South Africans were not pushing for black majority rule.[85] Unable to denounce Rhodesia's remaining 'friend', Smith had to pretend that the friendship meant more than it did.

In Pretoria, on 14 September, Vorster presented the Kissinger proposals to Ian Smith and two accompanying ministerial colleagues, David Smith and Roger Hawkins. According to Flower, who was also present, the Rhodesian ministers showed 'a surprising readiness ... to settle once and for all'.[86] There was some argument over the timetable but none at all about a return to legality and the appointment of a multiracial Council of State to act as a transitional government and to prepare a programme for majority rule. Smith then returned to attend the RF annual congress in Umtali on 15-16 September, knowing that his own party had not been forewarned of his readiness to settle and that perhaps a majority would oppose him. His own supporters had prepared themselves to the extent of persuading 'Mac' Knox, a former party chairman, to stand against Des Frost. Yet they, like the party officers, were not informed of the extent of Smith's commitment on 14 September.

The grass roots of the RF remained firmly embedded in the past. Des Frost told an interviewer in early June that 'a very big proportion' of RF members agreed with his views; namely, that black majority rule was not inevitable and that the races 'must have the right to run their own affairs'.[87] The branches which sent resolutions to the September congress confirmed Frost's assessment of party feelings by demanding that the government uphold residential segregation, institute provincialisation, and maintain the RF's principles when implementing the Quenet recommendations. Frost told the opening session of congress that 'a large proportion of the party firmly believe that the Government is watering down our principles and our policies'. His examples included a decision to allow limited multiracial sport at government schools, the reception of the Quenet Report, and the failure to implement provincialisation. Frost rehashed his habitual complaints by urging the government to take the party into its confidence and arguing that the RF must collectively determine its political direction to restore the determination and unity of purpose of the UDI years. He was preaching to a sympathetic audience which lacked the power and the will to impose his demands, and which – like him – did not fully comprehend what was happening in Salisbury, in southern Africa, or in the Western capitals. Frost believed, for example, that provincialisation need not interfere with external negotiations for a settlement, and seemed quite pleased that Ian Smith might now meet Dr Kissinger so that the Americans would better understand the Rhodesian point of view. If in his heart he feared for Rhodesia, and knew in his mind that

Smith could not be trusted,[88] Frost had not yet despaired of the situation. After all, he did not know that the game was up. What he did understand was that the delegates would never agree to depose the Prime Minister.

Ian Smith produced another masterly performance. Colin Barlow's Avondale branch had proposed two resolutions: one reaffirmed the party's basic principles and the other gave Smith full power to negotiate 'for the future of all the people of Rhodesia'. Both were passed unanimously after the Prime Minister received a standing ovation for a seventy-five-minute speech ending with an appeal: 'Are you coming with me or not? For God's sake let's be honest.' Being honest did not, of course, mean telling the party that he was under irresistible pressure to submit, let alone that he was poised to do so. Hitherto he had always preached defiance and ridiculed the Jeremiahs. Hadn't he told an audience in Que Que in early August that it was nonsense to talk of Rhodesia fighting a 'no-win war'? Hadn't he also denounced surrender?

After the tremendous effort of the past 10 years to preserve Western civilisation, Rhodesians have no intention of handing over to anyone. We are not that kind of people.[89]

At Umtali in September, however, he was warning the RF that it might have to change its policy for the good of the country. Honesty meant no more than facing up to this fact, without revealing just how fundamental the change might have to be.

Significantly, Smith felt strong enough to admonish Frost and his supporters, sure in the knowledge that they could not produce a credible alternative, either as a leader or a policy. Des Frost did retain his post as Chairman, which indicated that the right was not altogether demolished. Frost's victory also suggested that a majority wanted some kind of rein or watchdog placed on Ian Smith. There may have been another factor: the congress might have jibbed in choosing the genial 'Mac' Knox because he was such a demonstrable lightweight. Not that Smith was disturbed by the re-election of Frost because he had rarely been troubled by the Chairman's hostility. Nor did it bother the Prime Minister that the majority of delegates at Umtali thought that his mandate meant no more Than 'the go-ahead to represent Rhodesia and look at what is on offer'.[90]

The Prime Minister added the loyal Jack Mussett to his reliable ministerial team for the second Pretoria meeting. Henry Kissinger delivered his bleak message on Sunday, 19 September. Basically, he told the Rhodesians that, if they persisted, they were completely on their own in a deteriorating situation. He could not even agree that the Rhodesians might simply renounce UDI and start all over again. They must accept the principle of majority rule, and certain transitional arrangements, including a timetable. If they did not, the Americans, the British, and the South Africans would leave them to their fate. Smith wriggled and bartered during the seven hours of talks, won some minor concessions, and emerged convinced that Dr Kissinger had been decent and honourable, and that the South Africans were the real villains in the destruction of white Rhodesia.

The Rhodesians returned to Salisbury in the early hours of Monday morning. The Prime Minister met the cabinet on Tuesday and Wednesday where, he admitted, he experienced some 'difficulties' because Lardner-Burke, Cowper, and Sutton-Pryce pressed him hard on the reasons for submitting to the Kissinger package. Caucus gave him an even rougher passage. After the meeting, which lasted six hours, Smith said there was no acrimony or irresponsible talk and that he was 'very pleased with the performance of my caucus'. Asked whether the decision was unanimous, he replied: 'I am satisfied that it was.' He did not divulge that John Wright, a young farmer from the Eastern Districts, had stomped out of the meeting declaring his total opposition to the Kissinger plan. Wright rejected the argument, spelt out in a confidential document which listed eighteen favourable selling points, that the Kissinger package 'was an achievement for evolution and responsibility and a defeat for extremism. It is not in any sense a sell-out or capitulation.'[91] The long and grim faces which left the caucus room on 23 September knew very well that they had surrendered.[92]

Ian Smith spoke to white Rhodesia for twenty minutes on Friday night, 24 September.[93] His task was to sell a surrender. So he began by assigning responsibility:

It was made abundantly clear to me, and to my colleagues who accompanied me [to Pretoria], that as long as the present circumstances in Rhodesia prevailed, we could expect no help or support of any kind from the free world. On the contrary, the pressures on us from the free world would continue to mount.

He went on to explain that, while he had Dr Kissinger's assurance of their common purpose to preserve Rhodesia from communism, there was a difference over methods and 'we were not able to make our views prevail'. The West was determined to impose its own solution and, having been told what rejection of this solution would mean, the cabinet and caucus decided upon acceptance. He was certainly not guilty of any betrayal:

I would be dishonest if I did not state quite clearly that the proposals which were put to us in Pretoria do not represent what in our view would be the best solution for Rhodesia's problem.

Smith also stressed the 'positive' side. First, he had Kissinger's 'categorical assurance' that sanctions would be lifted and that 'terrorism' would cease. Rhodesia's acceptance of the package was conditional upon the implementation of these undertakings. Secondly, there would be an immediate injection of capital to stimulate the economy. Thirdly, there would be certain financial provisions 'to retain the confidence of the whites'.

Before he imparted the bad news the Prime Minister provided a general background which, once again, sought to place both himself and the Pretoria agreement in a better light. He wanted to demonstrate his own consistency, to allay fears of a sudden Marxist take-over, and to convince the whites (and everybody else) that he and they could still influence the outcome. Smith emphasised that the proposed Council of State, with its equal numbers of blacks and whites and a white chairman, would normally reach its decisions by consensus – in accordance with the cabinet system – or by a two-thirds majority. The Council was the supreme body and its decisions on the design of the constitution would 'determine whether Rhodesia remains a stable, democratic and progressive country'. He stressed that this constitution 'will be drawn up in Rhodesia by Rhodesians, and will not be imposed from outside'. A 'Rhodesian solution' was bound to be more acceptable to the white community because it might protect them from the extremism associated with the external nationalists and their foreign supporters. Smith then enunciated one of his positions on majority rule (the one detested by the RF's right wing but which presented him as moderate and reasonable):

I have stated in public many times that I believe I echo the views of the majority of both black and white Rhodesians when I say that we support majority rule provided that it is a responsible rule.

He conceded that some might regard the timetable of two years to be too short but claimed that there were 'advantages', which he did not specify, in reaching finality as soon as possible.

Smith then read out the terms of the Kissinger package: first, Rhodesia agrees to majority rule within two years; second, there would be an immediate meeting between the Rhodesian government and African leaders at a mutually-agreed place to organise an interim government; third, the interim government should consist of a Council of State – half white and half black with a white chairman without a special vote – with legislative and supervisory functions including the drafting of a new constitution, and of a Council of Ministers whose functions would include delegated legislative authority and executive responsibility and which would have an African majority, an African

First Minister, and a white Minister of Defence and Law and Order; fourth, the British and Rhodesian governments would enact enabling legislation to implement the terms; fifth, sanctions would be lifted and hostilities would cease upon the formation of the interim government; sixth, there would be a trust fund to promote economic development and to underwrite the guarantees by the interim and subsequent governments of pension, property, and investment rights.

The Prime Minister concluded with a homily, directed mainly at his own people. He recognised that his statement 'will be the cause of deep concern to you all', but Rhodesians had to adapt to change. Rhodesians could be satisfied in knowing that all the races had 'built up a magnificent country where the prospects are second to none in Africa'. Race relations remained 'friendly and relaxed' – despite 'terrorism' – and black and white must now act with restraint to create the right atmosphere for constitution-making. He urged his compatriots to exploit the opportunity to achieve a Rhodesian solution, to dedicate themselves to the success of the operation, to demonstrate 'the great fighting spirit' which had earned the 'tremendous respect' of the world over the past ten years, to maintain morale and confidence, and not to be unworthy of past sacrifices by falling into 'any premature despondency'. It was proper in these circumstances for the leader to demonstrate his own faith by offering his services 'in helping to guide the destiny of Rhodesia' (in other words, to seek to retain as much of the past as possible). He had, after all, received messages of support from 'so many Rhodesians'. It was even more appropriate that his final remark was borrowed from Winston Churchill: 'Now is not the end; it is not even the beginning of the end; but it is perhaps, the end of the beginning.' Characteristically, Ian Smith had offered another false hope. He had, in fact, been talking about the beginning of the end.

Most of the immediate reactions of the white community were variations on the 'wait-and-see' attitude which characterised majority white opinion over the following years.[94] The *Sunday Mail* conducted a survey in Salisbury and quoted the following as a 'typical comment' of the whites who were interviewed: 'If it looks like working we'll stay. If not, we'll pack and leave.' Nearly all those interviewed were stunned. They either had no idea of what was coming, or had refused to face up to what they suspected. A farmer in Chipinga, descended from Pioneer stock, described the announcement as 'a shock' and said he never thought he would live to see the day of black majority rule. Others, equally shattered by the prospect, put on a brave show. Fawcett Phillips said he accepted the terms – with reluctance – because there was no alternative. Des Frost even said he was 'reasonably optimistic', although he did warn that a lot depended on the black Rhodesians who were involved in the negotiations. The far right, on the other hand, was uniformly pessimistic, angry rather than surprised. Roy Buckle of the United Conservative Party spoke of Smith's 'enormous impertinence and audacity' in explaining – with obvious sincerity – how he had discharged his trust by 'selling us out to black majority rule in, he hopes, less than two years'. Len Idensohn addressed a meeting of 400 people attacking this 'incredibly evil speech'. Church leaders in Bulawayo all welcomed the news: the Catholic Bishop was the most enthusiastic, the Anglican Dean was relieved 'that we now know where we are going', and the Revd Quentin Smith for the Methodists managed both to praise the terms of the settlement and to congratulate 'our Prime Minister for the lead he has given the country over the last years'. The General Secretary of the white Trade Union Congress remembered his constituents, and demanded firmer guarantees for skilled workers while Lardner-Burke's son joined a noisy demonstration of young men outside the parliament. A lone middle-aged man registered a silent protest. Dressed in the camouflage uniform of the Security Forces he held a brief vigil outside Smith's official residence, his head on his chest, his hands clasping a bush cap and a white stick.

The business community generally welcomed the speech. In July the government-controlled Rhobank had tried to be optimistic by pointing out that commodity prices were improving, and that the balance of payments would be helped by the cutback in holiday and emigration allowances.[95] But the share market was unimpressed and had plunged to its lowest point in four years. In contrast, two months later, mining and industrial shares had already risen in Salisbury in anticipation of Smith's announcement while Rhodesian government bonds in London doubled in value between 20 and 24 September. This confidence soared on the weekend after the announcement. Any settlement would be good for business, and a settlement which upset the far right could be very good indeed. The Chairman of the Salisbury Chamber of Commerce, and the leaders of ACCOR and ARnI all predicted an expansion of economic activity. Even Roy Wright, the Mayor of Salisbury, a right-winger who had travelled a long way since his early post-war days as an international socialist, looked forward to the prospect of replacing plant and machinery. His main worry was that the projected higher cost of living would push up interest rates. His caution was shared by investment analysts. Double-digit inflation could occur, they said, if the government eased the brakes after the removal of economic sanctions.

Apart from the 'I told you so' reaction of the far right, and the mutterings from the right wing of his own party, all of which he continued to ignore, the Prime Minister had escaped unscathed. Five ladies from Bulawayo expressed a common view when they indignantly responded to a Centre Party stalwart who suggested that Smith should be excluded from any future role in Rhodesia: their hero 'has tried to do everything he could to make a better life for all Rhodesians and, indeed, has succeeded to a very large extent'. Ian Smith's reputation remained unshaken among those who believed he would never let them down, and for whom any loss of mastery might only be tactical or temporary. An 18-year-old dental nurse suggested that 'he probably has something up his sleeve. He looks too happy.' In reality, Smith was deeply unhappy but even his liberal opponents were gracious rather than triumphant in acknowledging the wisdom of conceding defeat. Friend and foe alike applauded his 'statesmanship' and credited him with a 'tremendous diplomatic success'. For all their fighting talk, and their reputation as fighters, most Rhodesians were beginning to see the futility of a prolonged and, at best, indecisive war. They wanted peace, comfort, and the good life. They did not like the Kissinger package and were angered and perplexed by the refusal of the African nationalists to welcome its terms but, as materialists rather than moral crusaders, they would settle for any price 'Smithy' could obtain.

6

'Everything to fight for'

I

Four days after Smith's public capitulation the *Rhodesia Herald* printed a letter from a Territorial soldier. The writer asked a question which – in one form or another – had probably occurred to all of Rhodesia's fighting men:

Is it worth doing my next call-up in two months' time, because I don't want to lose my life or perhaps spend it in a wheelchair, only to see the leaders of this country sitting around a table with terrorists?[1]

It was a question which Reg Cowper, who had replaced Van der Byl as Minister of Defence in September 1976,[2] felt bound to address. He agreed that 'reading the [Pretoria] agreement in cold print might have been a traumatic experience for Rhodesians'. Cowper claimed, however, that there was 'everything to fight for in the new situation': the elimination of 'terrorism' and the creation of a stable society 'where black and white can live side by side'.[3] His response suggested that the RF was about to lurch in a new direction. In one sense it did. During 1977, having previously insisted upon retaining white rule and racial discrimination, the governing party participated in the initial dismantling of both. By the end of 1977 the RF had breached every major principle which it had been formed to uphold. By then, too, the RF was arguing that defeating 'terrorism' was essential in order to protect an acceptable form of African rule which *might* preserve the essence of civilised standards in Rhodesia.

Reg Cowper was not destined to follow the RF into this position. He joined a breakaway section of the party's right wing which remained captive to its illusions that a military victory was possible, and that the old order could be maintained. Ian Smith, however, understood that 'terrorism' would never be eliminated by purely military means. After years of neglect he proceeded during 1977 to provide some kind of leadership by endeavouring to translate the Kissinger package into an acceptable and workable agreement with moderate blacks. Typically, he was neither far sighted nor courageous enough to act decisively or graciously. Nor was he correct in claiming, as he always liked to do, that everything which happened during 1977 – culminating in his decision in November to enter settlement negotiations with the internal nationalists – fulfilled all his predictions and his plans. Even so, Smith did complete a successful transition from the unbending supremacist to the clever bargainer. He had begun to move in early 1976. By the end of 1977 he was ready to extract the best terms from his weakened position and to seek what was called an 'internal settlement'.

There were four important developments within Rhodesia, occurring largely in chronological succession, which preceded Smith's formal entry into the settlement negotiations at the end of 1977. First, there was the confusion in the months immediately following the September surrender: the war continued to escalate; there appeared to be some progress towards ending discrimination; the Rhodesian government regained the initiative following the failure of the Geneva Conference in October-December to implement the Kissinger package; and most Rhodesians assumed what became their customary posture of ignoring the world around them and of allowing themselves to be kept ignorant. Secondly, the military leadership privately acknowledged that it was now engaged in a holding operation, reorganised its hierarchy, endured the further complications of the call-up, and became more directly involved in white politics. Thirdly, the split in the RF in March-April 1977 opened the way for a realignment in white politics which was sealed in the general election of August 1977 and which provided Smith with a mandate to negotiate a qualified transfer of power to moderate black leaders. Fourthly, towards the end of 1977, when the war was spreading deeper into the country, more Rhodesians called for peace while sharper and discordant voices demanded tougher action against 'terrorism'. This chapter will follow these developments while endeavouring to show how the Rhodesians came to accept the fact of change, without ever facing up to its implications, and contimied to fight a war the original rationale of which had disappeared.

II

The all-party Geneva Conference on Rhodesia, called by the British government after Smith's formal surrender, assembled on 28 October 1976.[4] The Rhodesian government and several nationalist delegations spent the next seven weeks trading insults and jockeying for position. Back home, most white Rhodesians were so immersed in the war, domestic politics, and the daily round of living that they quickly tired of the

Geneva negotiations. They largely ignored the various settlement 'plans' and the procession of official visitors from Britain and the United States during the first half of 1977. The weighty matters, which so intrigued and obsessed outsiders, assumed a different importance when translated into the world of white Rhodesia.

Ian Smith made sure of their domestic impact by successfully exploiting the failure of the Geneva Conference – which adjourned on 14 December 1976 – to restore his relations with South Africa.[5] The Prime Minister projected himself at Geneva as the model of sweet reasonableness in the face of great provocation. The nationalists – Muzorewa, Ndabaningi Sithole, Mugabe, and Nkomo (the latter two being formally allied since 9 October in the Patriotic Front) – were demanding that the Kissinger package be either scrapped or amended. So long as Smith declared his willingness to implement the package, the whole package, and nothing but the package, he was assured of diplomatic and material support from the South Africans against the Marxists of the Patriotic Front and their backers in the Front Line States.[6]

The Rhodesian government also profited domestically from the willingness of the British and American governments to make further concessions to the Front Line States and the Patriotic Front. David Owen, the British Foreign Secretary, and Cyrus Vance and Andrew Young from the new Carter Administration, were convinced that no settlement should or could work without the participation of the Patriotic Front. When the Geneva Conference faltered, Ivor Richard, the British Chairman, sought approval for a revised plan. He wanted to appoint a transitional government headed by a British resident commissioner and including a council of ministers and a national security council, each of which would be two-thirds black in membership. Smith rejected this plan on 24 January and the Geneva Conference, which had not reconvened after 14 December, was officially closed. The Prime Minister's reply to Ivor Richard became his standard response to every British-American initiative thereafter: he objected to the Security Forces being placed under British and, ultimately, 'terrorist' command; and he refused to accept that 'a few thousand terrorists, the majority of them mere schoolboys', assisted by the black Presidents, should decide the fate of six million 'ordinary' Africans (and, more to the point, of 270,000 white Rhodesians).[7] The British, Smith could say, had reneged on Kissinger. Clearly neither the British, nor the new American Administration, nor the Front Line States, nor the Patriotic Front could be trusted to devise and implement an acceptable settlement. Instead, the Richard plan and the later Anglo-American proposals could be used – overseas and in Rhodesia – as a justification for proceeding with an 'internal settlement'.

Meanwhile, the entry of hundreds more guerrillas into the country coincided with Geneva and the rainy season. The foreign press claimed that there were 2,000 operating inside Rhodesia by the end of October 1976, and that another 8,000 were poised to enter from Mozambique.[8] On 8 December a spokesman for the Security Forces informed a press briefing that there were about 1,500 'terrs' in the country: 350 in Hurricane, 700 in Thrasher, 350-400 in Repulse, and up to 80 in Tangent.[9] The Security Forces responded with the first major external raid since Nyadzonia and thrust into both the Tete and Mapai regions, claiming huge victories which buoyed morale inside the country. The 'kill ratio' improved but 152 members of the Security Forces and 24 white farmers or members of their families were killed between mid-October and mid-March in the worst period of the war thus far. David Bashford, the son of the former Centre Party leader, was one of the victims. The young man was killed on Christmas Eve while on active service, a poignant reminder of his father's prediction in June 1969 that Smith would lead Rhodesia into the abattoir.[10]

The pressures were also being felt in other areas. The hastily-constructed PVs of 1974 had mushroomed. By the end of 1976 there were 41 established villages with another 138 in various stages of construction. A new protective unit (Guard Force) had been created and Internal Affairs had set up special Civil Action Teams (CATs) to locate and prepare sites. Individuals became 'experts' by virtue of their planning skills or their sheer enthusiasm. Keen developers forgot about the military priorities, and the conservatism of African peasants, and seized the opportunity to advocate the introduction of capitalist enterprise and European concepts of urban living.[11] For all the activity, Internal Affairs and the Security Force commanders were acutely aware at the end of 1976 that the government lacked the material and human resources to create enough 'secure' villages to withstand the increased rate of infiltration. Senior officials also knew that, apart from the limited success of the military objective, the PVs were a total liability. An Internal Affairs committee reported that the young white national servicemen in Guard Force showed evidence of low morale, irresponsibility, and ill-discipline. There were 'even incidents of brutal conduct', for which the committee blamed the 'sordid, frustrating and boring existence' of guarding PVs. It also complained that 'we are losing the people, physically, psychologically and emotionally', principally because Internal Affairs was identified with a hated system which had destroyed traditional agriculture without putting anything in its place.[12] This savage indictment echoed some of Williamson's sentiments in 1974. It also contradicted the official claims that the PVs were helping to turn the war in favour of the Security Forces and that a grateful peasantry were forging new and worthwhile lives under wise and benevolent leadership.[13] The report disappeared into the files, the PVs continued to fail, and the escalating war ensured that most white Rhodesians were never told the truth.

Ken Flower knew what the mounting pressures meant. He insisted that all the defence chiefs recognised that 'the "no-win" war of 1972-6 was becoming a "losing" war'. They understood that there could be no 'purely military solution', and that the role of the Security Forces from late 1976 was to contain 'terrorism' in order to maintain the government's bargaining position and to provide a breathing-space for a negotiated settlement.[14] In Flower's view, the public grandstanding by the nationalists at Geneva, and Smith's unhurried approach at home, were profoundly frustrating.

In his own mind, Ian Smith believed that the government was doing all it could to remove 'unnecessary racial discrimination'. On the eve of returning to Geneva in early December, the Prime Minister told a press conference that the government was 'aiming at a non-racial society'. A subsequent press statement catalogued some impressive progress in a number of areas: education, internal affairs, law and order, the railways, defence, local government.[15] Councils of government schools could now approve multiracial sport and social activities, steps were being taken to promote African prison officers and appoint black prosecutors and magistrates, hoteliers could apply to local authorities for permits to extend African drinking hours beyond 7.00 p.m., non-Europeans could be promoted to mainline engine drivers, African NCOs and warrant officers had already been selected to train for entry into the commissioned ranks of the Army. In addition, twenty-three Africans had been appointed to the rank of Patrol Officer in the police and enjoyed equal pay and conditions with their white counterparts.[16] Excusing any tardiness with the claim that 'some of these things are involved, complicated, and some of them do require legislation', Smith clearly believed that he was entitled to a sympathetic hearing both at home and abroad. He also assumed that reform was proceeding at a pace which the white electorate could tolerate. Anything faster was unnecessary and would be dangerous.

His constituency appeared to agree: Rhodesians at the end of 1976 remained anaesthetised by the illusion that nothing of substance need occur. The failure in October-December to implement the Kissinger package persuaded them that the present situation would endure, that the rest of the world would come to its senses, and that majority rule was tar away.[17] Geoffrey Fairbairn, who had returned to Rhodesia, explained this myopia as a case of 'insensate pride engendering ultimate downfall: quite like a Greek drama, except that most Rhodesians aren't particularly interesting people'.[18]

III

The Security Force commanders were concerned that the Rhodesian government was not making the best of the breathing-space created by the military operations at the end of 1976. They were worried, too, about the call-up system, the military chain of command, and the general state of white morale.

Reg Cowper was determined to settle the call-up issue. He realised that a regular army of about 6,000 men – including some 1,400 foreigners[19] – and the existing call-up system could not provide sufficient resources for the Security Forces to fight an all-out war. Cowper proposed, therefore, to widen and tighten the call-up.[20] In future, he said, no Territorial unit would go on active duty with its strength reduced to 60 per cent by exemptions and deferments. He believed that the private sector could afford further sacrifices and suggested it make more use of overtime and reduce leave entitlements. Cowper's problem was that Rhodesia was just too small to conduct both a military and an economic war on several fronts. This problem was compounded by the government's inability or unwillingness to decide its priorities and by the bureaucratic complexity which accompanied any government intervention.

On 30 November 1976 Cowper announced that, to compensate for a proposed phasing-out of the indefinite call-up, national servicemen would undertake a continuous call-up of three months after the completion of their initial training period of eighteen months.[21] He also decreed that intending tertiary students must first complete their training,[22] and that no 17-year-old male would be permitted to leave Rhodesia for further study. On 27 January 1977 he announced three further changes: the withdrawal of certain exemption certificates for those already attested into the Security Forces; the review of exemption certificates for national servicemen and for those in the 25-37 age group who had been called up for initial training; and the introduction of new call-up procedures designed to ensure greater equity and more rational planning in the use of resources. The Minister also confirmed the rumour that conscription would be extended to cover the 38-50 age group following the reregistration of the 25-37 year olds.[23]

Cowper related the January decisions to the government's 'stated objective of achieving an all-out effort in the pursuit of the anti-terrorist war'. These decisions also signalled his success in persuading cabinet colleagues that the needs of the Security Forces must be paramount. On his own admission, it took him three weeks to win their approval. It took them just one weekend to desert him.[24] The business and farming communities, which had previously tried to dissuade Cowper from his stand, now led the outcry against the January announcement. The RTA, RNFU, ACCOR, the Institute of Personnel Management, and ARnI criticised the Defence Minister for failing to rectify the existing anomalies, and for planning to conscript the 'captains of industry' (the 38-50 age group), thereby putting Rhodesia at risk in the economic war. Mike Daffy, the President of ACCOR, said that his members had lost confidence in Cowper's ability to solve the manpower problem.[25] There was certainly abundant evidence of hardship and anomalies. A plant manufacturing agricultural equipment allegedly lost $400,000 in 1976 because 60 per cent of its skilled staff were on continuous call-up. A Salisbury branch of Barclays Bank had lost eighteen of its twenty white staff to a recent call-up. The Directorate of Manpower discovered that 6,000 men had either not been called up or served just once during 1976.[26] Everyone wanted to blame the Minister of Defence, and his bluff, uncompromising approach to a delicate issue. The press thought he should go.[27] So did Ian Smith. Cowper eventually resigned on 12 February and the government – yet again – modified the call-up system.

There was to be a new body – the National Manpower Board – to deal with those 'exceptional cases' which might justify a modified commitment 'from an economic standpoint'.[28] Local exemption boards would continue to be the first port of call for claims. They would still be empowered to grant ninety-day deferments but the Board alone had the power to grant exemptions. Although the Prime Minister stressed that the criteria would be more stringent than before, it was evident that the government had buckled under private sector pressure and rebuffed the 'total war' approach of its own right wing. The Board itself was described as 'an impartial non-Government body'. The Chairman, a former Customs Adviser to the Prime Minister, was now involved in private enterprise and the other members had a similar interest in the 'economic standpoint'. Cowper's later complaint – that the government had watered down the agreed proposals of 27 January and was not prepared to use the country's fullest military capacity[29] – certainly seemed justified.

The government took the opportunity in mid-February to reshape the ministerial and bureaucratic structure. In addition to its adjudicating functions, the National Manpower Board was also expected to advise the government on the general use of manpower. Responsibility for the National Service Act was assigned to the Labour ministry which was now designated the Ministry of Manpower, Industrial Relations, and Social Affairs. Rowan Cronje was appointed to the post and, within days, was attending a seminar organised by the Directorate of Manpower to explain the working of the system.[30] Cronje learnt that 200 people were still employed on collecting call-up statistics and creating a database, ten months after it had been established by Cowper. Perhaps he was heartened to hear the marketing manager of International Computers boast that the computers were now achieving 'a 95 per cent accuracy on most people'. Significantly, the leaders of the private business sector who attended the seminar agreed that, with a more tactful and approachable minister, it might now be possible to balance the economic and defence needs. The government was confident that the bungling and inequities were not endemic. After all, it pointed out, the employer returns and the computers had uncovered 2,000 'eligibles' in the 25-37 age group who had no military commitment and had no reason to postpone their responsibility. The mistakes and inadequacies of the past would now be overcome.

Another problem for the defence chiefs was the state of their own organisation. There had long been talk of combining the Security Forces under one commander and of the need for better co-ordination in counter-insurgency activity. The problems of duplication – evident in the proliferation of intelligence-gathering and interpreting services[31] – were magnified by the emergence or expansion of special forces (Selous Scouts, Grey's Scouts, PATU, Guard Force, Police Support Unit), and aggravated by the service rivalry common to all military and paramilitary organisations. These rivalries were in part responsible for the delay in developing a unified command because the Air Force under Air Marshal McLaren had long been concerned about an Army takeover.[32] One option, discussed privately among senior Army officers, had been to appoint a Supremo on the Malayan model where General Templer was given full political and military powers.[33] A more appropriate step – given Rhodesia's British traditions – was to retain the political apparatus and to aim for a more centralised and, it was hoped, more efficient chain of military command. Smith took the first step on 14 March when he appointed his loyal friend, Roger Hawkins, to be Minister for the new post of Combined Operations.[34] The second step was the appointment of Walls as Commander of COMOPS on 23 March – on the day Lamont was deported from Rhodesia – and of McLaren as Deputy Commander and executive officer of the headquarters staff.[35] Hawkins said that 'our greatest problem was the lack of decision' and the object of these moves was to prepare Rhodesia for a war 'in the fullest sense'.[36] So, theoretically, there was now a central authority to control the special forces, plan a general strategy, and act as a clearing house for all the problems arising in the sub-JOCs and JOCs.

A common criticism of the new arrangements was that there were 'too many Chiefs and too few Indians'. The complaint was certainly justified in the case of the civilian managers of the war. On 17 May Roger Hawkins addressed a luncheon meeting of Catholic businessmen where he outlined the responsibilities of the ten ministries and three statutory bodies directly involved in the war effort.[37] Hawkins wanted to show that everything was logical, clear-cut, and well understood. His audience was probably sceptical: they knew about the empire-building practices and jealousies of Rhodesia's civil servants, and of a growing tendency during the war to blame someone else for mistakes. They must, for example, have wondered how the plans for civil defence could have worked. Hawkins explained that, while Internal Affairs was responsible for civil defence, Combined Operations was responsible for 'some aspects' in the war zone – including homestead defence – and co-operated with other ministries, 'the adviser on war supplies', and several elements of private enterprise. It was a recipe for more committees, more overlaps, and more demarcation disputes. In practice, the Ministry of Combined Operations alternated between supervision, centralisation, independent action, duplication, and inertia. Perhaps the saving grace was that the call-up kept so many civil servants busy in the bush or on urban security.

The civilian and military war managers met in the maze of rooms and corridors which comprised COMOPS headquarters at the Milton Buildings in Salisbury. Hawkins explained to the Chichester Club that under Walls and McLaren, who also had their own personal staff, there was a top-level planning group chaired by an Army brigadier (the Director-General of Combined Operations) and which included a Senior Assistant Commissioner from the BSAP, a senior officer representing both CIO and Special Branch, a Senior Provincial Commissioner from Internal Affairs, and an Air Force Group Captain (Director of Operations). This committee – which was assisted by the Joint Planning Staff, run by aspiring Indians and lesser Chiefs – was expected to plan and direct the operational plans, and to plan and supervise the Commander's plans and directives. Simultaneously, the former OCC was enlarged into the National Joint Operations Command (NATJOC) consisting of the Commander of COMOPS, the Commanders of the Army and the Air Force, the Commissioner of Police, the Director-General of CIO, and the Secretaries of Internal Affairs and Combined Operations. NATJOC, in turn, was responsible to the War Council which was chaired by the Prime Minister and included some NATJOC members and the civilian ministers directly involved in the war. From the top to the very top, to the top of the very top, and down to a myriad of lesser committees in the Milton Buildings and in the headquarters of the services, a small society had indulged in some creative administration to fight a guerrilla war. The much-vaunted Rhodesian flair for invention and innovation had produced a bureaucratic labyrinth.

A serious flaw of the committee 'system' was that COMOPS and

Combined Operations became immersed in detail at the expense of developing an overall strategy. As a result, the inter-service rivalries and duplication increased rather than decreased.[38] Internal Affairs and the police continued to plan and act separately in several spheres; the police continued to resist Army attempts to pre-empt their role in maintaining internal order; and the various external and internal intelligence-gathering organisations within Military Intelligence, Special Branch, CIO, and the Selous Scouts continued to argue about their precise and proper roles.[39] One thing was indisputable: the further the war progressed the more apparent it became that the Security Forces, like Rhodesia itself, were composed of different factions which had quite different notions of what the struggle was all about.

Walls regarded himself as a victim of the new arrangements. He had been due to retire in July 1976 and Major-General John Shaw would then have succeeded him. Shaw's death in the helicopter crash of December 1975 brought Hickman's name forward, whereupon Smith asked Walls to remain on as Army Commander. When he was appointed Commander of COMOPS Walls asked for written authority recognising his overall control over military operations, and insists that Smith promised to give him a signed document. Walls had also hoped for a promotion to full general, thereby placing him above the recently-promoted Lieutenant-General Hickman, who succeeded him as Army Commander, and above Frank Mussell, the new Commander of the Air Force. Walls never received a written authority or a promotion, for which he blamed Smith's alleged fear of all potential rivals. Smith denied that he was ever worried about Walls supplanting him, or that he promised to give him written authority. Smith thought that Walls was unjustifiably obsessed about being made a full general when neither the size of his responsibility nor his capacity warranted such a promotion.[40]

Notwithstanding the differences in these versions of the Walls appointment, the outcome was hardly a satisfactory one either for the cause of a unified command or for Walls himself. No major decision could be imposed without the intervention of 'the headmaster', and the Commander of COMOPS frequently had to visit 'the study' to obtain authority to manage the disagreements and the disagreeable, even to the extent of calling on the Prime Minister to secure the removal of a 'use-less' police sub-JOC commander who was protected by the Police Commissioner. Walls also had continuing problems with Hickman over the Selous Scouts because the Army Commander – quite understandably – resented the assignment of special forces to COMOPS and, in par-ticular, the cosy relationship between Walls and Reid Daly. The new unified command was neither united nor effectively commanded. And Walls, an approachable and warm-hearted man, simply lacked the prestige, vision, and drive to overcome the pettiness, the committee system, and the bureaucracy.

A point of more immediate importance in early 1977 emerged in an editorial comment by the *Rhodesia Herald* on 28 March:

Until now [the war] has been accepted as basically a Police operation with military support, against criminals. Now it is to be a military operation, mainly by the Army, with Police support.

In one sense the *Herald* was merely giving belated recognition to a development manifest soon after Altena. Yet the public acknowledgement was important because it coincided with the ascension of Walls and of Army spokesmen as significant *political* figures in white Rhodesia.

Their elevation followed naturally upon the expansion of the war and their role in combatting insurgency. The generals maintained their view throughout 1977 that the job of the Security Forces was to provide Rhodesia with a strong bargaining position from which to negotiate a settlement, and they made it clear that the ultimate solution must be a political and not a military one.[41] There was another important concern. Speaking at a passing-out parade at the RLIs Cranborne Barracks in Salisbury, John Hickman explained the Army's political role in terms of resisting the 'ludicrous demands' of the Patriotic Front. Hickman assured his audience that, as Commander, he would not be party to any recommendation which threatened the effectiveness, professionalism, or integrity of the Army. Nor would he allow it to be replaced by 'an undisciplined shower of terrorists, many of whom cannot read the alphabet, let alone a map or simple operational order'. The Army should remain neutral, owing its allegiance to the President and to Rhodesia and not to any political party. To do otherwise 'would be tantamount to signing the death warrant for a civilised nation'. Hickman's concern – to protect the white-controlled Army from any black-controlled government – was itself blatantly political. So, too, was the underlying assumption that the Army's sovereignty was itself a guarantee for whites under majority rule, a theme which was to become more pronounced during 1978-9.[42]

Apart from self-preservation, the Security Force commanders were deeply worried about falling white morale. Whereas Colonel McVey had suggested on 8 December 1976 that morale was 'very, very good', and was 'fantastic' among those on continuous service, Ken Flower reported that the Army Chief of Staff told the War Council on 15 December 1976 that most officers in the field expected the 'vast majority' of those on indefinite call-up to emigrate once fhey were released from continuous service.[43] One suggestion was that a statement from Smith might minimise the departure rate. It was also recognised that air and ground strikes on external 'terrorist' bases boosted confidence because they created the impression of taking the fight to the enemy. P. K. van der Byl later claimed that, when he was Minister of Defence, he had advocated another morale-boosting enterprise: closing off 'subverted' TTLs, excluding all foreign journalists, and giving the RAR a free hand to kill all 'terrorists' and anyone remotely suspected of collaboration.[44] Abused by the Chipinga farmers for allegedly supporting a 'no-win' strategy, Van der Byl sounded a clarion call when addressing badly-disabled soldiers at Tsanga Lodge near Inyanga in June 1977:

We will contest every hill and every river, every river and every town, every crossroad and every bridge. Inevitably and unavoidably, the land will suffer. Indescribable chaos and irreparable destruction will follow but come what may we will uphold the ideals for which these men fought. We cannot let them down. This war can be won and if all Rhodesians remain united with God's help it will be won.[45]

Whether 'PK' ever convinced anyone with his oratory is unknown. But the young men who kept asking the question 'What are we fighting for?' needed something more concrete. The government tried to answer them in mid-1977 in a statement issued to all Security Force personnel and civilians in the operational areas: to defend your country, family, and homes; to safeguard your future (the RF's 1974 election slogan was quite useful even if, to some, it sounded somewhat hollow); and to ensure that you have a positive say in any settlement proposals and a right to reject them if they are unsatisfactory. The Security Forces were promised that there would be no sell-out, and that they were not fighting to hand over to a government which would not protect their rights.[46] Judging by the RF's huge electoral victory some five weeks later, the argument was probably effective.

John Hickman saw the matter in a different light. He told a civilian audience in early July that morale in the field was 'very high'.[47] Problems occurred when the men went home. Hickman and Derry MacIntyre (now a Major-General and Chief of Staff for Administration), believed that there was a malaise infecting civilian life in Salisbury.[48] Men who fought fearlessly and with purpose in the bush became anxious and uncertain at home. The senior Army officers tried to arrest this tendency with direct appeals to the civilian population. Opening the Umtali Show on 19 August, just two weeks before the general election, Hickman praised the local citizens for 'staying put' and said that their determination was 'an object lesson to us all'. The lesson he wished to impart to urban Rhodesia was that, by remaining calm and rational, re-cognising that the enemy was 'communist imperialism', and standing up to the enemy's 'psychological machinations', Rhodesians would not fail the young men who had already died for 'our cause'. Once 'terrorism' and communism had been defeated – 'and win we will' –

there would be dramatic economic growth and exciting opportunities to fulfil personal ambitions. The key was not to spread alarm and despondency but to follow Umtali's example and stand firm.[49] Hickman's remarks were manifestly political in tone and content. Like the other commanders and senior officers, he thought he had two obligations: to reassure the white communities about the progress of the war and to stiffen their backbone in the face of adverse migration figures, higher casualty rates, and irritation over the call-up system. By the end of 1977, when they were disheartened by the failure of the politicians to push ahead with a political solution, some Army officers were openly boasting of a more important role: they might be called upon to create the conditions for a settlement.

IV

The escalation of the war, the arguments about the call-up, and the state of the settlement negotiations all influenced a critical debate within the RF in January-March 1977. The specific issue was Smith's attempt to amend the Land Tenure Act. Criticised on the white left for undertaking 'too little, too late', the Prime Minister's determination to reform the Act brought the long-standing conflicts within the RF into the open, irrevocably split the party, and signalled the Prime Minister's formal abandonment of the RF's most sacred principle.

Despite its humiliation at the Umtali congress in 1975-6, the right-wing faction of caucus and in the party organisation had no intention of conceding defeat. It continued to advocate different versions of provincialisation and criticised the government's acceptance of the Quenet report. Rumours of dissent occasionally surfaced in the press, and were strenuously denied.[50] One story concerned a dinner held at an MP's house near Salisbury in July 1976 where the guests – including Des Frost – insisted that they were merely discussing ways and means of providing 'a clear and dynamic political lead' for the country's youth. In fact, they canvassed the possibility of a new leader but Smith soon learnt of their plans and the waverers fell back into line.[51]

The hard core resumed their scheming soon after Smith accepted the Kissinger package. One of the conspirators was Colin Barlow. The MP for Avondale, Smith's personal dentist and a former disciple of the 'old man', had become thoroughly disillusioned by what he saw as the dishonesty and treachery of his mentor. Barlow's associates included a number of MPs from rural seats who, when in town, used to stay together at the George Hotel in Avondale. Tipped off by a friend inside Special Branch that his rooms and telephones were bugged (which was probably true), Barlow resorted to whispering in corridors as various friends planned their desperate moves to save Rhodesia from Smith, Kissinger, and majority rule. Barlow recalled one bizarre proposal to eliminate Smith altogether, a plan which he claimed was frustrated only by the inability to raise the foreign currency demanded by the intended assassin.[52] A more credible option was to persuade Walls to seize power. Barlow, Cowper, and Sutton-Pryce reportedly urged him – as the one man with the status to rival the Prime Minister – to place Smith under house arrest and to appoint a military junta and a ruling national council. The conspirators even had a speech prepared by a West German which Walls was supposed to read when announcing his seizure of power. According to Barlow, Walls got 'cold feet' in late January 1977 when the President of ACCOR denounced the Cowper plan for extending the call-up. Walls's own explanation was that Barlow and his friends could never convince him that their constitutional schemes would work. Significantly, however, the General, who believed that his own rooms were bugged, was prepared to listen to those who might fulfil his own ambition 'to do something for Rhodesia'.[53]

In the meantime, Smith had forced a show-down. On 23 February 1977 the Prime Minister reviewed the progress made in removing racial discrimination and announced a further package of proposals which included amendments to the Land Tenure Act.[54] The changes would open all white agricultural land to purchase by members of other races, and residential 'non-racial urban areas' could be established after consultation between a local authority and the Ministry of Local Government. No alteration was contemplated for the TTLs, African townships would still be protected, and white residential areas, not declared non-racial, would remain exclusive.[55]

Although the changes in rural land ownership were largely symbolic – very few blacks could afford to buy white farms – the right denounced this blatant breach of the party's principles. Two caucus meetings were held in mid-January, and everyone who attended tried to be tight-lipped about the sharp divisions which were emerging.[56] Des Frost, 'surprised and perturbed' by the news of Smith's planned amendments, assumed at this stage to include urban residential land, tried to pre-empt his leader by summoning a special national executive meeting on 27 January, the day on which Cowper made his ill-fated statement on the call-up system and three days after Smith rejected Ivor Richard's proposed settlement. The meeting endorsed the Prime Minister's proposed reforms, and Frost went immediately to South Africa for a holiday leaving his forthright deputy, Harold Coleman, in charge. Coleman accused Smith of violating the RF's policies and principles, and the MPs of betraying their election pledges. He said that, contrary to Smith's claims, there was an alternative to the reforms being forced upon the

Rhodesians: namely, the full implementation of the RF's policy of provincialisation. Coleman called upon the RF MPs to honour their election undertakings. Twelve of them did so and left the caucus over the land tenure issue,[57] convinced that between six and twelve others shared their opposition to the amendments,[58] and knowing that they had strong support from their party, constituency, and branch officials.

Their arguments in the subsequent debates were often emotional, hypocritical, and specious.[59] Denunciations of 'appeasement', 'capitulation', and 'criminal folly' accompanied evocations of the memory of Allan Wilson, Cecil Rhodes, and the resistance to Germany in the Second World War. One MP professed concern that the African middle class would be bought out by the whites. Another claimed that segregation of land was largely responsible for Rhodesia's 'excellent race relations'. A third member accused the government of sacrificing its responsibility for 'six million ordinary people' to appease 'a few thousand clerics and academics and intellectuals and press-ganged followers'. Sutton-Pryce offered the most considered and ingenious case for retaining the status quo. He argued that white society had a 'constitutional right ... to a part of the country' and that a permanent land base for each tribal grouping was the 'cornerstone' of the political stability needed to achieve an internal settlement. He believed that the issue was not racial discrimination but to ensure that, in the 'realities of power politics in Africa', each community in the second (provincial) tier of government was protected from a national government which could be dominated by a particular group. He also drew a distinction between immutable principles (such as the protection of a land base) and expendable policies (such as the retention of existing land boundaries). So, while he could agree that a government might change the size of the base, it was unacceptable to destroy that base altogether. The probability that economic factors would ensure continued white control of the best land was irrelevant. A central principle was at stake, and Sutton-Pryce sought to defend it in the manner of the fair and reasonable man.

Most MPs agonised over the decision.[60] John Gleig, who had won the close Mabelreign by-election in 1971, was torn between a heart committed to the principles of 1962 and a head which told him that the Act could not remain in its present form. Mark Partridge, speaking for the government, resolved his own doubts by trying to reconcile two different strands of white self-interest: first, reform was necessary in order to promote a settlement and African economic development; secondly, the proposed changes were not far reaching.

The Land Tenure Bill barely survived the rebellion. Under the 1969 constitution, an entrenched clause could not be amended except by the vote of at least two-thirds of the total composition of the lower house.

Twelve of the sixty-six members crossed the floor, and ten of the blacks decided to abstain, which meant that the government needed all the remaining thirty-eight white and six black votes to pass the legislation. Some of the six black MPs were very reluctant. One RF back-bencher had to receive medical treatment before the vote and, along with a minister, was helped into the chamber. Another Smith supporter arrived in a wheelchair following a severe heart attack. He had received a telegram from a constituent urging him to do his country a service by remaining in bed.[61]

The government's knife-edge victory did not end the crisis within the RF. Boosted by messages of support from their own branches and constituency councils and insisting that they had voted for a principle which only a party congress could revoke, the rebels maintained their RF membership and defied Smith's demand that they should honour their pledge, resign, and re-contest their seats. Instead, two of them went off to South Africa to rally support among the leading Nationalists. The rest observed a call by the national executive on 17 March for a 'cooling off' period pending a special congress to be held on 18 April. The delay did not help their cause. Smith assumed the initiative by securing the appointment of a party committee – chaired by his friend 'Boss' Lilford – to investigate allegations that the rebels and senior party officers had sought to undermine the government. The Prime Minister also exploited a fortuitous meeting with David Owen in Cape Town on 13 April by enlisting the rumours of a possible settlement to quell internal dissent.[62] The rebels went to the congress on 18 April knowing that they could not denounce an exploratory initiative without giving it some sort of trial and that Ian Smith was master of a situation where he could raise hopes without alleviating uncertainty.

Two critical resolutions were passed by the congress.[63] One, approved by 313 votes to 116, urged the government to negotiate a settlement in the best interests of Rhodesia and 'in doing so to *strive* to abide by the principles and policies of the party' (emphasis added). There was a clear implication that if, after doing his best for the party, Smith could not obtain a settlement in the prescribed terms then he was free to act as he saw fit. The other resolution, passed by 422 votes to 25, accepted the need for a settlement and urged the government to ensure that the rights of communities were 'meaningfully safeguarded'. Des Frost tried desperately to play down the extent of Smith's triumph.[64] He argued that no settlement should be implemented until approved by a referendum of the white electorate, and claimed (wrongly) that Smith had only just obtained the two-thirds vote necessary to negotiate a settlement. Frost could not, however, ignore some unpalatable facts. The party faithful were not prepared to renounce Smith's capitulation of 24 September, they had recognised that the principles of 1962 could not survive, and they had accepted that the issue was no longer one of resisting majority rule but of establishing safeguards for minorities.

Congress further cleared Smith's path by referring the matter of the dissidents to the party's standing committee where the Prime Minister had an assured majority. The standing committee met on 29 April and resolved to expel Coleman and the twelve MPs, and to silence Frost by restricting party comment in public to Smith and his ministers. The dissidents insisted that they had not been given a proper hearing and claimed that the standing committee had exceeded its powers. Frost himself was now in the extraordinary position of acting on behalf of a committee in opposing the rebels while he remained under investigation himself and was wholly sympathetic to the rebel position.[65] Two further standing committee meetings were called. One reinstated the twelve while affirming Coleman's expulsion, the other discussed the possibility of reconciliation with the six rebel MPs who attended. Eventually the twelve were invited to reapply for membership of the caucus. They, in turn, demanded that the Prime Minister reject the principle of black majority rule whereupon the standing committee expelled them all by the end of May.

Frost hung on until early July. He then resigned, bitterly accusing Smith of being 'tired and negative' and responsible for 'a total lack of leadership, planning and direction'. Rather than seizing the initiative, Smith waited until outsiders imposed their unacceptable terms and was 'now completely bankrupt of ideas'. The Prime Minister, who never worried about the propriety of casting the first stone, replied that Frost was 'completely two-faced'. He also asked – with some justification – why the chairman had stayed so long when he was so critical of the party leader.[66] Wilfred Brooks, whose pathological hatred of Smith had become his nemesis, also wondered why the rebels had taken so long to wake up.[67] The answer was that Frost, and all those hardline branch, constituency, and divisional chairmen who had resigned after March, knew that the price of upholding the RF's principles would be to risk political oblivion at the hands of a Smith-led RF.

Wilfred Brooks appreciated what it meant to challenge Ian Smith. In February 1976 he had publicly alleged that the Prime Minister had foreknowledge of the disappearance of Edson Sithole in October 1975 and had intentionally benefited politically by the abduction. Although the State withdrew a charge of criminal defamation, Smith engaged Chris Andersen, the country's top advocate,[68] to pursue Brooks through the civil courts. Whether or not Smith wanted him silenced, Brooks believed that the libel suit and the cancellation of advertisements in *Property and Finance* were all part of a communist conspiracy to destroy the right. The court case began on 6 June 1977, the day after Brooks heard that his son had been accidentally killed while on active service with a PATU stick. The defendant refused the offer of an adjournment and, according to his own version, addressed Mr Justice Pittman as follows:

I have been stripped of my paper, my company, my son; and I now face personal ruin. I have nothing more to lose – or be taken; but for my son's sake alone, and for the sake of the fathers of many sons, I appear today. He is probably fortunate to be out of the political cesspool that is our – once – beautiful Rhodesia.

Given the seriousness of Brooks's allegations, and the failure to substantiate them, it is hardly surprising that the Judge denounced the 'gutter press' and awarded Smith damages of $15,000.[69] Having turned down every opportunity to retract his indefensible claims, Brooks apparently decided to indulge his bitterness in an act of martyrdom. Des Frost, who had his own reasons for hating Smith, had more political acumen.

V

Frost's departure from the RF meant – to Smith – the elimination of the last 'malignant growth' in the RF. The Prime Minister's authority was fully restored. Now he needed another electoral mandate to confirm him as the spokesman for white Rhodesia and to authorise his negotiations for an internal settlement. On 18 July Smith called an election for 31 August.

In one sense it was a brave decision. Governments in conventional democracies are usually hesitant about calling an early election when the traditional indicators are unfavourable. The business confidence of September 1976 had collapsed into predictions of a continuing economic depression.[70] Net emigration was running close to 1,000 a month. An Umtali real-estate agent claimed in June that 1,500 people had left the border city – most of them young couples heading south or for Britain – and that there were 150 houses currently on the market even though prices were down by nearly 30 per cent since 1972.[71] A similar downturn in prices was evident in Salisbury although the market in Bulawayo and Gwelo remained steady despite the increasing emigration rate in those two cities.[72] The migration of professional workers was also having a noticeable effect throughout the country. By mid-1977 it was harder to find a suitable dentist, many families were obliged to seek a new family doctor, and the drain of anaesthetists was so serious that hospitals had to allocate priorities for operations.[73]

It was impossible to conceal the effects of the war. Promises of 'victory over terrorism' – while persistent – did not reduce the obligations of Territorials and Police Reservists in the under-38 age-group. From June 1977 they were formally required to serve a maximum of 190 days in one year.[74] Mark Partridge, then Minister of Defence, told the farmers in late July that 'the situation is critical, and ... the next six months will get worse'.[75] An Anglican, attending the Mashonaland Synod in August, would have heard Bishop Burrough reporting that 'terrorist activity' prevented Africans from meeting in six or seven large parishes, and had forced the closure of 200 Diocesan schools in the previous eighteen months.[76] Safety factors underlay the decision by the Anglo-American Corporation to withdraw its prospecting staff from the Midlands, Bindura and Kariba.[77] The war had caused the 60 per cent fall in holiday visits from outside Rhodesia over the previous two years. In July the Meikles Southern Sun Hotels group announced a loss of $2 million in the financial year ending in March 1977.[78] Every adult Rhodesian would have noticed the sharp rise in the cost of living (the index lifting from 162.6 in 1976 to 178.2 in 1977). In addition, there was the increase in sales tax (up from 10 to 15 per cent), the freeze on wage rises to a maximum of 5 per cent or $400 to apply until June 1978 and the 10 per cent income tax surcharge, all of which were announced in February 1977.[79] Rhodesians would also have been aware that the July budget approved an increase of 44 per cent in defence spending for 1977-8, and that the direct costs of the war now accounted for 26 per cent of annual government expenditure.[80]

Nor was the government endearing itself to the farming community by its failure to solve the call-up problems. Following representation from the RNFU, concerned about the movement of farmers from the 'sharp end', and especially about the effect of call-ups on one-man farms, the government designated some farming areas as 'super-sensitive' and therefore subject to special call-up concessions. Under a new scheme, explained in detail by Hawkins to the 1977 congress,[81] members of the Police Reserve would assume the first line of defence in the 'super-sensitive' areas and would not be called out of their district except for periods of relative calm and where there was an emergency in a nearby area. Farmers working one-man operations could transfer their Army or Air Force commitment to the Police Reserve and, along with other Police Reservists, would be excused stated periods of call-up and used only on a 'need basis'. Concessions were also granted to farmers in 'other' areas, reducing the time of their commitment and, in the case of the crop farmers, ensuring their availability for the growing season from October to March. Inevitably, there were qualifications, Hawkins admitted further concessions were impossible: 'we are so stretched with our Security Forces at the present moment that literally it is almost every man counts in this regard, and this is our problem.' As a result, specialists in the Army and senior NCOs, and farmers who belonged to a Territorial regiment drawn from the Eastern Districts, could not immediately be released to the Police Reserve. Farmers who remained uncertain about their commitment were further confused when the government, having intended to phase in the concessions, starting with the 'super-sensitive' areas, discovered that the Army – through a misreading of the map – had notified farmers in the 'other' areas that they could join the Police Reserve. The situation was complicated by two further factors: the definition of a 'super-sensitive' area did not coincide with the conventional police districts or Intensive Conservation Areas boundaries; and it was not clear whether the local 'Member-in-Charge' (the senior Police officer), or the senior Army officer, was empowered to determine the call-up commitment.

Despite all these problems, Ian Smith had an overriding need for a mandate to sabotage the British and American proposals, to give himself a free hand to negotiate an internal settlement, and to remove the rebels from parliament where, untrammelled by party discipline, they were having the time of their lives attacking the government.[82] In his national broadcast on 18 July Smith said he had called the election to obtain 'a clear and positive mandate' to proceed with a new five-point plan: a 'fair and just settlement' by the end of 1977, entrenching the safeguards necessary to maintain white confidence and to avoid the chaos of post-independence evident in Angola; a determination to strengthen the war effort, making it clear that Rhodesia intended to eradicate 'terrorism' and, if need be, by more ruthless methods; the maintenance of a viable economy; the establishment of 'a broad-based government', including black Rhodesians, in order to create the climate of trust to enable all Rhodesians to work together for a settlement; and the removal of any remaining discrimination considered 'unnecessary and undesirable'. Smith concluded his statement with a plea for unity, 'the cause of our incredible success' over the past ten years. The present 'tragic spectacle' of white disunity was inviting Rhodesia's enemies to employ the tactics of divide and rule. Now, more than ever, Rhodesians must unite to enter what he predicted would be 'the final lap of our settlement marathon'.[83]

The dissidents quickly formed the Rhodesian Action Party, chose Sandeman as leader, and, after promising to fight the RF for every seat, selected candidates for forty-six of the fifty constituencies. Although it affected an air of great confidence, the RAP did not expect to defeat the RF so much as prevent Smith from obtaining a two-thirds majority in the new house. There were good grounds for optimism. RF branches and constituency councils continued to resign *en masse* and were now joining the RAP.[84] The RAP's candidates generally conformed to the Rhodesian tradition of choosing presentable, well-qualified men of some standing in their immediate community. There were no obvious lunatics. The new faces included a former mayor of Salisbury, a managing director of an engineering firm, and a Matabeleland rancher who headed the Rhodesian Cattle Producers' Association and sat on the council of the RNFU. More important, the RAP knew it could strike a chord in white Rhodesia. Even loyal Smith supporters spoke openly about their favoured option of retaining unfettered white rule. Speaking on a party political broadcast, Rowan Cronje urged electors to vote with their heads and not their hearts, clearly indicating that the RF knew what its people preferred.[85] Besides, the RAP reckoned that fear for their jobs or their pensions would jolt many white artisans, lower-ranking civil servants, poorer widows, and the aged out of their blind faith in 'Good Old Smithy'. Finally, the RAP believed that its two principal platforms – an all-out effort to win the war and a three-tier system of government (local, community, and national) – met the widespread desire to stop being gentle with 'terrorism' and to provide the one genuine safeguard of permanent white rule. It was just a matter, according to the party strategists, of persuading the white electorate that it was 'not too late' to act decisively.[86]

The RAP, whose members had learnt most of their politics inside the RF, understood the value of scare tactics. One of the sensitive issues in mid-1977 was housing.[87] On 21 July the Salisbury City Council voted on the February recommendation of its town planning and works committee to evict the Adams family (who were Coloureds) from their newly-purchased home in the white suburb of Prospect, south of the railway line, The constitution did not distinguish between Europeans, Asians, and Coloureds but there was a restrictive clause in this particular title deed which forbade the transfer of the property to a person 'not wholly of European descent'. The matter was complicated because of a previous rumour that the government intended to allow certain southern suburbs to become 'non-racial urban areas' under the amended Land Tenure Act, a rumour vigorously denied by Bill Irvine, the right-winger who had become Minister of Local Government and Housing. For some eight months African families had already been moving into another white suburb – Houghton Park – in anticipation of a change in the law. When this issue was raised, and in the same week as the Council decision on the Adams family, Irvine made a strong statement promising the eviction of all illegal residents from Houghton Park by 31 August.

The RAP had expected to gain electorally from the open defiance of the Land Tenure Act and the movement of blacks into white suburbia. Paradoxically, the strategy failed precisely because of the movement of whites from some of the southern suburbs of Salisbury. At least 20 percent of the houses were standing vacant, and their white owners were distressed because potential European buyers were not prepared to pay the asking price of $13-15,000. On the other hand, there were willing black purchasers – like Ndabaningi Sithole – who were ready to pay well above the market value. Instead, therefore, of standing firm, demanding evictions, and supporting the RAP, the residents of the poorer suburbs simply wanted to move house themselves and, for the sake of recouping or maximising their investment, demanded a further liberalisation of the Land Tenure Act. The white shopkeepers were the most distressed. The manager of the Houghton Park butchery complained that trade had dropped off because of the exodus of Europeans. Empty houses meant fewer customers and, so far as he was concerned, African and Coloured buyers were every bit as good as whites. The RAP would not, therefore, necessarily win votes in Houghton Park by trying to enforce racial segregation.

The housing episode pinpointed the government's own sensitivity on the question of racial discrimination. At first, Irvine wanted the Salisbury City Council to conduct the evictions. When the Council refused, the police began interrogating African families in Houghton Park, allegedly to uncover the names of estate agents who were illegally letting or selling properties to blacks. While the RAP remained a threat it was more important to assuage presumed white fears and prejudice than to curry favour with moderate, well-off Africans. So, in an election which was to give Smith a mandate to negotiate with internal African leaders (including Ndabaningi Sithole), one of his ministers threatened to evict Sithole from a poorer white suburb on the grounds of his race. The government's first priority was to promote and protect the narrowly-conceived interests of the white electorate. When it became apparent that the electorate was not particularly fussed about breaches of the Land Tenure Act in Salisbury, the government quietly dropped its commitment to evictions.[88]

Its failure to make headway over the housing issue did not dent the RAP's confidence, which survived until two weeks before the election. Martin Meredith, a well-informed British journalist on Rhodesian affairs, claimed at the start of the campaign that the RAP might win between 30 and 40 per cent of the vote, adding that the party was not expected to gain more than six seats.[89] Meredith was soon reporting a different tale. He encountered artisans from Lochinvar – a southern suburb of Salisbury which housed many railway workers – who sounded like committed multiracialists. Less miraculously, he met a farmer's wife in Melsetter who said: 'We would all love to have the RAP system. But it's just not practical any more, is it?'[90] The RAP heard similar messages throughout the last two weeks, and felt their support ebbing away.[91]

Three factors help to explain this phenomenon.[92] First, the RF played a successful 'confidence trick' on the electorate. Meredith pointed out that Smith's formula for white survival – 'give them the parliament and keep the banks' – was so dangerous that the real intentions had to be obscured. The government, therefore, adopted a 'bewildering variety of ploys' to reassure the white electorate that nothing so radical was being contemplated. Evidence of these tactics may be found in several speeches delivered by senior ministers at separate public meetings around the country over a five-day period in mid-August.[93]

Hawkins, Partridge, and Van der Byl emphasised one or more of the following themes: any blacks who entered the broad-based government would be joining an RF government and would have no power base in parliament; the notion of one man-one vote must and would be resisted 'at all costs'; immediate majority rule was simply out of the question; any constitutional changes must first be approved by the white elect-orate in a referendum; there might be rough times ahead but 'we will win'; the Patriotic Front would never be involved in a settlement. Their audiences were interested only in assurances that Muzorewa and Sithole had genuinely renounced 'terrorism' and were not at all concerned that neither of them could conceivably join an 'RF government' or abandon the principle of a universal franchise. Nor did anyone query Van der Byl's preposterous claim that the Third World (minus the Front Line States) would endorse an internal settlement and oblige the West to follow suit. No one pressed Partridge to reconcile his stinging attack on majority rule with his party's policy of negotiating its implementation. In each case the audience wanted to believe the distortions and half-truths. And, on its side, the government wanted to dispel fears rather than invite the electorate to confront the new realities.

Another favourite tactic was to present two versions of majority rule. One, which the British and the Americans, the communists and the 'ter-rorists' wanted to implement immediately, would begin with one man-one vote and end in anarchy and chaos. The other, desired by realistic Rhodesians and moderate blacks and introduced in stages, would start with a broad-based government and culminate in a settlement where the economy and civilised standards of the old Rhodesia would still prevail. The trick lay in repeatedly denouncing the former version, stressing the 'positive' features of the latter, and avoiding any public acknowledgement of the central fact of any settlement: namely, that it would involve a transfer of power to black rule.

The RAP's scare tactics could not overcome this approach. Nor could the right counter 'the Smith factor', the second reason for the marked drift in its support. The farming communities began rallying behind him at the RNFU annual congress which he addressed some twelve days after announcing the election.[94] The Prime Minister told them that he was a Rhodesian, that he was ready to return to his farm if he wasn't wanted (but he was, so he wouldn't), and that, although he was always sincere in seeking a settlement, 'there is a limit beyond which we will not go'. He was among 'trusted people' so he could reveal that there was a contingency plan for evacuating the whites, but then Rhodesia's 'incredible' civil servants had contingency plans for everything and, in any case, he was thinking more of 'getting on and winning'. Smith also assured the farmers – in confidence – that Muzorewa's men were basically reasonable in private. When the session ended nearly all of the delegates cheered him. They did not notice, or care, that he had merely pandered to their expectations.

In public the Prime Minister gave another consummate performance.[95] He told the electorate that majority rule would come, that he did not like it, and that he would fight for the best possible form. He denied asking for a 'blank cheque' (when, in fact, he was): all he wanted was a mandate to ensure there would be safeguards and no sell-out. He blamed 'our friends' for forcing Rhodesia to capitulate, and then said it would be 'madness' to vote for the RAP and thereby alienate those same friends. Smith even told a joke, which his audiences liked: when African leaders say they want one man-one vote, don't believe them, because you should never believe public statements by a politician.

If the wit was heavy, and the message confused, the refrain was familiar. As in 1970 and 1974, the electorate was asked to endorse a man rather than a policy, a leader who knew what was best, who would achieve what could be achieved, and who would never let Rhodesia down. There were just two innovations: on this occasion the right rather than the left was the victim and, for once, 'Good Old Smithy' was leading the sheep in an unwelcome direction. A minor change, too, was the appearance of Janet Smith on the hustings for the first time since 1962. She spoke at a special women's meeting on the theme of 'adapt to survive', and told the only questioner that Rhodesians needed to change because if you have travelled a road for sixty years, 'and there's a ruddy great hole in that road, are you still going to go along it?'.[96] She received three cheers at the end, and there was 'one for Ian'. Every class of Rhodesian, and both sexes, wanted 'Smithy' to rule. Audiences loved him, and he responded to every cheer with another half-truth.

The third factor which explained the drift from the RAP was that the South Africans were obviously backing Ian Smith.[97] Pik Botha, the South African Minister of Foreign Affairs, visited Salisbury on four occasions between June and August, and twice after the election date was set. Smith went to Pretoria on the weekend before the election where he received a standing ovation at a rugby match and plenty of exposure on television back home. The RAP now knew it had lost.[98] All these visits were connected with the forthcoming Anglo-American plan and enabled the Rhodesian government to claim that the South Africans fully supported Smith's proposals for an internal settlement. The RAP's policy of defiance lacked any credibility without the endorsement of the South Africans. Instead, Pretoria backed Smith's attempts to persuade the British and the Americans to withdraw the proposal that the Security Forces be disbanded during the transition to majority rule. Indeed, the rumours leaked about the Anglo-American plan only helped Smith's campaign. His very public refusal to countenance either an immediate transfer of power or the emasculation of the Security Forces made it difficult for the right to portray him as weak and indecisive.

The left had few expectations in August 1977. After a year of trying, the CP and the RP finally agreed on 21 May 1977 to wind up their separate affairs and work together as the National Unifying Force (NUF).[99] Allan Savory, still a controversial figure, was elected leader. The party also produced a policy: it called for free and fair elections on the basis of universal suffrage, the safe return of any guerrillas who accepted a settlement and their incorporation into a national army, and the formation of a broad-based government to supervise the transfer of power. NUF dithered, however, over the question of whether to participate in the 1977 elections. Some members wanted a boycott to avoid splitting the anti-RAP vote, others wanted to vote for the RF to keep out the extremists, some wanted a boycott to avoid a crushing defeat and to maintain their principled opposition to participation under the 1969 constitution. The leadership eventually agreed to contest eighteen seats in an attempt to deny the RF an absolute majority and to establish its right to be involved in settlement negotiations. So NUF collected the familiar faces – Savory, NcNally, Diana Mitchell – and a few new ones, and entered the lists demanding the speedy end to white rule. It called for negotiations with the guerrillas and with the British and the Americans, and denounced the RF for its past failures and the RAP for its insane extremism. The left had found a role, which Ian Smith admitted was at least 'straightforward, simple and honest',[100] by giving selected Rhodesians the option of voting for a quick transfer of power, one man-one vote, and the possibility of peace through a settlement more acceptable to the West.

NUF polled just 4.5 per cent of the total vote on 31 August, obtaining over 20 per cent in two seats and over 10 per cent in five. Given that NUF contested those seats where it was thought to have the best chance, the result was certainly disastrous. Yet NUF surprised the pundits by outpolling the RAP in half of the sixteen seats where both parties stood against the RF and, whereas the RAP obtained just 9.3 per cent of the total vote, NUF's adjusted figure for contested seats was 10.6 per cent.

Clearly, the result was even more catastrophic for the right. Two-thirds of the RAP's candidates lost their deposits, supposedly popular rebel MPs suffered humiliating defeats, and, in spite of the brave assertions about soldiering on, a deep gloom settled upon the RAP's headquarters in Salisbury. For once there was a reluctance to comment but no one would have disputed Peter Nilson's assessment: 'it is the old story of Rhodesians putting their faith in one man and until this myth is destroyed I can only see it continuing.[101] Another 'old story' was about to be told. Destroyed at the polls, the RAP soon followed the familiar path of white opposition parties and set upon its own course of self-destruction.

The RF won 85 per cent of the vote and achieved its greatest electoral triumph just when it was on the point of capitulation. Ian Smith had smashed the right, the left was irrelevant, white Rhodesia was seemingly reunited, the formal Anglo-American Proposals – published on 1 September and described by Smith as 'crazy' and 'insane'[102] – could now be by-passed on the route to an internal settlement. The Prime Minister interpreted the result in the same way as other Rhodesians: when he spoke, he spoke for white Rhodesia.[103]

There was just one drawback. The RF, which once had stood for something, now appeared to believe in almost everything. Whereas the original coalition of 1962 had embraced the supremacists and those who wanted to retain white power for as long as possible, the coalition of 1977, having shed the diehards, had gained thousands of moderate and liberal-minded Rhodesians who knew that white rule was finished.[104] The traditional supporters of the left had lined up behind Ian Smith and were making their own arrangements with Bishop Muzorewa or Ndabaningi Sithole, the leaders of the 'internal' African parties. The corporations, local business houses, and professional organisations were no longer interested in white opposition politics. Their objective was to press Smith into further reforms and, to do this, they wanted to work with a government which could deliver the necessary changes. Not that the relationship was an easy one. When the 'Five white Presidents' – the institutional heads of commerce, industry, mining, farming, and tobacco – went to Geneva, the government delegation was deeply suspicious of their attempt to woo the nationalist parties.[105] In early June 1977 thirty-six prominent figures – including representatives of the corporations – published an open letter calling on the Prime Minister to end all racial discrimination.[106] Smith subsequently told a delegation that he would not be stampeded into action. Nevertheless, the government's links with business were now closer and easier, a symptom both of the changing face of the RF and of the diversity of interests which underlay the restored 'unity' of August 1977.

VI

Smith's post-election confidence could not hide the fact that the situation was becoming desperate. There were some 3,600 guerrillas inside the country at the end of September; Security Force casualties continued to rise;[107] Operation Grapple had been formed to cover the Midlands; and Salisbury itself had become an operational area – Salops – following the bombing of Woolworths in the capital on 11 August 1977 when eleven blacks died and some seventy people were injured. Rhodesia's leaders were not discouraged by these developments from making wild promises about the future. A senior Security Force spokesman claimed on 10 October that there was 'no shadow of a doubt that we are right on top and no suggestion that we are not winning the war'.[108] Given Flower's claim, quoted earlier, that the high-level view of late 1976 was that the 'no-win war' was becoming a 'losing war',[109] this opinion was either ignorant or reckless, and was certainly misleading. Ignorance probably explains the remark of the Deputy Commander of Op Hurricane who told a veterans' convention in Gwelo in late October that the 'terrorists' did not pose a military threat because they refused to make contact with the Security Forces.[110] The fact remains that the government and the Security Force chiefs were, in trying to sustain morale, creating a false sense of hope. Perhaps the experience of those who served in the bush should have made them more sceptical. Mutual deception, however, suited almost everybody.

But confusion did not. The complaints about the call-up system reached new heights after the election. The farming community might have been forgiven for thinking that it was the prime and even intended victim of incompetence and red tape. Stories were still surfacing in October 1977 of farmers being transferred to a district and of others from that same district being sent to replace those transferred.[111] Even the purged RF back-bench dared to express the discontent. One of the most outspoken was Wing Commander Rob Gaunt, whose father, the former Chief Censor, had been one of the original 'cowboys' of 1962. Gaunt moved on 12 October for the appointment of an independent commission of inquiry to investigate the procedures for registration, call-up, deferment, and exemption, and to consider the introduction of a system of national mobilisation.[112] Another ten RF back-benchers spoke in support, all of them careful not to appear too critical, and anxious to acknowledge some improvement in the working of the call-up system, while determined that the government should act upon the anger or disquiet expressed by their constituents. The complaints were familiar. Paddy Shields, representing the railway constituency of Raylton in Bulawayo, spoke on behalf of the apprentices who were still disadvantaged in relation to tertiary students. Another Bulawayo member drew attention to the 'very long standing, continuous low level erosion of public morale' over the 'significant number of people ... who successfully avoid their obligations'.

Cronje defended the call-up by claiming that human error rather than the system was the cause of any problems. He explained that responsibility was now divided between the ministries of Manpower, Combined Operations, Defence, Law and Order, and Internal Affairs. Manpower conducted the registration and initial call-up for training. All subsequent call-ups were handled by particular force and unit commanders, and their respective ministries. Combined Operations determined the initial allocation of men to a particular force, monitored the annual commitments of the various age-groups, and was responsible for transferring manpower between branches of the Security Forces. The other ministries took charge of the emergency call-ups – for example, Army and Air Force (Defence) and police (Law and Order) – and Manpower was responsible, through the exemption boards and the National Manpower Board, for granting deferments and exemptions. Cronje was convinced that these arrangements were 'entirely logical'.[113]

The Directorate of Security Manpower, armed with its computer and receiving additional data from quarterly employer returns and Exit/Entry cards from the Department of Immigration, assembled monthly statistics on service details at a force, unit, and individual level. Sets of statistics were then distributed to the unit and force commanders and to the Ministry of Combined Operations. A unit commander, upon discovering that one individual under his command had done 120 days and that another had served just fifteen, could rectify the position and ensure greater equality of service. A force commander (the Army Commander) could then oversee the equity issue between units while the Ministry of Combined Operations could determine if there had been inequity between the forces. Cronje admitted that there had been problems within the Army: 'Statistics have exposed a non-effective pool of men in some units ... In other words a large pool of men liable for call-up for some reason or another have not been called up.' One way of avoiding this problem was the flow chart system, an idea initiated under Cowper's regime, revised on 10 October, and planned to become fully operational from 2 January 1978. Working in two-week cycles, instead of total periods of, say, fifty-six days followed by another block of thirty-two, call-ups would be for a fortnight or multiples of two weeks. Cowper's original justification for the flow chart system was that, in addition to giving advance notice to individuals and employers in order to reduce personal hardship and economic disruption, it would enable the unit commanders to meet the overriding consideration of operating efficiency.[114] Under more pressure to ensure balance, Cronje stressed the advantages to employers of an integrated call-up system where all forces were operating on the two-week system. Overall, his stock response was that, while the critics might argue about individual decisions over exemptions or deferments or point to human weaknesses in the operation, they could not complain about the system itself because the structural problems had all been ironed out.

Few Rhodesians were so sanguine or trusting. The system might – on paper – *appear* fair, logical, and workable. In practice, it remained inequitable and confusing. Cronje was wrong in assuming that structural and human factors could be separated. A unit commander might well have secured the call-up of one man for 120 days and have left another alone for fifteen precisely because the former was a useful soldier and the latter was not. If the price of equity was the operational *inefficiency* of a four-man stick than it was much too high. One solution was to abandon the entire notion of calling up civilians and employ more black or white professionals. Neither option was seriously pressed in 1977; and so the Rhodesians set about defending their way of life by constantly calling up their male residents while refusing to mobilise for war.

Gaunt was deliberately testing the government's commitment to total war. Whereas Cowper had directly challenged his colleagues to subordinate economic demands to military necessities, the Wing Commander chose a more circuitous route to advance the cause of national mobilisation.

One aspect that has concerned me for some time has been the Government's policy of trying to maintain an air of normality in a wartime situation. It is my contention that there are still far too many people and organisations who are unaware of the fact that we are fighting for our very survival.

Gaunt's supporters on the back-bench felt so strongly that they insisted on forcing a vote on Gaunt's proposed commission of inquiry. Cronje thought that an inquiry was unnecessary but he was overruled, and the whole government supported the motion.[115]

Some matters – affecting morale – could not be disposed of so easily. Rhodesians realised that more of their compatriots were emigrating (in fact 18,882 left the country permanently between October 1976 and November 1977 when net emigration reached 12,205). The letters and speeches became even more abusive. P. K. van der Byl said that, while he had compassion for those who had to leave to make a living, he had 'nothing but contempt' for those who left because they were afraid, or were tired of the call-ups: 'if the cause our soldiers died for should be lost, then an intolerable and shameful burden of responsibility will rest on the shoulders of those who fled and [will] haunt them for all of their days.'[116] John Hickman described the emigrants as the 'casualties of the enemy's psychological assault', the 'self-seekers and "dismal Jimmies"' who had taken their 'precarious loyalty' to other countries, and said they were 'more interested in their own self-comfort'.[117] Dennis Divaris was outraged. Accused of selling his assets preparatory to taking the 'yellow route', he made a personal statement to parliament, claiming that, as he was perennially engaged in buying and selling, any disposal of assets was normal. Besides, at 63, he had just completed an advanced infantry officer course at Gwelo and been invited to train national service recruits.[118] Wickus de Kock, who had every intention of leaving the country, was less upset about the rumours. He just resented being called 'yellow' for making a principled decision to reject majority rule.[119]

Other emigrants were understandably reluctant about divulging their plans, some of which were quite ingenious. Wealthy couples were allegedly arranging divorces because they could take out more of their assets as individuals and because a wife could claim maintenance for herself and any children by drawing upon her former husband's frozen assets in Rhodesia.[120] The government's response was to tighten every loophole as it appeared, and to go on the offensive by trying to attract former residents back to Rhodesia. Commenting on the mid-year figures, Eli Broomberg, then Minister of Immigration, gleaned some good news from the fact that 30 per cent of immigrants were returning residents.[121] On 30 October the government launched a new campaign to stem the flow of emigrants, a far cry from 'Settlers '74' which sought to attract immigrants. Under the slogan 'Once you're a Rhodesian, no other land will do', advertisements pointed out that the grass was no greener elsewhere. The level of unemployment, the weather, and living conditions in Britain 'would make a rat weep'.[122] Yet the employment situation in Rhodesia was also worrying: migration and harder economic times had forced business closures which, in turn, meant fewer jobs for low-skilled and inexperienced white school-leavers and national servicemen returning from call-up.[123]

Like it or not, and nearly all Rhodesians did not, their world had deteriorated since Smith's capitulation. The striking feature of their response was the degree of calm acceptance, matched by an unwillingness to address the consequences of their own surrender. This reluctance was evident in the failure to tackle the issue of racial discrimination. It was (understandably) less disruptive to allow matters to take their course, and the government and local authorities – ever afraid of offending presumed sensibilities – were in no hurry for change. Minor adjustments were possible, of the kind which Smith had envisaged at the end of 1976: junior black officers in the Army, the appointment of a black magistrate and of black prosecutors, the promotion of Africans into the middle grades of the public service. In July 1977 the two key figures at the RBC/TV – David Williams, the Chairman, and Harvey Ward, the Director-General – resigned following complaints about management methods and amidst claims that the extreme right wing had been ejected. Basil Watts, a businessman who became the new Chairman, signalled a new approach to broadcasting and television when he spoke of the need for reconciliation, better race relations, and a balanced reflection of Rhodesian life.[124] There was no suggestion, however, of a new outlook prevailing on the Salisbury City Council. A majority voted in mid-September to postpone debate for six months on the issue of turning the whole city into a non-racial area.[125] And, caught between two opposed viewpoints over the housing issue, the government in late October fined real-estate agents a derisory $50 on each occasion they let or sold a property to blacks in a white area. No action was taken against African tenants or purchasers.[126]

Other groups in society were impatient for a positive commitment to change. In September 1976 – just before the Smith surrender – a group of business and professional people, with strong Bulawayo connections, had published a declaration supporting African participation in govern-ment and the removal of discrimination. Rhodesians were asked to sign the declaration which, in April 1977, was modified to include support for David Owen's initiative and called for an immediate constitutional conference leading to the introduction of majority rule. Both versions of the September Declaration acknowledged the inevitability and immi-nence of majority rule.[127] In July 1977 Lady Wilson, the widow of a for-mer Speaker, formed 'Women for Peace', 'a fully multi-racial non-party political movement' dedicated to preparing the country for majority rule, supporting racial equality, and ending 'the bitterness and suffering of the war'.[128] Like NUF, the September Declaration and Women for Peace urged Rhodesians to think positively about majority rule: to recognise that it would come, to prepare for its eventuality by removing racial discrimination, and to create a welcoming spirit towards the new Zimbabwe.

The 'Five Presidents' of agriculture, commerce, industry, mining, and tobacco and their Private Sector Co-ordinating Committee were thinking along similar lines.[129] Yet the major business houses were slow in promoting Africans onto boards and into senior management.[130] Moreover, their 'Harmony' campaign of October 1977-January 1978 had all the hallmarks of do-gooding irrelevance. Financed by donations amounting to $25,000, the campaign was launched by the Co-ordinating Committee to achieve 'greater understanding, racial tolerance and an easing of racial tension'. Its message – 'You don't have to love your neighbour, just try to understand him' – was launched with a three-and-a-half-minute television commercial depicting blacks and whites working together in the Security Forces and in hospitals and a black child and a white child climbing a mountain together. Perhaps there was too much symbolism and emotion; the white singer of the Harmony jingle reportedly broke down and cried after recording it. The *Rhodesia Herald* claimed that there was an 'incredible reaction' to the campaign, and surveys conducted by the organisers claimed that, of 385 people polled, 74 per cent were in favour of its objectives. The euphoria lasted a few weeks but Harmony was an embarrassing memory by the time the campaign finished in January. It soon lost credibility because, apart from the creation of the Beverley Language Clinic which introduced whites to a new Shona or Sindebele word each day on radio, it could not promise any substantial or lasting impact. The issues in 1977 would not be resolved by people in suburban streets smiling at each other.[131]

Some, indeed, preferred to be very nasty. Each publicised 'terrorist' incident was greeted with howls of rage from white Rhodesians, none louder than the response to the news that 6-month-old Natasha Glenny was bayoneted to death near Chipinga on 29 September. Restraint was one of the first casualties of the civilised society when the war entered a more vicious phase after September 1976. Understandably, the white farmers were among the least inhibited. At the RNFU's 1977 congress a farmer raised the question which bothered most of his community: what was happening to the idea, mooted at previous congresses, of 'kangaroo courts' for the north-east? Hilary Squires, the Minister of Justice and Law and Order, blanched a little because such courts should not feature in a 'reputable society'. He explained that it was really a matter of facilities, and it just wasn't possible to go to every place where there was an incident 'and hang them from the nearest tree'. When told that there were plenty of trees, Squires responded – jokingly – that it was a question 'of carrying round the rope'. The future judge was unmistakably serious on the matter of vigilante farmers exacting retribution and forcibly recovering stolen stock. In such cases the 'reputable society' would not allow 'some little policeman' to arrest farmers who, while retrieving their stock, happened to shoot the alleged thieves.[132]

Compassion for the white victims of 'terrorism' was rarely matched by an equal concern for blacks. It was rare for anyone outside of NUF to ask questions about the rising number of blacks killed while allegedly breaking the curfew or 'running with terrorists'.[133] There was a ritualised reaction of shock and horror at the 'atrocities' inflicted upon 'innocent tribesmen' which, after the appearance of David Owen and Andrew Young on the Rhodesian scene, was coupled with denunciations of the various Anglo-American initiatives.[134] It was good politics to link Owen and Young to the 'terror' perpetrated by the Patriotic Front and, thereby, to condemn the Anglo-American plan for its callous disregard of millions of African peasants. Otherwise it was becoming hard to feel much for 'innocent' blacks when Rhodesians had enough worries of their own.

VII

By November 1977 fourteen months had passed since Smith's surrender, and nothing much had happened to sustain hopes for peace or for a settlement. Led by Ian Smith, the Rhodesians blamed everyone else except themselves. In the meantime, when all fit males between 18 and 50 were being regularly called up and exemptions and deferments had become harder to obtain, the war had entered deeper into every facet of Rhodesian life. School-leavers were forced to grow up very quickly, honourable men shot defenceless peasants, bank clerks drowned their fears in bars and night clubs, the lonely wives of serving men found solace in furtive encounters outside the marital bed, and more families shed tears and sent death notices to the press. Convoys were now regularly operating on some of the country's main roads, the police conducted random 'cordon and search' sorties in Salisbury, private security firms enjoyed a boom, and a number of white women were heard to complain about handbag inspections by black guards (not all of whom wore white gloves) as they entered shops and stores.[135] If Gaunt was right – that 'too many people' were unaware of the fight for survival – no one could escape the fact that Rhodesia was at war. In December 1976, in the four years since Altena, the death toll within Rhodesia's borders was 3,169 people of all races. Thirty-one more deaths were announced on the fifth anniversary of Altena and – in total – 3,046 men, women, and children of all races, including some fifty members of white farming families, were killed on Rhodesian soil during 1977.[136]

7

'Let this be a Rhodesian solution'

I

On 24 November 1977, fourteen months after his capitulation, Ian Smith announced that he was ready to negotiate with internal black political leaders for a transition to black majority rule based on the principle of an adult suffrage.[1] His objective was what he liked to call 'a Rhodesian solution'. Forewarned, cynical, or too bruised to care, the white electorate barely managed any reaction to Smith's statement. Attention, instead, was focused on some more exciting and palatable news. The Rhodesians had just launched a massive air strike against the ZANLA bases at Chimoio and Tembue in Mozambique.[2] The timing was impeccable. White Rhodesia could believe, and the internal black leaders might be persuaded, that the government now occupied a strong negotiating position.

Three African leaders were ready to enter negotiations. Smith claimed that they represented '85 per cent to 86 per cent of black Rhodesians'.[3] Of the three, Bishop Muzorewa, now leading the United African National Council (UANC), probably had the most popular support and was the least favoured by the government. Although, in 1974, he had previously demonstrated a commendable disregard for principle and a capacity for compromise, there remained doubts about his ability to control his followers and fears that some of them might stiffen his backbone. Senator Chief Chirau, the senior chief of Mashonaland and a deputy minister since April 1976, was the favourite son. A paid servant, whose party – the Zimbabwe United People's Organisation (ZUPO) – was secretly financed by the government, Chirau was conservative and reliable. It was unfortunate that he lacked popular support. The third politician, Revd Ndabaningi Sithole, was much brighter than the other two – which made him dangerous – but, having lost the leadership of ZANU to Robert Mugabe and, with it, his base in the bush, he was a virtual hostage to any internal settlement.

Smith turned to Muzorewa and Sithole at the end of 1977 because they represented his last hope for an internal accord which he could sell to the outside world *and* to his own electorate. The British and American governments were immediately sceptical and argued, on grounds of justice and practicality, that the externally-based guerrillas must be involved in any settlement. After all, the war had forced Smith into negotiations in the first place, and the war would not cease until the fighters were prepared to stop fighting. The 'boys in the bush' were uncompromising: their struggle was about the total and immediate transfer of power, the complete destruction of the white State and of the Security Forces, and the creation of a socialist economy and society. So long as the Patriotic Front held this position and felt it could win, then any form of negotiations – let alone a settlement acceptable to the whites – was out of the question.

Ian Smith obtained his internal settlement in March 1978, the white electorate voted itself out of power in January 1979, and the last white parliament rose on the following 28 February. Within this period, the war spread further throughout the country and beyond its borders. Despite the attempts to present an image of normality, the working days of all government departments were consumed by the war. The Department of Roads and Road Traffic, for example, now published casualty lists of employees killed on maintenance duty, and recorded that its work was almost entirely devoted to the building, securing, and repairing of roads, bridges, airfields, and PVs in the operational areas.[4] Combined Operations headquarters announced more than 2,600 deaths of people of all races on Rhodesian soil during 1978; nearly 300 white civilians were killed between January 1978 and February 1979, a figure inflated by the shooting down of two civilian airliners; the economy teetered then, surprisingly, began to recover; white morale plummeted and the call-up continued to infuriate; racial discrimination was partially dismantled; and some Protected Villages were disbanded.

The main theme of this chapter is that the Rhodesians accepted further and fundamental political change without adapting mentally to its consequences. A secondary concern is to show how the society which considered itself civilised plunged deeper into uncivilised thinking and behaviour as it tried to resist assault.

II

The formal negotiations for an internal settlement began on 2 December when delegations representing the government, the African National Council (Sithole), and ZUPO met at the Civil Service Training Centre in Salisbury. Muzorewa's UANC delegation was absent, having decided to observe a week's mourning for the victims of the Chimoio raid. The first full session was held on 9 December where Smith set out the eight 'safeguards' needed for a settlement:[5]

1. a justiciable Bill of Rights to protect individual freedoms and property rights;
2. an independent and highly competent judiciary;
3. an independent Public Services Board whose composition and functions would be entrenched;
4. an efficient civil service, police, defence force and prison service, all free from political interference;
5. guarantees that funds from government pension schemes would be paid and be fully remittable overseas, and that the rights of contributors to private pension funds would be observed;
6. retention of dual citizenship;
7. the requirement that the above provisions could only be altered by a majority of two-thirds plus one in the parliament;
8. the reservation of one third of the parliamentary seats for whites who would be elected exclusively by white voters.

The assumptions were clear enough: the country needed the whites in order to escape the fate of independent black Africa; the whites would leave unless they received certain guarantees; and Smith's purpose in entering the settlement negotiations was to secure black acceptance of his terms for a transfer of power.

The African parties had little difficulty in accepting the first six safeguards which had been informally approved in advance and did not inhibit future moves against discrimination or segregation. The exception was the question of control and composition of the Security Forces, and that matter was left over for later negotiation. Nor was there any real problem with Smith's seventh demand. The sticking-point was the eighth. Sithole flatly rejected the idea of a blocking third for whites, but he did agree to the reservation of twenty seats out of 100 for whites to be elected on a separate white roll. Muzorewa was prepared to concede a blocking third provided that the whites were elected on a common roll. Smith, with Sithole's support, argued that the UANC scheme would mean the election of 'black stooges' who would in no way represent white interests. A compromise was reached on 15 February: twenty seats would be elected on a separate white roll, eight would be chosen by a common roll from a panel of sixteen selected, initially, by the existing RF-dominated parliament, and an amendment of the entrenched statutory clauses would require the support of seventy-eight members.

The white opposition parties took these negotiations very seriously. On the left, NUF spent many hours defining its position. Anxious to remain neutral in the struggle between all the nationalists, aware that support for an internal settlement would identify it with the internal factions, and conscious of the need for international recognition, NUF decided to maintain a low profile and to wait and see. A contrary opinion gathered momentum during February when a settlement seemed imminent. According to this argument, the Patriotic Front's insistence on the violent overthrow of the system, its demand that the guerrilla armies become the basis of the new security forces, and its commitment to Marxism meant that the Front's leaders could not usefully be brought into the talks. On the other hand, Smith's acceptance of a universal franchise, the willingness of the internal nationalists to negotiate, the probability of a just settlement, and a genuine transfer of power all suggested that NUF should publicly endorse the proceedings.[6] NUF's council finally agreed on 18 February to maintain its previous position, and to content itself with formulating papers stating the principles upon which a settlement should be based. The debate showed just how difficult it was for the well-meaning left to reconcile aspiration and actuality. The ideal of a democratic, pluralist society would not work if it excluded the opponents of pluralism and liberal democracy. Recognising the problem, the wiser and harder heads insisted that the Patriotic Front would have to be part of any genuine settlement. Their view prevailed, and NUF stayed astride the fence in March 1978.

Whereas the left appeared indecisive, the right wing of white politics was resolute and single-minded. The RAP regarded any settlement which allowed majority rule as unacceptable. Well-attended public meetings in Salisbury and Bulawayo in January-February 1978 gave its supporters an opportunity to vent incoherent anger at Ian Smith and sufficiently worried the RF for its Chairman to undertake a tour of party branches.[7] The RAP wanted to persuade Rhodesians that they did not have to accept majority rule. Sandeman argued that there was 'a positive and constructive alternative policy' which would supplant worthless 'paper guarantees' with a stable and permanent 'pluralist democracy'.[8] By the end of April, however, the right was so divided over its own policy that the RAP split. Many former RF members, led by Sandeman and Des Frost, left in disgust at the unbridled racism of the party's rump which insisted that the 'pluralist democracy' must be permanently white dominated.[9] Even before the split, the right had failed to arouse people who, in the savage words of one RAP supporter, were 'walled-in, blinkered, blinded, brain-washed, bedazzled and beleaguered'.[10] The RAP had made no headway with Rhodesians who simply followed the 'gospel' according to Ian Smith.

Salisbury's white citizens had several other things on their minds in early 1978. Thirteen white civilians were killed between 7 and 18 January and three incidents, in particular, sent a shiver through the capital.[11] On Saturday, 7 January, at about 4.00 p.m., just one hour after the Security Forces began clearing some 200 holiday-makers from the Lake McIlwaine area 20 km from Salisbury, Sheila Gumming and her teenage daughter were murdered on Camrie Farm near Norton at the southern end of the lake. Two days later an elderly grandmother, her son, and two teenage boys were shot dead near Hartley, 80 km to the south-west of Salisbury. Colin Tilley, a 15-year-old schoolboy, was killed on 13 January when his parents' car was ambushed next to their farmhouse. The Tilleys lived just 2 km from the north-western border of the Salisbury municipality in an area occupied by market gardeners, horse-breeders, and retired folk. In each case, at least one black employee was subsequently charged with complicity, giving false information, or not assisting the authorities. In all cases the attacks were directed at 'soft targets', and were close enough to Salisbury to warn its white civilian population that the war might not always be fought elsewhere. The jitters were revived – briefly – on 31 January when two Lonrho employees were ambushed, robbed, and killed on the Arcturus road just to the north of Salisbury while they were delivering the wages. At first it seemed like the work of 'terrorists'. Reassuringly, a few days later, another white employee was charged with the murders.[12] The act was so well conceived and implemented that it was gratifying to have some long-standing assumptions confirmed: no black man could have done it.

The earlier January deaths had some important implications. One was the introduction of a dusk-to-dawn curfew in the white farming area lying between three TTLs and the northern city limits of Salisbury, extending, at one point, to within 20 km of the centre. The killings also created problems for the local tourist industry. Lake McIlwaine was a popular resort for Salisbury's residents and its game park remained closed for weeks after 7 January and the normally brisk weekend trade in boating and eating almost collapsed.[13] Indeed, by early 1978, it was necessary to be cautious in leaving Salisbury at all. Travellers north to Mazoe, Bindura, Shamva, Mrewa, Mtoko, Mermaid's Pools, or Arcturus were advised to do all their driving in daylight. Further afield, there were now convoys on all the main roads out of Fort Victoria, stretching as far north as Enkeldoorn, south to the South African border, east and north all the way up to Umtali, and extending to Chipinga and Melsetter. Convoys and petrol coupons had become the major factors preventing Rhodesians from enjoying their outdoor world.

Other changes were also interfering with the traditional way of life. The 'braai' now cost more because of a decision in late February to raise the wholesale price of beef by 10 per cent. Mark Partridge explained that the government could no longer protect the urban consumer at the expense of ranchers who had not received a price rise in four years and were the 'frontline troops on a voluntary basis'. Urban Rhodesians were soon telephoning their MPs to complain about the sudden increase, to accuse butchers of raising their charges by more than 10 per cent, and to denounce the continued freeze on wages. The General Secretary of the

Trade Union Congress had already warned that the long-term effect of the wage freeze would be a decline in living standards and the emigration of skilled manpower.[14] Similar prophecies greeted the news about the beef price. By raising beef prices and continuing to peg wages, the government exposed the divergent interests of consumers and producers, of town and country. It also demonstrated that avowals of Rhodesian patriotism did not imply a readiness to sacrifice expectations about the Rhodesian way of life.[15]

Price rises in Salisbury were common in the early part of 1978 though one commodity remained cheap and became more accessible as an indirect result of changes in discriminatory practice. African and Coloured families were moving – illegally but unmolested – into white housing areas in the city centre. Eleven African or Coloured brothels began operating at either end of Union Avenue which crosses the heart of Salisbury. Residents complained of cars cruising along the street and of being accosted by women in their quest for clients. The Municipality said it would act and occasionally the madams were fined, yet business flourished because the demand kept expanding. The patrons were predominantly white and it is unlikely that the steady stream consisted solely of foreigners or of locals who were committed multiracialists. At $5 a visit, it was inexpensive to exploit the more relaxed rules of the post-Quenet era.[16]

There were other ways in which the Christian society was breaching its own code of behaviour. Churchmen and other moralists were frequently torn between affirming Rhodesia's place in God's scheme of things and rebuking Rhodesians for testing His goodwill. The rising divorce rate continued to perplex them in early 1978. By then one marriage in just over three was being dissolved. The redoubtable Senator Mrs Maclean was not prepared to blame the war. She attributed everything to the 'permissive society': to sex before marriage, trial marriages, and to people laughing at virginity which, she said, 'led naturally to adultery and faithlessness'.[17] The Senator was responding to the *Report* of the Commission of Inquiry into the Divorce Laws,[18] which had been appointed by the government in August 1976 and had submitted its findings in September 1977. The *Report* was something of a hybrid: at once liberating, interventionist, and restrictive. It proposed no-fault divorce and extensive counselling, preserved some of the old rigidities by insisting on an intensive state involvement, and tried to maintain society's professed values while acknowledging the considerable deviation in practice. The Assembly had voiced concerns in 1977 about the *Report's* liberality, and the Senators followed suit in March 1978.[19] There was, nonetheless, a widespread recognition in right-wing circles and in the Women's Institutes that Rhodesia's divorce laws and procedures were archaic,[20] that the country had to take account of practicalities and acknowledge the disadvantages experienced by women. Some Senators went beyond the *Report* itself in their concern for the children affected by any divorce action. Their enthusiasm for change, however, was restrained by the old preoccupations with preserving Rhodesia from the 'evils' of easy marriage and easy divorce, and by a desire to maintain the steadying guidance of parents on the young.

Preoccupied with these and other matters, most Rhodesians ignored the settlement talks. Experience had taught them to be sceptical, and there was little attempt to keep them informed. The government's justification was similar to that used when refusing to disclose military information: secrecy was essential to ensure success and to confuse Rhodesia's enemies. The associated, unstated reasoning was equally familiar: an ignorant electorate would not panic. Both arguments underlay the expanded use of 'D notices' in January 1978 to stop the publication of further details about the government's policy of allowing the 'safe return' of former 'terrorists'. The government was worried about a possible hostile white response to a scheme which Smith himself had previously denounced.[21] It was better for the whites to hear a different kind of message. In November 1977, just two weeks preceding his announced intention of entering negotiations with the internal black parties, the Prime Minister had spoken of Rhodesia's '12 incredible years . . . we have prospered where we might have failed and grown stronger where we might have fallen into decline'.[22] Speaking in February 1978, at a ceremony at his old school, where he opened a $100,000 new building, Smith said that Rhodesians were fortunate: 'our black Rhodesians are among the best blacks that you can find anywhere in the world.'[23]

III

At 10.30 a.m. in Salisbury on 3 March 1978, in the presence of 100 members of the press and television corps, Ian Smith signed the 'Rhodesian Constitutional Agreement' (commonly known as the Salisbury Agreement) which formally began the transition from white rule.[24] Government officials, anxious 'to add a bit of history to the ceremony', brought along a water-colour etching of Cecil John Rhodes which normally hung in the Prime Minister's office. The Bishop, dressed in a Liberian costume, sat in front of the etching, and on Smith's right.[25] After two months of walk-outs and boycotts, and just twenty-four hours after threatening to present new proposals, he had acquiesced in an operation whose success depended upon his participation. Ian Smith, supported by the compliant Chirau and the eager Sithole, had – for the second time within four years – persuaded the Bishop to dump his radical wing and not to exploit his stronger bargaining position. Muzorewa could, of course, claim that he had won the important fight by securing Smith's acceptance of majority rule based on a universal franchise. Yet that victory was secured before the negotiations began, and was hardly Muzorewa's triumph. When, after signing the document, he called for three cheers, the other delegations ignored him. He looked and sounded faintly ridiculous and irritated the other black parties by endeavouring to present himself as the next Prime Minister. More importantly, few white Rhodesians were ready to take Muzorewa seriously or were willing – until it was too late – to give him the chance to sell himself to black Zimbabweans.

On one reading, the Salisbury Agreement seemed like an unqualified victory for Ian Smith. Critics noted how the preamble identified the principal objective as the removal of sanctions and the ending of the war, and not the introduction of a social democracy free of racial discrimination or the implementation of majority rule.[26] The Prime Minister, knowing that he had to sell the settlement to his own constituency, announced in a national broadcast on 12 March that 'our two over-riding objectives' in reaching a constitutional settlement were 'to bring an end to the war and to restore normal trading relations'.[27] The Ministry of Foreign Affairs sent a memorandum to its overseas representatives and other interested parties stressing that the agreement was 'based on the principle that a prosperous and stable future for Rhodesia can only be achieved by recognising, and meeting, *legitimate* black aspirations and understandable white fears' (emphasis added). By implication, the demands for 'a radical Marxist state' from 'intransigent extremists', who wanted the military overthrow of the settler state, were plainly illegitimate.[28]

Smith had obtained nearly all his proposed 'safeguards': a justiciable Declaration of Rights guaranteeing, in particular, property and pension rights; an independent judiciary and civil service; the Security Forces and prison service free of political interference; and the entrenchment of these provisions in the constitution which could not be amended without the support of at least six white MPs. The present all-white judiciary, for example, could remain intact for another seven years before the next retirement was due. The same applied to the Public Services Board which controlled civil service appointments and promotions. Although he failed to secure a blocking third of white votes to prevent constitutional amendments, Smith did obtain 28 reserved seats for whites for at least ten years in a house of 100. Twenty of the white MPs were to be elected by white voters and 8 by voters on the common roll from 16 nominated in the first instance by an electoral college composed of the present 50 RF MPs, and thereafter by an electoral college consisting of the 28 white MPs. Obviously, one man-one vote did not mean one vote-one value.

Smith may have been just one of four members of the new Executive Council in the new Transitional government (the others were Muzorewa, Sithole, and Chirau) but the requirement that decision-making proceed by consensus gave him, like the others, the right of veto. His wealth of experience also gave him an edge in exercising the Council's functions. These functions were to implement the decisions of the Transitional government, including all policy decisions relating to the new constitution, bringing about a ceasefire, determining the composition of the new military forces, removing all racial discrimination, releasing detainees, and reviewing prison sentences for political offences. The functions were so ill-defined that a Smith-dominated Council could either delay proceedings or find other reasons for keeping opponents in detention. The Ministerial Council, which was responsible for the daily governance of the country, and was to operate on the cabinet system except for the majority vote required of its decision-making, was based on an equal white-black membership where each portfolio would have a black and a white co-minister. Once again, the experience of the RF ministers was bound to give them an edge. Further, the existing RF-controlled parliament retained the power and the responsibility to enact constitutional, financial, and other legislation. Finally, Ian Smith confirmed in June 1978 that the white electorate would have to approve any new constitution at a referendum.

The fact remains that Ian Smith had signed away the purpose of UDI. The point of the preamble was to divert attention from what the RAP called a 'sell-out'. And the tactic certainly worked. Businessmen were relieved and looked forward to the end of sanctions. Even Father Lewis of the Rhodesian Christian Group was accommodating. He supported the settlement because it would give 'practical Christianity' and moderate blacks a chance.[29] Journalists, who conducted informal surveys in Bulawayo, Gwelo, and Salisbury, found that the majority of whites would 'wait and see'. There were two concerns, both of which were repeatedly raised with Smith at RF and civil servants' meetings in Gwelo on 28 March: would standards be maintained and would 'terrorism' end?[30] The *Chronicle* decided that 'terrorism' would not cease until there was a settlement with Joshua Nkomo. Down in Bulawayo, Robert Mugabe was not regarded as either desirable or threatening. Back in Salisbury, Wilfred Brooks was incensed. He referred to 3 March as 'the Day of Surrender' and 'black Friday' and, in a poetic moment, reflecting upon the weekend cloudburst which followed the signing, wrote that 'the heavens wept' while an ancient tree 'fell drunkenly and in disgust across the Enterprise Road'.[31] Brooks excused anyone who, having fought the good fight, now wanted to leave the country: *they* were not 'the rats' who had brought the country to its knees. Yet, even as he wrote, the country was standing tall. On Saturday, 11 March, the Rhodesian cricket team won its first and last major trophy in the South African competition. A 'dashing (white) Matabele', who cut short his Durban holiday, and a Rhodesian-born English professional combined for an heroic sixth-wicket stand to win the Datsun Shield one-day final against Eastern Province.[32] National pride soared, if only momentarily, even as the nation itself was about to disappear.

Smith's critics on the left in 1978 were understandably sceptical that the Salisbury Agreement signified any change of heart.[33] The 'wait-and-see' attitude, and the assumption that the blacks had the responsibility for making the settlement work, confirmed suspicions that the white electorate had not experienced any overnight conversion to majority rule or to dramatic reform. Nevertheless, some frenetic activity in March-April seemed to belie the early doubts. The Bishop went off to London to persuade David Owen to recognise the Agreement. The Executive Council was formally constituted on 21 March, the release of detainees began on 6 April (561 were set free by the end of the month), and executions for 'political' crimes were halted. The Council of Ministers was formed on 12 April and two of the more right-wing RF ministers (including Lardner-Burke who wanted to retire) did not join the new government. The Education Department also decided to introduce compulsory courses in Shona or Sindebele in three of the school years.[34] Three judges, including Chief Justice Hector Macdonald, resolved on 20 April that it was contrary to public policy to allow a master to inflict corporal punishment on his employees. In February a Bulawayo magistrate had sentenced a Plumtree rancher to ten months' jail (six months being conditionally suspended) for caning two juvenile employees. The two young Africans had consented to the caning, in preference to a report on theft being submitted to the police. The Appeal Court accepted consent as an argument in mitigation but was unmoved by the rancher's claim that the presence of 'terrorism' necessitated special steps to preserve discipline. Although it set aside the prison sentence (except for a conditional one month), and imposed an alternative $200 fine, it laid down that the courts were the proper authority for determining and administering punishment.[35]

Two events quickly revived the doubts about the internal settlement. First, David Owen and Cyrus Vance, the American Secretary of State, arrived in Salisbury on 17 April and received a cool response to their proposal for an all-party conference. Given that Muzorewa and Sithole were plainly unable to persuade the 'terrorists' to lay down their arms, and that a ceasefire would not eventuate without a conference and a broader-based settlement, the Salisbury Agreement could not attain one of its central objectives.

The second event, the 'Hove affair', highlighted the narrow view of the Agreement held by the white political and military leadership.[36] One of the three ministers nominated by the UANC was Byron Hove, a London-based lawyer, who had once described Smith as 'the Hitler of Southern Africa' and declared his support for a Nuremberg-type trial of white leaders. Hove was appointed Co-Minister of Law and Order and of the Public Service, and was to work with Hilary Squires. Almost immediately Hove declared that, while the Agreement provided for a judiciary free from political interference, he did not interpret the provision to mean 'that the present judiciary will be retained'. When asked how the BSAP might help to achieve an atmosphere conducive to majority rule and free elections, Hove replied that he would not tolerate any police officer who went beyond his mandate. The police would have to change 'their conduct, activities and outlook'. On 16 April he made a speech in Bulawayo where he said that whites had to adjust to the idea of majority rule. He complained that government officials from the highest to the lowest had implemented unjust laws against blacks for a decade and that the police – including blacks- – were harassing the African population. He foreshadowed 'positive discrimination in favour of the African policeman' who had been 'discriminated against all these years' and called for a similar upgrading in the public service, saying that the Agreement would be meaningless if blacks were not given positions in the administration. Two days later Hove admitted that his remarks had caused consternation in the police and the civil service but claimed that he was working well with Squires and P. K. Allum, the Police Commissioner, and spoke warmly about the willingness of whites to make the Agreement work.[37]

The Executive Council, including the Bishop, agreed that Hove should be reprimanded for his outspoken comments and asked him to make a public withdrawal. Before Hove could respond, Walls and Squires made their own public statements attacking the Minister.[38] After complimenting the new ministers for acting 'pretty reasonably, sensibly and constructively', the Commander of COMOPS spoke of one 'notable exception'. Without referring to Hove by name, Walls said it was 'a pity' that the Minister spoke as he did: Hove's remarks had cast doubt on the validity of the whole Agreement by questioning that clause which protected the Security Forces from political interference. Knowing 'for an absolute fact' that the minister was not speaking on behalf of the Executive Council, Walls said he hoped that the new ministers would accept the Rhodesian tradition of collective responsibility, and that the Council would disassociate itself very clearly from this particular minister's views. Squires was equally emphatic. He told a police passing-out parade that any new government structure would be implemented in accordance with the Agreement or not at all. Any restructuring of the BSAP by political directive would be 'a gross departure from what was accepted' and 'should not be countenanced for a moment'. Squires reminded Hove that positions of command in the BSAP were earned by officers who took up service as a career: if this process was in any way truncated or abrogated then efficiency would be impaired, and the signatories of the Agreement did not want that to happen in Rhodesia.

Walls and Squires were responding to a 'ripple of alarm' which spread throughout white membership of the Security Forces.[39] Hove refused to apologise or recant. The Executive Council again discussed the issue and, despite Muzorewa's reluctance, called once more for Hove to withdraw his comments. A mild suggestion from the UANC that Walls should also be disciplined for speaking out was not taken seriously. Meanwhile, the police themselves bolstered Hove's case by their differential treatment of demonstrations. They did not intervene on 17 April when ZUPO supporters pelted raw eggs, tomatoes, and bananas at a car carrying Cyrus Vance and Andrew Young. Yet, on 24 April, some 400 black university students were diverted by a police cordon when they attempted to march into the centre of Salisbury to protest against the Agreement. Eighty students were arrested the next day when they assembled in Cecil Square bearing placards. Quick justice followed. Seventy-nine of them, all except one appearing before Rhodesia's sole African magistrate, were sentenced on the following day to three months' hard labour, conditionally suspended for five years.[40] Evidently there was a distinction between a violent expression of legitimate aspirations and a peaceful breach of the Law and Order (Maintenance) Act.

Hove continued to stand out and, after its third request for a retraction, the Executive Council dismissed him from the ministry on 28 April. There was considerable confusion about the events on that day: whether the Bishop participated in the decision, whether Hove's letter reached the Council in time.[41] The Council eventually reaffirmed its decision on 9 May leaving the Bishop, who reserved his position, in a no-win situation: if he resigned from the Transitional government, he could be accused of sabotaging the settlement and would lose his power base in the struggle against the external nationalists; it he remained, he could equally be accused of condoning racial discrimination, opposing substantive change, and propping up the old regime. The UANC wrestled with this embarrassing problem for several more days before an eight-hour meeting of its national executive decided on 14 May to stay with the Transitional government. The Bishop would save face by refusing to participate in Executive Council rallies which were to be held in centres around the country. He had already boycotted one meeting at Mrewa on 10 May and remained under the false impression that his absence would devastate his colleagues.

The Hove affair ended when the UANC decided to remain in the Transitional government: 'a victory', according to the Bishop, 'of reason over emotion'. The party nominated a replacement, the government continued to function, and the rumblings soon ceased. But the affair continued to have ramifications. First, it raised or confirmed doubts among whites and UANC supporters about the Bishop's capacity for leadership and judgement. Secondly, the dismissal removed the one UANC figure who carried any weight with the guerrillas, and probably eliminated any chance of significant numbers agreeing to lay down their arms. Thirdly, the affair demonstrated that most Rhodesians had not grasped the implications of accepting the Salisbury Agreement. They did not understand that even moderate blacks were bound to demand the rapid demolition of discriminatory practices and the advancement of Africans in government. Part of the problem was that men who had spent years denouncing change were now expected to preside over its implementation. Leaders, whose immediate and habitual response was to reassure the white electorate that nothing dangerous could or should happen, were not the best equipped to prepare the electorate for the massive changes which were about to occur. When Ian Smith and P. K. van der Byl were telling closed meetings during April-May that nothing much would change, and that majority rule would be delayed, they were helping to allay fears and prevent a mass migration. They were also doing their constituents a monumental disservice.

IV

The end of the Hove affair coincided with the deepening realisation that the internal settlement was not working. The Chaplain-General of the Army reported that the white troops were grumbling: they wanted blacks to be conscripted and they believed they were fighting for a lost cause.[42] In June-July the representatives of the overseas press were pronouncing the settlement a failure, partly because there was little evidence of ZANLA and ZIPRA guerrillas being prepared to lay down their arms. The correspondents were also reporting a further, consequential decline in white morale.[43] Mark Partridge, the Co-Minister of Agriculture, spoke to the farmers in late July about the 'great deal of uncertainty and some pretty low morale'. His explanation was that there was about to be a change of government and 'we have no confidence in that change'.[44] By August white Rhodesia was thoroughly disillusioned. Bill Irvine, a Co-Minister in the Transitional government, put it bluntly: the electorate would probably vote 'No' at the promised referendum and he could only agree with its assessment.[45]

Smith did have some comfort to offer: 'we have had 15 of the most wonderful years in our history.'[46] The missionaries and farmers might have disagreed. A spate of deaths were bearing out Walls's comment, made two days after the Smith speech, that the 'terrorists' had switched their attention from the TTLs to white civilians and economic targets.[47] Twenty foreign missionaries were killed in June, apparently in an attempt to close down mission schools in the rural areas.[48] The incident which aroused world attention and sent the Rhodesians into a frenzy was the massacre at Elim Mission on 23 June. Despite attempts to blame the Selous Scouts,[49] a ZANLA group was probably responsible for the murder of six women, three men, and four children at the Pentecostal school in the Vumba mountains. Caute records that the thirteen had been taken from their rooms to the playing fields and there 'beaten with logs, stabbed with bayonets, hatcheted, raped, mutilated in some cases'.[50] Pamela Lynn, who was just three weeks old, was bayoneted through the head. White Rhodesia was enraged. All its darkest prejudices and fears poured out in the next few days, diverted – momentarily – in Salisbury by the problem of obtaining tickets for the forthcoming rugby encounter with Northern Transvaal. Rhodesian minds managed to remain clear enough to draw an important distinction. Roger Hawkins and P. K. van der Byl referred in parliament to an incident on 14 May where fifty-two African civilians had been 'killed in cross-fire' when the Security Forces stormed a village near Gutu. The two ministers castigated African MPs for attempting 'to equate accidental and unintentional deaths in the field by cross-fire with deliberate cold-blooded murder which has not been equalled since the concentration camps of Dachau and Buchenwald'.[51]

Most Rhodesians were finding it difficult in 1978 to comprehend or forgive the failure of the blacks to compensate the whites for all their 'sacrifices' in accepting the Salisbury Agreement. There were several avenues available in late June and during July to express their general disenchantment. The RF caucus used the Address in Reply to denounce or chide the Executive Council for its lack of progress. The Chief Whip admitted that the criticism in the party room was both frank and wide-spread.[52] There was a by-election for Highlands North set for 21 July where, in a low poll, the RF share of the vote fell from 70 per cent in 1977 to 49 per cent, NUF improved from 20.5 to 32 per cent, and the RAP vote rose from 9.5 to 19 per cent. If, in one sense, the RF had little to fear because the opposition parties were poles apart, it was disturbing that even its own supporters were complaining about a lack of leadership and were obviously unhappy with the record of the Transitional government. Another opportunity to express disquiet was the annual congress of the RNFU held over 25-6 July.[53] The President of the Rhodesian Tobacco Association was forthright: morale was 'very low', in part because the government could not provide adequate farm protection just ten weeks before the start of the planting season. Roger Hawkins offered little comfort. He pointed out that emigration had cost '700 bayonets' from the Territorials since the beginning of 1978. The farmers also taxed the white co-ministers and, in particular, Cronje, over the maintenance of standards and the Executive Council's apparent inactivity. After one nebulous response, Cronje was given the plain truth: 'just like his Prime Minister, he has told us nothing.'

An occasional voice spoke out against the prevailing mood. Trevor Dollar, Chairman of the Chamber of Commerce in Gwelo and soon to become an RF MP, attacked the 'pathetically negative' attitude of 'many Europeans': the Executive Council must be supported against the unacceptable alternative; too much was expected of it too soon; there was now an opportunity of working with the Council, 'which has the backing and support of the vast majority of the African people', to build a multiracial state and prosperity for all.[54] Dollar's comments neatly pinpointed the problem: the whites thought that the onus was on the Executive Council to make a success of the internal settlement. In their view, the time to tackle racial discrimination was after the Transitional government had achieved a cease-fire.

The government began addressing the discrimination issue on 8 August when it declared that all public places, industrial sites, and trading centres would be open to all races and that legislation would remove the power of local authorities to provide separate facilities and ensure that enfranchised persons could vote in local government elections in their area of residence. An editorial in the *Rhodesia Herald* pointed out that the Transitional government was acting 'as if it had all the time in the world', and the President of ACCOR said bluntly that these measures 'did not add up to a row of beans'.[55] Some Rhodesians did try to do more. Members of the Rhodesian Medical Association, worried that African sensitivities might lead to the nationalisation of health services under majority rule, sought the appointment of black medical staff to European hospitals and the extension of medical aid schemes to cover more Africans.[56] The RNFU council failed to obtain the two-thirds majority necessary to change the name of the farmers' peak organisation,[57] but the *Rhodesia Herald* dropped the word 'Rhodesia' on 15 August, the Salisbury Chamber of Commerce elected its first African Vice-President in September, the Red Cross appointed a black Chairman on 1 October, and in November the State Lottery dropped the word 'Rhodesia' and the prestigious Salisbury Sports Club agreed to admit

African members. Slowly – very slowly – a few Rhodesians were beginning to break down the barriers.

Even the apparent successes of the Transitional government simply intensified the sense of gloom. On Sunday, 13 August, a television programme introduced Rhodesians to Comrade Max. He was the product of a campaign begun in April to use former 'terrorists' to assist in restoring or maintaining the government's control in the TTLs. Originally organised by Special Branch, the scheme soon created its own problems in the form of ill-disciplined and murderous 'private armies' which served the political objectives of the internal nationalists.[58] By early 1979, when transformed into the Security Force Auxiliaries and, on the recommendation of PSYOPS given the name of 'Pfumo re Vanhu' ('Spear of the People'), the 'Army' which supported the UANC did perform a valuable counter-insurgency function. The obsession with secrecy, however, meant that white Rhodesia was ill-prepared for the appearance of Comrade Max in August 1978. The former 'guerrilla',[59] wearing an animal skin Davy Crockett cap and denims and warmly embracing an ecstatic Bishop Muzorewa, declared that he was the new DC of the Msana TTL and was responsible for education and other civil services and for maintaining a free zone between the Security Forces and the Patriotic Front. While the aim of the programme was to prove that the cease-fire was working, the effect was a public relations disaster. The government had not explained its policy of employing former 'terrorists', nor did the programme explain that Comrade Max was under the command of the Security Forces and that the police and Internal Affairs remained responsible for normal administration in his area. Roger Hawkins announced that Max was just 'unsophisticated' about interviews and had got 'excited' and 'carried away'. Hawkins could not, however, allay white fears that the internal settlement would install the likes of Comrade Max in power. Illusions could protect morale but white confidence might not survive an encounter which confirmed the worst suspicions about reality.[60]

Ian Smith blamed the low white morale on the failure to achieve a cease-fire and on the bickering between and within the internal African parties.[61] Just after this interview, Smith flew to Zambia for a secret meeting with Joshua Nkomo. On 14 August the two 'Matabeles' reached a remarkable accord whereby Nkomo would return to Salisbury as Chairman of the Executive Council. CIO had been involved in setting up the negotiations and Flower, whose ambivalent role in the whole business suggests that he was uncertain just whose cause he was serving, implies that the deal might have worked.[62] Kaunda wanted it, Smith *may* have accepted it, Nkomo grasped at it, and Sithole and Muzorewa had become expendable. Whether or not the participants were sincere, two things at least are clear: when the details were prematurely disclosed in late August there was a blazing row between the two factions of the Patriotic Front and between Nkomo and Nyerere;[63] and the white Rhodesians, the last perhaps to know of their leader's machinations, were quite bewildered.

The country was then in mourning because the respected John Wrathall had died suddenly on 31 August.[64] Many young Rhodesians had something else on their minds. Fifty-nine school-leavers sent a letter to the *Herald* at the end of August asking the familiar question – 'What are we fighting for?' – and complaining that their elders could never provide a definitive answer. Ian Smith spoke on 1 September at the official opening of the Salisbury Show where he addressed that very issue: Rhodesians were fighting, he said, to restore peace and to maintain standards and an efficient economy.[65] The Prime Minister was warmly applauded.

Two days after Smith's speech, and eleven minutes after taking off from Kariba, bound for Salisbury with fifty-two passengers and four crew members on board, Captain John Hood of Air Rhodesia's flight RH825 radioed a distress signal.[66] His Viscount then disappeared near the Urungwe TTL. Wreckage was spotted from the air the next morning, and a ground search arrived soon after. Thirty-eight bodies were found in and around the aircraft, obviously victims of the crash. Another ten were heaped together a short distance away, all of them shot dead. Three survivors were found near the scene, and another five – who had walked off looking for help – were located later. A macabre story soon emerged. A heat-seeking SAM-7 missile had hit the inner starboard engine. Captain Hood almost executed a safe crash landing in a cotton field except for the last moment when the Viscount hit a ditch and broke up. The tail section broke away and eighteen lives were saved. Half an hour after the crash, and after the five had gone for help, a group of 'terrorists' appeared on the crash scene and ordered the remaining survivors to assemble whereupon they opened fire with their AK-47s. Three started running and got away, and watched as the 'terrorists' looted the aircraft before finally leaving.

For days on end, white Rhodesia was overwhelmed by shock, grief, and anger, a reaction strengthened by the further news that Umtali's residential suburbs were rocketed on the night of 8 September.[67] The demand for instant retaliation extended through the Security Forces, stopping only when it reached Walls.[68] The anger increased with the news that Nkomo had claimed credit for downing the plane – while denying that ZIPRA had killed any survivors – and had accused Air Rhodesia of ferrying troops and military equipment. A false report that he had laughed (or 'cackled') merely strengthened demands for revenge.[69] So did the stories of individual and family tragedies circulated in the media, spelt out in the condolence columns, and passed around by word of mouth. Although the names were not released it was reported that two of the ten murdered survivors were children and that another six were women. Eight of the ten, therefore, were the traditional 'innocents'. Cheryl Tilley, the sister of the schoolboy killed by 'terrorists' in January, did not survive the incident, nor did her fiancé. Captain Hood and his co-pilot died on impact and became instant heroes because of their skilful and valiant attempts to save the aircraft. Hood's own story saddened its readers. A Bulawayo boy, with 8,000 flying hours, he had two young daughters by a previous marriage. A happy photograph recorded his remarriage just three months prior to the crash. One prominent Asian family was especially devastated; eight of its members were killed. There were also the customary tales of distraught relatives waiting for news, of people who joined the flight unexpectedly, and of others who had a miraculous change of plans.

By coincidence, there was a routine meeting of NATJOC set down for 4 September where Ian Smith was expected to press for tougher military action against the 'terrorists'. Ken Flower observed that Walls kept the session within bounds but also noted that the sense of outrage 'took some time to develop'.[70] Outrage was certainly evident by 6 September when parliament met to debate the estimates. By then the execution of the ten survivors was uppermost in members' minds.[71] The killers became 'vermin', 'sub-humans', 'Neanderthal', 'animals'. Their pre-sumed backers – most notably Owen, Carter, and Andrew Young – were, in the words of the Afrikaner farmer who represented Karoi, 'dripping with blood – blood from the innocent and helpless'. The RF's Chief Whip assured the government that feeling was 'running high about this matter' as members canvassed the potential responses: more raids into Zambia, the imposition of martial law, a general mobilisation. Wing Commander Gaunt wanted a nation-wide curfew and the shoot-ing of any curfew-breakers as 'terrorists'. Ministers hastily assured their back-bench that there would be some form of retaliation. Irvine warned that Rhodesians 'will not let these innocents go unavenged' and promised the Patriotic Front 'that those who seek to ride the wind, will reap the whirlwind'. Ian Smith promised something more definite: on 9 September he told parliament that Rhodesian patience had been tested too far and it was now time to embark upon 'a positive and firm course'.

Calmer voices could not compete with the wrath of a society. Bishop Paul Burrough appealed to Rhodesians not to seek revenge and to remember that 'the most grievous suffering is still among the defenceless people in the tribal trust lands'. A spokesman for the mourning Asian family pleaded for peace and said he feared retaliation.[72] But the words urging caution, brotherly love, and reconciliation were ignored in the memorial services held around Rhodesia on the following Friday. The spirit of the Old Testament prevailed over the New. John da Costa, Dean of the Anglican All Saints Cathedral in Salisbury, observed that the 2,500 mourners who crammed into the cathedral, or listened outside, ignored one part of his sermon.[73] Looking directly at Smith and other senior figures in the front pew, the Dean spoke of the blameworthiness of politicians who made opportunistic speeches, and of men who called themselves Christians who treated other human beings as expendable and did not show enough real love and understanding. He also wondered how clergymen (such as Muzorewa and Sithole), who were supposed to be great reconcilers, could involve themselves in divisive politics. These comments were soon forgotten. What mattered was the Dean's tirade against those whose bestiality 'stinks in the nostrils of Heaven' and those leaders whose 'silence' in condemning the atrocities was 'deafening'.[74] Outside the cathedral two men held placards one of which told Smith what to say to Nkomo at their next meeting: 'GO TO HELL you MURDERING BASTARD'. The Dean and Bishop Burrough wanted the demonstrators to leave. Some of the crowd agreed. It was not the time or the place for political spectacle. Yet the RF back-bench, most of the electorate, the hot bloods in the Security Forces, and the demonstrators outside All Saints Cathedral all wanted that message delivered to the Patriotic Front.

For all the talk about reprisals, the immediate options were limited. Air raids or air-land attacks required careful planning and their financial cost and the loss of Western support might outweigh any emotional and military gains. A general mobilisation would simply be disastrous for the economy. The advantages of martial law were not so obvious either. According to Flower, all the officials on NATJOC opposed 'martial licence'. Walls was totally opposed to the concept: the Security Forces already possessed all the legal powers necessary to maintain law and order and the officials recognised that the war was being lost and that the answer lay in a political settlement.[75] A declaration of martial law might create an impression of positive action but would not reverse the deteriorating situation inside Rhodesia's borders. These political considerations eventually prevailed, and NATJOC agreed to implement a limited and ill-defined form of martial law coupled with a ban on the internal wings of the Patriotic Front and a public warning to Zambia and Mozambique about the continued harbouring of 'terrorists'. There was just one complication: Roger Hawkins, the ailing Minister of Combined Operations, when pressed to order executions under martial law, broke down and cried. Walls assumed the authority to confirm any death sentences and the white Co-Ministers of Defence and of Justice and Law and Order (Hilary Squires and Chris Andersen) were required to add their signatures.[76]

Smith announced the NATJOC decisions on 11 September.[77] He made his now-familiar denunciation of the British and American governments whom he blamed for the escalation of 'terrorism' and for the Elim and Viscount 'massacres', and he accused Julius Nyerere of being the 'evil genius' behind Nkomo. The Prime Minister admitted that his contacts with Kaunda and Nkomo had become unpopular but insisted that these negotiations had been in the best interests of the country and would resume if necessary. The 'stroke of fate' – as Smith called the Viscount incident – may have horrified him; it also saved him from having to sell Nkomo to a suspicious electorate.[78] Forced back upon his colleagues in the Transitional government, Smith made the best of the situation by calling upon the Rhodesians to exercise their virtues of ingenuity, energy, resourcefulness, and 'well-known and well-acclaimed valour'. They should accept his measures and eschew the desperate alternatives of capitulation or making a do-or-die stand.

He knew that his earlier remarks in parliament had fuelled some unrealistic expectations. The *Herald*, which had previously urged caution, described Smith's speech as a 'damp squib', and claimed that the overwhelming public response was one of bitter disappointment.[79] A minority opinion was that he could do little else. Relieved that Smith had not launched a programme of vengeance, NUF accused him of incompetent leadership and called for his resignation and the formation of a national government. The RAP was predictably contemptuous, and called for a 'ruthless prosecution of the war'. Ever hopeful, the party expected a surge in support following Smith's apparent failure to read the mood of the electorate. Once again, it was disappointed. In no time, the electorate resumed its customary position of accepting that 'Smithy' was doing his best.

The Security Forces immediately provided the government with a useful statistic. A press release on 15 September announced that the Security Forces had 'notched-up their highest kill rate against internal terrorists for any two-week period since hostilities began in December 1972'.[80] A total of 165 'communist terrorists' had been 'exterminated' and thirty-eight collaborators or recruits had been 'eradicated'. The other 'good' news was that martial law was being progressively imposed. The government's position, however, was highly ambivalent, as evidenced in a long press release issued on 27 September. For while it was anxious to bolster white morale by demonstrating that special courts martial were providing swift and effective 'justice' and that the priority was to combat 'terrorism' rather than to observe the niceties of law and order, the government also wanted to prove that martial law need not affect law-abiding citizens, did not mean 'the arbitrary and traumatic interruption of civil life', and did not affect the ordinary working of the law, the administration, business, or parliament.[81] COMOPS had, however, announced that all cases must be heard in camera, allowing the special courts martial to exercise their sweeping powers of trying and sentencing offenders and of destroying property and possessions without facing public scrutiny.[82] At the end of the year the government issued another statement denying that it was conducting 'kangaroo courts': only Company Commanders, Squadron Leaders, Police Superintendents, DCs, or equivalent levels could exercise martial law powers; no one below the rank of major or who was not a prominent local citizen could preside over the courts martial; court decisions were subject to stringent conditions and each death sentence had to satisfy the three-man Review Authority before being carried out.[83] The civilised society did not wish to appear uncivilised just because it was obliged to take uncivilised action against the barbarians.

Martial law was not the sweet revenge which so many Rhodesians craved. For that, they had to wait until well into October, when airborne raids hit three ZIPRA bases in Zambia. Variously described as transit centres, training grounds, or refugee camps, they were attacked because the political necessity for a morale-boosting action coincided with a growing feeling inside COMOPS that external strikes would prolong Rhodesian resistance and slow down the rate of penetration. CIO opposed the decision and it is possible that Flower was denied details of the operation because of a suspicion about his contacts with the British. His argument was that external raids would widen the conflict without necessarily assisting the Rhodesian cause.[84] The Viscount disaster, however, had thwarted the minority in NATJOC who wanted to push exclusively for a settlement. It was now imperative to take the risk. The result – in purely military and morale terms – seemed to justify the action. Over 1,600 ZIPRA members or supporters were killed in three separate raids, tonnes of weapons and material were destroyed, valuable intelligence was collected, and Rhodesian losses consisted of one helicopter, one dead soldier, and two injured airmen.

The important action – for boosting white morale – occurred early in the morning of 19 October. Four Canberras, eight Hunters, and four helicopter gunships – or 'K (Kill) cars' as they were known – attacked ZIPRA's 'Freedom Camp' at Westlands Farm just 20 km north of Lusaka. CIO had collected some useful intelligence and, armed with special Rhodesian-designed anti-personnel bombs, the invaders delivered a precise and devastating blow.[85] They also achieved a propaganda coup. After completing his bombing run on Westlands Farm, the Squadron Leader who commanded Green Section (the four Canberras) and whose call-sign was 'Green Leader', read out a prepared message to the Lusaka control tower. His words were delivered 'with clarity and determined emphasis':[86]

Green Leader: Ah, Tower, this is Green Leader. This is a message for the station commander at Mumbwa [the Zambian Air Force base alongside the civilian aerodrome] from the Rhodesian Air Force. We are attacking the terrorist base at Westlands Farm at this time. This attack is against Rhodesian dissidents and not against Zambia. Rhodesia has no quarrel – repeat no quarrel – with Zambia or her security forces. We therefore ask you not to intervene or oppose our attack. However, we are orbiting your airfields at this time and are under orders to shoot down any Zambian aircraft which does not comply with this request and attempts to take off. Did you copy all that?

Lusaka Tower: Copied.

Green Leader: Roger. Thanks. Cheers.

On Sunday, 22 October, three days after the attack, the RBC replayed excerpts from the tape taken from Green Leader's Canberra.[87] The segment was introduced with the comment that, for thirty minutes, the Rhodesians were 'virtually in control of Zambian airspace'. Then, in succession, the Rhodesian public heard Green Leader's prepared message to Lusaka Tower; a question from the air traffic controller asking if civilian aircraft might take off, whether 'you have no objections', and Green Leader's reply that there was no objection but 'hang on ... for a short while, half an hour or so'; a request that Green Leader should keep 'a listening watch on this frequency, so we can ask you what we want to ask'; a question 'What do I call you?' to which the reply was 'Green Leader'; Lusaka Tower's request to Green Leader (which was granted) that he should change frequencies – provided it was 'not inconvenient to you' (tape indistinct) – in order to obtain clearer messages; a further question about permission for two civilian aircraft to take off and the response to hold them for another ten minutes; Green Leader's request to the air traffic controller to contact Dolphin-3, the airborne command post which took over from the Canberra as the latter was heading back to base; and, finally, Dolphin-3's instructions that all civilian aircraft should not take off for ten minutes, that an incoming Kenya Airways flight could land at Lusaka, and that the Zambian Air Force must remain on the ground. The RBC commentary concluded:

As positive Rhodesian control of Zambian airspace was maintained with the assistance of the Lusaka controller, the Kenyan airlines flight was allowed to land after a short delay and all the Rhodesian military aircraft returned safely to base.

There was a 'final footnote'. It was reported that the captain of the Kenya Airways flight asked the control tower, 'Who has priority here anyway?' and was informed, 'Well, I think the Rhodesians do at this time.'

Judging by the public response, the repeated broadcasts on 22 October immediately lifted white spirits. Green Leader became a cult figure, and young 'Rhodies' sported T-shirts celebrating his exploits and proclaiming Zambia's humiliation. Peter Armstrong, a popular local author, who clearly had access to the full tape recording, quickly produced a novel where the raid on Westlands Farm was a central feature.[88] Armstrong also reproduced Green Leader's first message to Lusaka Tower. John Edmond, a New Zealand-born performer of 'troopie' songs, included Green Leader's speech in a number which immortalised the 'sky warrior': 'he is a man, a very special kind.' According to Edmond, Green Leader went into battle believing that his motherland 'had gone through hell', and that the choice was to 'kill or see the children killed'. The writer imagined the hero uttering the familiar complaint: 'my little country cries for peace; no one will hear her case at least.' Now he, and Rhodesia, would strike back: 'No one in the world to heed her. Tomorrow the world will know Green Leader.'

In fact the world was denied part of the story because the authorities released only a sanitised version of the original tape.[89] The cavalier of the skies, the avenging angel, was in reality an ordinary mortal. Like his crew he was tense and anxious as the Canberra screamed towards its target. Once the bombs had been dropped, and he looked down at the havoc he had helped to cause and searched for his prepared speech, Green Leader began shouting some 'choice obscenities'. Two sympathetic authors have pointed out that this reaction was 'not unusual in such a combination of exhilaration and stress'.[90] Still, if broadcast, his words might have tarnished the image projected inside Rhodesia.

Beautiful! Jesus Christ, you want to see all those fuckers ... The fucking bombs were beautiful ... Fucking beautiful ... Roger, let me just get on to the fucking tower and give them our bloody message. Where's this fucking piece of shit? ... Fucking hundreds of the cunts. Fucking magnificent ... Jesus, those fucking Kaffirs everywhere ... Yah, they've got the K-cars in there. They'll have a beautiful time. They're like fucking ants running around there ... Just check that tape recorder ... OK, let me try and get this spiel off ... Lusaka Tower, this is Green Leader.

The representatives of Christian civilisation – even under extreme pressure – were not really meant to think or talk in that way. Fortunately, after Green Leader had read his message to Lusaka Tower, and it was obvious that the Rhodesians controlled the airspace, the voices on the tape, including those reporting from the K-cars, became calm, authoritative, and businesslike. The language improved and the Rhodesia which believed itself to be civilised was back in command.

V

In addition to obtaining a cease-fire, the Executive Council had three important functions to perform in 1978: to pursue international recognition, supervise the removal of racial discrimination, and to prepare a constitution and independence elections. The Bishop introduced a fourth: the opening up of the Protected Villages.

Brigadier Campling, who commanded Op Hurricane in 1978, acknowledged in June that the internal 'Afronats' had persuaded the Council to open the PVs by 31 December 1978, the first projected date for 'independence'.[91] Concerned about the effectiveness of PVs in Hurricane, Campling was even more worried about the new policy: the 'Communist Terrorists' (CTs) would claim a propaganda victory, the morale of farmers would fall, and it would be more difficult to hold an election. By 31 August, when he issued orders for a phased opening of selected PVs, Campling recognised the need to enhance the credibility of the Transitional government.[92] Significantly, his two priorities were to prevent the CTs from claiming a triumph and to mollify those white farmers who were bound to feel more vulnerable. Campling suggested that the DCs should hold confidential meetings with the farmers of the Centenary/Mount Darwin/Mtoko area to explain that the exercise was designed to release more members of Guard Force for defensive duties on white farms. The deliberate lie was a way of saving face. There was a much stronger case for PVs in 1978 than in 1974,[93] except that the whites lacked the manpower and commitment to make them work and that – on this occasion – the Bishop's political needs had to override white conservatism. Reluctantly taken, the decision to open the PVs meant bowing to necessity while trying to present a defeat as a victory, all the time being primarily concerned about the implications for white morale and for maintaining physical control of the TTLs.[94]

Smith and Sithole arrived in the United States on 7 October to pursue the higher matter of international recognition. Joined later by Muzorewa and Chirau, the Executive Council had discussions in the State Department with the British Ambassador and the Acting Secretary of State. The mission agreed to the idea of an all-party conference. Although the visit to the State Department on 20 October coincided with the Zambian raids, which were not well received by the Carter Administration,[95] and although he got little more than a sympathetic hearing Smith regarded the mission as 'a clear victory for us' because the United States had agreed to a conference 'without preconditions'.[96] Meanwhile, at home, the Rhodesians were misled by the media into believing that new ground had been broken in the quest for a settlement, a cease-fire, and international recognition.

One of the anticipated propaganda victories of the Washington visit totally misfired. Before leaving for the United States, Muzorewa announced on 10 October that all racial discrimination in Rhodesia would be abolished: he said, 'I am so happy I could jump off the roof.'[97] Rhodesian liberals, the Catholic Commission for Justice and Peace, and outside commentators promptly pointed out that the war was not being fought to give blacks access to white suburbs, hospitals, and schools and that the inability to pay represented a formidable barrier to racial integration.[98] The liberal critics had a point. Rowan Cronje himself described the decisions as 'a victory for moderation. It was a compromise.'[99] He said that the ultra-left and the extreme right would not be satisfied because the aim was to meet the aspirations of black Rhodesians without arousing the fears of the whites. While the Bishop had spoken for the aspirations, Cronje addressed the apprehensions. He pointed out that the opening of the white residential areas would be subject to certain conditions: no more than one family (defined as one set of parents and their children) may live on each property and the character and standard of these areas must be maintained. Cronje also announced an ingenious system for preserving the European composition and character of the existing white government schools. High fee-paying schools would enrol only those children who were proficient in English, were approximate to the average age of their appropriate class, and whose parents owned or leased property in a zoned area. A second form of protection was to be the community school, an idea borrowed from India, whereby a community could purchase its school from the government, appoint its own board of governors, and maintain its exclusive identity. So while racial discrimination might have disappeared in name, differentials in income would, in one way or another, maintain the Rhodesian way of life.

There were always 'mechanical problems' which slowed down the rate of change. The Umtali Town Clerk said that, until the Land Tenure Act was formally repealed, the Umtali Council was not going to allow Africans to buy or lease in European residential areas even though there were plenty of vacant houses.[100] An Asian and Coloured school in Southerton, Salisbury, remained half-empty and closed to Africans because the Education Act remained in force.[101] The parcel of eight bills, designed to remove land, local government, health, and education discrimination from the statute books, was not introduced until late December, when the Transitional government also announced increases of up to 200 per cent in school fees and disclosed that only property owners and certain classes of occupiers would have the vote in local government elections. The education legislation was delayed beyond the start of the 1979 school year with the result that in Waterfalls African children and their parents arrived at schools which had places but no authority to fill them. Cronje said he had no intention of breaking the law so the children had to be sent away.[102]

No matter what laws were being changed there were elements on the RF back-bench who maintained the spirit of the past. One MP said that blacks looked upon the Transitional government as the means of providing 'peace and stability, universal employment, full cooking pots, a two-day week and three wives for every male'.[103] While ostensibly supporting the repeal of the Land Tenure Act, Don Goddard spoke in favour of racial discrimination which, he believed, was introduced so that 'we might live under the most harmonious conditions that we find ourselves in Africa'. He said that attacks on the Land Tenure Act were inspired by political opportunists and were supported by world leaders who imagined that discrimination was responsible for all the ills of the black man. He assured the African MPs that repeal meant 'the end of paternalism in Rhodesia':

... no longer does the white man carry the black man on his shoulders, now it is a question of every man for himself – buddy, you stand on your own two feet and those of them who are intelligent enough to realise it will see that it is a retrograde step, as opposed to being the marvellous thing they imagine it will be.[104]

Goddard was unrepentant, even when he was disowned by his own side. He was worried that the high fee-paying schools would eventually become all-black and argued that where blacks numbered more than 40 per cent (no matter which social class they came from) standards were sure to fall. He also opposed the Bill to end discrimination in public premises, believing that it would lead to enforced integration.[105]

For all these qualifications, the decision to abolish racial discrimination was, in terms of the Rhodesian past and of what it meant to the whites, quite revolutionary. The RF had won its elections promising to maintain standards by continuing to segregate services on grounds of race. Integration evoked images of European children sitting in classes with older, less-advanced Africans, of overcrowded and dirty hospitals serviced by under-qualified medical staff, of clean and neat suburbs becoming littered with filth, full of noisy extended families, and where the sewerage, general plumbing, and electricity services had collapsed, The majority of Rhodesians retained these images after October 1978: having accepted that change was inevitable, they hoped for the best and expected the worst.

Alongside the preparations to remove discrimination, the relevant ministers and law officers were attempting to write a new constitution. The original timetable – set in July 1978 – assumed that an independence ceremony would be held at midnight on 31 December. Smith announced on 29 October that this timetable had to be revised because of certain complications. The delay was caused, principally, by the attempts to ensure that the safeguards of 3 March would hold firm after independence. Muzorewa and Sithole knew that any hold-up would further undermine their credibility among blacks, a prospect which did not seem to trouble the white constitution-makers. Eventually, after a long and bitter exchange on the Executive Council over the delay, the Council announced on 30 November that majority rule elections would be held no later than 20 April 1979. Two further decisions highlighted white control over the transition and the determination to shore up white power. One was the proposal to create a 'Government of National Unity', providing for the proportional representation of all parties which secured five or more seats in the Assembly elections. Assuming that the RF won the white seats, its representatives would be assured of nearly one-third of the ministerial posts. The second decision was to name the new country 'Zimbabwe Rhodesia'. Even as they were dismantling the past, Rhodesia's leaders wanted to preserve its symbols. The effect was to undermine the standing of their supposed black allies and, thereby, to lessen the credibility of the internal settlement. And, for once, a compensatory gesture towards the feelings of white Rhodesia did not inspire any real gratitude. Every faction of white politics greeted the name of 'Zimbabwe Rhodesia' with incredulity, dismay, or laughter.

The whites-only referendum was held on 30 January 1979. The campaign was held against a background of a further deterioration in the security situation. Morale plummeted in the capital city when a rocket attack on 11 December led to the destruction of twenty-eight bulk storage oil tanks in Salisbury and a consequent loss of vital fuel supplies and a big increase in petrol prices. It was hardly comforting to learn later that the attack had been initiated by an African who had casually driven to the scene in a taxi and that the airport fire engines – which were properly equipped for such emergencies and situated close by – were required to remain on airport duty. The news over December-January was almost uniformly bleak:[106] the authorities had been obliged to extend martial law to cover 70 per cent of the country; twenty-six white farmers and fifty-eight members of the Security Forces were killed in this period; there was a record net emigration of 2,771 whites in December; and Rollo Hayman, the Co-Minister for Internal Affairs who was responsible for organising the April elections, resigned because he thought the new constitution would not win international recognition, would not end the war, and would lead to a Marxist takeover.[107]

The referendum campaign itself was spirited enough even though the result was a foregone conclusion. Aside from the meetings addressed by Smith, the audiences were generally small. Smith's constant refrain was that a 'No' vote would embarrass 'our friends', that Rhodesians could not expect a better deal, that the proponents of the 'No' cause were unable to offer a workable alternative, and that, like it or not, and he did not, the whites would have to accept black rule. He was, at times, uncompromisingly blunt. But the old Smithy was never far away, telling audiences what he 'honestly believed', accusing the opposition of delivering 'a complete pack of lies', and practising his own conjuring tricks.[108] He admitted that there were no absolute guarantees for the whites. Nevertheless, he urged an audience of 1,200 in a Bulawayo hall to support the new constitution on the ground that the rest of the world had rejected it for being 'so good' in giving 'the white man too much'.[109] So the voters could support a constitution which needed world recognition to achieve its objectives, precisely because the world had rejected it. Smith then shamelessly declared that there was a 50-50 chance of international recognition, without ever presenting any justification for his optimism. A few right-wingers and young troopies were less gullible than the traditional RF loyalists and Smith was repeatedly heckled at the most hostile meetings he faced since becoming Prime Minister.[110] He was safe, however, because a sense of resignation had spread throughout white Rhodesia. A woman who attended a Smith meeting in Umtali summed it up: 'We don't like it (the new constitution), but there is no alternative.'[111]

The right-wing opposition tried hard. The Save Our Nation campaign was launched at a meeting in Salisbury on 5 January when the RAP and other bodies joined with Strath Brown of the defunct Rhodesia Party and people who had not before declared any political affiliation.[112] Within days, however, the opposition was divided. Whereas the RAP types and Len Idensohn's RNP opposed any form of majority rule, Save Our Nation merely rejected the proposed 1979 version because it would not mean international recognition or the end of sanctions, and because it would result in a mass white exodus, a longer delay in obtaining peace, and the formation of a minority black government. Its analysis was accurate and compelling but its expectations were quite unrealistic. Somehow a 'No' vote was supposed to force the present parliament to achieve peace, a return to legality, the lifting of sanctions, and a restoration of black and white confidence. Somehow the 'surrender' of power could be delayed until the Transitional government had completed the commitments made under the Salisbury Agreement.[113]

The RAP's solution was characteristically straightforward: reject the constitution, install a federal system, form a large professional white army, remove the call-up, stop worrying about the unattainable international recognition, believe that South Africa would support a stable government and oppose a Marxist take-over, support UDI, and win the war. Voting 'No' would still mean a bad time for Rhodesians, but at least they will 'have kept something worth fighting for' and there was 'every prospect of getting back on top of the security situation'.[114] It was a policy full of beguiling simplicities, promising what could never be delivered. Moreover, it blatantly misrepresented Rhodesia's potential saviour. Pik Botha immediately set the record straight: the South African government was not favourably disposed to the RAP's solution and had not taken sides in the debate. Pretoria believed that the Salisbury Agreement was a step in the right direction.[115] Just as it had done in the 1977 election, South Africa removed the RAP's 'guarantee' for a 'white Rhodesia'.

NUF's reaction to the referendum was outwardly sensible. Whatever the outcome, the war would continue, there would be no peace. The way ahead was to seek a return to legality and to participate in an all-party conference. How, then, should NUF members vote in the referendum? The council considered five forms of advice: vote 'No'; vote 'Yes'; abstain; vote 'No' or abstain; spoil the ballot paper. After a long debate it was decided to treat the referendum as a 'non-event': to vote 'No' might look like opposition to majority rule; to vote 'Yes' might be construed as support for a racial constitution. On the other hand, these intrepid and articulate liberals could hardly opt out altogether. Why not go to the polls and write a letter on the ballot paper supporting a return to legality? In the real world, only the impotent are pure.[116]

The referendum was white Rhodesia's last community debate. As the *Herald* observed on the eve of the poll, the campaign was confused and frustrating because of the extravagant claims and counter-claims, and because both the 'Yes' and 'No' cases were based on speculation and hope.[117] The 'No' supporters tried hard to evoke a sense of guilt and obligation. Save Our Nation published several advertisements under the heading 'THE GOVERNMENT IS ASKING YOU TO VOTE FOR THE SAME THINGS RHODESIANS HAVE DIED FIGHTING AGAINST'. In one, a young war widow, who had a six-month-old baby and a two-year-old son, told how she answered her little boy's question 'Why did Daddy die?' by telling him that 'the joking, fun-loving guy' who was his father, and who could never do enough for others, had been killed fighting for the future of his country. She asked the electorate to ensure that her husband had not died in vain.[118] The 'Yes' campaign could hardly counter this kind of advertising. Mark Partridge openly admitted in a letter to his Salisbury constituents that a 'Yes' vote did not guarantee Western recognition or the end of the war. He just hoped that 'men of goodwill' would get together to confound 'the communists' and that God would assist Rhodesians to achieve what was right and honourable.[119] As for winning the referendum, the RF relied upon the name of 'Good Old Smithy' and upon its perception that the electorate was sick of the war.

It was indeed a tired, defeated, and sombre electorate – 71.5 per cent of the 94,000 registered voters – which, on 30 January, produced 57,269 'Yes' votes (84.4 per cent of the returned ballot papers) in favour of a constitution which none of the whites actually wanted.[120] The 'Rhodesian solution', the cause of such hostility abroad, did not inspire any great enthusiasm among its presumed white beneficiaries.

Ian Smith interpreted the 'Yes' majority as evidence of the coolness and realism of the Rhodesian electorate. An irate 'Proud Rhodesian Patriot' from Fort Victoria explained the outcome in a different way: the 'No' case had been defeated by the 'money-grubbers', by those 'enslaved by their charismatic idol', or by those who tried to buy six months' time while they prepared to emigrate or believed that Rhodesia would not go the same way as the rest of Africa.[121] Disillusioned by the 1977 election result, the far right in early 1979 railed against what it saw as the cowardly and supine behaviour of the white electorate. Ina Bursey of the RAP accused Rhodesians of selling their soul to the devil, and said they deserved 'to reap the fruits of the whirlwind'. As a parting shot she announced that the RAP would be dissolved – which it was on 3 February – and asked that the 'No' voters should be allowed to depart in peace carrying their hard-won assets.[122] The RAP had scored just one minor victory in the poster war. When the Transitional government issued an advertisement declaring that 'if you vote "No", Nkomo and Mugabe will dance in the streets of Moscow', the RAP responded: 'if you vote "Yes", [they] will dance in Cecil Square: better they dance in Moscow.' Neither side seemed aware that in 1979 Robert Mugabe was unlikely to receive or welcome an invitation to visit the Soviet Union.

On 31 January, the day after the referendum, a number of senior officers of the Security Forces attended a dinner at Cranborne Barracks to mark the 17th anniversary of the formation of the RLI.[123] It was a convivial evening, until Ron Reid Daly, the Commander of the Selous Scouts and a former RSM of the RLI, asked if he might make a speech. Reid Daly had just learnt that his telephone had been 'bugged', apparently on the orders of Lieutenant-General Hickman, the Army Commander. The saga began in mid-1978 when a disenchanted Scout alleged that some of his colleagues were collecting 'black and white gold' (guns and ivory) in the 'frozen areas' from which other units were excluded, and were then selling the goods to contacts in South Africa. Special Branch was called to investigate the activities of a particular individual who, forewarned of the raid, reportedly cleaned up the ivory 'factory' at the Inkomo Barracks near Salisbury. Lieutenant-Colonel John Redfern, the Director of Military Intelligence, then approached Hickman who, in August 1978, approved a plan to bug Reid Daly's office and to investigate his files.[124] Major Des Fountain, Director of Military Counter-intelligence, ran the operation which, far from assuming sinister overtones, quickly degenerated into farce. A captain in the Selous Scouts, who was supposed to monitor the bug, went out on operations and did not arrange a replacement. As a result, the listening device did not have a listener. Redfern himself 'forgot' about the operation until 29 January 1979 when a signals officer found the bug while he was moving the telephones from Reid Daly's office into some newly-completed barracks. Reid Daly was incensed, claiming that a spy could have overheard his calls to an agent in Zambia, thereby admitting that he used an open line to communicate with his agents. Walls tried to calm him down, promised an investigation, and asked him not to take any action pending its findings. If Reid Daly had intended to exercise restraint that resolve disappeared during the dinner at Cranborne Barracks.

Later described as being 'emotional and overwrought', Reid Daly turned to Hickman, the guest of honour, and began: 'I want to say to you Army Commander for bugging my telephone, thank you very much.' Raucous cheers prevented him from going any further: only a few of those present were sober or informed enough to realise that Reid Daly was not joking. He repeated his sentence, the company went silent, and he concluded: 'if I ever see you again it will be too soon.' Within moments the Army Commander and the Commander of the Selous Scouts were shouting at each other and squaring up for a fight. After Major-General MacIntyre and Colonel Bate, the Commanding Officer of the RLI, helped to pull them apart, Hickman demanded that Reid Daly be arrested for insubordination. A hurriedly-convened meeting of senior officers agreed that Reid Daly should be court-martialled. The case was eventually heard in camera, Reid Daly was reprimanded, and he later resigned from the Selous Scouts.[125]

On the morning after the fracas in the Officers' Mess, a 'family gathering' attended an anniversary ceremony at the Cranborne Barracks. Members of the RLI, former members, and next of kin listened to a reading of the Roll of Honour and watched the unveiling and dedication of 'The Trooper', a 300 kg memorial made from cartridge cases commemorating those who had died in the war.[126] Next day – 2 February – all eight anti-discrimination Bills were gazetted whereupon African children were admitted to formerly white government schools for the first time in Rhodesia's history. The large majority of white citizens of Salisbury would not have detected much difference. Schools reported only a handful of enquiries or provisional enrolments. In Umtali, the Town Clerk was unmoved by the changes. He said that six black families who had shifted into formerly white residential areas would not receive light or water until the municipality had actually sighted the *Gazette*. Given that the *Gazette*, issued on a Friday, would not reach Umtali until Monday, the six families had a whole weekend to ponder the thinking of a civilised white bureaucracy.[127]

VI

On 12 February 1979 another civilian Viscount was brought down by a heat-seeking missile just after taking off from Kariba. All fifty-nine people on board were killed outright. Sixteen days later – on 28 February – Ian Smith addressed parliament for the last time as Prime Minister.[128] He spoke mainly about Britain's 'treachery' and 'vindic-tiveness' and about the 'tragic stroke of fate' which meant that Rhodesia claimed its rightful independence at a time when it could be 'dragged down in the morass of British decadence and decline'. He praised 'those great Rhodesians' who contributed 'to what will go down in history as one of the most memorable stands against dictatorial aggression and oppression'. The voice occasionally faltered, the speaker was obviously overcome. When he finished, he slumped back into his seat, his head bowed. David Smith, the Minister of Finance, took his hand. There was a deep hurt but no sense of guilt. Everyone else had got it wrong.

8

'In a hell of a turmoil'

I

One election began and another ended the period from April 1979 to March 1980, the decisive months when political power was transferred from Rhodesia to Zimbabwe. The Rhodesians administered both operations, thereby ensuring the efficient demolition of their own authority. Neither election was wholly free or fair, yet neither could have been held at all without the painstaking efforts of Rhodesia's electoral officials and the massive call-up of white males to help protect the voters, the officials, and the ballot boxes. Rhodesia buried itself with considerable integrity and maximum bureaucratic effort.

The Rhodesians hoped that the international community would recognise the Bishop's government which was elected in April 1979. The UANC did obtain 67 per cent of the vote in a 64 per cent poll, or around 40 per cent of the total potential vote.[1] Muzorewa was more popular electorally than either the British Prime Minister or the American President, let alone those Commonwealth leaders who had abandoned the democratic process. Mrs Thatcher, elected to office with the British Conservatives in May, might have agreed, but the Foreign Office and various Commonwealth advisers persuaded her that the Patriotic Front must be brought into the fold before the 'Rhodesian problem' could be finally laid to rest. The Americans and the British withheld recognition when the Muzorewa government took office on 1 June 1979, and the Lusaka Commonwealth Heads of Government Meeting in August approved a plan for a constitutional conference at Lancaster House in London to try to negotiate an acceptable settlement. The main players all agreed to attend the Conference which opened on 10 September. Lord Carrington, the British Foreign Secretary, became the new ringmaster. He was supported behind the scenes by Presidents Kaunda and Machel who, as victims of increased Security Force raids in late 1979, pressed the Patriotic Front into abandoning its more hardline positions. An agreement was eventually signed on 21 December 1979. By then, Lord Soames, the British Governor, had already arrived in

Salisbury to preside over the transition. A formal cease-fire came into effect on 28 December and the guerrilla leaders returned to Salisbury in triumph and a number of their followers entered Assembly Points around the country. A Commonwealth Monitoring Force and other officials arrived to oversee the election in which the Patriotic Front contested the ballot as two distinct parties: Mugabe's ZANU(PF) and the PF (Patriotic Front).[2] On 4 March 1980 Mugabe's ZANU(PF) was declared the outright winner.

Exhausted by the war and ready for peace at (almost) any price, Rhodesian society in 1979 exhibited unmistakable signs of military failure, moral decline, and political disintegration. At the military level, the JOC and sub-JOC commanders and the farmers in their Area Co-Ordinating Committees in Op Thrasher and Op Repulse seemed to be fighting separate wars of survival. The superiority evident in the external raids of 1976-8 was less obvious in the 1979 assaults on ZANLA positions in Mozambique which either failed to meet all the objectives or cost too much in money and casualties, and which heightened tensions within NATJOC and COMOPS. Several plans devised by the Selous Scouts to assassinate Nkomo in Lusaka failed to materialise and, though a subsequent SAS mission in April 1979 destroyed his headquarters, there is evidence that Nkomo was forewarned and made his escape.[3] Despite the continuing assertions about winning the war, martial law had to be extended over 90 per cent of the country by September 1979, and there was persistent talk in military and civilian circles from mid-1979 of forming columns to secure the escape routes to Beit Bridge and of whites selling up, cutting losses, and leaving in droves. The wilder ones – forgetting that they were part of a civilising mission to the Dark Continent – announced their intention to shoot their way out of the country and leave it in a state of permanent and total darkness.

Moods and attitudes veered sharply during 1979-80 as the Rhodesians reacted to events now beyond their control. They managed – almost simultaneously – to offer a grudging or cautious acceptance of change while maintaining an undiminished commitment to the symbols and substance of the past. They never seemed to be quite sure whether the civilised society should condone or resist the transfer of power from white or black, and then from Muzorewa to Mugabe. Somewhere between 28 February and 1 June 1979 – between the last sit-ting of the white parliament and the installation of a black government – the Rhodesians lost what was left of their common cause save that of defeating 'terrorism', of surviving, and of preserving what remained of the Rhodesian way of life. Their leaders, meanwhile, faltered, dithered, or abdicated; and white Rhodesia spent its final year either drifting or hurtling about in confusion.

II

Potentially, the most damaging event for military morale during 1979 was the dismissal of the Army Commander on 6 March. Soon after the Reid Daly incident on 31 January John Hickman had left for South Africa on holiday and in the hope of repairing his failing marriage. Met at the airport on his return, Hickman was ordered to present himself at Army Headquarters where Hilary Squires, as Co-Minister of Defence, levelled three allegations against him: that, prior to his departure for South Africa, Hickman had been found – drunk and almost naked – at the scene of a motor car accident near Smith's official residence;[4] that he had given a false name to the police; and that his behaviour had been consistently inappropriate for the Commander of Rhodesia's Army. Hickman went off to consult his lawyer. Before he could respond, Squires announced that the Army Commander had been dismissed from the Army. The local press was silent, probably silenced.[5]

It is possible that Hickman's record of opposition to Walls and to the government was a factor in his dismissal. The former Army Commander had a reputation for being 'anti-establishment', and for saying just what he thought about a succession of 'hopeless' Ministers of Defence.[6] Hickman always believed that his attacks on the competence of the country's military and political leadership were primarily responsible for the campaign to remove him from office. In his view, the Reid Daly outburst on 31 January was a deliberate attempt to set him up, while the allegations about his private life – including those of the farmers stretching back to the time when he commanded Op Hurricane – were all deliberate fabrications. Flower claimed that, even admitting the substance if not the details of the allegations, the charges against Hickman's personal behaviour were 'irrelevant' in assessing his capacity to remain as Army Commander. Flower thought that the military and political leadership were happy enough to find an excuse to get rid of him.[7] John Hickman, he said, had upset too many important people for too long.

Whatever the truth of the matter, the senior commanders were relieved that the strained relations between Walls and Hickman would no longer complicate the conduct of the war. In any case, the Reid Daly-Hickman episode was overshadowed in command circles during 1979 by rumours that the Director-General of CIO was a British MI6 'mole' and that he was sabotaging external operations. The 'evidence' against Ken Flower was that he had close personal connections with British intelligence officers; that, in line with British government policy, he had always opposed external raids; that well-planned raids in 1977-9, and especially during 1979, were thwarted because the enemy was forewarned at the last minute (and, conversely, that where CIO was not fully informed or involved, or Flower was in London for the Lancaster House Conference, a raid could be very successful). A number of very senior Army, Air Force, and police officers claimed after the war that Flower was definitely a British agent – or that they were suspicious of his activities – and that, as a consequence, he was deliberately excluded from planning discussions.[8] Equally, some of Flower's closest former confidants, who are not usually included in the charges of treason and who had their own reasons to resent him, were adamant that he was completely innocent.[9] Ian Smith insisted that he had confronted Flower with the allegations and pronounced himself satisfied with the response: namely, that while it was essential to exchange information in the intelligence world, he – Flower – had never divulged anything detrimental to Rhodesian interests.[10]

Flower's position in NATJOC during 1977-9 was decidedly ambivalent. Convinced from about 1974 that Rhodesia had no long-term future, inclined to take a broader view of trends in southern Africa, and holding beliefs close to those of the Centre Party, Flower's objective was to secure the best deal in the inevitable transfer of power. Yet his sense of self-importance, his conviction that he could manipulate a solution, and his unwillingness to let go of a powerful position kept him serving a cause which he knew would fail. Flower had become an outsider within the military and political leadership: his abilities, intellectual interests, and secretive demeanour were not easily approved or understood by many Rhodesians, especially among the 'head-crackers' and those who believed in talking straight. Whether Flower was also guilty of other offences cannot, on the available evidence, be answered here. It can be said, however, that implementing a different and longer-term definition of Rhodesian interests from the one prevailing in NATJOC, and communicating with other intelligence agencies and their masters, were not – in themselves – acts of treason.

The important point here is that the very existence of the allegations or suspicions of treachery during 1979 (and earlier) suggests that COMOPS and NATJOC did not always constitute a happy band of pilgrims. Yet, just as Hickman's summary removal did not have the feared, damaging repercussions on the morale of the lower ranks of the Security Forces, so the rumours about Flower either did not penetrate far beyond the upper echelons or, where they did, failed to unsettle those who were too busy at the 'sharp end' or were too baffled to make sense of the gossip and the scuttlebutt. The fighting members of the Security Forces were much more interested in finding a convincing reason for continuing the war, and a more effective means of waging it. Intrigues at the top were relevant only to the extent of undermining confidence in the capacity of the military commanders to give a clear lead and a sense of purpose.

For its part, the RF had every intention of supplying decisive political leadership. Formed to defend white Rhodesia, the RF proposed in 1979 to continue representing and protecting what it perceived to be white interests. There was to be no pretence of developing policies appropriate to an African-governed society except in so far as Africans might threaten European standards or influence. It was predictable, therefore, that when the RF selected candidates for the new Assembly it should turn to the stalwarts of the past to safeguard the future. Squires, Irvine, Van der Byl, Moseley, and Stuttaford had impeccable credentials for representing the old Rhodesia (though former RAP members might disagree).[11] They had demonstrated a flair for the headmasterly lecture, for the racial insult, and for spotting communistic tendencies lurking within a progressive suggestion.[12] Mark Partridge was also given a seat, a reward for dogged loyalty, and Jack Mussett, put forward and rejected as one of the final eight Assembly members, was handed a Senate seat after years of dependability.[13] David Smith decided to withdraw from politics but was drafted into the Muzorewa ministry because of his expertise and amenable disposition. Ian Smith indulged in his customary public musing about retirement, and then answered the call of his RF colleagues to remain in politics to help the next government handle the British and to reassure the white electorate with his presence.

Sixteen of the twenty Assembly seats were uncontested. Voting in the remaining four was conducted on 14 April, on the day the SAS conducted its ill-fated raid on Nkomo's headquarters in Lusaka and just prior to the common roll elections. A few 'independents' were nominated but the liberals and supremacists decided, for different reasons, that participation was both irrelevant and futile. Even so, the average poll was 60 per cent. There was only one serious contest, for the Salisbury seat of Kopje, which had a high proportion of Coloureds and Asians and where a Coloured businesswoman stood against Divaris who achieved 71.4 per cent of the vote. The other RF candidates won with 79.8, 84.0, and 87.7 per cent of the votes respectively. No one, therefore, could dispute the RF's claim to speak for that large majority of whites who were not ready mentally to migrate from Rhodesia to Zimbabwe.

In one respect RF Rhodesians did respond to the new circumstances. Whereas they might have been puzzled or appalled by the intricacies of black politics and were especially worried about the behaviour of the Muzorewa and Sithole private armies, there was a common view about the election itself. First, it must happen; secondly, there must be a high turnout; thirdly, it must be, and be seen to be, 'free and fair'.

Having decided that the April common roll elections should – and would – be regarded overseas as a black referendum on the internal settlement, the Transitional government spared nothing in the quest for a high poll. It undertook a massive advertising campaign to emphasise the importance of voting and adopted rules for the election – such as not requiring formal registration and allowing migrant labour to vote – which materially helped its chances of a high turnout.[14] NATJOC passed a resolution recognising 'the crucial importance' of obtaining 'as high a percentage poll as possible' and, after warning against active canvassing, ordered all JOCs to ensure that the election was 'free and fair' (in other words, that voters could get to the polls).[15] In an effort to counter expected 'terrorist' sabotage and intimidation, all eligible males were called up for the election period in the greatest mobilisation of whites in the history of the war. Civil servants, including the Secretary for Education, the Deputy Secretary of Internal Affairs, the Chairman of the National Election Directorate, and a BSAP member of the Directorate, figured prominently in the campaign. A. J. Smith, the Secretary for Education, informed all teachers that they had a civic duty to instruct people to vote and to explain that their vote was secret.[16] These interventions were excused on the ground that the advice was 'non-political' because no one was being urged to support a particular party. In fact, government officials *were* giving 'political' advice because the whites had converted the very act of voting into a political issue. Rhodesia's much-vaunted apolitical civil service, so often contrasted with the politicised administrations of black Africa, was – in this respect – a myth.[17]

Private enterprise also became heavily involved in the campaign for a high turn-out. Members of ACCOR reminded employers that, while they should not tell their black employees who to vote for, they might wish to emphasise the importance of voting, explain the system of voting, and give their workers time off to vote.[18] The President of the RTA urged tobacco farmers to assist wherever possible in achieving a high poll. His argument was that an 'effective vote' might help to end sanctions and enable everyone to get on with the main business of farming.[19] There were innumerable reports during the voting period – 20-25 April – of farmers and urban employers ferrying their labour force to mobile or stationary polling booths, and of African workers learning that their continued employment depended on their attendance at the polls. Denis Norman, the President of the RNFU, effectively confirmed these reports when he congratulated the agricultural community after the election for its vital part in obtaining a high poll.[20]

Depending on their approval or rejection of the internal settlement, contemporary commentators pronounced the April elections to be either 'substantially free and fair'[21] or 'a gigantic confidence trick'.[22] Claire Palley tried to be judicious: 'it would be unsafe to regard these elections as more than indicating some considerable support for Bishop Muzorewa, but obtained in circumstances ot undue influence.'[23] Her comments stand up well in view of the Bishop's miserable showing in the 1980 elections (when 'undue influence' operated against him). Yet, whether he was a surrogate for the Shona who wanted Mugabe's party or was seen as a man of peace and moderation, the Bishop did win a clear majority of the popular vote in April 1979. On that basis, he was entitled to become the Prime Minister of Zimbabwe Rhodesia.

It was, inevitably, the Rhodesians who misread the signs. Many of them interpreted Muzorewa's clear victory and 'the festive air and carnival-like spirit' at the polls as evidence that the Africans wanted the internal settlement and had 'massively' rejected the 'external leaders'.[24] The advent of an African government was also expected to hasten the end of the war. The press contributed to this short-lived optimism by trumpeting the extravagant claims of senior officials at Combined Operations Headquarters. The lead article of the *Sunday Mail* on 20 May was headed 'WAR-TORN TERRORISTS COME HOME IN PEACE'. 'Hundreds' more were reportedly anxious to return: 'their morale is broken.' An accompanying statement – that 301 'terrorists' had been killed during the previous week – constituted the real news: the death toll was rising because the guerrillas were now pouring into the country.

Convinced that Muzorewa needed the whites (which he did), it was a short step to believe that the Bishop should not, and need not, attempt to alter the existing balance of racial power. Things might go on much as they had done before. Muzorewa encouraged these assumptions when he announced his new Government of National Unity on 30 May. Five of the seventeen cabinet posts and two of the seven deputy ministries were taken by former RF ministers. Ian Smith was appointed Minister without Portfolio, David Smith took Finance (to the great relief of the business community), Irvine became Minister of Agriculture – the RNFU was pleased enough that he was white – and Van der Byl, Andersen, Cronje, and Walker were the other inclusions. They were all 'sound' RF appointments, so Rhodesia's interests would be well guarded.

At midnight on 31 May Ian Smith ceased to be Prime Minister of anything. He regretted nothing that he had done, lamented what others had done to his country, and, for all his professed quiet confidence, believed in his heart that 'Rhodesia' was entering a dangerous path too quickly.[25] Two days later Combined Operations Headquarters issued a stark reminder of where the old path was heading: a monthly record of 891 people of all races (including five white civilians) were killed during May.[26] Smith's immediate legacy had been to protect and insulate his own constituency. When Zimbabwe Rhodesia was formally launched on 1 June its white enclave retained a disproportionate political presence, a profound commitment to its past, and little idea of what to do next.

III

The whites had neither the time nor the inclination to develop any sense of loyalty to Zimbabwe Rhodesia. Perhaps, for his part, the Bishop truly believed that the 'victorious minute' of midnight on 31 May 1979 signalled 'the assumption of nationhood'.[27] He was deluded because his government would never acquire the legitimacy needed to end the war, achieve international recognition, or remove economic sanctions. Ironically, and unjustly, RF Rhodesians blamed the Bishop for failing to achieve these objectives. They said he was weak and had become too vain. True, a stronger and wiser man might have demanded a more favourable inheritance. On the other hand, it ill-behoved those who had cast him into the role of puppet to accuse him of failing as a leader. Their reward for having sacrificed a pliable moderate, by denying him credibility among his own people, was the election in 1980 of a man assumed to be an uncontrollable extremist.

Even if they were not enthusiastic about the Bishop, the Rhodesians did give the country half a chance. The rate of white emigration declined from a net loss of 12,900 whites between June 1978 and February 1979 to one of 4,569 between June 1979 and February 1980.[28] Thousands had postponed their departure plans in the hope that the new government might achieve peace. Their optimism, and the Bishop's prayers, were not fulfilled: the white casualty rate remained close to that of the bleak months of 1978, forty-four farmers or members of their families were killed between 1 June and the cease-fire, total net livestock losses between April and November 1979 were in the region of 47,118-64,796,[29] the cost of the war rose to $1.1 million a day, and the raids into Zambia and Mozambique, which coincided with the Lancaster House Conference, did little to ease the threat already inside the country. On 26 June 1979 a Military Intelligence paper concluded that corridors leading to the north and south of Salisbury from ZANLA's 'secured bases' in the eastern TTLs could eventually sever the lines of communication; in that case, Salisbury 'will ultimately fall'. External operations were essential to prevent the 'terrorists' from 'topping up' their forces in the corridors.[30] The paper did not concern itself with ZIPRA although many of the raids late in 1979 were designed to halt Nkomo's planned conventional assault upon the main cities. Other secret documents, which were more widely distributed, indicated that the strategists had already

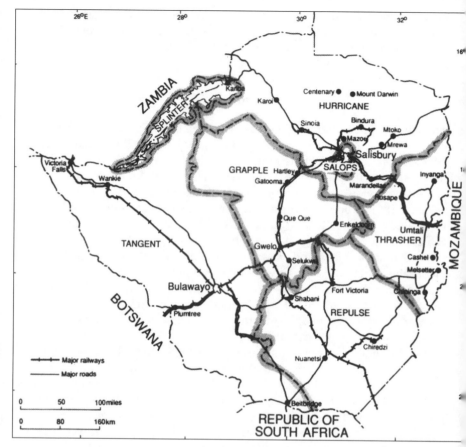

MAP 8.1. *The Operational Areas, 1979*

distinguished between expendable areas and those designated Vital Assets Ground (including the richer commercial farming land),[31] and were implicitly acknowledging that the government did not control a number of districts. So, notwithstanding all those confident assertions about never having lost the war, the Security Force commanders in 1979 were preparing for a losing operation. They were fortunate that peace broke out when it did.

The advent of the Muzorewa government did not improve the quality of life. The government announced that from 1 August the fuel ration would be cut by a further 10 per cent, a holiday fuel allowance of 1,000 km would be withdrawn, and grants permitting residents of small towns to visit larger centres for shopping would be more strictly controlled.[32] Fuel costs, combined with rationing, had seriously eroded an

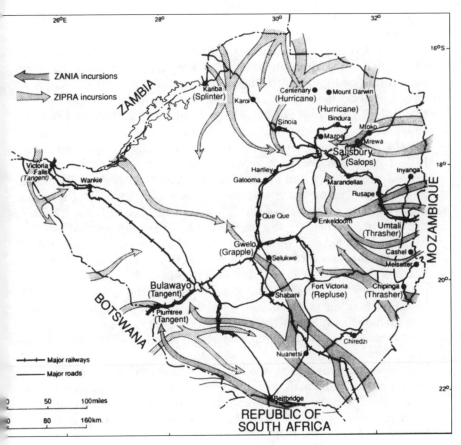

MAP 8.2. *The Direction and Extent of Guerilla Incursions, 1979*

Source: Map prepared by Military Intelligence, July 1979

important aspect of the Rhodesian way of life.[33] The rate of erosion accelerated after David Smith's self-styled 'budget of war' of 26 July 1979. By then the war was consuming 37 per cent of the budget and the Minister of Finance therefore reimposed the income tax surcharge and increased it to 10 per cent.[34] He did scrap a special defence levy and doubled the holiday allowance for overseas travel, but compensated by stopping the practice of accumulating travel funds over two years. Whatever he did, however, the Rhodesians continued to take holidays outside the country.[35]

There was little relief in sight for those subject to call-ups. During 1978 a committee, headed by 'Mac' Knox, the RF Chairman, investigated the possibility of abolishing the call-up system altogether and of expanding the professional Army. These proposals were considered too revolutionary, expensive, and impractical and were quietly shelved.[36] The Transitional government did reduce the initial period of national service to twelve months, tried to cut back the commitments of the older age-groups, and had hoped that the introduction of black conscription would appease the whites. The critics, however, were unimpressed. In March 1979 J. G. Hillis, the President of ARnI, attacked the lack of consultation on the call-up of the 'over-50s' who, he said, ran the factories in the absence of younger men. Hillis said he was 'frankly appalled' as he looked back over the years when a similar lack of consultation had caused 'unnecessary and avoidable difficulties'.[37] Speaking in Que Que in May he called on the government to 'ease the burden on the white minority'. The Chairman of the Midlands Chamber of Industries was even more forthright: the military had 'the intermittent use of Rhodesia's white youth for many years' and, in the process, impeded or frustrated the careers of young whites. Industry had suffered principally because there had been a delay in developing the talents of future managers and technicians. And now, because of the failure to provide sufficient training programmes for blacks, Zimbabwe Rhodesia would have to look to white youth or expatriates for the necessary skills.[38]

Whereas it was easy enough to abuse an RF back-bencher in the Smith government, or to whinge to white co-ministers in the Transitional administration, the leaders of commerce and industry and most private individuals felt more restrained when Muzorewa took office. The frustrations, however, continued and were complicated by other factors. In June 1979 Ken Winsor, a Gwelo Town Councillor and President of the Motor Trades Employers' Association, was charged under the Law and Order (Maintenance) Act with conduct likely to expose the police to contempt or disesteem: that is, he had uttered two four-letter words to a white Chief Inspector after being stopped at a road block in the curfew area of the Gwelo industrial sites. Winsor was generally angry because the 50-9 call-up in Gwelo was not working efficiently and because he did not like the police assuming a paramilitary role. He was especially provoked on this occasion by what he saw as officious behaviour in administering an unnecessary curfew.[39] Yet, given the rejection of the Knox proposals and the prospect of more disturbances in industrial areas following the expansion of the war in late 1979, there was no real alternative to the call-up system, to urban curfews, or to the expanded role of the police. Dr Mutiti, the Bishop's Minister of Manpower, admitted on 10 August 1979 that the situation was 'becoming ever more acute'. He was addressing the annual congress of the Motor Trade Association in Salisbury where he restated the predicament which Reginald Cowper had confronted in 1976-7: every man possible must be spared for the war effort, but no business must be forced to close because its manpower had been called up.

Meanwhile the war goes on, and unless it is fought with all possible vigour, there will be no future for Zimbabwe Rhodesia as we know it. Conversely, if the manpower of the civil sector is over-taxed by call-ups, the economy will collapse and once again there will be nothing worth fighting for.[40]

White youths and the older male age groups from the urban areas perennially asked themselves whether the call-up was worth it. The farmers, traditionally depicted as the bedrock of the RF, had no reservations about continuing the fight against 'terrorism'. Nor were they greatly worried by the arrival of the Muzorewa government. Their leaders in the RNFU, several of whom had supported the RP in the mid-1970s, were happy to co-operate with black ministers. In keeping with the changed circumstances, they sought at the 1979 annual congress – and successfully on this occasion – to change the name of the organisation from the RNFU to the CFU. The farmers were now too preoccupied with self-preservation to worry much about their past attachments or even the future of Western civilisation. The continuing war, the political uncertainty, the drought of 1978-9, stock theft, escalating input costs, and poor financial returns had combined to promote a deep sense of gloom. Once again, agriculture appeared to be in crisis and the consensus was that, without peace and better commodity prices, the situation would become very grave. In this context, arguments about majority rule and maintaining standards seemed less pressing.

If peace was not an immediate prospect in mid-1979 at least the farmers were heartened by the tough attitudes of the new ministers. An immediate favourite was Francis Zindoga, the Minister of Law and Order, who was applauded at the annual congress in July 1979 when he reminded the delegates of his earlier public refusal to distinguish between 'terrorists', stock thieves, and *mujibas*.[41] Zindoga had issued orders to the Security Forces to take 'appropriate measures' and promised legislation to impose tougher penalties on stock thieves. An Afrikaner farmer was sceptical: he had heard promises of strong action for fourteen years and – since 1976 – every congress 'has been left rather like an empty shell'. He, too, was applauded when he demanded that the Minister say what would be done – now – to stop the harassment of the farming community. Zindoga's response would have pleased (and even amused) RAP supporters:

Ladies and gentlemen, this is Africa. What was done in white Africa and was criticised abroad, if it is done in black Africa, there is no criticism. Therefore the measures we intend to take are stiffer than the measures 14 years ago.

Individuals and minorities had always wanted to take the gloves off, and the Catholic Commission for Justice and Peace often accused the Security Forces of doing so. The country now had a Minister of Law and Order who told irate farmers in Victoria Province to give him the names of officials who were preventing them from acting as they 'would like to do'. Although Zindoga had the 'correct' approach, another Afrikaner farmer insisted that 'we can't go backwards and take the law into our own hands': the farmers must be given proper legal authority and not rely upon ministerial statements made at meetings around the country. Zindoga understood the problem: first, the farmers did not wish to be known as 'a bunch of murderers' (which, he said, they were not); secondly, the police were telling the farmers that, if they acted in the manner of black Africa, 'we will have no option but to put you behind bars'. The Minister responded by emphasising that, while the government was not giving a licence to kill indiscriminately, it was determined to eliminate stock theft. To this end, it would impose stricter legal penalties and sanction any actions by the farmers which were necessary to 'defend' themselves.[42] Clearly, Zindoga was shaping up as the best RF minister the farmers had ever had.

Nor could the farmers object when the Muzorewa government followed the RF practice of treating them as a protected species subject to special favours. Pricing policies provided a good example. When, in April 1979, the Transitional government announced its pre-planting prices, setting a return of $66 a tonne for maize, the farming community erupted. On 22 May some 450 farmers descended upon Salisbury to attend a public meeting which was unprecedented for its ugly mood and for the unbridled criticisms of the government. A proposal to boycott the delivery of crops to market was defeated by 154 votes to 103, and the RNFU leadership successfully dissuaded the meeting from passing a vote of no-confidence in the Co-Ministers of Agriculture.[43] But the councils of both the RNFU and the RTA had, for the first time, totally rejected the pricing policies of the Ministry of Agriculture and the meeting unanimously demanded a re-negotiation. The resentment crossed racial boundaries. The President of the African Farmers' Union was applauded when he declared that the farmers were 'all chaps together in the operational area'. David Spain, the Vice-President of the RNFU, provided a succinct explanation of this unity in hostility. He pointed out that average input costs in agriculture had gone up by 66 per cent since 1972 whereas prices had risen by just 21 per cent. A Lomagundi representative complained that the Ministry was working from a model which presupposed that a farmer in his area would produce 55 bags of maize per acre and sustain a net loss of $40 an acre just to do so.[44] Farming in general, and maize-planting in particular, had become uneconomic. The RNFU council continued to press for a higher return and, in the following August, the Muzorewa government announced that the pre-planting price for maize had been raised to $75. A black-led government, anxious to ensure food supplies and desperate for the white farmers to remain on the land, had become an attractive proposition for the farming community.

Living in constant fear for their lives and their livelihood, the farming community was apt to explode in the face of bureaucratic arrogance or excessive regulation. One attack, made at the annual congress of the Grain Producers' Association, was so strong that Bill Irvine felt obliged to defend his civil servants in the Agriculture ministry by claiming that, while they might disagree with RNFU members and even be wrong, the officials did not deserve to be publicly castigated.[45] Some farmers were in no mood to forgive, especially when they read of four incidents reported in their national journal in September 1979. One man was advised to leave his farm in 1977, which he had occupied for seventeen years, following five separate raids and the destruction of his crops and tobacco barns. Working in Salisbury to pay off his debts, he had just received a court order demanding the forfeiture of his furniture. Another farmer, a victim of stock theft, faced the prospect of losing all his cattle to pay his debts. A third received a court summons while undergoing a call-up.[46] A fourth had lost $184,000 in twenty-two months and was trying to farm in an area where three-quarters of its original properties were now unoccupied. Liable for unit tax, payable to his local Rural Council, the farmer could not meet the debt of $430 and, under the law, the Council was required to sue him for the outstanding sum. He responded angrily:

They pin medals on you . . . and then summons you for your last penny. These views have been expressed by hundreds of farmers. They are not going to pay. They are saying, 'To the hell with it.'[47]

The question of the unit tax had been raised at the annual congress in July.[48] It was a 'thorny one' because farmers, who were members of Rural Councils, were obliged to pursue their fellows. According to Mrs Guild, who chaired both her Farmers' Association and the Rural Council in the Mtoko district, the defaulters fell into three categories: those who had left the country, those who could not continue farming because of 'terrorist' attacks, and those who had been deliberately evacuated. The Rural Councils should not, in her view, be required to levy the tax on the second and third groups, and she asked that the matter be negotiated with several ministries including Combined Operations, Law and Order, and Finance. The President of the RNFU intervened to say that the matter had been discussed with Local

Government six weeks earlier but the Ministry had not yet notified the farmers of its outcome. He assured Mrs Guild that the Ministry of Agriculture was not to blame, and Irvine confirmed that it was a Local Government matter which should be discussed with the Rural Councils. Confronted every day with the twin battles of staying alive and maintaining viability, it is no wonder that the farmers were unimpressed by the bureaucratic, legalistic, and taxing procedures of the authorities.

Some were none too pleased either with the performance of their own organisation. After five years of debate, the farming bodies had eventually accepted a pension scheme for their African labour which many farmers felt had been forced upon them by the RNFU council. Against this background, there was renewed resentment when the council sought to transfer the farmers from the old Masters and Servants legislation and bring their operations within the ambit of the Industrial Conciliation Act. The council wanted to achieve this objective before the election of a black government and to establish the operation of a 'responsible' Industrial Board before any post-majority rule attempts to lift the minimum wage to 'uneconomic levels'. The issue was discussed at the 1978 annual congress. Sixteen branches and producer associations met between 7 and 13 November 1978 and nearly 80 per cent of those present approved the new arrangements. Within one month the matter was being debated in parliament and the relevant amendment was enacted by the end of the year. The speed of the exercise demonstrated both the influence of the RNFU council over the Transitional government, and the bureaucracy's own capacity for swift action where it was subject to the right sort of pressure. Many farmers, however, were furious. They had not been adequately informed or consulted. The due democratic process, which in the past had effectively prevented change, had not been followed. The Selous branch placed a resolution before the 1979 congress calling on the council to hold a referendum before it committed members to any major changes in the policy of the industry, and to circulate full details of its intentions.[49] The congress eventually accepted a compromise motion (by 85 votes to 29) which removed the formal requirement of a referendum but pressed the point about supplying details and communicating branch responses. The critics were not happy about the outcome because their real objective was, in the words of a Marandellas farmer, to show that 'we don't like being pushed around'. Rhodesia's white farmers could tolerate almost anyone, or anything, provided they were treated as a protected species.

IV

Mrs Thatcher agreed at the Commonwealth Meeting in Lusaka in early August to withhold recognition of the Muzorewa government. Britain would convene an all-party constitutional conference at Lancaster House and supervise fresh elections leading to internationally-accepted independence. A draft proposal, published on 14 August, the day before COMOPS announced another forty-eight deaths in the war, laid down that any settlement must be 'comparable to those on which Britain has granted independence to other former dependent territories'.[50] In effect, the British told the white minority that its privileged position under the Zimbabwe Rhodesia constitution could not be maintained. A *Herald* suggestion that Mrs Thatcher was 'really a Labour Prime Minister in drag' reflected the general disappointment of whites in Rhodesia, although members of NUF, the CPU council, and of the business community did welcome Lancaster House as an opportunity to achieve an internationally-accepted settlement, a genuine peace, and the end of economic sanctions.[51]

On 5 September, three days after the Zimbabwe Rhodesia flag was first unfurled at Rufaro Stadium in Salisbury, and five days before the Lancaster House Conference was due to start, the Rhodesians launched Operation Uric, their biggest-ever raid into Mozambique. The action was concentrated in the Mapai area, to the south-east, where the aim was to destroy ZANLA and FRELIMO forward bases, to halt further infiltration through Op Repulse, and to attack lines of communication. The Rhodesians met their stiffest resistance thus far on external operations.[52] Two helicopters were lost. One of them, a South African Puma and piloted by South Africans, carried eleven Rhodesians who were all killed by a rocket attack on the helicopter.[53] One of the victims was Corporal LeRoy Duberley, the full back of the national rugby team. There were poignant scenes the following Saturday in Durban when Zimbabwe Rhodesia met Natal in the Currie Cup. A trumpeter played the Last Post and the Reveille, several young Rhodesians laid Rhodesian national flags on the ground behind the goal posts, Duberley's replacement wept as he pulled on the No. 15 jumper, and the Rhodesians threw themselves into the game and won by 19-15 in a thrilling finish. Attempts before the match to obtain a call-up exemption for Duberley had failed, prompting the distraught President of the Zimbabwe Rhodesia Rugby Union to ask 'Goddamit, what is this war all about?'[54]

The Lancaster House Conference convened on 10 September, just after the Security Forces had returned from Mozambique. The British had assembled a formidable team and a clear agenda: the Conference would first agree on a constitution, then settle the transitional arrangements involving the formation of an interim government and the holding of new elections, and, finally, endorse a cease-fire plan which required the two sides to disengage, to collect their forces at bases around the country, and accept the presence of a small Commonwealth monitoring force. The Patriotic Front, which had a very clear notion of what the war was all about – 'the total liquidation of colonialism in Zimbabwe' – arrived in London convinced that the intention was to deny them a sweeping victory. The Salisbury government came with many advisers and an unattainable objective: formal recognition and the lifting of economic sanctions.[55]

Ian Smith was a member of the Bishop's delegation, included because Muzorewa regarded him as the leader of white Rhodesia. Ken Flower, now advising and bolstering the Bishop, was everywhere, often in the company of Air-Vice Marshal Hawkins who was still Salisbury's accredited representative in South Africa. Walls, Peter Allum – the Police Commissioner – and Flower's deputy, Derrick Robinson, also went to London for long periods. Under McLaren, the Deputy Commander of COMOPS, who was left in charge and was more of a 'hawk', the Security Force commanders felt less constrained about ordering cross-border raids. Meanwhile, CIO had organised another presence in London. The former British paratrooper who had participated in the Chitepo killing in 1975 arrived with orders to plan the assassination of Robert Mugabe.[56]

In two respects Lancaster House reminded Rhodesians of Geneva: there were the corresponding elements of theatre in the verbal brawls, threatened walk-outs, and grandstanding; and there was that same sense of living in two worlds, one removed and remote in the northern hemisphere and the other – claiming more lives and property each day – which was pressing and immediate. On the day, for example, when Lord Carrington first addressed the delegates in such elegant surroundings in London, a hastily-formed battalion set out to secure the area between Mount Darwin and Rushinga. The commanding officer was an Australian veteran of the Vietnam War, all except one of his officers were white, and the troops were half-trained black recruits.[57] The existence of 'Digger Force', its limited supplies, the orders to shoot all curfew-breakers, and the fact that it suffered as many casualties as it inflicted were all testimony to the desperate situation confronting the Rhodesians in late 1979. Lancaster House may have been remote but, whatever the rhetoric about winning the war, or not losing, the Rhodesians needed Lancaster House to produce a solution.

The whites in London had their own reasons for feeling out of touch. Installed in a five-star hotel in Kensington, they were shocked by the prices, and a little bemused by the traffic jams and by the presence of so many wealthy Arabs in the streets.[58] They also felt frustrated by the ability of the Patriotic Front to overshadow the Bishop and his squabbling ministers.[59] Worse still, instead of walking out of the Conference and clearing the way for Carrington and Muzorewa to reach a settlement, the Patriotic Front never implemented repeated threats to withdraw. Even when the Front accepted the constitution in mid-October, the whites in London expected that it would reject the transitional arrangements or, failing that, the cease-fire. There was also consternation when it became apparent in December that Carrington would achieve his desired 'first class solution' of a settlement involving all the parties.[60] Paradoxically, the very success in 'plastering' Zambia and Mozambique, operations which so pleased the warriors in Salisbury, had ensured that its backers would do almost anything to keep the Patriotic Front at the conference table.

Two developments in London during the first two months were of the greatest significance for white Rhodesia. Lord Carrington needed Salisbury's quick approval of the constitution so that he could use the threat of a separate settlement with Muzorewa to put pressure on the Front. The immediate issue for the Muzorewa delegation was Carrington's proposal to remove the 'safeguards' by giving the Prime Minister power over senior appointments in the public service, the police, and the armed forces, and by dropping the whites' power to block constitutional amendments. The Bishop and his fellow black delegates were happy to agree and thereby obtain some credibility for standing up to Ian Smith. David Smith supported Muzorewa. He was also a member of the official delegation and was beginning his own migration from Rhodesia to Zimbabwe which eventually took him beyond the Bishop and into Robert Mugabe's first ministry. Chris Andersen and Rowan Cronje, who had gone to London but were not part of the official delegation, lined up with David Smith, making the atmosphere among the whites 'a bit tense'.[61] On 21 September the official delegation voted by eleven to one to approve the removal of the blocking mechanism. To the victors, the real issue was the removal of formal white privilege and the acceptance of Zimbabwe; to the loser, Ian Smith, it was a question of keeping civilised standards and retaining white confidence. Isolated and rejected, the former Prime Minister never forgave the deserters.

Nor did he spare the Bishop: he was 'like wet putty' in the hands of the British and 'the most inept politician – no, man – I've ever met'.[62] The inexcusable acts were to abandon the safeguards and to agree to resign in favour of a British Governor without first obtaining the removal of economic sanctions. Angered by Muzorewa's weakness as a negotiator with the British and by the 'treachery' of his fellow RF members in London, Smith spoke of using the existing blocking mechanism to oppose Carrington's constitution. Others back in Salisbury stood firmly by him. John Landau, now the RF Chief Whip in place of Divaris, said that there would be no sell-out of white interests. Bill Irvine threatened to stop the constitution from passing through the Zimbabwe Rhodesia parliament if it did not provide real safeguards for the whites.[63] Yet, as Ian Smith appreciated, Muzorewa's commitment to the new constitution had seriously damaged the cause. Even Hector Macdonald deserted. The supposedly reactionary Chief Justice arrived in London in mid-November to tell the Bishop that he could implement the new constitution without having to resort to parliament.[64]

The second important development in London was Smith's own surrender speech. On 8 November he announced that 'the time has come to tell our people back home that to continue the fight would now be sterile, even counter-productive'.[65] Defeated in London, he was not prepared to carry on the struggle in Salisbury. P. K. van der Byl told an RF fête in Bulawayo that their leader had fought a 'lonely battle', treacherously abandoned by those who had been wined and dined by the British.[66] Smith himself was already gloomily predicting that the Patriotic Front would 'walk' an election.[67] Returning to Rhodesia in time for the 14th anniversary of UDI, the first where he did not strike the Independence Bell at a midnight ball, Ian Smith might also have sensed that his own status within the white community was diminishing. Peter Walls was looking the better proposition if the Rhodesians had to fight their way to Beit Bridge. In any event, white Rhodesia did not publicly commemorate 11 November. An RF spokesman said that such a celebration did not seem to be appropriate.[68]

A foreign correspondent noted in mid-November that the London talks had 'provoked little interest and even less enthusiasm among the whites'.[69] The Rhodesians understood that they could not determine their own future, they were understandably afraid of the unknown, and they had known too many false dawns. It was better to concentrate on survival, to ignore the unwelcome news, and just pray for the best. The farmers, however, needed to be more involved. The Patriotic Front wanted a fundamental redistribution of land and thus it was important to support the British proposal to protect white farmers from expropriation. The Front backed down in mid-October after the Americans agreed to provide financial support for resettlement schemes. The CPU's next concern was that land might be resettled for political rather than planned, productive purposes. A three-man delegation went to London and used its extensive contacts there to emphasise the key role of commercial farming in making the country self-sufficient in food and a food exporter.[70] The CPU stressed that it favoured the resettlement of under-utilised agricultural land. The organisation's leadership in the late 1970s was acutely aware of the need to adapt to the new circumstances and saw that, by working *with* the government of Zimbabwe and pressing the economic advantages of commercial agriculture, it could better protect the interests of viable white farming. Like the other 'economic presidents', Dennis Norman was considerably better attuned to black politics than the RF leadership.

Peter Walls was also amenable to change, a fact which greatly pleased the British government because his involvement and support were essential for a peaceful transition. The strategy was simple: invite him to London, make a fuss of him, and persuade him that 'we need your cooperation, my dear chap, to make this thing work, and so that we can get what we all want'.[71] In addition, the Foreign Office wanted Walls to restrain the wild boys back in Salisbury whose persistent raids were doing more damage to Mozambique and Zambia than was necessary to keep the Patriotic Front at the negotiating table. So, the General was fêted in London when he arrived on 14 October. He saw Mrs Thatcher at Downing Street, had tea with the Queen Mother, lunched with Ken Flower at Whites, and was forever having private chats with Lord Carrington, an apparent intimacy signalled by each calling the other 'Peter'. Walls himself believes that he was not influenced by all the attention, though few Rhodesians in London shared this assessment.[72] It obviously helped that Walls had long been committed to a political solution, was out of his depth in high politics, and was naive enough to accept verbal assurances from the British government. He left London on 13 December convinced that the British had no intention of allowing the Patriotic Front (or, at least, Robert Mugabe) to come to power. Walls had not understood that the British regarded a coalition government as the best solution, nor realised that the Foreign Office expected Mugabe to form the majority party. Perhaps he just misinterpreted Carrington's elliptical style of speaking, and could not believe that an aristocratic Tory would countenance a Marxist coming to power in Zimbabwe.[73] Anyway, Walls had convinced himself that Mrs Thatcher had given him 'all sorts of assurances', including the promise of an open and direct line to her if anything went wrong: 'I thought she was playing it straight.'

Walls should have understood the signals. It was, after all, Ken Flower who suggested that he should visit 'the lady' (Mrs Thatcher) and Walls claimed to know that Flower had MI6 connections. Yet, whatever he might think of Flower's motives, it made sense to seek assurances from the British Prime Minister. Muzorewa approved the visit, whereupon the General asked if he could bring a friend in order to keep an eye on things, suggesting that he was not quite so naive and trusting as he appeared. After some hesitation, Walls was told he could bring anyone, provided it was Flower. But the Director-General of CIO did not arrive in time for the Thatcher meeting. He was fog-bound and delayed in Paris, an explanation which Walls did not accept.[74] So there were no supporting witnesses except Sir Anthony Duff, the Deputy Under-secretary of State at the Foreign and Commonwealth Office, who later went to Rhodesia as Deputy Governor. The guarantees which Walls sought to invoke in late February 1980 were never converted into writing and could not be independently verified. This point should have been obvious during his secret meeting with Soames in the House of Lords just before the Governor departed for Salisbury. When Walls raised the matter of the election Soames said that he was not a party to any deals. So far as the Governor was concerned, the first horse past the post would be declared the winner. The General then spoke of certain assurances, and Soames remarked that he had received no such instructions.[75] Walls should have recognised then that he could not expect any intervention from London.

But not everything was lost. Against the wishes of the Patriotic Front, the Lancaster House constitution gave Rhodesian citizens automatic rights to Zimbabwean citizenship, even if they had arrived after UDI. The whites were assigned 20 seats in the 100-member House of Assembly, those 20 could elect the 10 white Senators in an upper house of 40, and this provision could not be altered within seven years except by a unanimous vote of the lower house. Separate white representation was, at best, a mixed blessing: it helped to reassure the majority of whites who remained in Zimbabwe yet the existence of those seats, and the behaviour of their RF occupants, became the single most important impediment to racial reconciliation in the early 1980s. An unqualified gain at Lancaster House was an agreement to pay existing pension entitlements which could be remitted to persons ordinarily resident outside Zimbabwe. The Declaration of Rights specifically protected private property from expropriation, guaranteed compensation where under-utilised land was compulsorily acquired, and allowed the remission of compensation payments overseas. These provisions could not be amended for ten years save by a unanimous vote in the House of Assembly. It was possible, therefore, to adopt a brave front. But for anyone who had joined the RF in 1962, approved UDI, and accepted Zimbabwe Rhodesia only because of its safeguards, these assurances must have looked very slender. On 4 December two RF MPs vented their anger when the Zimbabwe Rhodesia parliament voted itself out of existence. Donald Goddard walked out before the vote was taken,[76] and Mark Partridge defiantly shouted 'No' and called for a division.

The Rhodesians were not entirely happy with the transitional and cease-fire arrangements. It was galling having to acknowledge the appointment of a British Governor, and when Lord Soames arrived on

12 December – in anticipation of a final settlement – the public cheering was left to a tearful Sir Humphrey Gibbs, the Governor at UDI, and a gathering of liberals who paraded their old flags outside the official residence. Shrewd observers like Ian Smith also recognised the danger inherent in the Bishop standing aside: in African eyes, his self-sacrifice would be interpreted as weakness. No one was very confident that the Patriotic Front would observe the cease-fire or agree to bring all its forces into the proposed sixteen Assembly Points. The Rhodesians were reluctant to acknowledge that the Front was also taking an enormous risk. Despite the requirement that the Security Forces should be confined to their bases, Mugabe and Nkomo knew that the guerrilla forces inside the Assembly Points would be a sitting target for a conventional attack. Their fears were well founded. The staff of COMOPS began planning an attack from the moment the idea of Assembly Points was first mooted. Here, at last, was an opportunity of assaulting large numbers of 'terrs' congregated inside the country.[77] Mugabe and Nkomo were also worried that the Governor, in relying upon the Security Forces to maintain order during the elections, would give them a licence to manipulate the vote and harass the Front. If the Rhodesians were apprehensive, so were their opponents, and both sides had good reason to be so.

Notwithstanding all these anxieties, the parties signed their agreement on 21 December, the seventh anniversary of the attack on Altena Farm. Almost everyone could claim some sort of victory. Lord Carrington had deflected a right-wing revolt in the Tory party and his deft footwork and blunt ultimatums had secured agreement on the substance of the British plan for the constitution, the transitional arrangements, and the cease-fire. The Patriotic Front sensed it could win an election so long as the Security Forces were kept under control and the British Governor played fair. The Bishop announced that 'The Winner' had delivered the peace he had promised to his people. Walls felt sure that the Patriotic Front would never come to power. And all the main players could cheat while believing that the others would be held in check.

The cease-fire came into effect at midnight on 28 December. On that day COMOPS announced another 30 deaths: 4 members of the Security Forces (including a 19-year-old white officer), 19 'terrorists', 5 'terrorist collaborators', and 2 civilians 'caught in the crossfire'. A further 26 African farm workers had been hurt in a landmine explosion. It was also reported that the Commander of ZANLA had died on Boxing Day as a result of a car accident in Mozambique. Walls and Ian Smith were convinced that Josiah Tongogara was a force for unity between the two wings of the Patriotic Front, and between black and white, and that he was murdered because of a power struggle within ZANLA.[78] It was a story which made the front page without distracting the whites from the things which really mattered: Zimbabwe Rhodesia had recently lost a cricket match in Johannesburg against the invincible Transvaal by the indecent margin of an innings and 34 runs; the Salisbury cinemas were showing *Midnight Express, The Deer Hunter, Jack and the Beanstalk,* and *The Muppets;* the rains had started; sanctions had been lifted (prompting an Umtali complaint that Salisbury – 'Bamba Zonke' – had received the full benefit of the $10 million worth of newly-imported goods for Christmas);[79] and real-estate prices were set to soar.

Besides, the Commonwealth Monitoring Force – consisting of Australian, British, Fijian, Kenyan, and New Zealand troops – had begun to arrive. In one respect, it was a miniature version of the American servicemen's invasion of Britain and Australia during the Second World War. Several Rhodesian women quickly formed liaisons with British and Australian men who were more 'caring' and 'attentive' than the Rhodesian males.[80] Quick marriages and brief affairs (including one between the wife of a senior Rhodesian Army officer and a senior member of the Commonwealth Forces), and the proud discovery that a member of the foreign press liked 'our curvy, healthy lasses', signalled the end of isolation. Years of voluntary exile had narrowed personal opportunities while encouraging a craven respect for anybody who would say something flattering. A journalist from the London *Daily Express* was quoted because of his opinion that Rhodesian girls of British stock 'are the most beautiful in the world'. Compliments of this kind were eagerly reported. Not so welcome were the criticisms offered by the Rhodesian girls themselves. One woman, described as a 'thirty-one-year-old divorcée', had the temerity to accuse Rhodesian men of being narrow-minded, of preferring to drink with other men, and pestering unescorted women. According to one paper, 'a host of top glamour girls' rushed to defend the 'natural, carefree – and real men' of Rhodesia.[81]

V

Just after the cease-fire was announced, a group of Rhodesians who had attended the Lancaster House talks met informally at their London hotel. They discussed the likely outcome of the common roll elections which were set for the following 27-9 February. Harold Hawkins delivered what became the convenient and conventional wisdom: the Patriotic Front could not possibly win. It was hoped and expected that the Bishop would secure an outright majority or head a coalition government. The Special Branch representative in London disagreed with the Hawkins assessment. He predicted that the Patriotic Front would keep some of its forces outside the Assembly Points in order to intimidate the black electorate.[82]

This minority view was reinforced on 3 January when, in Salisbury, PSYOPS predicted that the Patriotic Front would win forty-eight seats. On 13 January John Redfern, the Director of Military Intelligence, warned of the possibility of a Patriotic Front victory unless the guerrillas were contained in the Assembly Points and prevented from intimidating the local population.[83] While not even the most pessimistic were yet forecasting an outright Mugabe victory, Redfern knew that thousands of ZANLA 'terrorists' had in fact remained outside the Assembly Points after the cease-fire and were well placed to 'canvass' rural support.[84] The Rhodesians were also aware that a proportion of those who entered the Assembly Points were *mujibas,* some of whom turned up with rusty weapons held together by wire and who failed the test – imposed to determine who was a bona fide guerrilla – of stripping and reassembling an AK within a certain time limit. By mid-January the commanders of the Security Forces, and more independent observers, believed that intimidation was widespread, and that ZANLA guerrillas who remained outside the Assembly Points were the main perpetrators.[85] According to Walls, he had a blazing row with Soames when the Governor decided to give Mugabe an extra Assembly Point. Telling him that he was 'a drunken, dishonest old bastard', Walls stormed out of their meeting and did not visit the Governor again until after the election.[86]

A number of middle-ranking and junior officers decided on a course of counter-action. A Military Intelligence paper on 21 January outlined six tasks for the period ending on 31 March 1980: to form a combined planning centre to co-ordinate the military operations of the Security Forces and the South Africans; to oppose the Patriotic Front and prevent it winning the election; to create the right circumstances for a UANC victory; to achieve a high poll in UANC areas and ensure a low poll in areas hostile to the UANC; to install and consolidate a UANC government; to eliminate ZIPRA and ZANLA. A CIO officer merely queried the assumption that the South Africans were prepared to do more than help the whites to escape in the event of a disaster. On 23 January a further Military Intelligence paper predicted a victory for 'one party of the P(atriotic) F(ront) or a coalition involving one or both parties' which could mean a concerted rush on Salisbury from the Assembly Points, the disarming of the Security Forces and of private citizens, the occupation of strategic points and the summoning of 'friendly' powers to assist the Front in asserting its authority. Some 'constructive' suggestions were offered in another paper circulated on 29 January to all JOCs, the Selous Scouts, 1 SAS, and 1 RLI. The areas designated as Vital Assets Ground must be protected to preserve strategic points, to retain European confidence, and to enable the Europeans in turn to influence their labour to vote against the Patriotic Front. To ensure that Salisbury did not go 'sour', tanks should be deployed around the city, armoured cars and mounted infantry should go on parade, fly-pasts should be organised, and military bands should play numbers with an African flavour. This paper also contained the important message that the Assembly Points must be 'neutralised' and flares set for lighting them at night.[87]

The status and influence of these documents remain unclear. What they suggest is that officers in Military Intelligence were alert to the prospect of an unacceptable result and were arguing for drastic pre-emptive action. Members of Special Branch and junior officers attached to COMOPS were also concluding by late January that Muzorewa was not holding the electorate. This view was dramatically affirmed on 29 January when Robert Mugabe returned to Salisbury and a tumultuous welcome by a crowd of some 250,000. The Bishop also realised that his support was evaporating and tried to recover it by branding ZANU(PF) with satanic images, the main effect of which was to project himself as a panic-stricken loser. Ian Smith was no help. He was openly advising the whites to persuade their employees to vote for Nkomo.[88]

Righteous indignation about the intimidatory practices of ZANU(PF) supporters, and fears that a Marxist victory could lead to reprisals as well as the destruction of the Rhodesian way of life, inspired a number of Security Force members to practise their own dirty tricks. Several attempts were made to portray ZANU(PF) as godless and brutal, nearly all of which exposed the perpetrators as crude and incompetent amateurs. A particularly callous, and futile, action occurred on Sunday, 3 February, when Security Force personnel attacked a bus carrying guests returning from a wedding. Thirteen Africans were killed outright, and three died later. COMOPS issued a statement referring to follow-up operations against 'the terrorist faction responsible', and the Security Forces produced a dead ZANLA body and the tell-tale evidence of Australian-made matches thereby connecting the attack with ZANLA 'terrorists' quartered at Assembly Point Echo nearby. If, indeed, anyone believed such a clumsy fabrication, the logical conclusion was to vote for ZANU(PF) to avoid any repetition.[89] On 14 February, the day on which the RF candidates romped home in the six contested white seats for the Assembly, two black Selous Scouts tried to implicate ZANU(PF) in anti-Christian activity by placing bombs and forged papers near two churches. Their main achievement was to blow themselves up. Other 'dirty tricks' included a counterfeit issue of the Catholic paper *Moto*, which made some scurrilous allegations about Mugabe and ZANU(PF), followed by a bomb attack on the Catholic Mambo Press in Gwelo. Presumably, the electorate was supposed to conclude that ZANU(PF) had retaliated because *Moto* had given the party a bad press. Another bomb – found by ballistics experts to be a fake – was placed on the steps of the Catholic Cathedral in a suitcase containing anti-Church slogans. On yet another occasion PSYOPS, using an unmarked Dakota, managed to drop a bundle of leaflets reading 'Don't vote for Godless Marxists' directly onto the heads of members of the Commonwealth Monitoring Force.

Three further incidents might have had serious consequences.[90] First, early on 6 February, two ZANU(PF) houses, including Mugabe's newly-acquired residence in Mount Pleasant, were attacked with grenades and small arms fire. Secondly, on Sunday, 10 February, when Mugabe was leaving Fort Victoria after a rally, a device containing 40 kg of high explosive was detonated beneath a culvert on the airport road. Mugabe escaped unharmed, the passengers in two escort vehicles were lucky to survive, and repair teams were left with a 3-metre deep hole. P. K. Allum, the Police Commissioner, was livid: 'MY policemen' were in one of the escort cars. Allum also resented being expected to provide the 'cover-up' for botched operations, and he demanded that Flower forbid any further action.[91] Like many CIO and Special Branch officers, Allum detected the hand of the Chief Superintendent whose branch of CIO was allegedly responsible for the removal of Edson Sithole in 1975 and who was assumed to be acting on Flower's orders. Flower denied that CIO had authorised the attacks, a credible response given his own inability from 1979 to control the various special forces supposedly under his command or influence. The Director-General himself was accused of foiling the third operation. On 17 February the ZANU(PF) leader was due to speak at Bulawayo where elaborate plans had been made to assassinate him. Warned of the security risk, Mugabe made a last-minute decision against leaving Salisbury.

The most audacious of the plots of January-February 1980 was Operation Quartz. The objective, which was clearly behind the Military Intelligence paper of 29 January, was a simultaneous attack on the ZANLA Assembly Points to coincide with an assassination attempt on Mugabe at Mount Pleasant, on Simon Muzenda (his deputy) in his house at Highlands, and on the ZANLA leadership quartered at the Audio Visual Centre next to the university grounds.[92] The South African Air Force, as well as the Zimbabwe Rhodesia Air Force, together with the SAS and the Selous Scouts, would constitute the main strike force. The plotters reasoned that they could take out the leadership and enough of the trained forces to set ZANLA back twenty years. They were not worried about an existing Rhodesian or Commonwealth presence at the Assembly Points: 'our blokes', at least, would have had some seconds' warning 'and would have known what to do'. Nor were they worried about the political implications: 'we were only in the military business' but 'would probably have got away with it anyway'.[93]

The plans for Quartz depended on four things. First, there was the need for intelligence. By mid-February, the Rhodesians knew enough about the various targets in Salisbury and around the country.[94] Secondly, Quartz banked on South African assistance which, in addition to the equipment already supplied to the Security Forces, would take the form of air strikes and, if necessary, involve ground troops. Lord Soames had already agreed to allow some 400 South Africans to enter the country to 'protect' Beit Bridge. Following an outcry, the force was suppos-edly withdrawn at the end of January but some troops remained inside the country and a larger contingent was poised to cross the border. Thirdly, the success of Quartz depended on Nkomo's willingness to enter a coalition with Smith and Muzorewa. For all their apparent insen-sitivity, the planners of Quartz recognised the necessity of securing a political settlement after the military action. It suited this strategy, there-fore, that ZIPRA forces had already begun joint training exercises with the Zimbabwe Rhodesia Security Forces and they were to be given the choice of coming on side once Quartz was launched against ZANLA.

Fourthly, and critically, Quartz was formulated on the assumption that Mugabe would return to the bush, either because he was defeated by the ballot box, or because the British had annulled the election, or because ZANU(PF) had been proscribed. Quartz had not been conceived to counter a Mugabe victory: rather, it presupposed ZANU(PF)'s defeat or isolation, followed by a desperate attempt to renew the war which would thus legitimate a pre-emptive strike against an outlaw. So, when on 3 March Walls realised that Mugabe had won the election, he refused to countenance a military assault (however much he might question the validity of the electoral process) because he recognised that the political consequences for the Rhodesians would be disastrous.

An intriguing question raised by these plans to kill Mugabe and to attack ZANLA is whether those involved ever thought through the political implications of a short-term success. The Nkomo option would have created its own problems with those whites who had never for-given him for the Viscount attacks. Nkomo's relations with Muzorewa were notoriously difficult and his own political base was limited to Matabeleland, parts of the Midlands, and Mashonaland West. Even Nkomo, who rarely allowed ideological considerations to divert him from his struggle for the highest office, and who felt hurt by ZANU(PF)'s decision to fight the election separately, would have jibbed at turning upon his former Patriotic Front ally. The 'Father of Zimbabwe' would surely have supported the overwhelming international condemnation of any military strike against Mugabe's forces and which caused

Monitoring Force casualties. Finally, white Rhodesia might have been less than grateful if – as seems probable – the war resumed and sanctions were reimposed.

An equally intriguing aspect was the attitude of those in authority. The Police Commissioner later denied any knowledge of Quartz, although he did know of the separate assassination plans for Mugabe.[95] Walls publicly claimed that he first heard of 'a coup' when he visited the United Kingdom after Zimbabwe's independence. He then proceeded to explain why he had refused to order an operation – whose existence he had denied – by saying that no coup would have lasted forty-eight hours once Mugabe had won. Walls also admitted that, as a soldier, he had been bound to consider every option.[96] Flower later insisted that a coup was never likely because people such as himself would have known of the preparations.[97] Yet Flower did know of the plans, which were given to him in detail by a white Special Branch officer who later served in Mugabe's CIO. Flower also claimed that no one at 'the highest level' ever thought that a coup was practicable or had seriously contemplated organising one. He admitted that there had been one occasion, just before the election, when the junior commanders let off steam at COMOPS in front of two British officials, and that there was some 'rather wild chatter' in the lower ranks. But Flower emphasised that the senior officers were never involved.[98] Yet senior officers in the Army, the Air Force, and the police did know of the planning since the previous August, and in some cases had sanctioned it. Either the Director-General of CIO was drawing a distinction between involvement and knowledge, or he had his own reasons for denying what he knew to be the case.

High-ranking Rhodesians in January-February shuttled between what they preferred and what they could have, and were not certain which way to turn. Allum, for example, detested 'terrorism', but was opposed to 'dirty tricks', partly because the operators were so barbaric and incompetent, partly because he believed that the authorities had a duty to keep the election on course, and partly because he understood 'the game was up'. Two days before the election results were announced, an Assistant Police Commissioner, accompanied by Flower, presented Allum with a plan to substitute ballot boxes stuffed with Muzorewa votes. Allum ordered the Assistant Commissioner from the room: he was outraged by the immorality of the proposal – 'it would have been irresponsible of me to say go ahead and fix the vote' – and, bearing in mind the previous fiascos, what concerned him 'most' was that 'news of the plan would get out'.[99] Whether he would have found it 'responsible' to approve a workable plan is another matter. The point is that, in opposition to those in the Security Forces who intended to fiddle the ballot or to render it irrelevant, there were all those white electoral officials, DCs, and police, so fulsomely praised by the British Election Commissioner and less publicly acknowledged by initially-sceptical observers,[100] who were fiercely determined to demonstrate their own integrity and efficiency. One Rhodesian might believe that the ends justified the means, and another might think that the means should reflect the ends. The latter, who practised the virtues which supposedly distinguished all Rhodesians from the uncivilised behaviour of the corrupt, were among those abused by the angry elements on 4 March.

Perhaps the most difficult thing to explain about the behaviour of high-ranking whites in early 1980 is that so many of them apparently failed to predict a Mugabe victory. Walls, for one, remained outwardly optimistic. Returning from Lancaster House in December 1979, he summoned a meeting of JOC commanders and informed them that Muzorewa would win and that Mrs Thatcher would not allow a 'Marxist terrorist' to take power. To make sure, he ordered everyone present to work for a Muzorewa victory.[101] From that moment Walls kept assuring his forces that everything would be all right, believing he could play the Thatcher trump if the cards started to fall the wrong way. In late January, for example, he told an Internal Affairs meeting that the UANC would win, a proposition which puzzled a young DC from the Midlands who knew that the PF controlled the TTLs in his district, that ZANU(PF) held Que Que, and that the UANC did not dare campaign in either area.[102] Walls made a similar statement to a business group just two weeks before the election,[103] and, with a week to go, Flower reportedly told CIO officials that Muzorewa would win.[104] Peter Allum – armed with several charts based on the April 1979 elections – informed NATJOC on 26 February that Muzorewa would take the most seats.[105] He based his assessment on the assumptions that those women and townspeople who voted for Muzorewa in 1979 would do so again, and that the black workers on white farms would be protected from any intimidation occurring in the TTLs.

Allum's judgement was supported by one Special Branch estimate, prepared on 24 February, which outlined the 'best' and 'worst' results in terms of seats as in Table 8.1. And if there happened to be a 10 per cent swing to the UANC, the 'best' result would improve to 37 seats for the Bishop against 24 for ZANU(PF).[106] This estimate clearly took no account of a letter purportedly written by Mugabe to Machel, and allegedly intercepted at Salisbury airport by Special Branch on 17 February. The ZANU(PF) leader provided a frank and measured account of the election campaign, predicted that he would win 56 seats, complained that the Security Forces were using the intimidation argument to persuade the Governor to ban ZANU(PF), and forecast that the Security Forces and the South Africans would not stand idly by and allow his party to win.[107] If the letter was genuine, then one section of Special Branch had evidence which challenged the assessment of another. Allum, who never saw the letter, said that he was obliged to become an amateur psephologist because Special Branch never gave him consistent and unambiguous advice.[108] Ron Peters, who commanded Special Branch in Salisbury, invariably gave the same, clear assessment that ZANU(PF) would win. He told Walls that ZANLA was not allowing Muzorewa's UANC to operate in his province, and that he had reported this information to the Police Commissioner who refused to forward these reports to NATJOC.[109] Peters also claimed that, at a seminar attended by senior uniformed, CID and Special Branch officers, Allum made it clear that he was primarily interested in the opinions of uniformed officers who confirmed the Commissioner's judgement about Muzorewa's chances.[110]

TABLE 8.1. *A Special Branch Prediction of the 1980 Election Results*

Party	Best	Worst
UANC	32	26
ZANU(PF)	30	30
PF	17	23
ZANU(Sit)	1	1

The failure to predict Mugabe's landslide victory, and the total collapse of Muzorewa's Shona vote, led to all kinds of accusations against Allum, CIO, and Special Branch.[111] The allegation was that Flower, Allum, and Walls, and other unnamed persons, had conspired to fore-stall Op Quartz by telling the Security Forces and white civilians that everything was 'under control'. It was easy enough to assemble motives: Flower was working for MI6 (and, on this reckoning, the British wanted Mugabe and/or Nkomo to win); Allum, a practising Catholic, was a closet liberal who was sympathetic to the Catholic Justice and Peace Commission which, in turn, favoured Mugabe; and Walls had been bought by the 'duchessing' conducted at Lancaster House.

The evidence for a conspiracy is of two kinds. First, there was the public display of confidence about the result. Yet there was nothing necessarily conspiratorial about trying to bolster morale. Allum visited BSAP stations around the country telling his men not to give up hope: 'I couldn't have said anything else, it would have been treasonous to undermine them.[112] Secondly, and more seriously, there was the failure to press the case for abrogating the election or proscribing ZANU(PF).

As early as mid-January the Security Force commanders in Victoria and Mashonaland East provinces were so concerned that they were collecting affidavits for submission to NATJOC and the Governor. On 30 January Allum wrote to Robin Renwick, the Governor's Political Adviser, providing detailed instances of widespread unlawful practice but he did not recommend any retaliatory action.[113] Just prior to the election there was a meeting in Muzorewa's official residence where it was agreed to call upon the Governor to postpone the election. The task was assigned to the Commissioner of Police and he was given affidavits acquired from contacts inside the Monitoring Forces attesting to widespread ZANU(PF) intimidation. When Walls and Soames renewed their relations at a dinner in Walls's house after the elections, the Governor swore that neither he nor Robin Renwick saw any affidavits from the Commissioner of Police. Finally, on 26 February, when NATJOC heard Allum's prediction of a Muzorewa victory, it had an overwhelming case of intimidation to present to the Governor. Instead, it passed a resolution noting that 'it would not be in the nation's interests' to recommend that the Governor should exercise his powers, a position which, NATJOC also noted, had already been communicated to Walls by Robin Renwick. NATJOC made a similar response when it received reports of widespread intimidation from the commanders of Hurricane, Thrasher, and Repulse on the first two days of the election. Those in authority simply did not want to know, or did not know how to act upon their own information, or still believed that Mugabe could not win.

Did Allum and Flower and, to a lesser extent, Walls conspire against *Rhodesian* interests by not insisting on action against intimidation?[114] One thing is clear: Allum and Flower did not conspire together. They utterly detested each other and could not have worked jointly for any reputable (or disreputable) purpose. Relations between them had long been tense, probably because of the ambiguous status of Special Branch which Flower controlled for some operations but which remained the responsibility of the Police Commissioner. The real weaknesses of the conspiracy thesis, however, are that it is based on a highly questionable version of *Rhodesian* interests, and presupposes that these high-ranking Rhodesians had a clear idea of what they were doing. Quite separately, Allum and Flower had reached the conclusion that the country's best interests lay in holding elections, accepting the result, and ensuring world approval. It hardly mattered that both men were affected by contradictory pressures. Flower wanted to 'see it through', he also wanted to help Muzorewa, and his strongest preference was to bring Nkomo into a coalition. Allum, like Flower, did not want Mugabe to win, he loathed the 'cowboys' who practised 'dirty tricks', he would 'cover up' as required but refused to back unworkable and potentially embarrassing schemes, and he wanted to do the honourable thing. What mattered was that two views had emerged in January-February over the approach to the election: one, for practical and moral reasons, said it should proceed; and the other, on moral grounds (the extent of intimidation) and for practical considerations (the success of intimidation), said it should not. In effect, white Rhodesians were conducting their last debate about how a civilised society should behave.

The participants were very confused, and none more so than Peter Walls. Ian Smith could not understand why the Security Force commanders did not simply tell Soames that either he should call off the election or that they would do it for him.[115] A more politically astute and tactful military leader might have engineered a stronger British response to the intimidation charges. One effect of his row with Soames was that Walls could not press the case. Yet Walls never quite knew what to do. The British sensed his vulnerability to the domestic pressures and, being aware of Quartz and of Walls's possible role in launching the operation, kept in close – almost daily – touch to ensure that he did not do anything 'daft'.[116] Like Allum, Walls wanted to appear honourable: he would act if 'the lady' agreed to invalidate the election; short of Mrs Thatcher's intervention, he would assure everybody – from the Governor's Political Adviser, to Samora Machel,[117] to Ken Flower – that he would abide by the result.

It would be fair to conclude that most high- (and low-) ranking Rhodesians looked upon their world much as Walls did. He saw that too much was happening at once; he could see so many conflicting options and only a limited capacity to implement any of them; he knew what he wanted, knew he could not have it, knew he wanted to stay in Rhodesia, and knew very little about what Zimbabwe was, or could be, like. A member of the British Observer Team in Bulawayo encountered so many whites who, more so than Walls, were 'wishing for a lost world'.[118] Andrew Campbell thought that the older ones were 'a somewhat kindly but sad lot', and that the young 'dont [sic] have much grip on present day realities'. He found resentment against Britain for not 'backing us up', a deep-seated hostility towards Mugabe, an ambivalent attitude to Nkomo, and official support for Muzorewa. Campbell's papers confirm the general view of even sympathetic outsiders: in January-February 1980 most Rhodesians were bewildered and apprehensive, and wanted to be reassured. Not surprisingly, therefore, they failed to predict Mugabe's win because they did not want it, and because they did not want to believe, or could not interpret, the evidence which was all about them.

VI

The hotels in Salisbury had filled up with journalists, Commonwealth and national observer teams, official and unofficial delegations, and with individuals from across the political spectrum who arrived expecting to denounce the skulduggery of either the 'racists' or the 'communists'. A contingent of British police was also flown in just before the common roll election and 565 'Bobbies' were dispersed to the polling stations on the assumption that the natives (white as well as black) knew of their honesty and would respect their impartiality. The whites, who were irrelevant to the result, if not to its acceptance, were called up in their thousands. They had already chosen their twenty white MPs. Nick McNally of NUF had tried to assemble a 'non-party party' to contest the election but the heroes of the RF's defeat – such as Ian Smith, Van der Byl, Partridge, Irvine, and Goddard – were elected to protect white interests in the new Zimbabwe. Meanwhile, the Rhodesians were a trifle bemused by the sudden international attention and the arrival of so many expense accounts. Nonetheless, they performed according to the scripts written elsewhere. Drunken young 'Rhodies' and stony-faced housewives denigrated 'the munt' and denounced 'the devious British', and the 'really fine types' countered these images by showing themselves to be thoroughly decent and liberal.[119]

On 27 February, the first day of the common roll elections, Ian Smith held a meeting in his Salisbury house which was attended by the Security Force commanders, P. K. van der Byl, and 'other' white politicians. (Allum and Flower were not present.)[120] Smith asked Walls, who was sitting on the couch opposite him, whether he had a contingency plan in the event of Mugabe winning the election. The General said – repeatedly – that Mugabe 'won't win'. Pressed by Smith, Walls admitted that there was a plan and that Mugabe would be stopped. The other commanders nodded in agreement. Walls's own plan had already been implemented. He had written to Mrs Thatcher, sending his letter through the South African Ministry of Foreign Affairs, and was confident that this approach, which ignored the Governor, would lead to the abrogation of the elections.

For the next three days long voting queues gathered at the polling stations throughout the country. No one died violently while attempting to vote, although the democratic process was enlivened by the repetition of the 1979 (false) rumours about missing ballot boxes and double voting. A clever suggestion, allegedly put about by ZANU(PF), was that Mugabe voters should turn up on the first day, Nkomo supporters on the second, and Muzorewa on the third. On that basis, the 400,000 voters on Day Three were either courageous, deaf, or lived in the more remote areas. The ballot boxes were collected and taken to the provincial centres – thereby preventing any identification of the results by district or polling station – and counting started on Monday morning, 3 March.

By late that afternoon it was clear that Mugabe had won a landslide victory. ZANU(PF) secured 63 per cent of the vote and 57 seats, Nkomo's PF won 24 per cent and 20 seats, and the Bishop's UANC collected just 8.3 per cent and 3 seats. Hurried meetings were called in Salisbury, rumours flew around the country, and members of the SAS, the Selous Scouts, and the RLI waited expectantly. Peter Walls then made a fateful decision. He went in the evening to the television studios just near the Borrowdale Racecourse. A pre-recorded message from Soames called for calm. Mugabe then spoke and pleaded for the acceptance of the results and for no recriminations. Walls was not certain until the last moment whether to speak, or what he should say. He was 'in a hell of a turmoil'.[121] Finally, he agreed to appear in front of the cameras. After claiming to represent the Security Forces, and those members of ZIPRA and ZANLA who had acknowledged the authority of the Governor, he went on:

Anyone who obeys the law will have our backing and will have nothing to fear. At the same time, anybody who gets out of line or for whatever reason starts disobeying the law will be dealt with effectively and swiftly and, I may say, with quite a bit of enthusiasm ... We are looking forward in a spirit of reconciliation to maintaining law and order.[122]

It was a chilling, significant statement. Walls was warning the country against violence; in joining with Mugabe on television he was telling the observant who had won; and he was also announcing that there would be no coup. Having failed to persuade Mrs Thatcher to intervene and cancel the election, and having committed himself to so many people, he really had no alternative except to acknowledge the result. Like everyone else, Walls had not anticipated the collapse of the Bishop's vote in Mashonaland and, contrary to his alleged statement to Smith on the first election day, he had no plan to counter a decisive electoral victory for Mugabe.

Despite all the rumours, and the obvious implication of the Mugabe and Walls speeches, large sections of the white electorate were stunned when the results were officially released on the morning of 4 March. It was a measure of its mental isolation that so much of the electorate seemed incapable not only of predicting the result – after all, even those all-knowing internationalists who descended on Salisbury in early 1980 were no wiser[123] – but of accepting what was obvious from at least 27 February and what was told to them on 3 March. The announcement on 4 March finally obliged the majority to come to terms with reality. There would be no coup, the 'garden boys' and the 'nannies' would now govern the country, and whites could continue to live in Zimbabwe because the new rulers were not interested in retribution.

9

'Fourteen great years'

I

Just after the election results were announced, the wife of a Mount Darwin farmer described her new world as 'heaven – sheer bliss. We can actually sleep through the whole night.'[1] Earlier, Ian Smith had told his wife, Janet, that he was quite optimistic. He had just left a private meeting with Robert Mugabe who assured him that Zimbabwe would not destroy the wonderful legacy left by Rhodesia.[2] In public, Smith was more cautious, advising the whites not to run: they should 'wait-and-see'.[3] But on one subject he was unrepentant. There were no regrets about UDI and no regrets about resisting 'terrorism': the Rhodesians had been given 'fourteen great years'.

The headstones in the white cemeteries indicated that some boys died before they were old enough to appreciate their good fortune. And a number of grieving relatives and friends might have found Smith's statement a trifle emphatic. There were many other ways in which the last of the 'great years' had become less attractive: the emigration of friends, the call-ups, petrol coupons, handbag inspections, restricted holidays, convoys, security fences, shortages, rumours, gloomy news broadcasts, bad whisky, and awful wine. The war years also meant more divorces and more drinking, a pace of life which assumed no tomorrow,[4] where the young were enticed into day-long parties and quick marriages, and their elders into brief and bizarre relationships, where decent men and women experienced a hardening of the soul and snarled at each other, at blacks, and at the rest of the world.[5] The end of the war was, indeed, 'heaven'. Relieved rather than angry, the farmer's wife was not one of those Rhodesians who, in the words sung by Clem Tholet, would 'fight through thick and thin'. By 1980 she belonged to the majority. And, ironically enough, for people like her, the collapse of the 'great years' marked the restoration of part of the Rhodesian way of life.

Surely, therefore, it was worth asking whether the war had been fought in vain? After all, by 1980 the Rhodesians had seemingly lost all they had been fighting for: their political power; their formal, privileged access to land, housing, jobs, education, and health services; their assurance that everything from economic policies to the political culture, from the attitudes and priorities of public officials to the content of television programmes, would reflect or meet their expectations. Notwithstanding a brave defiance, 'Godless Marxism' had apparently triumphed over 'Christian civilisation'. On the other hand, there was a good case for the proposition that, just as the guerrilla war had hastened the process of political change, forcing Smith into the surrender of September 1976, so the armed resistance by the Security Forces had not only delayed the 'terrorist' victory but had forced the 'terrorists' into the constitutional process. This argument was probably too subtle to console those RF stalwarts in 1980 whose resistance to 'terrorism' and political change was avowedly absolute. They had fought the war to prevent change, not to make change less unpalatable. Besides, too much had been invested in resistance to permit many Rhodesians in 1980 to admit that the fighting was a mistake, or that the Rhodesians were actually in danger of defeat if the war had continued beyond 1979. It was more reassuring to insist that 'the British', 'the West', or an 'international conspiracy' had deprived the Rhodesians of victory. Certainly there would be no acknowledgement that the reviled Centre Party liberals – and their predecessors and successors – had been right all along. Nor was there any possibility of Front supporters publicly addressing the sensitive question – frequently asked by the far right – of whether the sacrifice had all been worth while.

This reaction to the Mugabe election victory suggests that the war and political change had not had any immediate, significant impact on the mental attitudes of the majority of whites. Nevertheless, the war did have profound implications for individuals and families, and especially for those who lived in the rural areas. The most important, overall effects of the war, however, were to divert attention from the political and legislative changes of the late 1970s and to confirm some cherished assumptions about the essence of Rhodesian-ness while – sometimes – undermining their credibility. Opposition to 'terrorism' had helped to unite a society even as internal discord, emigration, and pragmatism were exposing its fragility. This apparent paradox – of solidarity in the midst of disharmony – poses the broader question of how far the war and the advent of majority rule had changed the Rhodesia of 1970. The objective of this chapter is to address the several facets of that question.

II

The statistics of death and injury provide one clue to the individual and family experience of the war.[6] In all, COMOPS reckoned that there were at least 20,350 war-related deaths on Rhodesian soil between December

1972 and December 1979: 468 white civilians, 1,361 members of the
Security Forces (just under half of them white), and, in round figures,
10,450 'terrorists' and 7,790 black civilians.[7] Allowing for the certain
understatement of black civilian deaths and the high casualties inflicted
on external raids,[8] these figures show that, while the African population
bore the brunt of the war, the European minority had shed proportionately more blood.[9] The school honour rolls recorded some other stark
facts: there are at least 52 names listed at Prince Edward School, 35 at
Guinea Fowl, 27 at Churchill, 23 each at St George's College and
Plumtree (Walls's old school), and 21 at Umtali Boys' High School.[10]

A further clue to the cost of the war is contained in the death notices
and in the 'Roll of Honour' and 'In Memoriam' columns in the press. A
few wondered if fathers and sons, husbands and brothers, had died in
vain.[11] Others clung to the Christian hope of meeting again. 'Mum and
Dad' often recalled happier times; and, occasionally, 'Mum' and 'Dad'
appeared in separate notices, a reminder that the Christian society could
not force people to live together until death. If some families seemed
unsure about the value of the sacrifice, others at least knew its purpose.
Trooper Des Washington 'died for Rhodesia'. So did Gordon Jackson.[12]
Delville Vincent, who was killed early in the war on 3 April 1973, was
buried in the tiny cemetery attached to the Anglican church at
Umvukwes. The inscription on his grave records that he died 'In defence
of Rhodesia'. A headstone in the cemetery at Chipinga said that Ken
Cremer, who was killed on 15 August 1978, was 'Rhodesian'. No prefix
was needed. Yet by 1980, 'Rhodesia', the focal point of all this sacrifice,
had gone. The bereaved who might, as a last resort, justify a death as an
offering to a noble and living cause, had lost even that last crumb of
comfort.

Another grave in Chipinga records the death of four people in a
single landmine incident on 6 July 1976. Shirley Wickstead, a 15-year-old
schoolgirl, was the sole survivor. She lost both her legs and, overnight,
became a celebrity for her cheerfulness and courage in the face of such
shocking injuries. Douglas Bader, the legendary British war hero, sent
her a message of encouragement and so did several of Rhodesia's
leaders. Dale Collett, a highly-decorated Selous Scout, was another
patient at St Giles Rehabilitation Centre who was fêted in the local press.
Ian Smith was photographed standing next to him. It suited the cause to
praise his spirit. It also suited his future convenience that the Salisbury
Municipality altered the kerbs in the main streets to allow for the easier
passage of wheelchairs.[13] By late 1979, St Giles was providing physiotherapy for 190 patients a month (compared with 20-40 in 1970-2), so that
there were plenty of potential users of the new facility.[14]

The war crippled others in a different way. Early in the morning on

5 January 1980 Bruce Verdal-Austin, the DC of Mudzi to the north-east of Mtoko, and his assistant, Graeme Duncan, together with a third European, left Mudzi to drive the 140 km to Salisbury. The DC had spent the previous day drinking. After four hours' sleep he helped to consume a bottle of cane spirit on the trip into Salisbury. Jeered and abused by busloads of ZANLA guerrillas as they entered Salisbury, the men had breakfast on arrival and then drank beer before leaving for Mudzi early in the afternoon. On the way back, Verdal-Austin and Duncan began firing automatic rifles into the air before shooting at African cyclists and pedestrians, at a small car, and at a bus carrying over fifty black passengers. Two Africans in the car later died, and several others were injured. The Land Rover was stopped by a police roadblock at Mrewa and Verdal-Austin and Duncan were arrested and subsequently charged with murder and attempted murder.

The facts of the case were not disputed. The sole issue was whether the crimes could be described as politically inspired, in which case the two men would have been freed under the Amnesty (General Pardon) Ordinance of 1980. In rejecting their plea, the court concluded that, by firing first into the air, and not using the more effective weapons in the vehicle (namely, cannons and a machine gun), the accused were hardly providing evidence of 'wanting to blow the whole thing [the cease-fire] sky high' and of wanting to launch 'a full-scale, gloves-off' fight. Sentencing both men to ten years in prison, the court accepted that they were intoxicated, that they were under strain, and had no actual intent to kill.

The mitigating argument of strain was the most revealing. Verdal-Austin had been in the service for twenty-two years. He had spent the war in some of the hottest zones and was hit by landmines on five occasions (four on the same day). Morale at Mudzi was poor: the DC's base camp was inadequately protected, there had been two heavy ZANLA attacks before the cease-fire, there was constant drinking and fighting within the camp, the DC's own ministry had decided that his area could not be properly administered, no senior officer from JOC Hurricane or sub-JOC Mtoko had visited Mudzi during Verdal-Austin's tenure, and a Special Branch officer had told him that the post was considered expendable. Both men had recently lost a friend in an ambush, Duncan was required to help collect the charred bodies after the first Viscount incident, and both had lived in daily fear of attack, were constantly drunk, exhibited signs of deep anxiety, and felt isolated and 'abandoned'. Although the court rejected the political motive, there was uncontested evidence of anger and frustration directed at Lancaster House and ZANLA. Neither of the men had proved to be strong or resourceful; hurt, bitter, and drunk, they had let off their anger in a senseless orgy of shooting. The war had driven the weak to take a terrible revenge.[15]

Verdal-Austin's experience was hardly typical, but parents, the police, and the Army were concerned in the late 1970s that more young whites were turning to alcohol and drugs.[16] In June 1979 Chief Superintendent Hartley from the Drug Squad told a university seminar that there had been a rise in dagga smoking and alcohol abuse.[17] Chief Superintendent Rogers, head of the drug squad, made a similar point in May 1980.[18] Both argued that a fondness for the outdoors, and Rhodesia's isolation, still protected the young from hard drugs. Alcohol consumption, however, had reached dangerous proportions. It was clearly a factor behind the deadly games of Russian roulette which became something of a vogue towards the end of the war. One game in January 1980 left a young Grey's Scout dead in a Salisbury bar.[19] Another unsavoury manifestation was the increasing incidence of drunken behaviour among young whites in the cities and towns. In Salisbury the problem regularly exploded in four inner-city bars in 1978-80 and led to fights amongst themselves, considerable property damage, and physical and verbal abuse of black waiters and any other Africans in the vicinity. One city hotel manager, who had served in the British Army for twenty-two years, said he had never seen anything like the incidents where whites would enter 'African bars' and 'set about any Africans with anything they could lay their hands on'.[20]

There is some – largely anecdotal – evidence of a longer-term dislocation caused by the war. Chris Cocks, who had served in the RLI, told a sad tale about the fate of his companions after 1980: two committed suicide, one drowned in his own vomit, two were convicted of drug smuggling, one died of natural causes, one joined the Seychelles coup of 1984, one faced an arm amputation, and one (himself) had to visit a psychiatrist. Those he did not name included some who had gone on fighting elsewhere and the rest who had returned to civilian life where the majority were 'just drifting'.[21] Whether Cocks was reliably reporting from a representative sample, and whether the war was directly responsible for the behaviour of his associates in the 1980s, are not questions which can be answered authoritatively here.[22] Probably some men simply coped better than others. The young whites who patronised the (diminishing) number of bars and night clubs in Harare in the early 1980s might have fostered the impression of a generation unhinged by the war. A closer inspection suggested that the rowdiest were often those whose promising military careers as 16 year olds were cut short by the outbreak of peace. Few of the rowdies had been present when shots were fired in anger and it was probably too early in 1980-1 to determine whether the war had permanently disabled their lives. The evidence which emerged in interviews during the 1980s was that the former troopies, for whom the war was already life's great experience, reacted just like ex-soldiers everywhere: they either preferred to reflect in solitude or sought the company of those who shared their experience. They recalled the past with a blend of affection and sorrow, pride and disillusionment. And they were more disposed to remember the laughter, the mateship, and the thrills than the boredom, the hurt, and the fear.

Their consolation was that, unlike the American or Australian veterans of Vietnam, they had not been forced to slink back into their own society as an embarrassment. Outsiders might sneer at the men and women who fought bravely for a discredited cause but the Rhodesians, during and after the war, honoured their heroism.[23] Yet when the Americans and the Australians finally decided to acknowledge their Vietnam veterans they did so within societies which had physically survived the trauma of defeat. The Rhodesian veterans, convinced that they had not lost, no longer owned a country which permitted them to march.

There is also evidence that the war helped other whites to mature or to grow in self-esteem. During 1978 a young officer in the RLI found himself leading some 'nasties and drunkards' who were eventually turned into 'a most effective fighting unit'. One of his men, who was considered a 'sissy' at Umtali Boys' High School, led a troop with the highest 'kill ratio' in the Commando. The officer also noted how school-leavers and apprentices soon dispensed with their civilian sensibilities: they could sit on the bodies of dead 'terrs' and calmly cut open a can of beans and eat the contents. A few of them 'avoided the heroics'; some were loners and unloved or just 'aggro'; the majority, the Rhodesians rather than the foreigners, were stable and level-headed, just 'ordinary boys' who learnt to overcome their fears when in battle. Admittedly, the young officer himself was once ordered back to Salisbury to restore his nerves after spending ten consecutive days of hitting the ground first when the helicopters of a Fireforce unit attacked guerrilla positions. But he left the Army after independence a seemingly well-adjusted farmer.[24]

Given the nature of the war, however, it is hard to believe that the whites were not brutalised – or, at least, temporarily desensitized – by their experience. Bishop Burrough, who was critical of the Security Forces as well as of Z1PRA and ZANLA, was convinced that the war did terrible damage to all sides.[25] The freedom fighters terrorised villagers, butchered alleged 'sell-outs', massacred innocent families, and desecrated the churches. The defenders of Western civilisation tortured their captives, murdered civilians, burnt villages, and calmly dispatched prisoners in preference to long trips back to base.[26] whites customarily argued that horrible things inevitably happen in war and that, in any case, the 'terrorists' more frequently crossed the line of what was forgivable.

A white Special Branch officer justified the torturing of blacks with the argument that the 'terrs' would surely disembowel any African suspected of collaborating with the Security Forces.[27] Ken Flower, who was ultimately accountable for CIO's 'dirty tricks',[28] did not excuse his Organisation for employing the Revd Arthur Kanodareka, a leading figure in Muzorewa's UANC, to supply poisoned clothing to young recruits which consigned them to a slow and agonizing death. 'For more years than I would like to tell . . . [m]any hundreds' died in this fashion. Instead, Flower pinpointed Kanodareka as the real villain in 'a most sordid tale of treachery and betrayal', When Kanodareka was murdered near Salisbury in late 1978 a number of prominent whites attended the funeral of this presumed victim of nationalist faction-fighting. They did not know that CIO had ordered the assassination because the scheme was 'so diabolically successful' that Kanodareka had to be eliminated to avoid an inevitable exposure. Flower likened the killing to the hunter finishing off the wounded animal 'to stop further suffering'. The simile was inaccurate though telling. Flower wanted to seize the higher moral ground because the image of the civilised society, and of civilised men, had to be sustained even when it was thoroughly compromised. So the reverend gentleman was the truly guilty one, and his removal – forced on CIO because his controller reported that he had become greedy and ill-disciplined – became morally justified.[29] In effect, the war had forced a society which proclaimed moral absolutes to allow individuals and their organisations to indulge in moral relativism.

The divorce courts provide further evidence of how difficult it had become to adhere to the absolutes. Marriages in the towns and cities collapsed sooner and at a faster rate (rising from 1 in 5 in 1970 to 1 in 4 by the mid-1970s, and to 1 in 3 by 1979),[30] family tensions became more visible, and charitable institutions reported increased evidence of affairs and domestic violence. Indeed, while the stated standards of moral behaviour had never been universally practised, the internal critics were quick to claim that the war years had promoted moral decay. The upright Harvey Ward, the former Director-General of RBC/TV, blamed the political defeat of 1976-80 on what he saw as the abandonment of Christian principles, symbolised by the growing practice of abortion.[31] The story of John Hickman might also have attracted his attention, if only because few of the general's fellow officers were qualified to cast the first stone. According to Smith, who was emphatic and repetitive on this point, Walls himself had to be reprimanded for his past errant behaviour.[32] Other senior Army officers, and their wives and mistresses, swapped beds and lovers with a blatant disregard for the Seventh

Commandment. Smith's own explanation – 'I was told that these things happened in wartime'[33] – meant that, at worst, John Hickman was just a more extravagant sinner at a time when a number of the martial leaders of Rhodesia had lost sight of their inherited morality.

Even though few Rhodesians probably escaped unscathed from the moral pitfalls, Harvey Ward exaggerated the extent of the moral collapse. The war did not cause the Rhodesian world to fall apart, the majority of Rhodesians did not plunge into the abyss, and Rhodesia did not become an *ancien régime* weakened by corruption and disintegrating at the centre. More importantly, Ward confused cause and effect in explaining political defeat in terms of abandoned Christian principles. For it was the expectation of defeat and the implications of majority rule which encouraged so many Rhodesians to look after themselves and to abandon the preferred codes of conduct.

A few senior civil servants saw an opportunity in 1979 to repatriate their full pensions, took the money, and fled. The twenty-two members of the Fraud Squad, bolstered in numbers and expertise by the call-up which enabled the squad to draft accountants, was kept fully occupied by the activities of the currency swindlers. Minor cases – for example, where residents supplied Rhodesian dollars to visitors in exchange for foreign currency paid abroad – were never pursued unless the activity became too conspicuous.[34] The major cases – where businessmen tampered with invoices, set up dummy companies, made 'arrangements' with companies overseas, or tried exporting precious stones – were tackled with the utmost vigour. Statistically, there was a sharp increase in this form of crime and in its detection. In 1974, 35 cases involving illegal transactions in gold and precious stones were taken to court; in 1978 and 1979 the figures were 111 (involving 147 accused) and 226 (259 accused) respectively.[35] The Police Commissioner in his 1979 *Report* said that the 'large increase' could be 'attributed to the uncertainty with which many view the future and is indicative of the lengths to which people will go to remove assets from the country'.

Some of Rhodesia's lesser notables were caught, including Rodney Simmonds, whose failure to repatriate funds cost him $35,000,[36] and Jurick Goldwasser, a former Bulawayo Mayor and RP candidate in 1974, who was one of three men convicted of exporting $560,000 by falsifying invoices. Two senior civil servants – a Chief Customs Security Officer and an Under-Secretary in the Ministry of Defence – were convicted of over-invoicing a number of arms deals to the value of about $1 million. A third man, Ted Muller, a South African-born managing director of a subsidiary of the Rennies company, had once dined with Ian Smith at Independence House as a reward for his sanctions-busting activities.[37] Although Army officers and NCOs came under suspicion for presenting large bills for trucks bought in South Africa, more official attention was given to the rumours of 'bigger' names which were rife in 1977-9. Walls and MacIntyre were both investigated, and Ian Smith employed CIO to examine allegations about his ministers. Suspicion rested heavily on one Smith minister but, it was claimed, there was not enough evidence to charge and convict, though it was known that he (and others) had made special arrangements with Jewish businessmen in South Africa.[38] Rumours also abounded that Smith himself, and 'Boss' Lilford, had illegally moved cattle to South Africa and had acquired large properties there.[39] Both men vigorously and persistently denied the allegations which, in the absence of any supporting evidence, are more significant for what they reveal about the togetherness of white Rhodesia in the late 1970s. Things were just beginning to fall apart, and the accusations were flying about. Yet if the men at the top were not the brightest, nor the most sensitive, the vast majority of them were not crooked either.

Thousands of whites did, however, commit what the 'true' Rhodesians condemned as the ultimate selfish and unpatriotic act: they emigrated. Given that there were an estimated 232,000 Europeans in mid-1979 compared with 228,296 in 1969, that there was a slow-down in emigration in the second half of 1979, and that 14,284 Europeans had arrived in Rhodesia between January 1977 and November 1979 (admittedly, they were mainly returning Rhodesians and whites on short-term contracts), the statistics were not universally depressing. But, in December 1975, official estimates were that the European population numbered 278,000 and, challenging the far right's faith in permanent white supremacy, the estimated black population of 7.1 million in 1979 raised the ratio of black to white from 21 :1 in 1969 to 30 :1. The more alarming fact was that 46,722 whites had left the country in the period of 1977-9.[40] Just as the largest categories of immigrants in 1970 were adults between 25 and 39 years of age and children under 14 years – when there was a net immigration of 6,331 Europeans – so the same categories dominated the emigration statistics in 1979. Whereas in 1970 the loss of the 'economically active' males was always worrying, in 1979 the Security Forces classified 'economically active' males as 'bayonets' whose departure was damaging. In 1974 Ian Smith declared that his government's 'greatest achievement' had been to reverse the net migration loss of the 1962-6 period by persuading 'good Rhodesians' that their country had a future.[41] Yet, by 1979, thousands of young families had deserted Rhodesia for material and personal security and the future of their children, or were too 'Rhodesian' to tolerate the transformation of their country into Zimbabwe. Either way, their vote of no confidence was unequivocal evidence that the war and political change had undermined the purported unity and solidarity of Rhodesian society.

Faced with the hardships and crises of the late 1970s, and determined to stay or unable – financially – to leave, more individuals and families looked inwards, or upwards, for the kind of reassurance which seemed unnecessary before the war. The Sunday believers of 1970 acquired a more intensive and pervasive faith in the late 1970s.[42] Parishes might complain about declining attendances – which they associated with rising emigration rather than increasing disbelief[43] – but the charismatic influence was reviving interest in the city churches and in non-institutional Christianity. One prayer group, the Esthers, who originated in South Africa in mid-1978, established 28 groups in the Eastern Districts and had 200 members praying for particular farmers and their families as well as mines, villages, and farms. Telephone chains were established, Operation Esther was linked to the Nation at Prayer organisation, and the believers – citing the peaceful outcome of the 1979 and 1980 elections and numerous cases of 'miraculous' survival under armed attack – were convinced that their prayers were answered.[44]

For those who needed more dramatic miracles there was the brief appearance of white spirit mediums, one of whom claimed to have reached Elvis Presley who obligingly sang 'Hound Dog' and 'Blue Suede Shoes'.[45] A less improbable source of comfort was the clairvoyant who had the good sense to focus upon ideologically-sound predictions. Bill McLeod came into vogue after forecasting the first Viscount disaster and Margaret Thatcher's election victory. In mid-1979 he foresaw Pik Botha becoming South African Prime Minister within two years, Castro falling within eighteen months, Muzorewa firmly in control by the coming November, and Edward Kennedy becoming the next President of the United States. In January 1980 McLeod announced that Muzorewa would win the February elections by a large majority, that Samora Machel would be deposed by a coup within two years, and that Walls would remain in the country for a long time. He did manage some successes, though it was hardly a master-stroke to predict that Ian Smith would win all twenty white seats in the new Zimbabwe parliament.[46]

McLeod retained his credibility into 1980 because more Rhodesians wanted to believe him. There was nothing new about this quest for reassurance. Since the early 1960s the Rhodesians had exhibited an almost pathetic innocence and gullibility in seeking approbation. In those happier times they wanted support for UDI, and to be told how race relations in Rhodesia were better than those of other mixed societies, that 'their' blacks were the happiest and most fortunate in Africa, and that they represented the last hope for Christian civilisation and moral rectitude. They also wanted to hear about the doom and gloom which had settled upon the outside world. By the late 1970s the need for reassurance had merely intensified and by then the Rhodesians had become especially vulnerable to anyone who offered good news, to say nothing of the well-wishers, cranks, killers, saviours, and would-be heroes who came to assist in the defence of Western civilisation, to tell the Rhodesians how wonderfully brave and good they all were, and to speculate when the Free World would come to its senses. One difference was that, while the messages were broadly similar, the Rhodesians became even less discriminating in their choice of messengers.[47] Another difference was a more explicit embrace of the supernatural.

III

Clearly, the war and political change had an immense though varied impact on families and individuals. Not surprisingly, the effect on communities and institutions was also mixed and wide ranging.

There were, for example, obvious and profound differences between the wartime experiences of rural and urban Rhodesia. Contacts between the two Rhodesias were certainly close: Territorial soldiers from the cities served in the small communities, members of those communities moved into town for safety, the farmers' representatives were constantly lobbying the government, rural and urban MPs sat together on the RF back-bench, Walls and other senior police and Army officers regularly visited the farming districts. Yet the farmers themselves were convinced that Salisbury never really understood what it was like living in the war zone. The Vice-Chairman of the Grain Producers' Association, speaking at the farmers' protest meeting on 22 May 1979, accused the planners in the Ministry of Agriculture of not knowing

... what it is like to be constantly armed, to be always prepared to be under attack ... to wake up in the middle of the night to the sound of gunfire and rockets and the smell of burning ... to see one's fields alight ... to face the tired and frightened labour force in the morning when all their possessions have been burnt, and to see the dead being carted away.[48]

A number of rural districts were emptied by the war. In 1975 there had been 225 family units on private farms in the Melsetter and Cashel districts and 150 families lived on the estates; by the end of 1978 there were 108 families on the farms and 62 on the estates.[49] Twenty-four homesteads were destroyed in the district during 1977, 13 whites and 39 African employees were killed in 1978, and there were 1,053 'terrorist' incidents in 1976-8. By 1979 some 30 per cent of farms in the Eastern Districts had been abandoned and nearly 70 per cent of the remainder did not have a resident farmer. Another 'bad' area was Mtoko. A farming representative told the CPU's annual congress in July 1979 that just 50 of its 93 farms were still occupied, 10 were being maintained on a caretaker basis, and 33 had been abandoned (10 of them in the Mayo district).[50] Several farmers from Tokwe informed the same meeting of their intention to vacate their area east of Gwelo. Theft had reduced their herds by 25 per cent and they wanted to avoid any further murders in the district. Denis Norman, the CFU President and a former RP supporter, warned the government at this congress that unless remedial action was taken to ensure law and order no farmers would be left at all.[51] Yet the incidents and deaths continued throughout 1979. Some 80 farmers or members of their families were killed between 1 January and 31 December (116 were killed in 1978), and 44 died between the election of the Muzorewa government and the end of the year. Although the fatal attacks occurred over several parts of the country, a high proportion of them were concentrated in the area around Umtali and west towards Marandellas in the latter part of 1979.[52]

The greatest dread of all in the farming communities was to detonate a landmine and then, while staggering dazed and numb from the vehicle, to be fired upon by waiting 'terrorists'. It was impossible to know when and where other attacks might occur, although some occasions were more dangerous than others: for example, travelling on dirt roads which led only to white-owned farms or on any road at all from late afternoon; visiting the labour compound to check on a reported illness or fight; paying the labour force. Living alone or being elderly increased the risk but no one was certain of immunity. The assumption that hard or Afrikaner employers were more vulnerable might have been true in some areas such as Centenary and Mayo. By 1978-9 the one guarantee against attack was to collaborate with the enemy, always assuming that each group of ZIPRA and ZANLA guerrillas both knew of the arrangement and respected it. Garfield Todd admitted that he co-operated with the guerrillas (which, given his views, was hardly surprising), and there is uncorroborated evidence of prominent RF families who achieved a *modus vivendi* with the insurgents. Special Branch uncovered one case where a manager of a tea estate in the Eastern Highlands was caught in the act of meeting with ZANLA guerrillas.[53] For those who could not contemplate such treasonable (or pragmatic) behaviour the only options were to take every possible safeguard and to co-operate with the neighbours.

To counter the daily threat to their lives, the farmers took precautions which changed their work patterns and curtailed their enjoyment of life. They were inundated with advice from area co-ordinating committees, DCs, sub-JOC commanders, Territorial Army officers, the police, farming organisations, private security firms, neighbouring farmers, and several self-appointed experts.[54] In response, the farmers trained their households to respond to attack. They also acquired, assembled, or constructed alarm systems, security fencing, external lighting, special inside curtains, bunkers, 'safe areas' inside the house, guard dogs, rocket, grenade, shrapnel, and bullet screens and blast walls, flares, beacons, and observation posts, emergency sources of rations, power, and communications, and remote-control defensive firing systems. To repel a rocket attack, for instance, farmers were advised by the RNFU to build a screen wall of hard gauge steel woven mesh, set 8 metres from the house. An RPG-7 rocket was usually fired within a 150-500 metre range and, fitted with a night sight, was designed to plunge a molten plug into a tank. The plug could – on detonation – penetrate 90" of earth and sandbags, 18" of reinforced concrete, 15" of granite rock, or 13" of steel armour-plating. A blast wall, unprotected by a screen and placed close to the house, would stop grenades and rifle fire but a rocket could then explode right next to the house and have no open space in which the blast could dissipate. A screen wall would detonate the rocket thus enabling a 9" brick wall to stop the molten plug.

The elaborate defence systems converted the farm houses into fortresses. Peter Storrer's seed potato farm, situated above Troutbeck near Inyanga in the Eastern Highlands and just 5 km from the Mozambique border, was mortared three times during the war. On one occasion the house came under such heavy and accurate fire that the second-storey roof was destroyed. Storrer's response was to install the full range of available security measures: 'Bright Lights' patrolled the farm and perimeter of the house;[55] Guard Force units were stationed on the property; the house was surrounded by a security fence; inside the fence three vicious dogs ran loose at night; the living quarters of the house were sandbagged and curtains blacked out the house after dark; Storrer kept a minor arsenal of small arms including weapons of Soviet and Chinese origin; the Agric-Alert was placed in the 'control room' which also operated a system of explosive devices set in the ground to provide a 360-degree coverage for the house. The devices consisted of Adams grenades, canons, and rockets which could be set on automatic fire lasting twenty minutes or operated manually and directed at selected areas. Mrs Storrer once accidentally fired the mechanism, a timely error which proved that the system worked and let the district know its capability. The Storrers were not attacked after the accident.[56]

Mounting a defence system involved costs over and above government assistance. In January 1979 the Farm Protection Advisory Service divided homestead security into three sets of priorities: the top requirement of a safe area, grenade screening, bulletproof walls, a fence alarm system, hedge, outside lighting, Adams grenades, a switch-off device for household lighting, and fire precautions would cost $2,000; the next priority of RPG-7 screening, extra Adams grenades, an electric fence, and an intercom linking the house, barns, and the labour compound would require an extra $500; the third priority of a reinforcing fence, an emergency lighting system, a beacon light, and other aids would account for another $500. The sum total was $3,000 but the wealthier farmers of Centenary and Marandellas spent thousands more protecting their homesteads, barns, and equipment.[57] Retired folk, living on small holdings near Ruwa, found the cost prohibitive and, not being a priority district, could not expect government assistance. They had to hold lotteries and jumble sales to raise the money for a minimum defence system which, on one occasion, led to the startling revelation that a respectable lady of the district maintained a drawer-load of French underwear (which was snapped up by female African buyers).[58]

Co-operation with the neighbours meant that farmers who had lived as strangers fought together in PATU sticks or in the Police Reserve where they established a new togetherness which helped to minimise political and cultural differences. British-born farmers learnt to respect their Afrikaans-speaking neighbours and farmers' wives formed friendships in canteens or in radio operations rooms. And the nerve centre of their togetherness was not 'Rhodesia' but the district or the Agric-Alert network. For at night, in those moments of darkest despair or greatest fear, with the children huddling in a corridor and rockets, mortars, and automatic fire crashing around the house, it was the Agric-Alert which helped a family to know that it wasn't alone.[59]

The war changed women's lives in the rural areas. Margaret Strong, the wife of a former RNFU President, reminded the farmers' annual congress in July 1979 of some of the innovations: the fences around the homes, followed by the grenade screens, the protective walls around the bedrooms, the gun belt around the waist. In her area of Sipolilo, Val lectured on First Aid, Helen did administrative work for the police, Mary raised funds to convert buildings at the police camp, the women on radio duty learnt to talk confidently in a new vocabulary, while Barbara – after six landmine explosions on their farm, four homestead attacks, and the loss of their tobacco and maize crops and a seedbed pump – was adamant about staying put. After referring – ironically – to the 'halcyon days' of the early 1970s, when farmers' wives merely ran the home, shouted at the children, arranged the flowers, and played bridge and tennis, Mrs Strong observed that the wives were now helping to run the farms while husbands were on call-ups, their marriages had acquired an 'added closeness', and all would say that their greatest burden was 'worry': not about the running of the farm but about 'the safety of her loved ones' in the bush, on the roads and the farms, and in the home. She also recognised that rural women had a new priority by 1979: 'We pray with all our hearts that this war will soon end, and with it an end to all the suffering and bloodshed.'[60]

Generally, the rougher the experience the tighter the community became. The reverse, however, was not always true. Although the Trelawney district, which was situated south-east of Sinoia, was not so directly affected by the war, there was an obvious closeness among its people. And even the close-knit communities had their disagreements and animosities. Peter Storrer, who retained some traditional Australian prejudices, drew a distinction between the 'Poms' (unacceptable) and 'Englishmen' (acceptable) in the Inyanga district.[61] Ruwa South, a small district some 20 km south-east of Salisbury, had so many squabbles that the chairman of the Civil Defence Committee urged each section to 'BECOME A COMMUNITY' and to 'forget irritations and any other form of disagreement'.[62] The problems of the Goromonzi-Ruwa district were greater than average because it was so difficult in the less affected areas to strike the right balance between taking realistic precautions and causing general panic. These difficulties were heightened in Ruwa because the poorer smallholders felt alienated from the bigger farmers and wealthier folk who had money in neighbouring Salisbury.[63]

The closeness of the rural communities extended into their neighbouring towns and villages. The rocket attacks on Umtali of 1976-9, and the parcel bomb threat in November 1979, created a bravado which evoked memories of the British at Dunkirk arid during the London Blitz. 'Come to Umtali and get Bombed': the message, carried on T-shirts where it was emblazoned over a beer bottle, was typical of a brand of wartime humour which sought to make light of danger. It also reinforced the assumption that 'Umtali' was special, well deserving – like Malta in the Second World War – of its own decoration.[64] Though every effort was made to preserve normal services and lifestyles, it was impossible to hide the fact that there was a war on.[65] Empty houses stood as stark reminders of the dangers and of the problems created by departing residents who had left properties which were vulnerable to theft and damage.[66] Umtali's white schoolchildren had repeated drills in preparation for the expected attacks, arrived late because of convoy delays, left early to join convoys, and missed out on sports days because other schools decided that it was too dangerous to visit Umtali.[67] Similarly, in Fort Victoria, where Centenary was hardly mentioned in the local press in 1973, the residents became accustomed by 1978-9 to stories of lucky escapes from 'terrorist' attacks near the town, to gritty remarks from farming families in the area labelling persistent attacks as 'just one of those things', and to visiting dignitaries attempting to rally spirits by claiming that morale went up in proportion to the distance from Salisbury.[68] It was impossible to maintain an air of normality after Fort

Victoria became the headquarters of JOC Repulse. By 1978 the local shopkeepers and hoteliers – so dependent on South African visitors to nearby Lake Kyle and the Zimbabwe Ruins[69] – were complaining that their tourist industry was the worst affected by the war. Others were protesting about a much more important matter: the continuing poor television reception.[70] The local press – in Gwelo as well as Fort Victoria – tried to counter the encircling gloom by filling its pages with 'normal' news: that is, with the round of social events and with information about club activities ranging from bridge, darts, and kennels to riding, rugby, racing, and bowls.[71]

Rhodesia's cities were inconvenienced by the war but, apart from Umtali, did not live with a daily threat. The attack on Woolworths in August 1977, the murders near the capital in early 1978, the bombing of the petrol dump in December 1978, and a series of minor incidents during 1979 warned of what could happen in Salisbury. There were other reminders of Rhodesia's problems: the cordon-and-search operations in the city streets, the shortages in the supermarkets, the call-ups, the ubiquitous camouflage uniforms, and the nightly news bulletins from COMOPS. Much to the amusement or distress of visitors from the rural areas – who frequently accused their urban cousins of spreading rumours or of concentrating on making money[72] – some of Salisbury's residents were apt to imagine that experiencing minor inconveniences placed them in the heart of the war zone. At the same time, the Rhodesians of Bulawayo and Salisbury managed to maintain much of their normal social, sporting, and working patterns. If migration and the call-ups restricted their opportunities to see good theatre in the late 1970s – though nothing dented their confidence in its quality – the restaurants, night clubs, cinemas, and television could always keep them entertained.

On the other hand, urban Rhodesians felt they were peculiarly vulnerable to the general downturn in the economy in the late 1970s. All sections of white society experienced a decline in real living standards between 1975 and 1980, a direct result of the war and of effective economic sanctions. Real Gross Domestic Product per head of the country's whole population rose by 11.5 and 9.7 per cent respectively in 1971 and 1972; and there were negative growth rates in each year from 1975 to 1979 (the worst being -7.4 per cent in 1977).[73] There was a 'bottoming-out' of the general economic downturn in 1979 – despite a sharp fall in the value and volume of agricultural output – because of the surge in industrial output, a 20 per cent rise in the value of mineral production, buoyant retail sales, and a 30 per cent jump in activity in the construction industry. The fact remained that the economy was merely clawing its way back to pre-war levels. In real terms, for example, the booming retail sales of 1979 had just reached 1973 levels. Overall, the world recession, the war, and sanctions had caused negative growth for five years, and a decline of 24 per cent in real income per head of population between 1975 and 1979.

The above figures made no distinction based on location or race. Other evidence pinpoints those areas where the urban white population in particular experienced a fall in living standards. The CPI figures together with income statistics indicate that, while urban Africans suffered more than whites from the inflationary pressures of the 1970s, the real income of urban whites fell in the latter part of the 1970s. The racial breakdown of earnings ceased in 1978 but it is known that in 1975-7, when the CPI for higher income urban families rose by 20 per cent, total European, Asian, and Coloured earnings rose by only 16 per cent.[74]

TABLE 9.1. *Consumer Price Index, 1964-1979: Higher Income Urban Families*[a]

Year	Food	Clothing and footwear	Household stores	All items
1964	100,0 (100.0)	100.0 (100.0)	100.0 (100.0)	100.0 (100.0)
1970	115.1 (116.1)	107.3 (105.1)	106.2 (114.3)	115.6 (112.4)
1975	153.6 (153.2)	146.6 (132.4)	141.1 (172.7)	149.2 (141.8)
1976	167.3 (166.7)	157.8 (143.6)	156.3 (197.7)	162.6 (160.7)
1977	183.8 (185.7)	173.3 (161.1)	172.2 (236.5)	178.2 (180.0)
1978	205.3 (204.3)	183.4 (167.6)	183.0 (255.5)	190.0 (197.6)
1979	228.4 (229.1)	197.0 (194.5)	195.7 (290.5)	210.6 (223.1)

[a] Lower income urban families given in brackets. Although the official practice of making racial distinctions was steadily abandoned during 1978-9, these figures roughly divide white (higher) from black (lower).

Further evidence is available in the household budget survey conducted for the period December 1977-January 1978.[75] The findings indicate that, whereas household income in Bulawayo, Gwelo, Salisbury, and Umtali rose by 23 per cent, expenditure increased by 26 per cent between 1975-6 and 1977-8. There was also a noticeable shift in expenditure patterns with a higher proportion of household incomes being spent on taxation, education, and servants' wages. On the income side, there was no change in proportionate contributions to the family income between 1968 and 1977-8: wives continued to provide about 13 per cent of joint income. Whereas in 1968 heads of household earned $298 a month, their wives received $45. In 1977-8 the figures were $649 and $96 respectively. The latter survey also showed some quite marked disparities between the cities. The white residents of Salisbury could save an average of $84 a month, and those of Umtali $44, but their counterparts in Bulawayo and Gwelo barely broke even. While the lower income groups in all cities continued to live beyond their means, the lowest group in Bulawayo (averaging an income of $351 a month) spent $60 in excess of wages. Significantly, too, whereas some 36 per cent of households in Salisbury received in excess of $900 a month, the comparable figures for the other three cities ranged between 19 and 24 per cent. The survey also suggested that the Rhodesians of Salisbury and Bulawayo remained fervent home buyers – nearly two-thirds in both cases were buying or already owned their own home – while the remaining third preferred to rent houses rather than flats. In Gwelo and Umtali the average figure for home ownership was just 40 per cent.

The 1977-8 survey indicates that the differences in white income and status, within and between cities, remained unaltered in the 1970s. Although it may not have taken sufficient account of probable increases in expenditure over the Christmas period, the survey also confirmed that the lifestyles of urban Rhodesians were being eroded in the late 1970s. The evidence, however, was never entirely consistent. The tourism figures suggest that, despite the economic downturn and the currency restrictions, Rhodesians tried to travel abroad though there was a 24 per cent fall between 1972 and 1979 in the number of residents who spent more than one night out of the country.[76] On the other hand, the Rhodesian cricket umpires reported that their numbers had dropped from 83 in 1973 to 45 in 1978 and, though they attributed the decline to emigration, bad health, and the use of bad language, it is obvious that sport in general – for most Rhodesians, a central feature of their way of life – had suffered because of sanctions, the war, and call-ups.[77] A contrary indication was that, in spite of the slow-down of Salisbury's residential and commercial building boom after 1975, locally-generated capital was responsible for a steady development of a construction programme, which was duplicated in Bulawayo, Gwelo, Fort Victoria, and Sinoia.[78] In Salisbury new low-density suburbs were built, older ones were expanded, and – in the earlier 1970s – the construction industry produced new insurance and finance blocks, hotels, factories, the Seven Arts Theatre in Avondale, the Earl Grey administrative building, as well as the new municipal offices – the Rowan Martin Building – the ceilings and upper floors of which began almost immediately to collapse. A principal beneficiary of the boom was the swimming pool construction industry. Even though pool building peaked in 1975 the major firms continued to flourish during the subsequent recession. Twelve companies remained in the business in 1980, the number of pools in Salisbury had risen from about 8,000 in 1970 to about 17,000, and the firms were now installing pools in the middling and even the poorer white suburbs.[79] The desire for status and pleasure, the availability of capital, the continued dislike of multiracial municipal pools, and the capacity of most companies to install a pool within two weeks, had stimulated the building programme. And one result was that the outsider's image of white Rhodesia – of a luxurious lifestyle symbolised by the days spent round the family pool – was, in Salisbury, closest to reality at the point when Rhodesia ceased to exist.

IV

The war touched and affected the lives of every white Rhodesian in the late 1970s. The war, and the advent of majority rule, the implemented or foreshadowed changes in discriminatory law and practice, and the tightening of economic sanctions, were also responsible for weakening the bonds which held Rhodesia together in 1970, for changing the patterns of white politics, and for eliminating or threatening key elements in the Rhodesian way of life. Paradoxically, even as their world appeared to turn upside down, as the ideologies of the 1960s ceased to be relevant, the Rhodesians found a bond in their opposition to 'terrorism' and an old 'comforter' in their self-deception and self-image. The war and political change had both exposed or created disunity and promoted a new form of accord. The effects were uneven as well as contradictory. For there were communities, families, and individuals who discovered that their world tilted rather than somersaulted after the surrender of 1976.

Despite all its suffering during the war, rural Rhodesia emerged in better shape in 1980 than most other sections of white society. One reason was that the political changes of the late 1970s did not immediately impinge upon the rural communities. Moreover, unlike the skilled white workers, whose jobs were taken by blacks or by whites brought into the country on contract, the farmers were not easily replaced and were protected by the Lancaster House arrangements. The amendment of the Land Tenure Act in 1977 had made little difference to land distribution. Roger Riddell argued in 1980 that the 1976 figures still applied: namely, that there were 675,000 farming units in the TTLs located within 16.3 million hectares at 24 hectares per unit, and there were 6,682 white farms taking up 15.2 million hectares at 2,290 hectares per farm. Riddell went on to suggest that this inequitable access to land was 'accompanied by growing overpopulation, landlessness, land deterioration, and increasing poverty in the African areas alongside serious underutilization of land in the European areas'.[80] The white farmers answered this criticism by citing their greater contribution to agricultural output and to exports. The CFU pointed out in a promotion booklet in 1980 that commercial farmers (nearly all of them white) were responsible for 85 per cent of gross output expressed in dollar terms.[81] They also listed the 'wasteful' farming methods in the TTLs, the degree of soil erosion, and the high African birth rate as factors both justifying the retention of the white farming lands and explaining the 'failure' of African agriculture. These familiar claims and counter-claims about white land ownership and usage highlighted the obvious fact that nothing substantial had occurred before 1980 to reduce the privileged position of white farming. And, so long as the Lancaster House provisions remained (restricting land transfers to 'willing seller-willing buyer' arrangements, and to special national needs), that situation was bound to continue.

No community in the country was cosseted like the farmers. In the past, organised agriculture had marshalled support on the basis of its contribution to exports, the savings in food imports, and its role in the RF. After 1972, and especially from 1976, the security argument rivalled the economic case: a farm, abandoned because it was considered too dangerous to be inhabited or because it was no longer economically viable, created even bigger security risks for the neighbours, and a possible free passage for the 'terrorists' into the 'softer centres' of white Rhodesia. Apart from the tax concessions and specialist services, the government provided millions of dollars in loans just to keep them on the land. At the end of 1970 total short-term credit extended to farmers by commercial banks, the Agricultural Finance Corporation, and other private companies amounted to $59.5 million; in 1975 the figure was $111.1 million; in 1979 it was $128 million (for March 1978 and March 1979 the figures were $152.9 million and $135 million respectively).[82] In addition, the government paid heavy compensation for losses derived from the war. The National Co-Ordinating Committee, set up in November 1978, provided over $10 million in eighteen months in accordance with the Victims of Terrorism (Compensation) Act. Little regard, it seems, was given to the recurrent and widespread unprofitability of farming. In 1976, after a good season, the Ministry of Agriculture concluded that thirty farms in a sample of ninety remained 'below a respectable level of viability'.[83] Bill Irvine told the farmers' annual congress in July 1979 that few farmers made sufficient profit in 1978-9 to finance their next season's crops, that just one-third of them earned enough to pay income tax, and that unrecoverable debt had doubled in two years.[84] But the farmers were like royal game and so, though always dissatisfied, white agriculture remained intact in 1980.

Urban Rhodesians, on the other hand, were beginning to feel the changes which were occurring in three of the citadels which the RF had been formed to protect: the separation and privileged status of the residential areas, health care, and education.

A major difference was that, by 1980, white residents of several suburbs in Bulawayo and Salisbury were sharing streets with black families. An influx of blacks into 'flatland' was transforming the residential character of inner Salisbury north of the railway line. Property transfers listed in the *Herald* over the October-December period in 1979 indicate that almost every sale in Waterfalls involved an African purchaser and that half of the house buyers in Hatfield, a quarter in Mabelreign, and a few in Marlborough and Highlands were black. White patients in Andrew Fleming Hospital in Salisbury were also more likely in 1980 to be tended by African nurses, though not by black doctors, and more African civilians were being treated there in preference to being sent to, or applying for, Harari Hospital. The whites grumbled in early 1980 about declining standards, overcrowded hospitals, and ill-trained or insolent black nurses. They were concerned about the net loss through migration of twenty-two European physicians and surgeons and of 249 nurses and midwives in the period between January and November 1979.[85] Along with members of the medical profession, they were afraid that a black government would introduce a nationalised health system, thereby lowering standards and promoting further emigration. Yet, given that white infant mortality rates continued to fall during the 1970s and that the whites maintained their traditional way of dying,[86] it would seem that any changes in the specialist skills available to whites had not made much impact on the vital statistics. Separate and quality health care remained an issue with urban whites but they never experienced the total breakdown or partial withdrawal of medical services which affected most TTLs during the later war years. Nor had the political changes after 1976 significantly affected the education of their children. There had been an increasing trickle of black children into the exclusive private institutions and a substantial movement into the government schools in the poorer white (or ex-white) suburbs of the major urban centres. Even so, critics of the inequalities of the Rhodesian education system could still – in 1980 – argue that white privileges remained intact.[87] They could also point out that the one major change affecting white schoolchildren during the 1970s was the introduction of the rudimentary teaching of African languages.

Although dismissed by the critics as often inconsequential, these changes in the residential, health, and education arrangements were sufficient for urban Rhodesians, of all political persuasions, to think they were living through revolutionary times. For the poorer whites, whose needs were earmarked in 1970 by Ralph Nilson, the RF Chairman, as needing special protection, the turnabout in 1977-80 in the residential areas and in the removal of racial barriers to entry into government schools must have seemed cataclysmic. And, unlike the farmers, they lacked the economic and organisational strength to shore up their position in the face of the additional demands for the rapid and extensive Africanisation of the lower and middle levels of the economy.

The most obvious and significant change since 1970, however, was the loss of executive and legislative power. Back in 1962 the RF had argued in opposition to the whitehead government that there was no guarantee, under majority rule, of the whites being able to control their own destiny. No doubt, virtually all of the RF's long-standing supporters in 1980 maintained that perfectly legitimate position. No doubt, too, in 1980 the implications of losing control were more foreseeable than actual. Nevertheless, the advent of Robert Mugabe signalled the final collapse of a constitutional and legislative system which, in 1970, was considered critical to the survival of white Rhodesia and which, through the artifice of the internal settlement, had endured after the election of Bishop Muzorewa.

Less obviously, there had been some important shifts of power within the white political structure since 1970: first, from the politicians to the military; and, secondly, from both to the 'Five Economic Presidents'. The first change was both temporary and partial. It began during 1977 when the war so dominated Rhodesian life that the Security Force commanders became politicians and Walls rivalled Smith as a popular hero. It ended in 1980 when Ian Smith re-emerged as the sole leader of the whites after Walls refused to implement Quartz and Mugabe's policy of reconciliation removed fears of physical reprisals. The second shift was permanent and more fundamental. The leaders of the economy began to assume a quasi-political importance following the Kissinger intervention in 1976, and their status was reinforced by the new Zimbabwe government which needed their co-operation to sustain export growth, the sanctions-created import substitution industries, and domestic food supplies. Conversely, the skilled artisans and the civil servants, who had solidly supported the RF and who greeted the assurances of white ministers in 1978-9 with increasing scepticism, felt they were losing ground well before Zimbabwe's independence.[88] So although Ian Smith continued to serve a crucial role in white politics in the early 1980s – by shoring up old prejudices and offering comfort to the mentally dispossessed – the white economic leaders led the migrants from Rhodesia into Zimbabwe. They were accompanied by one set of stalwarts from the past (the farmers), having conveniently unloaded another (the artisans). And, in the process, they restored the influence with government which they last enjoyed in the whitehead years before 1962.

There were two further significant developments in white politics after 1970. First, while the divisions of 1970 became more open, the solid mass of the electorate – all except the far right – abandoned firmly-held positions. It was argued in Chapter 2 that the Rhodesians had always been divided over the fundamental question of whether or how long their country should remain under white rule. In 1970, at a formal party level, that division lay between the liberals of the non-racial Centre Party and the supremacists of the RF. The liberals argued for a representative democracy based on a qualified franchise and, in opposing the principle of African majority rule, supported the ideal of a non-racial meritocracy. The RF itself was polarised between those in the party machine who wanted to entrench segregation and white supremacy, and Ian Smith's followers who supported white supremacy for the foreseeable future while opposing segregation as a permanent solution and preferring the principle of advancement upon merit. So, while the overwhelming majority in 1970 opposed any transference of power to blacks in the foreseeable future, that majority was fundamentally divided on the issues of perpetual white rule and provincialisation. The effect of the war and of the surrender of 1976 was that the liberal minority in 1977-9 – leading figures in organised agriculture, mining, industry and commerce, long-time supporters of the Centre Party, and reconstructed members of the all-white Rhodesia Party of the early and mid-1970s – now favoured a prompt transfer to majority rule. A large minority – consisting of unreconstructed RF supporters and followers of the far right, angry troopies and a sprinkling of wealthy farmers, lower-level civil servants, Afrikaners, Greeks, artisans, and retired folk – wanted to retain white power and persisted with the notion of political segregation. The majority of Rhodesians – also representing a cross-section of Rhodesia's communities – fluctuated between a begrudging acceptance that white supremacy was finished and the despairing hope that 'Smithy' could still pull something out of the bag. A principal effect of these developments was that the RF dropped all pretence of being a grass-roots party, governed from 'below'. If it had been a participatory democracy, then the official policy of 'provincialisation' would have been implemented before the war escalated in 1976 and those who eventually supported the RAP would have remained the dominant force within the RF. Another principal effect was to raise the temperature of the political debate, particularly within the right where the angry and bitter exchanges during and after 1975-6 made a split both inevitable and a useful purgative.

The second development was that, by 1977, the RF had come to occupy the middle ground of white politics,[89] thereby sustaining the illusion that white Rhodesia remained a solid and single entity. Many of the liberals and moderates in fact abandoned the left after 1977 and openly supported Smith as the only white leader capable of engineering the desired change. Many of the right-wingers marched out of the RF, but the large rump continued to follow Smith – sensing that to oppose him would mean their political oblivion – while remaining highly critical of the surrender. Unable, however, to replace or supplement the principles of 1962, the RF could not bind its real and notional followers to a common cause save that of resisting 'terrorism'. 'Good Old Smithy' remained a rallying-point but he had nothing to offer once the internal settlement failed to win international and guerrilla approval. In effect, therefore, by 1979 most Rhodesians were just hanging on in hope and, having discarded their ideological baggage, they were now the supreme pragmatists who were prepared to 'wait and see'.

These realignments in white politics occurred against a background of considerable tension within Rhodesian society. For divisions merely widened and multiplied when the Rhodesians began losing their control over events. Catholics argued with each other because the Commission for Justice and Peace apparently ignored the atrocities committed by the 'terrorists';[90] Anglicans argued about the right-wing stand of Senator Father Lewis and about their relationship with their fellow black communicants; businessmen continued to criticise unionists for failing to understand the need for African advancement; skilled workers complained of conspiracies to undermine their living standards; everybody at some time, and the farmers repeatedly, attacked the civilian and military bureaucracies for arrogance, over-regulation, and incompetence; and the 'true' Rhodesians verbally assaulted the 'dismal jimmies' and the liberals who doubted whether 'Rhodesia' was worth fighting for or who dared to question the achievements of Ian Smith or the Security Forces.

Some of the more serious forms of friction occurred when the normal inter-departmental and inter-service rivalries exploded into blazing rows and accusations of disloyalty. The administration of the PVs was repeatedly undermined by arguments about jurisdiction, about the manner of exercising authority, and about the quality of the administrators. Several ministries, branches within ministries, and elements of the Security Forces became involved: COMOPS, Guard Force, Internal Affairs, Health, Agriculture, Water Development, Natural Resources, Works, and Local Government and Housing. There were repeated clashes between the developers and those who emphasised the primary purpose of security. These differences, in turn, were affected by personnel changes resulting from the call-up, by the lack of resources, and by the different interests of individuals and their ministries.[91] One particular source of rivalry was the question of supervision. Having developed its own protective unit, including an air wing, Internal Affairs objected to the arrangement whereby Guard Force was assigned the principal role of defending PVs which Internal Affairs was expected to administer. Senior officials in Internal Affairs did not disguise their contempt for Guard Force which, they suggested, was composed of the scum of African volunteers and inexperienced white lads from the cities. At the same time, most branches of the Security Forces could always find common ground in denigrating Internal Affairs. One head of Special

Branch described the monthly reports from Internal Affairs as 'consistently awful and unreliable' and dismissed the DCs as 'little tin gods' who were remote from their people.[92] A favourite target was Don Yardley, the Secretary of Internal Affairs in the late 1970s. Puffed with self-importance, and wearing on parade a paramilitary regalia he had designed for himself, Yardley was hardly in a position to criticise Guard Force for an obsessive concern with appearances.[93]

One factor which conspired against harmony within the Security Forces was that the rapid formation and expansion of units during the war, and the formation of JOCs and sub-JOCs under Army command, created a myriad of small empires and attendant jealousies. The Selous Scouts constituted the most controversial of these empires. While ZANLA and ZIPRA feared and hated them more than any other unit, leading figures in the Army, Internal Affairs, Special Branch, and CIO deeply resented the secrecy and privileges of the Selous Scouts. Reid Daly's very success in raising the profile of the Scouts, and of himself, was the undoing of both. There were constant complaints about the pretensions of this 'jumped-up Sergeant-Major' and about his penchant for strutting around the parade-ground.[94] Other units were jealous of the mystique attached to the Scouts, of Reid Daly's direct line to Walls, and of his apparent immunity from bureaucratic constraints. They were angry that the reputation for brutality and excessive killing had rebounded on the rest of the Security Forces. They were contemptuous of the kind of arrogance, bungling, and poor planning which forced the Scouts to abandon a bulldozer inside Mozambique after it had broken down because they had refused to take an engineer with them,[95] which obliged the SAS to take over the responsibility for assassinating Nkomo, and which led to the risible efforts by the Scouts to discredit Mugabe during the 1980 elections. The comic mistakes did not allay the anger.

The Reid Daly-Hickman confrontation on 31 January 1979, and the Hickman dismissal on the following 6 March, highlighted a fundamental problem which confronted a small population thrust into a long and widening war. Very simply, there was a limited pool from which to recruit senior officers. Men who might have commanded companies or battalions found themselves in charge of brigades; men who were qualified to be colonels became generals. Walls himself was the clearest example of what happened when the war got out of hand. Thrust into a role for which he was not prepared, the Commander of COMOPS was criticised for his lack of political acumen and his overall strategic deficiencies. Younger officers looked at Walls, liked his warm personal style, and yet wondered aloud whether his leadership was of the right calibre. When they looked at the alternatives, it was time to shudder.

It is difficult to estimate the impact of inter-service tension and leadership failings on the performance of the Security Forces. The conventional wisdom is that despite the repeated claims that the Rhodesians fought the war by forming committees,[96] and despite the fact that some of these committees fought each other, the Rhodesians managed to sustain an effective counter-insurgency operation under deteriorating conditions. The weakness at the top may have been countered by the skills and determination of the Air Force, the special units, and many of the junior officers and ordinary ranks. The more critical point here, however, is that, faced with a war which challenged white rule and threatened every feature of the Rhodesian way of life – except its climatic advantages – the leading warriors and some of the bureaucrats busied themselves with personal feuds and empire-building. The image, and self-image, of a united and single-minded Rhodesia was plainly untrue at the leadership level during the last years of the war.

The Rhodesians in 1970 liked to contrast the efficient working of their civil service with the administrative chaos elsewhere in Africa. In view of the tensions affecting the bureaucracy, the enforced and increasing regulation of Rhodesian society (not matched, according to right-wing critics, by the effective regulation of 'our black Rhodesians'), and the enormous pressures imposed on white civil servants who themselves were subject to call-ups, it was inevitable that the machinery of government would not meet all the demands placed upon it. A small white society, which had deliberately excluded the assistance of the black majority, lacked the human and material resources to maintain both a wartime and a peacetime administration. Continuity (the majority of the departmental secretaries in 1970 remained in office until 1979-80), the quality of the initial senior appointments, and a determination of the Public Services Board to maintain standards in appointments and promotions meant, however, that there was no prospect of collapse. But it was hard to govern well in places where it was nearly impossible to govern at all. Although the authorities publicly denied that there were any 'liberated areas' in 1979, the planned defence of 'vital strategic assets' and Verdal-Austin's complaints about his own district being expendable were just some of the substantial hints that ordinary government had effectively ceased in some areas. Veterinary reports, highlighting the spread of disease from 1973 and its rapid escalation after 1976, provided direct evidence of the breakdown of government services throughout the TTLs where the guerrillas effectively halted cattle dipping.[97] Annual departmental reports – from roads and traffic to education to the police – told much the same story: a mounting death toll among departmental employees and a breakdown of services. The Police Commissioner reported in 1979 that cattle theft had reached uncontrollable proportions: a 64 per cent rise in cases over 1978; a 100 per cent increase in the total value stolen; and a recovery rate of just 16.3 per cent. The news was not all bad. The call-up provided additional manpower for patrols and road-blocks which assisted in the prevention and detection of housebreaking and theft in 1979.[98] Nevertheless, while every attempt was made to maintain government services, each department had to admit that the war had forced a scaling down of activities or a reordering of priorities. Civilised government may not have ceased but the government's authority was substantially diminished.

Yet nothing, it seems, could curb the bureaucratic instinct. Having completed the fiendishly complicated forms applying for stock theft compensation, and waiting for the police and Ministry inspectors to submit reports, farmers could face months of delay before securing payment under the Victims of Terrorism (Compensation) Act. Following protests, the government agreed to expedite claims and to appoint the farmers themselves to act as inspectors. Not to be outdone, the bureaucracy devised elaborate procedures for appointing farmers as inspectors, a complex system for claiming petrol (evidently the farmers could not be trusted), and intensely detailed instructions to inspectors on how to fill in the forms." Even if the farmers – once again – were able to manipulate the system, and if at other times they successfully operated the time-honoured methods of phoning officials they knew, chatting to the local police member in charge, or contacting a white minister or MP, it remained that the yards of 'red tape' lengthened in rough proportion to the growing inability of a stretched civil service to administer all of Rhodesia.

One traditional feature of Rhodesian life – the role and status of women – which was superficially affected by the prospect of 'total war', did not permanently change during the 1970s. Minority attempts to call up the white female population never attracted much support. The women's service within the Security Forces numbered about 400 who worked mainly as clerks, telephonists, and cypher, radio, and computer operators. Apart, however, from the busyness of women involved in war charity work, one of the striking features of Bulawayo and Salisbury life in 1978-9 was their largely uninterrupted patterns of 'feminine' social activity: managing the home, delivering or collecting the children, shopping and playing bridge or tennis, chattering with friends over tea or drinks. Derry Macintyre regretted what he called 'all this idle behaviour', arguing that Rhodesia should have followed the Israeli example and mobilised both sexes.[100] Given Rhodesia's British antecedents, its entrenched masculine assumptions about gender roles, and the desire to maintain normality, such a step was inherently unlikely.

Some women did, however, experience a temporary change of status during the war. Margaret Strong, in her speech to the farmers' congress in July 1979, had drawn attention to the way in which white women in the rural areas were assuming full responsibility for running farms while their husbands were away on call-up.[101] Women in urban Rhodesia also acquired more responsibility during call-up periods and immediately faced some new problems. One woman told a panel discussion, organised by the Mashonaland branch of the Nursery School Association in mid-1977, that children experienced behavioural problems after their fathers left. Another said that children resented 'continual domination and discipline from the mother'. Two men on the panel gave the wives some useful warnings: men returning from the bush found it hard adjusting to domestic life; don't send mail listing domestic problems; a man was likely to feel usurped if his wife proved to be too accomplished (especially in mechanical matters).[102] The war might, therefore, increase responsibilities but it should not be allowed to upset the traditionally supportive role. Mrs Pruitt had told the Salisbury Mothers' Club on 12 October 1976 that men were driven to dominate, subdue, multiply, exercise authority, keep, and guard. Woman, she said, had been created as a companion to meet man's needs: 'she is God's love gift to man.'[103] The family and women's magazines – *Home and Country, Talk,* and *Illustrated Life and Talk* – maintained this theme during 1979 by constantly reminding women of how to be better wives and mothers, and more desirable and undemanding lovers.

Discriminatory laws and practice irritated a minority. A woman could not, for example, prevent a man who had maintenance obligations from leaving the country and, although this disability was hardly unique to Rhodesia, it caused serious hardship in a society which had a high divorce and emigration rate.[104] In 1976 a divorcée of five years, aged 39, discovered another aspect of Rhodesian conservatism when her gynaecologist insisted that she obtain the prior approval of her ex-husband before the doctor would undertake a sterilisation operation.[105] A few Rhodesian women – like their counterparts elsewhere – had to contend with both female and male prejudice. In October 1976, a woman active in liberal politics wrote in her diary:

Funny how in politics I have discovered over and over again, a woman has to be twice as good as any male because she not only has the competition of the male but the rivalry of the other women to overcome.[106]

The same woman complained to Nick McNally, the President of NUF, in August 1979 that she had not been consulted about the composition of a delegation to meet a black minister. She accused McNally of needing a male companion 'to satisfy your own and the chauvinistic tendencies of most other men in the political arena'.[107] For all the changes of the 1970s a woman's place in urban Rhodesia was still the home.

V

One of the principal effects of the crises of the late 1970s was to reinforce the unifying assumptions and values of earlier years. For most Rhodesians – urban and rural – turned desperately, defiantly, or unthinkingly to their old convictions about Rhodesia itself. Drastic political change, the loss of direction, the evidence of moral decay, the curtailed freedoms, the restricted lifestyles, the physical dangers: nothing seemed to shake their view that the Rhodesians constituted the last bastion of Christianity and Western values, that they were decent folk who believed in democracy, a brave people who could take on the world, an ingenious people who could survive and triumph if only the world would come to its senses. Their political leaders and the media successfully persuaded a receptive public to believe that abnormal and undesirable events need not disrupt the normal and pleasant patterns of Rhodesian life. And, where disruption occurred, Rhodesians were assured of the justice of their cause and the certainty of its triumph.

Three widely-held beliefs, which survived intact through the 1970s, were that Rhodesian racial policies were quite different from those of South Africa; that most Africans benefited from, and even preferred, the forms of segregation and discrimination which did exist; and that Rhodesia continued to have the best race relations in the world.[108] One particular incident appeared to confirm the third assumption. A truck carrying former guerrillas crashed and caught fire near Cherington Tilley's home in Borrowdale just after the 1980 elections. Tilley, who lost his son in January 1978 and his daughter in the first Viscount disaster, leapt from his car and, risking his own life, dragged several of the guerrillas to safety and then righted the vehicle with his tractor to enable the two bodies to be recovered.[109] The reassuring thing was that outsiders noticed these acts by 'true Rhodesians'. The *Outpost* published a fulsome letter from a British policeman sent to Zimbabwe after the 1980 elections who had seen two soldiers helping a seriously ill African woman: it 'showed me that the white Rhodesian had a natural affection for the black Rhodesian and has not allowed the long war to change it'.[110]

Oddly enough, the war may also have lent credence to the third assumption by thrusting the whites into closer contact with black members of the Security Forces. The need to collect and disseminate intelligence may have brought more whites (and especially those civilians subject to call-up) into a better understanding of the customs and worldview of those who had, hitherto, been the exclusive property of the presumed specialists in Internal Affairs. Farmer organisations, the business houses, and the Rhodesia Promotion Council made a point of currying favour with African leaders in 1978-9 or, as they preferred to put it, of 'getting to know you', an approach to which the Muzorewa ministers warmly responded.[111] These contacts proved to members of the business community that race relations in Rhodesia were excellent, notwithstanding the selfish demands or the loutish behaviour of white artisans and some of the hot-headed young troopies.[112] Yet they could hardly claim the credit for the Mugabe government's policy of reconciliation which said more about the good nature of the new rulers, and their common-sense intention to exploit white skills, than it did about the legacy of race relations handed over by the whites.

In any case, the third assumption and its corollary – that Rhodesia's blacks were the happiest in Africa – was rooted in a deep though convenient misunderstanding. For years before 1972 white Rhodesians believed that acquiescence in discriminatory practices implied approval. The blacks wanted to remain separate and preferred stable white government. After 1972 they were intimidated or misled into opposition by agitators and 'terrorists'. So the war was caused by 'Communist-trained thugs' seeking 'to force their philosophies on an unwilling and peace-loving, indigenous population', and was perpetrated by the 'cowardly terrorists' who were 'terrified of the security forces and make every effort to avoid contact with them'.[113] Rhodesian Front whites simply had no idea of the bitterness and mistrust created by their elected government.[114]

They had even less idea of how to adjust their thinking to a new order. A spate of letters to the press in July 1979 reflected the prevailing attitudes. The busloads of Muzorewa supporters who greeted their leader every time he arrived at Salisbury airport were criticised for wasting valuable petrol. There were calls for greater equity in bearing the costs of the war by imposing a poll tax on poorer blacks who did not earn a taxable income. There were constant reminders that whites had 'built' the country and had provided schools, clinics, dip tanks, beer halls, and bus services as part of their 'repressive racist colonial imperialism'. One writer warned that charitable gifts would not be so readily available in 1980. Another suggested that Zimbabwe Rhodesia's new flag should retain the Rhodesian white and green and add 'two other colours favoured by our African community'. Others found it perversely comforting to believe that the inheritors of 'this once great country' would surely make a mess of it.[115] Racial goodwill, therefore, as practised by a number of whites, seemed to depend on their capacity to dictate the terms. When the whites lost control it was apparently consistent to become ungracious.

Meanwhile, it was comforting to know that those who had helped to destroy Rhodesia were just hypocrites who oppressed their own people in Birmingham or in Alice Springs. The outside world, feared for its immorality in 1970, was despised for its amorality in 1980. Andrew Young, Jimmy Carter, David Owen, Jim Callaghan, Lord Carrington, Malcolm Fraser, Lord Soames, the British Foreign Office, the Commonwealth, Western capitalism: the hate list grew rapidly after 1976 as the Rhodesians blamed self-interested parties in the West for their predicament. The myopia reached every level. Ian Smith was convinced that a crisis in the Middle East would save Rhodesia because the West would need all its allies in protecting Israel and in thwarting the Soviet Union.[116] The government-controlled radio and television and the supposedly 'leftist' Argus Press kept up two morale-boosting themes during 1978-9: Rhodesia had its problems but things were far worse everywhere else; and, apart from the war (and its unfortunate habit of dominating conversation), Rhodesians were busy doing the ordinary, everyday things of living, working, and playing. When the Vice-President of the RTA and his wife visited Australia in September 1978, Mrs Bertie Palmer made the astonishing discovery that Ian Smith 'is the darling of most Australians'. Mrs Palmer had also learnt an important lesson during her travels; namely, that when Rhodesians discovered how difficult it was to adjust to 'strikes, demonstrations, muggings and the rest', they would realise 'that there is no place like Rhodesia'.[117] The whites who travelled, and those who stayed at home, rarely allowed any experience to interfere with the received wisdom. Isolation and conviction helped to sustain unreal expectations.

Mental attitudes could stay fixed because the war confirmed much of what the Rhodesians believed about themselves. They did prove to be brave and resourceful in combating fearsome odds. Various units of the Security Forces, and various individuals, performed brilliantly. They were also ingenious, perhaps the best proof being their defence against economic sanctions. Although successful sanctions-busting necessarily involved willing external parties, the Rhodesians were notably adept at finding new buyers and sellers. The price of isolation was having to buy at a premium and sell at a discount but, as the pressure mounted from 1976 to close off their options, they never failed to uncover business partners. Geoff Ellman-Brown, the former accountant and minister in the Todd government, was one of the country's principal sanctions-busters. Asked what happened when hostile British and American organisations exposed their operations, he replied: 'Oh, they nosed around and got something; we nosed around and got something else.' His view, shared by Jack Quinton, another former Todd minister, was that sanctions did not work.[118] Whether it was Jack Malloch's air charter firm carrying out its regular 'meat run' to African states, or Stan O'Donnell, the Australian-born former Secretary for Foreign Affairs, undertaking arms-buying trips in Europe and Latin America, or Mark Rule running a highly successful company selling minerals, or the 'Scottish Mafia' running the Reserve Bank and the Treasury and safeguarding the currency and the economy, the Rhodesians exhibited levels of enterprise and skill remarkable for such a small society.[119] The economic situation may have become perilous by the end of 1979 but a number of them lauded their survival as evidence of character and virtue.[120]

Inventiveness was another much-prided quality. The Rhodesians were ingenious in protecting themselves from death and in devising weapons to kill others. Just as the Security Forces often borrowed and adapted counter-insurgency tactics to suit their own purpose, the Rhodesians developed their own versions of the Israeli Uzi, the 'Dam Busters' bomb, and the 'Stalin Organ'. The landmine, which had the potential to break the farming community, became less of a threat following the invention of the 'Rhino' (short for 'Rhino-sore-arse') and the protected Land Rover in 1973.[121] By separating the wheels from the chassis, and providing special armour on the sides, the invention of the 'Leopard' and the 'Crocodile' barricaded troops against both landmines and ambushes, and the especially designed 'Puma' enabled the Rhodesians to lead the world in landmine detection.[122]

The war confirmed other qualities, including the ability to laugh at their own predicament. The critics did not always understand that the cartoons and one-liners, at once defiant, bitter, irreverent, and self-deprecating, reflected a very human need to shrug off death and defeat.[123] The racism was often ugly: a T-shirt in early 1979 might carry the message 'Say No to the SettleMunt. Sometimes it was relatively benign: the last white man was urged to turn off the lights before leaving the country. It could be quick and unsubtle: the wits in early 1980 decided that 'Comrade' was the Russian word for 'kaffir'. During 1979 a few individuals, who had worked on the PV programme, organised an elaborate joke at the expense of the UN and the moral improvers. With the support of a Catholic nun, they distributed condoms in a north-eastern TTL, ostensibly to determine whether conservative rural communities could be induced to practise birth control. The real objective was to monitor excessive use of condoms as an indication of a 'terrorist' presence in the area. The practitioners derived considerable amusement from the exercise, which they designated Operation Field Undertaking in Condom Kinetics, and prepared an academic paper for a UN conference.[124]

Assured of their personal qualities and the rightness of their stand, the Rhodesians found it easy to overlook or justify actions by the government or the Security Forces which appeared to violate their avowed concern for practising good government and for maintaining the appropriate (in Africa) values of a Western democracy. All except the liberals and some members of NATJOC condoned, indeed welcomed, the introduction of martial law. Typically, however, whereas other societies in other situations might well have rested their case on the circumstances confronting their security forces, the Rhodesians wanted it both ways: to impose an arbitrary and draconian system while clothing its application in bureaucratic and legalistic procedures to maintain the facade of British justice.[125]

The political censors usually argued that the civilised society had to shed some freedoms in order to preserve its existence. By December 1979 'D notices', the Emergency Powers regulations, COMOPS regulations, the Criminal Procedure and Evidence Act, the Official Secrets Act, the Law and Order (Maintenance) Act, and the Censorship and Entertainments Control Act could all be used to alter news, stifle information, and intimidate journalists.[126] The arguments underlying these regulations and practices were always the same: the need to protect vital security information and to maintain morale. Their main effect was to attack the very principles which the Rhodesians were supposedly defending. The *Chronicle* argued on 9 December 1978 that 'the national mania for sealed lips on almost every subject will be the death of the remaining freedoms in this country'. A more common complaint was that attempts to suppress the news had an adverse effect on morale. Right-wingers on the RF back-bench made this point back in 1973 when the government tried to censor unfavourable news in the wake of Altena. In January 1979 a senior police officer in Gwelo was sharply rebuked by the local newspaper editor after he issued a warning against rumour-mongering. The paper argued that rumours flourished when the news was bad and was accompanied by excessive secrecy.[127] Everyone agreed that gossip was harmful but, in the absence of sufficient information, rumours hurtled around the white communities in 1978-9, distorting and exaggerating unpalatable facts, and inducing the alarm and despondency which censorship was intended to circumvent. Conversely, attempts to impose the 'good' news required Territorial soldiers, businessmen, farming families, and members of Internal Affairs – or any white civilians possessing reasonable powers of observation and in contact with the economic or the security situation – to ignore the obvious fact that morale-boosting assessments and promises were flawed, misleading, or flagrantly dishonest.

At one level, the deception disguised government failures while insulating the Rhodesians from some unpleasant facts about the 'ordinary Af'. Between 1973 and 1978, the whites were asked to believe that rural Africans pleaded to be admitted to PVs and welcomed the facilities, economic opportunities, and security which PVs provided. The government, the press, and the Rhodesian public either repressed or ignored the conflicting evidence. A former Provincial Commissioner admitted in a confidential document in June 1977 that the PV policy had 'not been completely successful'.[129] Brigadier Campling's secret memorandum of June 1978 admitted that 127 of the 158 PVs in Hurricane had failed to achieve their military objective or had alienated their African population.[130] Assessments of that kind were not publicised. Little prominence was given to a short statement in December 1978 from the Ministry of Information announcing that all the villagers had left the opened PVs in the Mrewa, Mtoko, and Mudzi districts. A continued 'terrorist' presence was blamed for the failure of these 'growth points'.[131] So the failure of PVs was not so much admitted as explained: that is, the Rhodesians simply lacked the resources to implement a system which would have worked. The original lie – that the system had been completely successful – was never confronted or was soon forgotten.

The most deleterious effect of the incessant propaganda was that the Rhodesians were ill-prepared mentally for the changes of 1978-80. For if the whites had been forced to confront the changes which were supposed to accompany the internal settlement, if they had not been side-tracked into thinking that the war was really about the defeat of 'terrorism', if they had not regarded the April election of 1979 merely as a step towards international recognition, the end of sanctions, and the defeat of 'terrorism', they might have grasped the simple point that their old privileged world was finished. If, too, the years of isolation had not taken their toll, if 'our superior system of education' had actually prepared the young for living in a different Africa,[132] they might also have understood that their desired privileged world was always doomed. At least the left and the far right had always understood the significance of the surrender of 1976, whereas the large majority was persuaded that, by defeating 'terrorism', nothing of significance would change. So most whites were stunned on 4 March 1980 precisely because they had been repeatedly assured, and wanted to believe, that the 'terrorists' could never win and that the ordinary African would never vote for 'Marxism'. Deceived by their own leaders, and colluding in their deception, the whites had only themselves to blame. Unlike the right and the left, they were active players or willing victims.

VI

On 18 April 1980, ten years and two days after Clifford Dupont's inauguration as the first President of the Republic of Rhodesia, Revd Canaan Banana was installed as the first President of the new Zimbabwe. Standing beside him was Robert Mugabe, the former 'Marxist terrorist', and now Zimbabwe's Prime Minister. Mugabe's recently acquired friend

– Lord Soames, the last Governor of Southern Rhodesia – was nearby, and so was the Prince of Wales. Ian Smith did not attend the ceremony but David Smith, Mugabe's Minister of Finance, did. A white Chief Superintendent had a brief to watch one of the special guests. Bob Marley, the Caribbean reggae singer, whose song 'Zimbabwe' echoed through the Rufaro Stadium the following night, was under suspicion for using drugs. His 'type' was considered a threat to the country's innocence and the Chief Superintendent intended to arrest him for the slightest hint of a transgression.[133] There were in fact remarkably few hitches or incidents. While the family of a young DC mourned the anniversary of his death in an ambush,[134] and other whites were contemplating migration or trying not to notice, Zimbabwe was launched in an atmosphere of great rejoicing. It was a far cry from the formal, and largely unnoticed, ceremony in April 1970, and from the annual festivals on 11 November where Ian Smith struck the Independence Bell in the midst of all those dinner suits and ball gowns. It was also a world far removed from the one Clifford Dupont had visualised where the Rhodesians would demonstrate the greatness he saw within them. The 'fourteen great years' had become the distant past.

Conclusion

There are three concluding observations to be made about the Rhodesians' experience of the war years. First, the white minority could not for long have withstood the combined pressures of the war and economic sanctions as they were applied in the late 1970s. White Rhodesia lacked the resources for a sustained fight. Honest men and women acknowledged this fact even though a number of them in prominent positions refused to be frank with the white electorate. Those who continue to think that Op Quartz could have rescued Rhodesia from becoming Zimbabwe, who insist that the war was still winnable in 1979, share a fairly harmless fantasy. Its persistence, however, is the best surviving evidence of how the Rhodesians had acquired the harmful habit of lying to themselves and to each other.

Secondly, a combination of factors – the lack of resources, the intolerable pressures, the absence of any common commitment to fight to the death – weakened Rhodesian resistance in the 1970s by creating or fostering tensions and uncertainties. Old divisions surfaced, new ones emerged, and the society which Clem Tholet said would 'fight through thick and thin' was never collectively sure what it was fighting for after 1976. Once the government accepted the principle of majority rule it removed the bonds which united three-quarters of white Rhodesia. From that point, the opposition to 'terrorism' became all-important and, paradoxically, more unifying. Nevertheless, from 1976 it was apparent that the perceptions of what mattered about the Rhodesian way of life were so varied that there could be no uniform conception of the war beyond a hatred of 'terrorism'.

Thirdly, the society which claimed to stand for certain principles, principles which critical outsiders interpreted as racial or class privilege, was composed of people whose common interest was that they came, and stayed, for a good material existence. Most of them were decent ordinary folk who, as a whole, never dreamed beyond their immediate security and happiness. Young and old alike, they experienced a warm inner glow when thinking of their Rhodesia but this recent invention of few or shallow traditions could, and did, so easily fall apart.

II

The falling apart accelerated in the months and years following 4 March 1980. Rhodesia simply dispersed as the whites left the country in their thousands. A white population of 232,000 in mid-1979 had become about 80,000 in 1990. When 72 white senior police officers retired between May and June 1980 – 36 of them having served for eighteen years or more – the police journal gave three reasons why so many of them also planned to leave the country: fears for their individual safety, concern about the standard of living, and a conscientious objection to Marxist rule.[1] These factors were often cited in the following decade when individuals and families, who had once boasted that nothing would shift them, who had survived the worst years of the war and buried their dead in Rhodesian soil, tried to explain their departure. A basic concern was the rate of Africanisation which especially affected the career prospects of their children. A more subtle influence was the emigration of friends, or the declining membership of favourite clubs, or the appearance of blacks in cherished watering holes. For some, it was the surprise of discovering that the policy of reconciliation did not mean the preservation of the status quo. For others, it was the shock of a racial insult, or the propaganda on radio and television, or the failure of the police to attend a burglary.

The ideologues, the Afrikaans speakers, and the committed Rhodesians were among the first to go. The route to South African carried young ex-troopies, generals and colonels, skilled artisans, professional men, retired civil servants, and some farmers. The South African Defence Force eagerly accepted former members of COMOPS, the SAS, and the Selous Scouts but soon found it hard to emphathize with English-speaking Rhodesians who wanted revenge for the past or who felt and behaved as outsiders. Des Frost moved more easily between the two worlds. After all, he could return to the Cape of his boyhood. The major change was that this gruff and blunt individual, frustrated as RF Chairman because he could never get the measure of Ian Smith, became a born-again Christian. It now merely amused him that the new white owners of his former farm near Marandellas had placed a ZANU(PF) sign on the gate. In 1989 Des Frost wanted to bury the past: the bitterness of 1978, the hatred of Smith, was dead.[2] Other RAP types like Rodney Simmonds maintained their rage though, instead of joining the Conservative Party in South Africa, Simmonds stressed the importance of white unity and strongly supported the National Party. Reg Cowper prospered in business, faltered, and then recovered. Many of the old RF – like 'Mac' Knox, Jack Mussett, and Hilary Squires – also crossed the Limpopo. So did Colin Barlow, one of the RF's bright young men of the future and the RAP's leading zealot. Barlow left Avondale on the day the 'terrorist' leaders returned to Salisbury. He then set up a successful dental practice in a suburb of Johannesburg. Peter Walls, the object of Barlow's campaign in 1977 to launch a coup against Ian Smith, occasionally joined him to watch Currie Cup rugby.

Walls was not a willing emigrant. He had reluctantly agreed to Mugabe's request to head the new Joint High Command to manage the integration of ZANLA, ZIPRA, and the Rhodesian Security Forces. In 1980 he wanted to retire. Though Walls repeatedly denied claims of harassment from angry whites, including the allegation that a member of the RLI had flung thirty pieces of silver at his feet during a post-election parade, he needed to escape the pressures of command. Walls knew, however, that he had to stay on, partly because he represented some sort of security for the whites, and partly because he wanted to supervise the return of South African equipment lent to the Security Forces in the last months of the war.[3] Naive as ever, and perhaps disappointed that Mugabe as well as Smith had refused to make him a full General, he made his very public remarks in August 1980 about Quartz and about the future instability of Zimbabwe. The Mugabe government subsequently banned his re-entry to the land of his birth.[4] Lacking any real business acumen, and having failed to acquire and shift large sums out of the country, Walls eventually worked for a former Rhodesian SAS commander in Johannesburg and lived quite modestly in a suburban house jammed with memorabilia.

It was perhaps easier to leave Zimbabwe than it was to settle in South Africa, Britain, or Australia. The reunions and the memories were happy enough. In 1990 the Rhodesia Association of South Africa celebrated the centenary or the flag-raising at Salisbury with a week of festivities at a resort near Messina close to the Zimbabwe border. The resort was renamed 'Rhodesianaland', a newspaper was published, the roads were given the street names of Salisbury and Bulawayo, and there were dinners, re-enactments, and much nostalgia. It was, in different ways, comforting to recall the years of resistance, the comradeship, and humour of the war, and the perfidy of supposed friends who had helped to bring Rhodesia down. It was reassuring to repeat stories of how 'THEY' had made a mess of their bountiful inheritance. Yet, for the settled as well as the unsettled, the loss of a country, the rootlessness, had created a confused mental world. The one certainty was that Rhodesians should not feel any guilt. They told each other to be proud of all that had been achieved in ninety years, and to be proud of defending their country against 'terrorism' and economic sanctions. Their consolation is that they are the Rhodesians who will 'never die'.

The Rhodesians who remained in Zimbabwe, perhaps imprisoned by the currency regulations, or guided by their sense that things – for them

– would be no better elsewhere, had to contend with a decline in ordinary urban services, the scarcity of parts for their cars or swimming pools, a sharp rise in the rate of inflation, the restricted holiday allowances, the barrage of ZANU(PF) propaganda, the visible signs of corruption, the possibility of a one-party state, and their isolation from the mainstream of politics. For most, their individual worlds did not turn upside down; rather they were cocooned in little white islands within Zimbabwe. If it appeared that life had resumed some kind of normality, their mental world existed apart from its surroundings. Alone with friends – all of them white – they muttered their unhappy thoughts, or laughed at the latest perceived absurdity, or recalled a happier past. There were, of course, many consolations. No one, after all, could legislate against the climate.[5] The sunshine, the colours of the jacaranda, and the bougainvillaeas were just as bright and warm as ever. Petrol rationing had ceased in 1980 and there were no more call-ups. The racial tension of the early 1980s gradually eased, the video clubs provided an alternative to the government-controlled media, Reps and the local theatres struggled along, a number of country and sporting clubs survived (albeit with depleted memberships), international sporting ties were resumed, the shops were reasonably if erratically stocked, and the local wines had noticeably improved. And, even though some of the younger ones yearned to get out into a bigger and more exciting world, the hedonists of Harare could still find much to entertain themselves.

The pragmatists were quick to adjust. Farmers and businessmen were soon preoccupied with the kind of problems which had absorbed their energies in the 1970s. There were the familiar grumbles: high input costs, shortages of foreign exchange, the difficulty of obtaining machinery and parts, bureaucratic delays. But so long as the government respected the role of white commercial farming, and so long as it allowed capitalist enterprise a reasonable rein, then the survivors of Rhodesia could live well in the new Zimbabwe. The radical critics complained,[6] the black peasantry demanded more land, and the black urban workers wanted higher wages and some of them called for control of the commanding heights of the economy. The Mugabe government, however, insisted on observing the Lancaster House terms for the required ten years, and the most relevant of those terms protected white farming lands from expropriation. In that period the security of the white farmers was both a symbolic and practical guarantee of continued white privilege. Co-operation with the government, therefore, made good sense.

A number of Rhodesians – exemplified by David Smith, Chris Andersen, and Denis Norman – went beyond pragmatism and became ardent, practising Zimbabweans. So did people like Diana Mitchell who had long associations with liberal politics. It is unclear whether these former Rhodesians have fully completed their migration. A degree of ambiguity probably persisted, and more obviously among those liberals who had higher expectations of black rule, and who applied exacting standards. It was also irritating that the pro-Zimbabwean whites who came after Independence on short contracts, and who were bent on doing good and righting the wrongs of the past, never had the commitment to the country of those born Rhodesians who had endured ostracism for their liberal views.

The war years continued to affect others who remained. Two men pursued an old feud. When Ken Flower transferred his allegiance to Robert Mugabe, P. K. Allum, who stayed on as Commissioner of Police, accused him of planning to murder the Prime Minister.[7] Allum eventually went to Natal – where he was not always welcome among former BSAP officers – and Flower retired to his hill-top house on the outskirts of Harare to tell his version of the past. Murders and suicides continued to eliminate the prominent and the anonymous alike, all of them in some way victims of the 1970s. 'Boss' Lilford, Smith's close confidant from the RF days, was killed at his home near Harare in November 1985. Lilford, aged 77, managed to wound one of his assailants before being overpowered, beaten, and shot in the head. ZANLA hotheads and ZIPRA dissidents cut a swathe through the respective farming communities of Goromonzi and Matabeleland. Other whites experienced unsettled periods. Marc de Borchgrave had walked off Altena Farm in 1978. His marriage broken, his life as a farmer finished, he tried his hand at several commercial ventures. John Hickman, a private citizen since March 1979, subsequently lost a son in the war, worked with an engineering firm, was jailed by the Zimbabwe government on fraud charges, became a born-again Christian, and eventually entered the swimming pool business in Harare.

Ian Smith's position was always ambiguous. While many of his associates departed for South Africa, he continued to farm, to attend parliament, and to be gloomy. In 1980 he was given two bodyguards at a time when Mr Mugabe evidently needed sixty. By 1990 he lived – unguarded – in a tastefully furnished house near the centre of Harare and next to the heavily fortified Cuban Embassy. Throughout the 1980s Smith clashed repeatedly with the government, the most spectacular occasion leading to his suspension from parliament in April 1987 after making speeches in South Africa attacking the imposition of sanctions and urging the Republic to defy political change.[8] Convinced that he had a role in representing and protecting Zimbabwe's whites, Smith fought the 1985 election (the last one held under the Lancaster House agreement providing for twenty white seats) as if nothing had changed.

'Ladies and Gentlemen, let us be honest about this': and there would follow a pessimistic account of African rule and much praise of his own stand in the past.

The old troopers – P. K. van der Byl and Mark Partridge – stood by him. Others, loyal followers in the 1970s, had left the RF, the renamed Conservative Alliance of Zimbabwe (CAZ), because like Dennis Divaris they had decided that the whites must align themselves with the new order.[9] Bill Irvine, the hardline anti-communist, whose opinions belonged to the RAP, led the rebels. He was joined by the once-deferential John Landau, the former RF Chief Whip and armaments manufacturer. On one occasion in 1980 Landau entered Smith's office whereupon he was summarily though politely dismissed by 'the old man'. He bowed his head and said 'Thank you, Sir'.[10] Irvine and Landau, two doughty opponents of the Lancaster House terms, had apparently undergone a Pauline conversion on their way to political preferment under ZANU(PF).

III

One obvious question is whether these Rhodesian experiences bore, or bear, any messages for whites in South Africa. Despite frequent Rhodesian warnings that South Africa would be next, and the underlying presumption that the two situations were parallel, it was widely assumed in the late 1970s and the 1980s that the South African experience was, and would be, very different. For a start, South Africa was richer and stronger, capable of withstanding a sustained economic and physical assault. The whites could also claim more than three centuries of continuous history; most of them knew of no other home and would fight with more determination. Further, the African National Congress was not so well placed to organise and sustain a liberation war, even if it had enjoyed the continued material support of the Soviet Union.

The split in Afrikanerdom in 1982, the severe economic downturn in the 1980s, and the advent of the De Klerk government, were among the factors which undermined much of the conventional wisdom about the capacity and commitment to survive. The National Party leadership, which had long been aware of its inability to determine South Africa's future, grasped the opportunity presented by the changes in Eastern Europe, Angola and Namibia, to announce its decision on 2 February 1990 to remove the bans on the black opposition groups. This decision, which was equivalent to the Smith surrender speech of 24 September 1976, confirmed that the National Party, like the RF by 1977, occupied the centre of white politics and was opting for a negotiated transfer of power in a manner which preserved civilised standards and a privileged lifestyle. By 1992 the National Party – much in the manner of Smith at the whites-only referendum of 1979 – was accusing its white opponents of being unrealistic. On the other hand, the Rhodesian example offered little solace to a South African President who was confronted by an apparently formidable opposition on the far right and which, unlike the RAP, had the numbers and the military connections to defend the laager, to disrupt the negotiating process from within and to assault it from without, even to the point of conceiving – and implementing – its own version of Op Quartz.

Yet, in the end, the Right in South Africa proved to be no more threatening than it had been in Rhodesia, except that in its various manifestations it contributed significantly to the violence of 1990-94. Arguably, however, the important parallels and contrasts go beyond particular political events and configurations. First, the process of change in both Rhodesia and South Africa exposed, accelerated and created divisions within and between the white communities. The common cause in South Africa, which was once identified with the National Party, openly disintegrated during the 1980s and was formally dissolved in February 1990. When it became evident that the National Party government and the African National Congress intended to achieve a peaceful transfer of power, and to push ahead with an election in April 1994, there was no possibility of resurrecting that common cause. Instead, the whites headed in different directions, much as they had done in Zimbabwe immediately before and after 1980.

Secondly, the white communities of South Africa were not prepared emotionally or mentally for the advent of a Mandela-led government after the elections of April 1994. The rhetoric and reality of supremacy and separation were so embedded that the National Party faithful could not easily undertake a migration to the New South Africa. Like their Rhodesian counterparts in the early 1980s, many imagined that the policy of reconciliation meant that little would change. At the same time, for every Bill Irvine, there are one hundred imitators south of the Limpopo, just as there are thousands of white liberals who welcomed the demise of apartheid while remaining apprehensive about the long-term prospects of a democratic state. Moreover, white South Africa did not experience the sudden loss of all political power which bewildered or shattered the Rhodesians. Unlike the CAZ which, for most of the 1980s, remained a whites-only party contesting the whites-only seats prescribed by the Lancaster House constitution, the transformed National Party was obliged to broaden its appeal by seeking – and winning – Coloured and even some black support. As a result, it may have a longer life at the centre of South African politics, extending beyond its current role in Nelson Mandela's Government of National Unity. If that is so, then those whites who cannot resist Africanisation or buy privilege, or who do not command the heights of the economy, may still enjoy that sense of participation and belonging which was denied to the Rhodesians.

The fact remains that, whereas white nationalism in southern Africa has not proved to be sufficiently adhesive, it has been sufficiently intrusive to prevent all of the true believers from adapting to different circumstances. The consolation for the white nationalists of South Africa is that, in contrast to the Rhodesians, they are much better placed to hold their reunions inside a country they can still call home.

Notes

Introduction

1. For an elaboration of the usage of 'terrorist', 'terrorists', 'terrs', 'guerrillas', and 'freedom fighters' see the Glossary.
2. For an elaboration of the interchangeable usage of the terms 'Rhodesians' and 'white Rhodesians' see the Glossary and below.
3. *Rhodesia Herald* (25 Nov. 1971).
4. The full title of Mugabe's party is Zimbabwe African National Union (Patriotic Front). The 2 main African nationalist parties – ZANU and the Zimbabwe African People's Unon (ZAPU) – formed the Patriotic Front in 1976. ZAPU fought the 1980 election separately as the Patriotic Front and won 20 seats against the 57 won by ZANU(PF).
5. Ian Smith, quoted in M. I. Hirsch, *A Decade of Crisis: Ten Years of Rhodesian Front Rule (1963-1972)* (Salisbury, 1973), p. 22.
6. K. Good, 'Settler Colonialism in Rhodesia', *African Affairs*, 73 (1974), p. 22.
7. The Rhodesians wrote and talked incessantly on this theme. Scarcely a day would pass during the parliamentary sessions of 1970-9 without a white minister or back-bencher denouncing the world or praising Rhodesia's stand against perfidy. For a more subtle version of this approach see P. Berlyn, *Rhodesia: Beleaguered Country* (London, 1967), or H. P. W. Hutson, *Rhodesia: Ending an Era* (London, 1978). For a vigorous foreign friend see R. Moore, *Rhodesia* (New York, 1977),
8. Variations on this theme will be found in M. Loney, *Rhodesia: white Racism and Imperial Response* (London, 1975); E. Windrich, *Britain and the Politics of Rhodesian Independence* (London, 1978); D. Caute, *Under The Skin: The Death of white Rhodesia* (London, 1983).
9. Colin Barlow, 'Letter to Constituents', Dec. 1970, Barlow Papers (in the owner's possession).
10. National Archives of Zimbabwe (NAZ), MSS 548/1/2-3; 549/5/1-2.
11. For examples of a more narrow form of listening see Caute, *Under the Skin*, and the 2 books by Denis Hills: *Rebel People* (London, 1978) and *The Last Gays of white Rhodesia* (London, 198).
12. The best account of the manoeuvres, and one which is combined with a narrative of modern Rhodesian history, will be found in M. Meredith, *The Past is Another Country: Rhodesia: UDI to Zimbabwe* (London, 1980).
13. In particular, the authors regret that they were unable to consult Ian Smith's papers which are held at Rhodes University in Grahamstown.
14. *Braai(vleis)* is an Afrikaans word meaning barbecue.

15. Readers will note the frequent use of quotation marks without attribution
16. *Talk*, 2/1 (Feb. 1979); Interview (Hancock): Clem Tholet, 4 Jan. 1991. The album, which included 'Rhodesians Never Die', sold a record 27,000 copies in Rhodesia.
17. See especially the Introduction and ch. 6 of E. Hobsbawm and T. Ranger (eds.), *The Invention of Traditional* (Cambridge, 1983).

1.   We're all Rhodesians*

    * Clem Tholet and Andy Dillion, 'Rhodesians Never Die'.

1.   Rhodesia, *Parliamentary Debates (Parl. Debs.)*, House of Assembly (Ass), 85, col. 1510, 14 Sep. 1973.
2.   R. Blake, *A History of Rhodesia* (London, 1977), p. 278. Blake had used the phrase to describe Rhodesia in the early 1950s.
3.   For a substantial demographic analysis of the White population at an earlier point see P. J. M. McEwan, 'The European Population of Southern Rhodesia', *Civilisations*, 13 (1963), pp. 429–41. This chapter is much indebted to McEwan's work.
4.   Rhodesia, Central Statistical Office (CSO), *Census of Population, 1969* (Salisbury, 1971).
5.   The figures in this paragraph are taken from ibid., pp15–16 and tables 17, 20 and 22.
6.   In Australia in 1914, when the country committed itself enthusiastically to an imperial war, an event which many of its nationalist historians consider marked the birth of the 'Australian nation', the Australian-born constituted some 80 per cent of the white population.
7.   Comparative figures are available in United Nations, *Demographic Yearbook* (New York, 1972), table 31.
8.   The term 'munt', originating from the word for 'person', was generally used derogatively although the term had so entered the vocabulary that, in casual conversation, some whites employed it as a descriptive noun.
9.   G. Kay, *Rhodesia: A Human Geography* (London, 1970,), p. 31; McEwan, 'European Population', pp. 436–7.
10.   C. B. Metcalfe, *A Guide to Farming in Rhodesia* (Salisbury, 1971), p. ix. Metcalfe had himself migrated to Rhodesia from the Sudan in 1956 and worked with Conex (the Department of Conservation and Extension in the Ministry of Agriculture). The book was published under the auspices of the Rhodesia National Farmers' Union.
11.   A sundowner, as the name implies, was a drink taken in the early evening. The term also applied to a cocktail party.
12.   Kay, *Rhodesia*, p. 30.
13.   See, for example, G. Arrighi, 'The Political Economy of Rhodesia', in G. Arrighi and J. S. Saul, *Essays on the Political Economy in Africa* (New York, 1973), ch. 7; c. Stoneman and L. Cliffe, *Zimbabwe: Politics, Economics and Society* (London, 1989), pp. 17–18.
14.   B. M. Schutz, 'European Population Patterns, cultural Persistence and Political Change in Rhodesia', *Canadian Journal of African Studies*, 7 (1973), pp. 9 and 24.

15. McEwan, 'European Population', p. 431.
16. For a history of the Jewish community see B. A. Kosmin, *Majuta: A History of the Jewish Community of Zimbabwe* (Gwelo, 1980).
17. Interview (Hancock): Rowan Cronje, 3 Feb. 1981. Cronje was a dominee (cleric) who became a leading Smith minister in the 1970s. The prominent Afrikaner areas included Charter, Chipinga, Gutu, Cashel, Melsetter, Rusape, Odzi, and Marandellas.
18. Interviews (Hancock): D. Divaris, 2 July 1985; A. Pilavachi, 16 Jan. 1974. Pilavachi, an Egyptian-born Greek Cypriot, regarded UDI as a boon in breaking the stranglehold of British businessmen but felt alienated from his 'natural' community by his background and business achievements.
19. K. Hodder-Williams, *white Farmers in Rhodesia, 1890-1965: A History of the Marandellas District* (London, 1983), esp. ch. 8. For an exchange of letters on the subject of teaching Afrikaans in government schools see *Umtali Post* (30 Jan. and 11 Feb. 1970).
20. Interview (Hancock): Rodney Simmonds, 12 Mar. 1980. Simmonds, the former RF MP for Mtoko, complained that the sudden migration of Afrikaners reduced his chances of re-election when he stood for the RAP in 1977.
21. See Kay, *Rhodesia*, p. 69. Kay's 11 towns did not include Sinoia, and he listed Que Que and Redcliff separately.
22. Ibid., pp.69ff.
23. R. Tredgold, *The Rhodesia that was My Life* (London, 1968), pp. 98, 101; Interview (Hancock): 20 Mar. 1974. The remains of Cecil John Rhodes are buried at Matopos.
24. 'Joint Memorandum Submitted by Salisbury's Peri-Urban Town Councils', 20 Oct. 1969; Highlands Town Management Board, 'Local Government in Greater Salisbury' (Salisbury, n.d.). Copies in the authors' possession.
25. For the parliamentary discussion on this issue, and the related outpouring of regional loyalties, see *Parl. Debs.*, Ass. 79, cols. 1719-45, 12 Aug. 1971.
26. *Census of Population, 1969*, p. 13 and table 51.
27. *Parl. Debs.*, Ass. 81, cols. 262-3 and 268, 8 June 1972; Public Services Association, *Record* (Mar. 1970 and June 1971).
28. Much of this paragraph is drawn from C. M. Brand, 'Race and Politics in Rhodesian Trade Unions', *African Perspectives* (1976), 55-80.
29. In 1973 there were 17 registered white unions (3 of which had black sections), 14 multiracial unions, and 19 African unions.
30. Rhodesia, Ministry of Labour, *Annual Report* (1970-1).
31. *Granite Review*, 12/5 (1971), p. 33,
32. For accounts of the dispute see *Rhodesia Railways Review* (1968-9); *Parl. Debs.*, Ass., 76, cols. 909-12, 5 Nov. 1969; cols. 1548-50, 1553-4, 18 Nov. 1969; *Rhodesia Herald* (22 Oct., 18 Nov., 20-2 Nov. 1969).
33. See the comment by the Gwelo No. 1 Branch of the RRWU in the *Rhodesia Railways Review* (Jan. 1969).
34. NAZ, Andrew Dunlop, Oral/DU 2, pp. 33-4, 43.
35. The history of the new Association is well documented in its journal, the *Locomotive Express*.

36. *Umtali Post* (14 Jan. 1970); *Chronicle* (26 Jan. 1970). Two of the 10 members of the executive council of the AEU were members of the Alliance though the General Secretary, Doug Muller, admitted that 80 union members had petitioned them to resign.

37. Chamber of Mines, *Annual Report* (1970); Association of Rhodesian Industries (ARnI), *Annual Report and Proceedings of the Annual Congress* (1970).

38. *Rhodesian Financial Gazette* (30 Apr. 1971).

39. Ibid. (26 Nov. 1971).

40. For a sample of Newington's views see *Parl. Debs.*, Ass. 79, cols. 98-112, 2 June, and cols. 1982-8, 18 Aug. 1971. Divaris claimed that Newington's outspoken criticisms of the government in caucus over the position of European workers led to Smith's attempt to remove him as Deputy Speaker. Caucus rebuffed the Prime Minister on this issue. (Interview (Hancock): Divaris, 2 July 1985.)

41. Rhodesian Front, *A Report on the Proceedings of the National Congress* (Sept. 1970), p. 31, copy in the authors' possession. This particular phrase formed part of Clause Eleven of the RF's founding principles in 1962.

42. *Parl Debs.*, Ass. 81, col. 770, 20 June 1972.

43. These points were made, for example, in ARnI, 'Report of the Economic Affairs Committee' (June 1971). This report was compiled after one of the Association's regular meetings with the Minister of Finance.

44. NAZ, ORAL/235, pp. 46-7.

45. Ibid., p. 49. See also the interview with Jack Quinton, who was appointed by the RF to chair the Sabi-Limpopo Authority, but who shared a common political background with Ellman-Brown: NAZ, ORAL/QU 2.

46. P. K. van der Byl, a senior RF minister, speaking at the Sinoia Show on 31 July 1970: *Rhodesian Tobacco Journal* (Aug. 1970).

47. This view was expressed by a statutory body, the Agricultural Marketing Authority, quoted in John Alistair McKenzie, 'Commercial Farmers in the Governmental System of Colonial Zimbabwe, 1963-1980', Ph.D. thesis (Harare, 1990), p. 153.

48. See, for example, RNFU, *Report of the Annual Congress* (1970), pp. 33-7, 43-9; NAZ, HA/1/17/7/2 (the papers of George Hartley, a former RF-elected Speaker of the Legislative Assembly and, later, a Senator); and McKenzie, 'Commercial Farmers', esp. chs. 2-3.

49. *Rhodesia Herald* (30 Apr. and 5 Nov. 1971); McKenzie, 'Commercial Farmers', pp. 161-5.

50. See the editorials in *Rhodesian Tobacco Today* for Jan. and Mar. 1970, and July 1971.

51. Beryl Watkins, Chairman [*sic*] of the Church Women's Association, reporting from the Annual General Meeting held in Salisbury, *Anchor* (July 1970).

52. Metcalfe, *Farming in Rhodesia*, pp. 1-2. See also J. B. Hattle, (Department of Meteorological Services), *Zimbabwe's Climate* (Harare, n.d.). Hattle's pamphlet, which was published by the Zimbabwe Tourist Board, pointed out that the mean annual temperature of the four main urban centres fell within the range of 17-19.5 °C, making them roughly equivalent to Sydney,

Los Angeles, and Cape Town, slightly warmer than Johannesburg, Rome, and Mexico City, appreciably warmer on average than London, and slightly cooler than Durban.

53. Not every British visitor approved. Some have complained of the harsh light, the drying heat, and the drought conditions, preferring, it seems, cold, fog, drizzle, and persistent greyness. See Blake, *A History of Rhodesia*, p. 5.

54. Rhodesia, Ministry of Information, Immigration and Tourism, *Rhodesia in Brief* (Salisbury, 1971).

55. Ibid., p. 54.

56. Rhodesia, CSO, *European Expenditure Survey* (Salisbury, 1969).

57. The real estate statistics cited below have been compiled from the monthly figures for 1971 produced by the Record of Transfers (Pvt.) Limited.

58. *Census of Population, 1969*, tables 35 and 88. Statistics for car ownership are difficult to obtain because of government restrictions on releasing registration figures after UDI. A survey conducted by the local press suggested that just 6 per cent of Rhodesian whites over 16 years of age did not own a motor car in early 1973. *Umtali Post* (24 Jan. 1973).

59. G. Kay, 'A Socio-Geographic Survey of Salisbury, Rhodesia', *Zambezia*, (1974), pp. 77-80.

60. Interview (Hancock): R. Jackson, 13 July 1989. Jackson Pools is now the largest pool-construction company in Harare. Bob Jackson, a Glasgow-born plasterer by trade, has worked in the pool-building business since the mid-1960s. He claimed that the business 'took off in 1968-9 and that the largest company was by 1970-1 building up to 1,000 a year. The principal factors behind the boom were: the favourable climate, the low cost ($800-1,000), the availability of funds held in the country after UDI, the desire 'to keep up with the Joneses', and the opening of public pools to non-racial use. In 1963, for example, there were some 400,000 visits to Salisbury's municipal pools; in 1966 the figure was 346,577; in 1970 it was 239,087: Salisbury Municipality, *Minute of His Worship the Mayor* (Salisbury, 1963-70). The fact remains that just under two-thirds of detached European houses in Salisbury did not have a pool in 1970. On the other hand, the survey quoted in n. 58 claimed that there were 39,000 private pools in Rhodesia in early 1973.

61. See *Chronicle* (22 Jan. 1970), for the argument that class and employment created distinct communities of interest in Bulawayo which, in turn, should be instrumental in determining the electoral boundaries of white seats.

62. For material on Rhodesia's divorce laws see B. Goldin, *Unhappy Marriage and Divorce: The Problem in Rhodesia* (Salisbury, 1971); D. R. Seager, 'Marital Dissolution in Rhodesia: A Socio-Legal Perspective', M.Phil. thesis (Salisbury, 1977).

63. *Illustrated Life Rhodesia* (13 July 1973).

64. National Federation of Business and Professional Women of Rhodesia, *Profiles of Rhodesia's Women* (Salisbury, 1976).

65. The RF did select female Senators but rejected the one serious candidate for the Assembly in the 1970s – Olive Robertson (who contested an allegedly

unwinnable seat in 1962) – because she 'talked too much'. (Interview (Hancock): Des Frost (former RF Party Chairman), 17 May 1989.) Frost's own wife was appointed to the Censorship Appeals Board.

66. The evidence relating to Janet Smith's influence is contradictory and elusive. Jack Quinton, a prominent businessman and former politician, who dined several times with the Smiths, described her as 'extremely rightwing', claimed that she had 'a tremendous influence' on her husband, that she 'worried' him into taking UDI, and would tell him to 'mind his own business' if he tried to interrupt her at the dinner table. NAZ, ORAL QU/2, p.93. Advisers close to Smith deny that he relied on her opinions, while the authors – perhaps affected by their impressions of Smith himself and of the way in which so many male Rhodesians tended to assume the role of decision-makers in any household – doubt that Smith relied on the advice of anyone except Ken Flower and Jack Gaylard, two senior civil servants.

67. See the monthly round-up of branch activities contained in the June 1970 issue of *Home and Country*. See also the 'Report of the 44th Annual Congress of the National Women's Institutes of Rhodesia' (1971).

68. *Home and Country* (Sept. 1970).

69. *Umtali Presbyterian Bulletin* (June 1970).

70. NAZ, ORAL/RU 3, p. 43. A record of interview with George Rudland, a former RF Minister of Agriculture.

71. Salisbury Municipal Employees' Association, *Bulletin* (July/Aug. 1970).

72. Rhodesia, Ministry of Health, *Annual Report* (1970), p. 28.

73. Africans paid about 10 per cent for hospitalisation in Africans-only institutions. Harari Hospital in Salisbury, which was used by the Africans, was better equipped in 1970 than the European Salisbury Central Hospital.

74. *Gwelo Times* (5 Nov. 1970).

75. For further comments on the high road toll see ibid. (28 Jan. 1971 and 29 Nov. 1973).

76. Noni Niesewand in *Illustrated Life Rhodesia* (13 Aug. 1970).

77. See the comments of a visiting American educationalist, quoted approvingly by the headmaster, in the *Prince Edward School Magazine* (1970).

78. *Chaplin School Magazine* (1972).

79. McEwan noted that 68.6 per cent of European society had obtained a school-leaving certificate: 'European Population', p. 432. See also table 30 of the 1969 Census for the figures of whites who had obtained post-school qualifications.

80. This point was made in interviews with several prominent Rhodesians in the late 1970s and early 1980s; for example, by D. J. Lewis, former Rhodes Scholar, Oxford cricket Blue, and member of the Rhodesian Promotion Council. (Interview (Hancock): 4 Mar. 1980.)

81. See the annual reports of the Secretary for Education, 1964-70, and especially for 1965-6.

82. For such views see the Headmaster's Report in the *Prince Edward School Magazine* (1970).

83. For RF reactions to the report in 1974 of the government-appointed and management-dominated Commission of Enquiry into Further Education in

the Technical and Commercial Fields see *Parl. Debs.*, Ass. 89, 8 and 10 Apr. 1975.

84. Quoted in R. Riddell, 'Education for Employment', Catholic Institute for International Relations, *From Rhodesia to Zimbabwe*, 9 (London, 1980), pp. 8-9.

85. These figures are based on the following: CSO, *National Accounts and Balance of Payments of Rhodesia* (1971); *Annual Report of the Secretary for Education* (1970); *Annual Report of the Secretary for African Education* (1973).

86. For a history of white education see N. Atkinson, *Teaching Rhodesians: A History of Educational Policy in Rhodesia* (London, 1972). By 1970 the brighter students were taking their O levels in the Fourth Form and their A levels in the Upper Sixth while others were taking M levels in order to obtain entry into South African universities.

87. The government schools enrolled boarders, maintained strict codes of disci pline, insisted on uniforms, and encouraged parent involvement.

88. Rhodesia, Ministry of Education, 'Suggestions for Teaching History in Primary Schools' (1970). African as well as European children were to receive this view of the past.

89. *Fort Victoria Advertiser* (14 Aug. 1970).

90. For a history of the University College see M. Gelfand, *A Non-Racial Island of Learning: A History of the University College of Rhodesia from its Inception to 1966* (Gwelo, 1978).

91. For an example of these views see the speech by Ian McLean, Minister of Labour and Social Welfare, opening the Loyal Women's Guild Conference in late July 1970: *Outpost* (Oct. 1970).

92. R. Gary, *The Story of Reps: The History of Salisbury Repertory Players, 1931-1975* (Salisbury, 1975), p. 191.

93. One of these companies – the Wankie Dramatic and Choral Society – was entirely African.

94. *Umtali Post* (2 Feb. 1970 and 12 Feb. 1973); Cary, *The Story of Reps*, p. 180.

95. C. J. Wortham, 'The State of the Theatre in Rhodesia', *Zambezia*, I (1969), pp. 47-53.

96. G. M. Jackson, *The Land is Bright* (Salisbury, 1974).

97. Ibid., p. 132.

98. Not that the Rhodesians lacked talent. Some of their past greats had worn South African caps including Colin Bland who was perhaps – in a sport prone to unprovable hyperbole – the most outstanding cover field in world cricket history.

99. *Illustrated Life Rhodesia* (2 Nov. and 28 Dec. 1972).

100. Two of the perennial complaints from the rural areas were that progress was slow in building transmitters and that the quality of reception in the marginal areas was poor.

101. *Look and Listen*, 4/52 (1970).

102. *Illustrated Life Rhodesia* (12 Mar. 1970).

103. Ibid. (1 June 1972). The former censor denied that she was a 'typical' censor because she accepted the reality of pre-marital sex and the necessity for some abortions.

104. Rhodesia, Ministry of Internal Affairs, Board of Censors, *Catalogue of Banned Books, Periodicals, Records etc from 1 December 1967 to 31 December 1972.*

105. *Report of the Commission of Inquiry into Termination of Pregnancy* (19 Feb. 1976), Cmd. R.R.2-1976, p. 7.

106. Occasionally, cases would surface in court or were mentioned in the police annual reports. See, for example, *Chronicle* (8 Jan. 1969), for a case involving indecent assault on three African males, and Rhodesia, British South Africa Police (BSAP), *Annual Report of the Commissioner of Police* (1973). There was a reported case of bashing in 1973 when a 'known homosexual' was beaten to death by two drunken whites – a middle-aged Irish engineer and a 19-year-old policeman – who were each given 4 years imprisonment for culpable homicide: *Illustrated Life Rhodesia* (3 May 1973).

107. *Illustrated Life Rhodesia* (13 Aug. 1970); Rhodesia, BSAP, *Annual Report of the Commissioner of Police* (1970).

108. *Parl. Debs.*, Ass. 79, col. 166, 3 June 1971; 80, cols. 2155-8, 8 Aug. 1972 (Fawcett Phillips).

109. Rhodesia, *Annual Report of the Secretary of Justice* (1975). According to a UN survey for 1970, which calculated the ratio of final decrees to population figures, the Rhodesians had 2.05 decrees per 1,000 compared with the United States (3.51), England and Wales (1.17), Australia (0.5), South Africa (2.06): United Nations, *Demographic Yearbook* (New York, 1971), table 37. See also Goldin, *Unhappy Marriage and Divorce*, and Seager, 'Marital Dissolution in Rhodesia'.

110. Except where otherwise stated, the material for this paragraph is taken from Rhodesia, BSAP, *Annual Reports of the Commissioner of Police* (1969-70).

111. Interview (Hancock): Ron Peters (formerly of the Criminal Investigation Department), 30 Aug. 1989.

112. An account of the Fisher and Diggeden cases may be found in A. Hardy, *Some Famous Rhodesian Trials* (Bulawayo, 1981), chs. 4 and 8.

113. The case was discussed in the *Rhodesian Financial Gazette* (4 and 18 June 1971).

114. Quoted in I. Linden, *The Catholic Church and the Struggle for Zimbabwe* (London, 1980), p. 87.

115. Ibid., p. 116; Diocese of Mashonaland, 'Statistics' (1977). Copy in the authors' possession.

116. Interview (Hancock): 21 Aug. 1989. Burrough, a former Oxford rowing Blue, had been a POW in the Second World War, a missionary in South Korea, and the chaplain to the immigrant community of Birmingham before going to Rhodesia.

117. *Link* (Nov. 1970).

118. Ibid. (June 1970), quoting a letter from the Bishop to the Minister of Lands on 1 May 1970.

119. Linden, *The Catholic Church*, pp. 131-2. For the Anglican position see M. Lapsley, *Neutrality or Co-option: Anglican Church and State from 1964 until the Independence of Zimbabwe* (Gweru, 1986), esp. app. 5.

120. For statements by Clutton-Brock and Lamont see *Moto* (Apr. and May 1970, Mar, 1971). For a discussion of Moto, which was published by the Catholic Church, see Linden, *The Catholic Church*, pp. 69 ff.

121. This position did not affect its contribution to African development through the Church's programme of training African artisans at Morgenster School.

122. CSO, *Monthly Digest of Statistics* (July 1971). See also P. S. Harris, *black Industrial Workers: The General Problems of Low Pay* (Gwelo, 1974), ch. 1.

123. *African Times* (29 Apr. 1970).

124. *Parl. Debs.*, Ass. 79, col. 262, 4 June 1971 (Peter Nilson, brother of Ralph Nilson, then Chairman of the RF).

125. Quoted in L. W. Bowman, *Politics in Rhodesia: white Power in an African State* (Cambridge, Mass., 1973), p. 141.

126. Public notices excluding or separating blacks were usually more subtle than those of South Africa. Peter Niesewand observed that the first 'Europeans Only' signs appeared in Bulawayo in 1971, and noted that there were about half a dozen in Salisbury (mostly adorning toilets): *Guardian* (London) (29 Sept. 1971). The more common exclusion notice in Rhodesia read 'Right of Admission Reserved'. In 1974 the Post Office introduced separate queues for the 'Personal Transactions Counters' and 'Messengers' Counters', thereby expecting to separate the Europeans from African messengers. For a survey of discriminatory laws and practice in the early 1970s see D. Davies, *Race Relations in Rhodesia: A Survey for 1972-73* (London, 1975).

127. *Rhodesia Herald* (7, 9, 14-15 Sept. 1970).

128. According to the parents and pupils of one Midlands high school, the communists would obtain a foothold in their institution if multiracial sport was allowed: 'we shall be sandwiched and crushed at their leisure.' ('Memorandum to Petition signed by Parents and Pupils at Thornhill High School, Gwelo', 1967. NAZ, HA/17/6/17.)

129. *Fort Victoria Advertiser* (15 Jan. 1971); *Rhodesian Financial Gazette* (31 Dec. 1970 and 8 Jan. 1971).

130. Bishop Lamont was more concerned about the 'fearful apathy' of the African population: they just 'sit idly by and permit their lives to be planned for them'. *Moto* (Apr. 1971).

131. *African Times* (8 Apr. 1970). The paper was first published in 1966.

132. *Umtali Post* (14 Oct. 1970).

133. *Home and Country* (June 1970).

134. 'Minutes of a Meeting of the Meyrick Park and Mabelreign Women's Institute', 23 Sept. 1970, NAZ, WO6/4/1/I7:

135. Rhodesia, BSAP, *Annual Report of the Commissioner of Police* (1971).

136. Ibid. (1970). When a white girl of seven was raped by an African there was an immediate demand (which was not met) for the introduction of the death sentence in such cases: *Gwelo Times* (19 Mar. 1970).

137. *Rhodesia Herald* (28-9 Nov., 2 Dec. 1969).

138. In Fort Victoria, alone, there were 44 predominantly white-run welfare associations in 1970: *Fort Victoria Advertiser* (6 Feb. 1970).

139. Market Research (Rhod.) (Pvt.) Ltd., 'Political Party Study' (1969), prepared for J. Walter Thompson Company, Central Africa, Pvt., Ltd. Copy in the authors' possession.

140. *Umtali Post* (21 Oct. 1970 and 1 Sept. 1971).
141. For the role of locally-produced novels in helping to develop 'the awareness of a new and distinct Rhodesian identity' see A. J. Chennels, 'Settler Myths and the Southern Rhodesian Novel', Ph.D. thesis (Harare, 1982).

2. 'The even progression of life'*

* Editorial, *Rhodesia Herald* (25 Nov. 1971).

1. The date of 2 March soon faded from the memory, assisted by a government decision that Republic Day should be a movable feast, celebrated on the second last Monday of October (a holiday), and an order that government schools (which, in 1970, were virtually alone in acknowledging the occasion) should hold appropriate ceremonies on the previous Friday to allow Rhodesia a three-day holiday weekend: *Rhodesia Herald* (19 Oct.), *Umtali Post* (21 Oct. 1971). The two more important commemorative days – Pioneer Day and Independence Day – preserved their respective fixed dates of 12 September and 11 November. The Rhodesia and Founders Days, which created a four-day weekend, were normally assigned the second Monday and Tuesday of July.
2. There were 90,704 registered voters: 81,572 were white, 2,487 were Asian or Coloured, and 6,645 were black. Some 85 per cent of the total cast a vote.
3. An account of these talks may be found in E. Windrich, *Britain and the Politics of Rhodesian Independence* (London, 1978), chs. 6 and 8.
4. The Rhodesian Printing and Publishing Company, which published the *Rhodesia Herald* and the *Sunday Mail* in Salisbury, the *Chronicle* and the *Sunday News* in Bulawayo, and a number of provincial papers, was a subsidiary of the South African-based Argus Press. Members of the RF despised the Argus Press for being 'left-wing' and 'disloyal', and they supported the introduction of the *Rhodesian Financial Gazette* in 1970 to counter its 'insidious influence'. (Interview (Hancock): W. R. ('Sam') Whaley, 19 May 1980.) The main objections to the Argus Press were that its editors gave more space to the opposition than allowed by the government-owned radio and television, that it pressed hard for a settlement with the British, and that it frequently criticised the government's judgement and competence. In fact, the RF's complaints were grossly overstated: the *Chronicle* may have remained more liberal than the *Herald* but neither could be described in 1970 as supporters of the 'left-wing' Centre Party. For a radical analysis of the Rhodesian media see E. Windrich, *The Mass Media in the Struggle for Zimbabwe: Censorship and Propaganda under Rhodesian Front Rule* (Gwelo, 1981).
5. *Rhodesia Herald* (17 Apr. 1970).
6. Dupont always denied the charge that he attended a cabinet meeting to press his opposition to the proposed *Tiger* constitution of 1966, and claimed that he always acted with propriety as head of state: C. Dupont, *The Reluctant President* (Bulawayo, 1978), pp. 188-9, 200; NAZ, ORAL DU/4, p. 68.

7. Dupont, *Reluctant President*, pp. 214-15; *Rhodesia Herald* (17 Apr. 1970).

8. Windrich, *Britain and the Politics ofRhodesian Independence*, p. 73.

9. *Rhodesian Financial Gazette* (6 Nov. 1970).

10. Rhodesia, Ministry of Finance, *Economic Survey* (Salisbury, Apr. 1971).

11. Interview (Hancock): David Young, 2 Feb. 1982. David Smith became the third member of the 'Mafia' when he was appointed Minister of Finance in 1976.

12. The next two paragraphs rely heavily on Interviews (Hancock): David Young, 2 Feb. 1982; John Cameron, 4 Feb. 1981; Mark Rule, 1 July 1984. Cameron, like Ellman-Brown, received the ICD for his services to sanctions-busting. He was a senior figure in ACCOR, a banker, and a director of finance and agricultural machinery companies. Mark Rule headed an organisation which was responsible for selling Rhodesia's minerals. For an attempt to write a thrilling account of tobacco sanctions-busting see P. Armstrong, *Tobacco Spiced with Ginger: The Life of Ginger Freeman* (Borrowdale, 1987).

13. Interview (Hancock): John Cameron, 4 Feb. 1981.

14. See n. 21 below.

15. For a critique of the constitution see C. Palley, in *Africa Research Bulletin (ARE)*, P, S, and C, 6/5 (1969), 1416C-7A.

16. A critical account of the RF's legislation may be found in R. Austin, *The Character and Legislation of the Rhodesian Front since UD1* (London, 1968).

17. For a description and critical account of the original 1960 Act passed by the whitehead government see R. Tredgold, *The Rhodesia that was My Life* (London, 1968), pp. 229-33. Tredgold resigned as Federal Chief Justice over the issue.

18. For two accounts, sympathetic to the Taugwena, see G. Clutton-Brock, *Rekayi Tangwena*, 'Let Tangwena Be' (Salisbury, 1969), and H. Moyana, *The Victory of Chief Rekayi Tangwena* (Harare, 1987).

19. Rhodesia, Ministry of Information, Immigration and Tourism, 'The Ministry of Internal Affairs', *Meet the Ministry*, 2 (Salisbury, 1970).

20. Rhodesian Front, *Principles and Policies* (Salisbury, 1962).

21. One reason for the surprise was that 66 per cent of the electorate had approved the 1961 constitution, although many may have voted 'Yes' in the belief they were voting for independence. Two electoral rolls were created under this constitution: the Europeans were mainly registered on the higher-qualification A-roll; and the Africans, who were mainly registered on the B-roll, elected 14 UFP members in a low turn-out. The African nationalists boycotted the election.

22. B. Schutz, 'The Theory of Fragment and the Political Development of white Settler Society in Rhodesia', Ph.D. thesis (Los Angeles, 1972), pp. 178-9. Schutz, who surveyed 113 of a possible 166 divisional, constituency, and branch chairmen, and conducted other random surveys, found that RF activists began their working careers in Rhodesia as semi-skilled or skilled artisans and had worked their way up to managerial, professional, or higher administrative positions: ibid., p. 201.

23. L. W. Bowman, *Politics in Rhodesia* (Cambridge, Mass., 1973), pp. 102-5.

24. R. Blake, *A History of Rhodesia* (London, 1977), p. 343.

25. Bowman, *Politics in Rhodesia*, pp. 92 ff.

26. For example, 'Minutes of (the) Committee Meeting of the RF', Victoria Lowveld Branch, 30 Apr, 1969. NAZ, MSS HA 17/7/1.

27. Interviews (Hancock): Rodney Simmonds, 12 Mar. 1980, and Des Frost, 17 May 1989; (Godwin and Hancock): Reg Cowper, 9 May 1989. Cowper represented the Wankie constituency.

28. Bowman, *Politics in Rhodesia*, pp. 104 – 5. Bowman was replying to the argument by C. A. Rogers and C. Frantz, *Racial Themes in Southern Rhodesia: The Attitudes and Behavior of the white Population* (New Haven, Conn., 1962) who had concluded that Europeans became more conservative the longer they lived in Rhodesia, and had assumed that the categories of 'liberal' and 'conservative' meant something 'substantively different' in Southern Rhodesian politics.

29. For Cary's biography see NAZ, ORAL CA/4.

30. For Dunlop's own account see NAZ, ORAL/DU 2; A. Dunlop, *The March of Time* (Salisbury, 1977).

31. D. C. Lilford was a wealthy rancher and a Smith confidant who has been regarded as the RF's principal financial backer and kingmaker. Barbara Field, the widow of Winston Field, argued that the RF's largest sums came from the Marandellas district, and denied that Lilford was so important: NAZ, ORAL/FI2, pp. 19-20.

32. Lardner-Burke won the Gwelo seat for Huggins's United Party in 1948, lost it when standing for Garfield Todd's United Rhodesia Party in 1954, and won it back in 1962 when standing for the RF.

33. Wrathall was elected for Todd's party in 1954, opposed Todd in 1958 when he was overthrown by the conservative faction of the UFP, and was elected for the RF in 1962.

34. Cf. D. Cowderoy and R. C. Nesbit, *War in the Air: Rhodesian Air Force, 1935-1980* (Alberton, 1987), pp. 13-14.

35. Interview (Hancock): Sir Roy Welensky, 7 May 1974. An early right-wing criticism of Smith may be found in *Citizen* (1 Apr. 1955).

36. P. Berlyn, *The Quiet Man: A Biography of the Hon. Ian Douglas Smith, ID Prime Minister of Rhodesia* (Salisbury, 1978), ch. 1. This biography is the most detailed and personal of those published so far but the subject still awaits a close, comprehensive, and critical analysis.

37. 'Mr. Smith has been so deeply committed to the white-dominated Rhodesia he knows and loves that he has failed to see, or failed to recognise, the tension which this society breeds', J. Barber, *Rhodesia: The Road to Rebellion* (London, 1967), pp. 194-5.

38. For a summary of Smith's contradictory positions, and a critical appraisal of him by a whitehead loyalist, see M. I. Hirsch, *A Decade of Crisis* (Salisbury, 1973), pp. 18-30.

39. R. Hodder-Williams, 'Rhodesia's Search for a Constitution: Or, Whatever Happened to Whaley?', *African Affairs*, 69 (1970), p. 217.

40. The Five Principles, which the Labour government inherited from the Tories, and which were to be the basis for independence negotiations,

required unimpeded progress to majority rule; guarantees against retrogressive amendments; an immediate improvement in the political status of
the African population; progress towards ending racial discrimination; and
the acceptability of any agreement to the Rhodesian people as a whole.
There is a comprehensive discussion of the principles and of NIBMAR in
Windrich, *Britain and the Politics of Rhodesian Independence.*

41. *Rhodesian Financial Gazette* (23 Dec. 1970).
42. Rhodesia, *Report of the Constitutional Commission* (Apr. 1968), p. 1.
43. Whaley, later an RF-appointed Senator, was a senior partner in a Salisbury
    legal firm which included Jack Howman, an RF minister who had been
    restored to cabinet after resigning when Field was overthrown. The other
    members of the Commission were Stan Morris, a former Chief Native
    Commissioner who became Chairman of the Public Services Board in 1965
    and, later, an RF-appointed Senator until he was dropped for 'liberal' ten-
    dencies; Robert Cole, a Bulawayo lawyer, one of Whaley's friends, and an
    RF member; Chief Sigola, a member of the Chiefs' Council and former
    member of the Monckton Commission which reported on the Federation;
    and Charles Mzingeli, an old warhorse from African trade unionism and
    the Southern Rhodesia Labour Party, a fighter – in his words – for the 'bot-
    tom dog' – who had parted company with the nationalists in the late 1950s.
    See Hodder-Williams, 'Rhodesia's Search for a Constitution', pp. 223-4.
44. Interview (Hancock): Whaley, 19 May 1980.
45. For accounts of this process see Bowman, *Politics in Rhodesia*, pp. 134-7.
46. The full story of Harper's departure from the cabinet has yet to be told.
    Officially, he was dropped as an alleged 'security risk': K. Flower, *Serving
    Secretly: An Intelligence Chief on Record. Rhodesia into Zimbabwe 1964 to 1981*
    (London, 1987), p. 97. Allegations have also been made involving torrid
    bedroom activity, the presence of a foreign agent, undercover work by
    Rhodesian intelligence, and secret tape recordings. The story is a bizarre
    one deserving a full disclosure.
47. Copy in the authors' possession.
48. Hodder-Williams, 'Rhodesia's Search for a Constitution', pp. 231-2.
49. Given that the 'No' vote on the separate question of the republic was just
    18.99 per cent, it would appear that the far right remained in the fold on
    that issue.
50. Rhodesian Front, *A Report on the Proceedings of the National Congress*
    (Bulawayo, Oct. 1969), pp. 28-30. Copy in the authors' possession.
51. See the booklet entitled *Provincialisation* by R. Howman, Deputy Secretary
    of Internal Affairs between 1962 and 1969, and brother of Jack Howman,
    the RF minister, which was published as Cambridge African Occasional
    Paper, No. 4 (Cambridge, 1986).
52. Rhodesian Front, *Report of the National Congress* (1969), p. 5.
53. The Mashona land Rural Division was in a strong position to dominate,
    being responsible for over half the RF's revenue. Interview (Hancock): Des
    Frost, 17 May 1989.
54. Rhodesian Front, *Report of the National Congress* (1969), pp. 4-8.
55. Rhodesian Front, *Report of the National Congress* (1970), pp. 3-5.

56. Ibid., pp. 26-9.
57. Rhodesian Front, *General Election, 1970: A Handbook for Candidates and Constituency Chairmen*, pp. 5-6. Copy in the authors' possession.
58. Market Research (Rhod.) (Pvt.) Ltd., 'Political Party Study' (1969).
59. I. Hancock, *white Liberals, Moderates and Radicals in Rhodesia 1953-1980* (London, 1984), p. 138.
60. Ibid., p. 122.
61. Interviews (Hancock): Colin Barlow, 26 Apr. 1989; Des Frost, 17 May 1989; Rodney Simmonds, 17 May 1989. The party organisation had agreed to back Lord Graham and George Rudland – a former Agriculture Minister – for Senate seats but Smith apparently ordered the Assembly members not to support them.
62. NAZ, Harvey Ward, Oral/246, p. 60. Some of the responsibility for projecting Smith may also belong to Ivor Benson, who was imported from South Africa in 1964 – 5 as an information adviser to the Rhodesian government.
63. Ibid., p. 66; Interview (Hancock): Frost, 17 May 1989.
64. Hodder-Williams, 'Rhodesia's Search for a Constitution', p. 234.
65. The information and interpretation of the next three paragraphs draw upon Hancock, *white Liberals*, chs. 6-7.
66. Quoted, ibid., p. 114.
67. This paragraph is largely based on J. A. McKenzie, 'Commercial Farmers in the Governmental System of Colonial Zimbabwe, 1963-1980', Ph.D. thesis (Harare, 1990) esp. pp. 101-3, 149, and 152-3.
68. Interview (Hancock): Pat Bashford, 24 Apr. 1980. The Intensive Conservation Area committees, which were first constituted under the Natural Resources Act of 1941, often went beyond their brief to protect land use and became involved in politics. See, for example, McKenzie, 'Commercial Farmers', p. 196.
69. *Sunday Mail* (26 June 1969).
70. Rhodesia, Ministry of Internal Affairs, Circular Minute Number 8/68, copy in the authors' possession. The document is partly reproduced in Flower, *Serving Secretly*, pp. 294-8. One former Secretary of Internal Affairs later claimed that Nicolle had originally favoured the *Fearless* terms, and wrote this document to support his political masters and to build up morale in a department which had expected the terms to be implemented. (Interview (Hancock): Don Yardley, 17 Feb. 1982.)
71. Howman, *Provincialisation*, p. xxiii. Even the notion of hardliners must be qualified. One of the most notorious of the self-professed 'oppressors' lost control over the 'disturbed' Shamva district in the early 1960s because he took off every afternoon to play golf. (Interview (Hancock): R. C. Wollacott, 7 Feb. 1982.)
72. This paragraph draws upon Flower's book, *Serving Secretly*, four long interviews Hancock had with Flower (19 Jan. and 4 Feb. 1982, 3 July 1985, and 9 July 1987), and interviews in 1985 and 1989 with a number of former CIO officers.
73. This issue is discussed in Chapter 8.

74. Interview (Hancock): David Young, 2 Feb. 1982. Young himself was born in Scotland in 1921, graduated from St Andrews University, served in India, Burma, and Malaya in the Second World War, joined the Southern Rhodesia Treasury in 1947, served in the Federal Treasury between 1953 and 1963, and returned to Southern Rhodesia following the break-up of the Federation. Young retired soon after independence in 1980.

75. For disputes in 1970 see the December issue of *Record*.

76. A list of the awards given on the fifth anniversary of UDI will be found in Rhodesia, *Government Gazette*, 68/57 (11 Nov. 1970).

77. One of the complaints against Winston Field was that he put 'UFP types' onto boards, the major example being the appointment of Jack Quinton to chair the Sabi-Limpopo Authority. Field was under the mistaken impression that expertise was more important than party affiliation.

78. Copy in the authors' possession.

79. Rhodesia, Ministry of Information, *Government List* (1973). The more obvious of them included Howard Bloomfield, Mike Butler, Nick Cambitzis, Des Frost, C. A. Heurtley, Esmond Micklem, Cecil Millar, R. G. Pascoe, and Senator Strong.

80. Windrich, *The Mass Media in the Struggle for Zimbabwe*, part ii. For the prevailing philosophy see especially the annual reports of the Rhodesian Broadcasting Commission for 1970 and 1971, and the speech by J. M. Helliwell, the Chairman of RBC/TV, at the Midlands Show reported in the *Gwelo Times* (3 Apr. 1970).

81. Interviews (Hancock): Simmonds, 13 Mar. 1980 and 17 May 1989.

82. Apart from the interviews with Simmonds, details of the affair were obtained from the *Rhodesia Herald* (21 Mar. 1968); *Regina* v. *Rodney Guy Swayne Simmonds* (typescript in the authors' possession); 'Confidential Statement to all Members of the IAA', 19 Apr. 1968, signed by L. G. Leach, Secretary-Treasurer (copy in the authors' possession); Interviews (Hancock): R. C. Wollacott, 7 Feb. 1982; Don Yardley, 17 Feb. 1982.

83. Rhodesian Front, 'Memorandum submitted to Caucus by (the) Sub-Committee for Information, Immigration and Tourism', 5 Sept. 1970; 'Minutes of a combined meeting of the Executive Sub-Committee on Immigration and Tourism and the Caucus Committee on Immigration', 27 Nov. 1970; 'Minutes of a Meeting of the Executive Sub-Committee on Immigration and Tourism', 12 Feb. 1971. Copies in the authors' possession.

84. *Parl. Debs.*, Ass. 79, cols. 1746-8, 1767-9, 12 Aug. 1971.

85. *Property and Finance* (Sept. 1971).

86. *Moto* (9 Oct 1971).

87. *Rhodesian Financial Gazette (9* July 1971); Interview (Hancock): Frost, 18 May 1989.

88. *Rhodesia Herald* (8 Oct. 1971).

89. *ARE*, P, S, and C, 8/11 (1971), 2292C-5C.

90. *Rhodesia Herald* (25-6 Nov. 1971); *Rhodesian Financial Gazette* (26 Nov. 1971).

91. *Property and Finance* (Dec. 1971).

92. Flower, *Serving Secretly*, pp. 99-100; Interview (Hancock): Flower, 9 July 1987.

93. Hancock, *white Liberals,* pp. 161-2.
94. Spokesmen for the white Churches, including prominent Catholic clergy (but not the bishops), adopted a similar stance. *Moto* (1, 8, and 22 Jan. 1972).
95. A, Muzorewa, *Rise Up and Walk: An Autobiography* (London, 1978), ch. 10.
96. NAZ, MSS CE 2/6/1.
97. An account of Judy Todd's detention may be found in J. Todd, *The Right to Say No: Rhodesia 1972* (Harare, 1972).
98. Reports of the violence may be found in the *Rhodesia Herald* (13-15, 17-22 Jan. 1972).
99. United Kingdom, *Report of the Commission on Rhodesian Opinion,* Cmnd. 4964 (May 1972), p. 125.
100. *Rhodesian Financial Gazette* (10 Mar. 1971).
101. Rhodesia, *For the Record,* 17 (23 May 1972). Privately, Smith and his ministers accused 'left-wingers' in the British Foreign Office of delaying the departure of the Pearce Commission for Rhodesia in order to give the opposition the chance to organise. Smith also believed that when Lord Harlech, a senior Commissioner, had returned briefly to London he was instructed by Edward Heath, the British Prime Minister, to obtain a 'No' vote which was Labour's price for supporting British membership of the European Economic Community. (Interview (Hancock): Smith, 11 July 1989.)
102. An editorial in the *Rhodesia Herald* (24 May 1972) urged the government to heed the warning given by the African 'No'.
103. This issue was raised by Newington. See *Parl. Debs.,* Ass. 81, cols. 1244-6, 20 July, and col. 1283, 21 July 1972.
104. *Parl. Debs.,* Ass. 82, col. 434, 22 Aug. 1972.
105. This point was made by Senator van Heerden: *Parl. Debs.,* Ass. 83, cols. 867-8, 7 Dec. 1972. Ministers were entitled to speak in both houses.
106. *Rhodesia Herald* (26 Oct., 7 and 11 Nov. 1972).
107. Ibid. (14 Feb. 1973); Secretary of the Sinoia Town Council to C. D. Hedderwick, 2 Mar. 1973, copy in the authors' possession.
108. *Umtali Post* (7 Feb. 1972).
109. 'Report of the Planning and Co-Ordinating Committee on Legislation Necessary to Implement Government Policies set out in the Caucus Document on Policy (SECRET)' (n.d.), Barlow Papers.

3. 'Only a pinprick in our sides'*

* C. Kleynhans, Centenary farmer: *Rhodesia Herald* (29 Dec. 1972).

1. The following 3 paragraphs draw heavily upon police reports and interviews Hancock had with Marc de Borchgrave (4 July 1989) and Margaret (formerly de Borchgrave) Nel (9 May 1989). See also *Rhodesia Herald* (22-3 Dec. 1972).
2. For a brief discussion of the choice of target see D. Martin and P. Johnson, *The Struggle for Zimbabwe: The Chimurenga War* (London, 1981), p. 73. It was widely assumed at the time that Altena was selected because of de Borchgrave's allegedly poor labour relations. Another possibility is that the choice was a random one. See also the transcripts of interviews conducted

with Josiah Tungamirai and Rex Nhongo in 1984 for the Granada Television *End of Empire* series. Whatever his record as an employer, the fact remains that De Borchgrave's labour force later captured and handed over a wounded guerrilla who had been involved in an ambush.

3. For an account of this process see Martin and Johnson, *The Struggle for Zimbabwe*, ch. 5.

4. Another 4 members of the Security Forces died while off duty and 29 were killed in 'accidents'.

5. A formerly busy hotel, located near the Chirundu border post, was an early victim of the closure which the owner, who went into liquidation, described as a 'monumental blunder': *Sunday Mail* (23 Feb. 1973).

6. ZANLA was the military wing of ZANU; the Zimbabwe People's Revolutionary Army (ZIPRA) was the military wing of ZAPU.

7. The Territorials were civilians who had completed a period of military service but remained liable for call-up.

8. These figures have been taken from *The Military Balance, 1971-1972* (London, 1972), which was produced by the International Institute for Strategic Studies. For further analyses of the Security Forces see L. H. Gann and T. H. Henriksen, *The Struggle for Zimbabwe: Battle in the Bush* (New York, 1981), pp. 30-3, and P. L. Moorcraft and P. McLaughlin, *Chimurenga!: The War in Rhodesia, 1965-1980* (Marshalltown, 1982), ch. 4.

9. *Parl. Debs.*, Ass. 79, col. 501, 10 June, and col. 1094, 29 July 1971; 82, cols. 869-70, 30 Aug. 1972 (Jack Howman, Minister of Defence). Women could serve in a civilian capacity, and Howman did not rule out the possibility of drafting them should the need arise.

10. Quoted in the BSAP magazine, *Outpost* (Oct. 1972). A stick normally consisted of four men. PATU sticks were drawn from the Police Reserve.

11. D. Cowderoy and R. C. Nesbit, *War in the Air. Rhodesian Air Force, 1935-1980* (Alberton, 1987), p. 35.

12. Rhodesia, *Annual Reports of the Secretary for Defence, the Commander of the Army and the Commander of the Air Force* (1972), p., 3.

13. Ibid., and *Outpost* (Jan. 1973). The Army Commander pointed out that whereas, in the previous years, 66 per cent of white recruits were school-leavers, that figure had fallen to 37 per cent in 1972. The Commander blamed the pay scales for the wastage and recruitment problems.

14. For a history of counter-insurgency in this period see A. R. Wilkinson, *Insurgency in Rhodesia, 1957-1973: An Account and Assessment*, Adelphi Papers, 100 (London, 1973); K. Flower, *Serving Secretly* (London, 1987), ch. 6; Moorcraft and McLaughlin, *Chimurenga!*, ch. 2.

15. Martin and Johnson, *The Struggle for Zimbabwe*, pp. vii and 10, Martin and Johnson point out that the first Chimurenga occurred with the uprisings of the 1890s and the second – variously translated as a revolution, war, struggle, or resistance – began at Sinoia on 28 Apr. 1966.

16. The full details might have amused or depressed them. Lt.-Col. (later Major-General) Derry MacIntyre claimed that the Rhodesians prepared in depth for one joint venture, and arrived at the rendezvous at the appointed time armed with detailed maps and full military equipment. When the

Portuguese commander finally turned up – late – he was carrying just one item: a Shell road map of Mozambique. (Interview (Hancock): 24 Jan. 1978.)

17. This phrase was used by Lardner-Burke, the Minister of Law and Order, when proposing a further extension of the State of Emergency. *Parl. Debs.*, Ass. 79, col. 460, 10 June 1971.
18. Flower, *Sewing Secretly*, p. 105.
19. L. H. Gann, 'Rhodesia and the Prophets', *African Affairs*, 71 (1972), pp. 35-6.
20. *Rhodesia Herald* (19 and 21 Aug. 1972).
21. Gann and Henriksen, *The Struggle for Zimbabwe*, pp. 30-1.
22. In 1972 the 90 per cent of white recruits into the Rhodesian Army were described as 'Rhodesians': *Annual Reports of the Secretary of Defence etc.* (1972), p. 4.
23. Ibid., pp. 5 and 11. The Army was less confident about the degree of morale and discipline both of which, it acknowledged, were being eroded by low pay and certain kinds of static duty.
24. *Outpost* (Oct. 1972).
25. Rhodesia, *Annual Report of the Commissioner of Police* (1972).
26. After retiring as Army Commander, Putterill joined the Centre Party and became an outspoken critic of the RF government. Clifford Dupont later revealed that Putterill once told him that he refused to acknowledge Dupont as his Commander-in-Chief because his loyalty was reserved for the Crown: NAZ, DU/4, p. 75.
27. Rower, *Serving Secretly*, p. 114.
28. Cowderoy and Nesbit, *War in the Air*, ch. 1.
29. Interview (Hancock): Flower, 4 Feb. 1982.
30. A surprising exception was Ron Reid Daly, the Commander of the Selous Scouts, who crossed Hickman on several occasions. Reid Daly said that Hickman had the best military brain in the Army. (Interview (Godwin): 1 Dec. 1982.)
31. Interview (Hancock): MacIntyre, 24 Jan. 1978. For 'official' pen portraits of Walls, Hickman, and MacIntyre see *Fighting Forces of Rhodesia*, 4 (1977), Walls and Hickman, and 6 (1979), MacIntyre.
32. *Flower, Serving Secretly*, pp. 111-12, 120-5.
33. Another landmine buried near the farm was detonated some weeks later by a truck carrying over 20 troops. The driver was killed instantly.
34. According to De Borchgrave, the rocket which hit his bedroom was fired by a man known as Misfire who was subsequently captured, tried, and executed for the death of Corporal Moore. De Borchgrave also claims that, at his trial, Misfire expressed regrets about hurting the child but none at all about trying to kill de Borchgrave. He threatened that his spirit would return to kill his intended victim. In June 1974 De Borchgrave had a very narrow escape when an elephant charged him and he believes that the local Africans, convinced that Misfire's spirit had tried and failed, pronounced that he was now safe. From that moment, De Borchgrave said, he never had any further (guerrilla) problems at Altena. (Interview (Hancock): De Borchgrave, 4 July 1989.)
35. *Rhodesia Herald* (25 and 29 Dec, 1972); *Illustrated Life Rhodesia* (11 Jan. 1973).

The editor of the *Rhodesian Farmer* claimed on 19 Jan. 1973 that the drought was the sole 'emergency' facing agriculture. The drought was, in fact, the worst in 25 years: Rhodesia, *Annual Report of the Secretary of Agriculture* (1973), p. 2.

36. See, for example, the editorial in the *Rhodesia Herald* (23 Dec. 1972).

37. Ibid. (1 Jan. 1973).

38. Ibid. (29 Dec. 1972).

39. *Sinoia News* 5/8 (Mar. 1973).

40. *Rhodesia Herald* (5-6 Dec. 1972). The Herald's first report of the statement on 5 Dec., which began on p. 1, relegated this remark to p. 3.

41. T. Kirk, 'Politics and Violence in Rhodesia', *African Affairs*, 74 (1975), esp. pp. 19-22.

42. Interview (Hancock): De Borchgrave, 4 July 1989.

43. *Parl. Debs.*, Ass. 83, col. 1126, 30 Mar. 1973.

44. Ibid., col. 1084, 29 Mar. 1973.

45. Ibid., col. 1228, 30 Mar. 1973.

46. Interview (Hancock): 16 Feb. 1981.

47. Interview (Hancock): 24 Jan. 1978.

48. Interview (Godwin): Walls, 3 Dec. 1982.

49. *Umtali Post* (10 Dec. 1975) (R. C. Wollacott). See also M. Meredith, *The Past is Another Country* (London, 1980), pp. 107-9, and H. Ellert, *The Rhodesian Front War: Counter-Insurgency and Guerrilla War in Rhodesia 1962-1980* (Gwera, 1989), pp. 58 ff.

50. 'OC Special Branch to All Provincial Special Branch Officers and all Special Branch Stations', 4 Dec. 1972, copy in the authors' possession. Special Branch certainly did not have the detailed understanding of D. Lan, *Guns and Rain: Guerrillas and Spirit Mediums in Zimbabwe* (Harare, 1985).

51. Interview (Godwin): Dr Louise Westwater, Deputy Secretary, Ministry of Health, 16 Mar. 1982. Westwater claimed that the same DC was later blamed for not reporting the danger signals.

52. Interview (Hancock): D. Yardley, 17 Feb. 1982.

53. Interview (Godwin): D. Bennison, Officer Commanding Special Branch, 1976-80, 4 Dec. 1982.

54. Interview (Godwin): 3 Dec. 1982. See also his contemporaneous comments reported in *Assegai* (the Army's magazine) in Dec. 1972 and in *Rhodesia Herald* (22 Dec. 1978).

55. One hundred farmers and residents of Centenary signed a petition calling for the closure of St Albert's: *Rhodesia Herald* (27 Jan. 1973), *Sunday Mail* (28 Jan, 1973).

56. The following summary and analysis of RF views is based upon the speeches during the first post-Altena security debate: *Parl. Debs.*, Ass. 83, 29-30 Mar. and 4-5 Apr. 1973.

57. Ibid. 85, col. 2215, 7 Dec. 1973.

58. *Rapport* (4 Feb. 1973).

59. *Parl. Debs.*, Ass. 83, col. 1118, 29 Mar. 1973 (Dr Colin Barlow).

60. Savory owned a game reserve in the area which, along with other properties, was included in the expropriation announcement of 14 Nov. 1971.

Savory denied that he left the RF over the issue, insisting the decision to acquire private land, and then to lease it to other individuals, was just the final straw. For a debate on this issue, and some thinly-veiled charges concerning Savory himself, see ibid. 81, 26 July, 2 and 9 Aug. 1972.

61. See especially ibid, 83, cols. 1187-206, 30 Mar. 1973; 85, cols. 142-64, 22 Aug. 1973.

62. Ibid., col. 1199, 30 Mar. 1973.

63. J. K. Cilliers, *Counter-Insurgency in Rhodesia* (London, 1985), p. 64.

64. *Outpost* (Sept, 1973).

65. Interview (Godwin): 1 Dec. 1982.

66. *Outpost* (Feb. 1973).

67. Cilliers, *Counter-Insurgency in Rhodesia*, p. 141.

68. There were occasions where the phrase had a literal as well as a metaphori cal significance. MacIntyre recalled the case of a captured spirit medium being paraded before kraals by the Security Forces. The gentleman howled in agony as a vigorous tugging movement demonstrated his very human qualities to the watching and listening tribespeople. (Interview (Hancock): MacIntyre, 24 Jan. 1978.)

69. For other measures, see Wilkinson, *Insurgency in Rhodesia*, p. 17.

70. *Rhodesia Herald* (9 Feb. 1974).

71. *Parl. Debs.*, Ass. 83, col. 1224; 84, col. 366.

72. *Rhodesia Herald* (20 Sept. 1974).

73. Ibid. (29 Nov. 1974).

74. *Parl. Debs.*, Ass. 83, cols. 1207 and 1212, 30 Mar. 1973. The speakers were Danie Brink and Dennis Fawcett Phillips.

75. For the government's account of the move – released to the press – see *Rhodesia Herald* (27 July 1974).

76. Ibid. (6 Sept. 1974); Cilliers, *Counter-Insurgency in Rhodesia*, p. 86.

77. *Parl. Debs.*, Ass. 88, cols, 981-8.

78. *Rhodesia Herald* (25 July 1974). It will be noted that the DC had also acknowledged that the government was not in full control of a pivotal TTL.

79. *Parl. Debs.*, Ass. 88, col. 986.

80. This phrase was the title chosen for a booklet published in May 1975 by the Catholic Institute for International Relations in London on behalf of the Catholic Commission for Justice and Peace in Rhodesia. *The Man in the Middle* depicted the experiences of villagers caught in the zone between the warring parties.

81. *Rhodesia Herald* (15 Aug. 1974).

82. *Parl. Debs.*, Ass. 88, col. 167, 30 Aug. 1973.

83. See, for example, the comments on conditions in Nyachuru village by Dr Pat Hill, who had been working in Chiweshe for two years: *Rhodesia Herald* (31 July 1974),

84. J. M. Williamson, 'Protected Villages: Chiweshe TTL (CONFIDENTIAL)', 21 Nov. 1974, copy in the authors' possession.

85. See, for example, A. G. Mann and C. T. McCabe, 'Proposals for consolidation in the Mtoko Tribal Trust Land (Restricted)', 25 May 1976: Du Toit Papers (in the owner's possession). McCabe was then a Senior Research

Officer with the Ministry of Agriculture and Mann was the Chief Geologist for Falcon Mines. Both were doing their national service with Internal Affairs, and were regarded in official circles as authorities on PVs.

86. The government and several leading business houses financed and promoted two pro-settlement black groups during 1973 – the African Settlement Convention and the National Settlement Forum – which attracted an assortment of opportunists and chancers. These attempts to create a credible alternative to the ANC might have seemed devious to the nationalists' supporters. Arguably, the actions were evidence more of a gullibility born of ignorance and blind faith. See I. Hancock, *white Liberals, Moderates and Radicals in Rhodesia 1953-1980* (London, 1984), pp. 165-7.

87. *Parl. Debs.*, Ass. 83, col. 1380.

88. Ibid. 84, cols. 637-54.

89. The party held a long post-mortem and blamed a number of factors but the National Secretary summed up the problem: 'Almost any candidate would have looked inadequate in terms of the political weight that the Prime Minister carries.' (Mark Doyle, 20 June 1973, NAZ, SA22/10/7.)

90. Hancock, *white Liberals*, ch. 9.

91. *Property and Finance* (Nov. 1972). See also *Sunday Mail* (27 Aug. 1972).

92. Interview (Hancock): Jim Sinclair, 23 Jan. 1981. Sinclair was an RP candidate for Norton in 1975 and a prominent farmer who eventually became President of the Commercial Farmers' Union (previously the RNFU).

93. Alexander's speeches and comments may be followed in the *Sinoia News*. See esp. 5/8 (Mar. 1973).

94. Interview (Hancock): D. Yardley, 17 Feb. 1982. This particular piece of gossip – which its narrators clearly considered to be important – was repeated to the authors some 10 and 15 years later by farmers from the north-east, by former senior officers in Internal Affairs, the police, the Army, and other branches of the civil service.

95. For accounts of the election see T. Kirk and C. Sherwell, 'The Rhodesian General Election of 1974', *Journal of Commonwealth and Comparative Politics*, 13 (1975), pp. 1-25; Hancock, *white Liberals*, pp. 185-9.

96. Mitchell suggested that the three of them should hold a preliminary ballot, and that the winner should stand alone against the RF. This proposal was rejected because the RP seemed more interested in destroying Savory.

97. *Rhodesia Herald* (25 May 1974), Another, unidentified estimate in the same issue put the figure at $2-3,000. The government introduced a grant scheme in July 1974 providing up to $4,000 for the defence of each farm and homestead. See J. A. McKenzie, 'Commercial Farmers in the Governmental System of Colonial Zimbabwe, 1963-1980' PhD thesis – (Harare, 1990), p. 212.

98. A. J. Venter, *The Zambezi Salient: Conflict in Southern Africa* (London, 1975), pp. 121-4.

99. For an editorial praising the Centenary spirit shown on this occasion see *Rhodesia Herald* (23 July 1973).

100. McKenxie, 'Commercial Farmers', pp. 200-1.

101. Interview (Hancock): 4 July 1989. An unhappy experience in Malta had originally made De Borchgrave suspicious of the police. He was especially angered by an incident where a Special Branch officer arrogantly walked onto Altena Farm and paid the labour a few dollars for assisting the authorities in the capture of one of Delville Vincent's killers. The objections were that the police had placed his labour at risk for a derisory sum and that De Borchgrave had not been consulted.

102. Sinoia News, 6/2 (Sept. 1973).

103. *Parl. Debs.*, Ass. 83, esp. cols. 1105-9, 29 Mar. 1973.

104. Ibid., col. 1106. Irvine was quoting a statement from the Ministry of Defence. See also the Minister's comment, ibid., cols. 1303-5, 4 Apr. 1973.

105. Lardner-Burke to Allan Savory, 2 May 1973, NAZ, SA/22/1/3.

106. *Parl. Debs.*, Ass. 83, col. 1306, 4 Apr. 1973 (Howman) and *Annual Reports of the Secretary of Defence etc.* (1972).

107. *Umtali Post* (9 Dec. 1970). In 1972 a Jehovah's Witness was fined $50 for failing to attend a military parade: ibid. (29 May 1972).

108. Ibid. (22 June, 18 Oct., and 28 Nov. 1973); *State v. du Chattlier,* Rhodesian Law Reports (1973), part 2, pp. 341-9.

109. It may have been acceptable where the alleged brutality was directed against whites. See the letter sent by Mrs V. Arnold of Bulawayo to Lt-General Walls in which she claimed that a white sergeant had kicked one of the white recruits and forced others to strip and 'make love' to their rifles in front of 400 young men: NAZ, SA/22/1/3, 22 Jan. 1974.

110. Niesewand's own account of this affair may be found in P. Niesewand, *In Camera: Secret Justice in Rhodesia* (London, 1973).

111. *Gwelo Times* (17 May 1973, 17 Jan. and 25 May 1974).

112. See, for example, the statements by Walls, ibid. (22 Oct. 1973), and by Smith in *Parl. Debs.*, Ass. 85, col. 2215, 7 Dec. 1973.

113. Flower, *Serving Secretly*, pp. 140-1, 262, 300-2. The authors understand that the account of CIO involvement recorded by B. Cole, *The Elite: The Story of the Rhodesian Special Air Service* (Amanzimtoti, 1984), pp. 243-6, is reasonably accurate. The Rhodesians handed over control of the Movement to the South Africans in 1980 when it became 'the monster' which caused so much havoc in Mozambique.

114. See R. Reid Daly, *Selous Scouts: Top Secret War* (Alberton, 1982), esp. chs. 2-3. Ken Flower, who was involved in the creation of the Scouts and who had been impressed by the success of 'pseudo gangs' in the war against Mau Mau in Kenya, was one of many critics in the Security Forces of the expanded role of the Scouts later in the war: see *Serving Secretly*, pp. 124-5. For material designed to boost respect and mystique – after the Scouts went 'public' – see, for example, the articles by Chris Reynolds, *Rhodesia Herald* (9, 11, 14 Mar. 1977).

115. Cilliers, *Counter-Insurgency in Rhodesia*, p. 22.

116. *Rhodesia Herald* (21 Sept. 1973).

4. This void in our national life'*

   * A. P. Smith, Minister of Education, announcing that the government had chosen Beethoven's 'Ode to Joy' as the music for Rhodesia's National Anthem: *Rhodesia Herald* (27 Aug. 1974).

1. For accounts of this episode, and of CIO's involvement, see D. Martin and P. Johnson, *The Chitepo Assassination* (Harare, 1985); P. Stiff, *See You in November* (Alberton, 1985), ch. 9; K. Flower, *Serving Secretly* (London, 1987), pp. 147-8. Flower was more forthcoming in interviews with Hancock when, like other former CIO officers, he acknowledged the general accuracy if not the embellishments of the 'Taffy' account in Stiff's book. 'Taffy' was a former British paratrooper who was employed by CIO on special missions.

2. The authors understand – from CIO sources, who may not be quoted – that Sithole and his secretary were killed soon after they were 'lifted' outside the Ambassador Hotel. The men allegedly responsible for the operation were part of the so-called 'Z' Branch of CIO which was commanded by Chief Superintendent M. J. P. McGuinness.

3. A popular and probably revealing Rhodesian joke of the time was that the train was named 'the Chatter-Nigger-Choo-Choo'.

4. The 'Big Push' may also have been designed to demonstrate to sceptical Rhodesians that the Security Forces were both committed to, and capable of, defeating 'terrorism'. See J. MacManus, in the *Guardian* (8 Aug. 1975). MacManus also claimed, presumably on his own observation, that the war still ran a poor second to the subject of sex as a topic of conversation in Salisbury in Aug. 1975.

5. This statement was made by Mike Edden, an Assistant Commissioner of the BSAP, who also claimed that Hurricane 'had been won'. Record of a Briefing, 3 Nov. 1976, copy in the authors' possession.

6. Flower, *Serving Secretly*, pp. 159-61.

7. Sithole was originally charged with planning to assassinate Muzorewa, Nkomo, and Dr Elliott Gabellah. A special court was assembled and heard, instead, charges against Sithole of heading ZANU's military wing. He was found guilty but was released on Smith's orders on 4 Apr. 1975 in response to South African pressure. The story is partly documented in *ARB*, P, S, and C, 12/3–4 (1975).

8. This point was made by a former Rhodesian Minister of Defence who thought that the SAP were otherwise 'useless': Interview (Godwin and Hancock): Reg Cowper, 9 May 1989.

9. An editorial in the *Sunday Mail* (3 Aug. 1975), urged Mr Vorster not to withdraw his forces but to 'send more'.

10. Muzorewa was notionally the leader of the ANC but, by late 1975, Muzorewa and Nkomo each claimed the leadership and Nkomo's ZAPU remained a separate party using the ANC title. Meanwhile, Sithole and Mugabe were contesting the leadership of ZANU outside Rhodesia. For greater enlightenment on what he called the 'African National Confusion' see M. Sithole, *Zimbabwe: Struggles within The Struggle* (Salisbury, 1979), pp. 110 ff.

11. *Parl. Debs.*, Ass. 87, cols. 62-6, 19 June 1974.
12. *Rhodesia Herald* (20 Sept. 1974).
13. SASCON was formed in 1974 and existed alongside the Rhodesian National Movement which, temporarily, fused the United Conservative Party and Idensohn's Rhodesia National Party. For SASCON's views and its public rallies see *Property and Finance* throughout 1975 and the *Sunday Mail* (20 May 1975), and the *Rhodesia Herald* (8 Aug. and 17 Dec. 1975). A tiny Nazi-style party, allegedly drawing from existing groups, was launched in Bulawayo in early 1976 to 'spearhead white resistance to ... terrorism and to combat the spread of degenerate, morale-sapping liberalism in Rhodesia': *Chronicle* (31 Jan. 1976).
14. Rhodesian Party files, 'Report of a SASCON Meeting', 10 Oct. 1975. These files were consulted in Harare but are now located at the University of Cape Town.
15. *Rhodesia Herald* (11 Dec. 1975).
16. *Group News* (Oct. 1975). This paper was published by the Rhodesian Christian Group whose principal spokesman was Father Arthur Lewis.
17. The following paragraphs relating to the sub-committee draw mainly upon the following: Caucus Sub-Committee on Planning and Co-ordination of Policy, 'The Constitutional Future of Rhodesia' (Feb. 1976), Barlow Papers; Interview (Godwin and Hancock): Barlow, 23 May 1989.
18. There were just 50 RF members of the Assembly. The 51st vote may have come from Colonel George Hartley, the Speaker, or been shared by the Chairman and Deputy Chairman of the RF, none of whom were elected MPs.
19. Chris Andersen, a gifted young advocate of Afrikaner stock, first entered parliament in 1974. Smith claimed that he had deliberately brought Andersen into politics in his search for talent. (Interview (Hancock): Smith, 26 June 1980.) Andersen eventually became a senior minister under Smith, broke with his leader at Lancaster House in 1979, and was one of the first white leading politicians to identify with the Mugabe government.
20. This account of the congress is based on interviews Hancock had with Sutton-Pryce, 8 Mar. 1980; Simmonds, 12 Mar. 1980; Smith, 26 June 1980; André Holland, 13 Jan. 1981; and Barlow, 26 Apr. and (including Godwin) 23 May 1989. The debate was secretly recorded in *Report on the Proceedings of the National Congress* (1975), copy in the authors' possession. See also *Rhodesia Herald* (19, 25-6 Sept. 1975); *Sunday Mail* (28 Sept. 1975).
21. Resolutions at RF congresses could either be carried, rejected, withdrawn, or left to lie on the table.
22. *Property and Finance* (Oct. 1975).
23. Interview (Hancock): Ken Flower, 9 July 1987.
24. *Rhodesia Herald* (17,31 Oct., and 1 Nov. 1975).
25. Interview (Hancock): Smith, 26 June 1980.
26. *Sunday Mail* (2 Nov. 1975).
27. The following two paragraphs draw upon I. Hancock, *white Liberals, Moderates and Radicals in Rhodesia* (London, 1984), pp. 195-9.

28. The five Front Line States were Angola, Botswana, Mozambique, Tanzania, and Zambia. Angola and Tanzania did not share any borders with Rhodesia.

29. J. Strong and S. Firks, 'Trip to Zambia, 1-7 April 1975', copy in the authors' possession.

30. The Commission was chaired by Sir Vincent Quenet, who had retired in 1970 as the Judge President of the Appellate Division of the High Court. The other ten members were three white businessmen, a former (RF-supporting) President of the RNFU, a white female former sports star, two African Chiefs (who, in 1976, were added to Smith's ministry), an African Purchase Area farmer, and two black women involved in welfare work.

31. *Rhodesia Herald* (9 July 1975).

32. Rhodesia, *Report of the Commission of Inquiry into Racial Discrimination* (Apr. 1976), Cmd. R.R.6-1976. Unless stated otherwise, the material for the following paragraphs is drawn from the *Report*. The Commission eventually received 252 written submissions and took oral evidence from 207 individuals. The evidence presented to the Commission was extensively reported in the local press.

33. *Rhodesia Herald* (6 Dec. 1975).

34. See, for example, the statement by the Chairman of the Public Services Board, ibid. (19 Nov. 1975).

35. R. C. Riddell and P. S. Harris, *The Poverty Datum Line as a Wage Fixing Standard: An Application to Rhodesia* (Gwelo, 1975); D. G. Clarke, *Agricultural and Plantation Workers in Rhodesia* (Gwelo, 1977), pp. 35-8; R. Riddell, *Alternatives to Poverty: From Rhodesia to Zimbabwe,* i (n.d.), pp. 12-3.

36. *Illustrated Life Rhodesia* (23 June 1975).

37. Ibid. (27 Nov. 1975 and 22 Jan. 1976).

38. *Rhodesia Herald* (27 Nov. 1975).

39. For the above paragraph see *Rhodesia Railways Review* (Oct. 1975 and Feb. 1976); *Locomotive Express,* 37 (1975) and 41 (1976). For a less strident view see the testimony to the Quenet Commission of Howard Bloomfield, President of the Associated Mineworkers of Rhodesia: *Rhodesia Herald* (4 Dec. 1975).

40. The Act received the Assent in Oct. 1975. For the main parliamentary debate see *Parl. Debs., Ass.* 91, cols. 1433-506, 28 Aug. 1975. See also I. Linden, *The Catholic Church and the Struggle for Zimbabwe* (London, 1980), pp. 210-11.

41. Ibid., pp. 181-205, provides a useful coverage of the Commission's activities.

42. P. Burrough, *Angels Unawares* (Worthing, 1988), pp. 48 ff.

43. See the article by Canon Fenwick in *Link* (Nov. 1975).

44. Rhodesia, BSAP, *Annual Reports of the Commissioner of Police* (1973-5). The reports also noted an increasing number of contraventions of the Exchange Control Act and of major fraud cases. *The Annual Report* for 1974 recorded an increase in the use of drugs – notably LSD – among young whites.

45. Helped by a white warder, McIntosh escaped from Salisbury's maximum security prison in Feb. 1975 only to be returned to Rhodesia by the

Portuguese authorities in Mozambique, who were tricked into the hand-over by the Rhodesian police.

46. *Rhodesia Herald* (29 Apr. 1975).
47. Ibid. (8 May 1975).
48. *Umtali Post* (30 June 1975).
49. Interview (Hancock): David Young, 2 Feb. 1982.
50. Rhodesia, *Annual Reports of the Secretary of Roads and Road Traffic* (1973-5).
51. *Parl. Debs.*, Ass. 90, cols. 806-30, 10 July 1975 (John Wrathall).
52. *Umtali Post* (30 June 1975), reporting the survey by the President of the Umtali Chamber of Commerce.
53. *Rhodesian Financial Gazette* (4 Jan. 1974).
54. *Umtali Post* (10 Apr. 1974).
55. Manicaland Development and Publicity Association, 'Report of the Proceedings of the Twenty-Ninth Annual General Meeting', 17 Sept. 1975. In the same year it was reported that South African hoteliers on the Natal coast were experiencing a boom because of the influx of Rhodesian holiday-makers: *Rhodesia Herald* (11 July 1975).
56. For the criticisms of the Bill see *Parl. Debs.*, Ass. 90, 16-17 July 1975.
57. *Rhodesian Tobacco Journal*, 27/7 and 10 (1975).
58. *Parl. Debs.*, Ass. 90, col. 1400, 25 July 1975 (Rodney Simmonds).
59. *Rhodesian Tobacco Journal*, 27/12 (1975).
60. Except where otherwise stated, the next three paragraphs are drawn from RNFU, *Report of the Annual Congress* (July 1975).
61. *Parl. Debs.*, Ass. 90, col. 1446 (David Smith).
62. Ibid., cols. 1415-16 (John Gleig).
63. Rhodesia, CSO, *European Expenditure Survey, 1975/6* (Apr. 1978).
64. Rhodesia, CSO, *Monthly Digest of Statistics* (1970-5).
65. Record of Transfers (Pvt.) Ltd. (1975).
66. S. D'Arcy, a former resident who left Rhodesia in 1970 and had returned for a visit in 1975, claimed that it was 'still possible to live on a medium income in a style for which you would need to be in the millionaire class in Britain', *Guardian* (29 Mar. 1975). Comparisons are difficult to establish but a British millionaire would certainly have pocketed a lot of change after buying the lifestyle in Britain which the medium white income could afford in Rhodesia.
67. *Record* (Mar. 1975).
68. *Parl. Debs.*, Ass. 92, cols. 327-37, 17 Feb. 1976 (Reg Cowper, Minister of the Public Service).
69. For local discussion of the mercenary issue see *Sunday Mail* (12 Jan. 1975); *Rhodesia Herald* (15 Jan. 1975); and *Chronicle* (28 June 1975). The Aug. 1975 issue of the Army magazine *Assegai* listed a series of objections to the use of foreign soldiers, alleging that they lacked discipline and a sense of loyalty.
70. *Rhodesia Herald* (8 July 1975).
71. Ibid. (8 Feb. 1974).
72. For criticisms of the call-up in late 1975 see ibid. (25 Oct. and 27 Nov. 1975); *Chronicle* (23 Oct. 1975); *Umtali Post* (24 Nov. 1975).
73. *Rhodesian Financial Gazette* (4 Jan. 1974).

74. *Rhodesia Herald* (1 Feb. 1974).
75. *Lomagundi News* (15 Feb. 1974).
76. *Chronicle* (7 July 1975).
77. *BSAP Annual Reports* (1972-6).
78. Rhodesia, CSO, Monthly *Migration and Tourism Statistics* (1972-5).
79. *Rhodesia Herald* (1 Jan. 1974).
80. Ibid. (21 Jan. 1974).
81. *Parl. Debs.*, Ass. 90, col. 1070,18 July 1975.
82. Ibid., col. 1124, 22 July 1975.
83. Rhodesia, Ministry of Foreign Affairs, Information Section, *Fact Paper,* 1/75 (2 Apr. 1975).
84. One such visitor was Eric Butler, a member of the extremist anti-communist and anti-Semitic Australian League of Rights, who was welcomed in Rhodesia as representative of Australian opinion.
85. For the parliamentary debate see *Parl. Debs.*, Ass. 90, cols. 1587-639.
86. *Rhodesia Herald* (12 July 1975) (John Bowles).
87. National Federation of Women's Institutes, The *W.I. Jubilee Book, 1925-1975* (Salisbury, 1975).
88. *Chronicle* (29 Sept. 1975).
89. *Gwelo Times* (2 Oct. 1975).
90. C. D. Williams (ed.), *Careers Guide for Young Rhodesians* (Salisbury, 1976).
91. Board of Censors of Rhodesia, *Catalogue of Banned Books Periodicals Records etc,* (1978). The same body produced a different title in 1978 from the volume issued in 1972.
92. *Sunday Mail* (25 Nov. 1973). Wright was later described as 'a charming gentleman, of very high principle': *Chronicle* (22 June 1977).
93. Ibid. (16 Jan. 1975).
94. Some of the dissatisfaction emerged during a parliamentary debate. See *Parl. Debs.*, Ass. 85, cols. 2045-50, 4 Dec. 1973. One MP, who admitted that he had not seen the film, and said he would not do so, declared that the decision was not 'a blow' to Christianity but to Rhodesia.
95. *Gwelo Times* (31 Jan. 1975).
96. Ibid. (6 June 1975).
97 The individuals were, respectively, Ian Robertson, Gerald Peckover, Simon Hobday, Gay Erskine, and Colin Dowdswell. Two other Rhodesian golfers – George Harvey and Denis Watson – won the World Pairs championship in Bogota, Colombia: *Illustrated Life Rhodesia* (27 Nov. 1975).
98. Rhodesia Cricket Umpires' Association, *News Sheet,* 11 (1975). See also 6 (1973).
99. R. Cary, *The Story of Reps* (Salisbury, 1975), p. 201.
100. *Umtali Post* (17 Jan. 1975); *Illustrated Life Rhodesia* (20 Feb. 1975).
101. RTV, 'Diary Panel Survey' (Apr.-May 1975).
102. The quotations in this paragraph are taken from the *Rhodesia Herald* (27-8 Aug. 1974).
103. *Umtali Post* (27 Aug. 1974).
104. See especially *African Times* (12 Mar., 2 Apr., 25 June, 16 July 1975, and 11 Feb. 1976).

105. The figures in this sentence were obtained from unpublished official records.
106. *Rhodesia Herald* (19 Dec. 1975) (quoting from Walls's Christmas message published in the Dec. issue of *Assegai*). A similar view was put by P. K. van der Byl: *Rhodesia Herald* (1 Jan. 1976).
107. The bad news is drawn from reports in the *Chronicle, Rhodesian Financial Gazette, Rhodesia Herald,* and the *Sunday Mail* from late Dec. to early Jan. 1975-6. The other three Army men killed in the crash were Colonel David Parker, the Commanding Officer of 2 Brigade of the RLI, Captain John Lamb, and Captain Ian Robertson. An Air Force NCO, Sergeant Pieter van Rensberg, was also killed. The pilot survived the crash which occurred in broad daylight north of Cashel and near the Mozambique border where the helicopter hit an unmarked transmission line. Shaw was a controversial figure within Army circles, disliked – by some – for his drinking and his manners; the loss of Parker and Lamb, on the other hand, was generally regarded as a grievous blow.

5. 'It is perhaps, the end of the beginning'*

   * Ian Smith, quoting Winston Churchill, on the night he announced his government's surrender to the principle of majority rule: *Rhodesia Herald* (25 Sept. 1976).

1. The foreign-based companies refused to allow their names to be associated with inferior packaging: hence the new names.
2. For the coverage of the garbage and cigarette debates see *Rhodesia Herald* (5 Jan.-19 Feb. 1976); Salisbury City Council, 'Minutes of a Meeting of the Health and Environmental Services Committee', 3 Feb. 1976; 'Minutes of a Council Meeting', 19 Feb. 1976.
3. *Rhodesia Herald* (7 Feb. 1976). For the full official text of Smith's speech see Rhodesia, *For the Record* (Feb. 1976).
4. *Rhodesia Herald* (20 Mar. 1976). See also J. Nkomo, *Nkomo: The Story of My Life* (London, 1984), pp. 156-8 and app. B.
5. James MacManus, in the *Guardian* (29 Feb. and 1 Mar. 1976).
6. 'Holiday and Travel Supplement', *Rhodesia Herald* (16 June 1976).
7. Record of an Army Briefing, 12 Nov. 1976, copy in the authors' possession.
8. *Rhodesia Herald* (22 Jan. 1976).
9. For the ANC version and Smith's response see ibid. (20 Mar. 1976). For the negotiations and the positions adopted by each side see Nicholas Ashford in *The Times* (London) (22 Mar. 1976) and M. Meredith, *The Past is Another Country* (London, 1980), ch. 10.
10. *Rhodesia Herald* (20 Mar. 1976) and *Sunday Mail* (21 Mar. 1976). For an example of the conventional interpretation of Smith's speech see P. L. Moorcraft, *A Short Thousand Years: The End of Rhodesia's Rebellion* (Salisbury, 1980), p. 1: 'The Rhodesian leader prophesied that white rule would last for a thousand years.'
11. *Rhodesia Herald* (23-4 Mar. 1976).
12. Ibid. (23 Mar. 1976).

13. Rhodesia, *For the Record*, 34 (5 Mar. 1976).
14. Interview (Godwin and Hancock): Walls, 31 May 1989.
15. Interviews (Hancock): Smith, 4 Feb. 1981; Flower, 3 July 1985,
16. *Rhodesia Herald* (14 Mar. 1976).
17. Ibid. (27 Mar. 1976).
18. This quotation and the quotations in the following three paragraphs are drawn from Rhodesia, *For the Record*, 35 (27 Apr. 1976).
19. Rhodesia, Ministry of Information, Press Statement, 5 May 1976.
20. Record of an Army Briefing, 7 Aug. 1976, copy in the authors' possession.
21. A few, like A. A. Black of Umtali, were prepared to ask the obvious question: 'With our admitted military superiority, why can we not bring the war to a swift and successful end?': *Umtali Post* (9 July 1976). Black was replying to earlier and similar boasts by MacIntyre delivered at a Lions Club dinner in Umtali on 3 July.
22. The admission books of St Giles Rehabilitation Centre in Salisbury show that half the admissions in 1976 involved bullet wounds, parachute accidents, and landmine incidents. In 1972-3 there were 20-40 patients receiving physiotherapy a month; the figure was 190 a month during 1979. The rise in admissions began in 1976.
23. For a triumphant account of the raid see R. Reid Daly, *Selous Scouts* (Alberton, 1982), pp. 178-222. The official Rhodesian announcement and some of the critical reactions to the raid may be found in *Rhodesia Herald* (11-12 Aug. 1976) and *ARB*, P, S, and C, 13/9 (1976), 4132A-3C, 4134C-5C. See also Meredith, *The Past is Another Country*, pp. 239-41.
24. Later accounts adopted 'the *appropriate* legal arguments' to describe the raid as a 'reprisal' rather than 'hot pursuit' in order '*to justify Government policy convincingly*' (emphasis in the original). Typically, every effort was made to demonstrate that Rhodesia had conformed to the civilised, international codes which legitimised aggression. See Rhodesia, Ministry of Foreign Affairs, Information Section, 'Background Briefing: Extra-Territorial Military Action', 15 Sept. 1976, copy in the authors' possession.
25. Accounts of the Umtali affair and of Rhodesian reactions may be found in the *Rhodesia Herald* and the *Umtali Post* (10-13 Aug. 1976) and the *Gwelo Times* (12 Aug. 1976). See also Meredith, *The Past is Another Country*, pp. 238-41, and J. MacBruce, *When the Going was Rough: A Rhodesian Story* (Pretoria, 1983), chs. 1-2. 'James MacBruce' was the composite name chosen by the 4 authors of this account of the Eastern Districts during the war. A *shumba* is a lion and, given that 'Lion' was a popular brand of beer among whites, the unwary might just have misinterpreted the war cry as a demand for beer. On the other hand, even the unwary in Umtali would have understood that 'true' Rhodesians never drank alone, and would be ordering 'a couple of Shumbas'.
26. The most serious incidents occurred in Oct.-Nov. 1979 when three bombs exploded in or near city shops. Two women were killed in one explosion.
27. 'Holiday and Travel Supplement', *Rhodesia Herald* (16 June 1976).
28. Ibid. (21 July 1976).
29. This arrangement did not help those young men who, because of their

current commitment, could not prepare for or sit university entrance exams in time for the 1977 academic year: *Parl. Debs.*, Ass. 93, col. 166, 24 June 1976 (J. Landau).

30. Rhodesia, Ministry of Information, Text of a Broadcast by the Army Commander', 4 May 1976.

31. For the story of the call-up in 1976 see *Parl. Debs.*, Ass. 93, cols. 1169-77, 21 July 1976 (Reg Cowper).

32. For examples of editorials in the *Rhodesia Herald* summarising complaints and recording community dissatisfaction see 8 Apr., 12 May, 2, 5, and 7 July 1976.

33. *Sunday Mail* (23 May 1976).

34. *Parl. Debs.*, Ass. 93, col. 271, 29 June 1976.

35. *Chronicle* (3 Aug. 1976).

36. *Parl. Debs.*, Ass. 93, 23-5 June, 29-30 June, 1 July 1976.

37. For a criticism of the system of moving farmers out of one area – to be replaced by farmers moved from another – see the comments by a leading RNFU figure from the Eastern Districts: *Umtali Post* (18 June 1976).

38. *New York Herald Tribune* (15 May 1976); *Rhodesia Herald* (19 and 23 June 1976).

39. *Parl. Debs.*, Ass. 93, cols. 139-40, 24 June 1976.

40. For the Carr case and the Authority's attitude see *Rhodesia Herald* (1, 2, and 9 Aug. 1976). If white university students were more advantaged than black apprentices they, in turn, could feel that black students – being excluded from the call-up – were getting preferential treatment. The 1976 intake at the University of Rhodesia was the first where blacks outnumbered whites, and the university itself explained that the requirement to complete national service before entering university was one reason for the change: *Sunday Mail* (9 May 1976).

41. *Parl Debs.*, Ass. 93, col. 327, 29 June 1976 (Dr Hamilton Ritchie).

42. Ibid., col. 1659, 29 July 1976.

43. *Rhodesia Herald* (19 Apr. 1976); Umtali Post (21 Apr. 1976).

44. *Daily Telegraph* (London) (24 Apr. 1976).

45. *Umtali Post* (30 Apr. 1976); *Sunday Mail* (2 May 1976).

46. All the statistics quoted here on emigration are drawn from Rhodesia, CSO, *Monthly Digest of Statistics* (Feb. 1977).

47. *Parl. Debs.*, Ass. 94, cols. 228-9, 5 Aug. 1976 (E. Broomberg). The Department, which sent a letter to prospective emigrants asking why they planned to leave, did admit that few were likely to confess their concerns about the call-up or about the war.

48. See, for example, Colin Barlow, ibid., col. 208.

49. Interview (Hancock): D. Smith, 9 Feb. 1982.

50. An article in the *Rhodesian Financial Gazette* (14 May 1976) pointed out that the effects of the extended call-up and increased defence expenditure were not all unfavourable: hotels in the operational areas could expect more business from the troops and the economy's infrastructure and individual companies would benefit from the greater spending on communications.

51. The budget speech may be found in *Parl. Debs.*, Ass. 93, cols. 1007-32, 15 July 1976. In mid-1976 the Rhodesian dollar bought £1.00 stg.
52. Ibid., cols. 1049-55, Divaris described the Finance Bill as the 'Emigration Promotion Budget'.
53. For the reactions in the white communities see *Rhodesia Herald* (17, 19-22, 31 July 1976).
54. Fares for trips beyond Rhodesia could be paid in Rhodesia, and were not deducted from the holiday allowance.
55. 'Holiday and Travel Supplement', *Rhodesia Herald* (16 June 1976).
56. See n. 53 above.
57. In late June the Speaker of the Legislative Assembly ruled that the words 'freedom fighter' and 'guerrilla' were 'seditious and treasonable' and there fore unparliamentary: *Parl. Debs.*, Ass. 93, cols. 181 and 241, 24 and 25 June 1976.
58. Ibid., col. 17, 23 June 1976 (Es. Micklem).
59. Ibid., col. 1558, 28 July 1976 (R. H. W. McGee).
60. By 17 Aug. 106 curfew-breakers and 306 other blacks, 'running with terrorists', had been killed since 1972: ibid. 94, cols. 859-60, 18 Aug. 1976. In releasing these figures, P K. van der Byl remarked: 'I believe from initial reports that there may be a few more in the pipeline today.'
61. See the report prepared for the Catholic Commission for Justice and Peace in Rhodesia, *Civil War in Rhodesia: Abduction, Torture and Death in the Counter-Insurgency Campaign* (London, 1976), part iv; *Parl. Debs.*, Ass. 94, col. 899, 18 Aug. 1976. Partridge was replying to a debate initiated by the RF right wing on the 'nefarious practices' and 'irresponsible land use' of 'certain missions'.
62. D. Lamont, *Speech from the Dock* (Leigh-on-Sea, 1977); I. Linden, *The Catholic Church and the Struggle for Zimbabwe* (London, 1980), pp. 225-9; Meredith, *The Past is Another Country*, pp. 231-7. Lamont was eventually deported in Mar. 1977.
63. For Ian Smith's statement justifying the special courts see *Rhodesia Herald* (1 May 1976). A list of the cases heard in the special courts between 26 May and 30 July may be found in Catholic Commission for Justice and Peace, *Civil War in Rhodesia*, pp. 89-92. The number of death sentences imposed by these courts reached 29 by early 1977. *Rhodesia Herald* (5 Jan. 1977).
64. *Parl. Debs.*, Ass. 94, col. 759, 13 Aug. 1976.
65. G. Fairbairn, 'Diary', 12 May 1976, copy in the authors' possession.
66. *Sunday Mail* (9 May 1976).
67. Interview (Hancock): Flower, 9 July 1987. Flower was certainly in a position to know because of his role as Hickman's mentor and long-standing family friend.
68. *Rhodesia Herald* (15 May 1976), *Hout* is an Afrikaans word meaning 'wood' which, in the sense of wooden-headed, was used in southern Africa as another derogative synonym for Africans.
69. *Guardian* (2 June 1976).
70. *Rhodesia Herald* (30 July 1976), quoted in Catholic Commission for Justice and Peace, *Civil War in Rhodesia*, p. 16.

71. For the CP, the RP, and the NPA in mid-1976 see I. Hancock, *white Liberals, Moderates and Radicals in Rhodesia* (London, 1984), pp. 199-200.
72. *Rhodesia Herald* (20 May 1976).
73. Ibid. (2 June 1976).
74. For a summary of the recommendations of the Report, and of reactions to it, see ibid. (15 June 1976) and in *ARB*, P, S, and C, 13/6 (1976), 4067A-8C.
75. *Rhodesia Herald* (23 July 1976). The Zimbabwe government came up with an ingenious solution: it decided that a 'gardener' should be called a 'gardener'.
76. Rhodesia, Ministry of Information, 'Text of a broadcast by the Army Commander', 4 May 1976.
77. These words were used by Bill Irvine, the Minister of Local Government, when he opened a brewery at Victoria Falls on the Day of Prayer: *Rhodesia Herald* (20 May 1976).
78. 'Army in Profile', *Rhodesian Financial Gazette* (7 May 1976). For similar views about the police see *Rhodesia Herald* (29 July 1976) and *Rhodesian Financial Gazette* (30 July 1976).
79. G. Fairbairn, in the *Bulletin* (Australia) (7 Aug. 1976). The word *nong* was not commonly used in Rhodesia; its use here suggests that Fairbairn was quoting a former Australian Army officer who was serving in Thrasher.
80. Fairbairn, 'Diary', 14 May 1976.
81. See, for example, *Time* (12 Apr. and 2 Aug. 1976) and Patrick Keatley in the *Guardian* (20 Apr. 1976).
82. Interview (Hancock): Ian Smith, 26 June 1980.
83. *Rhodesia Herald* (30 June 1976).
84. *Sunday Mail* (2 Aug. 1976).
85. *Rhodesia Herald* (15 Aug. 1976).
86. For Ken Flower's account of Rhodesian-South African relations, and of the Kissinger mission, see *Serving Secretly* (London, 1987), ch. 9. The account here draws heavily upon this book and upon Hancock's interviews with Flower on 3 July 1985 and 9 July 1987.
87. *Sunday Mail* (6 June 1976).
88. See ibid., where Frost hedged on the subject of Smith being in step with the party's thinking and said that he would 'definitely' place his loyalty to the party and the country above his loyalty to the Prime Minister. Smith gave an interview to the same edition where he said that the right wing constituted 'a very small minority', and that he wanted a 'meritocracy' for Rhodesia.
89. *Rhodesia Herald* (6 Aug. 1976).
90. A summary of the resolutions and of the congress debates may be found in *Rhodesia Herald* (9, 16-17 Sept. 1976). This account is also based upon interviews Hancock had with Sutton-Pryce, 8 Mar. 1980; André Holland, 13 Jan. 1981; and Frost, 17 May 1989. Holland was the press liaison officer for the RF at the congress.
91. 'Presentation of the Pretoria Agreement (Confidential)' (n.d.), Barlow Papers.
92. *Rhodesia Herald* (22, 23, and 24 Sept. 1976).

93. Ibid. (25 Sept. 1976). The full official text may be found in Rhodesia, *For the Record*, 38 (24 Sept. 1976).

94. Material for the following paragraphs on white reactions has been drawn from *Chronicle* (25 Sept. and 1 Oct. 1976); *Property and Finance* (Oct. 1976); *Rhodesia Herald* (25 and 27 Sept., 1 and 12 Oct. 1976); *Rhodesian Financial Gazette* (24 Sept. and 1 Oct. 1976); *Sunday Mail* (26 Sept. 1976).

95. 'Business Herald', *Rhodesia Herald* (29 July 1976).

6. 'Everything to fight for'*

* Reg Cowper, Minister of Defence: *Rhodesia Herald* (1 Oct. 1976).

1. Ibid. (28 Sept. 1976).

2. According to Smith, Van der Byl was shifted to give full attention to his valuable European contacts. (Interview (Hancock): Smith, 4 Feb. 1981.)

3. *Rhodesia Herald* (1 Oct. 1976). See also his comment made during a tour of units: 'We are on top of the military situation and we must negotiate from a position of strength': *Chronicle* (11 Oct. 1976).

4. The proceedings of the Geneva Conference may be followed in *ARB*, P, S, arid C, 13/10-12 (1976), 4197B-203C, 4234A-9C, 4263C-5C.

5. See the statements by Mr Vorster, ibid. 14/1-2 (1977), 4299C-300B, 4335A-B.

6. By Apr. 1977 the South Africans were reportedly supplying Mirage jets and recoilless rifles to counter Eastern bloc assistance. See James MacManus in the *Guardian* (28 Apr. 1977).

7. For a comparison of the Kissinger and Richard plans, and for a report and analysis of Smith's reaction, see *ARB*, P, S, and C, 14/1 (1977), 4297A-8C; *Rhodesia Herald* (25 Jan. 1977). The estimated European population in June 1977 was 268,000: Rhodesia, CSO, *Supplement to the Monthly Digest of Statistics* (July 1978), table 1.

8. *Daily Telegraph* (28 Oct. 1976), *Observer* (London) (31 Oct. 1976).

9. Record of an Army Briefing, 8 Dec, 1976, copy in the authors' possession.

10. Quoted in I. Hancock, *white Liberals, Moderates and Radicals in Rhodesia* (London, 1984), p. 140.

11. The papers of Fred du Toit, formerly of Conex, contain several valuable documents on PVs. The most notable include: A. G. Mann and C. T. McCabe, 'Proposals for consolidation in the Mtoko Tribal Trust Land (Restricted)'; CAT, 'Report of the Siting of 12 Consolidated/Protected Villages in the Kandeya Tribal Trust Land (Secret)', June 1976; F. du Toit, 'Development of Consolidated Villages in Tribal Trust Lands', 11 Oct. 1976; D. Arkwrigrit (Internal Affairs, Department of Physical Planning), 'Protected Villages in the Operation Repulse Area (Secret)', 8 Dec. 1976; L. J. de Bruijn, 'Administration and Community/Social Institutions Organisation (Secret)', 9 Dec. 1976; C. T. McCabe, 'Report to the Chairman, Protected Village Development Committee, Internal Affairs (Secret)', n.d.; Internal Affairs, 'Minutes of a Seminar (Secret)', 24 Jan. 1977; 'Draft Report of the Protected Villages, Agriculture and Planning Group (Secret)', 25 Jan. 1977.

12. 'Draft Report', 25 Jan. 1977. See *Rhodesia Herald* (1 Oct. 1976) for the letter from 16 heads of the major Churches urging the government to remove the people from the PVs on humanitarian grounds.

13. Examples of this propaganda may be found in *Rhodesian Financial Gazette* (10 Dec. 1976); *Sunday Mail* (12 Dec. 1976 and 19 June 1977); Rhodesia, Ministry of Information, Press Statement, 7 Apr. 1977; *Fighting Forces of Rhodesia* (4 July 1977).

14. Flower, quoting a War Council memorandum of 15 Dec., in *Serving Secretly* (London, 1987), pp. 175-6.

15. *Rhodesia Herald* (8 Dec. 1976); Rhodesia, Ministry of Information, Press Statement and *Rhodesia Herald* (17 Dec. 1976).

16. Ibid. (27 Oct. 1976).

17. Bulawayo Chambers of Commerce and Industry, 'Transition (Strictly Confidential)' (end of 1976), NAZ, MSS SA 22/5/1/4. The great concern was that the 'average' Europeans would not, therefore, see any need to co-operate with Africans in creating a new system and, once independence was achieved, would leave Zimbabwe and take with them any chance of maintaining private enterprise.

18. Fairbairn, 'Diary', 14 Dec. 1976.

19. *Chronicle* (21 Dec. 1976). According to this report, 400 of the foreigners were American and the rest were drawn mainly from Britain, Western Europe, Australia, and South America. The *Chronicle* insisted that these men 'are no more mercenaries than the Americans who fought in World War II. They just happen to share our belief in a particular cause.' For a later report see *Sunday Mail* (29 May 1977) and for the disastrous experiment with some 200 former French *legionnaires* see H. Ellert, *The Rhodesian Front War* (Gweru, 1989), pp. 130-2.

20. For Cowper's own account of his views and policies see his personal explanation in parliament: *Parl. Debs.*, Ass. 95, cols. 1399-402, 2 Mar. 1977.

21. This decision especially angered Intake 146. They were already 'victims' of the May decision to extend the period of service to 18 months and were now required to serve a further 3: *Sunday Mail* (12 Dec. 1976).

22. Such students were, however, given an option: either they could complete one year of their basic training, be given a deferment, and serve during vacations, or they could complete two years of training and be free of all service obligations during their period of study.

23. For the full text and Cowper's comments on RBC/TV see Rhodesia, Ministry of Information, Press Statement, 27 Jan. 1977, and *Rhodesia Herald* (28 Jan. 1977).

24. Interview (Godwin and Hancock): 9 May 1989. Cowper claimed that, when Smith told him on the Monday after the announcement that the farmers and business leaders did not like the new scheme, he told the Prime Minister that it was not his job to please them.

25. *Rhodesian Financial Gazette* (4 Feb. 1977).

26. *International Herald Tribune* (28 Jan. 1977).

27. *Rhodesia Herald* (29 Jan. 1977) and *Rhodesian Financial Gazette* (4 Feb. 1977).

28. *Parl. Debs.*, Ass. 95, cols. 876-8, 15 Feb. 1977.

29. Ibid., cols. 1399-402, 2 Mar. 1977.
30. *Rhodesia Herald* (26 Feb. 1977),
31. Phillippa Berlyn – poet, dramatist, author, and journalist – who wrote several propaganda pieces for the Security Forces and who was intimately involved in several 'psychological' operations in the TTLs, claimed that there were 11 such services by 1979. (Interview (Hancock): 20 May 1980.)
32. *Sunday Mail* (26 May 1974).
33. Private information supplied by Geoffrey Fairbairn following his visit to Rhodesia in May-June 1976. Reid Daly claimed that the Supremo idea originated among those who had served in Malaya. (Interview (Godwin): Reid Daly, 1 Dec. 1982.)
34. Mark Partridge, who became Minister of Defence following Cowper's resignation, remained in that portfolio until Sept. when Hawkins added Defence to Combined Operations. The two civilian posts were not, it seems, regarded as of sufficient importance to lift the cabinet ranking of their Minister. Hawkins was listed seventh in seniority after the Sept. reshuffle.
35. In the vain hope of avoiding confusion, 'COMOPS' will refer to the Organisation commanded by Walls and 'Combined Operations' will refer to the
    ministry headed by Hawkins.
36. *Sunday Mail* (27 Mar. 1977),
37. Rhodesia, Ministry of Information, Press Statement, 17 May 1977. Hawkins's address to the Chichester Club in Salisbury covered eight pages of highly-detailed text which would have 'lost' the most attentive of audiences. The ten ministries were Combined Operations, Manpower, Justice and Law and Order, Internal Affairs, Defence, Roads, Agriculture, Water Development, Works, and Health. The statutory bodies were Posts and Telecommunications, Electricity, and the Railways.
38. For two critiques of COMOPS see J. K. Cilliers, *Counter-Insurgency in Rhodesia* (London, 1985), pp. 68-70, and R. Reid Daly, *Selous Scouts* (Alberton, 1982), pp. 260-4, 273-4.
39. Interview (Godwin): Lt.-Col. John Redfern, 6 Dec. 1982. Redfern had been Director of Military Intelligence.
40. Interviews (Godwin): Walls, 3 Dec. 1982; (Godwin and Hancock): Walls, 31 May 1989; (Hancock): Smith, 11 July 1989. Ken Flower basically confirmed the Walls version. (Interview (Hancock): 9 July 1987.)
41. For two early public pronouncements see *Rhodesia Herald* (4 Apr. 1977) (Walls) and *Sunday Mail* (15 May 1977) (Hickman),
42. Hickman's Cranborne speech was reported in the *Rhodesia Herald* (25 June 1977). The assumption was made more explicit at another passing-out parade later in the year at the RAR's Barracks at Balla Balla: ibid. (21 Oct 1977).
43. Record of an Army Briefing, 8 Dec. 1976; Flower, *Serving Secretly*, pp. 175-6.
44. Interview (Hancock): Van der Byl, 17 May 1980.
45. *Rhodesia Herald* (27 June 1977).
46. Rhodesia, Ministry of Information, Press Statement, 22 June 1977.
47. *Rhodesia Herald* (3 July 1977).

48. Interview (Hancock): MacIntyre, 24 Jan. 1978.
49. *Umtali Post* and *Rhodesia Herald* (20 Aug. 1977). The full text of Hickman's speech may be found in Rhodesia, Ministry of Information, Press Statement, 19 Aug. 1977.
50. See, for example, the statement by Dennis Divaris, Chief Whip, in *Rhodesia Herald* (3 Apr. 1976).
51. *Sunday Mail* (25 July, 1976), *Rhodesia Herald* (26 July 1976). Interviews (Hancock): Frost, 12 Jan. 1978; A. Holland, 13 Jan. 1981; Barlow, 26 Apr. 1989; (Godwin and Hancock): Barlow, 23 May 1989. André Holland hosted the meeting. Right-wingers believe that Holland – or another MP, regarded by all of them as a 'drunken little squirt' – leaked the details to Smith.
52. Interview (Godwin and Hancock): Barlow, 23 May 1989. Smith himself was unaware of the alleged assassination plot. (Interview (Hancock): 11 July 1989.)
53. Interview (Godwin and Hancock): Walls, 31 May 1989.
54. *Parl. Debs.*, Ass. 96, cols. 1135-4.
55. The specific changes were listed in Rhodesia, Ministry of Information, Press Statement, and *Rhodesia Herald* (1 Apr. 1977).
56. For the main developments in the ensuing crisis see *Rhodesia Herald* (13, 22, and 28 Jan. 1977; 24 and 28 Feb. 1977); *Sunday Mail* (27 Feb. 1977).
57. The 12 were Barlow, Cowper, Fawcett Phillips, Hope Hall, McGee, Newington, Nilson, Olds, Sandeman, Rodney Simmonds, Sutton-Pryce, Wright. At least two members, Cowper and Sandeman, were as much concerned about the prosecution of the war as the issues of land tenure and provincialisation (Cowper himself not being enamoured of the latter). (Interviews (Hancock): Sandeman, 27 May 1980; (Godwin and Hancock): Cowper, 9 May 1989.)
58. Sutton-Pryce believed that 10 others were on the verge of joining them (including Archie Wilson who was soon to become a minister) but Simmonds believed that there were only six more potential rebels. (Interviews (Hancock): Sutton-Pryce, 8 Mar. 1980; Simmonds, 12 Mar. 1980.)
59. *Parl. Debs.*, Ass. 95, 1-4 Mar. 1977.
60. Just one RF MP – Chris Andersen – was publicly disappointed that the legislation did not open up urban land to African purchase.
61. The drama of the debate and the final vote may be followed in the *Rhodesia Herald* between 1 and 5 Mar. 1977.
62. Owen later pronounced himself well pleased by the Rhodesians' co-operative spirit. (Interview (Hancock): Owen, 31 July 1980.)
63. For a report on the congress see *Rhodesia Herald* (19 Apr. 1977); *Sunday Mail* (24 Apr. 1977).
64. *Rhodesia Herald* (19 and 23 Apr. 1977); *Sunday Mail* (24 Apr. 1977).
65. Frost did have one victory in this period. After accusing Colonel Fothergill, the RF's Administrative Secretary, of spying on him for Smith, Frost issued a 'Me-or-Him' ultimatum, and Fothergill resigned: *Rhodesia Herald* (20 May 1977); Interview (Hancock): Frost, 17 May 1989.
66. For these exchanges see *Rhodesia Herald* (4 July 1977).
67. See *Property and Finance* (Feb.-May 1977).

68. See Chapter 4 n. 19.

69. *Property and Finance* (Feb. 1976); *Rhodesia Herald* (7-8 and 11 June 1977); *Rhodesian Patriot*, 3-4 (Oct.-Nov. 1977). (*Property and Finance* was last published in May 1977 and was succeeded by *Rhodesian Patriot*.) Smith, who had originally asked for $25,000, promised to give the $15,000 to an unspecified 'worthy cause'.

70. See, for example, the comments by J. A. C. Girdlestone of ARnI: *Sunday Mail* (5 June 1977).

71. *International Herald Tribune* (21 June 1977).

72. *Financial Gazette* (1 Apr. 1977).

73. Figures and comments on the departure of all kinds of professional workers may be found in *Rhodesia Herald* (19-20 Feb, 31 Mar., 1, 5, and 19 May, 11 Aug. 1977). But it was not all gloom. The civic fathers of Umtali recognised that, whoever was in power, 'people will still need services'. The city intended proceeding with its $1.3 m. sewerage project: *International Herald Tribune* (21 June 1977).

74. *Rhodesia Herald* (4 June 1977). The maximum requirement for the 38-49 age group was 70 days.

75. RNFU, *Report of the Annual Congress* (July 1977), pp. 121, 126.

76. *Rhodesia Herald* (30 Aug. 1977).

77. Ibid. (21 July 1977).

78. *Sunday Mail* (17 July 1977). Government assistance – consisting of a $1.5 m. grant to the hotel industry, petrol allowances, and cheap bus fares to tourist centres to encourage resident holiday-makers – offered temporary respite. Bed nights in Inyanga and Umtali (but not in the Vumba) rose in Aug. 1977, compared to the same month in 1976, in what was traditionally a poor month for the Eastern Highlands: Manicaland Publicity Association, 'Report on Proceedings of the 31st Annual General Meeting', 28 Sept. 1977.

79. CSO, *Consumer Price Index for Higher Income Urban Families* (1964-1984); *Parl. Debs.*, Ass. 95, cols. 1217-25, 24 Feb. 1977.

80. Ibid. 96, cols. 647-81,14 July 1977.

81. RNFU, *Report of the Annual Congress* (1977), pp. 116-19.

82. Interview (Hancock): R. Simmonds, 12 Mar. 1980. This interpretation of Smith's motives is largely based on an interview Hancock had with him on 26 June 1980

83. Rhodesia, Ministry of Information, Press Statement, 18 July 1977.

84. See, for example, the *Umtali Post* (16 May 1977) for the story of the Umtali East Constituency Council which deserted Jack Mussett, one of Smith's most loyal ministerial supporters and the owner of a furniture shop in Umtali.

85. *Rhodesia Herald* (19 Aug. 1977).

86. Interview (Hancock): Sandeman, 27 May 1980.

87. The following analysis of the housing issue is based on the coverage in the *Rhodesia Herald* and the *Sunday Mail* between 22 July and 5 Aug. 1977. For another interpretation see D. Hills, *Rebel People* (London, 1978), pp. 207-8.

88. Old habits died hard. A spokesman for Irvine's ministry, when explaining that property owners could insert restrictive clauses, said – by way of

example – that such restrictions 'could apply to dogs, people of Jewish descent, only to those of wholly European descent, and so on'. It was an unfortunate juxtaposition which Ian Smith declared was irresponsible and which prompted Irvine to say that many of his friends were Jews. See *Rhodesia Herald* (2 and 5 Aug. 1977).

89. *Sunday Times* (London) (24 May 1977). See also the prediction by Heidi Holland that the RAP would win 35 per cent of the vote (40 per cent in some constituencies): *Illustrated Life Rhodesia* (18 Aug. 1977).

90. See *Sunday Times* (7, 14, and 21 Aug. 1977).

91. Interview (Hancock): Sandeman, 27 May 1980.

92. Part of this argument draws upon a shrewd analysis by Martin Meredith on the eve of the poll: *Sunday Times* (28 Aug. 1977).

93. Press reports of their speeches may be found in *Rhodesia Herald* (17 – 20 Aug. 1977) and the *Sunday Mail* (21 Aug. 1977).

94. RNFU, *Report of the Annual Congress* (1977), pp. 69-83.

95. For examples of the Smith speeches see *Rhodesia Herald* (12-13 and 17 Aug. 1977); *Sunday Times* (14 Aug. 1977).

96. *Rhodesia Herald* (24 Aug. 1977).

97. In keeping with the better, post-Kissinger relationship, Smith referred to 'my friend the South African Prime Minister' when speaking at the RNFU's 1977 annual congress. He vehemently denied that the South Africans were 'pressurising us unnecessarily' and urged Rhodesians to be 'fair' and recognise the pressures upon South Africa itself: RNFU, *Report of the Annual Congress* (1977), pp. 70-1, 75.

98. Interview (Godwin and Hancock): Barlow, 23 May 1989.

99. For a brief account of NUF in 1977 see Hancock, *white Liberals*, pp. 203-7.

100. *Rhodesia Herald* (1 Sept. 1977).

101. Ibid.

102. Published by the British government as a white Paper, the Proposals nominated Field Marshal Carver as Resident Commissioner and set out seven elements: a surrender of power by 'the regime' and a return to legality; a transition to majority rule in 1978; free elections based on a universal suffrage; a British transitional administration; a UN presence during the transition; an independence constitution abolishing discrimination and protecting human rights and judicial independence; and a development fund to revive the economy. The Proposals also provided for the formation of a national army 'based on the liberation forces' but including 'acceptable elements' of the Rhodesian Security Forces (and excluding the Selous Scouts who were to be disbanded). *ARB*, P, S, and C, 14/9 (1977), 4571A-7B.

103. *Rhodesia Herald* (1 Sept. 1977).

104. For an analysis of the RF as a 'centrist' party see H. H. Patel, 'white Power in Rhodesia: The Rise and Fall (?) of the Rhodesian Front', paper presented to the ASSA Congress, Salisbury, 1978.

105. Flower, *Serving Secretly*, p. 173.

106. *Rhodesia Herald* (3 June 1977). See also Hancock, *white Liberals*, p. 206.

107. After averaging over 30 deaths a month in the early part of the year, and

falling to below 20 in mid-year, the average monthly death-rate rose above 30 from Sept. 1977,

108. *Rhodesia Herald* (11 Oct. 1977).

109. Flower, *Serving Secretly,* p. 175; Interview (Hancock): 9 July 1987.

110. *Chronicle* (24 Oct. 1977).

111. See, for example, *Parl. Debs.,* Ass. 97, col. 997, 12 Oct. 1977 (S. N. Eastwood).

112. For the debate on this issue see ibid., cols. 978-1007, 1081-105, 12-13 Oct. 1977.

113. Ibid. col. 1084, 13 Oct. 1977. See Cronje's speech for a full account of the call-up system as it operated – on paper – in late 1977.

114. Rhodesia, Ministry of Information, Press Statement, 27 Jan. 1977.

115. A committee was eventually appointed, headed by 'Mac' Knox, the former Party Chairman, who returned to the post after Des Frost resigned from the RF in mid-1977. The committee's report is discussed briefly in Ch. 8.

116. *Rhodesia Herald* (27 June 1977).

117. Ibid. (20 Aug. 1977).

118. Interview (Hancock): Lt.-Col. B. J. Harper, 14 July 1988. Anyone who saw the RF Chief Whip arriving at Thrasher headquarters wearing wide-legged starched shorts, puttees, and hobnailed boots might have wondered at the value of his contribution. Apparently, a parliamentary colleague had advised Divaris that he should wear his best uniform to create the right impression.

119. *Parl. Debs.,* Ass. 96, cols. 418, 483-5, 495, 20 June 1977. When De Kock arrived at Beit Bridge, he received a thorough 'going over' from the Customs authorities (who were known to him from his prior ministerial visits), indicating that someone at the top was feeling vindictive. Later, when fearing a similar treatment on his own departure, Cowper left his family behind and booked himself into accommodation at the border when, to his surprise, the officials waved him straight through. (Interview (Godwin and Hancock): Cowper, 9 May 1989.)

120. *Rhodesia Herald* (27 June 1977).

121. *Sunday Mail* (26 June 1977).

122. *Guardian* (13 Dec. 1977).

123. *Rhodesia Herald* (9 Oct. 1977).

124. Ibid. (1-3 June and 5 July 1977); *Sunday Mail* (5 July 1977); NAZ ORAL/246, pp. 76-8 (interview with Harvey Ward). One critic suggested that these changes at the top merely reflected power struggles between those who were prepared to work within the confines set by the RF: E. Windrich, *The Mass Media in the Struggle for Zimbabwe* (Gwelo, 1981), p. 46.

125. For a scathing criticism of this decision see the editorial in the *Rhodesia Herald* (17 Sept. 1977).

126. Ibid. (29 Oct. 1977).

127. Copies in the authors' possession.

128. *Rhodesia Herald* (21 July 1977).

129. This Committee was set up in 1972 on the initiative of the RNFU and though it was little more than a dining club in its early years it became an important lobby group in the late 1970s. See J. A. McKenzie, 'Commercial

Farmers in the Governmental System of Colonial Zimbabwe, 1963-1980',
Ph.D. thesis (Harare, 1990), pp. 196-7.

130. Interviews (Hancock): Brian O'Connell, 2 May 1980; Sir Keith Acutt, 9 Feb.
1981. O'Connell was an accountant and company director with close personal business contacts with the major business houses in Salisbury. Sir
Keith Acutt was Chairman of Anglo-American Corporation in Rhodesia.
(Rio Tinto did appoint an African director to its board in 1977.)

131. For material on the Harmony campaign see *Rhodesia Herald* (9-10, 13 Sept.,
1, 11 Oct. 1977, 12 Jan. 1978).

132. RNFU, *Report of the Annual Congress* (1977), pp. 92-3.

133. A surprising exception, at first sight, was the right-wing Senator Father
Lewis who, in a rare display of solidarity with Bishop Paul Burrough, ques
tioned the behaviour and sensitivity of the Security Forces in the killing of
innocent blacks in two particular incidents: Rhodesia, *Parliamentary Debates
(Parl. Debs.)*, Senate (Sen.), 9/8, cols. 270-5, 1 July 1977.

134. See, for example, the *Rhodesia Herald* (21 Dec. 1976), for reactions to the
death of 27 tea plantation workers in the Honde Valley.

135. *Rhodesia Herald* (4 Oct. 1977); *Sunday Mail* (20 Nov. 1977).

136. *Rhodesia Herald* (22 Dec. 1977).

7.   'Let this be a Rhodesian solution'*

   * Ian Smith reportedly addressing the second session of the internal settlement talks
   in Salisbury where he rejected the idea of a British involvement: African National
   Council (Sithole), 'Minutes of the Second Constitutional Talks', 9 Dec. 1977, copy in
   the authors' possession. Although the minutes kept by the Sithole party must be
   treated with caution, a white official close to the talks has confirmed that they
   accurately summarised the government's position.

1. *Rhodesia Herald* (25 Nov. 1977).

2. The two-day attack of 23-4 Nov. was regarded by members of COMOPS
as the most successful external raid ever conducted by the Rhodesians:
they inflicted over 2,000 casualties (including civilians), destroyed or
captured tonnes of arms, ammunition, fuel, and documents, and seriously
affected ZANLA's plans for the coming rainy season. On the Rhodesian
side, one man was killed and another eight were injured. (Interview
(Hancock): David Padbury (a career Army officer attached to the
COMOPS staff in 1979-80), 14 Feb. 1982; *Rhodesia Herald* (29 Nov. 1977).)
For a remarkably fair summary of the comments and criticisms of the raid
see Rhodesia, Ministry of Foreign Affairs, Information Section, *Reaction to
the Rhodesian Attacks on Chimoio and Tembue Camps*, parts i and n (30 Nov.
and 1 Dec. 1977).

3. Rhodesia, Ministry of Information, 'Prime Minister's Press Conference',
24 Nov. 1977. *The Herald* report of 25 Nov. referred only to the figure of 86
per cent.

4. Rhodesia, *Annual Report of the Secretary of Roads and Road Traffic* (1978); C. P.
Barnes, 'Logistics of Security Work in Rhodesia', paper presented to the
Construction Engineers' Conference, Dec. 1978, copy in the authors'

possession. Interview (Godwin): a senior officer of the Ministry of Roads and Road Traffic, 11 Oct. 1982.

5. The principles underlying these proposals were set out in Rhodesia, Rhodesian Government Policy Statement, *Safeguards for a Settlement* (Mar. 1977). See also Rhodesia, Ministry of Foreign Affairs, Information Section, 'Weekly Background Briefing', 43/77, 13 Dec. 1977, copy in the authors' possession.

6. I. Hancock, *white Liberals, Moderates and Radicals in Rhodesia* (London, 1984), pp. 208-9. Papers presented to the NUF council (Feb. 1978), by A. Warner, L. Leach, L. Reynolds, N. McNally, E. A. B. Dickinson, W. Friedman, and M. Rosin (copies in the authors' possession). The strongest supporter of a change was Nick McNally, a Salisbury lawyer and one of the original members of the Centre Party, who had contested the 1974 and 1977 elections as an RP and NUF candidate respectively. McNally was elevated to the bench after Independence.

7. Interview (Hancock): 'Mac' Knox, 14 Feb. 1978.

8. *Rhodesia Herald* (23 Jan. 1978). Five hundred people attended an RAP meeting in Salisbury, addressed by Sutton-Pryce, Nilson, and Wright, where the former MPs were criticised for failing to break with Smith much earlier. For a report and photograph of this latter meeting see ibid. (3 Feb. 1978).

9. Ibid. (20 Apr. and 1 May 1978).

10. Ibid. (22 Feb. 1978).

11. An account of the January killings may be found in D. Caute, *Under the Skin* (London, 1983), pp. 176-80.

12. The deaths were first announced by Combined Operations headquarters, which made its customary reference to 'follow-up operations'. The *Rhodesia Herald* headline on 1 Feb. 1978 referred to Terror Ambush'.

13. *Rhodesia Herald* (23 Jan. 1978).

14. Ibid. (21 Feb. 1978).

15. A debate on the beef price may be found in *Parl. Debs.*, Ass. 97, cols. 2421-40, 24 Feb. 1978.

16. *Rhodesia Herald* (6 and 24 Jan. 1978).

17. *Parl, Debs.*, Sen. 10/21, cols. 729-30, 7 Mar. 1978.

18. Rhodesia, *Report of the Commission of Inquiry into the Divorce Laws* (23 Sept. 1977), Cmd. R.R. 16-1977. The Commission, which had a strong religious bias in its membership, drew heavily upon the Australian Family Law Act of 1975 which was then considered to be ahead of its time in Western divorce legislation.

19. For the parliamentary debates on the *Report* see *Parl. Debs.*, Ass. 97, cols. 1869-906. 1 Nov. 1977: Sen. 10/20, cols. 724-71, 7-8 Mar. 1978. Senator Maclean, the wife of a former DC, was one of the authors of J. MacBruce, *When the Going Was Rough* (Pretoria, 1983).

20. Over 100 women discussed the *Report* at a meeting convened by the Salisbury Women's Institute: *Rhodesia Herald* (24 Jan. 1978).

21. For material on the expanded use of 'D notices' see *Rhodesia Herald* (21 and 27 Jan. 1978) and *Sunday Mail* (8 Jan., 5 Feb. 1978).

22. Rhodesia, Ministry of Information, Press Statement, 10 Nov. 1977.

23. *Sunday Mail* (5 Feb. 1978).
24. The full text may be found in *Rhodesia Herald* (4 Mar. 1978).
25. Ibid.
26. See, for example, Catholic Commission for Justice and Peace, 'An Analysis of the Salisbury Agreement', 15 Apr. 1978. For a defence of the agreement, and some self-promotion, see N. Sithole, *In Defence of the Rhodesian Constitutional Agreement: A Power Promise* (Salisbury, 1978).
27. Rhodesia, Ministry of Information, Press Statement, 12 Mar. 1978.
28. Rhodesia, Ministry of Foreign Affairs, Information Section, *Fact Paper,* 1/1978 (25 Apr. 1978), copy in the authors' possession.
29. 'Occasional Letter of the Rhodesian Christian Group', Easter 1978.
30. *Chronicle* and *Rhodesia Herald* (4 Mar. 1978); *Gwelo Times* (9 and 31 Mar. 1978). On 21 Apr. the *Fort Victoria Advertiser* began a campaign of its own – which had little support in the town – to persuade Smith to retire.
31. *Rhodesian Patriot,* 8 (Mar. 1978). The Enterprise Road is a major arterial road in the capital city which bifurcates the suburb of Highlands and heads towards the north-east.
32. *Rhodesia Herald* (13 Mar. 1978).
33. Catholic Commission for Justice and Peace, 'An Analysis of the Salisbury Agreement', p. 8.
34. *Rhodesia Herald* (2-3 Mar. 1978); *Umtali Post* (3 Mar. 1978). In a country which had millions of Shona speakers, one of the factors which delayed this decision was the lack of machines and language tapes for whites-only schools.
35. *Rhodesia Herald* (21 Apr. 1978).
36. Two accounts of the affair may be found in Caute, *Under the Skin,* pp. 241-4; and K. Flower, *Serving Secretly* (London, 1987), pp. 201-7.
37. *Rhodesia Herald* (15, 17, and 20 Apr. 1978). Hove's stand received a surprising endorsement from the editor of the *Gwelo Times* (20 Apr. 1978).
38. *Rhodesia Herald* (20 Apr. 1978).
39. Interview (Godwin and Hancock): Walls, 31 May 1989. Walls claimed that there were also murmurs among the black members of the police and the Army.
40. *Rhodesia Herald* (25-7 Apr. 1978).
41. Hove released a copy of the letter in London. It answered the charges by claiming that discrimination and harassment did exist and insisting that one of the objectives of the Agreement was to remove such conditions. His response, while perfectly reasonable, would not have satisfied Walls or Squires and Hove plainly did not see why he should meet their objections: ibid. (10 May 1978).
42. Ibid. (20 May 1978).
43. See, for example, *Financial Times* (London) (8 June 1978); *Spectator* (London) (10 June 1978); *The Times* (22 June and 24 July 1978).
44. RNFU, *Report of the Annual Congress* (July 1978), pp. 117-18.
45. *Rhodesia Herald* (23 Aug. 1978).
46. Ibid. (16 June 1978).
47. Ibid. (18 June 1978).

48. *ARB,* P, S, and C, 15/6 (1978), 4897B-8C; Caute, *Under the Skin,* pp. 249-58. The denominations affected were the Catholics, Baptists, Pentecostals, and the Salvation Army.

49. Individuals and organisations have accused the Selous Scouts, the Rhodesian-backed Mozambican rebels, and even the RLI of complicity in the Elim massacre. So far these suppositions have not been supported by hard evidence. The authors have been assured by members of the political and military hierarchy, including those who regularly practised 'dirty tricks', that the Rhodesians were not responsible. In the absence of other evidence, they are inclined to accept that a ZANLA group was responsible.

50. Caute, *Under the Skin,* p. 254.

51. *Parl. Debs.,* Ass. 98, col. 326, 27 June 1978 (Van der Byl). Hawkins's speech may be found in cols. 321-4.

52. Interview (Hancock): Divaris, 2 July 1985; *Rhodesia Herald* (22 June 1978); *Parl. Debs.,* Ass. 98, 21-2, 27-9 June 1978; Sen. 11, 2-3, 21-2 June 1978.

53. RNFU, *Report of the Annual Congress* (1978), esp. pp. 84-8, 117-18, 137, 147-8.

54. *Gwelo Times* (20 July 1978).

55. *Rhodesia Herald* (9-10 Aug. 1978).

56. In June 1978 a committee appointed by the Rhodesian Medical Association warned that any attack on private medicine and the medical aid societies would undermine standards and promote emigration. See Rhodesian Medical Association, 'Report of the Committee formed to investigate the future of Medicine under African Majority Rule', June 1978, copy in the authors' possession; and *Sunday Mail* (24 Sept. 1978). For critical comments on this report – claiming that it sought to maintain the *status quo* whereby the privileged (predominantly white) population obtained quality personal care and that it ignored the black rural areas and the urban poor – see John Gilmurrary, Roger Riddell, and David Sanders, *The Struggle for Health,* From Rhodesia to Zimbabwe Series, 7 (London, 1979), pp. 55-6.

57. RNFU, *Report of the Annual Congress* (1978), pp. 15 ff. The vote was 80 to 52 in favour of a change to the 'Commercial Farmers' Union' The opposing argument was that Rhodesia 'wasn't finished yet'.

58. See, for example, the well-founded criticisms of the Catholic Commission for Justice and Peace, *Sunday Mail* (24 Dec. 1978).

59. Turned 'terrs' who joined the government were elevated into 'guerrillas'.

60. *Sunday Mail* (13 Aug. 1978); *Rhodesia Herald* (14 Aug. 1978); *(Herald* (17-18 Aug. 1978); *Parl. Debs.,* Ass. 99, cols. 169-76, 16 Aug. 1978; cols. 1193-4, 7 Sept. 1978 The Prime Minister himself was closely questioned at a caucus meeting and later reassured an RF fête that the television film was full of exaggerations and distortions. The government tried to blame the media but the press pointed out that it was the government which had stage-managed an affair which had backfired: *Sunday Mail* (20 Aug. 1978).

61. *Rhodesia Herald* (14 Aug. 1978). Smith made this statement in an interview with the BBC.

62. Flower, *Serving Secretly,* p. 209. Flower's account of this episode provides

another example of Smith's capacity for deception because he acted without consulting his partners in the Transitional government.

63. *ARB*, P, S, and C, 15/9 (1978), 4994A-C; 10. 5036A-7C.

64. Almost immediately after Wrathall's death was announced there were rumours that he had committed suicide, followed by suggestions of financial impropriety or mismanagement. A prominent member of the judiciary repeated the gossip to Hancock in 1980 as if the information was established fact. The currency given the story in 1978-80 tells much about the levels of self-esteem, discretion, and trust within the upper reaches of the Christian society.

65. *Herald* (2 Sept. 1978).

66. The following account is based mainly on local and international press reports: *Herald* (4-9, 11-12 Sept. 1978); *Sunday Mail* (10 Sept. 1978); *ARB*, P, S, and C, 15/9 (1978), 4994A-7B. A summary of the Civil Aviation report may be found in the *Herald* (4 Jan. 1979).

67. Another rocket attack as launched on the following 15 Oct.

68. Interview (Godwin and Hancock): Walls, 31 May 1989. Walls claimed that Norman Walsh, the Deputy Commander of the Air Force, almost resigned because Walls refused to countenance an immediate air raid on Lusaka.

69. Nkomo's own account is probably accurate. Questioned about the weapon used to bring down the Viscount, and not wanting to admit that ZIPRA had SAM-7 missiles, Nkomo made a reference to throwing stones and then laughed at his own evasive answer: J. Nkomo, *Nkomo: The Story of My Life* (London, 1984), p. 167

70. Flower, *Serving Secretly*, pp. 210-11.

71. *Parl. Debs.*, Ass. 99, 6-9 Sept. 1978.

72. *Herald* (9 and 11 Sept. 1978).

73. Interview (Hancock): 4 Jan. 1982.

74. The sermon was distributed commercially as a record and sold over 26,000 copies. The proceeds went mainly to war-related charities. It will be recalled that Tholet's album, which included the song 'Rhodesians Never Die', sold 27,000 copies.

75. Interview (Godwin and Hancock): Walls, 31 May 1989; Flower, *Serving Secretly*, pp. 211-12.

76. Interview (Godwin and Hancock): Walls, 31 May 1989.

77. *Herald* (12 Sept. 1978).

78. Flower, *Serving Secretly*, p, 210. See also W. Lloyd, 'War and Peace: Can Rhodesia be saved?', *Commerce* (Sept. 1978), p, 14.

79. *Herald* (9 and 12-13 Sept. 1978).

80. Rhodesia, Ministry of Information, Press Statement, 15 Sept. 1978; *Herald* (15 Sept. 1978).

81. *Herald* (27 Sept. 1978).

82. For an early criticism of martial law see Catholic Commission for Justice and Peace, 'The Declaration of Martial Law in Rhodesia' (n.d.), but published before the end of 1978, copy in the authors' possession.

83. *Herald* (22 Dec. 1978).

84. Flower, *Serving Secretly*, pp. 213-15. Flower dated the subsequent deteriora-

tion in his relations with COMOPS to the Walls claim that he – Flower – had tried to sabotage the raid. The issue of Flower's loyalty is discussed in Chapter 8.

85. For a detailed and partly technical account of the raid from a Rhodesian point of view, see D. Cowderoy and R. C. Nesbit, *War in the Air* (Alberton, 1987), pp. 116-30, See also P. Stiff, *See You in November* (Alberton, 1985), ch. 15. There were many subsequent arguments over the status of Westlands Farm as a transit, refugee, or training camp.

86. Cowderoy and Nesbit, *War in the Air,* p. 128.

87. Copy in the authors' possession,

88. Peter Armstrong, *Operation Zambezi: The Raid into Zambia* (Salisbury, 1979). The book first appeared in Mar. 1979 and a second impression was published in April. Armstrong described the raid as 'the greatest morale booster – actually hitting the problem at its roots': *Illustrated Life and Talk* (11 Apr. 1979).

89. Fuller versions of the tape may be found in D. Martin and P. Johnson, *The Struggle for Zimbabwe* (London, 1981), pp. 296-7, Cowderoy and Nesbit, *War in the Air,* pp. 127-9, and, especially, in P. L. Moorcraft and P. McLaughlin, *Chimurenga!* (Marshalltown, 1982), pp. 182-9. The authors possess a copy of the original tape.

90. Cowderoy and Nesbit, *War in the Air,* pp. 127-8.

91. 'The Strategy of Protected Villages (Secret)', app. A to JOC Hurricane, G (Ops), 15 June 1978, copy in the authors' possession.

92. 'Points to be covered by JOC Hurricane'; 'Guidelines to District Commissioners (Secret)', apps. A and B to JOC Hurricane, G (Ops)/1/1, 31 Aug. 1978, copies in the authors' possession.

93. This point was made in the *Chronicle* (11 Oct. 1978).

94. Seventy PVs were soon opened, most of them in the Mudzi/Mtoko/Mrewa/Mount Darwin areas where Campling said that the system had failed: *Herald* (11 Sept. 1978). Ironically, the Mugabe government re-established some PVs in the late 1980s in response to the spill-over of dissident activity in Mozambique into the north-eastern corner of Zimbabwe.

95. It was customary for the Security Forces to claim that they determined the timing of the external raids. Whether Smith benefited by being out of the country and whether the Security Force commanders wanted to make their own point to the Americans remains unclear.

96. *ARE,* P, S, and C, 15/10 (1978), 5032A-5B; *Herald* (30 Oct. 1978).

97. *Herald* (11 Oct. 1978).

98. *ARE,* P, S, and C, 15/10 (1978), 5033A-B; *Sunday Times* (15 Oct. 1978); *Herald* (24 Oct. 1978).

99. *Herald* (11 Oct 1978).

100. *Sunday Mail* (12 Nov. 1978).

101. Ibid.

102. *Herald* (17-18 Jan. 1979).

103. *Parl. Debs.,* Ass. 99, col. 1627, 6 Dec. 1978 (D. S. Parkin).

104. Ibid., cols. 1913-14, 9 Jan. 1979. Goddard was elected for Matobo in 1977 when he defeated an RAP MP. He sat in the Zimbabwe parliament in the

early 1980s where his uninhibited style contributed to a tense racial atmosphere.

105. Ibid., cols. 2121-5, cols. 2164-5, 11 Jan. 1979.

106. The good security news was the successful importation of 11 US-designed Huey helicopters which would greatly assist the movement of troops.

107. Smith responded to Hayman's resignation by hurling the ultimate Rhodesian insult: Hayman, he said, was planning to emigrate. Hayman denied the allegation (though he did eventually emigrate), resigned his seat of Mazoe, and lost the subsequent by-election to 'Paddy' Millar, the former President of the RNFU, who stood for the RF.

108. For Smith's speeches, delivered in the major centres throughout the country, see *Herald* (12-13, 16, and 19 Jan. 1979). For his pre-election broadcast see ibid. (30 Jan. 1978). For a different view of Smith's behaviour see Richard West, 'Grand-dad's Army', *Spectator* (20 Jan. 1979): 'Nobody could accuse Mr Smith of trying to hoodwink the whites or offer them false hopes.' West's view was supported in Don Knowler, 'Ian Smith Lays it on the Line', *Star* (Johannesburg) (29 Jan. 1979).

109. *Herald* (19 Jan. 1979).

110. For one rowdy Smith meeting in Salisbury see ibid. (20 Jan. 1979).

111. *Umtali Post* (12 Jan. 1979). For similar views in the Midlands see the *Gwelo Times* (25 Jan. 1979).

112. Strath Brown had first stood for the RP in the Sinoia/Umvukwes by-election of Feb. 1974.

113. *Herald* (25 Jan. 1979).

114. Ibid. (18 Jan. 1979).

115. Ibid. (25 Jan. 1979).

116. To adapt an aphorism of Gough Whitlam, a former Australian Prime Minister. See also Hancock, *white Liberals*, pp. 209-10.

117. *Herald* (29 Jan. 1979).

118. *Umtali Post* (26 Jan. 1979).

119. Partridge, 'Letter to Constituents', 19 Jan. 1979, copy in the authors' possession.

120. A by-election, held on the same day for the seat of Gwelo, gave Trevor Dollar, the RF candidate, 85 per cent of the vote in a 64 per cent poll.

121. *Fort Victoria Advertiser* (9 Feb. 1979).

122. *Herald* (31 Jan 1979).

123. Material for the next two paragraphs was drawn mainly from the following interviews: (Hancock): MacIntyre, 25 Mar. 1980; Hickman, 16 Feb. 1981; Flower, 3 July 1985; (Godwin and Hancock): Redfern, 16 May 1989; Walls, 31 May 1989. The account of the RLI dinner was confirmed by an officer who preferred not to be cited. For a bland review of these events see R. Reid Daly, *Selous Scouts* (Alberton, 1982), pp. 421-30.

124. Reid Daly later claimed that the bug was planted because Military Intelligence thought that the investigating officer – Danny Stannard, a known friend of Reid Daly's – was involved in a cover-up. (Interview (Godwin): 1 Dec. 1982.)

125. The matter did not rest there. An Assistant Police Commissioner investi-

gated the bugging because the Army officers had broken the law in that the telephone was a Post Office appliance and CIO alone had the authority to plant devices. The police decided that there was insufficient evidence to sustain a prosecution. Meanwhile, Reid Daly appealed against the court martial decision and, having lost his case on 16 Dec. 1979, took out a civil action against eight of the officers allegedly involved, citing each in conjunction with the hapless Bishop Muzorewa who, at the time of the action, was Minister of Defence, Reid Daly's civil action lapsed when he failed to appear again in Zimbabwe.

126. *Herald* (1-2 Feb. 1979).
127. Ibid. (3 Feb. 1979).
128. *Parl. Debs.*, Ass. 99, cols. 3089-97; *Herald* (1 Mar. 1979).

8. 'In a hell of a turmoil'*

* Peter Walls describing his feelings just before speaking on television on 3 Mar. 1980: Interview (Godwin and Hancock): 31 May 1989.

1. C. Palley, *Zimbabwe Rhodesia: Should the Present Government be Recognised?* (London, 1979), p. 35.
2. The title 'Patriotic Front' is used in this chapter to denote the two parties (and
   most Rhodesians in early 1980 continued to link Nkomo and Mugabe): 'PF' refers to Nkomo's party.
3. The assassination attempts are discussed in R. Reid Daly, *Selous Scouts* (Alberton, 1982), pp. 348-68; B. Cole, *The Elite: The Story of the Rhodesian Special Air Service* (Amanzimtoti, 1984), pp. 270-96; K. Flower, *Serving Secretly* (London, 1987), p. 219. Cole, among others, evidently holds Flower responsible for warning Nkomo though it is possible that another CIO officer in Salisbury passed on the message following high-level political intervention.
4. There are several, graphic versions of this incident. One, given a circulation in Army circles, was that just before the accident the Army Commander had called out the Guard at the nearby King George VI Barracks (the Army headquarters) and, scantily attired, insisted on conducting a full inspection. Hickman denied all the allegations during two interviews with Hancock on 16 Feb. 1981 and 13 July 1989.
5. The British press was less restrained and carried stories about Hickman's reputation and claimed that he had received five prior warnings from senior colleagues: *Observer* (London) and *Sunday Telegraph* (London) (11 Mar. 1979); *Guardian* (29 May 1979).
6. Interviews (Hancock): Hickman (16 Feb. 1981, 13 July 1988); *Sunday Telegraph* (11 Mar. 1979),.
7. Flower, *Serving Secretly*, p. 220; Interview (Hancock): 3 July 1985.
8. Walls claimed that the American CIA and South African officials had informed him of Flower's dual loyalties: Interview (Godwin and Hancock): 31 May 1989. For published references to the existence of an MI6 mole see Cole, *The Elite: The Story of the Rhodesian Special Air Service*, pp. 296 and 414.

9. Regrettably, the authors are bound by an undertaking not to divulge their sources. It can be said, however, that one reason for an anti-Flower feeling among former CIO officers is that they were distressed that he published his memoirs.

10. Interview (Hancock): Smith, 11 July 1989. One of the authors received a similar response to a question asked with considerable subtlety: 'Ken, were you a spy?' (Interview (Hancock): Flower, 9 July 1987.)

11. Alex Moseley and Wally Stuttaford, both from Bulawayo, would have been on the right of the RAP if they had been prepared to lose their parliamentary salaries and join the rebel MPs in early 1977.

12. Interview (Hancock): P. F. ('Paddy') Shields, 29 Jan. 1981. Shields, a former railway worker, active trade unionist, and a self-styled RF moderate, claimed that he was frequently assailed at caucus meetings, especially by Irvine, for his 'communistic leanings'.

13. The RF nominations for the 20 white seats were Andersen, Butler, Cartwright, Cronje, De Klerk, Divaris, Du Plessis, Elsworth, Irvine, Landau, Micklem, Millar, Moseley, Partridge, Shields, Ian Smith, Squires, Stuttaford, Walker, and Van der Byl. The successful nominations for the remaining eight in the Assembly were Ankers, Gawler (a new face), Wing Commander Simmonds, Holland, Parkin, Eastwood, Dollar, and Scott. The unsuccessful were Beaver, Crook, du Toit, Gaunt, Gleig, Goddard, Mussett, and Air Marshal Wilson. The ten Senate nominations (all elected) were Crook, Mussett, Wilson, Christie, Gaunt, Ritchie, Heurtley, Abercrombie, Fleming, and Whaley (the last four being previous RF Senators). No women were nominated.

14. See Palley, *Zimbabwe Rhodesia*, pp. 26-7, for a critique of the adjusted electoral procedures. It should be pointed out that voters were not registered for the 1980 elections on the ground that the task was beyond the officials in the time available.

15. Military Intelligence File, MI/100/1, fo. 179. This file and other official files cited in this chapter are part of a collection taken out of the country in 1980. Official numbers and identification are provided where they are available. The authors regret that they are not permitted to reveal the location of these documents.

16. *Herald* (5 Apr. 1979).

17. This paragraph draws some of its examples and argument from Palley, *Zimbabwe Rhodesia*, pp. 20-2.

18. 'Up to Date', *Commerce* (Mar./Apr. 1979).

19. *Rhodesian Tobacco Today* (Feb. 1979).

20. Commercial Farmers' Union (CFU), *Report of the Annual Congress of the CFU* (July 1979), p. 46. As pointed out below, the approval was given at this congress to change the name from 'RNFU' to 'CFU'.

21. *Rhodesia, Second and Third Interim Reports of the Electoral Supervisory Commission* (25 Apr. and 23 May 1979).

22. United Kingdom, Parliamentary Human Rights Group, *Free and Fair?: The 1979 Rhodesian Elections*, A Report on Behalf of the British Parliamentary Human Rights Group (May 1979), p. 52.

23. *Zimbabwe Rhodesia*, p. 34.
24. See, for example, the editorial in the *Gwelo Times* (26 Apr. 1979).
25. *Herald* (31 May 1979).
26. Ibid. (2 June 1979).
27. Ibid. (1 June 1979).
28. CSO, *Monthly Digest of Statistics* (Mar. 1980).
29. The first figure was compiled by the JOCs, the second by the police (copies of these statistics in the authors' possession). The attention to detail – at the height of the war – was itself remarkable; the disparity more so. The Ministry of Agriculture and the CPU considered the police statistics to be the more reliable.
30. Military Intelligence Directorate, 'Intelligence Conclusions (SECRET)', 26 June 1979.
31. See J. K. Cilliers, *Counter-Insurgency in Rhodesia* (London, 1985), pp. 249-52.
32. *Herald* (26 July 1979).
33. Some average comparative petrol costs in Sept. 1979 – per gallon and in Rhodesian dollars – were: Rhodesia $2.27, Britain $1.45, Australia $0.96. France was the only Western country to reach $2.27. (*Illustrated Life and Talk* (12 Sept. 1979).)
34. Zimbabwe Rhodesia, *Parl. Debs.*, Ass. 100, cols. 463-95.
35. In 1979 178,711 Rhodesian residents returned to the country after spending more than one night outside. The figures in 1977 and 1978 were 176,027 and 174,059 respectively. These figures include business trips and all races, although the overwhelming majority of travellers were certainly white. (Zimbabwe Rhodesia, CSO, *Monthly Digest of Statistics* (Feb. 1980), table 2.)
36. *Herald* (8-9 Dec. 1978).
37. Ibid. (22 Mar. 1979).
38. Ibid. (16 May 1979).
39. *Gwelo Times* (8 June and 26 July 1979); *Herald* (7 July 1979). Winsor originally pleaded 'Not Guilty', and threatened to charge the police with committing several irregularities. He eventually changed his plea to 'Guilty', apologized to the magistrate for having 'cracked', and was fined $50.
40. Zimbabwe Rhodesia, Ministry of Information, Press Statement, 10 Aug. 1979.
41. The *mujibas* were teenagers and even younger children who acted as the 'eyes and ears' of the guerrillas.
42. This discussion may be followed in the CFU, *Report of the Annual Congress* (1979), pp. 100-6.
43. One of the co-ministers was Mark Partridge who seemed destined to alienate everyone affected by whatever portfolio he administered.
44. For an account of this meeting see *Herald* (23 May 1979) and *Rhodesian Tobacco Today* (May 1979).
45. CFU, *Report of the Annual Congress* (1979), p. 62.
46. *Farmer* (21 Sept. 1979).
47. Ibid. (28 Sept. 1979).
48. CFU, *Report of the Annual Congress* (1979), pp. 73-5.
49. Ibid., pp. 21-9.
50. *ARB*, P, S, and C, 16/8 (1979), 5389A.

51. See, especially, *Herald* (6-9, 15-16 Aug. 1979).
52. For two accounts of the raids varying in perspective and reliability see Cole, *The Elite: The Story of the Rhodesian Special Air Service*, pp. 327-39, and D. Cowderoy and R. C. Nesbit, *War in the Air* (Alberton, 1987), pp. 161-73.
53. By Sept. 1979 the South Africans had become even more involved in the war through the supply of Mirages, helicopters, crews, technicians, and combat troops. For one of the many denials of South African involvement see Walls's statement in the *Herald* (3 Dec. 1979) which he later retracted by saying that the involvement was considerable. (Interview (Godwin and Hancock): 31 May.) For material on the South African involvement in Op Uric see Cowderoy and Nesbit, *War in the Air*, pp. 162-4. The COMOPS communiqué acknowledged that one South African airman was on board the Puma, Cowderey and Nesbit claim that there were three, whereas Cole does not mention any South Africans being present.
54. *Herald* (8 Sept. 1979).
55. For a full list of delegates and reports of the Conference see United Kingdom, 'Southern Rhodesia, *Report of the Constitutional Conference, Lancaster House* (Jan. 1980), Cmnd. 7802. The Zimbabwe Rhodesia government reproduced the report as two documents: Cmd. ZR 3 and 18.
56. P. Stiff, *See You in November* (Alberton, 1985), ch. 19. In this chapter 'Taffy' outlined an elaborate plan to detonate a bomb in a hotel foyer. Flower and other CIO sources told Hancock that 'Taffy's claims were accurate in that CIO did consider the assassination option' but they insisted that the account in Stiff's book 'romanticised' the importance and the extent of the operation.
57. Interview (Hancock): Lt.-Col. B. J. Harper, 14 July 1988.
58. *Daily Telegraph* (20 Sept. 1979).
59. See Flower, *Serving Secretly*, p. 234. Flower claimed that the Zimbabwe Rhodesia delegation (consisting of the UANC, Sithole's ZANU, Chief Ndiweni's new party, and the RF) was so factionalised 'that the British dare not disclose the real nature of their plans to anyone other than the Bishop and the three or four of us working closely with him'.
60. For Salisbury reactions see ibid., p. 315.
61. Interview (Hancock): David Smith, 9 Feb. 1982.
62. *Spectator* (London) (27 Oct. 1979); Interview (Hancock): Ian Smith 26 June 1980.
63. *Herald* (24 and 29 Sept. 1979).
64. Rower, *Serving Secretly*, p. 243.
65. *Herald* (9 Nov. 1979).
66. Ibid. (10 Nov. 1979); Interview (Hancock): Van der Byl, 17 May 1980.
67. The prediction was quoted in the *Spectator* (27 Oct. 1979) and, according to Colin Legum and David Martin, *Observer* (18 Nov. 1979), was repeated on another occasion. Smith later denied making this forecast when, during the election campaign in 1980, he was trying to bolster white morale. He remembered it when Mugabe won the election as evidence of his considerable prophetic powers.
68. *Herald* (12 Nov. 1979).

69. Nicholas Ashford writing in *The Times* (16 Nov. 1979). Ashford, like Chris Ashton (Australian papers), Martin Meredith *(Sunday Times)*, James MacManus *(Guardian)*, Christopher Munnion *(Daily Telegraph)*, and Xan Smiley *(Spectator)* were the best reporters of white moods and opinions during the later 1970s.

70. For Denis Norman's public statement of this position see *The Times* (27 Nov. 1979).

71. Interviews (Hancock): Flower, 9 July 1987; (Godwin and Hancock): Walls, 31 May 1989.

72. Interview (Godwin and Hancock): Walls, 31 May 1989. Smith was adamant that Walls had been given 'the treatment', and had succumbed to the flattery. (Interview (Hancock): 11 July 1989.)

73. Interview (Godwin): Sir Robin Renwick, 27 Oct. 1989. In 1979 Renwick was an official with the Foreign and Commonwealth Office who later went to Rhodesia as an adviser to Soames.

74. Flower, *Serving Secretly*, pp. 246 and 314. Walls believes that Flower's absence was deliberate. (Interview (Godwin and Hancock): 31 May 1989.)

75. Interview (Godwin and Hancock): Walls, 31 May 1989.

76. Goddard had just been returned to parliament replacing Theunis de Klerk, a prominent Afrikaner, who had been ambushed and killed in the Nuanetsi area on 20 Sept.

77. Interview (Hancock): David Padbury, 14 Feb. 1982.

78. Interviews (Godwin and Hancock): Walls, 31 May 1989; (Hancock): Smith, 11 July 1989. Flower, on the other hand, claims that the Mozambicans had invited Walls and himself to check the facts 'and we were satisfied that there had been no foul play': *Serving Secretly*, p. 252.

79. *Umtali Post* (21 Dec. 1979).

80. It is probable that unpublicised friendships were also established with the New Zealand contingent. It is unlikely that similar relationships were formed with the Fijians or the Kenyans although the Kenyans, in particular, found other sources of amusement.

81. For coverage of this issue see *Sunday Mail* (2, 9, and 16 Mar. 1980).

82. This paragraph is based on information provided by two former CIO officers.

83. 'An Assessment of the Threat to ZR prior to the Elections 27-29 Feb. 1980 and the Immediate Post-Election Period', MI/108. This file number includes several documents, some of which are listed separately in n. 87. below.

84. A Military Intelligence assessment on 23 Jan. claimed that 4,100 ZANLA and 1,400 ZIPRA combatants remained outside the Assembly Points. This assessment in fact understated the position.

85. Sir John Boynton, the British Electoral Commissioner, explained that intimidation 'took many forms, from acts of violence to more subtle methods of persuasion'. For Boynton's description of the various methods see United Kingdom, Southern Rhodesia, *Independence Elections, 1980, Report of the Electoral Commissioner, Sir John Boynton* (Mar. 1980), Cmnd. 7935, p. 17. For a critical view alleging that the Rhodesians exaggerated the extent and intensity of intimidation in Matabeleland see the 'Final Report of Election

Supervisors for Matabeleland North' (n.d.), Greenhill Papers, Rhodes House Library, Oxford, MSS Afr. S. 1748 (4), pp. 16-31.

86. Interview (Godwin and Hancock): Walls, 31 May 1989. This story was partially confirmed by a senior Western diplomat who, in an interview with Godwin, denied that Walls used such strong language.

87. 'Suggested short term strategy for Z(imbabwe) R(Rhodesia): 21 January to 31 March 1980', MI/113; Peter Foggerty (CIO), 'An Assessment of the Threat to Zimbabwe Rhodesia prior to elections 27-29 February and the Immediate post Election Period' (n.d.), MI/108; 'Assessment of Threats that might develop up to and immediately following February elections', 23 Jan. 1980, MI/108; Major Lindner, 'Intelligence Appreciation: the 1980 election'. All these documents were marked 'Top Secret', and the last-named was ordered to be destroyed by 29 Feb. (the last day of the common roll election).

88. See *Herald* (1 Feb. 1980) for Smith's statement and the UANC's angry reply.

89. Ibid. (4-5 Feb. 1980). Some reports denied that the victims were identified with any particular party but it was widely assumed that they were Muzorewa supporters.

90. According to Barbara Cole, these incidents formed part of Operation Hectic: Cole, *The Elite: The Story of the Rhodesian Special Air Service*, pp. 413 ff.

91. Interview (Godwin): P. K. Allum, 12 Nov. 1989; Allum, 'Memo to Self', 16 Feb. 1980. Allum Papers (in the owner's possession).

92. A highly-selective account of the plans for Quartz, may be found in Cole, *The Elite: The Story of the Rhodesian Special Air Service*, pp. 413 ff.

93. Interview (Hancock): David Padbury, 14 Feb. 1982.

94. A document marked 'Top Secret', which was signed by the Officer in Charge (OC) of Special Branch in Matabeleland and sent to Branch headquarters in Salisbury on 30 Jan. 1980, consisted of extensive reports on three Assembly Points covering such subjects as topography, guard placements, weapons, the quality of camp discipline, and the number of personnel.

95. Interview (Godwin): Allum, 12 Nov. 1989.

96. *Herald* (12 Aug. 1980); Interview (Godwin): 3 Dec. 1982. In effect, Walls confirmed that the original strategy was to act in protection of a Nkomo-Muzorewa coalition, a point emphasised by John Ellison of the London *Daily Express* who first broke the story of Quartz which he repeated after the furore created by Walls's public reference to the planned coup: *Daily Express* (London) (14 Aug. 1980) and *Herald* (19 Aug. 1980). The controversy over Walls's public statements in Aug. 1980 is briefly discussed in the Conclusion.

97. Flower, *Serving Secretly*, pp. 264-6, 276; Interview (Hancock): 3 July 1985.

98. Granada Television, Transcript of End of Empire series (1984), copy in the authors' possession.

99. This interpretation of Allum's motives and his account of the ballot-rigging episode emerged during an interview with Godwin on 12 Nov. 1989. Flower, *Serving Secretly*, p. 264, recounts this incident by ignoring the Police Commissioner's role and asserting that he decided to call the operation off.

Other informants 'blamed' Allum for the decision. It is significant that Flower, in claiming responsibility, was primarily concerned that the Rhodesians would not get away with it.

100. *Report of the Electoral Commissioner, Sir John Boynton*, pp. 61-2. Although he believed that the British presence persuaded the administration to become committed to the exercise, and although he was critical of some administration attitudes, Geoffrey Greenhill conceded that the election was organised 'by and large with resolve and efficiency': 'Final Report of Election Supervisors for Matabeleland North', p. 18, Greenhill Papers.

101. Interview (Hancock): Ron Peters, 30 Aug. 1989. Peters, formerly of the Criminal Investigation Department (CID), was OC Special Branch, Salisbury, in late 1979.

102. Interview (Hancock): Ian Rich, 15 Feb. 1982.

103. *Financial Times* (5 Mar. 1980).

104. This information was provided – separately – by two former CIO officers who asked not to be named.

105. MI, A/8/32.

106. Interview (Godwin): D. Bennison (formerly OC Special Branch), 4 Dec. 1982. A copy of the document is in the authors' possession.

107. Security Report, Special Branch, 17 Feb. 1980.

108. Interview (Godwin): Allum, 12 Nov. 1989.

109. Interview (Godwin and Hancock): Walls, 31 May 1989. Peters recalled that this conversation with Walls did take place. (Interview (Hancock): Peters, 30 Aug. 1989.)

110. Interview (Hancock): Peters, 30 Aug. 1989. Allum confirmed to Godwin that Peters, 'a down to earth character', and the most realistic and reliable of the senior Special Branch officers, had predicted a Mugabe victory.

111. Walls claimed that Special Branch reports led him to predict Muzorewa's victory: *Herald* (12 Aug. 1980).

112. Interview (Godwin): Allum, 12 Nov. 1989.

113. MI, A/8/32.

114. One of the accusers is Lt. Col. John Redfern. (Interview (Godwin and Hancock): 16 May 1989.)

115. Interview (Hancock): Smith, 11 July 1989. Smith, who had received assurances from Soames that the British would move against intimidation, learnt just before the election that no action was possible because 'Peter' Carrington had decided against it.

116. Interview (Godwin): Sir Robin Renwick, 27 Oct. 1989.

117. Walls and Flower flew on the weekend prior to the election to Mozambique where everyone agreed to accept the electorate's verdict,

118. Campbell Papers, Rhodes House Library, Oxford, MSS Afr. S. 1761(1), pp. 19-21. Campbell was a former member of the Colonial Service and of the Colonial Office and had served as Chief Secretary in Malta and as an Assistant Under-Secretary of State in Defence.

119. Interview (Hancock): Keith Shann, 3 Mar. 1980. Shann was a highly respected Australian diplomat who was a member of the 11-man Commonwealth Observer Group. He was speaking in particular of a

Rhodesian lawyer and former national sporting star, who was active within professional groups in promoting better race relations, but whose first-night contribution to the war effort as a 'Womble' had ended prematurely when he reportedly fell asleep in a ditch outside one of the houses he was guarding (his own).

120. Interview (Hancock): Smith, 11 July 1989.
121. Interview (Godwin and Hancock): Walls, 31 May 1989.
122. For different versions of this off-the-cuff speech see *Herald, The Times, Daily Telegraph* (4 Mar. 1980).
123. For some predictions close to the polls see *Daily Telegraph* (23 Jan. and 22 Feb. 1980); *Sunday Times* (3 and 24 Feb. 1980).

9. 'Fourteen great years'*

* Interview (Hancock): Smith, 11 July 1989.

1. *Sunday Mail* (9 Mar, 1980).
2. Interview (Hancock): Ian Smith, 11 July 1989.
3. *Herald* (8 Mar. 1980). The regional press confirmed that the panic and 'stunned disbelief of 4 Mar. had given way to the traditional 'wait-and-see' attitude: *Gwelo Times* (6 Mar. 1980); *Umtali Post* (7 Mar. 1980).
4. War, according to Mrs Twiss, the Headmistress of Arundel, the prestigious Anglican girls' school in Salisbury, made the young want to pack a maximum experience into the minimum time: *Arundel School Magazine* (1978), p. 6.
5. For two examples of the bitterness see the letters written by Denzil Dunn after his son was killed and Wilfred Brooks's comment on Dunn's letter: *Rhodesia Herald* (24 and 29 Sept. 1977). See *Umtali Post* (29 Sept. 1978) for a letter from Andrew and Milly Botha of Umtali referring to their 'unkind' treatment upon announcing their intention to emigrate.
6. There is no published information relating to war-related suicides or attempted suicides. The authors are aware of at least two suicides in May 1977 which involved civilians who had been affected by their involvement in 'Smith's war'. For one of the cases see H. Holderness, *Lost Chance: Southern Rhodesia, 1945-58* (Harare, 1985), pp. 231-2.
7. These figures were supplied by a former member of COMOPS. Inevitably, the Security Forces and the two armies of the Patriotic Front produced different sets of statistics. The authors have accepted the Security Forces' figures for white deaths on the ground that any attempt to fake them would have been exposed by the uncensored death notices in the press and by the inability to hide such deaths from families and communities.
8. It was widely assumed in the early 1980s that the overall number of war-caused deaths exceeded 30,000. See, for example, P. L. Moorcraft and P. McLaughlin, *Chimurenga!* (Marshalltown, 1982), p. 222.
9. On the other hand, the whites made – proportionately – their greater sacrifice in the two World Wars: 732 died in 1914-18 and 742 in 1939-45.
10. These figures have been taken from the incomplete lists supplied by I. P.

MacLaren (ed.), *Some Renowned Rhodesian Senior Schools: 1892-1979* (Bulawayo, 1981), and I. P. MacLaren (ed.), *More Rhodesian Senior Schools: Part Two, 1950-1982* (Bulawayo, 1982).

11. *Herald* (13 Feb. and 29 Sept. 1979, 5 March 1980); D. Caute, *Under the Skin* (London, 1983), pp. 295-6.
12. *Herald* (21 Feb., 1 Mar. 1980).
13. This point was made to one of the authors by Mr Justice Pittman who himself had lost a leg at El Alamein. (Interview (Hancock): 3 July 1980.)
14. St Giles Rehabilitation Centre, 'Physiotherapy and Occupational Therapy Register', 1970-9.
15. Interview (Hancock): R. Wollacott (formerly Internal Affairs), 7 Feb. 1982. For an account of the trial see *Herald* (10-15, 18 Apr. 1980). See also Caute, *Under the Skin*, pp. 391-2.
16. The problem was not confined to the young: doctors and pharmacists were reporting the abuse of pills (especially by housewives) while the number of deaths from cirrhosis of the liver had risen from 24 in 1970 to 31 in 1978. See *Herald* (28 Oct. 1978) and Zimbabwe Rhodesia, *Report of the Secretary of Health* (1978), table 2.
17. A report of his remarks appeared in the journal of the Women's Institutes, *Home and Country* (July 1979).
18. Interview (Hancock): 14 May 1980.
19. *Herald* (9 Feb. 1980); B. Moore-King, *white Man black War* (Harare, 1988), p. 35.
20. *Herald* (12 Oct. 1979); Caute, *Under the Skin*, pp. 364-5.
21. C. Cocks, *Fireforce* (Alberton, 1988), pp. 9-10.
22. For further examples of similar post-war experiences see Moore-King, *white Man black War.*
23. The decorations awarded for part of the period, 1977-9, are listed in P. L. Moorcraft, *Contact II: Struggle for Peace* (Johannesburg, 1981), pp. 179 ff.
24. This paragraph is based on an interview conducted by Hancock on 29-30 June 1983 with the officer who requested not to be named. For a description of sickened troopies, reacting to the shooting of civilians in a Mtoko village, see Moore-King, *white Man black War*, pp. 22-34.
25. P. Burrough, *Angels Unawares* (Worthing, 1988), pp. 20-1; Interview (Hancock): 21 Aug. 1989.
26. See Cocks, *Fireforce*, p. 236, for a reference to killing prisoners. Cocks served in the RLI from Jan. 1976 until Jan. 1979. For the charges of brutality which most annoyed the Rhodesian government see Catholic Commission for Justice and Peace, *The Man in the Middle* (London, 1975). For further charges – and denials see *Parl Debs.*, Ass. 97, cols. 1175-8, 14 Oct. 1977; *Rhodesia Herald* (24 Nov. and 3 Dec. 1977). The government, in turn, published several documents and pictures detailing 'terrorist' acts. See especially Rhodesia, *The Anatomy of Terror* (May 1974) and *Massacre of the Innocents* (Jan. 1978).
27. This sentence is based on Hancock's interview with a middle-level Special Branch officer in Salisbury on 2 Mar. 1980.
28. Former senior CIO officials – who cannot be quoted – were privately very critical in discussing the activities of their own killer squad. The planners, it

seems, were more honourable than those who implemented the plans.

29. K. Flower, *Serving Secretly* (London, 1987), pp. 137-8; Interview (Hancock): 7 July 1987. Further information on this case was obtained from a former middle-ranking CIO officer who wishes to remain anonymous.

30. For evidence of the concern about the effect of war on marriages see the statements by a marriage guidance counsellor, a divorce lawyer, and an Army chaplain in *Herald* (28 Oct. 1978). Of the ten Army wives who were interviewed by a magazine in 1974, three had divorced by 1977, four experienced marital difficulties, and the other three were being treated for nervous disorders. *(Illustrated Life Rhodesia* (31 Mar. 1977).)

31. NAZ, ORAL/246, pp. 79 and 83. Presumably Ward was offended by the mildly liberal Termination of Pregnancy Act in 1977. The Act legalised abortions in cases where the woman might suffer permanent physical dam age, where the child might be born with mental or physical defects, or where conception followed unlawful intercourse. The RF voted for the bill, the African MPs opposed it. See *Parl. Debs.*, Ass. 97, 4, 6-7 Oct. 1977.

32. Interview (Hancock): Smith, 11 July 1989.

33. Ibid.

34. The country did not have the resources to prosecute the thousands of Rhodesians who had become petty criminals. Besides, the unforeseen consequences could be embarrassing. A noted and otherwise upright business man committed suicide in Nov. 1976 after being exposed for a private deal amounting to $700.

35. Rhodesia, *Annual Reports of the Commissioner of Police* (1977-8); Zimbabwe Rhodesia, Zimbabwe Rhodesia Police, *Annual Report* (1979). Mr Justice Beck found that he was trying between 20 and 30 whites each year for serious breaches of Exchange Control regulations. (Interview (Hancock): Mr Justice Beck, 10 Feb. 1982.)

36. Interview (Hancock): Simmonds, 17 May 1989.

37. Interview (Hancock): D. Stannard, 4 Feb. 1981. Stannard was the police officer responsible for prosecuting Muller. Muller's prison sentence was reduced to two years because he co-operated with the authorities, though he was especially bitter because some of his other local associates, three of whom were later charged for breaching Exchange Control regulations and who made far more money, seemed to suffer less. Some of Muller's letters from prison, which were made available to the authors, spoke of his disillusionment with the Rhodesian government for an excessive punishment 'after all I have done for them'.

38. Interviews (Hancock): Stannard, 4 Feb. 1981; Flower, 3 July 1985 and 9 July 1987; Colin Barlow, 26 Apr. 1989. According to Ian Smith, the CIO investigation merely discovered that one of his ministers was 'where he shouldn't have been at night'. (Interview (Hancock): 26 June 1980.)

39. A former RF MP, now living in South Africa, has collected information which, he alleges, 'proves' that Smith smuggled funds out of Rhodesia. In its present state, the existence of the file is more important for what it reveals about the bitterness of the far right.

40. Zimbabwe Rhodesia, CSO, *Monthly Migration and Tourist Statistics* (Nov.

1979), tables 1, 6, and 8; Zimbabwe, *Report of the Secretary for Health* (1980), table 1.

41. *Rhodesia Herald* (11 Apr. 1974).
42. Interview (Hancock): Burrough, 21 Aug. 1989.
43. 'Minutes of the Church Council', All Saints, Gatooma, 5 June 1979, NAZ, MS 548/1/2.
44. J. MacBruce, *When the Going was Rough* (Pretoria, 1983), ch. 14.
45. *Illustrated Life and Talk* (1 Aug. 1979).
46. *Illustrated Life Rhodesia* (12 Oct. 1978); *Illustrated Life and Talk* (18 July 1979); *Herald* (2 Jan. 1980).
47. One of the visitors welcomed into the country in 1978 was an American negro, Ralph Moss, who was immediately credible because he declared that blacks were better governed in Rhodesia than in any other part of Africa. The government provided excellent accommodation in the white suburbs for Mr Moss, and his white assistant, and never seemed to question his claims of wielding enormous political influence in the United States. Perhaps not enough white ministers or officials had ever encountered an upwardly mobile black and were, therefore, easily seduced by one who adorned himself with flashy ornaments and who enjoyed a permissive Western lifestyle.
48. *Herald* (23 May 1979).
49. *Farmer* (16 Mar. 1979).
50. CFU, *Report of the Annual Congress of the CFU* (1979), p. 73. See also *Farmer* (16 Mar. 1979) and CFU, 'Statistical Survey of Cattle Holdings by ICA in Standard Livestock Units (as at 31 March 1979) and Farm Utilisation (as at May 1979)', copy in the authors' possession. The CFU document, which assessed farm occupancy and stock losses in the first half of 1979, calculated that over 35 per cent of farms in Cashel, Headlands, Inyanga, Mayo, Melsetter, Mtoko, Nuanetsi, Odzi, and Umtali North and South were unfarmed, and that the stock losses in Mayo and Odzi were 85 and 59 per cent respectively.
51. CFU, *Report of the Annual Congress of the CFU* (1979), pp. 103-4.
52. Some families had more reason to grieve than others. Ben Stander of Nuanetsi, his son, and a nephew died in separate ambushes in 1978-9. Another nephew lost both his legs below the knee while on patrol with a PATU stick. See *Rhodesia Herald* (28 June 1978), *Herald* (17 Aug. 1979); Caute, *Under the Skin*, pp. 358-9.
53. Transcript of the *End of Empire* series, Granada Television (1984), copy in the authors' possession; T. A. Wigglesworth, *Perhaps Tomorrow* (Salisbury, 1980); Interview (Godwin): D. Bennison, 4 Dec. 1982. The authors possess considerable, unproven anecdotal evidence of such collaboration, as well as material relating to the suspicious destruction of one property in the Eastern Highlands belonging to a liberal farmer who may have been the victim of either a renegade ZANLA gang or, more probably, a Security Force attack.
54. Samples of this advice from the Du Toit Papers include: Agric-Alert (Pvt.) Ltd., 'Early Warning VHP Radio System: Operating Manual', revised edi-

tion (May 1977); RNFU, Circulars marked 'Confidential', dated 4 July and 12 Nov. 1977 and 17 Jan. 1979; Chief Superintendent, Officer Commanding Police, Gatooma District, 'General Recommendations for Increasing Security Precautions (Restricted)' (n.d.); RNFU, 'Homestead Protection Course', Feb. 1979; Goromonzi Civil Defence Committee, 'Resume for Section Wardens of Ruwa South C.D. Area (Confidential)', 6 Feb. 1979; F. P. du Toit, 'Short Notes [over 20 pages] on Rural Homestead Defence', Autumn 1979; DC, Goromonzi, 'Labour Problems Arising from Terrorism' and 'Compound Complex Protection and Militia (Confidential)', 3 July 1979.

55. 'Bright Lights' were hired or voluntary white guards who often accompanied farmers around the farm or guarded the homestead at night.
56. Interview (Hancock): Peter Storrer, 29 May 1980.
57. Interview (Hancock): Des Frost, 17 May 1989.
58. Newsletters of the Ruwa Area Co-ordinating Committee (1978-9), Du Toit Papers; Interview (Godwin and Hancock): Flo du Toit, 16 May 1989. Mrs Du Toit had been an active member of the RF and of the Women's Institutes.
59. Tt [the Agric-Alert system] probably did more for our morale among our community than any other single thing': J. Sinclair, President of the CFU, in CDU, *Report of the Annual Congress* (July 1981), p. 30.
60. CFU, *Report of the Annual Congress* (1979), pp. 57-8. Mrs Strong used only first names when referring to the duties undertaken by the women in her area.
61. Interview (Hancock): Storrer, 29 May 1980.
62. 'Resume for Section Wardens of Ruwa South', 6 Feb. 1979, Du Toit Papers.
63. Arguably, nearby Goromonzi did not really pull together until after the war when ex-ZANLA combatants acquired two farms in the district and began killing and harassing their white neighbours. (Interview (Hancock): A. Carle, 10 Feb. 1982. Mrs Carle, a former RF activist in the district, is the wife of a Goromonzi farmer.)
64. Umtali was awarded the Meritorious Conduct Medal in Feb. 1979.
65. See MacBruce, *When the Going was Rough*, ch. 15, for the efforts to ensure that electricity, water, sewerage, road maintenance, RSPCA, and rural council services continued to function.
66. *Umtali Post* (25 Apr. 1977).
67. MacBruce, *When the Going was Rough*, ch. 3 and p. 203. Arundel School in Salisbury tried to be an exception: hockey and tennis teams, accompanied by armed escorts, went to Umtali during 1979. Arundel's headmistress argued that those who set themselves up as leaders should not be brainwashed into abandoning a normal life: *Arundel School Magazine* (1979), pp. 8-9.
68. *Fort Victoria Advertiser* (8 Jan. and 24 Mar. 1978, 5 Jan. 1979).
69. The Rhodesian title – 'Zimbabwe Ruins' – was replaced after Independence by 'Great Zimbabwe'.
70. *Fort Victoria Advertiser* (20 and 27 Oct., 3 Nov. 1978).
71. For an example of a round-up of news see *Gwelo Times* (27 July 1978).
72. *Umtali Post* (2 Feb. 1979).

73. The Standard Bank Group, *Economic Bulletin – Zimbabwe*, 21 (June 1980).

74. Rhodesia, CSO, *Supplement to the Monthly Digest of Statistics* (July 1978), table 6.

75. Zimbabwe, CSO, *Higher Income Expenditure Survey, 1977/18* (n.d.). The survey covered 677 household budgets: Salisbury 201; Bulawayo 220; Gwelo116; Umtali 140.

76. There was, however, a fall of 90 per cent of those who spent less than one night abroad, suggesting that day trips for business or pleasure were a thing of the past. There was also an 81 per cent decline in the same period for visitors entering Rhodesia. (Zimbabwe Rhodesia, CSO, *Monthly Digest of Statistics* (Feb. 1980), table 2.)

77. Rhodesia Cricket Umpires' Association, *News Sheet* (14 Mar. 1978). Rugby suffered a similar fate. In 1974 there were 49 clubs fielding 103 teams; in 1978 the figures were 32 and 49 respectively: J. Winch, *Rhodesian Rugby: A History of the National Side, 1898-1979* (Salisbury, 1979), p. 109. For a sombre assessment see *Illustrated Life and Talk* (5 Dec. 1979).

78. For a survey of the building programme see the Supplement to *Illustrated Life Rhodesia* (3 Mar. 1977).

79. Interview (Hancock): R. Jackson, the managing director of Jackson Pools, 13 July 1989.

80. R. Riddell, 'Zimbabwe's Land Problem: The Central Issue', in W. H. Morris-Jones, *from Rhodesia to Zimbabwe: Behind and Beyond Lancaster House* (London, 1980), p. 3.

81. CFU, *Information* (Salisbury, 1980).

82. Rhodesia/Zimbabwe Rhodesia, CSO, *Monthly Digest of Statistics* (Dec. 1971, 1976, 1980); Zimbabwe, CSO, *Supplement to the Monthly Digest of Statistics* (Dec. 1980).

83. Ministry of Agriculture, Economics and Marketing Branch, 'Agricultural Economics and Markets Report, July-December 1976', Dec. 1977, p. 10. The sample represented the results achieved 'by a moderately large number of farmers scattered throughout the country': ibid., p. 8.

84. CFU, *Report of the Annual Congress* (1979), p. 61.

85. Zimbabwe Rhodesia, CSO, *Monthly Migration and Tourist Statistics* (Nov. 1979), tables 10 and 11.

86. Although the 93 white deaths in vehicle accidents were overtaken for fourth place by the 298 European deaths caused by 'homicide and injury inflicted by other persons', the whites – as in 1970 – succumbed mainly to cardio- and cerebral vascular disease or various forms of cancer: Zimbabwe Rhodesia, *Report of the Secretary for Health* (1979), table 2.

87. R. Riddell, *Education for Employment*, From Rhodesia to Zimbabwe Series, 9 (London, 1980), pp. 55-6.

88. *Rhodesia Railways Review* (Feb. 1979); *Record* (Jan. and Oct. 1979).

89. For an extended commentary on this theme see H. H. Patel, 'white Power in Rhodesia', paper presented to the ASSA Congress (Salisbury, 1978).

90. For one priest's critical view of the Commission see Father Hannan, SJ, in NAZ, Oral/HA 11 (1977).

91. A number of sources to support this point are cited in n. 11 of ch. 6.

92. Interview (Godwin): D. Bennison, 1 and 4 Dec. 1982.

93. Interviews (Hancock): R. Wollacott, 7 Feb. 1982; Don Yardley, 17 Feb. 1982.

94. A typical anti-Reid Daly comment was that he was 'really a warrant officer'. (Interview (Godwin): Brigadier Bruce Campling, 27 Nov. 1982.)

95. Interview (Godwin and Hancock): Redfern, 16 May 1989.

96. Interview (Godwin): Reid Daly, 1 Dec. 1982.

97. See J. A. Lawrence, The Effects of the War on the Control of Diseases of Livestock in Rhodesia (Zimbabwe)', *Veterinary Record* (26 July 1980), pp. 82-5.

98. Zimbabwe, Zimbabwe Rhodesia Police, *Annual Report of the Commissioner of Police* (1979), pp. 5 ff. There was, for example, a 22.39 per cent decrease from 1978 in cases of housebreaking.

99. Interview (Godwin): a former senior officer of the Ministry of Agriculture, 15 Mar. and 14 Apr. 1982.

100. Interview (Hancock): MacIntyre, 25 Mar. 1980.

101. Three farmers' wives told a similar story to the *Herald* (15 Feb. 1980).

102. *Rhodesia Herald* (11 May 1977).

103. *Highlands and Greendale Times* (Oct. 1976).

104. *Illustrated Life and Talk* (23 May 1979).

105. *Illustrated Life Rhodesia* (28 Oct. 1976).

106. D. Mitchell, 'Political Diary', 13 Oct. 1976, Mitchell Papers.

107. Diana Mitchell to N. McNally, 24 Aug. 1979, NUF Files.

108. For an official expression of these views see Rhodesia, Ministry of Foreign Affairs, International Organisations Section, *A Case for Rhodesia* (29 Apr. 1976). Among those who openly stated this view in 1980, D. J. Lewis of the Zimbabwe Rhodesia Promotion Council made his pronouncement as crowds of Africans were celebrating Mugabe's victory in the streets below his office. (Interview (Hancock): 4 Mar. 1980.)

109. *Herald* (22 Apr. 1980); Caute, *Under the Skin,* p. 178. Caute described Tilley's action in 1980 as a 'peculiar sequel' to the personal tragedies of 1978.

110. *Outpost* (Mar. 1980).

111. See, for example, the speech by Dr Silas Mundawarara to the 1979 CFU annual congress: CFU, *Report of the Annual Congress* (1979), p. 37.

112. Interviews (Hancock): Brian O'Connell (an accountant who had long been prominent in business organisations), 27 Feb. 1980; D. J. Lewis, 4 March 1980.

113. See Rhodesia, *Anatomy of Terror; Massacre of the Innocents.*

114.]. A. McKenzie, 'Commercial Farmers in the Governmental System of Colonial Zimbabwe', Ph.D. thesis (Harare, 1990), p. 299, quotes a former President of the RNFU who reported after the Geneva Conference that the intensity of African feelings about the RF government surprised the Smith delegation.

115. See *Herald* (2-3, 16-17, 25, 27, 31 July 1979).

116. Interview (Hancock): David Young (former Secretary of the Treasury), 2 Feb. 1982.

117. *Rhodesian Tobacco Today,* 2/1 (1979).

118. NAZ, Oral/235 (Ellman-Brown), pp. 58-51.

119. For Malloch see *Sunday Mail* (9 Mar. 1980) and H. Ellert, *The Rhodesian Front War* (Gweru, 1989), pp. 132-6. Interviews (Hancock): O'Donnell, 13 May 1980; John Cameron, 4 Feb. 1981; David Young, 2 Feb. 1982. Young made the point that Rhodesia was greatly assisted by its capacity to raise short-term loans, although it did experience difficulty in trying to enter the medium- and long-term markets.

120. Interviews (Hancock): Cameron, 4 Feb. 1981; Jack Quinton, 10 June 1980.

121. See P. Stiff, *Taming the Landmine* (Alberton, 1986), chs. 4-8. Stiff also provides statistics for the war period demonstrating the greater survival capacity of individuals sitting in mine-resistant or mine-protected heavy vehicles in contrast to those in mine-protected light vehicles, unprotected heavy vehicles (African buses), and unprotected light vehicles: ibid., pp. 84-5.

122. Not every invention was successful. The authorities confiscated a gun developed by some Afrikaners in Enkeldoorn which consisted of a 2″ pipe loaded with wadding and rusty nails, a breach block, a car spark plug, a tyre valve, a toy balloon, and an acetylene generator. The weapon exploded in all directions during a demonstration and nearly killed the local dominee and an inspector from the Dangerous Devices Committee. (Interview (Godwin and Hancock): Fred du Toit, 16 May 1989.)

123. For collections of cartoon humour see C. K. Edwards, *1965 1979: A Cartoon History of Rhodesia* (Salisbury, 1979) and particular works such as *Meet the Rhodesians, Life with UDI,* and *More Life with UDI.*

124. Interview (Godwin and Hancock): Fred du Toit, 16 May 1989.

125. For an example of Rhodesian legalism see the reports of the case brought by the Catholic Commission for Justice and Peace which sought – unsuccessfully – to establish that a condemned individual had a right of appeal to the President to exercise the prerogative of mercy: *Herald* (27-8 Apr., 3 and 23 May, 14 June, 1 Aug. 1979).

126. For a fuller account see the statement by the President of the Rhodesian Guild of Journalists in the *Sunday Mail* (16 Dec. 1979),

127. *Gwelo Times* (18 Jan. 1979).

128. Chennels argues that it was possible to obtain accurate information about the war in a small society, that this information bore 'little relation' to media accounts, and that the whites were willing to be misled: A. J, Chennels, 'Settler Myths and the Southern Rhodesian Novel', Ph.D. thesis (Harare, 1982), pp. xvi-xxii.

129. Rhodesia, Ministry of Internal Affairs, 'Value of Protected and Consolidated Villages (Secret)', 22 June 1977, copy in the authors' possession.

130. The Strategy of Protected Villages (Secret)', app. A to JOC Hurricane, G (Ops), 15 June 1978, copy in the authors' possession.

131. *Herald* (9 Dec. 1978).

132. Interview (Hancock): D, J. Lewis, 4 Mar. 1980.

133. Interview (Hancock); Chief Superintendent Rogers, 14 May 1980.

134. Gerald Ross, the son of a former Native Affairs Department officer and Secretary of Information, who helped to draft the UDI document, was killed near Nkai on 18 Apr. 1979. He was one of three DCs to die in the war,

and one of two to be killed by 'terrorists' (the third having been accidentally shot by his own side).

Conclusion

1. *Outpost* (May 1980).
2. Hancock interviewed Frost in the RAP offices in Salisbury on 12 Jan. 1978 when he was suspicious, uncommunicative, and very bitter. Frost abruptly ended the interview saying that the questions were offensive. By the second interview, which took place on 17-18 May 1989 near Cape Town (the second day at his suggestion), Frost was open, gentle, and benign. He died soon after.
3. Interview (Godwin and Hancock): Walls, 31 May 1989.
4. *Herald* (12 Aug. 1980).
5. Interview (Hancock): Ian Smith, 11 July 1989.
6. See, for example, I. Mandaza (ed.), *Zimbabwe: The Political Economy of Transition, 1980-1986* (Harare, 1987), and C. Stoneman and L. Cliffe, *Zimbabwe: Politics, Economics and Society* (London, 1989).
7. In dismissing the allegation Flower referred to Allum as 'that shit'. (Interview (Hancock): 4 Feb. 1982.)
8. Smith subsequently won a legal action seeking reimbursement of his salary. The case led to a confrontation between the judiciary and the legislature because the Speaker initially refused to obey a court order. The outcome was a victory for the rule of law. Ironically, throughout the 1970s, Ian Smith had warned the Rhodesians that the rule of law would be the first victim of majority rule.
9. Interview (Hancock): Divaris, 2 July 1985.
10. The occasion was an interview Hancock was conducting with Smith on 26 June 1980.

Bibliography

Preliminary note

This bibliography does not list all the works consulted (in the case both of Rhodesian and non-Rhodesian sources) but is intended to indicate the range of sources available. In keeping with the themes of this book, an arbitrary and not altogether satisfactory distinction is drawn between texts which directly reflect Rhodesian viewpoints or circumstances and academic books and articles which seek to explain Rhodesian behaviour.

Official papers and reports

Parliamentary Debates, Assembly and Senate.
Rhodesian Government *Gazette.*

Ministries

Annual Reports (Agriculture, Defence, Education, Health, Internal Affairs, Justice, Roads and Traffic).
Ministry of Agriculture, Economics and Marketing Branch, 'Agricultural Economics and Markets Reports'.
Ministry of Finance, *Economic Surveys.*
Ministry of Foreign Affairs, Information Section, 'Background Briefings'.
– *Fact Papers.*
– *Focus on Rhodesia.*
Ministry of Information, *Government Lists.*
– *For the Record.*
– *Meet the Ministry* series.
– Press Statements and Texts of Broadcasts.
– *The Case for Rhodesia* (several revised editions).
– *Anatomy of Terror* (May 1974).
– *Massacre of the Innocents* (Jan 1978).

Other

Annual Reports of the Commissioner of Police.
Annual Reports of RBC/TV.
Board of Censors, *Catalogue of Banned Books Periodicals Records etc.* (1972, 1978, 1980).
Central Statistical Office, *Census of Population* (1969).
– *Consumer Price Index for Higher Income Urban Families* (1964-84).
– *European or Higher Income Expenditure Surveys* (1968, 1975/6, 1977/8).
– *Monthly Digests of Statistics.*

- *Monthly Migration and Tourism Statistics.*
- *Supplements to the Monthly Digests of Statistics.*
Record of Army Briefings.
Report of the Commission of Inquiry into Termination of Pregnancy (19 Feb. 1976), Cmd. R.R.2-1976.
Report of the Commission of Inquiry into Racial Discrimination (Apr. 1976), Cmd. R.R.6-1976.
Report of the Constitutional Commission (Apr. 1968).
Report of the Commission of Inquiry into the Divorce Laws (23 Sept. 1977), Cmd. R.R.16-1977.
Rhodesia, *Second and Third Interim Reports of the Electoral Supervisory Commission* (25 Apr. and 23 May 1979).
Rhodesian Law Reports.

Other reports and documents

Annual Reports (ACCOR, ARnI, the Chamber of Mines, the RTA).
Commercial Farmers' Union, 'Statistical Survey of Cattle Holdings by ICA in Standard Livestock Units (as at 31 March 1979) and Farm Utilisation (as at May 1979)'.
Granada Television, *End of Empire* (Transcript).
Manicaland Development and Publicity Association, 'Report on the Proceedings of the Annual General Meetings'.
Market Research (Rhod.) (Pvt.) Ltd., 'Political Party Study' (1969), prepared for J. Walter Thompson Company, Central Africa, Pvt., Ltd.
Record of Transfers (Pvt.) Ltd.
Rhodesian Front, *Reports of the Proceedings of the National Congress.*
- *General Election, 1970: A Handbook for Candidates and Constituency Chairmen.*
Rhodesia National Fanners' Union, *Reports of the Annual Congresses.*
Rhodesian Medical Association, 'Report of the Committee formed to investigate the future of Medicine under African Majority Rule', June 1978.
St Giles Rehabilitation Centre: Admission Book, Physiotherapy and Occupational Registers.
Salisbury Municipality, *Minute of His Worship the Mayor.*
Williamson, J. M., 'Protected Villages: Chiweshe TTL', 21 Nov. 1974.

Manuscript Collections

Private
P. K. Allum; C. Barlow; R. Cowper; F. du Toit; G. F. Fairbairn.

Archives and libraries
C. Campbell, Rhodes House, Oxford; Centre Party, National Archives of Zimbabwe and University of Cape Town; G. Greenhill, Rhodes House, Oxford; G. Hartley, National Archives of Zimbabwe; D. Mitchell, University of Cape Town; B. W. S. O'Connell, National Archives of Zimbabwe; National Unifying Force, University of Cape Town; Rhodesia Party, University of Cape Town; C. A. R. Savory, National Archives of Zimbabwe.

Interviews

National Archives of Zimbabwe: W. J. Cary; A. J. Dunlop; G. Ellman-Brown; B. Field; Father Hannan SJ; J. H. Howman; J. Quinton; G. Rudland; G. S. Todd; H. Ward.

Newspapers

African Times; Chronicle; Fort Victoria Advertiser; Gwelo Times; Lomagundi News; Moto; People; Rhodesia Herald (Herald from 1978); *Rhodesian Financial Gazette; Sinoia News; Umtali Post.*

Periodicals

Anchor; Arundel School Magazine; Assegai; Chaplin School Magazine; Economic Bulletins (Standard Bank); *Fighting Forces of Rhodesia; Granite Review; Group News* (Rhodesian Christian Group); *Highlands and Greendale Times; Home and Country; Illustrated Life Rhodesia; Illustrated Life and Talk; Link; Locomotive Express; Look and Listen; News Sheet* (Rhodesian Cricket Umpires' Association); *Outpost; Prince Edward School Magazine; Record; Rhodesia Railways Review; Rhodesian Farmer (Farmer* from 1978); *Rhodesian Patriot; Rhodesian Tobacco Journal; Rhodesian Viewpoint; St George's Chronicle; Talk; Umtali Presbyterian Bulletin.*

Rhodesian texts

Armstrong, P., *Operation Zambezi: The Raid into Zambia* (Salisbury, 1979).
– *Tobacco Spiced with Ginger: The Life of Ginger Freeman* (Borrowdale, 1987).
Berlyn, P., *Rhodesia: Beleaguered Country* (London, 1967).
– (ed.), *Rhodesian Homeowner's Handbook* (Salisbury, n.d.).
– *The Quiet Man: A Biography of the Hon. Ian Douglas Smith, ID Prime Minister of Rhodesia* (Salisbury, 1978).
Bolze, L., and Martin, R., *The Whenwes of Rhodesia* (Bulawayo, 1978).
Bond, F., *The Incredibles: The Story of the Rhodesian Light Infantry* (Salisbury, 1977).
Burrough, P., *Angels Unawares* (Worthing, 1988).
Carney, D., *The Whispering Death* (Salisbury, 1969).
Cary, R., *The Story of Reps: The History of Salisbury Repertory Players 1931 to 1975* (Salisbury, 1975).
Catholic Commission for Justice and Peace in Rhodesia, *The Man in the Middle* (London, 1975).
– *Civil War in Rhodesia: Abduction, Torture and Death in the Counter-Insurgency Campaign* (London, 1976).
– 'The Declaration of Martial Law in Rhodesia' (typescript, 1978).
Cocks, C., *Fireforce: One Man's War in the Rhodesian Light Infantry* (Alberton, 1988).
Cole, B., *The Elite: The Story of the Rhodesian Special Air Service* (Amanzimtoti, 1984).

– *The Elite: Rhodesian Special Air Service: Pictorial* (Amanzimtoti, 1986).

Dibb, C. E., *Spotted Soldiers* (Salisbury, 1978).

Dunlop, A., *The March of Time* (Salisbury, 1977).

Dupont, C, *The Reluctant President: The Memoirs of The Hon. Clifford Dupont, GCLM, ID* (Bulawayo, 1978).

Early, R., *A Time of Madness* (Salisbury, 1977).

Edwards, C. K. (ed.), *1965 1979: A Cartoon History of Rhodesia* (Salisbury, 1979).

Flower, K., *Serving Secretly: An Intelligence Chief on Record. Rhodesia into Zimbabwe 1964 to 1981* (London, 1987).

Gelfand, M., *A Non-Racial Island of Learning: A History of the University College of Rhodesia from its Inception to 1966* (Gwelo, 1978).

Goldin, B., *Unhappy Marriage and Divorce: The Problem in Rhodesia* (Salisbury, 1971).

– *The Judge, The Prince, and the Usurper – From UDI to Zimbabwe* (New York, 1990).

Greenfield, J. M., *Testimony of a Rhodesian Federal* (Bulawayo, 1978).

Hardy, A., *Some Famous Rhodesian Trials* (Bulawayo, 1981).

Hirsch, M. I., *A Decade of Crisis: Ten Years of Rhodesian Front Rule (1963-1972)* (Salisbury, 1973).

Holderness, H., *Lost Chance: Southern Rhodesia, 1945-58* (Harare, 1985).

Holroyd, A., *War Without Honour* (Hull, 1979).

Howman, R., *Provincialisation,* Cambridge African Occasional Paper, No. 4 (Cambridge, 1986).

Jackson, G. M., *The Land is Bright* (Salisbury, 1974).

Joyce, P., *Anatomy Of A Rebel: Smith of Rhodesia: A Biography* (Salisbury, 1974).

Lamont, D., *Speech From The Dock* (Leigh-on-Sea, 1977).

Lardner-Burke, D., *Rhodesia: The Story of the Crisis* (London, 1966).

Lewis, A., *Rhodesia Undefeated* (Salisbury, 1976).

– *Christian Terror* (Salisbury, 1978).

Lovett, J., *Contact* (Salisbury, 1977).

MacBruce, J., *When the Going was Rough: A Rhodesian Story* (Pretoria, 1983).

MacLaren, I. P. (ed.), *Some Renowned Rhodesian Senior Schools: 1892-1979* (Bulawayo, 1981).

– *More Rhodesian Senior Schools: Part Two, 1950-1982* (Bulawayo, 1982).

Metcalfe, C. B., *A Guide to Farming in Rhodesia* (Salisbury, 1971).

Moorcraft, P. M., *Contact II: Struggle for Peace* (Johannesburg, 1981).

Moore, R., *Rhodesia* (New York, 1977).

Moore-King, B., *white Man black War* (Harare, 1988).

National Federation of Business and Professional Women of Rhodesia, *Profiles of Rhodesia's Women* (Salisbury, 1976).

National Federation of Women's Institutes, *The W.J. Jubilee Book, 1925-1975* (Salisbury, 1975).

Niesewand, P., *In Camera: Secret Justice in Rhodesia* (London, 1973).

Parker, J., *Rhodesia: The Little white Island* (London, 1972).

Partridge, N., *Not Alone: A Story for the Future of Rhodesia* (Gwelo, 1972).

Peck, A. J. A., *Rhodesia Accuses* (Salisbury, 1966).

– *Rhodesia Condemns* (Salisbury, 1967).

Pitman, D., *You Must Be New Around Here* (Bulawayo, 1979).

Prominent Rhodesian Personalities 1978 (Salisbury, 1977).

Randolph, SJ, Father R. H., *Church and State in Rhodesia 1969-1971: A Catholic View* (Gwelo, 1971).

Redgment, J., *Introduction to the Legal System of Zimbabwe* (Belmont, 1981).

Reid Daly, R., *Selous Scouts: Top Secret War* (Alberton, 1982).

Rhodesian Farmer Publications, *Farmer at War* (Salisbury, 1979).

Rhodesian Front, *Principles and Policies* (Salisbury, 1962).

Skeen, A., *Prelude to Independence: Sheen's 115 Days (Cape Town, 1966)*.

Skelton, K., *Bishop in Smith's Rhodesia: Notes from a Turbulent Octave 1962-1970* (Gweru, 1985).

Stiff, P., *See You in November* (Alberton, 1985).

– *Taming the Landmine* (Alberton, 1986).

Strong, J., and Firks, S., 'Trip to Zambia, 1-7 April 1975' (typescript, n.d.).

Stumbles, A. W. R., *Some Recollections of a Rhodesian Speaker* (Bulawayo, 1980).

Todd, J., *An Act of Treason Rhodesia 1965* (Zimbabwe, 1982).

– *The Right to Say No: Rhodesia 1972* (Harare, 1987).

Tredgold, R., *The Rhodesia that was My Life* (London, 1968).

Wigglesworth, T. A., *Perhaps Tomorrow* (Salisbury, 1980).

Williams, C. D. (ed.), *Careers Guide for Young Rhodesians* (Salisbury, 1976).

Winch, J., *Rhodesian Rugby: A History of the National Side, 1898-1979* (Salisbury, 1979).

Non-Rhodesian documents

Africa Contemporary Record.

Africa Research Bulletin, Political, Social, and Cultural Series, and Economic, Financial, and Technical Series.

United Kingdom, Parliamentary Human Rights Group, *Free and Fair?: The 1979 Rhodesian Elections,* A Report on Behalf of the British Parliamentary Human Rights Group, May 1979.

United Kingdom, *Report of the Commission on Rhodesian Opinion,* Cmnd. 4964, May 1972.

– Southern Rhodesia, *Report of the Constitutional Conference, Lancaster House* (Jan. 1980), Cmnd. 7802.

– Southern Rhodesia, *Independence Elections, 1980, Report of the Electoral Commissioner, Sir John Boynton* (Mar. 1980), Cmnd. 7935.

Books and articles

Arrighi, G., and Saul, J. S., *Essays on the Political Economy of Africa* (New York, 1973).

Astrow, A., *Zimbabwe: A Revolution that Lost its Way?* (London, 1983).

Atkinson, N., *Teaching Rhodesians: A History of Educational Policy in Rhodesia* (London, 1972).

Austin, R., *The Character and Legislation of the Rhodesian Front since UDI* (London, 1968).

Barber, J., *Rhodesia: The Road to Rebellion* (London, 1967).

Blake, R., *A History of Rhodesia* (London, 1977).

Bowman, L. W., *Politics in Rhodesia: white Power in an African State* (Cambridge, Mass., 1973).

Brand, C. M., 'Race and Politics in Rhodesian Trade Unions', *African Perspectives* (1976), 55-80.

Caute, D., *Under the Skin: The Death of white Rhodesia* (London, 1983).

Cilliers, J. K., *Counter-Insurgency in Rhodesia* (London, 1985).

Clarke, D. G., *Agricultural and Plantation Workers in Rhodesia* (Gwelo, 1977).

– *Foreign Companies and International Investment in Zimbabwe* (Gwelo, 1980).

Cowderoy, D., and Nesbit, R. C., *War in the Air: Rhodesian Air Force, 1935-1980* (Alberton, 1987).

Dachs, A. J., and Rea, S], Father W. F., *The Catholic Church and Zimbabwe, 1879-1979* (Gwelo, 1979).

Davies, D., *Race Relations in Rhodesia: A Survey for 1972-73* (London, 1975).

Ellert, H., *The Rhodesian Front War: Counter-Insurgency and Guerrilla War in Rhodesia 1962-1980* (Gweru, 1989).

Evans, M., *Fighting Against Chimurenga: An Analysis of Counter-Insurgency in Rhodesia 1972-9,* Historical Association of Zimbabwe, 37 (Salisbury, 1981).

Frantz, C. A., and Frantz, C., *Racial Themes in Southern Rhodesia: The Attitudes and Behavior of the white Population* (New Haven, Conn., 1962).

Frederikse, J., *None But Ourselves: Masses vs Media in the Making of Zimbabwe* (Harare, 1982).

From Rhodesia to Zimbabwe (Series), Catholic Institute for International Relations (London, 1979-80).

Gann, L. H., 'Rhodesia and the Prophets', *African Affairs,* 71 (1972), pp. 125-43.

– and Henriksen, T. H., *The Struggle for Zimbabwe: Battle in the Bush* (New York, 1981).

Gifford, P., *The Religious Right in Southern Africa* (Harare, 1988).

Good, K., 'Settler Colonialism in Rhodesia', *African Affairs,* 73 (1974), pp. 10-36.

Hancock, I., *white Liberals, Moderates and Radicals in Rhodesia 1953-1980* (London, 1984).

Harris, P. S., *black Industrial Workers: The General Problems of Low Pay* (Gwelo, 1974).

Hills, D., *Rebel People* (London, 1978).

– *The Last Days of white Rhodesia* (London, 1981).

Hodder-Williams, R., 'Rhodesia's Search for a Constitution: Or, Whatever Happened to Whaley?', *African Affairs,* 69 (1970), pp. 217-35.

– 'white Attitudes and the Unilateral Declaration of Independence: A Case Study', *Journal of Commonwealth Political Studies,* 8 (1970), pp. 241-64.

– 'Party Allegiance among Rhodesians in Rural Rhodesia – a Research Note', *Journal of Modern African Studies,* 10 (1972), pp. 130-9.

– *white Farmers in Rhodesia, 1890-1965: A History of the Marandellas District* (London, 1983).

Hutson, H. P., W., *Rhodesia: Ending an Era* (London, 1978).

Kay, G., *Rhodesia: A Human Geography* (London, 1970).
– 'A Socio-Geographic Survey of Salisbury, Rhodesia , *Zambezia*, 3 (1974), pp. 77-80.
Kinloch, G. C., *Racial Conflict in Rhodesia: A Socio-Historical Study* (Washington, DC, 1978).
Kirk, T., 'Politics and Violence in Rhodesia', *African Affairs*, 74 (1975), pp. 3-38.
– and Sherwell, C., 'The Rhodesian General Election of 1974', *Journal of Commonwealth and Comparative Politics*, 13 (1975), pp. 1-25.
Kosmin, B. A., *Majuta: A History of the Jewish Community of Zimbabwe* (Gwelo, 1980).
Lan, D., *Guns and Rain: Guerrillas and Spirit Mediums in Zimbabwe* (Harare, 1985).
Lapsley, M, *Neutrality or Co-option: Anglican Church and State from 1964 until the Independence of Zimbabwe* (Gweru, 1986).
Lawrence, J. A., 'The Effects of the War on the Control of Diseases of Livestock in Rhodesia (Zimbabwe)', *Veterinary Record* (26 July 1980).
Leys, C., *European Politics in Southern Rhodesia* (Oxford, 1959).
Linden, I., *The Catholic Church and the Struggle for Zimbabwe* (London, 1980).
Loriey, M., *Rhodesia: white Racism and Imperial Response* (London, 1975).
McEwan, P. J. M., 'The European Population of Southern Rhodesia', *Civilisations*, 13 (1963), pp. 429-41
McFarlane, L. J., 'Justifying Rebellion: black and white Nationalism in Rhodesia', *Journal of Commonwealth Political Studies*, 6 (1968), pp. 54-79.
Mandaza, I. (ed.), *Zimbabwe: The Political Economy of Transition, 1980-1986* (Harare, 1987).
Martin, D., and Johnson, P., *The Struggle for Zimbabwe: The Chimurenga War* (London, 1981).
– *The Chitepo Assassination* (Harare, 1985).
Meredith, M., *The Past is Another Country: Rhodesia: UDI to Zimbabwe* (London, 1980).
Moorcraft, P. L., *A Short Thousand Years: The End of Rhodesia's Rebellion*, rev. edn. (Salisbury, 1980).
– and McLaughlin, P., *Chimurenga!: The War in Rhodesia* (Marshalltown, 1982).
Morris-Jones, W. H., *From Rhodesia to Zimbabwe: Behind and Beyond Lancaster House* (London, 1980).
Mosley, P., *The Settler Economies: Studies in the Economic History of Kenya and Southern Rhodesia 1900-1963* (Cambridge, 1983).
Murphree, M. W., Cheater, G., Dorsey, B. J., and Mothobi, B. D., *Education, Race and Employment in Rhodesia* (Salisbury, 1975).
Murray, D. J., *The Governmental System of Southern Rhodesia* (Oxford, 1970).
Muzorewa, A., *Rise Up and Walk: An Autobiography* (London, 1978).
Nkomo, J., *Nkomo: The Story of My Life* (London, 1984).
Palley, C., *Zimbabwe Rhodesia: Should the Present Government be Recognised?* (London, 1979).
Phimister, I. R., 'Zimbabwean Economic and Social Historiography Since 1970', *African Affairs*, 78 (1979), pp. 253-68.
Ranger, T., *Peasant Consciousness and Guerrilla Warfare in Zimbabwe: A Comparative Study* (Harare, 1985).

Riddell, R., *Alternatives to Poverty: From Rhodesia to Zimbabwe*, i (n.d.).

Riddell, R., *Education for Employment*, From Rhodesia to Zimbabwe Series, 9 (London, 1980).

Riddell, R. C, and Harris, P. S., *The Poverty Datum Line as a Wage Fixing Standard: An Application to Rhodesia* (Gwelo, 1975).

Roberts, R. S., 'Epiphenomena of the Struggle', *Zambezia*, 10 (1982), pp. 143-50.

– 'Essay Review: The Armed Forces and Chimurenga: Ideology and Historiography', *Heritage of Zimbabwe*, 7 (1987), pp. 74-91.

Rogers, C. A., and Frantz, C., *Racial Themes in Southern Rhodesia: The Attitudes and Behavior of the white Population* (New Haven, Conn., 1962).

Schutz, B. M., 'European Population Patterns, Cultural Persistence and Political Change in Rhodesia', *Canadian Journal of African Studies*, 7 (1973), pp. 3-25.

Stoneman, C. (ed.), *Zimbabwe's Inheritance* (London, 1981).

– (ed.), *Zimbabwe's Prospects: Issues of Race, Class, State, and Capital in Southern Africa* (London, 1988).

– and Cliffe, L., *Zimbabwe: Politics, Economics and Society* (London, 1989).

Venter, A. J., *The Zambezi Salient: Conflict in Southern Africa* (London, 1975).

Wilkinson, A. R., *Insurgency in Rhodesia, 1957-1973: An Account and Assessment*, Adelphi Papers, 100 (London, 1973).

Windrich, E., *The Rhodesian Problem: A Documentary Record, 1923-1973* (London, 1975).

– *Britain and the Politics of Rhodesian Independence* (London, 1978).

– 'Rhodesian Censorship', *African Affairs*, 78 (1979), pp. 523-34.

– *The Mass Media in the Struggle for Zimbabwe: Censorship and Propaganda under Rhodesian Front Rule* (Gwelo, 1981).

Wortham, C. J., 'The State of the Theatre in Rhodesia', *Zambezia*, 1 (1969), pp. 47-53.

Theses and unpublished papers

Barnes, C. P., 'Logistics of Security Work in Rhodesia', paper presented to the Construction Engineers' Conference, Dec. 1978.

Chennels, A. J., 'Settler Myths and the Southern Rhodesian Novel', Ph.D. thesis (Harare, 1982).

Kennedy, D. K., 'A Tale of Two Colonies: The Social Origins and Cultural Consequences of white Settlement in Kenya and Rhodesia, 1890-1939', Ph.D. thesis (Berkeley, Calif., 1981).

McKenzie, J. A., 'Commercial Farmers in the Governmental System of Colonial Zimbabwe, 1963-1980', Ph.D. thesis (Harare, 1990).

Patel, H. H., 'white Power in Rhodesia: The Rise and Fall (?) of the Rhodesian Front', paper presented to the ASSA Congress, Salisbury, 1978.

Schutz, B., The Theory of Fragment and the Political Development of white Settler Society in Rhodesia', Ph.D. thesis (Los Angeles, 1972).

Seager, D. R., 'Marital Dissolution in Rhodesia: A Socio-Legal Perspective', M.Phil. thesis (Salisbury, 1977).

Index